SIMON & SCHUSTER MEGA CROSSWORD PUZZLE BOOK

Series 19

300 never-before-published crosswords

Edited by John M. Samson

G Gallery Books

New York   London   Toronto   Sydney   New Delhi

Gallery Books
An Imprint of Simon & Schuster, Inc.
1230 Avenue of the Americas
New York, NY 10020

First Gallery Books trade paperback edition September 2019

GALLERY BOOKS and colophon are registered trademarks
of Simon & Schuster, Inc.

For information about special discounts for bulk purchases,
please contact Simon & Schuster Special Sales at
1-866-506-1949 or business@simonandschuster.com.

The Simon & Schuster Speakers Bureau can bring authors to your live event.
For more information or to book an event, contact the Simon & Schuster
Speakers Bureau at 1-866-248-3049 or visit our website at
www.simonspeakers.com.

Designed by Sam Bellotto Jr.

Library of Congress Control Number:

Manufactured in the United States of America

11 12 13 14 15 16 17 18 19 20

ISBN 978-1-9821-0964-6

COMPLETE ANSWERS WILL BE FOUND AT THE BACK.

FOREWORD

MIX-UP IN THE NURSERY by Harvey Estes

Ten nursery-rhyme characters are mixed up in the sentences below.
Each may be found in an anagram of consecutive words. For example, "When pulling up the anchor, jerk hard on it" contains the words "anchor jerk," which is an anagram of "Jack Horner." Match each character to its corresponding sentence.

Margery Daw
Cock Robin
Old King Cole
Solomon Grundy
Mistress Mary
Simple Simon
Little Bo Peep
Jack Sprat
Tommy Tucker
Mother Goose

I have noticed that in poems, slim people are seldom mentioned.
When he walks into the room, egos begin to need massaging.
I found the captain's log locked in a file cabinet.
I tend to resist smarmy sales pitches.
I heard everyone in my ward rage against the proposed tax increase.
If you hear the pope belittle himself, it is an act of humility.
They sent my truck to me without charging for the driver.
The person who is godly mourns no action of his own.
Where Robert Downey Jr. sat, pack animals could be seen moving about.
Placing a corncob in rock salt prevents insect infestation.

The Margaret Award winner is GETS CREATIVE by Wren Schultz.

JOHN M. SAMSON

1 ELVIS SIGHTINGS   by Harvey Estes

Elvis has left the building . . . and is lurking below.

ACROSS

1 Come together
6 Climber
10 Healthy look
14 Argue against
15 Unyielding
16 Unit price word
17 Customs document
19 Miranda in "I, Frankenstein"
20 Org. with many schedules
21 Sangfroid
22 Worth emulating
23 Blot on the landscape
25 Pop up
26 Narrow-mindedness
29 Special Forces cap
32 Blood line
33 Cone starter
34 "I second the motion!"
35 iPhone letters
37 Gun, slangily
38 "Decorates" with tissue, for short
39 Auth. unknown
40 TV's Uncle Miltie
41 Hilton's guest of a guest
45 Like marshland
46 Response to "Do you mind?"
50 "Scarborough Fair" quartet
51 Done for
53 Darth, as a boy
54 Art Deco name
55 It can turn and hold
57 Ball game buy
58 Walk nervously
59 Certain fisherman
60 Says further
61 Dish medium
62 Takes a load off

DOWN

1 Bandleader Shaw
2 Lighthearted
3 Put down
4 Ford Explorer, e.g.
5 Go for lunch, for example
6 Leigh in "A Streetcar Named Desire"
7 Place for a pupil
8 Victory margin
9 Aunt in "Bambi"
10 Crystal-rich rocks
11 Sack lingerer
12 Like stop signs
13 Musical symbol
18 Ending for love
22 Participant's words
24 Compact Chevy pickup
25 Like some twins
27 Chris in "Captain America"
28 Honolulu gift
29 Mother of Solomon
30 Given authority
31 Turned over again
35 Green-eyed monster
36 Hawaiian fish
37 Jupiter's wife
39 The von Trapps sang in this range
40 Pepsi employee
42 Fire remnants
43 Insult response
44 Kind of poem
47 Rescues, with "out"
48 Atlas enlargement
49 Stadium levels
51 Booty, in slang
52 Typewriter type
55 Site for three men in a tub
56 Neckline type

BAND TOGETHER   by Harvey Estes
Nothing holds us together like rock and roll!

ACROSS

1 Touches with a baseball
5 "Doggone!"
9 Muscle cramp, for one
14 Low cholesterol spread
15 Villain in "Othello"
16 Big name in tech stocks
17 Cafeteria list
18 Blue funk
19 Nostalgic fashion trend
20 Ointment for poison ivy
23 Shoemaker Thom
24 Accumulates excessively
25 Mother of Jesus, with title
28 Pat oneself on the back
30 Terre ___, Indiana
31 Avoid responsibility
36 Wheel connector
37 Oprah's role in "The Color Purple"
38 ". . . ___ they say"
39 Fuel for some trucks
41 Clean with a broom
42 Shaker filler
43 Mists
44 Narcotics Anonymous member
48 Teri of "Mr. Mom"
49 Pie with cheese and bacon
54 Loosen, as a knot
55 Morales of "Jericho"
56 "Night and Day" Porter
58 Crooked
59 "If all ___ fails . . ."
60 Santana's "___ Ways"
61 Lights in the night sky
62 "Mahogany" vocalist Diana
63 Okay but not great

DOWN

1 Male cat
2 Trump impersonator Baldwin
3 Rowlands of "The Notebook"
4 They were made for each other
5 Feeling of apprehension
6 Took to the police station
7 Opposed to, to Li'l Abner
8 Shopper's bag
9 Uncle in "A Christmas Carol"
10 Madonna-and-child depiction
11 Full of activity
12 New England catch
13 They orbit planets
21 Vineyard measure
22 ___ apso (terrier type)
25 State fish of Connecticut
26 Metered motorcar
27 Lounging slipper
28 Seem suitable for
29 Train track
31 Fuzzy fabric
32 They attract bargain hunters
33 Two-toned cookie
34 Web surfer
35 Spinning toys
37 Nominee list
40 Abstains from
41 Gilbert on "The Talk"
43 Fluctuates
44 Shades of blue
45 Kirsten of "Spider-Man"
46 Former Chicago Bears coach Mike
47 More like slippery winter roads
48 Hawaiian skirt material
50 Look lecherously
51 Capital of Norway
52 De ___ (again)
53 Wallach and Whitney
57 Band that joins together four answers

3 HERE'S THE SCOOP   by Howard Barkin
The alternate title can be found at 62 Across.

ACROSS

1 Average ___ (regular people)
5 Sci-fi monster of 1958
9 Bring to the shop for repair
14 It keeps the wheels rolling
15 Vishnu incarnation
16 Sidestep
17 Precipitous plunges*
19 Olympic decathlete Johnson
20 Composer known as "The Devil's Violinist"
22 Pokémon GO, for example
23 Serve in the role of
26 On the level
28 "Rhapsody in Blue" composer
32 Bump jumped by a waterskier
33 Without ice, at the bar
34 Seeks the affection of
36 Fridge forays
39 One in a Northern factory?
40 Bat stickum*
42 Uncut, as video footage
43 Up to this point
45 Rickman who played Snape
46 Archaeological finding
47 Laptop with a Retina display
49 Country where Tamil is spoken
51 Riles up
54 One on the plus side
55 Used to be
56 Those taking selfies in front of landmarks
60 Spy's retrieval
62 1993 Dan Aykroyd and Jane Curtin film/TITLE
66 Cross the goal line
67 Diamond-shaped flier
68 Wear out
69 Overly caffeinated, perhaps
70 Inedible fare
71 Big name in decking

DOWN

1 One of the Brady sisters
2 Blocked tic-tac-toe line
3 Ernie of the links
4 Ignore the negative qualities (of)
5 Place for misbehaving sailors
6 Big Island flow of 2018
7 Portent
8 Herb used in Italian cuisine
9 Inga in "Young Frankenstein"
10 Eggs, scientifically
11 Makers of square meals?*
12 Utopian
13 A bit bookish, perhaps
18 "The Incredibles" son
21 Word starting four U.S. states
23 Moorehead in "Citizen Kane"
24 Rapper/singer Green
25 Result of speeding, often*
27 Alias, initially
29 "Lawrence of Arabia" setting: Abbr.
30 College of the Gaels
31 Yuletide songs
35 Hollywood Walk of Fame honor
37 Word of gratitude, in Göttingen
38 Sign of exertion at the gym
40 One rambling on and on
41 Darth Vader's boyhood nickname
44 "Little Jack Horner" ending
46 Angela on "9-1-1"
48 "Shark Tank" panelist, often
50 Latticework strip
51 "If only!"
52 First lady after Rosalynn
53 Acts like a vacuum
57 Agitate
58 ÷, when spoken
59 Ooze
61 Before, in verse
63 Go public with
64 Dr. of G-funk
65 "___ and the City" (2008)

NEXT OF KIN   by Richard Silvestri
A recent family reunion inspired this theme.

ACROSS

1 Henley team
5 Pertaining to hearing
10 Dietary concern
14 Swear words?
15 Jobs in the computer business
16 Terrible tsar
17 Middle Eastern bread
18 Jukebox output
19 Mantel piece
20 Napkin?
23 Directional ending
24 X follower
25 Lend an ear
29 Insurance filing
32 Kon-Tiki Museum site
33 Garden sticker
34 North Pole toymaker
37 Pumpkin?
41 Get hard
42 Unrestrained
43 Elton John musical
44 "La Vita Nuova" writer
45 "___ on the Keys"
47 Ermine in summer
50 The youngest Cratchit
51 Firkin?
59 Ready for business

60 Spelunking spots
61 "___ Named Sue"
62 Used to be
63 Full of energy
64 Leap at the ballet
65 Pewter component
66 Made over
67 Belligerent deity

DOWN

1 Men in blue
2 One way to travel
3 Ides rebuke
4 Sound of impact
5 Away from the bow
6 180° manuever
7 Casino city
8 State
9 Word of comparison
10 Early morning hour
11 "Halt!" to a salt
12 Fashion sense
13 Three-time Masters champ
21 Social gathering
22 "Three Sisters" sister
25 Red-ink entry
26 Man, for one
27 Narrow opening
28 Beat
29 Decided on
30 Traditional tales
31 MGM motto opener
33 Easy run

34 Make the cut?
35 Fill the hold
36 Custard concoction
38 There's one at home
39 Long time
40 D.C. ballplayer
44 Mended with a needle
45 Locked lips
46 Little rascal
47 Show displeasure
48 Melville's first novel
49 It may be light or grand

50 Fountain in Rome
52 Mark for life
53 Mall event
54 Poet of ancient Rome
55 Punjab prince
56 Taxi alternative
57 Place for pigeons
58 Seeing things

5 BARELY PASSING   by Richard Silvestri
A grade of "D" is better than an "F" . . . but not by much.

ACROSS

1 Yokel
5 Dudish footwear
10 Biological pouches
14 Strong as ___
15 "The Hollow Men" poet
16 Sticking place
17 Flash of brilliance
18 Pat's TV partner
19 Wander about
20 One renting a college building?
22 In the thick of
23 Hopper load
24 Mexican munchie
26 Tranquil
30 Red Skelton character
32 Privileged group
33 Milkman's story?
38 Off-limits item
39 Cankers
40 Good enough
41 Really like Sir Isaac?
43 Orange yield
44 Scottish Highlander
45 Raised a red flag
46 Diamond, essentially
50 Prairie home material
51 Cantata melody
52 Dimwitted "Simpsons" bully?
59 Carpeting
60 Homeric epic
61 Piece of property
62 Passing notice
63 Safety outlet
64 Hampton Court attraction
65 Put together
66 Become a contestant
67 Jab

DOWN

1 Speakeasy risk
2 Bring to ruin
3 Transvaal settler
4 Occasion for proctors
5 Strict
6 Part of a service
7 "___ it the truth?"
8 Color variation
9 First team
10 "Blow!"
11 Evidence of baking
12 Split hairs
13 Angstrom or Celsius
21 Like a wolf, perhaps
25 Alcott girl
26 Email command
27 "Time Machine" people
28 Familiar sound
29 Rival of Harrow
30 December song
31 Property claim
33 Love to excess
34 Play the circuit
35 Analogous
36 Twine together
37 Looked over
39 Elegant pool entrance
42 It can be inflated
43 Shade of green
45 Marvel
46 Billiards maneuver
47 Caribbean resort
48 Inflexible
49 Moisten the meat
50 Nat Turner, e.g.
53 ___ Bator
54 Light air
55 Miner's hat feature
56 Incision evidence
57 Soup pasta
58 Cry out for

BY THE NUMBERS   by Lee Taylor
19 Down is the name of an orange.

ACROSS

1 Motors of Silicon Valley
6 Hang tough
10 Exchange
14 Total
15 Sicilian volcano
16 Rube Goldberg's Palooza
17 Emu relatives
18 Heated arguments
20 Gripe
21 ___ (Depp TV series)
22 British buddy
24 "Hit Me With Your Best Shot" singer Benatar
25 Humor can be this
26 Tyler of "Jersey Girl"
27 Underneath
29 Behaved like the Monkey Wrench Gang
33 It may be final
37 Egg-salad option
38 Cytoplasm component
39 Currants lack these
40 What NFL lineman have
41 Its bite is worse than its bark
43 Strawberry equines
46 Fros and bobs
47 Quick Kyrgios point
50 Flop
51 Boxing injuries
55 ___ (shipping container)
58 On the summit
59 Be a hostess with the mostest
60 The least bit
61 High time?
62 Beatnik's "Got ya!"
63 Regular joe
64 Be prone
65 Gas brand in Ontario
66 Assignation

DOWN

1 Supercharger
2 Lucy's BFF
3 Mount
4 ___ (lucky find)
5 Start of MGM's motto
6 Assist
7 Molecule part
8 Spoke sharply to
9 Relating to the ankle
10 Arc on a score
11 Let up
12 Cabinet wood
13 Unhealthy looking
19 Syracuse U. mascot
21 Daily grind?
23 Sex researcher Shere
27 Strong inclinations
28 ___ (Jeremy Renner film)
29 Brillo rival
30 Frasier opponent
31 Industry, slangily
32 Some patriarchs
34 Crossed (out)
35 Hurry-scurry
36 NY Rangers' home ice
39 Troon resident
42 Levine on "The Voice"
44 Hint of a gas leak
45 Em or Mame
47 One who acts for actors
48 Kayak alternative
49 "The Bridge" singer John
51 Baseball practice bat
52 Cinque Terre National Park locale
53 College football rankings
54 Sound at an egg toss
56 Advance
57 Long Island park
60 Fore's opposite

DENTAL DIRECTIVE   by Lee Taylor
. . . and that directive pertains to four long answers.

ACROSS
1 Fowl crops
5 Expert hand
11 NYC's Tappan ___ Bridge
14 Sal the mule's canal
15 Flagged a cab
16 Brown league
17 Europe, in the 2018 Ryder Cup
19 Ball prop
20 Carlos Santana, e.g.
21 Repeat offender
23 Will Ferrell Christmas film
24 Caress
25 More exposed
27 Ignited
28 Thunderstruck
32 ___ rock
33 **Dental directive: Part 1**
35 Whodunit discovery
37 Showing elegance
39 Bill with Hamilton
40 As of this day
41 **Dental directive: Part 2**
42 Barely manage, with "out"
43 Not too many
44 Dry, as wine
45 Not as well done
47 Anise liqueur
50 Ghostly form
51 Hunter's sauce
54 Father of geometry
57 Bagel topper
58 Blinds alternative
60 Copycat
61 Sing plainsong
62 Adam's apple locale
63 "Owner of a Lonely Heart" band
64 Pigpens
65 Thurber's "The Catbird ___"

DOWN
1 Cry like a baby
2 "Nessun dorma," e.g.
3 Snowy season, in verse
4 Forgetful with age
5 "Say it isn't so!"
6 Jet ___
7 Come apart
8 Easily influenced
9 Hung new wallpaper, e.g.
10 NFL receiver Beckham
11 Tubular pasta
12 At any time
13 Took a close look
18 Leading
22 Dr. Dre's earphones
24 Take off
25 "Silence!" in Roma
26 Standoffish
29 Windshield clearer
30 Call forth
31 Prevent
34 Capital of Panama?
35 School for future docs
36 Unpleasant and difficult
38 Stares open-mouthed
39 Quirks
41 Odd fellows
44 Some actors perform their own
46 Utah national park
48 Drifting
49 The Pont Neuf crosses it
51 Mason bee's nest material
52 It springs eternal
53 Says, "You're fired!"
54 Shropshire sisters
55 Concept
56 Fender bender outcome
59 Ketel ___ vodka

8 WHEN IN ROME by Gary Larson
In 1935, 23 Across introduced their first superhero, Doctor Occult.

ACROSS

1 City on the Rhine
5 Sporty Camaro
9 Part of a Latin trio
13 Alternatively
14 Contact lens cleaner brand
15 Metallic sound
16 Fifty-one cats?
18 Dispatch
19 Like baby aspirin
20 Reason for a siren
22 Suffix used with numbers
23 Six hundred stand-ups?
24 Eye sores
27 Start of a baseball song
28 Big name in private jets
29 Bordeaux wine
30 Ventilate
34 Son of Prince Valiant
35 Half-dozen monarchs?
37 Not only that but also
38 London landmark
40 Dead heat
41 Driver's warning
42 English poet John
44 No-no's
45 Five hundred and one martens?
48 For each one
49 At hand
50 Sign of an error
54 Match game?
55 Eleven hundred Trump namesakes?
57 Birchbark
58 Long stretches
59 Sack opener
60 "A Prayer for ___ Meany": Irving
61 Decisive time
62 Smooth sailing

DOWN

1 Round sound
2 Miscellany
3 Warning letters on internet sites
4 More hard-up
5 March marchers
6 Russo of "Get Shorty"
7 Solitary
8 Filmdom's John or Joan
9 The boy who cried wolf, for one
10 Kenyan nomads
11 Caper
12 Timetables, briefly
15 Auto-trim metals
17 Red-ink amount
21 When mammoths became extinct
23 1838 Mormon War vigilantes
24 Meat loaf serving
25 Hatcher of "Desperate Housewives"
26 2009 PGA Championship winner
27 Kesha's "___ Tok"
29 Old records
31 By and by
32 Fruity pastry
33 Appraises
35 Talkative
36 Palindromic diarist
39 Bygone Borders rival
41 Leave in the lurch
43 Considered
44 Campus bigwig
45 Music genre
46 Acquired relative
47 Scottish biscuit
48 Lacking imagination
50 Poet St. Vincent Millay
51 Crazy bone
52 Vitamin amts.
53 Glimpse
56 Chowder fish

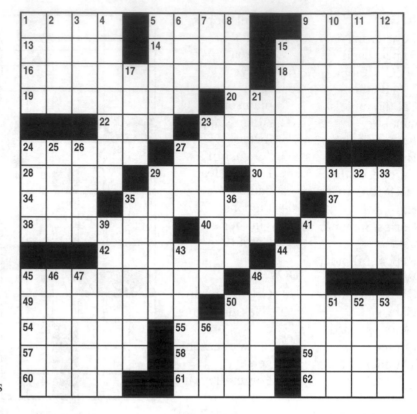

SPY GAME   by Gary Larson
44 Across had a film career that spanned seventy-seven years.

ACROSS

1 Priestly garb
4 "Horned" TCU team
9 Kind of fund
14 Bud's comedy bud
15 Cricket sound
16 Rapids transit
17 Jim Bakker's org.
18 Samurai's bushido, e.g.
20 Kind of bomb
22 Some Lowe's purchases
23 Entrance fee
27 Scoreboard trio
28 By and large
29 Mr. Chekov of "Star Trek"
31 Wanderers
35 Kid's ball material
36 They're in the back of the paper
40 Frost
41 Access
42 Elliptical path
44 "Arthur" Oscar winner John
49 Compass point
50 Christmas office tradition
54 "MADtv" regular Frank
56 Draft, maybe
57 Rainbow herbicide
61 Bother
62 "Goldilocks" playwrights
63 Sandwiches for dessert
64 Boy in a Johnny Cash song
65 "Ah, Wilderness!" mother
66 Early PC operating system
67 Nine-digit ID

DOWN

1 Peruvian wool
2 Numbers games
3 Watch brand
4 TV monitor?
5 Sorority letter
6 Suffix for fact
7 Scacchi in "Beyond the Sea"
8 Animal trail
9 Drag around
10 Golden Triangle land
11 Rattled
12 Lozenges, e.g.
13 Martha Stewart's "Men in Black II" role
19 London brume
21 French sea
24 Heads up
25 Intimate
26 Surround
30 Tokyo-based carrier
32 Astern
33 Sad song
34 Get the picture
36 Prom night wear
37 Mailroom machines
38 Gold of "Entourage"
39 Poor marks
40 Corn pone's cousin
43 Big-eye fly
45 Big pooch
46 Banded rock
47 Womb
48 Obscure
51 Rocker Brian
52 PlayStation disc
53 Surf sounds
55 Cross inscription
58 Homer's TV neighbor
59 Gunk
60 Twisty turn

"LET'S DANCE"*   by Kathy Matheson
Kathy pays tribute to a rock legend below.

ACROSS

1 "Let's Dance" singer (with 70-A)
6 "Waterfalls" trio
9 Create a lasting impression?
13 Indoor workout system
15 Sound of relief
16 Mountain goat's perch
17 Like some trivia
18 Ronan Farrow's mom
19 For fear that
20 Highest percentage of U.S. filmgoers*
23 Sister or mother
24 New Orleans-to-Miami dir.
25 "Elementary" actor Quinn
27 Georgia, to Georgette
29 Trial run at a car dealership
33 Airline to Stockholm
36 Earring spot
37 Absorb, as an expense
38 Ogres and trolls, e.g.*
42 Political commentator Navarro
43 Alphabet quartet
44 Handheld Sony game console
45 Reached out to
48 "Don't throw bouquets ___ . . ."
52 Late-night TBS show
53 Some online chats
56 Cheerios grain
57 Motor City bank run?*
62 C&W artist McEntire
63 Leslie on "Parks and Recreation"
64 Handled properly
65 Opera phantom's first name
66 Aperture
67 Materialize
68 "Insecure" star Rae
69 Patrick Mahomes target
70 See 1 Across

DOWN

1 Johnson in "Rampage"
2 Remove the stuffiness
3 Andean animal
4 Welsh form of John
5 Griminess
6 Break, in the corral
7 Place to hibernate
8 Spicy tea
9 Patisserie offering
10 More fashionable
11 Tapioca sources
12 Driver's lic. figure
14 Afternoon gatherings, in London
21 Got together
22 Military students
26 Monarch trap
28 Screening org. at ATL
30 Nix the wedding industrial complex
31 Junior
32 Shortening used in recipes?
34 Versace rival
35 Match audio with video
38 Eavesdroppers
39 Marijuana
40 French word?
41 Org. concerned about asbestos
42 Duke's conference
46 Godzilla creator Tomoyuki ___
47 Accomplished
49 Jarringly unfamiliar
50 Tiki bar drink
51 Automaker Bugatti
54 Arizona city or sight
55 Assembly guide "2"
58 UFC octagon
59 Model wife of 1 Across
60 Force in Times Square
61 Seized wheels
62 L.L.Bean rival

11 EXPERIENCING DIPLOPIA   by Christopher Liebel
The title explains itself at 57 Across.

ACROSS

1 Like 24-karat gold
5 "No ___, no foul"
9 Marshall Island test subject
14 West Wing office
15 Blue Bonnet product
16 Selection
17 Loutish
18 Organic fuel
19 Dispatch
20 Opens with a mouse*
23 Country ravaged by a 2010 earthquake
24 Some Michelangelo works
28 Pronouncement
32 Old radio tube
33 Outing for two couples*
36 Sportscaster Andrews
37 "You" homophone
38 Bad movie rating
42 Astronaut Grissom
43 Make like a hot dog
45 Hurried pace*
47 Russian folk dance
50 Rock band, Sonic ____
51 Role for Ronda Rousey in "Entourage"
53 Overhead coverings
57 Experiencing diplopia
61 Initiated
64 Explorer who says "Lo hicimos!"
65 Like the ol' days, proverbially
66 Bay window
67 Cut out
68 Hither
69 Violet variety
70 "The Chi" creator Waithe
71 Bygone monarch

DOWN

1 Yankee Stadium has a short one in right field
2 It may be irritated by strep throat
3 Bike spokes, e.g.
4 Chosen one
5 49 Down ingredient
6 Baldwin in "Beetlejuice"
7 "The ___ Slim Shady"
8 Theme
9 Phisherman?
10 Old term for a two wood
11 Eye
12 Prefix for function
13 Top seed's reward
21 Affectionate form of address
22 Obsolete PC monitor
25 Elizabeth II's favorite dog
26 Detestation
27 "Common ___": Paine
29 McKellen or McShane
30 Dementia pugilistica
31 Prickly
33 Well statistic
34 See 48 Down
35 Andrea Bocelli, for one
39 Uruguayan uncle
40 Dalton: Abbr.
41 So out it's in
44 Kleenex
46 Brain wave
48 With 34 Down, highly cognizant of
49 Taphouse serving
52 Emma Castro's brother
54 Double reeds
55 Plant life
56 Ceremonial meal
58 Protuberance
59 Show canines
60 It's mined and crunched
61 Jazz style
62 Baseball stat
63 Tom Collins ingredient

ACROSS

1 Engaged in hostilities
6 Unit of laundry
10 Suffragist Carrie Chapman ___
14 "Pal Joey" novelist
15 Points out
17 Hold sway
18 Plant to avoid contact with
19 Puente's favorite salsa partner?
21 Some bowls
22 Roadside warning sign
23 Pushrod pushers
26 In the rococo style
31 "Solve or spin?" asker
35 Shakespeare shrew's cry?
37 Mireille of "The Killing"
38 Work hard
39 Flash Gordon's merciless foe
40 Book about Hawke?
42 Lingerie item
43 Sit-down affair
44 LBJ or JFK
46 Pump product
48 Hinge problem
53 PGA motto?
58 Minute part
59 Grate stuff
60 It shows the lay of the land
61 Peanut Butter Cup inventor
62 Procedural part
63 "Lux et Veritas" school
64 Proof goof

DOWN

1 It comes straight from the heart
2 His and her
3 Ralph of "The Waltons"
4 Incandescent lamp gas
5 Rifle
6 Slimming surgery, briefly
7 Estimating words
8 Some tennis scores
9 Make public
10 "Pretty please?"
11 At the apex of
12 Brit breaks
13 Cluck of condescension
16 Associate
20 Johnny Reb's org.
24 Dog in "The Mask"
25 Overwhelm
27 Reputation
28 In the thick of
29 Watch over
30 Pushing the envelope
31 Rank competitors
32 "No" voter
33 "Your Song" singer
34 Straight ___ arrow
36 State emphatically
38 Form in layers
41 Cancel out
42 Draftsman's tool
45 Paul Anka's "___ Beso"
47 Aunt of Bart Simpson
49 Racing's Al or Bobby
50 Anesthesia of old
51 Playground retort
52 Comical bandleader Kay
53 Dr. Dre contemporary
54 Ceramic floor piece
55 Barber's stroke
56 Airline to TLV
57 Good Hope, for one
58 Jrs. superiors

13 THEMELESS by Alyssa Brooke
3 Down has been called "The First Lady of the musical comedy stage."

ACROSS

1 Track support
8 Tiny life form
15 Teri of "Desperate Housewives"
16 Guilt-ridden
17 H.W. Bush campaign slogan (with 36-A)
19 Handle
20 Neighbor of Leb.
21 Band together
22 Hawked
23 Beany's TV friend
25 German auto
26 Office slips
28 Object
30 "A Midsummer Night's Dream" fairy
32 Getting the most "aws"
35 Limbo need
36 See 17 Across
40 Slightest bit of money
41 Ready for battle
43 Dedicated lines
44 "Your Movie Sucks" author
46 Corp. recruits
47 NFL Hall-of-Famer Terrell
49 Golden Rule word
50 First word in a Bill Withers hit
51 Orange container
52 Get top billing
53 The big guns
56 Chin coverage
59 Chow
63 Like elbows boiled for 7 minutes
64 Football captain's choice
65 Zoo inhabitants
66 Excavate further

DOWN

1 Spring events
2 Odds, e.g.
3 "There's No Business Like Show Business" singer
4 One giving a lecture
5 Fall heavily
6 Guitar master Paul
7 Clears the board
8 El Prado's city
9 AOL or Earthlink, e.g.
10 Chinese dynasty
11 Postponed game
12 Everywhere
13 "The Divine Miss M"
14 Ford flub
18 Former U.S. capital
23 Last C of ACC
24 Walesa of Polish politics
27 It may swing
29 Trumpet muffler
30 "Dreams from My Father" memoirist
31 Benton of "Hee Haw"
33 Somewhat, slangily
34 Literacy volunteer, e.g.
37 Hardly a skyscraper
38 Nonpareil
39 Not so tough
42 Subjects of wills
45 Eager beaver
47 Some Mozart works
48 Placed in the Open
54 Flat rate
55 Pilaf ingredient
56 Chew the fat
57 José's huzzah
58 Toothpaste box letters
60 Impudence
61 Holiday threshold
62 Sam Houston, for 13 yrs.

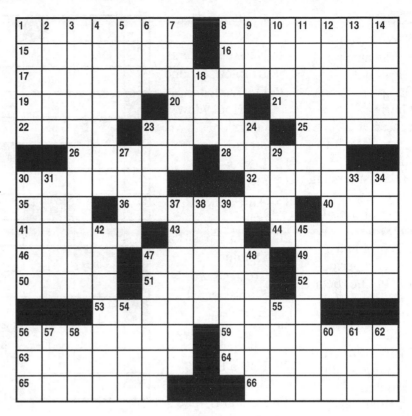

14 THE NAKED TRUTH   by Harvey Estes
As a stand-alone answer, 19 Across could be clued "laundry basket."

ACROSS

1 Served well
5 Come up short
9 Clean out
14 Samples
16 Glaringly sensational
17 Like feet with three parts
18 Heaviest fencing weapons
19 **Start of a nudist maxim**
21 Lid problem
22 Puberty period
23 Eta but not beta
26 Museum guide
29 "Be right with you!"
31 **More of maxim**
35 Printing widths
36 Geometry calculations
38 "Isn't ___ bit like . . .": Beatles
39 **More of maxim**
42 Think highly of
45 Call for
47 Wolf calls
48 First words in "Ozymandias"
50 Every 24 hours
52 **End of maxim**
57 No-frills
58 Quarantine
60 Unequaled
61 Dry rub alternatives
62 Hammer targets
63 Father of Deimos
64 Drug lord in "Scarface"

DOWN

1 Bedouin shirt
2 Supreme mil. leader
3 Series ender
4 Gives testimony
5 Not on the up and up
6 Chipped in
7 Reply to "That a fact?"
8 Nessie's waters
9 Krypton, for one
10 Dr. Teeth and Dr. Honeydew
11 Obsess over dress
12 Levels
13 QB stat
15 Agree out of court
20 Military position
23 Opinion
24 Treater's words
25 Slim-waisted flyer
27 "SNL" alumna Cheri
28 Half a Latin dance
30 Lounging robe
32 "That was close!"
33 Part of a pump
34 Tasty tubers
37 Stephen of "Breakfast on Pluto"
40 Offending the olfactories
41 Leads on
43 Medicine man
44 Corolla and Camry
46 Pakistani metropolis
48 Nationality prefix
49 Kind of jar
51 Sub stations
53 Award for Arijit Singh
54 Romanov ruler
55 Stereotypical canine
56 Alabama and Auburn, e.g.
57 Diamond corner
59 Decryption org.

15 SOLE-SEARCHING by Harvey Estes
A good one to solve with your sole mate!

ACROSS

1 Rocker Allman
6 Parting words
10 Southwestern art center
14 Beyond the fringe
15 Lucy Lawless TV role
16 Least of the litter
17 Place for rings
18 Like some airports: Abbr.
19 Song for Scotto
20 Sole
23 U-turn from SSW
24 Kidnap cattle
25 "Phooey!"
29 "Deck the Halls" phrase
30 Ancient Troy
31 Easily split stuff
32 Court records
36 Sole
39 Lays eyes on
40 Fin components
41 Crimean conference site
42 Porter's regretful miss
43 Ben of "Roots"
44 Small-time
47 Similarity suffix
48 Sole
54 Apple or orange
55 Type of code
56 Davis of "Do the Right Thing"
57 Israel's Abba
58 Spill the beans
59 Primary strategy
60 Eastern skillets
61 Frozen treat brand
62 "The Cat in the Hat" author

DOWN

1 Wear the disguise of
2 Lord over a kingdom
3 Jazz singer James
4 Steffi of courts
5 Apache chief
6 Lime, for example
7 Give a little
8 Works together
9 Bankhead in "Lifeboat"
10 Religious pamphlet
11 Of the ear
12 Cooling
13 Order to Rex
21 Hudson Bay prov.
22 "This ___ bust!"
25 Claim-stakers' word
26 Skin moisturizer
27 Marquee word
28 Gumption
29 High-pitched flutes
31 Kept track of
32 Yon
33 "Anything Goes" composer Porter
34 Haul around
35 ___ impasse (stuck)
37 Build a fire under
38 Visine dose
42 "Star Wars" name
43 By means of
44 Supercharger
45 Inflict
46 Roasting places
47 Many tracks
48 Goulash, for example
49 Count (on)
50 Man, for one
51 Seesaw sitter of verse
52 Cans for Brits
53 Simpatico sounds

16 ANIMAL FARM   by Jim Holland
. . . with apologies to George Orwell.

ACROSS

1 "The Alienist" author
5 Literary bear
9 Did a farrier's job
14 "Wake Me Up" singer Blacc
15 Guacamole tomato
16 "The Power of Positive Thinking" author
17 Taurine earthmover?
19 ___ up and up
20 Campaign tactic
21 Natural pain reliever
23 Ballerina's "pointe"
25 Art Deco artist
26 Ovine knot?
31 Outlay
35 Mauna ___
36 Unseals, à la Keats
37 Bring the puck down
38 Middle-earth creature
39 Free, in a way
42 Gob
43 Official decree
45 Calhoun or McIlroy
46 Do this on the side of caution
47 Literary dog
48 Anserine pie fruit?
51 Calendar row
53 Golfer known as "The Big Easy"
54 Soaring glider
59 In ___ (unborn)
63 Like a poltergeist
64 Porcinely stubborn?
66 Miniscule amount
67 "Picnic" playwright
68 Deadlocked
69 Rush-hour din
70 Fire residue
71 Startled responses

DOWN

1 Uber competitors
2 Reunion goer, briefly
3 Milk, to Penn
4 Have similar sensations
5 Motion beginning
6 Yucky stuff to step in
7 Comet, to some
8 Get tough
9 Fun and games
10 Chickeny kiss on the cheek?
11 ___ of office
12 Education range
13 Celebrity chef Paula
18 One with no class?
22 "Mork and Mindy" planet
24 Stephen A. Smith's network
26 Winter weather
27 1953 John Wayne flick
28 "Weird Al" parody of a Jackson hit
29 "___ got the whole world . . ."
30 Space City baseballer
32 Grit network film
33 Brenda in the comics
34 Cloth type
37 Heavenly shade
40 iPhone XS platform
41 Manitoba Indian
44 Bovine hair tuft?
48 One solution to a 44 Down
49 Giraffe relatives
50 Mar-a-Lago, e.g.
52 Triple-edged swords
54 Curry, for one
55 Dynamic beginning
56 Nation once headed by a shah
57 Señora's son
58 Waffles brand
60 Sedgwick of Warhol films
61 Smell of smoke
62 They can be even, ironically
65 ___ up (agitated)

DO THE MATH   by Jim Holland
Number-crunch these clues to discover a most original theme.

ACROSS

1 Big gap
6 Like Michael Jordan
10 Swindle
14 Sunny beginning?
15 Tight score
16 Luau lutes
17 O'Conner's SCOTUS successor
18 Curious to a fault
19 Choice provider
20 What clue* answers have in common
23 Lisbon–Madrid dir.
24 Not just anybody
25 Mexican political party
28 Good Hindu spirit
29 Gandhi and Jaising
31 Cheer up*
34 Like MGM's mascot*
35 Radius neighbor
36 Muslim prince
37 Dexterity*
41 Western red bark tree*
44 Greg in "Heaven is for Real"
45 Part of a Latin trio
46 So far
47 Acting pouty
49 ___ up (energize)
52 Hidden feature of each clue* answer
54 Pole, for one
57 His flagship was the "Scharnhorst"
58 Salon service or product
59 Hubbub of activity
60 Geek Squad client
61 Revival cries
62 4332.71 Jupiter days
63 Hansa and Hansson
64 Begets

DOWN

1 Man on the $10,000 bill
2 Oscar winner Mirren
3 "Stayin' ___": Bee Gees
4 Location
5 Lunar disappearing act
6 Rag-and-___ (London junk dealer)
7 Make ___ of (write down)
8 Mr. Clean competitor
9 Revered group member
10 Cadges
11 Presidential nickname
12 Deighton or Dawson
13 Wildcats in the Big 12
21 Aphrodite's realm
22 Make over
25 Hawaiian beer brand
26 Arrested
27 Grenoble river
28 Gradually exhaust
30 Motionless
31 UConn mascot
32 "Dallas" matriarch
33 Regarding
38 Marilyn Manson cofounder Gidget
39 "Reach for the sky!"
40 Wander
41 Popular Christmas depictions
42 Cole Porter's "I ___ Love"
43 Moonflowers
48 Villainous expression
49 Dogpatch dad
50 Intermediate, in law
51 Full-court ___
52 Always
53 "La Bohème" heroine
54 Lacking
55 Golf position
56 "13th" director DuVernay

18 PRODUCT PLACEMENT by Robert W. Harris

59 Across was known to give Harry a hard time.

ACROSS

1 Frau's counterpart
5 Taking out the trash, perhaps
10 Mrs. Fletcher, to friend Seth
14 S-shaped molding
15 Spicy Chinese cooking
16 Prefix with "lung" and "marine"
17 Insecticide used by New York's finest?
19 Batter's option
20 Chinese zodiac animal
21 "Downton Abbey" dog
23 Tuna variety
24 Identifying mark
25 Antiperspirant for frequent fliers?
27 ___ of omission
28 Okla. City, relative to Tucson
30 Glorifies
31 Super's concern: Abbr.
33 "Born from jets" automaker
36 Summers on the French Riviera
37 Bath soap for liberals?
40 Regard as
42 Patronize 43 Across
43 Website for handmade items
47 Virgil masterpiece
49 Proto suffix
51 Abbr. at Reagan
52 Furniture polish used on "All Things Considered"?
55 Bob and Carol and Ted and Alice
57 Openings
58 Capital of Spain
59 Potions Master at Hogwarts
60 Semis
62 Laundry detergent popular from 1945 to 1991?
65 Declare as true
66 Provide with a quality
67 Baseball's Hershiser
68 The first canvas-top "sneaker"
69 Former PGA Commissioner Beman
70 Zip

DOWN

1 Hip partner
2 Self-gratifying experience
3 Showing dependence
4 Wield the scepter
5 "Just Like Jesse James" singer
6 "M.J." of the LPGA
7 Radio studio sign
8 Mrs. Gorbachev
9 Salad green
10 Poke
11 Serene
12 Beach bonnets
13 Certain smooth fabrics
18 Surrender
22 Battle of the ___
24 Grp. founded by Robert Baden-Powell
25 Milkmaid's handful
26 Starbucks order
29 Stamp on a bad check
32 ___ like a log
34 Expression of disgust in Cologne
35 The hard stuff
38 Runner Zátopek
39 Mil. address
40 Keep from having
41 Seething
44 Poster paint
45 Directed
46 NFL stats
47 Polar parka
48 Confounded
50 "Frozen" princess
53 Monotonous tone
54 "A Woman Called ___" (1982)
56 Baseball's "Hammerin' Hank"
59 ___'Pea of "Popeye"
61 Class that's soon to leave: Abbr.
63 Brownish gray
64 In the manner of

19 BRIEF TOUR OF EUROPE* by Robert W. Harris
42 Down may be viewed in Jerusalem's Shrine of the Book.

ACROSS

1 Rolltop
5 Gangster's piece
8 Big name in car oil filters
12 Seed cover
13 4,840 square yards
15 "Kinky Boots" drag queen
16 Lillehammer spring holiday?*
18 Arab rulers
20 Slender
21 "Sara ___": Hall & Oates
23 "Skedaddle!"
24 Like Steve Austin
26 Brussels poem passage?*
28 Prefix for duct
29 Score for Taylor Hall
31 Put down
32 Copenhagen parent?*
35 Not active
36 6000-foot Greek peak
37 Custard ingredients
40 MCAT, for example
43 Granada vacation spot?*
48 Type of tax
51 Pale yellow Dutch cheese
52 Churchill's sign
53 Lisbon party gift?*
55 Shoot in the direction of
57 Simpson trial judge
58 1945 conference site
60 Par for the course
61 Corker
63 Esch-sur-Alzette fluid?*
66 Tip-off
67 "The Philistines" novelist Bates
68 "Ex Scientia Tridens" school
69 Tag on many yard sale items
70 Petition earnestly
71 Brain tests

DOWN

1 McGrew in a Service poem
2 Tending to wear away
3 T-bone alternative
4 Calvin of fashion
5 Furnace fuel
6 Book between John and Romans
7 Quake
8 Take to the cleaners
9 "Deep Space Nine" Ferengi
10 Adjusted the wheels
11 Matrimonial
14 Jay Gould's railway
17 Friends in Monterrey
19 Fireplace material
22 JFK's honorary Harvard degree
24 Hunk's pride
25 GI beds
27 Not quite right
30 Sounds of surprise
33 Decorative pattern
34 Process text
38 Seven-time Wimbledon champ
39 Sign between Taurus and Cancer
40 Lukewarm
41 Strange and intriguing objects
42 Qumran Caves discoveries
44 Make unsettled
45 Make trite
46 Widening a hole
47 Vietnamese New Year
49 Accept a proposal
50 Mendes in "Hitch"
54 Ceramic jar with a short wide neck
56 Outdoor game played with mallets
59 Spindle
62 George Sand's "Elle et ___"
64 Official record
65 ___ in dog

"PLAY BALL!" by Mark McClain
A good one to solve on Opening Day.

ACROSS

1 Writes in a rush
5 Mater lead-in
9 Rivera in MoMA
14 Website for DIYers
15 Bad state to be in
16 Concluded
17 World Cup org.
18 Gorilla's lack
19 Gave up, by treaty
20 Extremely unpleasant area?
23 All alternative
24 Oakland commuters' org.
25 Canoe for guests at a Polynesian resort?
32 Sweater size: Abbr.
33 TV's Warrior Princess
34 Gibbs of "The Jeffersons"
35 Lena in "The Reader"
37 "Don't play" symbols
40 Ireland's ___ Féin
41 Affair of the heart
43 Baum pooch
45 Hay burner
46 Typical amount of stuffing for quilts?
50 Opener for cop or call
51 Teacher's ___
52 Pile of orders from a whizbang sales rep?
58 Bone prefix
60 "Milk's Favorite Cookie"
61 Where Bhutan is
62 Reeves in "To the Bone"
63 Bearing
64 Offshoot group
65 Angler's moves
66 Popular Japanese seafood
67 Sierra Club logo, essentially

DOWN

1 Gordon of NASCAR
2 Sandusky locale
3 Veggie burger ingredient
4 Marshy lowlands
5 Sloth relative
6 Shakespearean king
7 Golda of Israel
8 Wings it
9 Proper behavior
10 Xenon, e.g.
11 Swirling water
12 "Who knew?"
13 Goofy
21 Cereal since 1954
22 Skosh
25 "All That Jazz" singer in "Chicago"
26 ___ savant
27 Hurricane category
28 Selassie disciple
29 Faucet repair item
30 Arm bones
31 Zingy taste
32 Utah city on the Colorado
36 Beneficial food element
38 "Mazel ___!"
39 Some acquired kin
42 Very merry
44 Provo neighbor
47 "SNL" airer
48 "Get lost!"
49 Celebratory phrase
52 Sch. support orgs.
53 View from Sandusky
54 Scottish dance
55 Geek Squad client
56 French Riviera city
57 Field on many forms
58 NBA Thunder logo letters
59 "Finding Dory" setting

21 STEWED AND BAKED   by Derek Bowman
The quote by Puddleglum below can be found in "The Silver Chair."

ACROSS

1 Feed the pigs
5 "60 Minutes" correspondent
10 Lateen or spinnaker
14 Sleek, slangily
15 Arapaho abode
16 Doing
17 Place to play ladder toss
18 Wee small hour
19 Mr. Coffee button
20 2010 Ben Affleck thriller
22 "The Entertainer" genre
24 **Start of a quote from Puddleglum**
26 "In Summer" singer in "Frozen"
27 "___' Nuff" (Black Crowes box set)
28 Fedora fabric
30 **Middle of quote**
34 Pitbull's "Climate Change" label
35 Major French port
36 Rome's ___ Veneto
37 Oh's "Grey's Anatomy" role
39 Spanish girlfriend
40 It's simply not right
41 **End of quote**
44 Scout's pride
47 Last
51 Adjective for 55 Across
52 Campaign staple
55 "Narnia" lion
56 Scalawag
57 "The Chronicles of Narnia" author
60 It can finish a round, briefly
61 Sugarloaf Mountain site
62 Kesselring's "Arsenic" partner
63 TiVo button
64 Tennis do-over
65 Having muscle pain
66 Yggdrasil of Norse mythology, for one

DOWN

1 Cure, in a way
2 Biblical mother of Levi
3 Like Big Brother
4 Ottawa leader
5 Vermont ski resort
6 Adidas product
7 Chest beater
8 Words from a wise monkey
9 Paul in "Stateside"
10 Not so blatantly obvious
11 #1 hit for Pat Boone in 1957
12 Tabloid twosome
13 Flockhart's "Brothers & Sisters" costar
21 Haggis ingredient
23 Social faux pas
25 Make a bundle on the farm
26 Seal hunter
29 Happy letters for 9-to-5ers
30 Brown trout?
31 Fires off
32 Statue garment
33 Convened
38 "Poker Face" singer
40 Christmas tree twinklers
42 Former AOL rival
43 "Be right there!"
44 Bar hustler
45 Hammer in "The Lone Ranger"
46 Bus stop
48 Prefix for sonic
49 Cleans up at the roulette table?
50 Fisherman in "Carousel"
52 Alan in "The Aviator"
53 Big name in Round Rock
54 Goody bag contents
58 Underhanded
59 Here, in Dijon

22 MATRIMONIAL MUSIC by Frances Burton
Paul wrote 20 Across for Peter Yarrow's marriage ceremony.

ACROSS

1 Tibia
5 Long green
9 Foibles
14 ___-my-thumb
15 S-curve
16 Sister of Polyhymnia
17 Love of the Latin language
18 Sarabi's warning
19 Brazil city
20 Paul Stookey tune
23 Libation station potation
24 Essential amino acid
25 Rod's mate
27 Dixie Cups tune
33 "S.W.A.T." network
36 Stash away
37 Forearm nerve
38 Jacket feature
41 Basket hoop
42 Hideaways
43 Rocker Cooper
44 Pass over lightly
46 Nay's opposite
47 The Platters tune
51 Suds
52 Comfort
56 Kingdom of ___ Vijaya
58 Bee Gees tune
62 Florida island near Naples
64 Radiate
65 First name in lexicography
66 Most of the Earth's surface
67 Falling-out
68 Musical combo
69 P.C. Wren hero
70 Choir voice
71 ___ souci

DOWN

1 Afghan
2 Comfy-cozy
3 Apple products
4 Scandinavian
5 Eye parts
6 Excited
7 The Red and the Dead
8 Good guy
9 Vindictive
10 Certain TD Ameritrade acct.
11 Barcelona locale
12 Lat. list shortener
13 Fish served meunière
21 Internet abbr.
22 Conservative e-zine on Twitter
26 "Enchanted" Levine heroine
28 Indian Zoroastrian
29 Wicked ways
30 Primate of Madagascar
31 Diversify
32 Irish
33 Dragon nail
34 "Eat, Pray, Love" setting
35 Battle of Britain fighters
39 Sympathetic response
40 Not to mention
45 Italian rice dish
48 Med. insurer
49 Neither mate
50 Sparkles
53 Athenian meeting place
54 Kind of gang not to join
55 Character
56 Air pollution
57 Le Mans event
59 Designer Wang
60 "Casablanca" croupier
61 Look through
63 Jellicle Ball attendee

TOTO by Max Carpenter
Old-school clue for 15 Across: Guido's high note.

ACROSS

1 Scottish chieftain
6 "Arabian Nights" bird
9 Red-headed Lindsay
14 Bleacher bum's sign
15 Common Core test: Abbr.
16 West Indies vacation spot
17 "___ of Winter" (1992)
18 Caboose, for one
19 Defies existence
20 Toto
23 Casey of Cooperstown
24 Lobster eater's wear
25 Touchscreen widget
28 Right angles
30 Recon unit
32 Prefix for vac
36 Blackguard
38 Tahrir Square locale
39 Toto
42 Shoelace tip
43 DVR model
44 Chicago-style pizza chain
45 Circus chair holders
47 Celebratory bash
49 Español envelope abbr.
50 Broadcasting ether
52 Slung mud at
57 Toto
60 Seeing things
62 Stooge with a bowl cut
63 It eats shoots and leaves
64 Strand, as a whale
65 Electrolyte trade-off
66 Stay afloat
67 "The Devil and Daniel Webster" author
68 Classic Jaguar model
69 Keeps as is

DOWN

1 Makes ice water
2 Bandleader's "Go!"
3 Blow away
4 "Memento" director
5 Leave the chrysalis
6 Call to mind
7 Snoopy's misfit brother
8 Ersatz chocolate
9 Unlike a type A
10 Roughly
11 Liszt's "___ Rhapsodies"
12 Hematology system
13 D.C. slugger, casually
21 Parliament of India site
22 Zilch
26 X-rated
27 Trudging footfalls
29 Stroke of the pen
31 Dana's "forbidden fragrance"
32 7.5-hour tests
33 "Nursery Suite" composer
34 Carriage dog
35 "Interesting . . ."
37 Staple of romcoms
40 Kind of flush
41 Vodka cocktail, for short
46 Part of RSVP
48 Whets the appetite
51 Altered recording
53 Disjointed
54 Rajah's wife
55 Finish by
56 Twosomes
58 "Falling Slowly" musical
59 Copped
60 Tidal recession
61 "___ haw!"

FRIENDS OF MOTHER GOOSE by Gayle Dean
Alternate clue for 9 Across: Lady's love.

ACROSS

1 Film editing transition
5 One who runs for Congress
9 "My Three Sons" dog
14 Andrea Bocelli number
15 "Bad Lieutenant" director Ferrara
16 Baklava ingredient
17 Follows closely
18 Humpty Dumpty
20 Twinklings
22 Lady Gaga dress size
23 Ex-lax?
24 Relief pitcher's goal
25 Rudder locale
27 Untouchable one
32 Worked on the "Pequod"
34 "I Remember Mama" papa
35 "Blecch!"
36 Smarmy
37 Sister of Terpsichore
39 Algonquian Indian
40 E. Waugh's "The Loved ___"
41 Dundee native
42 Gaol officer
44 Understands
47 Metcalfe of "Desperate Housewives"
48 Cupbearer to the gods
49 Answering machine button
51 Hall of games
54 Surmounted
57 Little Boy Blue
59 Ubiquitous abbr.
60 Maria Tallchief's tribe
61 Machu Picchu site
62 Barclays Center team
63 Swerved, at sea
64 Arabian Peninsula port
65 Tarzan's home

DOWN

1 African arroyo
2 Fe, to chemists
3 Tom
4 How the Amazon River flows
5 "En passant" captures
6 Diminishes
7 Salon goops
8 Expansion wing
9 The Merry Men, e.g.
10 Decayed
11 Phony beginning
12 Start of a Sunday morning talk show
13 Viking crematory
19 Seafaring Depp role
21 "The Witching Hour" author Rice
24 Jazzy improv
25 Drop like a roc?
26 Quaker "yours"
28 Like Pegasus
29 Miss Muffet
30 Fancy moldings
31 "___ You Lead": Streisand
33 Noise pollution unit
38 Gallivant
39 Emblem of Turkey
41 Garden plot
43 Cracked a bit
45 Nickel and dime
46 Critical
50 "Peanuts" character
51 Call on a yawl
52 Civil Rights activist Parks
53 Part of a bird's gullet
54 Was outstanding
55 Endgame's end
56 Lord High Everything ___
58 Greek celebration shout

25 ISOGRAMS AND UNIVOCALS* by Gayle Dean
17 and 57 Across are isograms. 37 Across is a univocal.

ACROSS

1 Organ parts
6 Onion relative
10 Piggy bank feature
14 Character type never seen in "Peanuts"
15 Monty Pythoner
16 Volcano top, frozen dessert bottom
17 Scientific study of fingerprints*
20 Dr. Dre's genre
21 Up in smoke
22 Results of hard work
23 Running mates?
25 Hoppers
26 Area near TriBeCa
27 Merle Haggard's "Misery and ___"
28 Floss flavor
32 Abnormal plant swelling
34 Sweet treat
36 "The Matrix" hero
37 Vulnerability*
40 Aussie bird
41 "Like a Rolling Stone" singer
42 Thumb-types
43 Sudan crosser
45 Yuletide quaff
46 "Catalan Landscape" painter
47 "___ the Roof" (1962 Drifters hit)
49 "Candy Land" mountain
52 Sheet fabric
55 Kennedy Space Center org.
56 "All Those Years ___": Harrison
57 In the public domain*
60 Antlered animal
61 UMW workplace
62 Baby who doesn't sleep at night?
63 Soprano who'll never sing?
64 Healthful retreats
65 Band section

DOWN

1 Sky pilot
2 Model of perfection
3 Single-minded
4 Nightmare street
5 One to give props to
6 They have their pride
7 Windows 10 Web browser
8 Architect's wing
9 Custodian's belt attachments
10 Acrimonious division
11 Maxwell of Bond films
12 Start of "The Raven"
13 Theater owner in "Burlesque"
18 Houston Texans' mascot
19 Goat-legged god
24 Fleshy fruit
25 First State statesman
27 Solzhenitsyn novel setting
29 Impossible to prevent
30 Harrier home
31 Coin flip
32 "The Dragons of ___": Sagan
33 Starbucks espresso shot size
34 Serious criminal
35 A big fan of ballpark figures?
38 Similar words
39 Computer geek
44 It's given at funerals
46 Command at the Iditarod
48 Dickens orphan
49 Combat challenges
50 Eyed amorously
51 Tracy K. Smith et al.
52 Essential
53 "Golden Rule" word
54 Scrutinize
55 Fashion designer Ricci
58 Boot Hill letters
59 Thunderstrike

CLUE BUILDER   by Harvey Estes
Combine three clues to get a fourth.

ACROSS

1 Geller of "Friends"
5 Gyro holders
10 Wistful word
14 Voting no
15 Al Yankovic's "___ Paradise"
16 Freddie the Freeloader, e.g.
17 Grab with a toothpick
18 Bob Marley, for one
19 Zenith
20 CHI
23 Dress reformer Bloomer
24 Noah's fleet?
25 Nancy's "Rhoda" role
28 Guitar master Paul
29 Janet, to Tito
31 Heavy
33 LL
36 Heavy volume
39 USMC barracks boss
40 Krabappel of "The Simpsons"
41 AX
46 Butting heads
47 Deli hero
48 Palindromic boy king
51 Nancy's hubby
52 A number of books
55 Killer in a cult classic
57 CHILLAX

60 Roast insert
62 Hub-to-rim lines
63 "To be" to Henri
64 Kind of code or rug
65 Start of a legal conclusion
66 Honky-___
67 "Hey, I never thought of that!"
68 Sure-footed animals
69 Former Chicago Cub Sammy

DOWN

1 Buckwheat or Alfalfa
2 Welcome airport monitor words
3 Kind of evidence
4 Prophetess
5 Layered dessert
6 Front end of my wit's end
7 Campbell in "House Party"
8 Daisy or sunflower
9 Put in irons
10 "___ the Arab" (Ray Stevens hit)
11 Badly balanced
12 Actor Vigoda
13 One Chicago nine
21 River to the Seine
22 Exploiter
26 Faculty boss

27 Bates' wife on "Downton Abbey"
30 Rifle range report
32 First homicide victim
33 Rip to bits
34 Cooler filler
35 Where they yell "Cut!"
36 Former Russian ruler
37 "A Fish Out of Water" fish
38 Gooey sandwiches
42 Ready for press

43 Empire of Nineveh
44 Ensembles
45 Penetrating reed
48 Name in a heart, perhaps
49 180 maneuvers
50 Kansas capital
53 Wild hogs
54 Art studio subjects
56 Track events
58 Bonneville Salt Flats locale
59 Court order
60 Reagan was pres. of this
61 Golf tutor

CLUE SPLITTER   by Harvey Estes
Take a clue. Split it up. Reuse it.

ACROSS

1 Racetrack figure
5 Athlete's words to the camera
10 Trucker on the radio
14 Florentine river
15 Refrigerator handle?
16 Chaplin of "The Crimson Field"
17 Bandleader in "Dirty Dancing"
18 Pal of Andy and Barney
19 Work with feet
20 MISTRUST
23 "Ice Age" mammoth
24 Like a Greek oracle
27 Resembling Rudolph
31 Underage heartbreaker
32 Prohibition, and more
34 Pipe elbows
35 MIST
41 Sitarist Shankar
42 Bikini, e.g.
43 Mimieux of "The Time Machine"
46 Port south of Tokyo
51 Butler or maid
53 Antony listener
54 RUST
58 Salon sound
60 Overplay
61 Prefix on European
62 Wile E. Coyote's favorite brand
63 Bit of broccoli
64 Plot in Genesis
65 Busy one
66 Urgency
67 Pink inside

DOWN

1 Steele's periodical

2 Cal Ripken was one
3 Incalculable
4 Absorbed
5 "Macbeth" trio
6 Reassuring words after an accident
7 With 26 Down, singer Elliot
8 Upright
9 Mime Marceau
10 Bargain with the prosecutor
11 Graveyard of the Old West
12 WSW opposite
13 Bang into
21 Seemingly forever
22 "Xanadu" group
25 "___ cost you"
26 See 7 Down
28 Weep aloud
29 Big name in New Age music
30 Not all there
33 "Go on!"
35 Prohibitionists
36 All-night party
37 Paycheck booster
38 Rattlesnake, e.g.
39 Yellowstone bugler
40 Greenery
44 Catch some rays
45 Tangle up
47 ___-than-thou
48 Plummer of "Pulp Fiction"
49 More steamed
50 Tennis follower
52 Gulf city
55 Nay and uh-uh
56 ERA or GNP
57 No better than
58 Down in the mouth
59 E-5 or E-6, e.g.

28 PLACES TO PARTY by Mark Feldman
33 Across is located in Times Square on Broadway.

ACROSS

1 Infant's bed
9 Iced coffee drink
15 Skin cream ingredient
16 Dawn goddess
17 Place for a launch party?
18 Light shades
19 Diving birds
20 Stun gun
22 Drift off
23 Hwys.
24 Cooler
25 ___ Appia
27 Place for a wrap party?
33 Performers at Carolines
36 "Over and done with"
37 Med. care providers
38 Buzzer
39 Rights grp.
40 Out of bounds
43 Peter ___ (Spider-Man)
45 Place for a pool party?
47 Logic game
48 Crumb
49 Orlando-to-Miami dir.
52 Short flights
56 Mrs. Gorbachev
58 Collar type
59 Starling relative
61 Place for a block party?
63 Magnifiers
64 1960s–'70s TV detective
65 Execute perfectly
66 Per some prescriptions

DOWN

1 Storybook elephant
2 One way to read
3 Fleeces
4 Hardens
5 Brown, e.g.
6 Puts in order
7 Gofer's job
8 Small amounts
9 Denim and lace
10 Bemoan
11 Dry
12 Walt Kelly's strip
13 Head honcho
14 Simplify
21 Its RSVP is a link
24 Lobbying grp.
26 "Eureka!"
27 Fiber used in rugs
28 Exercise
29 Entangle
30 Pawn
31 Leer at
32 Decant
33 Freshwater fish
34 Upscale hotel
35 Flanders of fiction
38 Myanmar, before 1989
41 Take the gold
42 Like Snow White
43 Model of excellence
44 Computer key
46 Knuckleheads
49 Restrained
50 Observation balloon, e.g.
51 Ceased
52 Maintain
53 Layered treat
54 32 tablespoons
55 Middling
57 Hip bones
58 Otherwise
60 Grassy area
62 "Ready Player ___" (2018)

ACROSS

1 Bewail
4 To ___ (without exception)
8 Indian prince
13 Indicator of intelligence
15 Author Zola
16 How Rogers danced with Astaire?
17 Son of Jacob
18 Home on the range
19 Way to go
21 Park, e.g.: Abbr.
22 Song of praise
23 Competition for truckers
25 Lou Gehrig's disease: Abbr.
26 Went gaga for?
30 With plenty of space
32 Particulate solution
33 Talkative one
34 Gets ready
35 Charity
39 No Mr. Nice Guy
41 Coil of yarn
42 Did a complete 180?
46 Communication for the deaf: Abbr.
47 Ahead
48 The out crowd
50 Common ID
51 Orpheus' instrument
54 Bellyached
56 Hotel offering
58 Ready to leave the garage?
60 Flying fish eaters
61 The utmost
62 Painter of ballerinas
63 Dethrone
64 "Get the picture?"

DOWN

1 Shuffle the troops
2 Irrationality
3 Tour de France stage
4 Type of hydrocarbon
5 PC alternative
6 Gelatin substitute
7 Biblical peak
8 Take up again
9 Early hrs.
10 Islamic warrior
11 Exam taken at Eton
12 In acccordance with
13 Colo. clock setting
14 Tired, poetically
20 Spots
24 Vertical, to a sailor
25 Ready for battle
27 Phileas Fogg's creator
28 Fatty liquid
29 Con artist
31 Deadly African snake
34 ___ wagon
36 Like some gas
37 Type of point mutation
38 Weekend TV show initials
40 Like some seals
41 Pack into a ship's hold
42 Salad type
43 Having doubt
44 In possession of
45 Straight
49 Oboes, e.g.
52 Start over
53 Brother of Jacob
55 Dah's partner
57 Contents of some bags
59 Real estate ad abbr.

30 SPORTS ACHIEVEMENTS   by Victor Fleming
A playful pun-and-games challenger.

ACROSS

1 Wildly excited
5 Tiny sweater?
9 Run after
14 Big wheel's wheels
15 Floor space, e.g.
16 Sty sounds
17 Town lot
18 Look like a creep
19 Make a scene
20 Hole-in-one?
23 Smidgeon
24 Circuit failures
28 Mary in "The Runaway Bride"
31 Scratch target
34 Hold
35 "Long Island" sound
36 FSU team, familiarly
38 Air-traffic overseer, initially
39 Ace?
42 Spot for travelers
43 Showed one's fallibility
44 Every seven days
45 Rules, briefly
47 June celebrants
48 Jell-O formers
49 Monk of yore
51 Bit of granola
52 Strike?
59 Bill's "Groundhog Day" costar
62 Leave unacknowledged
63 Man or boy
64 Plank
65 Dentist's request
66 Student stressor
67 Think piece
68 Unrest
69 Lowers, as lights

DOWN

1 European range
2 Supplied with an expensive coat
3 Catcher Narváez
4 Proceed with vigor
5 Was visibly afraid
6 Creme-filled cookie
7 Sandy ridge
8 House of Lords title
9 Sports hiree
10 Wild Bill of the Old West
11 Farm inhabitant
12 UPC cousin
13 Clairvoyance, for short
21 Dojo teaching
22 Groom's man
25 Get more gas
26 Became weepy, with "up"
27 Disciplines, in a way
28 Strive
29 Bakery items
30 Some nouns
31 Prefix with "red" or "structure"
32 ___ down (moderated)
33 Boors
37 Navigating aid
40 Law partner
41 Cheated on
46 Savings option for some
50 In want
51 Ferret's kin
53 Watch chains
54 Let out
55 Start to bank?
56 Ride seeker's cry
57 Symbol of silence
58 Does an alteration
59 Beame or Vigoda
60 Short digits?
61 Marx's "___ Kapital"

"ARE YOU KIDDING ME?" by Victor Fleming
Sometimes you just know when someone is trying to make you laugh!

ACROSS

1 Surly sort
5 Keanan of "Step by Step"
10 Thick serving
14 Cozy hideaway
15 Springsteen's "Born ___"
16 Cannes movie house
17 Fairy-tale villain
18 They joined the team
19 "I'm in" payment
20 **Start of many a joke (with 55-A)**
22 **End of many a riddle (with 54-A)**
24 Freudian error
25 Not at all eager
26 Physicist's work unit
29 Dinesen who wrote "Out of Africa"
31 Cornell football rival
32 Coldwater Jane, e.g.
33 Act the skinflint
35 Nectar drinkers
38 **Response to many a joke and riddle (with 41-A)**
40 ___-Turn (sign)
41 **See 38 Across**
42 Beach sweeper
43 Kind of hatch
45 Versifier's "before"

46 Word before liquor or shop
48 McDonald's founder
49 Engage a Singer
50 Den setup
52 Inquires
54 **See 22 Across**
55 **See 20 Across**
59 Yours, in Tours
60 "Theme From Rocky" composer
62 Wolf leader?
63 Mikkelsen on "House of Cards"
64 Apportion
65 Kite part
66 Callaway and Culbertson
67 Bartletts and Boscs
68 None other but

DOWN

1 Stop up
2 Pasta sauce giant
3 Light and fluffy
4 Ale and tea
5 Expert in coiffures
6 Was exceedingly careful
7 Synagogue vessels
8 Maestro's signal
9 Fit
10 Behave like jackals
11 Jewel box enclosure
12 Naysayers

13 Designer Geoffrey
21 "Must-invite" roster
23 Caesar's salutation
26 Work with copy
27 Newswoman Bakhtiar
28 Trivia champ's asset
30 Start of many a joke, when repeated
34 One who provides surety
36 Extremely urgent
37 Pot contents

39 Close one
41 Insurance lizard
43 British schoolboy's lid
44 Sticky notes
47 Third sign after Taurus
50 Map marking
51 Sum answer
53 Made sure of
55 Tom Petty's "Peace ___"
56 Hit on the head
57 Seed sheath
58 Bank, in a way
61 "___ Buttermilk Sky"

32 STAFF OF LIFE*   by Erik Agard
A hint to this puzzle's theme can be found at 71 Across.

ACROSS

1 Rachel Maddow's network
6 Citi Field denizens
10 Court king Arthur
14 Quantity of wisdom
15 Rapper who loves Coco
16 ___ Scotia
17 Capital of Yemen
18 Nam chim cuisine
19 Cinco de Mayo dip, for short
20 "Little House on the Prairie" actor*
23 Capital of Tanzania
26 Kitchen fat
27 Before, in odes
28 Pageant accessories
32 Squeezy snake
35 "Another Way to Die" songwriter*
38 Too many spoil the broth
40 Sunlit spaces
41 Interstitial prefix
42 Many Horn of Africa dwellers
43 Tyler and Dallas, e.g.
44 "On One" podcast host*
46 Ship letters
47 Space bar neighbor
49 Some Twitter communiqués: Abbr.
50 Raise to the third
52 Removes all traces of
55 "My Cherie Amour" singer*
60 Practice to perfection
61 "___ Up Everybody": Blue Notes
62 Plant named for an Austrian botanist
66 Four-H Club sponsor: Abbr.
67 Uttar Pradesh city
68 Oohed and ___
69 General ___ chicken
70 Birth datum
71 Staff of life

DOWN

1 UK pols
2 Sharks' home
3 Grandma's nickname
4 "Good job, tenor!"
5 Denote as one's own
6 Glove of diamonds
7 Reverb verb
8 Sign of joy
9 Sit on
10 Managed emotion
11 What pianos and guitars have in common
12 Trane Inc.'s systems
13 Per person
21 Coffee can contents, at times
22 No-goodnik
23 Eerie familiarity
24 Yammers for an audience
25 Gradual reduction
29 Target
30 Perform terribly
31 Betray uncertainty
33 "No objections here"
34 Size up
36 Currency in Laos
37 Sushi condiment
39 "R.I.P." singer Rita
45 Sized up
48 Elbow room
51 Eye parts
53 Restored building
54 Like a loud crowd
55 Close
56 Throw out
57 Union concern
58 New Orleans stew
59 Proximal
63 ___/her/hers
64 Beverage that sounds like a letter
65 Throw in the mix

33 "GOOD LUCK!"   by Erik Agard
Words in circles result if you (figuratively) 61 Across.

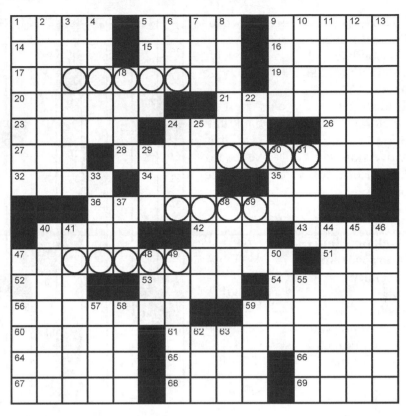

ACROSS

1 Scary storybook creature
5 Sun Ra's domain
9 Other name
14 Flak
15 High seas "hi"
16 Edmund Pettus Bridge site
17 Climb
19 Fruit cocktail
20 Eightsomes
21 Hybrid bathing suit
23 ORD
24 "I hear that!"
26 Contents of some towers
27 Lion locale
28 "La La Land," for one
32 Assent to a woman
34 Female sib
35 Greek letter associated with smallness
36 Ram
40 Ameslan speakers
42 Call ___ career
43 UGA athlete
47 Hostile missive to an editor
51 Long in "Friday"
52 Lose composition
53 Lionel Richie song
54 Anxious in a good way
56 Breathing aid
59 First name in tennis
60 Take care of
61 "Good luck!"
64 Taqueria sandwich
65 Farad, for one
66 Unengaging one
67 Early year
68 Dog food brand
69 ___ out (deduce)

DOWN

1 "Yay!"
2 Creole language
3 Lianas used in chairs
4 Obsolete anesthetic
5 Jax squad
6 Sound of relief
7 Saldana of "Avatar"
8 OTC antihistamine
9 Little league
10 Infosec breach
11 Not by the book
12 Stenberg of "The Hate U Give"
13 Pleasure from pain
18 Agenda line
22 Palindromic woman's name
24 With no changes
25 Shanks or slices
29 "The Sinner" network
30 Sloshed
31 Little fish, to big fish
33 Thom ___ (shoe brand)
37 LBJ's first AG
38 ___-bitty
39 Scot's negative
40 Talk unengagingly
41 Diner come-on
44 "I Shall Not Be Moved" poet
45 Dogs at a roast
46 Oft-cluttered rooms
47 "The Count of Monte ___"
48 "Go Set a Watchman" author
49 iPod accessory
50 Smell of sliced durian
55 Some Israelis
57 "___ girl!"
58 Washer contents
59 High school tests
62 AP Bio topic
63 Observance after Ramadan

34 CRIME-FIGHTER ELIOT by Betty Lopez
The answer at 66 Across does double duty.

ACROSS

1 Pound of lines
5 Consolidate
10 Talk with folded hands
14 Told stories
15 Doctoral hurdle
16 Seized item
17 Move slowly
18 Chris Rock, for one
19 Garbage pail, maybe
20 **Book on Eliot's interrogation specialty**
23 "March Madness" org.
24 Type of pressure
25 Apple product
27 Tigers of the SEC
29 Touch of chill
30 Dr. of G-funk
33 Inflation meas.
34 Most breezy
36 Metal container
37 **Subtitle of book (with 66 Across)**
40 Sheltered on the sea
41 Elite divers
42 Schoolyard retort
43 Question type
45 Data transmission letters
46 Take the tiller
47 "Addams Family" cousin
49 "What's that?"
50 What Eliot proved to be
55 Hendrix of '60s rock
57 Incandescent
58 Newsstand name
61 "My bad"
62 Move furtively
63 Barely got by
64 Arrest or bankrupt
65 Uses the keyboard
66 **Eliot/See 37 Across**

DOWN

1 Giants QB Manning
2 Insult, slangily
3 Kisses and makes up
4 For a specific purpose
5 Some slip-ons
6 Slangy suffix
7 Highway entrance or exit
8 Smooth-talking
9 Fantasy Islanders?
10 Vincent of horror flicks
11 Occasion for spinning vinyl?
12 Per person
13 In the distance
21 The ___ Lama
22 Pool dimension
25 Claude of the Harlem Renaissance
26 Heaps
28 Did some arm-twisting
29 Noel who played Lois Lane
31 Dishwasher cycle
32 Sci-fi forest moon
35 Start of a past-tense conjugation
38 Type of Marx follower
39 "Body Heat" actress Turner
44 Baseball's "Master Melvin"
46 Deli hero
48 Brown bread
49 Philips Arena team
50 Diamond foursome
51 Hard on the eyes
52 Money holder
53 Fine-tune
54 German sculptor Rehder
55 Task at hand
56 Paper promise
59 Guitar master Paul
60 Mag. execs

35 EMPTY NEST   by Betty Lopez
The square at the center of the grid is not a letter.

ACROSS

1 Squire in "Silas Marner"
5 "De-Lovely" star Kevin
10 Subtle suggestion
14 Cubemaster Rubik
15 Hospital helpers
16 Melville tale of the South Pacific
17 Cyclone path
19 Name on escalators
20 What TV advertisers buy
21 They're not serious
23 Blind spot's location
24 Pepper grinder
25 Start of a selection process
27 Spaceship sections
30 Energizes, with "up"
33 Sales aid
35 "Mona Lisa" feature
36 Laid up
37 Mild reproof
39 Rinks org.
40 Avoid capture
42 "Put ___ my bill"
43 "Weekend's almost here!"
44 That's what they say
46 Road anger
48 Model Banks
49 "___ black sheep . . ."
53 Sign of the future
56 Café employees
57 Jell-O pudding flavor
58 Topless beachwear
60 Biting
61 "Save Me" singer Mann
62 Brazil soccer great
63 "Frozen" queen
64 Last-ditch effort
65 Leave as is

DOWN

1 French Oscar
2 Shaw of swing
3 Quick drink
4 Missions from above
5 Himalayan capital
6 Old money of Milan
7 Neighbor of Mont.
8 Swan feature
9 Edmonton footballer
10 Tough on the streets
11 Tattler's threat
12 Film genre
13 Work on a salad
18 Greedy cry
22 Hast performed
26 Himalayan humanoids?
27 Kind of pool or court
28 Pertaining to most students
29 Narcissist's love
30 Marina sight
31 She, in Cherbourg
32 Damson orchard
34 What the title word "empty" means here*
37 ___ Haute
38 With sustained force
41 Spring break destination
43 China case items
45 "Dust in the Wind" band
47 Teri of "Young Frankenstein"
50 "The Cosby Show" actress
51 Sprain site
52 Black-ink item
53 Kind of hockey check
54 Cy Young winner Hershiser
55 Nincompoop
56 Some feds
59 "Hallelujah, ___ Bum"

60 ACROSS by Howard Barkin
17 Across was awarded the Lenin Peace Prize in 1959.

ACROSS

1 Pampering place
4 Bit for Rover
9 Deduce from facts
14 2013 Kentucky Derby winner
15 Spanish for "cheese"
16 Patterned sheer fabric
17 NAACP cofounder*
19 Farm trailer?
20 Aleppo's land
21 Viennese table offerings
23 "A Clockwork Orange" was initially this*
26 Teacher of Liszt and Beethoven
29 Take advantage of
30 Botanical added to some health drinks
31 Weakness for team players
34 Edmonton's Rogers Place, e.g.
38 Edward Snowden's former org.
39 Like divining rods*
41 Captain's recording
42 Hunter S. Thompson's journalism
44 Err on the balance beam
45 "Git, fly!"
46 Old World cont.
48 Sarcastic
50 Last page of animal alphabet books*
54 Pugsley's mother
55 Coming-___ film
59 Sign in the studio
60 March Madness tetrad/TITLE
63 Aussie buds
64 Sound like a bird
65 Horse or hound
66 Notification
67 "Battle of the ___" (2017)
68 "Green" prefix

DOWN

1 Scatters seed
2 Most "Hunger Games" participants
3 Word-shortening indicator
4 Public meeting place
5 2016 World Series player
6 Road classic
7 Whisper to the audience
8 Smiled for a selfie
9 "Such a pity . . ."
10 "No way, nohow"
11 "Diners, Drive-Ins and Dives" host
12 Bring joy to
13 Checkers side
18 Paper cup name
22 Rival of Texas A&M
24 Half brother of Hermes
25 Close-knit, as friends
26 Performed on "The Voice"
27 In addition to
28 Give for a time
32 One of a pair in the water
33 Masala, e.g.
35 Designed for K-12
36 Palindromic hour
37 Flabbergasted
39 "Be my guest"
40 E-book file extension
43 With more zing
45 Musical lines
47 Huge mythical creature
49 Dolls with long hair
50 By region
51 Completely fed up with
52 Rock fissures
53 "Rumble in the Jungle" locale
54 Manhattan museum
56 Stellar, slangily
57 Cinco de Mayo dip
58 "Then logically . . ."
61 Vote down
62 First-round draft pick?

SNACK ATTACK   by Howard Barkin
. . . providing a nice puzzle break, for those looking to sit a bit.

ACROSS

1 Drug at Woodstock
4 Car lifters
9 Rene of "Lethal Weapon 3"
14 Yellowfin tuna
15 Open-air courtyards
16 The blahs
17 Prefix for "stick" and "stop"
18 Packed in tightly
20 Fido, slangily
22 Misrepresent, as survey data
23 What "€" stands for
24 Chain offering a "Meat Mountain"
26 Lawmaking groups
28 Far, far away
31 Moines or Plaines preceder
32 Smokeless smoke
33 God, in Roma
34 "Beats me" gesture
38 Hours in a Jupiter day
39 Repetitive sound
42 Honor bestowed in the UK
43 Pond buildup
45 Make a rough less rough
46 Sport scored using electrical sensors
47 Headlight light
49 Burns slowly
51 Hoity-toity
55 Best strategy
56 "The Godfather" composer Rota

57 Take a short siesta
59 Jake's "11/22/63" love interest
62 Toy that must be shaken to reuse
65 Choose (to)
66 Give a thumbs-up to
67 First name in cosmetics
68 Vanna's longtime costar
69 Frequent barnacle hangouts
70 Eye sores
71 College URL suffix

DOWN

1 Reel in
2 "Git!"
3 Scatterbrain
4 "The Monkey's Paw" author
5 AAU member
6 Fitness regimen with "WODs"
7 Quit, as a habit
8 "For goodness' ___!"
9 Lincoln-era soldier
10 Let the dog run free
11 Shovelnose nose
12 Bolivian capital
13 Greek yogurt brand
19 Absolutely amazed

21 Kinnear in "Little Men"
25 Speak like this, he does
27 Squirrel or bird home
28 Self-referential, in slang
29 Mount Hekla loc.
30 Froths
35 Ali's "Rumble in the Jungle" tactic
36 Taxi alternative
37 Giggling foursome?
39 Got skunked?
40 "I Won't Back Down" singer
41 On the loose
44 It's missing from "virgin" drinks
46 Author Ferber
48 Lemons

50 They're fluttered by flirters
51 Kind of peek or preview
52 Book page
53 "I give up!"
54 Rudely gets attention
58 Drink garnish
60 Apple product
61 Rebuke to Brutus
63 "How cute!" sounds
64 2.0 average

38 OATER by Harvey Estes
A 100% whole-grain solving experience.

ACROSS

1 Eye drop
5 Put one's foot down
10 Hissers
14 Court order
15 Blade on a parking ticket
16 Dundee citizen
17 Faust of "Mission: Impossible — Fallout"
18 Hostile state
19 Jealous wife in Greek myth
20 Dobbin's oaty dinner
23 Rent collector
24 ___-cone
25 "What a relief!"
26 USNA grad
27 Beau Brummells
30 Come out
32 "The Butterfly ___" (Kutcher film)
34 Contended
35 Oaty General Mills product
39 Fashion designer Vera
40 Unpopped popcorn
41 It's worn
44 Malicious gossip
45 Bodybuilder's assets
48 Tango census
49 T or F, on exams
51 Kind of patch
53 Sometimes oaty treat
57 Mine, to Maurice
58 Husband of Bathsheba
59 Ram or rooster
60 Comedian's stock
61 Dirty look
62 Veep's boss
63 "Orinoco Flow" singer
64 Ditties for the deity
65 Loser of lore

DOWN

1 British dessert
2 Astronaut Collins
3 Size up
4 Examines a passage
5 Promise to give up
6 Triangle tone
7 Crude bunch
8 Office slips
9 "The Scarlet Letter" lady
10 ESPYS' Arthur ___ Award
11 Game plan
12 Overland routes
13 Put away
21 Successful, in "Variety"
22 Bearded turkey
28 Eat like a bird
29 IRS form
31 Santana's "___ Ways"
32 Vet
33 Hatcher in "Lois & Clark"
35 Female caped superhero
36 Metaphysics branch
37 Adds nutrients to
38 Nostalgic fashion trend
39 Amps × volts = ___
42 Arena shout
43 "Stop it!"
45 Capital once known as Angora
46 Source of steam
47 You may be blessed for this
50 Like a sourpuss
52 Get-up-and-go
54 "Rear Window" heroine
55 "The King and I" kingdom
56 Bring home

39 ILL AT EASEL by Harvey Estes
That's not a typo in the title.

ACROSS

1 Trudge along
5 Tossed salad type
9 Image maker
14 Leave in the dust
15 R.E.M.'s "The ___ Love"
16 "The Lion King" villain
17 King who married Jezebel
18 Lone Star State sch.
19 "The Second Coming" poet
20 Preparing to eat cereal?
23 Meadow
24 Rampaging
25 Soap scent
27 Prefix with corn or pod
28 Bad blood
30 "The Old Guitarist" painter
34 Outcomes
36 Aligned
37 Where many get in hot water
38 Their bad habits need kicking again
42 Spread
45 Evening gathering
46 Suntan spoiler
47 Mexican painter Kahlo
48 "Come and get it!"
53 An adv. modifies it
55 School in the hood?
57 Cross representations
59 Ages and ages
60 Alan of "And the Band Played On"
61 Belief summary
62 Forgetful actor's cry
63 "Da Doo Ron Ron" opening
64 "Jump" band Van ___
65 Shane portrayer
66 Second starter

DOWN

1 Wise Athenian
2 Lindsay in "The Parent Trap"
3 Japanese port
4 Red ink entry
5 Brigham Young team
6 Michigan neighbor
7 English channel (with "The")
8 Like the Earth, magnetically
9 Diller or George
10 Reuben bread
11 Admission of gluttony?
12 Fork over, with "up"
13 Planner of long trips
21 Trawling gear
22 Cellar contents
26 Tickle one's funny bone
29 Prewedding party
30 Jim and Tammy's old org.
31 Roth et al.
32 "Piano Man" Billy's morning eye-opener?
33 Norse pantheon
35 U-turn from NNW
39 Norse explorer
40 Change the décor of
41 Bulkhead
42 Take flight
43 Sang softly
44 Fidel Castro's brother
49 ___ vanilla
50 2014 movie about voting rights
51 Nash of humorous verse
52 "Outta sight!"
53 Saarinen's St. Louis design
54 "Cannery Row" madam
56 Jabba the Hutt's captive
58 JFK preceder

PANDA   by Anna Carson
There's a hint to the theme at 35 Across.

ACROSS

1 Place for valuables
5 Unrefined
10 Veep's boss
14 Compatriot
15 Bank job
16 "Othello" role
17 Need for a CPAP machine
19 Go across
20 Garfield, for example
21 Building front
23 Wither away
24 In search of
25 Stephen of "V for Vendetta"
26 Confronted
29 Steinbeck figure
32 "Get out!"
33 SEP, e.g.
34 With it
35 P and A, for example
37 Lisa Simpson, to Bart
38 Three R's org.
39 Penn and others
40 Work with acid
41 Whenever you want
43 Harrison of "My Fair Lady"
45 Thirst quencher
46 Get in the game
50 Black belt activity
52 Musical that won 11 Tonys
53 Olympian hawk
54 Go bargain hunting
56 Respect an anthem
57 Big name in cameras
58 "The very ___!"
59 Highlands girl
60 Unspoiled spots
61 Trial run

DOWN

1 Barack's daughter
2 Pass out
3 ___-de-lis
4 Blot on the landscape
5 Latin dance
6 Give in kind
7 "I ___ No Quitter": Shania Twain
8 U-turn from NNW
9 Military officer's wheels
10 Sign of late winter
11 50 Cent, for one
12 "My stars!"
13 Defense type
18 Cartoon skunk Le Pew
22 Molecular bits
24 Homestead Act's "160"
26 Showed initiative
27 Bana in "The Time Traveler's Wife"
28 Track event
29 "Horrors!"
30 Hot to trot
31 Modern location code
32 Offend the olfactories
35 No-___ poker
36 Fade away
40 Take advantage of
42 Rubs out
43 Acts follower
44 Islamic ruler
46 Food fowl
47 Staff exercise
48 Chromatic nuances
49 Be over by
50 Designer Lagerfeld
51 Oratorio highlight
52 Fine-tune
55 Put away

41 PEACE OUT   by Anna Carson
There's a hint about the theme at 52 Down.

ACROSS

1 And higher, price-wise
5 "My Fair Lady" race place
10 Start of a tot's song
14 Lovegood of Hogwarts
15 Not legit
16 Richard in "The Dinner"
17 Without serious thought
18 Gulf ship
19 Designer Cassini
20 One way to get through Nevada?
23 Grazing land
24 Some Fords
25 Pawns
27 Makeup mishap
28 Gin containers of old
31 Work with a steno
34 Kinkajou's home
35 Heart exam
38 Watering holes of female deer?
40 Mag. execs
41 "You bet!"
43 College units
45 Lucasfilm franchise sold to Disney
47 Nostalgic fashion trend
51 "Family Ties" mom
52 Expense record
54 Hill of San Francisco
55 Japanese warriors in public?
59 Pigeon sounds
61 Words before "forgiven"
62 Come to the surface
63 Morales of "Ozark"
64 Prolonged attack
65 MBA subj.
66 Becomes Jell-O
67 Fish stories
68 Slight progress

DOWN

1 Pizza topping
2 Debriefing and more?
3 Loosen, as a corset
4 Cargo that generates income
5 Make ___ (blog)
6 Prison weapons
7 Porter that could carry a tune
8 Ten C-notes
9 Emmy winner Banks
10 In the past
11 Remedy for ringing in the ears?
12 Gold-panning spot
13 Vacuum-pumps
21 Ban competitor
22 "Quiet down!"
26 Ex–Dallas Stars center Steve
28 Toyland tots
29 To some extent
30 Polo of "The Fosters"
32 Imogene of early TV
33 Okla., once
35 Pleasing smells
36 Run wild
37 Confederate ironclad?
39 Hit strings
42 Hesitation sounds
44 Locked down
46 Bentley of "American Beauty"
48 Again and yet again
49 Good sense
50 Use a compass
52 Peace symbol
53 Sites for dates
56 Like a cakewalk
57 Oscar winner Kazan
58 L.A. Dodger, for one
60 "___ for Silence": Grafton

ACROSS

1 Own (up)
5 Grille protector
8 Check out
14 Like a band, to Wings
16 Key with one sharp
17 "The Departed" director
18 Dog
19 Unit of angry soldiers?
21 Leather stickers
22 Steamed up
23 Mom of Tracee Ellis Ross
24 Where drives begin
25 Set the pace
26 Delt neighbor
27 Subscription cards, e.g.
30 Heels
31 Service groups
32 Well
35 Motions on oceans
36 Detour
39 Take it from me
41 Refrigerator section
42 Three, in Torino
43 "Love Story" composer
46 Oil can letters
47 Quick-witted
49 They share lots of DNA
50 Quite a bit
51 Do a how-to TV program on gardening?
53 Mesh
55 Incarcerated one
56 Serving tray
57 Most unfeeling
58 Creates a glaze
59 Solo in space
60 Favorites

DOWN

1 Old fogy
2 Concert ender, at times
3 Put away
4 Get rid of evidence
5 Like fish sticks
6 Bumpkins
7 "It's the end of ___"
8 Board opposite
9 Bird from down under
10 A taste of rum on the "Black Pearl"?
11 Came back
12 Casino game
13 Very in Vichy
15 Medium skill
20 Doing what needs to be done
26 "Fork over the money!"
28 French composer Erik
29 Teakettle sound
30 Relief pitcher's nail-biter?
32 Hail Mary path
33 Classified
34 Rack shape
37 Promotional come-ons
38 Proof part
39 Home of the Braves
40 Garden State capital
43 Property claim subject
44 Most fit
45 Dots in the water
48 "If only!"
49 Bacon unit
50 Della's angel character
52 Kind of mother
54 Dig

43 KC/DC by Harvey Estes
In honor of Kasie Hunt's news program "Kasie DC."

ACROSS

1 Duties for importers
8 Sings the blues
15 Bible's shortest book
16 Broadcast hours
17 Like a stranger to criticism?
19 Musher's transport
20 Chip features
21 SEP, e.g.
22 Easter display
23 "Now!" in a hospital
24 Jazz musicians who dig simple songs?
28 Got to second base, in a way
29 Tough nuts to crack
30 Tony and Oscar
31 Like some numerals
32 Introduction
35 Fed. agents
36 Noisy family reunion?
40 Keyboardist Myra
41 Top parts of suits
42 Skin layer
43 May Day sight
45 Grabs a few Z's
46 Remake of "Hamlet" by Orson Welles?
51 Like, on a menu
52 Plato's plaza
53 Aromatic herb
54 Pianist Gilels
55 Solitary sort
56 Even once
57 Coward on stage
58 Pat down a suspect

59 Title document
60 Griffith of "Matlock"

DOWN

1 A whole lot
2 Genesis brother
3 Hearty party
4 Fingered, briefly
5 Needle maker
6 Mill output
7 Aussie lassie
8 Bay of Bengal feeder
9 Takes the bus
10 Eye part
11 Romulans, to Kirk
12 Drop-in
13 Deep green
14 Puts under
18 Ready for press
22 Redgrave in "Shine"
23 Straphanger
24 Villainous Vader
25 "Ready or not, here ___ !"
26 Voluminous volumes
27 Takes place
28 Con
30 Nabokov protagonist
32 Part of LPN
33 Nice summer
34 Sounds from spas
36 Leafy veggie
37 "You wish!"
38 Hinted at
39 How to speak French?
44 Range in Arkansas
45 Bergen bumpkin

46 Knee neighbor
47 Straminsky of "M*A*S*H"
48 Collette in "Hitchcock"
49 "Satellite" singer Matthews
50 Film critic James
54 Aunt in "Bambi"

44 MERIT INCREASE by Andrew Tyler
For everyone who deserves a raise.

ACROSS

1. Lettuce variety
5. Brindled cat
10. Tiara display
14. Matinee figure
15. Last words of a Kilmer poem
16. Transactional analysis phrase
17. Sarah Palin portrayer Fey
18. Nashville legend Minnie
19. Guitar guru Hendrix
20. Cry like Alice in Wonderland?
23. Heated exchange of views
24. Nurse, in a bar
27. "Dizzy" singer Tommy
28. Cable trademark
29. Granola tidbit
32. Type of cracker
34. Coming or going, e.g.
36. Deck of the future
37. Cowboy's moniker
40. Christo's Central Park exhibit
41. Like a Mediterranean climate?
44. President Coin of "The Hunger Games"
46. Off the wall
47. Satirist Bombeck
50. "No kidding!"
51. Cracker shapes
53. Deli hero
54. Come to
56. Takes as one's own

58. Ang Lee movie about Blackbeard?
62. Do damage to
63. Long bones
64. Bus. school course
65. On top of that
66. At large
67. FedExed

DOWN

1. Short time
2. "Got it, dude"
3. Off-white
4. Sauvignon ___
5. Watering hole
6. Relaxed
7. They're spoiled
8. Deprived
9. Kennel noise
10. Soldier doll
11. Marathoner Zátopek
12. Some den leaders
13. Move among the moguls
21. Goof list
22. Brand of taco sauce
24. Army NCO
25. 401(k) relative
26. Boundaries
29. There's no air there
30. Dijon donkey
31. Some Hail Mary endings
33. Hacienda hello
35. "Merit" added onto 3 answers
37. Collette of "In Her Shoes"
38. Dutch cheese
39. Lucy Lawless role
42. Aware
43. Backslide, medically
44. First name in mysteries
45. Like sarin
48. Irish stew meat
49. Playing hooky
51. Darth, as a boy
52. Cold War abbr.
55. Cookie Monster's pal
57. Rock group
59. "Xanadu" band
60. "Double Fantasy" artist
61. Scale notes

45 SALUTE TO THE DODO   by Andrew Tyler
Raphus cucullatus . . . gone but not forgotten.

ACROSS

1 Hard knocks
5 "South Pacific" hero
10 Buffalo center?
14 Icon inscription
15 A driver pays it
17 No longer secret
18 Unseemly
19 He says "D'oh!"
21 "Sands ___ Jima" (1949)
22 "___ of Swing" (Dire Straits song)
26 "What's New ___": Tom Jones
30 City on the Illinois River
31 U-turn from NNW
32 Accolades
34 Turned on the waterworks
35 "Gimme all your dough!" source
38 Henry VIII's second wife
41 Flight part
42 Syllables from a laugher
45 Ark scrolls
48 Headlong rush
50 Great greed
52 Acrylic fabric
53 They sang "Doe, a deer . . ."
57 "Inventor's Guide": Step 1
60 "I" as in Ithaca
61 Superheroes have secret ones
62 Bird feeder fill
63 Places for prices
64 Beveled edges
65 Versailles verb

DOWN

1 Chess pieces worth 3 points
2 Joan Osborne hit
3 Basis of an argument
4 Power source
5 "___ Coming": Three Dog Night
6 Revealing dress
7 Silo contents, for short
8 Jumps over
9 Eventually becomes
10 Home of the BoSox, familiarly
11 Hypotheticals
12 "Play it again!"
13 "Go Set a Watchman" author Harper
16 Ripped off
20 "Boss" author Mike
23 "You ___ what you eat"
24 Bit of chill
25 Posed for pics
27 ___-de-sac
28 Computes the bottom line
29 Talks up
33 Minor argument
35 Gives hope to
36 Uma's "Pulp Fiction" role
37 Tanks and such
38 ___ loss for words
39 Veterans Day mo.
40 New Deal inits.
42 Lend a hand
43 New parent, at times
44 Able to feel
46 Part of a drum kit
47 Picturesque
49 Pat on the back
51 "Oh What a Circus" musical
54 Zeus, to Vikings
55 Former Nair rival
56 Moscow news agency
57 Best-seller
58 Oklahoma oil city
59 Take it easy, with "out"

RESIDENT PHYSICIAN   by Harvey Estes
"It" readers will know the answer to 63 Across.

ACROSS

1 Antioxidant berry
5 Trooper maker
10 "How 'bout ___!"
14 Jethro Bodine portrayer Max
15 Out to lunch
16 "Green Lantern" supervillain
17 Race place across the pond
19 Diamond covering
20 Freetown currency unit
21 Ovidian outerwear
23 Pinch
24 Book part
26 Firenze's land
28 It's built to order
32 Buck private's goal
35 Joe of "Apollo 13"
36 "Care to?"
37 Alt.
39 Verdi forte
41 Ball-___ hammer
42 Dead duck
44 Online sales
46 Cereal box no.
47 Riverbed clam?
50 Baltimore ballplayer
51 Painter's protection
54 Venom source
55 Establish as law
59 Pulls down
61 Actress Perlman
63 Where Pennywise lurks
65 ___-Frank Act
66 Words to live by
67 Voting no
68 Scand. nation
69 Hot spot
70 Trial run

DOWN

1 Cain's sib
2 Lighthouse locales
3 Fable fellow
4 Poignantly unexpected
5 Neither Rep. nor Dem.
6 Flue buildup
7 Spy plane or rock band
8 Whining noise
9 In thought only
10 "Animal Kingdom" network
11 Top draw at a concert
12 Called before the court
13 Palm apex?
18 Restaurant stack
22 Think obsessively
25 Nickname of a Bruin legend
27 PDQ, politely
29 Saved for later viewing
30 "You're ___ talk!"
31 Story conclusion
32 They're used in cribbage games
33 Nightclub offering
34 Leggy arthropod
38 Kill a bill
40 Isn't doing well
43 Rome, to Sinatra
45 Limping, maybe
48 Upright sort
49 Greet with loud laughter
52 Stretch one's neck forward
53 Makes a cardigan, say
56 Gillette razor
57 Many a dorm dweller
58 Genealogical work
60 Mad mood
62 Tack on
64 Resident physicians found in four answers

47 WAY OUT   by Harvey Estes
One of the dumbest movie remakes that ever o-curd.

ACROSS

1 Grating voice
5 "Mad ___ and Englishmen": Coward
9 Viper or calculator
14 Nobel Laureate Wiesel
15 Hospital division
16 "Later!"
17 Grand poohbah
19 English subways
20 It comes back to you
21 "Money" management
23 Tries to mislead
24 Curve on a score
25 Rinks org.
26 Down in the mouth
27 Had status
29 Diggs of "Private Practice"
30 Must, informally
32 Cuts away
33 Remake of a 1973 film starring 54-A and a 17-A?
37 Franks' partners
38 Large accounts
39 "Cosmo" competitor
40 "Wheel of Fortune" category
42 ___-de-lance
45 Furry sitcom alien
46 Faculty boss
47 Bundle up
50 Backward pass
52 Like some autobiographies
53 Say "somethin' "
54 Best Actress Oscar winner of 1969
56 C&W singer LeAnn
57 Robert Craig Knievel
58 Additionally
59 Cold forecast
60 Small sailing vessel
61 Bright night light

DOWN

1 Defies authority
2 Cher's portrayer in "Clueless"
3 Sounded wistful
4 River to the Rio Grande
5 Toward a pole, or away from one
6 A hundred sawbucks
7 "___ for Gumshoe": Grafton
8 Trump dossier compiler
9 In motion
10 Bk. of the Pentateuch
11 Charmingly sophisticated
12 Good for food, e.g.
13 Brawls in the backwoods
18 Best-seller
22 Firecracker flop
24 Doesn't fold
28 Eroded, with "away"
29 Very in Vichy
30 Trait bearer
31 Hurtful words?
32 Carrier in "The Aviator"
33 Practice deception
34 Pep talk occasion
35 Lacking color
36 Shade of white
37 Exercise caution
40 Gunpowder, for example
41 World War 2 admiral
42 Femme ___
43 Still
44 Flush
46 Clothing
48 Word before polloi
49 City on the Ruhr
51 Sarah Brightman album
52 Waxed
55 Knoxville hydroelectric org.

48 A DAY AT THE BEACH by Pam Klawitter

1 Down died on the same day President John F. Kennedy was assassinated.

ACROSS

1 In need of a trim
5 Works with a rope
10 Far from stern?
14 Buffalo's county
15 It's an obsession
16 Type of ant
17 Those who think alike are on the same one
19 Barclays Center team
20 Suffix for Gotham
21 Clean plates
22 Highest on the Mohs scale
24 Motion detector
26 Song line
27 Expiration date words
29 Sleep stoppers
33 "Grumble, grumble . . ."
35 Unantlered deer
37 Poly finish
38 Dish sites
40 High-speed hook-up, briefly
41 One in a pool
42 "Narnia" hero
43 Flue residue
45 Mind-blowing letters
46 "There's nothing to lose!"
48 In on
50 Give in to gravity
52 Minor slip-up
56 Most likely to survive, to Darwin
59 ___ Clemente
60 Lucky strike
61 Raw-silk color
62 Thimblerigs

65 A woman called Golda
66 A little creepy
67 Monthly expense for some
68 Starting from the date
69 Pharmacy weights
70 Some are padded

DOWN

1 "The Chronicles of Narnia" author
2 Address on a soapbox
3 "Murder by Death" star
4 Palomino prompt
5 Like lipstick after a kiss, maybe
6 "Critique of Pure Reason" author
7 NYC Marathon sponsor
8 To the point
9 Timbuktu expanse
10 Shore sculptures
11 Kid's fort site
12 "ER" extras
13 1990s PC game
18 Some August babies
23 Ticks off
25 Popular restaurant combo
26 Grandma's hand cleaner
28 Muscle mag pics
30 Numbered GPS lines
31 Convalesce
32 Sign of success
33 "Jeepers!"
34 Poly partner

36 Like some boats to China?
38 Inflamed
39 Nocturnal noise
44 Cantina wraps
47 Played catch
49 Part of an altar exchange
51 Significant ___
53 Diamond dinger
54 It's where the action is
55 Spray targets
56 Disaster aid initials
57 Treats a sprain
58 The Band Perry, for one
59 Modelesque
63 Coldwell Banker rival
64 Certain trader

A LITTLE ADDED TRASH TALK   by Pam Klawitter
A Broadway theater named after 14 Across houses "The Late Show."

ACROSS

1 Outward expressions
6 Interstate hauler
10 Auctioneer's word
14 "Toast of the Town" host
16 Low-grade school?
17 Cast doubt on Comey's tenure?
19 Tabloid fodder
20 Prompter opening
21 Some NCOs
22 Orion's love
24 "Humbug!"
25 Bit of anti-twister sentiment?
32 Center of a comparison
34 Non-HOV lane folks?
35 Cuba, to Carlos
36 Bit part
38 Salt finisher
39 Yet to be rented
40 Where to see the big picture
41 Toots one's own horn
43 Part of some portfolios
44 Marked-down flock?
47 It's a piece of work
48 RE/MAX alternative
49 Now, in Nicaragua
52 Super Bowl showtime
55 Functional math
59 Pyrotechnics show?
62 Ever so many
63 Animated film starring Boog the bear
64 Kate on the runway
65 Diet successfully
66 Artery implant

DOWN

1 Prefix for care
2 Words of confession
3 Shell Canada rival
4 Comet centers
5 WYSIWYG camera
6 Fries, often
7 Voldemort descriptor
8 The missing mitten
9 Written with five sharps
10 "Summertime" composer
11 Couturier Cassini
12 Ice-free
13 Ranch birds
15 Start of a stadium cheer
18 B-2 wing letters
23 Nobel Peace Prize site
24 Diddley and Derek
25 Spanish ladies
26 Square in Manhattan
27 Parisian legislature
28 Head lock
29 Suffolk County town
30 Nat, for one
31 Spreadsheet filler
32 It's baseless
33 ___-Am of "Green Eggs and Ham"
37 Certain passages
39 One with the keys?
41 Spy's favorite plant?
42 Illegal pickups
45 Like Sabin's vaccine
46 Copy Mrs. Sprat
49 Driver in "The Last Jedi"
50 Big Island destination
51 Barcelona bears
52 Syringe
53 Leaves wide-eyed
54 It can be dotted or crossed
56 Order in the court
57 Smooth things out
58 Decent chap
60 MapQuest parent
61 Men and boys

AT ODDS by Pam Klawitter

George Harrison played a 55 Across in "Norwegian Wood."

ACROSS

1 Homestead Act units
6 Julie of "Big Brother"
10 Some elephants
14 Comanche colt
15 "Kinky Boots" drag queen
16 NYC think tank
17 What the devil wears?
18 Australian gem
19 Poseidon's mom
20 The first replica?*
23 They're lost at the track
26 Sheedy and McBeal
27 Unlike NYC subways at rush hour*
32 Title holder
33 Goosebumps-inducing
34 Showy flower
35 Jazzed
36 Strap site
40 Fourth Estate
41 Winged
42 Response from a fence-sitter*
45 "You're shaking like ___"
47 Threw a Hail Mary
48 Red Solo cup, e.g.*
53 Twice-told ___
54 Heart of the matter
55 Bollywood instrument
59 Best Actor winner Jannings
60 Bulldogs by another nickname
61 JibJab offering
62 Aykroyd and August
63 Marquee
64 Some NCOs

DOWN

1 Droid download
2 Auburn, for one
3 Rivulet
4 Showed support for
5 Indy official
6 Dancing shoe
7 Bean Dance dancer
8 Joie de vivre
9 Disney lion queen
10 "The ___ Game": Joni Mitchell
11 In phone limbo
12 Like Niobe
13 Remains
21 Easter or Christmas: Abbr.
22 Links hazard
23 Laborious task
24 Moonlight bay?
25 New Rochelle college
28 Mideast land
29 Mountain Dew's parent
30 "Give it ___ already!"
31 Scotland Yard div.
35 Gold of "Entourage"
36 Golf tourneys
37 Robert in "Airplane!"
38 "May ___": Enya
39 Necessity
40 Fizzling-out sound
41 Stockpiles
42 Give a hand to
43 Flip-chart holders
44 DDT banner
45 "The World Is Not Enough" director
46 Anna Dewdney's red pajama wearer
49 "Rhyme Pays" rapper
50 "Unforgettable" singer
51 Popular emoticon
52 For fear that
56 Running game
57 Gumby creator Clokey
58 Hwys.

23 Down was previously head coach of the Jets, Patriots, and the USC Trojans.

ACROSS

1 Knacks
5 These, in Tijuana
10 Proffer
13 French winery
14 Bridge seat
15 "El Condor ___": S&G hit
16 Danube tributary
17 Solemn songbird?
19 Composure
21 Cheer up
22 Top-notch
23 Ursa Minor star
25 Tipsy egret?
29 Stir from sleep
30 Timesaving abbr.
31 Went belly-up
35 Temple mascot Hooter T. ___
36 Ad infinitum
40 Type of trader
41 Statistics
43 Anago or unagi
44 "To form ___ perfect union . . ."
46 Most-charming shorebirds?
50 Crécy veggies
53 Gets it
54 Offshore
55 Baby-shower gift
59 Baltimore helmet logo?
62 Vulcanize rubber
63 Salzburg setting
64 Beguiling
65 Server's point
66 Assent of man
67 Blue-ribbon beer
68 Holy Week's time

DOWN

1 "Lucky Jim" author
2 Pasadena bowl
3 Rip
4 Signs of a poor window washing
5 Wankel namesake
6 Did a laundry task
7 Cube holder
8 Off-road vehicle
9 Noted seashell seller
10 Storybook elephant
11 Question from Judas
12 Claire in "Les Misérables"
15 Chopin's homeland
18 Move, in Realtor-speak
20 Nick of "A Walk in the Woods"
23 Seahawks coach Carroll
24 Sauron's soldiers
25 Spur
26 Davenport locale
27 Extremist sect
28 Word on a nametag
32 Fanzine focus
33 Tupper of Tupperware
34 Hair salon stock
37 Not on the rocks
38 "___ fightin' words!"
39 Wise guys
42 Is in harmony
45 ___ chairs
47 Do a bank job
48 "The Elements of Style" elements
49 Take exception to
50 Braves announcer Chip
51 "I could ___ unfold": Shak.
52 Sends regrets, in a way
55 Zinger
56 Hose shade
57 Olympic luger Hamlin
58 Something to pitch
60 WWW access
61 Rita's "Fifty Shades Darker" role

52 EXTRA CHARGES by Bonnie L. Gentry

The National Museum of Natural History is the permanent home of 1 Across.

ACROSS

1 Famous blue diamond
5 Earthshaking event
10 Braggarts have big ones
14 Utah winter vacation spot
15 Bible book before Joel
16 "You got that right!"
17 Grand objective of NASA?
20 Internet connection need
21 Ask for votes
22 Email folder
25 Yummy but fattening
26 Gangster's hasty escape
29 Med school subj.
31 Vitamin-B component
35 Tree ring count, e.g.
36 Harden (to)
38 Civil Rights activist Parks
39 Exodus in North Africa?
43 Part of Julius Caesar's dying words
44 Words on a Wonderland cake
45 Games' companion
46 Loses one's poker face
49 Blue state majority, for short
50 Stereotyped teen's room
51 Limo window feature
53 Wild Turkey et al.
55 What Hercules became
58 Seat selection if you want legroom
62 1,000k race?
65 Tiger Woods' ex
66 Big house rooms?
67 Exam with an "arguments" section
68 Auto pioneer Ransom
69 It may follow a casing
70 Greed and gluttony

DOWN

1 Soccer Hall-of-Famer Mia
2 Eclectic collection
3 Combat vet's affliction
4 Becomes less jammed, as traffic
5 Kosugi in "Revenge of the Ninja"
6 One billion years
7 "We have met the enemy and he ___": Pogo
8 Tijuana address?
9 Vote by absentee ballot
10 It may end in PEZOLCFTD
11 Ginger Spice's real first name
12 Hops kiln
13 Pronoun for America
18 Do damage to
19 Last of a Latin trio
23 One of the sisters in "Frozen"
24 Norman Lear sitcom
26 Freckle remover
27 Cat's-eye cousin
28 Conductor from Mumbai
30 Tire or sneaker feature
32 Elaborate hairstyles
33 Has left for lunch
34 Mrs. Doubtfire, for one
37 Aromatic organic compound
40 Bidding events
41 Oscar : film :: ___ : TV
42 Put back into the freezer bag
47 Inconsequential quarrel
48 Quidditch ball
52 Little giggle
54 Opera diva nicknamed "Bubbles"
55 Snore-inducing
56 "National Velvet" writer Bagnold
57 Supermarket section
59 Pedro's emphatic okay
60 Provide temporarily
61 MDs for sinus sufferers
62 Rock's ___ Speedwagon
63 Sporting Kansas City org.
64 Ending for art or column

53 WHAT'S TRUE IS FALSE by Bonnie L. Gentry
Things aren't always what they seem to be.

ACROSS

1 Do some KP work
5 NASA part
9 They're checked in clubs
14 Doll that says "That tickles!"
15 Dairy-free spread
16 "You've Got Mail!" hearer
17 "Is there ___ against that?"
18 Jean in "The Da Vinci Code"
19 Spider-Man's adversary
20 "The Hustler," for one?
23 K.T. who sang "80's Ladies"
24 Workbench cutter
25 Bio. class
28 Pin the rap on a fall guy?
32 Triathlete vehicle
35 Caveat when expressing one's POV
36 Do pizza on the couch
37 Half of half of tetra-
38 3-D medical scan
39 College admissions stat
41 It may be inflated or brusied
42 Typeface selections
44 "Ugh, why did you share that with me!"
45 Nagasaki noodles
46 Injuries from an altercation?
50 Astringent fruit
51 "Hamilton" actress Phillipa
52 Some tournament rounds
56 Pennywise phobias?
60 It shares Everest with Tibet
62 Device that runs FaceTime
63 Tony's portrayer on "NYPD Blue"
64 "You crushed me"
65 Birthmarks
66 Email folder
67 "___ it" ("Get going!")
68 Fall setting
69 Droop-nosed jets

DOWN

1 "Whole New World" singer Bryson
2 Upper New York Bay island
3 Place to cybershop
4 Uncouth type
5 Asta's mistress
6 Royal or D-Back
7 Looks after
8 Sponge from a vine
9 Atkins diet no-no
10 "Schmancy!"
11 Feeling like an outcast
12 Most common card value in blackjack
13 Ticket office notice
21 Food Network chef Garten
22 Wide-eyed reaction
26 Pamplona pal
27 Joint component
29 Wine-and-cassis aperitif
30 Bowie's "Let's Dance" label
31 "___ pal and help me here"
32 Enthusiasts
33 How spring rolls are often cooked
34 Michael Jackson's nickname
38 Boulder winter hrs.
39 ABC early show, briefly
40 Indentation on a die
43 Polo field?
44 Walked en masse
45 Good for nothing
47 1990 Moldavia: Abbr.
48 Secant's reciprocal
49 PC "Oops!" key
53 Michelangelo sculpture
54 "You're the One That ___" ("Grease" song)
55 Tiny tantrums
57 A cappella voice
58 Most liked, casually
59 Match point score, perhaps
60 National Cancer Inst. parent
61 "Don't Bring Me Down" band

54 CUTTING CLASS by Greg Johnson
Test solvers liked the answer to 6 Down.

ACROSS

1 Web sensation
5 Unlikely to make the first move
10 Bulb unit
14 Pink-slips
15 Be aggressive in Texas Hold'em
16 Catcher Narváez
17 Salt used to treat icy roads
20 CPR practitioner
21 Horse groomer's focus
22 "You got that right!"
23 "Hmmm . . . don't think so"
24 Went feet first into second
25 Female cyborg of '70s TV
29 Household nickname
32 Like old-fashioned clothes
33 Phrase before "God"
35 Calorie counters' adjective
36 Paying job
37 Neatly arranged
38 Words of non-exactness
41 Prosper
43 Most-used English word
44 Sensitive firearm part
46 Happy gathering
47 Far from well
48 Widely assorted
51 Flower holder
52 Exasperated jigaw puzzler's cry
55 Roaring Twenties lingerie item
58 Casino conveniences
59 Specialty
60 Protected at sea
61 Biblical seafarer
62 Dentist's advice
63 Wolverine's super group

DOWN

1 Spice, club, or spray
2 Student stresser
3 Change states?
4 Error-fixing keyboard key
5 Attendance record blot
6 Response to "Are you awake?"
7 Tiny pets
8 "Sorta" suffix
9 Philistine seductress
10 ___ Champion
11 Brest friends
12 "And here it is!"
13 Ace, deuce, ___
18 Beatnik's "Got it!"
19 Group protecting a QB, in sports lingo
23 Like some GoFundMe goals
24 Horrible haze
25 Note above A
26 Kind of coffee with a kick
27 Convex navel
28 Basketry willow
29 Green garnish
30 Board meeting proposal start
31 Underground infrastructure
34 Towering

36 40 or 150 for sandpaper
39 A driver takes it
40 No-fuss oven cleaner brand
41 Gets rid of
42 New worker
45 Stretches of land
46 Blood brother?
48 Like Cinderella's stepsisters
49 Savvy about
50 Adult tube rating
51 Beach of Florida
52 Art house showing
53 Words of understanding
54 Mock election voter
56 D.C. insider
57 Caroline's "2 Broke Girls" roomie

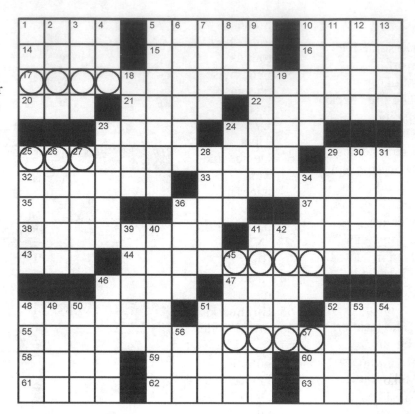

ACROSS

1 Player or Hoosier city
5 Public face
10 Branch division
14 Lard alternative
15 Cretan labyrinth builder
16 1965 Beatles album
17 Third Day creation
18 Ahead in the standings
19 Gathers info, with "around"
20 Observe a Christmas tradition
23 "Weird Al" Yankovic hit
24 Bucolic sprawl
25 Straw grass
28 Brother of a children's doll
33 Place to sample ziti and linguini
37 Paperless publication
38 "___ boy!"
39 Fun and games
42 Limerick's land
43 Sideshow worker
45 Does as a teakettle does
47 Device promoting gun safety
50 Enjoy a fine brandy
51 Underground commodity
52 Stern with a bow
57 Breakfast order/TITLE
62 Poster's POV comment

64 "___ With Music": Berlin
65 Bend, like wet lumber
66 It starts and ends at the same place
67 Swelling
68 Middle eye layer
69 Chilly forecast temps
70 Bowler's button
71 Spherical hammer part

DOWN

1 "Look for yourself!"
2 Apple : Siri :: Amazon : ___
3 Flinch, for example
4 "Super Mario Bros." dinosaur
5 "My turn to perform!"
6 Priceless Chinese vase
7 Poker payment
8 The G in Gmail
9 Looked (at)
10 Pointer's object
11 Conagra brand
12 Kind
13 Device that can calculate MPH
21 Gillette razor
22 Alice who sang "You'll Never Know"
26 Have a crush on
27 Pant-leg pullers
29 Fitness enthusiast's "six-pack"

30 Empty space
31 Mutt's warning
32 Be an accomplice
33 Deals formalized in writing
34 "Paperboy" parent
35 Sexy bit of burlesque
36 Sharp flavor
40 Pi-Sigma connector
41 First X or O in a game
44 Horror film blacksmith
46 Forklift's pallet
48 It gets the lead out
49 Like "True Grit" in 2010
53 Put in stitches
54 Tequila source
55 Be in harmony

56 "Washington Journal" TV network
58 Crime stoppers
59 NFL off weeks
60 Margarita wedge
61 Nouveaux-Mexique, e.g.
62 "___ Follow the Sun": Beatles
63 Sound from a pasture

DON'T BLAME MOTHER NATURE   by Mark Feldman

Rum, curaçao, pineapple juice, and cream of coconut are ingredients in a 43-A.

ACROSS

1 Detached
6 Planets and such
10 Video file format
14 ___ Nast
15 1979 exile
16 Like some history
17 Certain media barrage
19 Mention
20 Fixed in place, as a barnacle
21 Bibliophiles
23 Skyrocket
25 Loads
26 Chocolate Dairy Queen treat
31 Anatomical lint collectors
32 Fall flat
33 Galley need
36 Two found on Aaron Judge's uniform
37 Street cred
38 Zulu, for one
40 Letters after Sen. Coons
41 Confucian path
42 Mended
43 Colorful tropical drink
47 Pick
49 Cousin of a canvasback
50 Garage containers
52 Type of fiction
57 Docile
58 Very bright electric lamp
60 Soleil who was Punky Brewster
61 River to the Seine
62 Speciality
63 Over there
64 Early "Tonight Show" host
65 Like soy sauce

DOWN

1 Follower of John
2 "West Wing" actor Rob
3 Two make two
4 Keats creations
5 Fixations
6 Bone-related
7 Density symbol
8 Dig
9 Gossip
10 One who ridicules
11 Drama queen
12 Put away
13 Secluded valleys
18 They lack decorum
22 New Zealand yam
24 Weather (the storm)
26 Back
27 Author Bagnold
28 Mother of Good Queen Bess
29 Cause for a shootout
30 Nada
34 Egyptian deity
35 Boorish
37 Stadium cheer
38 Court officers
39 Bow
41 Justin Bieber's genre
42 Hogwarts villain
44 Guaranteed
45 "Suits" airer
46 One at ease
47 Like a well-used recliner
48 Sacred: Prefix
51 Actor LaBeouf
53 Director Kazan
54 Celebrated Coward
55 Farm newborn
56 Small whirlpool
59 Spanish she-bear

57 CUSTOM INSTRUMENTS by Mark Feldman
"If music be the food of love, play on." — Shakespeare

ACROSS

1 Book before Nehemiah
5 Jezebel's husband
9 Red carpet figure
14 Retain
15 Resting place
16 Key material
17 Instrument for a Saint Patrick's Day celebration?
19 Edge
20 Old Italian coin
21 Cornflakes condition, at times
23 A long time ago
25 Cheery tune
26 Instrument for a New Year's Eve party?
32 In shape
33 Flow stopper
34 Two-masted vessels
36 Milky gem
38 Beau
41 Nonclerical
42 Took off
44 Levin and Glass
46 Intel org.
47 Instrument for Nosey Parker?
51 Small case
52 Madonna's "La ___ Bonita"
53 Try again
57 Old strings
61 Part of a TV transmission
62 Instrument for a garage band?
64 Top-notch
65 Habit
66 Brother of Jacob
67 Lugs
68 Biblical plot
69 Cream

DOWN

1 Hosp. tests
2 Loser
3 Whirl
4 Simian's world
5 Volcanic fallout
6 Big house
7 '60s hairdo
8 Anklet
9 In a polite manner
10 In the future
11 Tribal knowledge
12 Work units
13 Tournament passes
18 Like sexist jokes
22 Bitmap image format
24 Nutritional figs.
26 Fiscal execs
27 River giant
28 Ever
29 Author Marsh
30 Banjo sound
31 "Clueless" actress Donovan
35 Peruse
37 "Project Runway" network
39 Put on edge
40 Some votes
43 Parlor art
45 Puzzle out
48 Pool tool
49 Tone quality
50 Corporate shark
53 Awestruck
54 Continental capital
55 Mine entrance
56 Egg on
58 About
59 Haole gathering
60 Blue material
63 "Baseball" director Burns

58 THEMELESS by Harvey Estes
The answer at 36 Across is serving double duty.

ACROSS

1 Fleece
5 Lay low
10 Works on a quilt
14 Cosmetics brand
15 Like a Bosc
16 Fast-food sandwich
17 Expresses awe
18 Tank buildup
19 Minute quantity
20 "Go Your Own Way" group (with 36-A)
22 Anesthetized
23 Eero Saarinen's homeland
24 Grovel
26 Editorial crew
28 Panama port
29 Rhubarb
31 Sparkle
32 Hayes of westerns
36 See 20 Across or 52 Across
37 Odysseys
38 On ___ with
39 Cavalry member
41 Spiff (up)
43 Stir them into liquids
48 Wades through puddles
50 Hung jury result
51 All in knots
52 A comfort food (with 36-A)
54 Mayberry moppet
55 Earmark
56 Fork over, with "up"
57 Small vessel
58 Kind of trail
59 Iodine source
60 Wiggly swimmers

61 "I Want You" singer
62 Salty septet

DOWN

1 Dismisses, with "at"
2 "Don't have a cow, boy!"
3 Parthenon figure
4 Emphatic first person
5 Salmon, at times
6 Play with excessive display
7 Verdi villain
8 Sports transaction
9 Needle feature
10 Chiseler
11 Vulnerable to washouts
12 Deciduous swamp tree
13 Rivals of the Buckeyes
21 Candy that sticks to your ribs?
22 Hagen of "Reversal of Fortune"
25 Washboard muscles
27 Goes over quickly
30 "Weird Al" Yankovic's instrument
32 Indoor range
33 Deep-dish dessert
34 Stately
35 Belgian lace city
37 Dare alternative
39 "Brokeback Mountain" director

40 Complex counterpart of Oedipus
42 Michael of "SNL"
44 "Them's the ___"
45 Many a homeowner
46 Lincoln Heights locale
47 What the lion does tonight, in song
49 Jazz vocalist Vaughan
53 Robert Mondavi Winery site
55 Sets in the den

59 THEMELESS by Harvey Estes

The name in the clue at 46 Across bears no connection to the puzzle's author.

ACROSS

1 Book after Job
7 Droll sorts
11 Class for EMTs
14 Country singer George
15 A lot, maybe
16 Dirt chopper
17 Snitch
18 On the battlefield
20 Trait bearer
21 Elongated cuttle-fish organ
22 Really enjoyed, as a joke
25 Fast online connection
26 Jazz great Fitzgerald
27 "Ghostbusters" goop
29 Nose activator
33 Medicinal doses
35 Height of happiness
37 Time of anticipation
38 Birmingham resource
40 She-sheep
41 Going over land
43 I's from Ithaca
45 Diggs of "Private Practice"
46 State ravaged by Harvey in 2017
48 Silver suffix
49 Atlantic crosser of old
51 Hitchcock classic
53 Dirty pool
57 Claim innocence of
58 Battery type
59 Points of view
62 Aberdeen river

63 "Downton Abbey" housemaid
64 ___ public
65 Coast Guard alert
66 "Son of Frankenstein" blacksmith
67 Put on board

DOWN

1 Winter time in L.A.
2 RMN's Veep
3 Florence's Uffizi, notably
4 Pass to the side
5 "Sneezles" poet
6 Chargers
7 Cry from a loser at season's end
8 Face defacer
9 Majesty
10 Splinter groups
11 In vogue
12 Sunbathing locale
13 Russo of "Ransom"
19 Hawk's hook
22 Reprise
23 Mariska's "Law & Order" role
24 Breakfast nook, e.g.
28 Long green
30 "Kashrut" subject
31 How Christian soldiers march, in song
32 Brand of peanut butter cup
34 Dear follower
36 "De Civitate ___": Augustine
39 Saber-___
42 AC pioneer Nikola
44 On account of
47 Auto suggestions?
50 Turn outward
52 "Death ___ proud": Donne
53 Passing things
54 Breakfast spread
55 Mandolin relatives
56 Word used in dating
60 Heir homophone
61 Pink Floyd guitarist Barrett

THEMELESS by Marie Langley
There appears to be a mini-theme at 23, 24, and 47 Across.

ACROSS

1 Slangy refusals
5 ___-Fella Records (former Jay-Z label)
9 For the future
14 Protected from the wind
15 Book of Mormon book
16 Hajj destination
17 Open cars
19 Starboard's opposite
20 "The Sound of Music" song
21 Observe Ash Wednesday
23 Lunar expanse (with 24-A)
24 See 23 Across
27 Quebec street
28 6–0, in tennis
31 Charged up
35 Honeybun
36 Stick in one's ___ (rankle)
37 No more than
38 False rumors
42 Cricket strikers
45 Optical range
46 Suffix for sheep
47 Inlets of 23–24 Across?
53 Invite forgiveness
55 Staff note
56 Now
57 Auto option
59 One who gives dough to doughboys
61 Constructive one
62 Garfield's sidekick
63 Herring species
64 Casts forth
65 First U.S. police agcy.
66 Deep desires

DOWN

1 "West Side Story" Shark
2 Above it all
3 Four-H Club "H"
4 Meal with questions
5 Hangers-on and others
6 Ace value in cribbage
7 Greek island
8 Lashes out at
9 Displaying love
10 Adjective for a cool cat
11 Environmental concern
12 It may be a plot
13 They're often raw
18 Bright
22 School zone sign
25 Math proof abbr.
26 Abounds
29 Cork's country
30 "Dawson's Creek" type
31 Behold, in old Rome
32 Angiogram, e.g.
33 Bamboo thicket
34 James Taylor's "___ Fool to Care"
39 Lyricists, notably
40 Rx amount
41 Crush underfoot
42 Chomped into
43 Racked by guilt
44 Sorority letter
48 Sycophant
49 Sphagnous
50 Donna Summer's "___ Radio"
51 Swell place?
52 Unhip types
53 National Mall shade providers
54 Swing a sickle
58 Do zigzags, maybe
60 Chihuahua cry

61 THEMELESS by Marie Langley
"I dood it!" was the signature line of 26 Down.

ACROSS

1 Auction stipulation
5 "The Jungle Book" star
9 Terrible twos, for one
14 Printed pause
16 White sale purchase
17 Keep on keeping on
18 Moorehead of "Bewitched"
19 "The Ranch" star
21 Half a laugh
22 Look suggestively
23 Made baskets
27 Random witness
31 Copier need
32 Ashtray remnant
33 Richard in "The Dinner"
34 Barely made, with "out"
35 Marseilles moms
36 Oratorio highlight
37 Barbecue entrée
38 They're not refined
39 Power networks
40 Atlas, for one
42 Potato peeler, e.g.
43 Long swimmers
44 Huge amount
45 Impending danger, proverbially
51 Poem division
52 Compact material
54 Reel person
55 Like a gut reaction
56 2018 Yankees skipper
57 Tide variety
58 Listen to

DOWN

1 Venom source
2 Ward of "Sisters"
3 Radio man Don
4 Wistful sound
5 Had no copilot
6 Out on a limb
7 Knock on the noggin
8 Hoofed mammals
9 Cry to actors on a set
10 Great esteem
11 Last of the Stuarts
12 Student of palms
13 Halves of ems
15 "One of Ours" novelist
20 Dry runs
23 Unsmiling
24 Newswoman Roberts
25 Year before AD began
26 Sheriff Deadeye portrayer
27 Baby food
28 Equip anew
29 Garter tosser
30 It gets a rise out of rye
32 "West Side Story" composer
35 Dough
39 Best Picture of 1982
41 Prior to
42 Increases in cost
44 Frat letter
45 Baylor University site
46 Not taken in by
47 Lacey portrayer Daly
48 Scout recitation
49 Drooling dog of comics
50 Gad about
51 Metered transport
53 Got hitched

AB WORKOUT   by Gary Larson
37 Across might get you home when you can't find a Lyft.

ACROSS

1 Babe in the woods
5 Fanatical
10 Cicatrix
14 Natural emollient
15 Amazon parrot
16 Tie up
17 Shell-seeking crustacean
19 Cut
20 Wacky doctor of radio
21 Old Olds
22 Type of jewelry heist
26 Director's cry
29 Inundated
30 Dentist's advice
31 Abba of Israel
32 Bygone title
36 St. Louis pro
37 Metered vehicle
40 Connect
41 Has chits out
43 Follows
44 Litmus reddeners
46 Swahili for "freedom"
48 Turkey's highest peak
49 A/C condenser base
53 Sporty Camaros
54 Personal partner
58 Go out with
59 Bazaar dish
62 Summers on the Seine
63 Ancient Aegean land
64 Archaeological find
65 Cold War foe
66 Descartes and Magritte
67 Flashed signs

DOWN

1 Former Saudi king
2 On the quiet side?
3 Contemptible one
4 Ruin
5 Wicker material
6 Some stations
7 Tavern
8 A Gershwin
9 Pinch
10 Dexterity
11 Play (to)
12 Capital of Ghana
13 Doctor's order
18 Deepest
21 S&L offerings
23 Regular visitor
24 Military plane acronym
25 Olive Oyl's mother
26 Retro hairdo
27 Manhandle
28 Heavy reading
31 Apply, as pressure
33 Arouse
34 "O patria mia" singer
35 Catch one's breath
38 Chill
39 Father of Sasha and Malia
42 Hit
45 Monthly bill, for many
47 Mins. and mins.
48 Top dogs
49 Autumn drink
50 Speak from a soapbox
51 Eminent
52 "Calvin and Hobbes" girl
55 Double-reed woodwind
56 Indistinguishable
57 Drops
59 Lady's man
60 Tiller's tool
61 Wayside stop

63 SHIFTING SELECTIONS   by Gary Larson
17 Across is a living memorial to John Lennon.

ACROSS

1 Boxer Riddick
5 National forest in California
11 Pensioned: Abbr.
14 Comparable
15 Affixes in a scrapbook, say
16 First mate
17 Strawberry Fields locale
19 Bedevil
20 Southern constellation
21 Broadcasts
22 Spark
23 Tricky football play
26 Big to-do
28 Email feature
29 Moist
30 Sure thing
35 First name in old horror films
36 Didn't attract attention
37 Wray of "King Kong"
40 Bad guy
41 Combine
42 Bit the dust
45 Exit
47 Like "flight attendant"
52 "M*A*S*H" actor
53 Bookkeeping entry
54 Rand McNally product
57 Caution sign warning
58 Hawaii's Road to Hana, for one
60 Farm mother
61 Slot spot
62 Not procrastinating
63 Election winners
64 Aim
65 Joins

DOWN

1 "Goldberg Variations" composer
2 ___-doke
3 Relax after work
4 Measure of disorder
5 Mudbath locale
6 Fit to eat, to Muslims
7 Easy ___
8 First Super Bowl MVP
9 Short-winded
10 Put it to
11 Studio effect
12 Very
13 Southwestern cuisine
18 Spanish for "Ralph"
22 Chap
24 Metabolism type
25 Aspect
26 "Good" cholesterol
27 Antipoverty agcy.
31 Be sick
32 Kind of approval
33 First name in pharmaceuticals
34 Lisa of "The Cosby Show"
36 For dieters
37 Tank-engine connector
38 Sancho's mount
39 "Of course"
40 Baseball's Blue
41 Rush site
42 1999 U.S. Open champ
43 Rat out
44 Funds
46 Alum
48 Puerto ___
49 Mushroom producer: Abbr.
50 Choice word
51 Gopher coll.
55 Ardent
56 Math groups
58 High school subj.
59 Red Cross supply

RARE BREED   by Gary Larson
52 Across was a Razzie nominee for Worst Actress of the Century.

ACROSS

1 Belly-wash
5 NYPD employee
9 Heathen
14 "When ___ Loves a Woman"
15 Cabeza, across the Pyrenees
16 Run off to the chapel
17 Pooch for a Muay Thai fighter?
19 Demean
20 Like yesterday's news
21 Played bumper cars?
23 PC key
25 Crowd sound
26 Popular music category
29 Pooch for a fashionista?
35 In the center of
37 Jimmy Stewart syllables
38 "Romeo and Juliet" setting
39 Kitchen set
41 Biological maps
42 "Brokeback Mountain" director
43 Kind of WWE team
44 Office fill-in
45 Pooch for a clinical scientist?
48 Method: Abbr.
49 Brazilian soccer legend
50 Anatomical pouch
52 "Butterfly" star
57 Fountain order
61 Hang
62 Pooch for a geologist?
64 Unmoving
65 Cuatro y cuatro
66 Victorian
67 Bad, bad Brown of song
68 Classic Jaguars
69 Fill to the gills

DOWN

1 Nordstrom rival
2 Leave out
3 "Dreamers" program
4 It's just over a foot
5 Simpson trial judge
6 Call in a bakery
7 The "S" in T.S. Eliot
8 Era
9 Olive cousin
10 Jessica of "Fantastic Four"
11 Bearded beast
12 Cathedral area
13 Distress
18 Superlative
22 Nevada gambling mecca
24 Like the moon
26 Bulletless gun
27 Nitrogen compound
28 Engine sounds
30 Milk supplier
31 Fox or turkey follower
32 Volumes
33 Hostile force
34 Woodworking tools
36 Expunge
40 Historic Boston event
41 Guy's date
43 Alcatraz nickname
46 Bleach brand
47 Big do
51 Whacks
52 "Two Hearts" singer Collins
53 Donovan's daughter Skye
54 Declare
55 Goose egg
56 Have a hankering
58 Ambience
59 Come together
60 Head start
63 68 George Foreman wins

65 TELEVISION SERIES   by Gary Larson
37 Down is Italian for "a little bitter."

ACROSS

1 Salad cheese
5 Leave in, as text
9 Get ready for a date
14 Milky white gem
15 Craving
16 Settle
17 Scenic stagecraft
19 Sell online
20 Footnote phrase
21 Did nothing
23 Double curve
24 Savior
26 Mechanics tool
30 Cunning
33 Pacific island
34 Procter & Gamble detergent
35 Skin cream ingredient
36 Bird-woman of myth
38 Carey or Barrymore
39 River mouth
40 "A Certain Age" author Janowitz
41 Delaware statesman
42 "Cape Fear" (1962) star
46 Barbecue fare
47 Hindu honorific
50 Technophobe
53 Criminal assistant
55 Adds and subtracts, verbally
56 Slang term for a hot dog
58 Filmdom's Mr. Chips
59 Like some glasses
60 "My treat"
61 Hoity-toity sorts
62 Mining finds
63 Concern for vets

DOWN

1 "All That Jazz" director
2 Olympic blades
3 "Soap" family
4 "Betsy's Wedding" star
5 Battle of Hastings locale
6 Transistor's forerunner
7 "Deviled" food
8 Taut
9 Like some deliveries
10 Stop working
11 Apple product
12 Letters
13 Gomer or Goober
18 "Crazylegs" Hirsch
22 Center of Orlando
25 Inscribe
26 Capital of Brazil?
27 Dork
28 Algonquian language
29 Goldie in "Shampoo"
30 Curtain-call group
31 Protected
32 Polo score
36 Attacks
37 Alabama Slammer ingredient
38 Insult, slangily
40 Keyboarders
41 Innocent ones
43 Form of acid
44 Like farmland
45 Puts down
47 Angioplasty tube
48 Goes here and there
49 Annoyed
50 Certain lights
51 Japanese noodle
52 Rat Pack nickname
54 Sporty car roof
57 Nasser's org.

66 EXCEPT AFTER C? by Scot Ober
Below are five exceptions to the rule.

ACROSS

1 "No way" man
5 Employed
9 Mischievous rascals
13 Like sexist jokes
14 Le Tour de France stage
15 Old phone feature
16 Campaigner's objective
17 Shortage
19 Arm art, for short
20 Ouse feeder
21 Wax like Webster
22 Marie Curie, e.g.
25 Dennis Mitchell's mom
27 Simian swingers
28 Atty.'s title
30 "Mr. Basketball" Holman
31 Airline to TLV
32 Toro's target
34 MLB VIPs
35 Upscale hotel employee
38 "Beat it!"
41 Word before or after "where"
42 Puts two and two together
45 Suffix for president
46 "Told ya!"
47 Wiped out
49 "Advise and Consent" author
51 CFO
54 Chatting with online, briefly
56 "Santa Baby" singer
57 Barely manage, with "out"
58 Jiminy Cricket's role
60 Made like
61 Chimney vent
62 Vichyssoise veggies
63 Arctic Ocean floater
64 At times, it's more
65 Down times
66 Highlands dialect

DOWN

1 In this precise way
2 160 square rods
3 Three-dimensional
4 Outer, at the outset
5 Female organs
6 Deposit boxes
7 Start to cure?
8 Oscar Bach's sometime art style
9 Best of all
10 Making money
11 One to follow at Indy
12 Foxy, in a way
14 Toys with text
18 Mesopotamia, today
20 Part of WASP
23 Put on the books
24 Conical home
26 Wormhole travelers
29 Sun. message
32 Viola's staff symbol
33 Grafton's "___ for Alibi"
34 "M*A*S*H" figure
36 Formerly known as
37 Haggard
38 Penguin captain Crosby
39 One-horse open sleigh
40 Claire Danes vis-à-vis Yale
43 Kiev river
44 "I'll Never Find Another You" group
46 Match sound to action
47 Contributes to Yelp
48 Coat in flour
50 Greets the judge
52 "Didn't surprise me!"
53 Shaving souvenirs
55 Bass organ?
58 Grey Cup org.
59 Fair-hiring initials
60 Japanese prime minister

ACROSS

1 Ne plus ultra
5 Dizzy's jazz style
8 Baseball crew
12 Disappearance of a five o'clock shadow
15 Cozy recess
16 1957 song by 56 Across
17 "I don't like your ___!"
18 2005 Prince hit
19 Conger and moray
20 "___ something?"
21 1972 song by 56 Across
24 Apple variety
27 Biting
28 Guide for a chair
31 Celt or Highlander
32 UK reference work
35 1975 song by 56 Across
38 Bachelor ___
39 Inks or clinks
40 Dahl of "Here Come the Girls"
41 Numbskull
42 Pioneer talk-show host
43 1960 album by 56 Across
50 Needing a rinse
51 Football coach Babers
52 Abdul Aziz ___ Saud
55 & & &
56 "Back in the U.S.A." singer
59 "In ___ of flowers . . ."
60 Successful Fagin trainee
61 Ballpark covering
62 Copycat
63 Royals manager Ned

DOWN

1 "What a pity!"
2 Loafer coin
3 "Spy vs. Spy" magazine
4 Pupil
5 Chaliapin and Pinza, notably
6 Egg head?
7 Chest muscle
8 Like Oscar Madison's room
9 Museum exhibit from Apollo 15
10 "Doctor Zhivago" producer
11 Flock in flight
12 Onion soup holders
13 Pirate on the "Jolly Roger"
14 Keel locale
20 Fisherman
21 Arrange in order
22 "Cool!"
23 "A Passage to India" heroine
24 Audible surprise
25 Turkish VIP
26 Starring role
29 Sheriff's subordinate
30 "You ___ kidding!"
31 Sporty Mustangs
32 Eligible for service
33 "The Cider House Rules" nurse
34 More waggish
36 King Tut's "cross of life"
37 "Sound of Music" backdrop
41 Drinks like a kitty
43 Halite
44 Ancient Aegean area
45 "Unsafe at Any Speed" author
46 Draw a conclusion
47 Hayseed
48 Beetle Bailey's status, often
49 N'awlins hero
52 Chafes
53 Brother of Bart and Brent Maverick
54 The Gray Lady's monogram
56 TurboTax alternative
57 Rose fruit
58 "Foucault's Pendulum" author

68 A GOOD WORKOUT by Mark McClain
Your muscles will feel better in the end.

ACROSS

1 Office personnel
6 Tan's "The Joy Luck ___"
10 Bridge seat
14 Capital of Siberia?
15 Clio, for one
16 One not to be trusted
17 Studio sign
18 Limbs
19 For two, on a score
20 Detailed objectives for a development team
23 Poughkeepsie campus
26 Work crew honchos
27 Complete
28 Embarrassing spat
30 Tiny quarters
32 Big Ten's Spartans
35 Journalist Hamill
36 "___ Changing" ("Dreamgirls" song)
37 Access point
38 Wood-shaping tool
39 They travel in borrowed shells
43 Barbershop symbols
44 A sister of Clio
45 Off the ship
48 Grammy category since 1987
49 Rapid-response police units
53 Manlis in "Dick Tracy"
54 Slips in a poker game
55 Wee bits
59 "A Death in the Family" novelist
60 Sedgwick of Warhol films
61 Engine booster
62 Firewood amount
63 Anti-DWI youth org.
64 Swine haunts

DOWN

1 1966 Herb Alpert album
2 Winery cask
3 Org. with many judges
4 45-B
5 Car with a black horse badge
6 Piano student's first key, briefly
7 Carrot on a stick
8 "Semper Fi" org.
9 Top choice
10 Pass, as time
11 Senate helpers
12 Remoulade, e.g.
13 Keyless lock
21 Lunchbox favorite
22 "___ and Lovers": Lawrence
23 Italian two-wheeler
24 Chipped in a chip
25 Model 8 Blackhawk car
28 Closes rudely
29 Short negligee
31 Terminate
32 2016 Disney film
33 Edna Ferber novel
34 Alpha ___ Minoris (Polaris)
37 Elicits
39 Triceratops feature
40 Melancholy works
41 Casserole fish
42 Acknowledges
43 Cool as a cucumber
45 Insurance giant
46 Irish county
47 Overwrought, informally
50 Part of a Happy Meal
51 ___ pro quo
52 Got some good out of
56 Numerical prefix
57 Pappy Yokum's grandson
58 Troubled telegraphy

69 INITIAL SETUP   by Mark McClain
A pencil is the only tool needed for this project.

ACROSS

1 Wedding party figure
6 Craggy peaks
10 Self-important
14 It may be one to ten
15 They play in Miami
16 Mephisto's realm
17 Large raptor
18 Former Dallas quarterback
19 Ms. Karenina
20 Free music source
22 They're not on the A team
24 One-time AP rival
25 Main drag
27 They cover their eyes
29 Working hard
30 Grand Central walkways
35 "You got me on my knees" song
37 Event places
38 Surgical assistant
41 The Doors album
42 Earthquake prefix
43 "The Planets" composer
44 Warren Buffett's birthplace
45 Croatian pasta
46 Headset, to hams
50 Misgivings
52 Judge ___ Bean
53 The Wolfpack of the ACC
57 It may be taught by a coach
60 Atlas datum
61 Not aweather
63 Restrict
64 Schnitzel meat
65 Musical based on "La Bohème"
66 Type of dress
67 Holler
68 Japanese salad plants
69 Bette Midler's "divine" nickname

DOWN

1 Handy
2 Garlicky seafood dish
3 Hogwarts friendly giant
4 "Enchanted" Hathaway role
5 Bassoonist's buy
6 Gas pedal
7 "Great Society" agcy.
8 Missile engine
9 Franklin namesake
10 "Inside the NBA" analyst
11 It might pop up or pull down
12 Radius partner
13 Tickled pink
21 Mom's ultimate reason
23 Scatters about
26 Narrow inlet
28 Post-snow mess
31 Make ___ of (write down)
32 Fall bloomer
33 Paella morsel
34 Govt. issued ID
36 Force defeated in 1588
37 Small carry-on
38 Barcelona bear
39 "Radio Song" group
40 Actress Vardalos
41 Pictures seen on utility poles
43 Epicenter
45 Gassed up
47 One of the Musketeers
48 Treats a cello bow
49 Modus operandi
51 Hokkaido seaport
53 Dark blue
54 Saskatchewan lake
55 "G.I. Jane" commando
56 Like giant sequoias
58 Geoduck
59 Violinist Haydn
62 Neuse River tributary

DOUBLE SHUFFLE   by Brian E. Paquin
Answers to clues* are anagrams of each other.

ACROSS
1 Olden days
5 Marching band instrument
9 Mosque leaders
14 Eddie's "Beverly Hills Cop" role
15 "Like ___ without a tail": Shak.
16 Kathmandu locale
17 Entered full-force*
19 Snap course
20 China's Zhou ___
21 "Get going!"
23 Tizzy
26 Big name in banks
27 Like natural hairstyles*
30 Napoleon's 1814 address
34 Little piggy
35 Slippery–eel connector
36 School papers
38 Perfume ingredient
40 "Every child. One voice." org.
42 On a cruise
43 "Apparently!"
45 Neighbor of Yemen
47 Tree goo
48 2007 animated superhero film
49 Contract winner, usually*
52 Font option, briefly
54 2017 category 5 hurricane
55 Hope and Centenary, e.g.
59 Company with a spokesduck
63 Task of a log driver
64 Capability*
67 Speak grandly
68 Speak wildly
69 Amazon's hands-free speaker
70 Genders
71 Elects (to)
72 Musical pause

DOWN
1 One of the Colonial Colleges
2 Farm team?
3 Honest-to-goodness
4 Hit song for Marty Robbins
5 Mai ___
6 Coffee container
7 Steps up to the plate
8 Forthwith
9 All thumbs
10 Superlative for country-style ribs*
11 Lhasa ___ (dog breed)
12 Request for permission
13 Jalousie part
18 Old pots and pans
22 Staffer
24 Psyche parts
25 Lie for a sand iron
27 Type of buddy
28 Allow to enter
29 Pulled behind
31 Finnish marathoner Virén
32 One way to play music
33 PDQ relative
34 Type of tube
37 "Spider-Man 3" supervillain
39 Ballpark figure*
41 Word form of "both"
44 Gusto
46 Broadcast
50 Veteran
51 More flaky
53 Big books
55 Musical pairs
56 Memo starter
57 Comet competitor
58 Afternoon drama
60 Pet problem
61 Hot tub sounds
62 Coagulate
65 Demolition compound
66 Grays, to George Noory

THEMELESS by Brian E. Paquin

22 Down was the only man to beat the great John L. Sullivan.

ACROSS

1 Objects of many internet romance scams
16 Silver-tongued scoundrels
17 Quit-smoking product
18 Canadian heavy weight
19 Spanish 101 verb
20 Cooties
23 Kiln
25 Arsenal contents
29 Lacking in funds
31 Thunderous applause
34 Assateague Island's wild animals
36 One way to serve strawberries
37 "Dragnet" alert
38 Only a few
40 "Life ___ cabaret . . ."
41 Looks through blinds
43 Cut loose
45 Holds in high regard
46 Spy plane
47 Pixels
48 Facebook security breach
52 MIT grad: Abbr.
53 Action figure, e.g.
56 Jessica in "Cape Fear"
58 Oak Island quest for many years
65 The Dalai Lama, e.g.
66 What Kojak licked

DOWN

1 Web portal introduced with Windows 95
2 "___ right?"
3 World sports org.
4 Money-minded rioters
5 "Airplane!" pilot
6 Horned heavyweight
7 Reed on "Dallas"
8 Olympic blades
9 School subj.
10 Best buds
11 Flatten
12 Say again and again
13 Crime boss
14 Bit of work
15 Not Hitchcock's dir.?
20 Like some living rooms
21 "With a little luck"
22 "Gentleman Jim" of boxing
24 Type of booth or bridge
26 4, 5, or 6, to Tiger
27 Cat skill
28 In theory
30 On edge
32 Cello's ancestor
33 Played a part
35 Tahini brand
36 Took a load off
39 Pish-___ in "The Mikado"
42 Result of jumping the gun
44 Origin of some syrups
49 Baptismal area
50 Italian name for Charles
51 Solemn toll
54 Big name in elevators
55 Himalayan "bigfoot"
57 Scottish Highlander
58 West Coast hrs.
59 Wall St. debut
60 Ipanema's city
61 Petition
62 Japanese salad green
63 Workout unit
64 Trauma ctrs.

72 HISTORIC DECLARATION by Gene Newman
A good one to solve on the Fourth of July.

ACROSS

1 Parka part
5 "The Wind in the Willows" protagonist
9 Sri Lanka royals
14 Control tower's "A"
15 Angelic corona
16 Convex molding
17 Historic Declaration author
19 Nothing to Caesar
20 Worried
22 Soprano Netrebko
23 Fife-and-drum drums
26 Like terra cotta
28 Pay strict attention
29 Bygone "cool"
32 Citi Field's predecessor
33 Muppet in a striped shirt
35 Printing process, familiarly
37 Sue Herera's CNBC show
40 M-1, for one
41 Scarf for Mae West
42 Jack of "Law & Order"
44 Suffix for chariot
45 Cold symptom
47 Dwell on gloomily
48 "Fedora" highlight
50 Birthplace of Venus
52 Prom problem
53 Paganini, by birth

56 Longshoreman
58 Boozehound
59 Loft tool
62 Lombardy capital
64 Monarch angered by the Declaration
68 Useful
69 Point de gaze
70 Mouth area
71 Uptight
72 Goddess of strife
73 Phoenix NBA team

DOWN

1 Pilgrimage to Mecca
2 Fiesta-taurina cheer
3 On holiday
4 Spring bloomer
5 Use a flail
6 Hops kiln
7 Plenty
8 Gift recipient
9 Yankee legend Guidry
10 Take to the sky
11 First signer of the Declaration
12 Skirt style
13 Large seabird
18 Blunder
21 Salt measure
23 Not here
24 Clifftop nest
25 Oldest signer of the Declaration
27 Equilateral parallelogram
30 Major river of Central Europe
31 Having reverence
34 Weird
36 Make the wild mild

38 Alamo hero Daniel
39 Winona in "Homefront"
43 Cheese and ___
46 Corned-beef dish
49 Grammy-winning Lorde song
51 Worships
53 Entire range
54 Crème de la crème
55 Protected bird
57 URL suffix for charities
60 Wine price factor
61 An ellipse has two
63 Word in an alumna's bio
65 Debtor's note
66 Charged atom
67 Qualifiers

36 ACROSS*   by Gene Newman
Clues* relate to 36 Across, or do they?

ACROSS

1 Type of tube or pilot
5 Losing project
9 A real bargain*
14 Scheherazade, for one
15 La Belle Epoch et al.
16 Sprite
17 Initial goal*
19 Omit, editorially
20 Alice's social
21 Pancake mixture*
22 Hurry
23 Roll-call call
24 Midlife ___
28 Norse death goddess
29 Judi Dench's title
33 "Back Street" novelist Fannie
34 Cinderella's debut event*
35 Gender
36 TITLE
40 Sine qua ___
41 Chart-toppers*
42 Zeal
43 Golfer Norman
45 Resort near Nice
46 Most slick
47 Apart from this
49 Chromosome component
50 Extinguish*
53 Twice the radius
58 Sluggish
59 Burnt offering*
60 Wells Fargo logo
61 Predeal investment
62 Richard in "The Dinner"
63 "Marine Coast" painter*
64 Coveted role
65 Burglar's booty

DOWN

1 President from Cincinnati
2 Albany-to-Buffalo canal
3 "Gravity" singer Bareilles
4 Butter meas.
5 Explosion remnants
6 Seeing red
7 Duck soup
8 Taoism founder Lao-___
9 Opera extra's prop
10 Askew
11 Departure
12 Amanuensis
13 Impolite stare
18 Gauguin's island
21 Stephenie Meyer heroine
23 Pitches in
24 Ravenclaw student Cho
25 Unconfirmed report
26 Peace goddess
27 Belarus, prev.
28 Impetuosity
30 Confidential stage line
31 Interoffice missives
32 Bring to bear
34 Pool table fabric
37 Medicine ___
38 Italian sub meat
39 Attempt
44 Babe Ruth, at birth
46 Caught
48 Smithfield Packing founder
49 Judicial opinions
50 Contemptuous reply
51 Golden Rule word
52 Work group*
53 Ophelia, for one
54 I preceders
55 "___ yellow ribbon . . ."
56 Lampshade shade
57 Dizzying dance
59 "Erie Canal Song" mule

74 REMEMBERING . . . by Mel Rosen
. . . a comedy icon who passed away in 2017.

ACROSS

1 Golden calf's maker
6 Weapon for Colonel Mustard
10 Rossum of "Shameless"
14 Commotion
15 Flapjack franchise
16 Heisman winner Flutie
17 **Start of a line by 46 Across**
20 Boxing official, for short
21 Mozart's "___ fan tutte"
22 Like hell?
23 Role of 46 Across
25 Chemical warfare gas
28 Apt. features
29 Victims of NFL sacks
32 Traffics
33 Quiet down
35 New Eng. campus
36 **Line: Part 2**
37 **Line: Part 3**
38 **Line: Part 4**
39 First name in dictation?
40 Love to extremes
42 "Home Sweet Home" lyricist
43 First character seen in "Zelig"
44 "I don't rightly reckon so"
45 Refreshment stands
46 "Back Home Again in Indiana" singer
49 How some kids spend the summer
52 "Chicken of the sea"
53 Diesel in "The Fast and the Furious"
56 **Line: Part 5**
59 Corrective coif
60 Churchill Downs, for one
61 Roaring Twenties car
62 The last word in churches
63 Goose liver spread
64 Resided

DOWN

1 Neil deGrasse Tyson subj.
2 Liniment target
3 Reduce sail
4 Thunder Bay's prov.
5 Political righties who once were lefties
6 Hair-tinting solution
7 2011 RBC Canadian Open winner
8 Detachable container
9 Louis Braille and Les Paul
10 Use an online matching service
11 Slam dance
12 Terpsichore, for one
13 Bela's "Son of Frankenstein" role
18 City on the Tiber
19 Like the name "Llewellyn"
23 Coolidge Dam river
24 Puckered plum
25 "Mad Men" milieu, casually
26 "The Cloister and the Hearth" author
27 ___ Hawkins Day
29 Waterfront structures
30 Precipice
31 Facets
33 Exhibited
34 2013 Rooney Mara film
38 Thailand neighbor
40 Inner self
41 Give the floor a quick clean
42 Like many films on torrent sites
45 King of Skull Island
46 Clarke in "Zero Dark Thirty"
47 Really vexed
48 Base horn
49 Gillette razor
50 The enemy, generically
51 Yield
53 Clamp
54 Hekla loc.
55 Soon to be served
57 Actress Longoria
58 180° from ENE

40 ACROSS   by Matthew Sewell
Twelve borderline answers relate to the title.

ACROSS

1 In need of a massage
5 Patient's record
10 Croissant
14 Kathryn of "Bad Moms"
15 "Our Gang" dog
16 Emollient ingredient
17 Plugging away
18 Not bottled
19 Versatile nuke
20 Encyclopedist Diderot
22 Free from
24 Neckline cut
25 Rarefied knowledge
27 Eldest von Trapp daughter
29 Welsh emblem on the £1 coin
30 Fair-haired guy
32 Quails
35 "I'm Real" singer, to fans
36 PhD exam
39 Less than bi-
40 Disdainful glance
43 Mahershala in "Moonlight"
44 Little jab
46 Rest one's dogs
47 Mine stratum
49 Immediate, in product names
51 Surfeit
52 UK humane org.
54 Junk pile
59 Make tracks
60 Indonesia's largest province
62 What a shin guard protects
63 Long-eared film sage

65 French nobleman
67 Paddock youngster
68 Naturalist on the California state quarter
69 Sun-___ tomatoes
70 One of the Baldwins
71 More than a quiz
72 Feb. 14 gift
73 Bullwhip

DOWN

1 Kind of tree
2 Daryl Hall's partner
3 Thick-skinned Spider-Man foe
4 Give the right to
5 USN rank
6 Playwright Ibsen
7 Room often entered headfirst
8 Easily comprehended
9 Cover letter head-slapper
10 Plow (into)
11 Fatigues color
12 Far from 4K
13 Flush
21 Tarot dealers
23 V8 Cafe owner in "Cars"
26 Kick up a fuss
28 Italian diminutive suffix
31 Chicago Jesuit school
32 Soccer trophy
33 Credited cowriter of "Imagine"

34 World's biggest encyclopedia
35 Deep black
37 Hoppy brew
38 Kettle cover
41 Cultural scattering
42 Lose it
45 Check in the mail: Abbr.
48 Righteous
50 Maple yield
51 Suitable for all ages
52 Mate bees with fleas?
53 Black Hills tribe
55 Chili powder herb
56 Virus carried by fruit bats
57 Former Fox News chairman
58 Stop-smoking aid

61 "High Voltage" band
64 Escort's offering
66 Big name in ice cream

61 ACROSS by Rich Proulx
Puzzlers will appreciate the answer at 61 Across.

ACROSS

1 Followers of prefixes
6 Mining target
10 Make turbid
14 Be on pins and needles, perhaps
15 Crowning achievement
16 Beige
17 Hawks
19 Charade
20 "People can die of ___ imagination": Chaucer
21 Sneaky ruse
23 Tiny, in Glasgow
25 Throws money around, literally
28 Sweet wine
30 Jobs for grads back in school
31 Meadow
32 German actress Sommer
33 Elects
35 Small songbird
39 "Love in the Dark" singer
41 Pluto, for one
42 Trap
43 Winona of "Stranger Things"
44 Swear
46 Peter III or Paul I
47 Citizens United, e.g.
49 "Y" wearer
50 Frequent flyers, once
51 Sharing feelings
56 Tiny
57 Arm-raising muscle
58 Corn syrup brand
60 Jazz home

61 Intellectual pastime
66 "What more ___ say?"
67 Sledder's need
68 Props
69 It's measured in kWh's
70 "Crikey!"
71 Nods

DOWN

1 Adage
2 Airline founded in 1930
3 Set aside
4 Harpo Marx, for one
5 Gully washer
6 See 41 Across
7 General Thade, e.g.
8 Gang lands?
9 Attack
10 Ties that bind
11 Lorena of the LPGA
12 Mashhad resident
13 Light unit
18 "Far out!"
22 Grounded flight?
23 Broccoli unit
24 Having mildew
26 Phi Beta ___
27 Emilio of "The Breakfast Club"
29 Like a meeting of the minds?
34 Russian vodka brand
36 Spycraft essentials
37 Seeing red
38 Brief
40 Muse whose name means "lovely"

45 Lets in on the joke
48 Swanky
51 Bring out
52 Mercury, for one
53 "It's a bird, it's a ___!"
54 Elba of "Luther"
55 Awkward
59 Lecher
62 Hi, in Fortaleza
63 Sneaky
64 With whom the buck stops?
65 Parseltongue sound

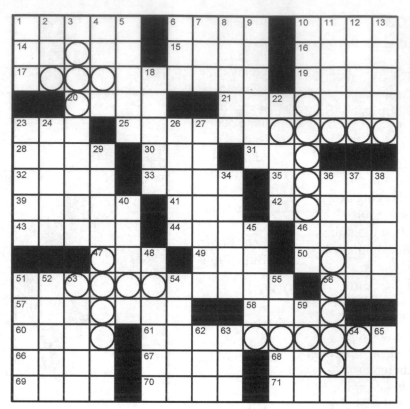

ACROSS

1 Big dos of the 70s
6 Medicare Rx section
11 Co. acquired by American
14 "The L Word" producer Chaiken
15 Child of the East and West
17 More unconvincing
18 2014 Bill Murray film
19 Dietary restriction
21 Observe shivah
22 Linking word
23 Cable service, e.g.
26 Word spoken with a hat tip
28 Considered
30 "___ Pagliaccio" (aria)
33 "The Big Bang Theory" network
34 First Lady of Song
35 Cold-blooded mousers
37 Easy tasks
40 Aloha State fruit
43 "The Sweetest Taboo" singer
47 Squeeze (out)
48 Blackjack table sight
49 Claw
51 Semiaquatic salamander
53 Kahlil Gibran's "earth poems"
55 CIA precursor
56 Basque cap
59 Skulks
61 Was logical
64 Aleve company
66 First felony conviction
67 Houston player
68 Prohibition
69 Essayist Nin
70 Butler who restored Tara

DOWN

1 Feel poorly
2 Sheet fabric
3 Add a second story
4 Washington singles
5 Mexican wrap
6 Unhealthily pale
7 Qty.
8 MLK title
9 Minor haircut
10 "Book 'em, ___!" ("Hawaii Five-O" catchphrase)
11 Neckwear organizer
12 Aspirant
13 Picnic invader
16 Vermin
20 Young'un
22 Gator tail
24 Shrimp boat
25 Curriculum ___
27 Slush pile contents: Abbr.
29 Nutmeg spice
31 AT&T offering
32 Tats
35 Move your mum
36 NAACP part
38 Two-year degs.
39 Champs-Élysées speed meas.
40 Pigsty
41 Japanese art of flower arranging
42 1994 Stephen Baldwin film
44 Altar server
45 Final course found in circles
46 Vocalized pauses
49 A pop
50 Weather map line
52 "___ bien, merci!"
54 Wired swords
57 "¿Cómo ___?"
58 Seabird with a forked tail
60 Launder
61 Group known for its hits?
62 Miss America ___ Franklin
63 Compete in super-G
65 Decay

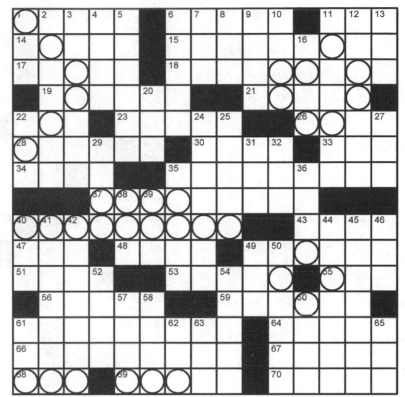

78 GIANT SOUNDS*   by Richard Silvestri
"...I smell the blood of an Englishman"

ACROSS

1 Having a musical key
6 Verne's circumnavigator
10 Ornamental stone
14 Ham it up
15 Turkish coin
16 Heaps
17 Big ray
18 Word of woe
19 Nut's partner
20 Bird of myth*
22 ___ Kappa*
24 Got lippy with
25 Irk
26 Have a go at
28 Afraid of nothing
32 Bunch of bills
35 Winter forecast
37 Neighbor of China
38 Like the Mojave
40 No longer hungry
42 Noah's scout
43 Challenge authority
45 Ape
47 Assault on the ears
48 Uses mucilage
50 Hidden hoard
52 Hall's singing partner
54 Cantina snack
58 Social blunder*
61 Dropped the ball*
62 Cross inscription
63 Mark of excellence
65 Take along
66 Don't lift a finger
67 Speck
68 Blake of jazz
69 No more than
70 Alter an Alsatian
71 Pulls (in)

DOWN

1 Office subs
2 City on the Missouri
3 They're forbidden
4 Bear witness
5 Almost ringers
6 Source of linen
7 Shale extract
8 Concord, for one
9 Cut to the bone
10 Talked on and on
11 Sunburn soother
12 Mental midget
13 Sundance Kid's love
21 Pastoral poems
23 Clarinet in "Peter and the Wolf"
25 Study of verse
27 Thunder or Lightning
29 Digital music player
30 "Avatar" humanoids
31 Hidden valley
32 Bend out of shape
33 Side by side?
34 Claim
36 Melodic subject
39 Rid of poison
41 Mirabile ___ (wonderful to say)
44 Take the plunge
46 Senate room
49 Lack of activity
51 Soak: Var.
53 Bar by law
55 Suspect's out
56 Soviet Union founder
57 Advances cautiously
58 Baklava dough
59 In a bit
60 River to the Caspian
61 Ravel
64 One-time link

NUTTY MUSIC   by Richard Silvestri
Clever clues and humorous wordplay from our nutty professor.

ACROSS

1 RR stop
4 "Friendly" action
9 Stop from flowing
14 One for the road
15 Words of wisdom
16 "My Fair Lady" lady
17 Nutty Fats Domino song?
20 Beats it
21 Man, for one
22 Came to a close
23 Call for attention
25 Indian chief
29 Night light
30 Whalebone
32 Aromatic seasoning
33 Fry a bit
35 River to the Rhone
37 Nutty Fab Four album?
41 YouTube offering
42 Old hat
43 Rocks in a glass
44 Indiana five
47 Sussex streetcar
51 Founder of Stoicism
53 Food sticker
54 Iota preceder
55 1988 Oscar winner
57 Go downhill
58 Nutty Dave Clark Five tune?
63 Come to terms
64 It may be blessed
65 Put to work
66 Father Time feature
67 Low temperatures
68 Always, in verse

DOWN

1 Zodiac symbol
2 Natural ability
3 Royal Navy foe of 1588
4 Faded away
5 Throws in
6 Miss
7 Freudian topic
8 Do over
9 Give a hand
10 "Luck and Pluck" author
11 One of Frank's exes
12 Six Day War weapon
13 Neverland resident
18 Keep an eye on
19 Renaissance family name
23 Way to go
24 1973 Woody Allen film
26 The third man
27 Shakes up
28 Parliamentary vote
30 On the contrary
31 They're picked by the picky
34 Resting on
36 Sheer, for short
37 Nursery rhyme trio
38 Blissful spot
39 Samoyed sound
40 Slalom track
41 Alternative to i.e.
45 Three or four
46 Middle manager?
48 Coast Guard job
49 Relaxed
50 Way
52 Earth tone
54 Sweetie pie
56 Pay attention to
57 Early in Cooperstown
58 Truck componenet
59 Time of your life
60 Madrid Mrs.
61 "___ had it!"
62 Professional charge

U PICK 'EM   by Jim Holland

Four fruits can be found below, ready to be picked.

ACROSS

1 Orchestra tuner
5 Hit the mall
9 Your Majesty
13 "Casablanca" actor
15 German sportswear company
16 "Goldfinger" fort
17 Some runners
19 Run in neutral
20 Invites
21 More cluttered
23 "Nautilus," for one
25 Dispense with modesty
26 Computer's tech specs
33 Encore!
34 Graphic puzzle
35 "The Talk" network
38 If not
39 Forewarning
40 Rorschach Test feature
41 Tennis call
42 "Hear! hear!"
43 Scrumptious in "Chitty Chitty Bang Bang"
44 Entirely trustworthy
47 Blue-pencil mark
49 "Vox populi, vox ___"
50 Run circles around
54 Braking maneuvers for skaters
59 "Blimey!" blurter
60 Lowlifes
62 "Hannibal" actor Esparza
63 Peddle
64 "Bat Out of Hell" singer Foley
65 "Crazy ___" (Alison Krauss song)
66 11th-grade exam
67 Abrasive heels

DOWN

1 Shamu, for one
2 Cote cries
3 Pen sound
4 They can be tight or loose
5 Bath, for one
6 "Hotel Rwanda" tribe
7 "Damien: ___ II" (1978)
8 "Back to the Future" destination
9 Snowmobile name
10 Exerciser shaped like a bowling pin
11 "Inside the Actors Studio" topics
12 Apply
14 Audits a course
18 Heisman winner Flutie
22 "The Scarlet ___": James Hurst
24 Sack stuff
26 City WNW of Paris
27 "Loverly" look
28 Showy, edible flower
29 "A curse on your family!"
30 Carney of "Penny Dreadful"
31 Overseas
32 Pharaoh of puzzles
36 "The Clown" novelist
37 Eyelid woe
39 Aaron Rodgers' asset
40 Lingerie item
42 Mooring post
43 "Could ___ Magic" (1957 hit)
45 "Good Food, Good Life" company
46 Group of badgers
47 Subsidiary of 15 Across
48 Airs
51 "Answer, please"
52 "24 Hours" novelist
53 "If you like ___ coladas . . ."
55 Weightlifting powder
56 Puebla pot
57 Argued a case
58 1040 IDs
61 Aug. hours in Denver

81 MISSING LINK   by Jim Holland
. . . and that missing link can be found below, but you'll have to find it.

ACROSS

1 Pound first
5 Smilodon features
10 Très ___ (stylish)
14 Way in or out
15 UNIVAC I predecessor
16 Audi logo, when connected
17 "I'm dependable"
19 1984 Nobelist for Peace
20 Calliope emission
21 La Rive Droite river
23 ___ Clemente
24 It opens toward the sea
26 Most creepy
28 Dumas title character
33 Golf instructor
34 Mrs. Charlie Chaplin
35 Austrian cake
38 Outdoor wedding rental
40 Like an NBA court
43 Meanie
44 Prognosticators
46 Opera highlight
48 Have problems
49 "Be grateful for what you have"
53 Oscar Night hopeful
55 When doubled, a dance
56 Org. for Dershowitz
57 Margaret Mead outpost
60 Dagwood's dog
64 Quaff with sashimi
66 Floored by a haymaker
68 "You said it!"
69 Urich "Vega$" role
70 El Paso school
71 Overlay with bacon
72 Inception
73 Gobblers

DOWN

1 Ben & Jerry's competitor
2 1940s suit
3 Rake
4 Only jockey to win the Triple Crown twice
5 Marsh
6 2018 y 2019
7 Love potion number of song
8 Venison vis-à-vis beef
9 Play opening
10 Shelter bed
11 Company newsletter
12 Jots, but not down
13 Count
18 Acid that builds proteins
22 Formerly, formerly
25 The whole ball of wax
27 Langston Hughes poem
28 Elects
29 On the house
30 Cash cow
31 Columbus Circle designer
32 Panama, for one
36 High school math
37 Slithery swimmers
39 Deanna of "Star Trek: TNG"
41 Byron's "before"
42 Reversi piece
45 Talking Stick team
47 Argentine barbecue
50 Tell a bedtime story
51 Grumble regretfully
52 Going nowhere fast
53 Twangy sounding
54 "The Audacity of Hope" author
58 Has legal possession of
59 England's last House of Stuart monarch
61 "Take ___ the Limit": Eagles
62 Noah's eldest son
63 Western assents
65 Terminus
67 Marbling in meat

82 OREGON DONORS by Harvey Estes
Three answers have benefited from Oregon donors.

ACROSS
1 Battle memento
5 Harasses newbies
10 Term for a horrible boss
14 Hearty partner
15 Digital dinosaur
16 Chick's ending
17 John McEnroe rival (with 38-D)
18 MC's spiel
19 Air chamber
20 Do touch-up work without the bother?
23 No longer available
24 Damp basement cause
26 Eyeballed
30 Insinuate
31 Beat to the tape
34 Drifts off
35 First-person pronouns aplenty?
39 Bellyache
40 Tahini ingredient
41 "That's disgusting!"
43 They're deep within the lines
48 Hurrying
51 Blackmore's Lorna
52 Elusive "Get Shorty" author?
56 Piercing wound
57 "Paper Moon" Oscar winner
58 Altar exchanges
59 The Who's Townshend
60 Pool stroke
61 Revolver brand
62 Deity on "Xena"
63 Pottery ovens
64 Work alone

DOWN
1 Gym class team
2 "As is" is one
3 State bordered by two oceans
4 Avis patron
5 Spouse or child, often
6 Mrs. Shakespeare
7 Popular pasta
8 Pulls down
9 Aiming aid
10 Salsa pepper
11 Pedagogue
12 Turncoat
13 Beer bust delivery
21 Runner aboard
22 Brain check, briefly
25 Triffids, e.g.
27 Milk ___
28 Where to look, in "Misty"
29 Lovers' lane event
32 Petri dish medium
33 Somebody
35 Cheese not connected to a German city
36 Snowball
37 Credits
38 See 17 Across
39 Murphy Brown's TV show
42 Marcher's syllable
44 Improv performers
45 Bringer of bad luck
46 Matriculate
47 Is responsible for
49 Nimoy's "I Am Not ___"
50 Painter Matisse
53 Not virtual
54 Exhibit ennui
55 Conduit bends
56 Évian, e.g.

83 "GOODBYE" by Harvey Estes
In 2005 the Minor Planet Center named asteroid 25924 after 66 Across.

ACROSS
1 Brings up the rear
5 Nonalcoholic bar
10 Modern junk
14 Riding
15 "Um . . ."
16 Bluefin
17 "Hitchhiker's Guide to the Galaxy" message (with 54-A)
20 Evasive tactic
21 Rodeo item
22 Grammy winner Bonnie
23 Office dupes, for short
26 Internet surfers
27 Diminished by
28 "Of course!"
29 Model Banks
30 Messengers of 17-A and 54-A
33 Soprano Gluck
36 Hostel visitor
37 Huge volume
41 Philadelphia heros
43 Still . . .
45 Ed in "Roots"
46 Future indicators
47 Red or black, e.g.
48 Queen in "Romeo and Juliet"
51 Mont. neighbor
53 I-95, e.g.
54 See 17 Across
58 Irene Cara cry
59 Minute openings
60 Site for a bell
62 Antioxidant berry
63 Games guru
64 Humdinger
65 Give a little

66 Author of book found at 17-A and 54-A
67 Additional

DOWN
1 Surgical tool
2 Like some 20th-century music
3 Hawn of "Private Benjamin"
4 Where to find scores of scores
5 Speak with your hands, so to speak
6 Mia in "Pulp Fiction"
7 VIP on the Hill
8 Fooled
9 Pt. of IMF
10 Alpha Centauri, for example
11 Not as strong
12 Mideast capital
13 Supporters of sailing
18 Loony
19 High in Le Havre
23 Guitar neck attachments
24 French pet name
25 Doth speak
31 Deli sandwich holder
32 "___ 'nuff!"
33 "Pequot" skipper
34 Suffer humiliation
35 Basketball defense
38 Emerson essay, with "The"
39 Some cigarettes
40 Irish

42 2017 category 5 hurricane
44 Canine comment
49 Athens opener
50 Red Cross supply
51 Overcome utterly
52 Positive reactions
55 2013 Senate Majority Leader
56 Campbell's "___ Little Kindness"
57 Goofing off
58 Four adjective
61 Feel sorrow about

FORMER LAB PARTNERS by Justin Andrew
September 13 is the day officially honoring 10 Down.

ACROSS

1 "Star Wars" knight
5 Early Spielberg film
9 Uneasy feeling
14 Mesopotamian land
15 Type of history
16 Loosen the ropes
17 Use an atomizer
18 Famous last words
19 Central Park's 843
20 **Place to get a reaction**
23 Swedish carrier
24 Silky dog
25 Regard with suspicion
30 Take stock of
34 Place for a chevron
35 Angler Walton
37 Slugs not found on the lawn
38 **Green-eyed lover (and former lab partner)**
42 Nothing but
43 In a lather
44 Green Day drummer ___ Cool
45 Take pleasure in
48 Questions after a mission
50 "Sweet Sixteen" org.
52 Show agreement
53 **Reaction uttered by 38 Across in 20 Across?**
60 "There it is!"
61 Fountain tools
62 Pale green moth
64 Moral man
65 For night owls
66 Some watch faces
67 Prepares to fire
68 Aphrodite's son
69 Go to market

DOWN

1 Kirk, to McCoy
2 "The Little Mermaid" prince
3 Cook's smidgen
4 Brainpower assessment
5 Fictional salesman of 1980s auto ads
6 Liberal follower
7 Current measure
8 Sucking sound
9 Disreputable docs
10 Patriotic cartoon figure
11 Gillette razor product
12 Stories from 5 Down
13 Kind of hall
21 Nintendo game character
22 Favorable vote
25 College choice
26 Ryan of "Pippin"
27 Like some talk or print
28 Belt alternative
29 Saved for later viewing
31 Overdo the acting
32 Blue cartoon character
33 Bumps and bruises
36 Mulgrew of "Star Trek: Voyager"
39 Staying out of sight
40 Greet, Maori-style
41 Lab wear
46 Cone toppers
47 Fundraisers pass it
49 Pastoral poems
51 Enough and then some
53 "___ no idea!"
54 Turn, as a ship
55 "The Sound of Music" baroness
56 Kind of book or end
57 "___ every life . . ."
58 "That smarts!"
59 Bring down
63 Venom source

85 SILENT TREATMENT   by Justin Andrew
You never say "Quiet on the set!" to this actor.

ACROSS

1 Six-time French Open winner
5 Turns over
10 Exec degrees
14 One-time great salt lake
15 Woman in a Left Banke song
16 Boy Scout recitation
17 Meter maid of song
18 Gung-ho
19 Follow the rules
20 **Start of a question about a silent performer**
23 Worn words
24 Dignify
27 Cowboy moniker
28 End of Caesar's boast
31 Cleverly skillful
32 Part of FDR
34 ___ fide
35 **End of question**
39 Topsoil, often
40 Stabler on "Law & Order: SVU"
41 "Now I see!"
44 Sad ending for love
45 Big pooch
48 Series starters
50 Big step
52 **Ironic response to question**
55 Film noir knife
57 Conical quarters
58 Infamous emperor
59 Fine-tune
60 Ethiopia's Selassie
61 Web surfer
62 Make better
63 Ravel's "Pavane for ___ Princess"
64 Sit before a lens

DOWN

1 Brigitte in "Les Novices"
2 Maryland's state bird
3 Like "Last Tango in Paris" in 1973
4 Toast necessity
5 The power to choose
6 Levi's mother
7 L. Frank Baum's Pingaree prince
8 Pet complaint
9 Gisele in "The Devil Wears Prada"
10 Satellite path
11 Population explosion
12 Fueled up
13 Retiring
21 Czech leader Václav
22 To boot
25 Place to wait
26 JFK posting
29 Cosmetics holder
30 As a whole
32 Penny dreadful, after inflation?
33 Norse port
35 Thick fog
36 1935 Garbo role
37 Plane's pace
38 Three-card game
39 Bloom of "The Producers"
42 Guy doll
43 "Queen of Soul" Franklin
45 This way
46 Thinks the world of
47 Label for many a photo
49 Home addition
51 Incurred
53 Friend of Barney Fife
54 Ward of "Sisters"
55 Librarian's admonition
56 Garden store purchase

86 THEMELESS by Harvey Estes
59 Across is an example of a portmanteau.

ACROSS
1 Persian Gulf land
5 Lane pickup
10 Polish partner
14 Citizen soldiers
16 Cry of frustration
17 "Friend" that becomes a nuisance
18 Cher's son Chaz
19 WW2 combat zone
20 U-turn from NNW
21 Off one's feed
23 Feet from floor to hoop
24 Flatter
26 Sea salt?
28 Bk. of the Pentateuch
29 Furniture piece by the boob tube
31 KFC servings
34 Instructions to a gofer
35 Bylaw, for short
36 Writer's deg.
37 Peter or Paul, but not Mary
42 Oxygen-dependent organisms
46 Keep up
47 Sticks in the billiard room
48 Circle in Washington
49 Vigilant
53 Source of needles
54 Cold war prog.
55 Haul
56 John of London
57 Rabble, for short
59 Time off spent locally
62 Road that led to Rome

63 Nevertheless
64 Broadway's first Tevye
65 Flunkies' responses
66 Highlands tongue

DOWN
1 Drive on
2 Calf catcher
3 Metal mix
4 Fine point of writing
5 Declines participation
6 Curfew setters
7 Latin I verb
8 Won't cooperate
9 Put into servitude
10 Show grief
11 Sneak into a shooting
12 Contemplation
13 Animated feature
15 Has a little
22 Dietary, in ads
25 Diane's "Chinatown" role
27 Back muscle
30 LAX listings
31 Grille protectors
32 Disavow
33 One who says, "I'm trying to find myself"?
38 Gas additive
39 New Mexico art colony
40 Davenport of tennis
41 Put a name to
42 Priest's assistant
43 Harem guards
44 Marley music
45 The Buckeyes coll.

50 "Doubt truth to be ___": Shak.
51 Inn array
52 Gifted person
53 Bad hair day problem
58 To's companion
60 Gore and more
61 Monogram of Prufrock's creator

87 THEMELESS   by Harvey Estes
Looks like Harvey slipped in a pun at 46 and 53 Across.

ACROSS

1 They've been had
8 Witty quips
15 Boise boy, e.g.
16 Picks
17 Open-air sitting area
18 Artists' works
19 Song with a sonnet and a bonnet
21 Fell off
22 Fixes
26 Important period
31 Literary contraction
32 Trait on the plus side
33 Washington gallery
35 Words used instead of "instead"
36 Star of "The Honeymooners"
37 Improvisational passage
38 Passes out
39 Tiger, for one
40 Tackles Carnoustie
41 Junkyard dog
42 Wear with pride
43 Slangy suffix
44 "Nightwatch" network
46 Tycoon in the cooling business? (with 53-A)
53 See 46 Across
56 Apple-pie order
57 Runs against
58 Kind of mail
59 Sketchers or skivvies
60 Stationery supplies

DOWN

1 "___ la France!"
2 Conception
3 Lincoln et al.
4 "Don't touch ___ dial!"
5 Skye of "Say Anything"
6 Monterrey mom
7 Crisp veggie
8 Baseball official
9 Coming up
10 Brightly colored
11 Site for a suicide barrier
12 Syr. neighbor
13 Wide spec
14 Serpent's sound
20 First homicide victim
23 Really loves
24 Old-timer
25 Queen Anne's house
26 Have the attention of
27 Lack of color
28 Moor of a Verdi opera
29 Rapper's farewell?
30 Party throwers
32 Chain in Chile
34 Discouraging words
35 McKellen of "The Da Vinci Code"
37 Spades, for example
39 Paul in "Scarface"
41 Soft touch
44 In pursuit of
45 Net user, perhaps
47 Mitigate
48 Spanish rodent
49 Iowa State location
50 Went lickety-split
51 River through Frankfurt
52 1976 World Series winners
53 Forum watchdog, for short
54 Earth Day mo.
55 4.0, for one

THEMELESS   by Harvey Estes
There's a mini-theme at 23 and 53 Across.

ACROSS

1 Greek house
5 RC, e.g.
9 Public square
14 City on the Tiber
15 Mireille of "World War Z"
16 Mechanic, at times
17 Unseen stimulant
18 Most of a monocle
19 Done for
20 Pain specialists
23 Baritone's vocal warm-up for "Don Giovanni"? (with 53-A)
24 RR terminal
27 The Buckeyes coll.
28 Harrow puller
30 Gunpowder holders
34 Watches a Netflix show
35 He framed Cassio
36 Often-dunked item
37 Den setups
41 Add by degrees
44 Gives a clue to
45 Verb for Popeye
46 Farm worker
47 "Nixon in China" role
53 See 23 Across
54 "The Maltese Falcon" star
57 Win for Magnus Carlsen
58 Mammoth tooth
59 Sidestep
60 "Be that ___ may . . ."
61 Gray matter product
62 "Lola" band
63 Big donors
64 At hand

DOWN

1 Fern leaf
2 Drive through Beverly Hills
3 Parisian passion
4 Pied-à-___
5 Ma is one
6 Joan Osborne hit
7 Middle of May?
8 Gives a hand
9 Following V-J Day
10 They get smacked
11 Pale drink
12 Kind of Buddhism
13 Gallery objects
21 1847 Melville work
22 Pigeonhole
24 Vacant look
25 Marisa in "The Big Short"
26 Torch job
29 Corp. bosses
30 Campbell of "Martin"
31 Stay home for supper
32 Rep with a cut
33 Left on a liner
38 Goes with
39 Big Island neighbor
40 Milky Way diagram
41 Like fool's gold
42 Whistle stops
43 "Diary of ___ Housewife" (1970)
48 "___ Teenage Werewolf" (1957)
49 Out to lunch, say
50 Norman Lear sitcom
51 Befuddled
52 Schindler with a list
53 Richard III's House
54 Put the question to
55 Bit of downhill gear
56 Solder component

89 THEMELESS by Harvey Estes
"Weird Al" fans will appreciate the clue at 52 Across.

ACROSS

1 Capone colleague
6 Audacious
15 Downy wader
16 Negligee jackets
17 "And there you are!"
18 "Cinderella" stepsister
19 Rock group whose song was satirized at 52 Across
21 Hour pt.
22 1 of 100 in D.C.
23 On the sly
28 Alarm
33 Dire destiny
34 Ice-cream brand
36 In isolation
37 Rubik of cube fame
38 Stop on the line
40 Seemingly forever
41 "Octopus's Garden" singer
43 Proscribed act
44 Sedgwick of Warhol films
45 Like some IMAX films
47 Thumbnail sketches
49 Higher ed. test
51 "Ooky" cousin
52 Song parody about composer Erik's clique?
59 Abacus, e.g.
60 Bright with warmth
62 The movie "Lincoln" is about the 13th one

63 Seeker's question
64 Business worth
65 Small particles

DOWN

1 Neighbor of Cal.
2 Noted lab assistant
3 The Andrews Sisters, for one
4 "Go on . . ."
5 Leaning letter
6 Read hastily
7 Type of gliding
8 Build up
9 Lightly sprayed
10 Baltic Sea country
11 Type of shark
12 Alternative word
13 Six of the Spaniards
14 Fed. retirement agency
20 Crimson-clad
23 That is, to Caesar
24 Top pole
25 Salvaging tool
26 Carl Sagan's place for Dragons
27 Thit and thas?
29 Words for one retiring
30 They sometimes swing
31 Comics orphan
32 Flunkies' responses
35 PlayStation maker

39 Drink diluter, at times
42 Applies another coat of gold
46 Wishful thinking
48 Home of hockey's Senators
50 Makeup maker Lauder
52 Matching
53 Help out
54 Salad fish
55 Holy water receptacle
56 Liberal pursuits
57 Breakfast spread
58 "Cheers" barfly
59 Catch some rays
61 Horror director Craven

59 ACROSS   by Gary Larson
38 Down has been called "The King of Cool."

ACROSS

1 Tach readings
5 Mosaic piece
9 Shells and shots
14 Coloratura's piece
15 Nivea rival
16 Like some jokes
17 King "It" guy
19 "The Age of Anxiety" poet
20 Mideast conflict site
21 Captain of the Nautilus
22 Anthem preposition
23 Home of SpongeBob
27 Sack
29 Peters out
30 Cartoonist Drake
31 Flinch, say
33 Place for a father-to-be: Abbr.
34 Width, for one
38 Major record label
41 Credit card come-on
42 First person
46 Put together
48 Hanks costar in "Forrest Gump"
50 Manning or Manning
53 Resting place
54 Latin bears
55 Response to "Are you hungry?"
57 Alleviated
59 Invent a bit of language
60 Discharge
61 Ballpark figure?
62 European tongue
63 "Cheep" homes?
64 Fleming and Holm
65 Song ender

DOWN

1 Toronto team
2 Oven setting
3 Goddess of wisdom
4 Without
5 Local
6 Hipbone-related
7 Kind of 8-Down surgery
8 Cataract site
9 Here, in Honduras
10 Piles
11 Gary Cooper title role
12 Another
13 Like word
18 Hip-hop's ___ Yang Twins
24 Clear the chalkboard
25 LBJ's daughter
26 Aware of
28 "Then what?"
31 Direct elsewhere
32 Chemical ending
35 Still competitive
36 Dermatologist's concern
37 A Bobbsey twin
38 "Bullitt" actor Steve
39 Pluck
40 Rolls up
43 Bend out of shape
44 Bad-mouth
45 Wander aimlessly
47 Homily giver
48 Perfumes
49 Big furniture retailer
51 Flora and fauna
52 For the birds
56 Dazzles
58 Skid row woe
59 Forensic TV franchise

91 ENDERS GAME   by Gary Larson
38 Down is recognized as the patron saint of messengers.

ACROSS

1 Major oil company
5 Stagehands
10 Electrical units
14 It's found in bars
15 Pi, e.g.
16 Bruce in "Middle Age Crazy"
17 Cool hunting dog?
19 S-shaped curve
20 Highway
21 Place for a barbecue
23 Kind of room
25 Amateur masseuse?
27 Evaluated
29 Half a 45
30 Miller, for one
31 Bunch
34 Like some internet talks
35 Macho acupuncturist?
38 Pinup's leg
41 Marked down
42 Dwindles
46 Delon in "Is Paris Burning?"
48 Founder of Detroit
50 Large water ouzel?
53 Demise
54 Train unit
55 Bean in "Jupiter Ascending"
56 Catalina, e.g.
57 Busybody valet?
62 They're caught in pots
63 Keypad key
64 Claudius I's successor
65 Future atty.'s hurdle
66 1974 Dustin Hoffman film
67 ER imperative

DOWN

1 Silvery gray
2 French king
3 Mozzarella, tomato, basil salad
4 Naysayers
5 Solving diagram
6 Printed
7 "The Addams Family" cousin
8 Devotion
9 More tender
10 Too cute, informally
11 Internet speed measure
12 Lead
13 Showed disapproval
18 Horse feed
22 100 kopecks
23 Chitchat
24 Manipulate
25 Sale prospects
26 Magazine revenue source
28 Like cotton candy
32 Like a renewable energy
33 Scratched (out)
36 Shot in the arm
37 Brushes up on
38 Last Judgment trumpeter
39 Jones and Smith, at times
40 Cartoon gorilla
43 Linus Van Pelt's security
44 Halloween decoration
45 MIT, for one
47 Least active
49 Conceit
51 Discussion group
52 Lying facedown
55 Active
58 RR stop
59 Desire
60 P&G detergent
61 It's "noble" in vineyards

"EW!" by Richard Silvestri
Potent punnery from this puzzling professor.

ACROSS

1 To boot
5 "Phooey!"
9 Possum player
14 Had regrets about
15 Way out
16 Dress with a flare
17 When moisture will form on the grass?
19 Delay, in a way
20 Fabergé objet d'art
21 Towel marking
22 Superlatively obese
24 Greets at the door
26 Bushy do
27 Bismarck played the trumpet?
33 Not out
36 Chapter of history
37 Mescaline-yielding cactus
38 Leads on
40 Give–go link
42 Point of view
43 Larry Ellison's company
45 Drop off
47 One of a Latin trio
48 Like an empty yarn store?
51 Tonsorial touch-up
52 Lorraine's partner
56 Brandy flavor
60 Letter from Greece
61 Important component
62 Lariat
63 What a sad feller may do?
66 Tick off
67 Neck and neck
68 Pebble Beach sand
69 Roof supports
70 Zip
71 Main man?

DOWN

1 Sign of spring
2 Fencing move
3 Marsh plant
4 Dedicated lines?
5 Train
6 Revolution center
7 Curry or Rice
8 André Agassi's love match?
9 Slick tricks
10 Found a perch
11 Long-tailed flyer
12 Son of Seth
13 Studio payment
18 Chopper noise
23 Not give ___ about
25 Prepared remarks
26 Together
28 Hindu honorific
29 Secondary rules
30 Potting soil
31 Sicilian hot spot
32 Moistens
33 Not very busy
34 Gold, in combinations
35 Brown house
39 Toys on tracks
41 Easy threesome?
44 Continental capital
46 Obvious
49 Supported the church
50 Vitality
53 Largest city of Ghana
54 Necklace material
55 "Aida" setting
56 Riyadh resident
57 Cleanser scent
58 It's played on a vina
59 Tabloid twosome
60 Still-life subject
64 Gabor in "Gigi"
65 Skid row woe

93 HOBSON'S CHOICE by Richard Silvestri
Six of one, half a dozen of the other.

ACROSS

1 York or Lancaster symbol
5 Romanian folk dances
10 Sunday celebration
14 Competent
15 Get away from
16 Norse explorer
17 Trying time at the start of a card game?
19 Dudley's "Arthur" costar
20 Obstinate one
21 Flying formation
22 Fill with joy
24 Use the microwave
26 Victory, in Berlin
27 World-renowned lip-reader?
33 Wharton degs.
36 Half a dance
37 Rodin work
38 Nest on a cliff
40 Zeta follower
42 Tomato blight
43 Many Dutch Golden Age paintings
45 School of thought
47 "Don't worry about me"
48 Beta vulgaris grove?
51 Hebrew prophet
52 Raises a glass to
56 Hot and bothered
60 Monk's title
61 OSS successor
62 Horn, for one
63 "Is Big Brother still watching us ... is he, George?"
66 Pizza place
67 Electrolysis particle
68 Draft status
69 Barbershop call
70 "Breaking Away" director
71 Geeky guy

DOWN

1 Police ___ gun
2 More than pudgy
3 Virgule
4 Sushi offering
5 Auto-da-fé victim
6 Merrie ___ England
7 Feel bad about
8 Slowly, on scores
9 Peter in "Being There"
10 Canasta play
11 Drought-stricken
12 Extent
13 Read at a glance
18 Cricket field shape
23 Banded quartz
25 Less taxing
26 Branch of physics
28 Haggard heroine
29 Pretentious
30 Bit of gossip
31 Sport in a ring
32 Tropical hardwood
33 Not fem.
34 Sister of Meg March
35 It may be gray
39 Be over by
41 Fire proof
44 By hook or by crook
46 Some prison guards
49 "Ivanhoe" heroine
50 Sound from Simba
53 Shooting script segment
54 Flooring specialist
55 Leaves for lunch?
56 Religious relic
57 Basilica center
58 Peak point
59 Shipped
60 Ice pack?
64 Set fire to
65 Took the cup

BODILY DISCOMFORT   by Lee Taylor
A careful construction with a fill-in-the-blanks theme.

ACROSS

1 Makeover
5 Drug that's smoked
9 Japanese cartoon art
14 Blues singer Redding
15 Biblical preposition
16 "Battle of the ___" (2017)
17 Have ___
20 Befuddling
21 Prefix for fab
22 Like Lowell's June day
23 Distant
24 Victimize
26 Put a ___
32 Be on the same page
33 Prepared to pray
34 Take a run
37 Skittered
38 Stands in line
39 Salad veggie
40 Pink Floyd frontman Barrett
41 Flavor
42 Arab country
43 "Here's ___!"
45 Jam
48 Plopped down
49 Age after Bronze
50 Kind
53 Coolest, slangily
57 Put your ___
60 More docile
61 Comedian Love
62 Length × width
63 Fashion
64 Squeaks (by)
65 Out of order

DOWN

1 Yellow Brick ___
2 Sicily volcano
3 Space cadet
4 Grew rigid
5 Famished
6 No matter which
7 Octagonal sign
8 Cuckoo announcement
9 Cleopatra killer
10 More accessible
11 Slangy rejection
12 D.C. subway
13 German city on the Ruhr
18 Senseless
19 Fends off
25 Maze runner, perhaps
26 Tuba's pitch
27 Like Hephaestus
28 Crossword diagram
29 Striped giraffe
30 Guild
31 Give it another go
34 Gunnysack fiber
35 Word of approval
36 Richard in "Chicago"
38 Get involved
39 Capacity of a links vehicle
41 Put on the feedbag
42 Misgiving
43 Fireplace fixture
44 Egyptian god of the underworld
45 Prepares flour for baking
46 Zagreb resident
47 What airplane seats are not
51 Country singer Lovett
52 Nut
54 Franc replacement
55 Slumgullion
56 Better safe ___ sorry
58 High dudgeon
59 French article

95 SHODDY CONSTRUCTION   by Lee Taylor

Don't let the title mislead you, this is hardly a shoddy construction.

ACROSS

1 "O Pioneers!" author Cather
6 Not us
10 Light fog
14 Tool for Everest
15 Franc replacement
16 Call ___ question
17 Over yonder
18 Sale advisory
19 Party in Hanalei
20 A chandelier caused this to crack?
23 Healthful berry
26 Neckwear for a 19 Across
27 Tattletale
28 This caused the stairs to collapse?
31 Snouts
32 It's treated with an inhaler
33 Squelched
35 Pi follower
36 Do something
38 Coniferous tree
39 Language spoken in Vientiane
42 Prepare to pray
44 Atelier fixtures
46 "Magic Burns" novelist Andrews
49 Result of a defective sand filter?
51 Groups of nine
53 Medical research org.
54 "You're ___ something!"
55 Shaky house add-on made with recycled tapes?
58 Lofty poems
59 Eternal City
60 Cliff home
64 Dole
65 Petri dish contents
66 Energizer mascot
67 Word before while
68 Gives one star
69 Dark suit

DOWN

1 Cleverness
2 Berlin pronoun
3 "Go Set a Watchman" author
4 On the stout side
5 Skating jump
6 Service needed at eleven
7 Wanton women
8 Guitarist Clapton
9 NBA Hall-of-Famer Malone
10 A thousand thousands
11 Nunavik natives
12 Position
13 Rowdies
21 Strasbourg is its capital
22 Not by any means
23 Way over yonder
24 Type of bar
25 Saxophone range
29 Originate
30 Pony up
34 Grow chompers
37 Senator Cruz
39 Boxer Spinks
40 Tons
41 Viking Ship Museum city
42 Israeli parliament
43 Worker during a power outage
45 Asserted oneself
46 Bacon, at times
47 Tractor with a bucket
48 Inceptions
50 Metro passengers
52 Latchet
56 Senate cover-up?
57 Truck compartments
61 Genetic info carrier
62 Neither Rep. nor Dem.
63 Private ___

96

THEMELESS by Alyssa Brooke

Netflix states 73% of video watchers say 34-A involves at least six episodes.

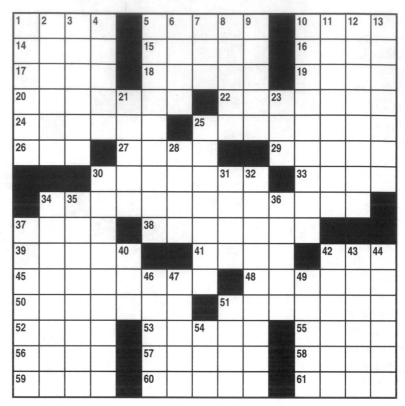

ACROSS

1 Pebble Beach hazard
5 "The Cloister and the Hearth" author
10 Apple of a sort
14 Obama's "The Audacity of ___"
15 Eggs on
16 NASA cancellation
17 Flock members
18 Nobelist Bohr
19 AMC series about Washington's spies
20 Breast-beating
22 Olivia Walton's portrayer
24 "Hold on!"
25 Bay Area city
26 "Chat" novelist McCarthy
27 Ste. Jeanne ___
29 Where the elated walk
30 Meteorological effects
33 Confessional list
34 OD'ing on "OITNB," e.g.
37 Went to the bottom
38 Home of Lions and Tigers
39 Song of David
41 Golfer's transport
42 Start for log or gram
45 Kind of grant
48 Super Bowl LII winners
50 Brewed drink
51 Ink source
52 Sound quality
53 NBA venue
55 Ax
56 Life of Riley
57 It may be local
58 Soon, long ago
59 Resign, with "down"
60 Car in a Beach Boys song
61 "I'll Cover You" musical

DOWN

1 "Monster" Oscar winner
2 Ivanhoe's love
3 "2001" extras
4 Cancun cash
5 Turn tail
6 Buffalo's lake
7 Mellow
8 Perry's secretary
9 City on the Ruhr
10 On the way
11 Denali, for one
12 In accord
13 Big birds
21 Excavated anew
23 Latin I verb
25 Pool error
28 Misty of "Hee Haw"
30 Completely involved
31 Little shaver
32 Record keeper
34 Layer beneath the finish
35 Kind of
36 Try to slug
37 Pixies
40 Wrestling surface
42 Skiing style
43 Spinal cord cell
44 Say yes
46 Change, chemically
47 Chocolate substitute
49 Make it
51 Words before "about"
54 Samuel's judge

97 THEMELESS by Alyssa Brooke
Prepare to groan when solving 36 and 57 Across.

ACROSS

1 Act badly
6 Physicist Niels
10 Some verse
14 Russian retreat
15 Balm ingredient
16 Bar request
17 Reel person
18 Like McCoy
19 Reid of "Josie and the Pussycats"
20 "Ender's Game," at first
22 Weight-loss pill
23 Playful bite
24 Holbrook in "The Firm"
25 Chow call
27 "No mo'!"
29 Bend a little
31 "May ___ of service?"
32 Ring
34 Daisy Mae's hubby
36 Description of 20-A when compared to novels? (with 57-A)
39 Surfer's need
42 Just out?
46 Wallach in "The Misfits"
47 Stew slowly
50 Prayer start
51 Student counselor, e.g.
53 Sign of a hit
55 Hasty escape
56 Yorke of Radiohead
57 See 36 Across
60 Trim back
61 Lady's man
62 Bara of silents
63 Peru native
64 "Hairy man" in Genesis
65 Perfected
66 Rosie O'Donnell's "Exit to ___"
67 Win in a walk
68 Like Carl Perkins' blue shoes

DOWN

1 He played Santa in "Elf"
2 ATM part
3 Beatle gardener?
4 Marvel superhero or Norse deity
5 Here we are
6 Anjou alternative
7 Kitchen staple
8 How Brando sounded in "The Godfather"
9 Swear by
10 Ready to be drawn
11 Gives a hand
12 Place for a stud
13 Wood furniture worker
21 Wrap choice
26 Orrin Hatch, for one
28 Duffer's warning
30 "Madam Secretary" star Téa
33 Ices, perhaps
35 Conk
37 Came clean
38 It's human
39 Hearty pastry
40 Veteran
41 Tammy Wynette hit
43 Part of TNT
44 Passed out
45 Summer cooler
48 Hair salon item
49 Melodic
52 Clarification starter
54 Solemn words
58 Coal porter
59 M or G

CAMELOT QUEEN by Tracy Bennett and Victor Fleming
... portrayed by four leading ladies.

ACROSS

1 Stay the course
5 Light head?
10 Auctioned off
14 Adele's range
15 ___ Oak (Faulkner's home)
16 Shallowest of the Great Lakes
17 Jackie in "Kennedy" (1983)
19 Do some road work
20 City saved by Joan of Arc
21 "Attack, Fifi!"
22 James Ryan's rnk.
23 CSI team's sample
24 With 46-A, Jackie in "Jackie" (2016)
26 White room's lack
28 Where the proverbial heart is
29 One may be split or tight
30 Quarter
31 Goalie's leg protector
34 Jackie in "The Kennedys" (2011)
37 "Place" of 1990s TV
38 "___ Buy Me Love": Beatles
41 Gardner of Hollywood
44 "Skin So Soft" brand
45 "Barefoot in the Park" star Charles
46 See 24 Across
48 Turkish honorific
50 "Not so fast!"
51 Egyptian water lily
52 Sought entry, in a way
54 Works of homage
55 Jackie in "The Butler" (2013)
58 Robin Williams role
59 Beatles tune covered by Alison Krauss
60 Exhilaration
61 Elementary school lavatory sign
62 Fusses over, with "on"
63 Lays down the lawn

DOWN

1 Chocolate dog
2 Pervasive
3 Gene Roddenberry series
4 Labor arduously
5 ___ sprawl
6 Woman of the Doones
7 Uncommon bills
8 Rarer than rare
9 Journalist Curry
10 Akin to mocha
11 Delphic seer
12 Like au pairs
13 Thought to be
18 Cherry and ruby
21 Robert Fulton's power source
22 Grp. for Rory or Tiger
24 Prohibited acts
25 Plentiful
27 Address for a lady
28 Sweet greeting
31 Henry in "The Manchurian Candidate"
32 Leggy shorebird
33 Roaring Twenties design style
35 League members
36 Instruction for a shy tot
39 Ribbed
40 Legally hear
41 Grace under pressure
42 Haitian hoodoo
43 Angioplasty focus
45 One way to go
47 Mammoth teeth
48 Fibula support
49 Soccer scores
52 Make a ski mask
53 Bar supplies
55 Prefix for section
56 Battle of ___ Jima
57 Network for Yankee games

99 CAMELOT KING   by Victor Fleming
. . . portrayed by three leading men.

ACROSS

1 Like Charles Barkley
5 Admire from ___
9 Kiosk kin
14 Durian quality
15 Hang fire
16 Place for a picnic table
17 Klebb of SPECTRE
18 "I'll ___ touch!"
19 Skillful
20 JFK in "The Kennedys" (2011)
23 Said without feeling
24 Take one's leave
29 In sync
30 Tony winner Salonga
32 Tom Joad, e.g.
33 Combat sport
36 Persil rival
37 JFK in "The Missiles of October" (1974)
40 Munro's pseudonym
41 Body in Jerusalem
42 Tommie of the 1969 Miracle Mets
43 Word that may or may not have an apostrophe
44 "___ People": Loesser
48 China shop purchase
50 Airline's offering on an overbooked flight
52 JFK in "Kennedy" (1983)
55 Take a knife to
59 Asteroid in "Ender's Game"
60 Durante's "___ Dinka Doo"
61 Studio sign
62 Bound bundle
63 Beaver skin
64 Secluded road
65 Last of a Latin trio
66 Eyelid affliction

DOWN

1 Lucrezia who married Alfonso d'Este
2 Fancies up
3 Get whipped by
4 Fastest flying insects
5 "Steal This Book" author Hoffman
6 Evildoer
7 Tennis score
8 Russo of "Outbreak"
9 Fifth wheel
10 Wee bit
11 Downed a sub
12 Projecting edge
13 Auction section
21 Show obeisance
22 Proverbs
25 What Brits call "crisps"
26 Of a feather, so to speak
27 Steppenwolf's "Magic Carpet ___"
28 Titleist holder
30 Margarita garnishes
31 Means justifiers
34 Premier Khrushchev
35 Quitter's word
37 Worker's reward
38 Furniture giant
39 Second rock from the sun
40 Remained unused
45 Sandra Bullock thriller of 1995
46 Like "Time"
47 More than fancy
49 Board for nails
50 "Twelfth Night" role
51 Initial stage
53 "Pee-wee's Playhouse" mail lady
54 Mine car
55 Kernel-covered core
56 Word with body or how
57 Untapped
58 Itinerary word

100

58 ACROSS by Tracy Gray
You may want to solve 58 Across first.

ACROSS

1 Shoestring neckties
6 It's a wrap
10 Gopher, for short
14 Cain's firstborn
15 The Band Perry, e.g.
16 Uppity one
17 Start of a proverb on winning (Spanish)
20 Shortening, in short
21 Novel ID
22 Peace Palace site (with "The")
23 Fruits named for a city in Spain (Italian)
26 "___ Beso" (Anka song)
27 Green lights
28 Sotheby's signal
29 CPR specialist
30 Vacuum flask inventor James
32 Gloria Allred, in brief
33 Canticles
34 Manager mom of actress Lindsay (Hawaiian)
38 Temporary state of mind
41 It's a wrap
42 "I haven't the foggiest!"
46 Clerical vestment
47 ___ Center (Chicago landmark)
48 These rocks melt
50 Ribbed fabric
51 1983 "Star Wars" sequel (Swedish)
55 Statue trunks
56 Levitator's command
57 Auto maker Ransom
58 Famous line from "Jerry Maguire"
61 Hershey Park attraction
62 Whiz-___
63 Used a nanny cam, perhaps
64 Flexible Flyer
65 Pianist Ciccolini
66 Cup of café

DOWN

1 Stayed in line
2 Award for a balk
3 Unsportsmanlike move
4 Earthy pigment
5 "Weeds" airer, in TV listings
6 Balance
7 Bonaire neighbor
8 "___ view your personal account"
9 Glacier on Mount Olympus
10 Narnia lion
11 Torn, as pantyhose
12 Accused person's flippant dare
13 They're given periodically to healthcare workers
18 Start on a popsicle
19 Fish that's high in Omega 3's
24 "Me neither!"
25 IRA type
31 Recipe verb
32 Boxing's "Louisville Lip"
33 Palindromic female artist
35 When both hands are up
36 Unorthodox
37 1958 Pulitzer winner James
38 Eleven Apostles, e.g.
39 Beef suet extract
40 Interfere
43 Garden structure for climbers
44 Horns in
45 VI, for 51 Across
47 Song for Renée Fleming
48 "We've gotten the green light!"
49 Journalist Huntley
52 Worked the theater aisles, slangily
53 Hellhound
54 Former Nittany Lions coach, familiarly
59 AKA, before a company name
60 Oahu hrs.

101 "STEP ON IT!"   by Pam Klawitter

The Merneptah Stele from 1208 BC can be found in the museum at 1 Down.

ACROSS

1 Boy Wonder's wear
5 Start of Oregon's motto
9 Hail damage
13 Solemn assent
14 Gulf Coast city
16 Isaac's firstborn
17 Mononymous model
18 If you get it, you've had it
19 Catch some Z's
20 One with a need for speed
23 Ryan in "Love Story"
24 Work up a sweat
25 Bit of evidence on "COPS"
32 911 at sea
35 ABC News anchor David
36 Scrat's snack
37 "A Chorus Line" producer
39 Philatelic item
42 Tag after
43 Kirk's communications officer
45 Sam twitched it on "Bewitched"
47 Answer sheet
48 Nothing out of the ordinary
52 Corrida critter
53 Pop singer McLachlan
57 What a mnemonic device may do
61 Comfy shoe
63 Narrow groove
64 Zaftig supermodel
65 Coin of Chile
66 Crotchety
67 Atomic number 10
68 Figure skater Paulsen
69 Some bank contents
70 1/3 a 1970 war film

DOWN

1 Egyptian Museum site
2 Jordan city once called Philadelphia
3 "Shalom"
4 Group of nine
5 Flik's friend
6 Bert in "Flying High"
7 Chatted with online
8 Athens rival
9 Abandoned
10 River to the Elbe
11 "Halftime" was his debut single
12 Belly
15 It's the truth
21 Littleneck
22 Brawny alternative
26 Hog genus
27 Thwack
28 Hoisting device
29 Heisman Trophy winner Walker
30 Lake bordering Ontario
31 Part of ROM
32 Center of San Antonio?
33 "Hawaii Five-O" setting
34 Rotated
38 Diplomatic etiquette
40 Tattoo word
41 Greek consonant
44 What the dim run around in
46 "You are something ___!"
49 Risky rendezvous
50 Showed contempt
51 Feel sorry about
54 Shakespeare title character
55 Joust wear
56 Mongoose relative
57 "Do You Know the Way to San ___"
58 Bear in the night sky
59 "Stanley & Iris" director
60 Chichén Itzá constructor
61 Tax pro
62 Sgt. Preston's horse

102

Billboard named 10 Down the #1 artist of the 2000s.

ACROSS

1 Lift up Killington
5 Pool predator
10 Falls away
14 "Samson et Dalila" solo
15 El Niño feature
16 Srta. in France
17 Holy Week beginning
19 Debtor's letters
20 Victim of a garden snake
21 Make right, perhaps
22 Zoom and fisheye
24 Make drinkable, as seawater
26 "Remnants" singer LeAnn
27 Strength training asset
32 Meter readout
35 Uber user
36 Former New Zealand bird
37 Black cat, to some
38 Feeder filler
39 Beatles album
40 Class for a Spanish speaker
41 Spot for a cast
42 Ice-cream brand
43 Global area of 6.888 million miles
47 Unpopular double features
48 Electrify
52 Show up
54 Purse weapon
56 Casino stockpile
57 Diego's days
58 Prime vacation property/TITLE
61 Lucy Maud Montgomery heroine
62 "Fiddler on the Roof" role
63 Name associated with "The Jackie Look"
64 Citi Field sluggers
65 Wild blue yonder
66 Vancouver gas brand

DOWN

1 Like some confessions
2 Word in the Boy Scout Law
3 One-time Fox News honcho
4 Colorado State mascot
5 Action-film feats
6 Drake's "Golden" ship
7 Ray in "The Green Berets"
8 Vitamin bottle letters
9 Pie fruits
10 Rapper whose name sounds like a candy
11 Was in flower
12 IBM's color
13 Short Congressional meeting
18 "Star Trek" crewman
23 Jealous Yeats heroine
25 Word from the corner
26 More inflamed
28 Off-white shades
29 César Franck's birthplace
30 Pudgy, with "poly"
31 Sounds like a small dog
32 Warring parties
33 Sandbox comeback
34 Less than eager
38 They're waiting in the wings
39 Try, as a case
41 Kind of hockey pad
44 Luther's "Ninety-Five ___"
45 Suffers from prurigo
46 One with a high hat
49 Rock stars, to many
50 Some are fine
51 "Unhand me!"
52 Levine on "The Voice"
53 Fork feature
54 Salon service, slangily
55 Part of a Molière play
59 "I see a ghost!"
60 Shad delicacy

103 TRIPLE DOUBLE by Pam Klawitter
It took four people dressed in black to bring the 10" 21 Down to life.

ACROSS

1 Tugs tug them
6 Kimono closer
10 Good War cards
14 Female vampire
15 Canadian tribe
16 Room on top
17 Late lunch hour
18 "The Road Taken" novelist Jaffe
19 Tiny carpenters
20 Line on a label
23 It might be found in a ring
24 Dinny's Alley
25 Giant of Cooperstown
26 Be a little shy
29 Metalworking tool
33 Add some bling
34 Puts one's foot down
35 Beat-up auto
38 Mount a diamond
40 Nice head
41 Shoreline features
44 Shampoo bottle directive
47 Neighbor of Burbank and Studio City
51 Bolivian bear
52 Semi compartment
53 RE/MAX competitor
54 ___ in "Idaho"
56 Ray Romano's "Ice Age" role
60 20% of forty and 40% of fifty
62 Flowing rock

63 Start of a counting-out rhyme
64 Canterbury clink
65 Baltic feeder
66 Cubic measure
67 Pita sandwich
68 "Ring Around the Collar" detergent
69 Sniggler

DOWN

1 Jostle the bucket
2 Nickname for a Harvard student
3 Underworld code of silence
4 Clean the whiteboard
5 When repeated, it's nothing new
6 Windshield clearers in winter
7 Former Yankee third baseman
8 Forward an email
9 Firesides
10 It might precede bad news
11 Clear soup
12 Young newt
13 NYC's are numbered
21 Ed Sullivan's mouse buddy
22 Louisiana, in Lyon
27 End of the shortest Bible verse
28 It's heard in the Highlands
30 Mike's spot

31 Cadiz calendar page
32 "Psycho" setting
35 "___, it's off to work . . ."
36 Hazzard County deputy
37 Factor in
39 A line in the sand?
42 Tickle Me Elmo toy company
43 Purple martin
45 Drag-racing org.
46 "Lady and the Tramp" cats
48 Half a Beatles "White Album" title
49 Vibraphonist Hampton
50 Swift stuff
55 Like some curtains and cliffs

57 Scandinavian capital
58 Montand in "Z"
59 Pass out
60 ___ McMuffin
61 Wray of "King Kong"

58 ACROSS   by Gary Larson
10 Down was the home of one of the Seven Wonders of the Ancient World.

ACROSS

1 Fishing equipment
5 Ethan Allen, religiously
10 Idina's "Frozen" role
14 Crowning
15 Make good on
16 Come down hard
17 Lays product
19 Arizona Indian
20 "World Series of Poker" home in Vegas
21 "The Merry Widow," for one
23 Tijuana turnovers
25 Not one's best effort, in sports
28 Han Solo's son Kylo
29 Kind of room
33 British royal
34 Cancels, with "out"
35 Sam's Club rival
36 "My boy"
37 Lake Okeechobee's state: Abbr.
38 Fellows
39 Bully
40 Contacts quickly, perhaps
42 Noted Warhol subject
43 Blackball
44 1965 march site
45 Elevator part
46 Related maternally
47 Sometime in the past
50 Cover again
53 Fired
57 Razor brand
58 Perform acrobatically to music
60 For men only
61 Taps instrument
62 Go (over)
63 French door part
64 The same age
65 Formal accessory

DOWN

1 Deep in thought
2 However, in textspeak
3 Lavish affection (on)
4 "Enough already!"
5 Sag
6 Common Market letters
7 X and XS
8 Northern Marianas capital
9 Used a keyboard
10 Temple of Artemis site
11 Hot stuff
12 School system VIP
13 Diva's solo
18 Magazine debut of March 3, 1923
22 Make fun of
24 Calculus calculation
25 Diamond corners
26 Fairy-tale figure
27 Year's record
30 ___-Sketch
31 Tonto's horse
32 "Chinatown" screenwriter
34 Big sizes, briefly
35 Corp. bigwig
37 Imperfections
38 Foal's mother
41 Response to "How's it going?"
42 "Fragile" masculine trait
43 Popular movie candy
45 Wispy cloud
46 "Goodness gracious!"
48 When doubled, a 1940s "Wow!"
49 Appealed
50 Gravelly voice
51 Jazz singer James
52 Neighbor of Pakistan
54 Cluster
55 Hose hue
56 Feat
59 Every man jack

105 FIRST PRIZE by Gary Larson
Three entertainment legends have more than one thing in common.

ACROSS

1 Club owned by Walmart
5 Diplomat Boutros Boutros-___
10 Clio winners
13 Carrier to Ben Gurion
14 Bow applications
16 Furrow
17 Multiple winner of 60 Across
19 Imitate
20 Sea off Greece
21 Darling
23 Multiple winner of 60 Across
25 Shot spot
27 Seating sections
28 Leave, briefly
29 "Beat it!"
31 "Three Sisters" sister
35 Fruity drinks
37 Cornerstone abbr.
40 Film genre
41 Coward of note
42 City near Anaheim
44 Family card game
45 Simple choice
49 James Bond, for one
51 Multiple winner of 60 Across
55 Revolt
56 1971 prison riot site
59 Plus
60 Recording Academy bestowal
62 New England catch
63 "What fools these mortals be" writer
64 Excited about
65 Have a go at
66 Kidney-related
67 Russian news agency

DOWN

1 Harper Lee's "Go ___ Watchman"
2 Skin lotion ingredient
3 National arbor of Bangladesh
4 Least candid
5 Popular red wine grape
6 Cupcake
7 Child's play
8 Schubert songs
9 Entirely
10 Ishmael's people
11 Lego brand for toddlers
12 Dutch painter Jan
15 Spread around
18 Salad topping
22 Unlawful firing?
24 Bygone theaters
25 Stuff in a muffin
26 Cancel
30 Gambling inits.
32 Purchase of 1803
33 Actress Lollobrigida
34 Eisenberg of "Deep Space Nine"
36 Cracks up
38 Domain
39 Double-cross
43 Main artery
46 Atkov and Cassini
47 Leonine loudmouth
48 Lighter fuel
50 Birdbrain
51 Pass
52 Big house
53 Not clear
54 Macho types
57 Old PC screens
58 Tumults
61 Major record label

"GIMME A BREAK!" by Gary Larson
The earliest known 13 Down appeared in the 8th-century Byzantine Empire.

ACROSS

1 Big name in pineapples
5 Filtered email
9 Armrest?
14 Race place
15 ___ Major
16 Nightclub charge
17 Purchase vampire protection?
19 Brick clay
20 Many a middle schooler
21 Summer TV offering
22 Grateful?
23 Exactly
27 Dockworker's org.
28 Portuguese monarch
29 Shape a death mask?
32 Perfume ingredient
35 Sanctimonious sort
36 Presentation graphics
38 Partygoer
41 Judge
45 Grant the use of one's horse?
47 Toothpaste type
48 Chaucer's Tabard
49 Canadian gas company
50 Garlic unit
52 Lugosi and Bartok
55 Ousted
57 Full of pep
58 Ring the ringside bell?
60 Faux pas
61 "Hogwash!"
62 Line up
63 Having a bite
64 Wash out
65 Dirty Harry's org.

DOWN

1 Off-leash area, often
2 Direct
3 Football foul
4 Cheer up
5 "O.K."
6 "Now!"
7 Simpleton
8 "No ___": Duran
9 Cicatrix
10 Bank deposit
11 Grand keys
12 Cosmic clouds
13 Explosive device
18 Parisian pronoun
24 Husband of Eurydice
25 Turkish honorific
26 Treat roughly
29 Plant Audrey's request
30 ___ and sciences
31 Blow off steam?
33 Dentist's word
34 Dobrev of "The Vampire Diaries"
37 Bus. bigwigs
38 Chinese e-commerce giant
39 "Wild Thing" rapper
40 Bikini wearer's mark
42 Google oneself
43 Sprite competitor
44 Went downhill
46 Silently acknowledged
50 EMT specialty
51 Plunders
53 Express
54 Djokovic, for one
56 Let up
58 Shoemaker's helper
59 Miss America Franklin

57 ACROSS* **by Gary Larson**
The cave at 24 Down is a U.S. national monument in Utah.

ACROSS

1 "Typee" sequel
5 Free TV spots, briefly
9 Sporty Mazda
14 Criticizes
15 Jessica of "Dark Angel"
16 Much of Chile
17 Footnote word
18 Nasty personality trait*
20 Pool contents?
22 Heir's concern
23 "I agree completely!"*
25 Flat floater
29 Joan of Arc, e.g.
30 Canadian crooner Michael
31 Connections
32 Archaeological find
36 Arise
37 Flatworms, scientifically*
39 Exorcist's concern
42 Charity ball VIP
43 Spaniard's "that"
46 Be bombastic
47 Bewitch
49 Diddly-squat
50 "American Beauty" star*
54 Comic Gabe
56 Jay Silverheels role
57 Post-matrimonial option for brides
61 Cry out
62 Cognizant
63 Drawn tight
64 To ___ (perfect)
65 Bill of fashion
66 Canadian gas company
67 Amount to make do with

DOWN

1 Paper-folding craft
2 Oath of omertà taker
3 Intros
4 Emily of "Hannah Montana"
5 Popular cooking spray
6 Cold shower?
7 Embarrass
8 Father Christmas
9 Slugger Williams
10 Like many summer TV shows
11 Juice suffix
12 Genteel affair
13 "Shoot!"
19 Convened
21 Disposable cup material
24 City south of Timpanogos Cave
26 Exercise target
27 Winter bug
28 Athletic supporter?
30 Bar snack bit
33 Fellow
34 Simpson judge
35 Bamboozle
37 "Isn't anyone interested?"
38 They fawn over fawns
39 Baseball manager Mattingly
40 Great time
41 Certifiable
43 Come (from)
44 Military missions
45 Birds in hanging nests
48 Frank acknowledgment
50 Dash abbr.
51 Buoy
52 Grannies
53 Black ___ cattle
55 Many Isner serves
57 Bag
58 Cobbler's tool
59 Kid's cry
60 Command for DDE

ORPHEUS ON EDGE   by Theresa Yves
Is he nervous or mendacious?

ACROSS

1 "Come to My Window" singer Etheridge
8 Cobbler containers
15 Sam Cooke's "___ Saturday Night"
16 Willa Cather heroine
17 **Start of a comment to Orpheus**
18 Cracks up over
19 Place for ring exchanges
20 Lena of "Chocolat"
22 Henri's here
23 Openings at a dermatologist's office
25 Enjoy some home cooking
27 **End of comment**
32 "Tell me ___ haven't heard!"
33 Classified ad abbr.
34 Last drumbeat?
35 Land for everyone
37 Ulster city
41 "Turn up the heat!"
42 3 on a pad
43 Bear up there
44 **Start of Orpheus' response**
49 Marine fliers
50 Joe of "Apollo 13"
51 Cribbage marker
52 Jessica of "Seventh Heaven"
53 Private languages
58 Small wheels
61 **End of response**
63 Begin, for example
64 "Invisible Man" author
65 Wet floors
66 Swell

DOWN

1 Mother of Buddha
2 Carbon compound
3 Big ape
4 Long story beginning?
5 Mountain guide
6 "Got it?"
7 Magazines
8 Louisiana county
9 Cognizant of
10 Sked info
11 Height
12 Undisturbed
13 Vitamin B3
14 Filling up
21 Fitting toy for a child?
24 Porter's pen name
25 Series ender
26 Like a literary Dodger
27 Part of SPCA
28 Alabama island near Florida
29 "Radio Song" group
30 Sound quality
31 Netman Edberg
36 Heavy metal rock group?
37 Made still
38 Musical based on "Exodus"
39 1040 digits
40 Cry before "You're it!"
42 Take in
44 Toxic condition
45 Menacing phrase
46 Wool type
47 Tut's underworld god
48 Area folks
52 Like Charles Barkley
54 Set down
55 AMEX rival
56 High-tech suffix
57 Enrapture, in slang
59 Key for indenting
60 Fair grade
62 Lilly of drugs

109 "GRIDIRON GAZETTE" MOTTO   by Theresa Yves
A sports analogy for journalists.

ACROSS

1 Ford frame
8 Puts to bed
15 "Praise God!"
16 Coming
17 Juice providers
18 Bowled over
19 **Motto at the "Gridiron Gazette": Part 1**
21 Before, in the past
22 Start of a footnote abbr.
23 Alaskan abode
27 Slightly
30 Platform article
32 St. Patrick's land
33 Peach center
34 Coin stampers
35 Baghdad resident
36 Alabama island
37 **Motto: Part 2**
40 Tears for Fears, e.g.
41 Ivan of tennis
43 Figure skater Rippon
44 Hamburger's one
45 Sneaker feature
46 Apply, as a patch
48 Bounders
49 Smeltery needs
50 Tour operator
51 Old Dixie org.
53 **Motto: Part 3**
59 Griffith of "Working Girl"
62 Receiver of waves
63 Cracker Jack prize
64 Put through the wash
65 "Good heavens!"
66 Not singly

DOWN

1 Vittles
2 Word with happy or zero
3 Italian wine city
4 Like margarita glasses
5 Contemptuous smile
6 Fearless
7 Talk trash
8 Skillet coating
9 Use a key on
10 Nile menace
11 More nutty
12 Kerouac's "Big ___"
13 Suffix for Israel
14 Baseball manager Yost
20 Remove with dynamite
24 Like a good egg
25 Part of LCD
26 Labor forces
27 Space mission name
28 Musical inability
29 "Yesterday!"
31 Island necklace
34 "Runaway" rocker Shannon
35 Belief system
38 "Deep Space Nine" character
39 Spread head
42 Line above the melody
46 More nimble
47 Marsh birds
48 Poolside convenience
52 Vital fluid
54 "My Way" lyricist
55 Tall story
56 Says further
57 Tells tales
58 Folk knowledge
59 "Rhoda" production co.
60 Suffix with green
61 Lille lily

110 SAY, SAY, SAY by Clarence Tyler
When read aloud, the theme only has one clue.

ACROSS

1 How old the universe is?
9 Aviator Earhart
15 Enthusiasm enhancer
16 Headquartering
17 Aisle, say
19 It may be spun
20 Feel remorse
21 Crafty one
24 He and she
25 Golf great Sam
28 They go into drives
32 Sked info
35 Lint traps, perhaps
38 Gin type
39 Isle, say
42 Ron Howard film
43 Lofty standards
44 "Weeds" org.
45 Hologram maker
47 Poison plant
49 Diggs flick
52 Like the good earth
56 En masse
61 Shooter ammo
62 "I'll say!"
65 Punches in
66 Rub the wrong way
67 Handles
68 Leather flower

10 Potato option
11 Editorial writer
12 Neeson of "Kinsey"
13 England's "Gloomy Dean"
14 Like sharp cheese
18 Gentle touch
22 Taking action
23 Bottled spirits
26 "And giving ___ up the chimney he rose"
27 Breaks bread
29 Tried to avoid a tag
30 Summer treat
31 Video game name
32 First name in stunts
33 "There!"
34 Gets off the fence
36 Biblical birthright seller
37 2014 movie about voting rights
40 Means
41 Bygone leader
46 Snappy comeback
48 Per ___ spending
50 "Wrong!"
51 "The Last Ship" network
53 Word in a genealogical table
54 "Chicago Hope" actress
55 Rob on the screen
56 One side of a vote
57 Type of wolf

DOWN

1 Barbecue rods
2 Kind of colony
3 As is proper
4 Brief belief summaries
5 Place for a stud
6 Will Smith title role
7 Amorphous mass
8 Brontë governess
9 Embarrass

58 Pear-shaped instrument
59 Fashionable
60 Banjoist Scruggs
63 Numero before quattro
64 Glass edge

111 SHOPPING CENTER   by Clarence Tyler
King Arthur sings 27 Down in the Broadway musical comedy.

ACROSS

1 Gives refuge to
8 Dish with layers
15 Asian environmental disaster
16 Ask on bended knee
17 Scrutiny
18 Safe keeping
19 Advocate for our nonhuman friends
21 Iowa metropolis
22 Trait bearer
25 "How could ___ so blind!"
26 Clock sound
30 Islands off Portugal
33 Explorer of southern Australia
35 Boxer's warning
36 Gut-related
40 Do an impression of
41 "Casablanca" pianist
42 Most like hot fudge
43 Despicable
44 TV spots
46 Little League official
47 The S of RSVP
49 Cosmo competitor
51 The neighbor's kids
53 Peggy in "Auntie Mame"
56 Shopping center found in four answers
57 Like a dark street
58 Salt's saint
59 Former netman Nastase
60 Esther of "Good Times"
61 Hip
62 President before Wilson
63 Bethlehem product
64 "My Way" composer
65 Popeye's ___ 'Pea
66 Present, for one
67 Kind of pressure

DOWN

1 Luck
2 "___ you serious?"
3 "Ta-___ Boom-der-e"
4 Slip
5 Davis in "Do the Right Thing"
6 Scolds, with "out"
7 Deli dangler
8 "Giant" heroine
9 Playwright Chekhov
10 Pilot's place
11 Takes into custody
12 It's got teeth
13 Kvetch
14 Fueled up
20 Soft toss
22 Comedian's stock
23 Book after 2 Chronicles
24 1996 crime film with ordinary people
27 Song from "Spamalot"
28 Guitar neck attachment
29 Was certain of
31 Dairy aisle section
32 Paulo or Pedro
33 It comes before the season
34 Follower of John
37 Avoid hitting this while singing "Lemon Tree"
38 Voice of Buzz Lightyear
39 "Jurassic Park" dominant life forms
45 PC key
48 Pole cover
49 Sends off
50 Leg. drama
51 Fly apart
52 Arrow shaft
54 Burning evidence
55 Clean energy type

112 SIX GUESSES*   by Victor Fleming
38 Across can be heard in the 2001 film "Bridget Jones's Diary."

ACROSS

1 Book of maps
6 Curved entrance
10 "The Big Easy"
14 On one's stomach
15 "Damn Yankees" heroine
16 Colorful gem
17 One with a safe job?*
19 Last name on "Dragnet"
20 "No pain, no ___"
21 Famous Bruin blueliner
22 Short pants?
23 Julius Erving, familiarly
25 Rabbit's foot, e.g.*
28 Former Brazil capital
29 Bandmate of the Edge
30 That woman
31 Fireplace leftover
32 Chief Wiggum's son
34 "Hop ___": Dr. Seuss
38 "It's Raining ___"
39 Folk rock's DiFranco
40 Psychology topic
42 Lyrical tribute
43 Illegal ignition
45 Spanish appetizers
47 Scores by FB's
48 River pollutant
50 Bitsy lead?
51 Court decision?
52 Swan song*

56 Tax collecting org.
57 Spots in the Seine
58 Pastor wannabes' sch.
59 "Well, if you insist"
62 Choir voice
63 Car cylinder seal*
67 Pasta sauce maker
68 Emmy-winning Falco
69 Ewe's trim
70 Guess (and a hint to starts of theme answers)
71 Lovett of rock
72 Movant or respondent

DOWN

1 BOLO
2 "La-la" preceder
3 Winter underwear*
4 "Diana" singer Paul
5 Golf pro ___ Pak
6 Eur. nation
7 2014 sci-fi film
8 Court employee
9 Gillette competitor
10 Start of a consoling phrase
11 Puccini opus
12 AFL part
13 "Tapestry" is one
18 Like many library books
23 Serious story
24 Part of a stairway
26 Dark
27 Difficult to please

29 Locust limb
33 Starter for "seven"
35 Liquid left after boiling greens*
36 Less conventional
37 Bothersome sorts
41 Fuel guzzler
44 Withdraws
46 Inverted Jenny stamp type
49 Orchard measure
52 Dishonest ones
53 Mosque deity
54 Ready following?
55 Thin, as a voice
60 Trunk closer
61 Workplace watchdog grp.
64 Actress Ruby
65 Polish off
66 Opportunity

113 SERIOUSLY by Tracy Bennett and Victor Fleming
Featured are four former "SNL" stars who stopped kidding around.

ACROSS

1 Swing states?
6 Musical epilogues
11 "Without further ___ . . ."
14 Reduce to mush
15 Ethiopia's Selassie
16 "A little one'll do ya"
17 "SNL" alum with a serious role in "Foxcatcher"
19 Ninth-grade subj.
20 Milky gems
21 "___ be so bold"
23 It attaches to the shirt
26 Pulls back
27 Like big brother
28 Citation maker
29 Affirming motion
30 Bell-shaped flower
32 Believer in Brahma
35 Zipcar parent
37 Brahmanic precept
39 Tree of Knowledge locale
40 Vichyssoise veggies
42 Lube a second time
44 Weeks in a Roman calendar?
45 Great Lakes tribes
47 Give ___ (cause)
49 Calumet Farm income source
51 "Voyager" captain Janeway

52 ___ around (cavorted)
53 Vanzetti's codefendant
54 "The Sound of Music" peak
55 "SNL" alum with a serious role in "Stranger Than Fiction"
60 "I've seen better"
61 Watsky song "Strong as ___"
62 "Marcovaldo" author Calvino
63 Barnyard wallowing spot
64 Crimean Peninsula city
65 Sporty car engine option

DOWN

1 "M*A*S*II" cops
2 Uncloseted
3 Cuprite, e.g.
4 Consecrate or pledge
5 Overlook, as faults
6 Odds-on favorites
7 Dinghy gear
8 Go kaput
9 Central Powers opponent
10 Unlikely to share
11 "SNL" alum with a serious role in "Punch Drunk Love"
12 The ___ Lama

13 Lady doctor?
18 "___ Tree": Joni Mitchell
22 Bellybutton type
23 Melodious
24 "___ a Parade": Arlen
25 "SNL" alum with a serious role in "Dream Girls"
26 Printing proof
28 References
31 Philadelphia Eagles owner
33 Brahma, for one
34 Striking group, at times
36 Loses control, in a way
38 Rickenbacker, for one
41 Supermarket chain
43 Theory course for Eng. majors

46 Saudi Arabia city
48 Either vowel in "humbug"
49 Pillow covers
50 Rental sign
51 "Amerika" author
53 Bed support piece
56 "Seriously funny!"
57 Part of EENT
58 British law deg.
59 London lavatory

114 TRUNKS by Harvey Estes
. . . but not the kind you swim in.

ACROSS

1 Ready to swing
6 Restorative sites
10 Retrievers
14 Lorna of literature
15 "Opera of Operas" composer
16 Retro hairdo
17 It may give you a rush
19 Race in a regatta
20 TRUNK
22 Type of analyst
23 Sounds of pounds
24 Steamed
26 Dermal decoration
30 Boxer Willard
34 With the intent
36 Cuts short
37 TRUNK
40 Part of an unwelcome phrase
41 Prefix with physics
42 Full of guile
43 Arizona desert
45 Gong shape
47 "Jungle Book" star
49 Little guys
54 TRUNK
58 Capitol topper
59 John Calvin, for one
60 2017 cat 5 hurricane
61 "Dawn" author Wiesel
62 To-be, in politics
63 Hard shipbuilding wood
64 Retreats
65 Table wines

DOWN

1 "Dilbert" cartoonist
2 Now
3 Villain for Rocky and Bullwinkle
4 In regard to
5 Tightens up
6 Indoor place to park a car
7 Proper companion
8 Get to
9 Consider it proper
10 Breaking point
11 Some miles away
12 Dessert cheese
13 Fish dish
18 As an upper limit
21 Lickety-split
25 Dog-___
27 Spelling of TV
28 Kadett maker
29 Start of a question of optics
30 Sports cars, for short
31 Shared currency unit
32 Suffix meaning "country"
33 In a way
35 Hits the spot
38 Vaughan of jazz
39 Big cuts
44 Took down a peg
46 Friend of Seinfeld
48 "Enough!"
50 Writer Calvino
51 Tones down
52 Part of CPI
53 Dissenting groups
54 Ready for press
55 Oral history
56 American poet Lazarus
57 Like a wafer

115 WITH A CRASH OF SYMBOLS   by Harvey Estes
The source of the lyric at 39 Down is "Nowhere Man."

ACROSS

1 Voting group
5 Kind of pad
10 Perry Mason story
14 Skye in "Gas Food Lodging"
15 Smash really bad
16 "Country Boy" singer Jackson
17 Coward on stage
18 Bakery emanation
19 Gaping mouths
20 Five-finger discounters
23 Avon and Cornwall
24 One of the martial arts
26 Nairobi's nation
27 Gobbler
30 Tropical eel
31 Land of O. Wilde
32 Watches a Netflix show
35 Three, for Sophia
36 Ecuador neighbor
38 Centaur, in part
39 Pianist Myra
40 **Reason why 20-A don't understand symbolism: Part 1**
42 **Reason: Part 2**
44 It's all in your mind
46 Daytime TV fare
49 Thai language
50 Neither solid nor liquid
54 Spacewalk, at NASA
56 Canadian oil company
58 Kind of battery
59 Naval Academy freshman
60 **Reason: Part 3**
63 Visibly embarrassed
64 Sights in the western sky
65 Diamond goofs
66 Hits hard

DOWN

1 Hopper
2 "Listen to me!"
3 Pithy witticism
4 Bloody Mary stalk
5 ESPN figures
6 Houston Texans' mascot
7 Half the alphabet?
8 Crib call
9 Platform part
10 Sporty Chevy
11 Dining option
12 Was dazed
13 Jr. naval officer
21 Shooter ammo
22 Dog food brand
23 Record flaw
25 Checks out
27 Home of Paris
28 Finish'd
29 Rigging support
33 Hoi polloi
34 Prove your worth
37 Versatile vehicle
39 "Isn't ___ bit like . . .": Beatles
41 Witchy woman
43 WBA stats
44 One of Santa's eight
45 More optimistic
47 BB, e.g.
48 Slim and trim
49 Leave alone
51 Turned traitor, with "out"
52 Bulldogs booster
53 Feedbag fare
55 Bottomless chasm
57 Not taken in by
59 Skip a turn
61 Lab warning
62 Genetic info carrier

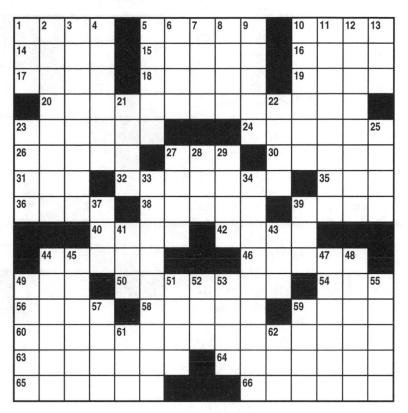

116

ACROSS

1 Briard's cry
5 The second step
13 Eros, by another name
14 "Any volunteers?" response
15 Stun
16 Responsibility for the Civic minded?
17 Canopy part
19 Slang
20 Beloved ones
22 Berra had a hand in it
23 1993 Janet Jackson film
27 Reunion attendees
29 Stay over
30 Your back?
31 Jack
32 Hooch
33 AQI part
34 Miguel Wattson is one
35 ___ con pollo
36 The Floss, for one
38 Place for butterflies
41 Play the hero
42 Down source
43 See 9 Down
45 Antennae
49 Students of yesteryear?
53 Giddy feeling
54 Join
55 April Fools' Day perpetration
56 Fail to get a good handle on?
57 Coachella shelter

DOWN

1 Move through the air
2 Epps or Dorsey of film
3 Move through the cracks
4 Revolutionary's battle cry
5 "¡___ favor, amigo!"
6 Cadence count
7 "Fifty Shades" protag
8 Fly
9 MVP of Super Bowl XXVIII (with 43-A)
10 Starfire and Beast Boy, for two
11 Chrysler logo
12 Suspicious of, for good reason
14 New Year's Eve sign
16 Winter wear
18 Summer wear
21 Tight one
22 Guiding spirit
23 Spin doctors
24 Monk's domain?
25 In
26 Brontë character
27 "Wonder Woman" antagonist
28 Movie mogul Marcus
32 French cheese
35 Ancient Greek wine vessel
36 No idler
37 "Fine"
39 Barbie's parent
40 Adoring verses
43 Ham's brother
44 Pint-size
46 Plant in health drinks
47 Tend toward one side
48 Blue message
50 Spare part?
51 Elephant suffix
52 Whence OutKast: Abbr.

117 THEMELESS by Erik Agard
The "P" in 26 Across stood for "Pay it no mind."

ACROSS

1 Plot giveaway
8 Prescribe
15 Saving face?
16 Sign of bad things to come
17 Kind of clue 61 Across is
18 Went up the charts
19 Fiji rival
20 Birthday suit
21 Spotify visuals
22 Hue that rhymes with "hue"
24 Show with a spinoff set in NOLA
26 Sylvia Rivera contemporary
32 They're shared in a pool
33 Former Cunard flagship
34 Language with a steamy logo
35 George on the "MacGyver" reboot
36 Towns
37 Poetry collection subset
38 Bordeaux buddy
39 "___ not and say we did"
40 LPGA player's wear
41 Tater tots?
44 "It didn't escape my notice"
45 Fearstruck
46 Kosugi in "Enter the Ninja"
48 Dededo's island
50 Biopic role for Hulce
55 Creative starting point
57 Mai tai venue
58 Talent show from "The Waltons," say
59 Nirvana album
60 Removes from the roster
61 Error

DOWN

1 Wearing kicks
2 Michael of "CHIPS"
3 Catan cards
4 Setting of 2011's "Butter"
5 Den mother
6 Lard
7 Beatles album
8 Friend of Harry and 11 Down
9 Where the Big Muddy flows
10 Finalize
11 Friend of Harry and 8 Down
12 Brand rep
13 Ready for a drive
14 Burnt ___ (BBQ delicacy)
20 Stacked squad, in NBA lingo
23 Golden Globe winner Welch
25 Evoker of LOLs on a group text
26 Sound Machine city
27 Like a supplement
28 Puts back to normal
29 Puzzle type
30 Some sports bets
31 Mag magnate
32 Genuine
36 Unleashed some frustration on
40 Number puzzles
42 Coronas, e.g.
43 Paul McCartney's sign
46 Boatload
47 Fine-tune
49 20 sources
51 Pimples
52 Provide job security for, say?
53 Not everyday
54 De ___ (excessive)
56 Pixar specialty
57 Cook, Curry, or Rice

ACROSS

1 Mell Lazarus comic strip
6 Dial duality
10 Play bass guitar percussively
14 "It's your pot"
15 Surrealist befriended by Farrow
16 Bank notes?
17 Playground retort
18 Thrift store wares
20 Cry after "Extra! Extra!"
22 Subtle
23 "Star Trek: TNG" android
24 Pitbull's "Climate Change" label
25 Burgess of Broadway musicals
27 "Roundball Rock" was its theme music
32 Hellenic vowels
33 Saint with a writing system named after him
34 Bring to light
35 Home city of rapper Paper Boi
38 Experience
40 "I have a dream" monogram
41 Lie in store for
43 Husky sounds
44 Therapy meetings
46 Helps with prep work
48 Denzel's 2010 title role
49 Be over-concerned
51 Like Willie Winkie
52 On easy street
57 "Wow, thank you so much!"
58 Undermine
60 Snorkeling site
61 Kimye's daughter
62 "Main Street" novelist
63 Home row starter
64 Van Morrison's "Brown ___ Girl"
65 Mother of Perseus

DOWN

1 "The Voice" prop
2 Stick-up man in "The Wire"
3 "Cash is king"
4 Malian sultan Mansa ___
5 Warring
6 Racy
7 Tatiana on "Orphan Black"
8 Rover bug
9 Mesencephalon
10 Great Plains language family
11 Fenced goods
12 Bavarian automaker
13 "Over here"
19 Start missing shots
21 Common batteries
22 Prepares in its bag
26 "Mr. Robot" airer
28 Vintner's adjective
29 Compile a short list
30 Bounce legend heard on Beyoncé's "Formation"
31 Stick for a field sport
33 James in "Brian's Song"
36 Affix with a hammer
37 Like some printers
39 Enjoy a half-smoke, e.g.
42 "Oh, really?"
45 Escort to the door
46 "___ better to have loved . . ."
47 Reaffirmed
50 Took another crack at
52 "Queen of Katwe" director Nair
53 Brothers of "Rag Mop" fame
54 Went to bat for, in the AL
55 2004 Brad Pitt film
56 Vicinity
59 Tongue suffix

119 THEMELESS by Erik Agard
Alternate clue for 9 Down: Nonce word in "Finnegan's Wake."

ACROSS

1 Rap's Run-___
4 Upscale clothing store
12 "Ruh-___!": Scooby-Doo
13 Money used for spring snow removal?
14 Adored one
16 "Listen to the man"
17 Would-be geneticist's study
19 Like witch noses
20 It stops when it's broken
21 The Brain's friend
22 Henri's house
24 Quirky
26 "That is . . ."
27 Brought to bear
31 Uptick
32 Swansea locale
33 "Horror of horrors!"
34 Entranceways
36 It's all the rage
37 Hot lines accessed by phone?
38 Resonator guitars
39 Journo's project
41 Equip
43 Fakeries
44 One with big plans?
47 Founder of Hawaii
49 Kensington kiss
50 Irreverent acts
51 "Bow, wow, wow, ___ Yale!"
52 Big Brown's Belmont finish
53 Simons of fashion

DOWN

1 Drab partner
2 Manmohan Singh's successor
3 Most exacting
4 Nickname for Greenwood, Tulsa
5 Popups, usually
6 Seat people, cutely
7 HBO crime drama set in Baltimore
8 Conditions
9 Mild, creamy cheese
10 Solidarity
11 Vortex
13 LaBeouf of "Disturbia"
15 Call for a card
16 "No more!"
18 Lion's gait
21 Mat decisions
22 "Amelia" director Nair
23 Score after deuce
25 You are, in Uruapan
27 "Stop right there!"
28 Pencil-pusher's need?
29 Car designer Ferrari
30 "Nobody ___ It Better": Simon
32 Like lotus leaves
35 NASCAR driver McGriff
36 E. ___ (bacteria)
38 Museum of Islamic Art home
39 "Ah, that's too bad!"
40 "Magic Mike" setting
42 "Draft Dodger Rag" singer
43 Cargo pallet
44 Gallic pals
45 Gummy bear flavor
46 Weekly clocking-out cry
48 ___ disadvantage

120 "LEND ME YOUR EARS" by Harvey Estes
Grant Mark Antony's request when solving this one.

ACROSS
1 Stuffing herb
5 Reversed
10 Sec
14 Think out
15 Pricey hotel room
16 Rob Reiner's alma mater
17 Set down
18 Mother of Elizabeth I
20 Songs laced with profanity?
22 Field of work
23 Gives the evil eye
26 Distinctive manner
27 Pack item, for short
30 ___ a time
31 Baltic Sea country
34 Nile reptile
35 Orson Scott Card novel about a real charmer?
39 Gardner in "On the Beach"
40 Heart-related
41 Office slips
44 USN officers
45 Gave a glowing review
49 Nativity display
51 Curly salad green
52 Higher-priced German magazine?
56 Spring cleaning event
58 Granny in "The Simpsons"
59 "East of Eden" brother
60 Outrigger, for one
61 One way to stand by
62 Enlivens, with "up"
63 Sandcastle destroyers
64 Bits of the Bahamas

DOWN
1 Cramps, e.g.
2 Out in left field
3 High spirits
4 Necessitated
5 One-time Pan Am rival
6 "Cats" director Trevor
7 Fender nick
8 Agenda listing
9 Fix program problems
10 Cellist Lloyd Webber
11 It comes in bricks
12 Birds do it
13 Stir up
19 Northern metropolis
21 June's portrayer in "Walk the Line"
24 The life of Riley
25 Racing car product
27 Reef buildup
28 Like krypton
29 Hems in
32 Middle X or O
33 "Softly ___ Leave You"
35 Even a single time
36 Talk about seeing stars?
37 Haute cuisine term
38 Rather conjectural
39 "Preacher" channel
42 Indian and others
43 Fetch
46 Abe of "Barney Miller"
47 Fifty-fifty
48 Airport hassles
50 At attention
51 Wired swords
53 Lou's "La Bamba" costar
54 "Atlas Shrugged" author
55 Tart plum
56 Clothing chain, with "the"
57 It may follow you

FAMOUS LAST WOOORDS by Harvey Estes
The locale of 19 Across is the Rockaway Peninsula in Queens.

ACROSS

1 MGM cofounder Marcus
5 I's in Ithaca
10 Coward on stage
14 It's all around you
15 On the ball
16 Gumbo veggie
17 Like new
18 Originator
19 Jacob ___ State Park
20 Boot
22 Able to come back
24 Sportscaster Ahmad
26 Swab a spill
27 Letter-ending word
29 Do an usher's work
33 Dismisses lightly
37 Marisa of "The Handmaid's Tale"
38 Eye rakishly
39 Kind of mail
41 Getting ___ years
42 Hiker's path
44 Critical court situation
46 Higher-ranking
48 Speed skater Ohno
49 "___ bad moon rising . . .": CCR
51 Haunted house hangings
55 Chart shunned by Flat Earthers?
59 "___ Never Walk Alone"
60 Morales of "Jericho"
61 Words of empathy
63 Key opening
64 "Gandhi," for one
65 Stalin's predecessor
66 Solemn procedure
67 Old strings
68 Cliff feature
69 Fall game?

DOWN

1 Not so believable
2 Medium alternative
3 Marine eagles
4 **Famous last words on a slippery mountain trail**
5 Real suffix
6 "ER" actor Epps
7 **. . . in a high wire act**
8 Playground comeback
9 ATM card feature
10 **. . . by a parachutist**
11 Steinbeck migrant
12 St. Patrick's land
13 Bringing up the rear
21 Diamond covering
23 Driving desire
25 The Black Keys et al.
28 Have a yen
30 Former Dodge model
31 Restraint for Justify
32 Windshield option
33 Lobster traps
34 Grimm villain
35 Buck character
36 Gullible guy
40 Trotsky or Jaworski
43 Give the slip to
45 Sneaky maneuver
47 Bar order
50 Roast host
52 "Calvin and Hobbes" girl
53 Tickle pink
54 Not so naïve
55 Projector load
56 Sports award
57 Cougar's retreat
58 Goody-goody
62 WSW opposite

122 A THROWAWAY PUZZLE   by Howard Barkin
Please recycle this one when you're done.

ACROSS

1 Sounds from a door knocker
6 Fix, but not in a good way
9 Covertly added to an email
14 Where a rock band rocks
15 Prenuptial agreement?
16 A state song (with "oe")
17 Album for clippings
19 Full of info
20 Expose
21 Capital on the Chattahoochee
23 Busy mo. for CPAs
25 Class event
29 One sharing puppy love?
34 She played Elizabeth in "Elizabeth"
35 ___ roll (hot)
36 Bagged leaves
37 Salt-throwing wrestlers
38 Efficiency adage
42 Fragrant compound
43 Sphere starter
44 "Hurray, Manolete!"
45 React to an uppercut
46 Place for odds and ends
49 Replace a lightbulb
51 And so on
52 More mousy
55 Geppetto's goldfish
59 Followers of Guru Nanak
62 Weigh-in insults/TITLE
64 Before surgery
65 Ltr. enclosure
66 Chennai's land
67 Funny girl Brice
68 Anonymous surname
69 Like some rock gardens

DOWN

1 Woofer's range
2 Place de l'Étoile sight
3 Fictional detective Wolfe
4 Slowly bother, as worries
5 Sugarhouse sight
6 Uncivil disobedience
7 One looked up to
8 Mini-racer
9 Language family that gave us "gumbo"
10 Like West Pointers
11 Animal seen in "Chik-fil-A" ads
12 Sounds accompanying shrugs
13 One rotation of the Earth
18 Devoid of fauna
22 Word between names in a bio
24 Tosh of reggae fame
26 Annoyed reply to "Are you awake?"
27 "Smallville" actor Annette

28 Avian homebuilder
29 Brings down the curtain
30 "Hang on!"
31 Wine judge
32 "Nixon in China" role
33 Sean who played Rudy
37 Nasal sound of derision
39 Fund-raiser that might offer tote bags to donors
40 Implement for heating sesame oil
41 Thermometer inventor Celsius
46 Croce's "You Don't Mess Around With ___"

47 Airline with seven U.S. hubs
48 Check ID?
50 Faint, as clouds
53 Honey Ryder's Bond film
54 Icicle anchor
56 Chaps
57 Yalies
58 "Agreed?"
59 Sunscreen inits.
60 Roth ___
61 Barbie's toy boy
63 Musical duo She & ___

123 VISIONARY   by Howard Barkin
If you get stuck, try seeing things a bit differently.

ACROSS

1 Part of EPA
5 Huge gap
10 Say you'll be there
14 Delicious leftover?
15 Mea ___
16 Rapier relative
17 Dr. No, for one*
19 Common investment
20 Urge into action
21 Upgraded circuitry
23 Exist
24 Stunning fish?*
27 Prince Charles' domain
29 Día de San Valentín gifts
30 Beats by ___ (headphones brand)
31 Mideast carrier
32 iPhone card
33 Talking bear of film
35 November sale day*
39 "Deliver Us From ___" (2003)
40 iPhone platform
41 Came to (with "up")
44 "That's revolting!"
47 Comic book artist
49 Nunavut resident
50 1998 Matt Damon role*
53 Quirky
54 Completely fooled
55 Ship fronts
57 Anthony Hopkins in "Thor"
58 Shockers/ TITLE
62 Came and ___
63 Nobelist Egyptian
64 Pioneer shock jock
65 Pesters
66 U-bolt cousins
67 Where F can mean "false" or "fail"

DOWN

1 Quick tennis point
2 Spread quickly online
3 Climactic police drama setting
4 Restaurant rating site
5 Mid-size battery
6 Fifth-century invader
7 Fazal in "Victoria & Abdul"
8 Bursts of speed
9 GranTurismo and GranCabrio
10 Sepulcher sight
11 Knocked the rest of the pins down
12 Walnut overlay
13 What cheap-jacks do
18 Thousands of $, slangily
22 Caught on (with "up")
23 Reverence
25 Gaston Leroux's phantom
26 More like a beanbag chair
28 Fanning in "The Beguiled"
32 Least substantial
34 Elie Wiesel book
36 Like some kites
37 Culkin in "Signs"
38 "Remember that favor I did you?"
42 Former children's clothing chain
43 Airport screen info
44 North, to Manhattanites
45 Like good eggs
46 On the Appalachian Trail
48 David Rudisha, by birth
49 Memo heading
51 Lets off some steam
52 Calendar box entries: Abbr.
56 Doing a needed task
59 Brown URL suffix
60 Cereal bran
61 Fast flier, once

124 SOUNDS THE SAME TO ME   by Anna Carson
Two down clues sound the same, but they're not part of the theme.

ACROSS

1 Rival of Ole Miss
5 Sarcastic taunts
10 Alaskan abode
14 Cookie king Wally
15 Having a lot to lose
16 "Shucks!"
17 That's French
18 Rental contract
19 Gallery on the Thames
20 Words after "Shall we change 'me' in this text?"?
23 Be tactful, sometimes
24 SDI weapon
25 Ice skating figures
27 Letter like an inverted "y"
29 Makes a union
31 "___ Italien": Strauss
32 "Wonderful Town" sister
34 Pass, as time
35 Product endorsement from the American Optometric Assn.?
39 Choir perch
40 Geronimo, for one
41 Furry sitcom star
42 Equips for war
44 Role models
48 "Aw, c'mon!"
50 Racket extension
51 Part of AARP
52 Where to find everyone's approval?
56 Some watch faces
57 Deep voice
58 On the summit of
59 Sheltered on the sea
60 "Full House" twin name
61 Prefix with scope
62 Farmiga of "Bates Motel"
63 Joanna of "Growing Pains"
64 Biblical garden

DOWN

1 Frequent Bogart costar
2 Social reformer Bloomer
3 Islamic
4 Home of some bubbly
5 Driver target
6 Structural member
7 Theodore Cleaver, to Wally
8 Bygone pump name
9 Blow a fuse
10 Name provider
11 Silver thread among the gold?
12 Leeway
13 Versatile vehicle
21 Conductor Boulanger
22 Spanish affirmatives
26 U-turn from NNW
28 Cowardly Lion Lahr
29 Breaks down
30 New Age music superstar
33 Cowboy actor Jack
34 "The Beverly Hillbillies" star
35 Milkweed sac
36 Word after "repeat"
37 Troop formations
38 "SNL" cast member Oteri
39 Indy 500 unit
42 Light wood
43 Nike rival
45 Took to the stump
46 Pooh's grumpy pal
47 Cross the threshold
49 In a fog
50 "The Beverly Hillbillies" star
53 Chalky white
54 Country in a Beatle song
55 Good Hope, for one
56 Restroom, for short

125 THEMELESS by Anna Carson
There's a bit of wordplay at 17 and 59 Across.

ACROSS
1 Just plain awful
10 Does some PR work
15 Kid's hideout
16 Dugout
17 Compassionate crown prince? (with 59-A)
18 Engage in rhetoric
19 Winding curve
20 Astonished
22 Small world's beginning
24 360-deg. curve
25 Record spiral
26 Soda fountain sound
28 Havarti additive
30 NY Met or LA Dodger
31 More sheepish
33 Diamond of note
35 Generation-X followers
36 Cozy
38 Compound
40 JFK info
43 "Goody Two Shoes" singer Ant
45 Increases
49 Attack deterrent
51 Designer Cassini
53 Kind of bar
54 To boot
56 Barker and Bell
58 Schoolyard retort
59 See 17 Across
62 Deutschland "and"
63 Old def. pact
64 Like a family tree
66 Will of "American Dreams"
67 Some plates
68 Rubberneck
69 Vapor visible above

DOWN
1 Divinity denial
2 El elevator
3 Second edition
4 Finish'd
5 Victuals
6 Greek column style
7 Performed better than
8 Greet and seat
9 Come off as
10 Scrub hard
11 "Here You Come Again" singer
12 Behind
13 When perdition freezes over
14 Tournament directors, at times
21 Giving the eye to
23 Synagogue chests
27 Elizabeth of "Transamerica"
29 Appomattox figure
32 Ballet dancer Nureyev
34 Roller coaster feature
37 Cowboy's date
39 Carrie's "Star Wars" role
40 Makes a pile
41 Most upbeat
42 Unprocessed info
44 Vacationer's purchase
46 Japanese warrior
47 Straighten out
48 Topiary dogs
50 Balance unsteadily
52 Café cry
55 Kind of change
57 Bloodhound's guide
60 Fem. opposite
61 Belgian river
65 Carrier in "The Aviator"

126 THEMELESS by Harvey Estes
Harvey came up with the clue for 12 Down on April 15th.

ACROSS
1 Brut product
11 Poses for pics
15 Lincoln, Jackson, and Cleveland
16 Shin neighbor
17 Androids
18 Land unit
19 Sault ___ Marie
20 Monkey's uncle, literally
21 Falsifies
23 Woo with music
26 Send in
27 Banned bug killer
28 Sylvan showplaces
31 Asks for alms
33 "Nonsense!"
34 Rocky top
35 Cosmetics holder
36 Hen at work
37 TV hubby of Phyllis
38 PC key
39 Skater Henie
40 Theatre on 9009 Sunset Blvd.
41 Don
43 "So ___ me!"
44 Macho dude
45 Zimbabwe neighbor
50 It's in hot soup a lot
53 "Foiled again!"
54 Caesar of comedy
55 "The ___ of Spring": Stravinsky
56 Proven over the years
59 Two words before "about"
60 China set for a cabinet display
61 Links numbers
62 Without rebuke

DOWN
1 Take ___ (skip)
2 Galway's instrument
3 Snuffy Smith's son
4 Logical beginning
5 Sends back to a lower court
6 Get testy with
7 More than unpopular
8 Latin I verb
9 Work in the bleachers
10 Calgary's ___ Plaza
11 Apolo Ohno, for one
12 Capital punishment?
13 Hawaii or Alaska, once
14 React to a haymaker
22 Boast
24 Jumping-off place
25 Piece of cake
29 Saturn satellite
30 Limbo need
31 One performing a fouetté turn
32 Insurance worker
33 Need air
35 Profitable produce
36 Allie's fiancé in "The Notebook"
37 MGM cofounder Marcus
39 Make a putt
40 Tailbacks, typically
42 Indiana cagers
43 Island birthplace of Joan Baez
46 More than large
47 On the move
48 She may cry "Uncle"
49 Put in later
51 Ides of March words
52 Nothing, to Nicole
57 Raincoat or computer
58 Ice-T's show, briefly

127 FIGHT CLUB   by Harvey Estes
Where the prices can't be beat, but the customers can.

ACROSS

1 Dharma's TV friend
5 Make fit
10 Throat clearer
14 New York college
15 Kind of bear
16 Traditional knowledge
17 Did the crawl
18 Where Socrates shopped
19 Chew like a mouse
20 Charges for joining a fight club
23 "___ a Million": Aaliyah
24 Slings mud at
26 Third Crusade sultan
29 Cardio med
30 Can tool
34 Furthermore
35 With 53 Across, Fight club motto with low 20 Across?
38 Wrist bone
40 Game tile
41 Battlefield cry
43 Cause ___
48 Places for canvases
52 Kind of wrench
53 See 35 Across
56 Voting no
57 Roasting places
58 Jazz singer James
59 French Christmas
60 Fender bender scars
61 Go after

62 "The Neverending Story" author
63 Home of the Ewoks
64 Prompter prefix

DOWN

1 Gadgets
2 Ivanhoe's lady love
3 Crown material
4 River to the Atlantic
5 On ___ with
6 Some setters
7 Honolulu hello
8 Capital on the Seine
9 "The Sound of Music" family
10 Barbary Coast resident
11 "I kid you not!"
12 Mistake removers
13 Cry like a kitty
21 At the ___ one's rope
22 Low boggy land
25 Jack of "Barney Miller"
27 Apple Touch, for one
28 Green Lantern's enemy
31 "Apocalypse Now" locale
32 Heroic saga
33 Russo of "Thor"
35 Like most paragraphs
36 Emery board
37 The "Ryan Express"

38 Thurman of "Kill Bill"
39 Made privy to
42 AFL counterpart
44 First among siblings
45 Untroubled
46 Summer cottage, often
47 Mesh gears
49 Lose ground
50 Baltimore footballer
51 Stimulate the economy
54 Not taken in by
55 Country in a Beatle song
56 Request to Sajak

COMING-OF-AGE PUZZLE   by Harvey Estes
24 Across was the site of the Manhattan Project.

ACROSS

1 St. Patrick's Cathedral has 21
7 Jefferson Airplane's music
15 Rainbow's end?
16 Toledo's waterfront
17 Address from the brass?
19 Supernova output
20 Catchall abbr.
21 Stop ___ dime
22 Bernadette of Broadway
24 Los ___, New Mexico
28 Parisian parent
30 ___ buddy
31 Advice to a homeowner with a burned-out lawn? (with 39-A)
36 Amazon smart speaker
37 Avis rival
38 ___ noire
39 See 31 Across
41 Lipstick shade
42 Creep (along)
43 Lighten up
44 Fishing footwear
48 "___ yer ol' man!"
49 Fruity coolers
50 Stretch the truth
56 Taylor Swift song for grammar schoolers?
59 Bullring VIP
60 Materialize
61 Broadway opener
62 Precisely right

DOWN

1 Cosmetics company
2 Severe sentence
3 Vegan protein source
4 Hit the helipad
5 Place for a pool table
6 Oktoberfest mugs
7 "On top of that . . ."
8 Pushrod pushers
9 "Runaway Bride" hero
10 ___ Plaines
11 Odometer button
12 Mount the soapbox
13 1995 Horse of the Year
14 Faints, with "over"
18 Nucleic acid
22 Veep's boss
23 Racket extension
24 Help with the heist
25 Lomond, for one
26 Queens stadium name
27 Frame of mind
28 Homer Simpson's wife
29 Suffix with sermon
31 Overly diluted
32 Bassoon's little brother
33 Fashion designer Wang
34 JFK predictions
35 Swear by, with "on"
37 Med. plan options
40 Taxing mo.
41 Halloween wear
43 Hit the links
44 Bulb info
45 Kind of committee
46 Big name on the farm
47 City on the Ruhr
48 Highway warning
50 Suffix with cyclo
51 Brontë heroine
52 Mid-voyage
53 Piecrust ingredient
54 Waffle choice
55 Gone out with
57 ___ kwon do
58 "Deep Space Nine" changeling

129 GRADUATION DAY by Harvey Estes
Mussorgsky composed 31 Down as a memorial to Viktor Hartmann.

ACROSS
1 Rare entrée, at times
6 "To ___ it may concern"
10 It's blown in the winds
14 Sci-fi "home team"
15 White House staffer
16 Ready, to Rimbaud
17 Plane parking place
18 React while watching "The Onion Movie"?
20 Where to find graduated bobs
22 Contact piece
23 NY hrs.
24 Cleared the board
27 Regard
29 Poison in espionage flicks
30 Union commander at Gettysburg
33 List keeper
34 Where to find graduated tax schedules
40 Normandy city
41 Elroy's pooch
42 "Conga" singer
45 Reach out
50 Athlete that cuts ice
51 Wall St. group
53 Hand cream ingredient
54 Where to find graduated cylinders
57 Homage
59 Nellie's "South Pacific" love
60 Wine list info
61 Disastrous fate
62 Piano adjuster
63 Put up, as money
64 Hill builders
65 Explanation preceder

DOWN
1 Pinto's place
2 Conical homes on the plains
3 Like a roving knight
4 Rile up
5 "Critique of Pure Reason" author
6 Insects with narrow waists
7 Part of a drum kit
8 Baltic Sea tributary
9 Melodic sequence
10 Modus ___
11 More forward
12 Finish'd
13 UFO crew
19 Reddish hartebeest
21 Mocha's country
25 Red rind contents
26 Game rooms
28 Cassowary cousin
29 Loafer coin
31 Mussorgsky's "Pictures ___ Exhibition"
32 Bad-mouth
34 Poker's "pocket rockets"
35 Poe's Amontillado container
36 Whale or dolphin
37 About 33%
38 Judy in "Tomorrowland"
39 Henhouse raider
43 Professional charges
44 "Invincible" fleet
46 Rabbi's text
47 Jerry Seinfeld's pal
48 Court figures
49 Mirage site
51 "My Fair Lady" race place
52 Holds back
55 Party to
56 Snowman of Asia
57 Olive played by Duvall
58 Royal jelly producer

130 "HERE'S THE KEYS!" by Tracy Gray
A song from "Rubber Soul" inspired this theme.

ACROSS

1 It may cover all the bases
5 Southern Slav
9 Horse's stride
13 Caribbean sea color
14 "Bonjours" opposite
16 Nashville stage concert
17 Beatles song lyric (with 61-A)
19 "Eat Up Every Moment" sloganeer
20 NYC stage awards
21 "Here's the keys!": Arnie Cunningham
23 Make money hand over fist
25 Platoons
26 Have ___ on (claim)
29 Dot.com address
30 "Here's the keys!": Luke Duke
35 Trans-Siberian Railway city
39 Home of BYU
40 2015 Verizon acquisition
41 Govt. security
42 50-oared ship of myth
43 "Here's the keys!": Jim Douglas
45 Bar topic
47 Brown meat with high heat
48 Morning sickness symptom
51 Created a band
56 "Here's the keys!": Ronny & the Daytonas
59 United Airlines hub
60 Berry touted as a superfood
61 See 17 Across
63 Goose egg
64 Divorce
65 Deckhand
66 Activist Brockovich
67 Many, many moons
68 Teddy bear–like "Star Wars" character

DOWN

1 Mount in Galilee
2 Jordan seaport
3 His cube was a craze
4 Check recipient
5 ___ Paulo, Brazil
6 "Every Student Succeeds Act" dept.
7 Full-bodied
8 Paddington and Pooh
9 Proceed independently
10 Plant louse
11 Pressing items?
12 Blood classification
15 Like fingerprints
18 San Diego County's San ___ Mtns.
22 South, in Spain
24 Peeples or Vardalos
27 Dullsville
28 Blackthorn drupes
30 Transcript fig.
31 Botch
32 Eggy holiday quaff
33 Darwin's theory
34 Lifestyle magazine of French origin
36 Underworld
37 Ex–Knicks coach Jackson
38 It's tapped in frats
41 Remote location?
43 Nubby woolens
44 Knucklehead
46 Hearing-impaired com.
48 More congenial
49 "Pong" creator
50 Shake on it
52 One and done, for one
53 Colorful parrot
54 Muse of lyric poetry
55 Jeter of baseball
56 Veg out
57 Its logo is a smiling TV set
58 Kitchen appliance
62 Trauma centers, for short

131 FINAL REARRANGEMENTS by Tracy Gray
That's a new clue for 19 Across!

ACROSS

1 Do the math
6 Holy terrors
10 Trail mix
14 "Moody River" singer
15 Pants, in brief
16 Period following Passover
17 Tack found on harness horses
19 Middle name of Ricky Gervais
20 Silt, sand, clay soil
21 Plame affair scandal
23 Smack a homer, in baseball slang
26 Joan Collins role on "Batman"
27 Beers made with top fermentation
28 The Marx Brothers, e.g.
30 Show stoppers?
31 ___ Friday
32 Job for a grease monkey
33 TSA ___
34 Oral hygiene product
39 Stooge with a bowl cut
40 "Metamorphoses" poet
41 Org. that refunds
43 Swift steeds
46 Odette, by day
47 Spot on a radar screen
48 Plant secretion used for incense
50 Ford fob
52 Copious
53 Home of the Quechua
54 Source of indigo
55 "The Intercept" journalist
60 Walk wobbly
61 The rain in Spain
62 Missouri River tributary
63 Turnblad in "Hairspray"
64 The first canvas-top "sneaker"
65 Iceberg lettuce chunk

DOWN

1 "Dancing With the Stars" network
2 Homer's "Stupid me!"
3 Homophone of 2 Down
4 Wiggily and Remus
5 Sri Lankan export
6 Tabloid twosome
7 Hospital scan
8 Save it for a rainy day
9 Girl in a #1 Everly Brothers song
10 Heaven-sent
11 1998 Masters winner Mark
12 Like some vacation homes
13 Primps
18 #1 Blondie hit
22 "Pippi Longstocking" author Lindgren
23 One-liner
24 "Frozen" snowman
25 Small wooded hollow
26 Secure with straps
29 Slugger's stat
32 Like clothes after a diet
33 Would-be kings
35 Beach accessory
36 Mendes of "Hitch"
37 Kimono material
38 Pennsylvania's "Flagship City"
42 Sneak a peek
43 Blinding
44 Totally unusable
45 Prescription sleep aid
46 Stored fodder
47 Black eye, e.g.
49 "Solve or spin?" asker
51 The CW superhero series
53 Leguminous plants
56 Spa slathering
57 Melancholy
58 Cobb salad ingredient
59 Michelle Obama ___ Robinson

132 LIGHTS THAT TURN by Victor Fleming
...and those lights are found in three answers.

ACROSS

1 Full to the gills
6 Up, in Yankee Stadium
11 Suds source
14 Make a jack-o'-lantern
15 North Pole discoverer
16 That, in Chihuahua
17 At full speed, to bards
18 American robin
20 Biathlete guns
22 Sound stage equipment
23 Santa fey?
24 Three-ring ___
27 Obama predecessor
28 Cedar Falls college
29 It's a blast
30 Hereditary class
31 Push-up muscle
32 "Happy motoring!" gas
33 Muddled situation
34 Yellowtail game fish
36 Unctuous
39 Con man's prey
40 Sponsor at Indy
43 Like some strays
44 Literary foot
45 Angry feeling
46 Bitty's partner
47 Archived documents
49 Hood's weapon
50 Least interesting
52 Culture-related
54 Newbie
57 Lennox rival
58 Mountain's end?
59 "Fiddler on the Roof" meddler
60 Landlord's sign of availability
61 Mark Rudd's org.
62 Joe Cocker's "You ___ Beautiful"
63 Mississippi quartet

DOWN

1 Gather
2 "Now We Are Six" author
3 Lights that turn (with 40 Down)
4 Up to no good
5 Brightest star in Cygnus
6 Natl. Poetry Mo.
7 Place to start driving
8 Ill-advised wager
9 Sheltered spot
10 One learning on the job
11 2016 Ryder Cup winners
12 Lends a hand
13 New parts of old jeans
19 Set out
21 Takes no action
25 Brandy sniffer
26 Hotel employee
30 "___-a-doodle-doo"
32 2017 award for Donald Glover
33 "___ Halls" (song by 51-D)
34 Diamond knit
35 Magazine for ENTs
36 Skoshes
37 Developed, as a player
38 Buck feature
40 See 3 Down
41 One learning on the job
42 They're often seen in laps
44 Recite monotonously
47 Painter Durand
48 What each star represents
51 "Caribbean Blue" singer
53 Managed care grps.
55 ACLU concerns
56 Classical beginning?

133 WRITING ON THE EDGE   by Victor Fleming
At times, being avant-garde ain't all it's cracked up to be.

ACROSS

1 Mort who wrote jokes for JFK
5 I Kings queen
10 Stare in amazement
14 Final Four grp.
15 Vietnam's ___ Tho
16 Hard-and-fast thing
17 **Writer's lament: Part 1**
19 Like a valedictory
20 Game stopper
21 Hawkeyes
23 Maris, to pals
24 Cardio–boxing exercise
26 "New York" director Burns
29 **Writer's lament: Part 2**
34 Wear gradually
36 Change a cornea
37 "Runaround Sue" singer
38 "Lazarus" singer Bowie
39 Stubborn–mule connection
40 Very cold
41 Lyft competitor
42 Letters above 0
43 Uneven, as leaf edges
44 **Writer's lament: Part 3**
47 T-man
48 Twi-nighter pair
49 Thanksgiving side
51 Betting setting
54 Skilled worker
58 Life partner
59 **Writer's lament: Part 4**
62 Admired one
63 Abraham's would-be sacrifice
64 Desert dignitary
65 Call by intercom
66 Eyed tubers
67 Grain storage locale

DOWN

1 Angry mood
2 When "My Shot" is sung
3 Scathe
4 Hen, hopefully
5 Backwater
6 Seven: Comb. form
7 School URL ending
8 Work on tables
9 Pull off
10 Age
11 General look
12 Strategize about
13 Aquatic shockers
18 Played the horn
22 Brit. honor given Sade in 2002
24 China cabinet display
25 Aziz of "Master of None"
26 Name anew
27 Pitcher Hideki
28 Long for
30 Expire
31 ___ vitriol (sulfuric acid)
32 Stage presence
33 All finished
35 Hindenburg, for one
40 Italian ice cream
42 One learning method
45 Shoe hue
46 Hal David's words
50 Pits
51 Desk tray item
52 Slave of Broadway
53 Visibility reducer
54 Just slightly
55 Automatic introduction?
56 Seed envelope
57 "Wedding Bell Blues" songwriter
60 Cough medicine amt.
61 Sports org.

134 DIAMOND FACETS by Jim Holland
"Take me out to the ball game . . ."

ACROSS

1 Kind of computer virus
5 Bite antidote
10 Workout target
14 Toast topper
15 Whirlpool subsidiary
16 Unctuous
17 Olivia's "perfect" musical asset?
19 Habeas corpus, e.g.
20 Shout to the sty
21 It goes from 32 to 63 mph
22 Recently departed
23 "Pants on fire" one
25 Part of QED
27 Guy in a string quartet?
31 Sack of diamonds?
35 Saperstein of basketball
36 Teen in black
37 Annie, for one
38 "The ___ Not Taken": Frost
40 Rises on hind legs
42 Familiar farm sight
43 Tank top
45 Greek salad cheese
47 Aquarium tool
48 "I want to be where ___!"
49 Quonset hut, to some?
51 Go in ankle-deep
53 Loser to Clinton
54 Pontiff, in Vatican City
57 Palm or its popular berry
59 Any Everly Brothers song, e.g.
63 Not quick to catch on
64 Send a fan letter to Sally?
66 Normandy town
67 "Kisses on the Wind" singer Cherry
68 "The Cornish Wonder" painter
69 Cheap commodity
70 Radial lugs
71 Pair of oxen

DOWN

1 Amazing reactions
2 Musical medley
3 Move, in Realtor slang
4 Mexican beer brand
5 Easy mark
6 Seek political asylum
7 Colombian rodent
8 Family reunion goers
9 "Real Time" host
10 Helpful hints about cooking Turducken?
11 Turkish currency
12 Came down to earth
13 Apple storage unit
18 Taking a good look at
24 Call off a mission
26 Chad's loc.
27 Webb of West End musicals
28 More or less
29 Approaches
30 Put the screws to
32 Horned pachyderm
33 "The House of Seven Gables" setting
34 Govt. security
37 Bone prefix
39 Sketch Yan's pan?
41 Corrected a first edition
44 JFK posting
46 "___ Me" (Martin/Tomlin film)
49 According to Franklin, three can keep one if two are dead
50 Greek sun god
52 ". . . by the ___ early light": Key
54 Verbal nudge
55 Utah ski resort
56 Some take it before running
58 Indigenous Japanese
60 "Finding Neverland" star
61 Olympic skater Kulik
62 Where Eve got snaked
65 Canadian sentence enders

65 ACROSS   by Jim Holland
Beginnings of three answers are hints to this theme.

ACROSS

1 Deep Throat, some thought
5 Don't eat this cake
9 Pare precipitously
14 Greek peak
15 Part of SATB, musically
16 Marilyn Monroe's birth name
17 "Arrangement in Grey and Black No.1"
20 Do not disturb
21 U. of Florida mascot
22 Keyboard key
23 Mushpie of "Bloom County"
25 New Testament letter
27 Mom or dad, but not both
32 Bath bathroom
33 Exec
34 "Green Acres" actress
38 Sgt. Snorkel's dog
40 They might put you in a hole
43 Ancient alphabet character
44 Celebratory expression
46 Steed with speed
48 Unit of wire measurement
49 "Through the Looking-Glass" character
53 Cover conspicuously
56 Fireman's tool
57 2015 Verizon acquisition
58 Quidnunc
61 "___ Billie Joe": Gentry
65 Rodgers & Hammerstein musical
68 Berlin river
69 "Monster" lizard
70 Sea dust, in diners
71 "Slammin' Sammy" of golf
72 Tournament position
73 Road runner

DOWN

1 Moonlight bay?
2 Site of Osaka's 2018 grand slam
3 "___ bigger than a breadbox?"
4 Windy one
5 "Do the Right Thing" pizzeria owner
6 Boxer Maskaev
7 Razor rival of Quattro
8 Playbill
9 Sleep apnea symptom
10 Abraham's nephew
11 Enlightened Buddhist
12 Pass the ___ test
13 "The Outcasts of Poker Flat" author
18 Poker giveaways
19 Gloomy Gus
24 Davis–Crawford conflict
26 Pentacle
27 Slothlike
28 Little bit
29 Chris of "Law & Order"
30 Chart type
31 Up, in a way
35 Displace, at Logan
36 Tending to business
37 Depend
39 Awestruck reactions
41 Sip tentatively
42 Thompson in "Pollock"
45 Was a top drummer
47 Full-figured
50 Dining memento
51 Antler features
52 Snake-haired Gorgon
53 They often get crossed
54 Lindsay in "The Shadow Within"
55 Naproxen's brand name
59 "Garfield" dog
60 Barbershop symbol
62 Genesis twin
63 Pinball penalty
64 Septi- plus one
66 ___ Breeze cocktail
67 Pet rock, e.g.

ACROSS

1 "The Nazarene" author
5 Turkish title of honor
9 Having less risk attached
14 Card game in which players bet against the dealer
15 Seeks the affection of someone
16 Returned from the Land of Nod
17 **Headline about Wilson's "Charlie & Co." debut?**
19 Toms and bucks
20 One of the Montagues
21 Make a higher offer
23 Saint-Lô soul
24 **Headline about Zappa's "Fast Times" acting?**
29 Around late December
31 Towel embroidery
32 Champs-Élysées, e.g.
33 Santa Clara tech company
35 Alpo's T-___ treats
36 **Headline about Principal's mishap on the "Dallas" set?**
41 Ballet move
42 Like many stages on Monday

43 1 or 92, in a popular Christmas song
44 Roth plan
47 Camelot lasses
51 **Headline about Sirtis' "Star Trek: Nemesis" comeback?**
54 Rome's ___ Veneto
55 Chancellor Merkel
56 Cries from the pews
58 Legalized gambling
60 **Headline about Archerd's "Variety" column ratings?**
63 Bring to bear
64 Final Four grp.
65 "Got it"
66 Nehi and Cheerwine
67 Norse god of thunder
68 ___-Frank Act

DOWN

1 Noisy quarrel
2 Dance of the Seven Veils dancer
3 Black Sea locale
4 Rhode Island's motto
5 Hole-making tool
6 Gunk
7 Invitation from a biker
8 Per se
9 Festive dances of Rio
10 Look for
11 Nonsense
12 Make do with

13 Hi-___ monitor
18 Stir up
22 ___-color pasta
25 Informed about
26 Wroclaw river
27 Scores at 57 Down
28 R.E.M.'s "Lisa ___"
30 Paddy crop
34 "Elementary" star Lucy
35 Diner orders
36 Brightest star in Lyra
37 Went over again
38 "You ___": Lady Gaga
39 Make like a bird
40 Prepares to shoot
41 Tough spot
44 Bullion bars
45 Arctic explorer
46 At an angle
48 Nevertheless

49 Connected
50 Wise-mouthed
52 Prefix meaning "within"
53 Non-evergreen conifer
57 Minute ____ Park
58 Guitar man Paul
59 Tic-tac-toe loser
61 Menorca's capital
62 Tasha on "Enterprise-D"

137 37 ACROSS   by Tracy Gray
"Never Gonna Give You Up" was a big hit for 20 Across.

ACROSS

1 Dentist's directive
5 Shakers and Quakers
10 Mope
14 "They ___ thataway!"
15 Intensify
16 Swenson of "Benson"
17 Website for handmade goods
18 Ratched or Houlihan
19 ___ and mean
20 Rick of rickrolling fame
22 Top limit
24 Sigma preceder
25 Like the Atkins Diet
28 Lyrical stanza
29 Barcelona bulls
31 Super-long period of time
32 Beelzebub
34 Dentist's directive
35 Part of ABA
36 Lodger
37 ABC hit reality show
40 Hangout for brothers and sisters
43 Steve Austin has a bionic one
44 Fill a freighter
48 "The buck stops here," e.g.
49 Self-importance
50 Jordan's "Red City"
51 WWW address
52 Caesar's comedic partner Fabray
55 ___ Lingus
56 Headquarters of 55 Across
58 Inverse trig function
60 Cause for alarm?
61 Animal in Katy Perry's "Roar"
64 Sorbet flavor
65 Radley competitor
66 Calendar notation
67 "Little Earthquakes" singer Tori
68 "Dress for Less" chain
69 Garden center rack purchases
70 It makes a real impression

DOWN

1 Assure under oath
2 Boys who sang "West End Girls"
3 About to happen
4 Texter's ta-ta
5 Panasonic subsidiary
6 Bird on the Aussie coat of arms
7 It's a real lifesaver
8 Simplest order of Roman architecture
9 "Inside the Third Reich" author
10 Medicinal unit
11 A smidgen
12 Kampala native
13 Conversational digression
21 Silly pair?
23 "Peer Gynt" playwright
26 Tread deterioration
27 BYOB service fee
30 Genesis
33 Popular tattoo spot
35 Hitting stats
36 Pom-pom hat
38 Doglike carnivore
39 Word following turkey or fox
40 Bottled water source
41 Cinco de Mayo fare
42 Short open jackets
45 Singly (with "one")
46 "You wish!"
47 From the heart
49 Bitter-tasting salad green
50 Pay-___-view
53 Play dough
54 Open-topped pastries
57 Wide-angle or zoom
59 Clothed
62 "I had no idea!"
63 Call it a day

138 "OH NO!" by Richard Silvestri

52 Down was popularized by Moon Unit Zappa in her song "Valley Girl."

ACROSS

1 Game played for marks
5 Shell out
10 Use an auger
14 Euphonium kin
15 Lashes
16 Middle Eastern gulf
17 Healthful snacks with added minerals?
19 Tubular pasta
20 A picky person picks it
21 Outstanding
22 Shot the breeze
24 Private aye?
26 Hardwood tree
27 Randall's neatnik role
29 Anticipates with alarm
33 Auction piece
36 Old Nick's bailiwick
38 Brilliance
39 Garment for Granny
41 Area DDE commanded
42 Candidate roster
43 Linger in expectation
44 "Madagascar" penguin
46 ___ even keel
47 Possessive people?
49 Nag
51 Vijay of the PGA
53 King in "Macbeth"
57 Freight train component
60 Above, in odes
61 Turmoil
62 Take it easy
63 Capitol Hill?
66 Words of understanding
67 Love to bits
68 Mall event
69 Nobleman
70 Worked the keyboard
71 Pub potations

DOWN

1 Hard
2 Chemistry Nobelist of 1911
3 Helps in a heist
4 Buddy
5 Cause of ruin
6 Freshwater fish
7 Elm City collegian
8 Family member
9 Ran 100 meters
10 Dickens biography on his wit and humor?
11 Skip over
12 Assess
13 Oklahoma city
18 Valhalla VIP
23 Big spread
25 One who struggles with addition?
26 Revolutionary War figures
28 At any time
30 Rock pioneer Freed
31 Bank deposit?
32 Tommy's gun
33 Ratio phrase
34 Sign of spring
35 Be worthy of
37 Lomond, for one
40 Line in a song
45 Chose from a menu
48 Reprove sharply
50 Continental currency
52 Disgusting
54 Ontario's Welland ___
55 Confuse
56 Things to count
57 Gymnastic maneuver
58 What Justify never did
59 Away from the wind
60 Grimm heavy
64 Prune
65 Olympics chant

139 SLOE GOING   by Richard Silvestri
Humorous wordplay from a puzzling math professor.

ACROSS

1 Makes presents presentable
6 Star starter
9 Out-and-out
14 Condor-minium?
15 Improvise with the band
16 Lasso loop
17 Map of Arctic ice?
19 Perfect Sleeper maker
20 President pro
21 ___ Corrida figure
22 On the couch
23 Sports schedule span
25 South American parrot
27 Long haul
29 After the event
33 Pal of Porthos
36 Infamous czar
38 Time for a revolution?
39 Chili bit
40 Sudden outburst
41 Epsilon follower
42 Chalet overhang
43 Notre Dame niche
44 Officious
45 Railroad support
47 Place for a guard
49 Shake your booty
51 Right, in a way
55 Secret stores
58 Circle dance
60 Einstein's birthplace
61 Grace
62 Caviar named for a London tailoring street?
64 Wine grape
65 Strings of islands?
66 Helmet feature
67 Not flat or sharp
68 Coal container
69 The other side

DOWN

1 Rides the breeze
2 U.S. Grant foe
3 Coffeehouse draw
4 Peach product
5 Military zones
6 Open a bit
7 Ricochet
8 911 responder
9 Open, as an envelope
10 Where bare feet are banned?
11 Civil suit subject
12 Town near Padua
13 Go through volumes
18 Use a whetstone
22 Movie shoot
24 Kidney pain that's the pits?
26 Dies down
28 Smoked herring
30 Pro shop purchase
31 Grub
32 Strong cart
33 Help a hood
34 Glum drop
35 Give birth to
37 Anatomical passage
40 Company division
44 Clam or oyster
46 A score
48 Name in spydom
50 Uniform color
52 Nightingale, for one
53 State of melancholy
54 Polishing powder
55 Syndicate head
56 Point after deuce
57 Knock on the noggin
59 Hot spot
62 Sixth man in the NBA
63 A, as in Austria

140 "IZZATSO?" by Jim Leeds
Some of these answers will surprise you.

ACROSS

1 Internal organs
8 "Obsessed" singer Carey
14 Origin of Panama hats
15 Airplane's black box color
16 Bureaucratic snarl
17 Lollygags
19 Showing sorrow
20 Dispense justice
22 Ladybug, for one
23 Suit, slangily
25 Racy message
27 Chihuahua, e.g.
28 Strong fabric
30 Windjammer
32 Texaco logo
33 Haul in
35 Olive genus
37 Jupiter's mother
38 Camel-hair brush material
41 Macaw in "Rio"
43 Curmudgeon
44 Wapiti
45 Not of the cloth
47 Coconut, e.g.
49 Thirst for
53 Worked on Broadway
55 Bit of sediment
57 Clodhopper
58 Napoli locale
60 Gush lava
62 Miltonian poem
63 Luker of Broadway musicals
65 Was intrinsic
67 First name of George VI
68 Purple finch color
69 Time sharer, e.g.
70 Windstorm

DOWN

1 Skilled (in)
2 Mountaineering tool
3 Like a thunderclap
4 Balinese or Birman
5 Cheese city
6 Ring enclosures
7 Sierra spurs
8 In, in the '60s
9 Bedouin
10 Stethoscope sounds
11 Rias
12 Rabble-rouser
13 Bit of liquor left in a bottle
18 Clairvoyants
21 Those making urgent appeals
24 Deux + trois
26 Pagoda roof material
29 Handle without care
31 Hawaiian volcano goddess
34 Vitae
36 Last two words in "Psycho"
38 Apt
39 Regretted
40 They're picked on the Big Island
41 Presidential guest house
42 Milky
46 Hollywood heavyweights
48 Portray
50 "My kingdom for ___!": Richard III
51 Bull riding venues
52 "You ___ bother"
54 Prepares onions
56 Art class
59 Part of a big plot?
61 Passing fancy
64 Put away a dish
66 Hirohito's title: Abbr.

141 ROYALS by Bonnie L. Gentry and Victor Fleming
Where kings and queens are found outside the castle.

ACROSS

1 Center of Disney World
6 Historical chapters
10 Strategize about
14 Desire strongly
15 "Please?"
16 Film pal of Stitch
17 Where to find kings and queens
20 Tennis or golf event
21 Olive in the funnies
22 Longtime local
23 Hard knocks
25 Wiped out, in a way
26 Boldly states
28 900-year-old teacher in film
29 Davy Jones' locker
30 Far Eastern desert
31 Object of reverence
35 Where to find kings and queens
38 Sapphire's mo.
39 Big hairdo
40 Decent grade
41 Shrewdness members
42 Job openings
43 Here, there, and everywhere
47 Skittles' partner
48 Cleared a windshield
49 Peridot's mo.
50 Calc forerunner
54 Where to find kings and queens
57 Words of enlightenment
58 Beehive, for one
59 Sports
60 Check for doneness
61 Thompson of the Warriors
62 Suitable for sticklers

DOWN

1 She loved Narcissus
2 Support
3 Put in an appearance
4 Bake slowly
5 Private eye, slangily
6 Primetime awards
7 Billiard cushion
8 Objectivist Rand
9 Registered
10 Part of a place setting
11 Confines
12 Trade name for naproxen
13 Pried, with "around"
18 Klutz's comment
19 Lavish party
24 They're seen in waves of grain
25 Country music guitar
26 Longing
27 Washington bigwig
28 Truly go-with
29 Mil. training site
30 Page
31 Tariff
32 Shoulder muscle, briefly
33 Albatross, symbolically
34 29-Down grads
36 Cassette player
37 Fit
41 Maintain
42 Nintendo competitor
43 Let in
44 Flat agreement
45 The Chi-___ (1970s R&B group)
46 Chamber work
47 Sarah Michelle Gellar role
49 China setting?
51 Edwin Drood's fiancée
52 Camaro ___ Z28
53 "Peer ___ Suite"
55 Between fa and la
56 Guerrilla Guevara

142 CIRCULAR REASONING* by Sarah Keller and Derek Bowman
37 Across is also celebrated in Canada, Australia, and New Zealand.

ACROSS

1 Water barriers
5 You could break out in this
10 Arthur ___ Courage Award
14 Same: Comb. form
15 Manly man
16 It may be common or proper
17 1988 Kevin Costner film*
19 Related
20 Conversed with
21 Sporty Mazdas
23 Puts out at home
24 Harmony
25 "Rick's Café Américain" proprietor
28 Injured a joint
32 "___ are meant to be broken"
33 Saint Basil's Cathedral feature*
34 Sermon ending?
35 Spy
36 Mars ___
37 December 26 observance in the UK*
40 Off-the-cuff
42 Smitten with
43 Without restraint
44 Ball-___ hammer
45 Baby powder
46 Sweet-talk
49 State trees of Georgia
53 Not quite shut
54 Mae West play*
56 Sound of a dog needing water
57 Court is called to it
58 June Allyson's "first" name
59 Splitsville residents?
60 "What the World ___ Now"
61 Word linked to clue* answers

DOWN

1 Amount owed
2 Caribbean color
3 Think (over)
4 Classy cravat
5 Blot
6 ___ and all (as is)
7 Reverberate
8 "That's it!"
9 "Horsefeathers!"
10 Tums, for one
11 Coal dust
12 Dance performed at luaus
13 Puts the kibosh on
18 Big men on campus
22 "I knew ___ instant . . ."
24 Prickly
25 Inappropriate offer
26 Philippine island
27 Assisting voice from Amazon
28 Winner of the 2019 Masters
29 Blue-blooded
30 Text alternative
31 Bowler hat
33 Salt Lake City neighbor
35 Mutually accepted
38 They're not domestic
39 Playwright Coward
40 "Stormy Weather" composer
41 Unscrambling device
43 Benefits from friends
45 Like "Scrabble" tournament games
46 Accessory for a dramatic entrance
47 Shield wielder in the "Iliad"
48 Dick's storybook partner
49 Fill the hold
50 "___ Want for Christmas Is You"
51 Glassworking oven
52 Smeltery waste
55 Choler

143 MORE CIRCULAR REASONING* by Sarah Keller and Derek Bowman
"We Can Do It!" is the slogan of 40 Across.

ACROSS

1 Scott Joplin tune
4 Alternative to a tablet
10 Jane Austen protagonist
14 Be outstanding?
15 "Let's do it!"
16 Popular gaming console
17 Prohibition libation*
19 Caution
20 Approximately
21 "Ode to a ___ Gun": S.N. Teed
22 Took into consideration
23 Geek Squad staff
25 Bubbly beverages
27 Like lips that "sink ships"
30 "Come on, out with it!"
34 Celeb tell-all
36 Arm & Hammer muscle
39 "Don't just stand there!"
40 Poster lady of WW2*
43 Scanned unit
44 Home of the Mud Hens
45 Banana Republic parent
46 "Sleeping Murder" sleuth
48 "The ___ of Love": Huey Lewis
50 Winfrey in "The Butler"
53 Blueprints
56 Reunion group
59 Try for a role
62 PRNDL part
63 Dodge Super Bee engine
64 Shirt stiffener*
66 Tied
67 Fashion designer Picasso
68 Small cobra
69 Words linked to clue* answers (with 70- and 71-A)
70 See 69 Across
71 See 69 Across

DOWN

1 The Iron Giant, for one
2 Cognizant
3 Nears
4 "Skedaddle!"
5 Ostrich relatives
6 Pride parade banner letters
7 Pet store purchases
8 Essential ___ acids
9 Waterman invention
10 "Beg pardon"
11 Degrees for CEOs
12 Less, to a Bauhaus artist
13 Chopped down
18 Popular snack cake
22 Atlas page
24 Lifewater bottler
26 Square dance step
28 Date night hire
29 Platform for Alexa
31 Lacking skills in
32 Vascular eye layer
33 Cop's target
34 Fedora feature
35 Smallest Greek letter
37 Sushi delicacy
38 Get ready
41 Like Mount Rushmore
42 Swear words
47 78 successors
49 Omar in "Traffik"
51 Like Yosemite Falls
52 "Howdy-do"
54 Stay for the night, slangily
55 Contact via video chat
56 Grammy winner for "Believe"
57 ___ Strauss & Co.
58 "Well said!"
60 Baseball's Moises
61 Send to blazes
64 4/15 specialist
65 Surfer's "Tubular!"

ACROSS

1 Smoothie fruit
5 Memorable saying
10 Beijing blight
14 Deck honcho
15 Little streams
16 Danish shoe company
17 Crime show extras
18 Radio, newspapers, etc.
19 Utah ski resort
20 "No trivial matter, that!"
23 Kiev locale
25 Waze ways
26 Wacky or radical ideas
30 "Cabaret" star Lenya
31 Send forth
32 Martin's "A Song of Fire and ___"
33 Move slowly
35 Non-___ (food label)
38 Do more than browse
39 False prefix
41 Proverbial spoiler
46 New team member
47 Theoretically, in a sense
48 Greenwich setting
52 Concert hall seating area
53 Donald Duck, to Louie
54 Most of West Va.
57 Blue dye
58 Corn pest
59 Catchall abbr.
60 ___ souci (carefree)
61 Bedside pitchers
62 Apple-cheeked

DOWN

1 "Agents of S.H.I.E.L.D." network
2 Pigeon sound
3 Remove by suction
4 Blink of an eye
5 Fashion designer Giorgio
6 Fuel for big rigs
7 "The Aviator" Oscar nominee
8 Smooth, to a fault
9 Morales of "Ozark"
10 Water scooter brand
11 "American Pie" singer
12 Rowing teams
13 Soccer successes
21 Broad
22 Sandpaper surface
23 Wrinkly fruit
24 Subject of "The Founder"
27 Bounded
28 Coal industry union
29 RSVP part
33 Letter before psi
34 Fictional Burgundy
35 Pinocchio's parent
36 West Point mascot
37 River to the Baltic
38 "Jolly Roger" first mate
39 "Big ___" (David Ortiz)
40 Internet scofflaw
41 Ryder in "Edward Scissorhands"
42 Where it all started
43 Takes great pleasure (in)
44 Shout
45 Comes on stage
46 Luau performances
49 Country bumpkin
50 Winter fall
51 Hell's half-___
55 Mass Appeal Records founder
56 Duplicitous

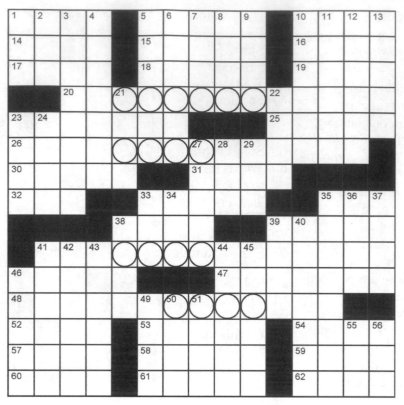

50 ACROSS   by Mark McClain
The golfer at 28 Down was the first person of color to compete in the Masters.

ACROSS

1 Kennedy coin
5 Whitish stone
9 Heavenly strings
14 Villa Maria College site
15 Terse denial
16 Unpleasant aromas
17 Literary Flanders
18 Dodge Viper engine
19 Quantum physics particle
20 "Jake and the Fatman" star
23 Bank assessments
24 Water tester
25 Gluten-free diet no-no
33 Davenport locale
34 Caustic solutions
35 Montmartre Mrs.
36 Piece for two
37 Consumer crusader Ralph
39 Dark, to the Bard
40 Bolivian bear
41 "Take ___" (Jazz standard)
42 Cravings
43 Flipped out
48 Angry state
49 Employs a Singer
50 "Tell everyone you know!"
56 Arcadian
57 Like much of Mongolia
58 Cheer
60 Omit a syllable
61 Pasture mom
62 Novelist Ferber
63 "The Caine Mutiny" captain
64 Business sign abbr.
65 Look as though

DOWN

1 Tailor's line
2 Get one's ducks in ___
3 "Darling" Julie Andrews role
4 Did a face-plant
5 Being displayed
6 Fertilizer ingredient
7 "Lemme ___!"
8 "The Mod Squad" role
9 Pals around (with)
10 Worshipful one
11 Sub ___ (secretly)
12 Egg on
13 W-9 Form info
21 Member of the 1979 Ryder Cup team (with 28-D)
22 Mink's cousin
25 Lehár's "The Merry ___"
26 Hugh Laurie series
27 Haven't paid for
28 See 21 Down
29 Shipboard assent
30 Fix firmly
31 With
32 Tightly packed
37 Skin care brand
38 ___ Maria
39 Visual pollution
41 What Fido shakes with
44 Angry outburst
45 Wearable souvenir
46 Taken to heart
47 "Gross me out!"
50 Uhura crewmate
51 ___ -dieu (prayer bench)
52 Kiri Te Kanawa, for one
53 Refrain syllables
54 Took a bus
55 Finished
56 Mandatory: Abbr.
59 Lassie's cap

146 THEMELESS by Brian E. Paquin
Alternate clue for 15 Across: Run-of-the-mill coffee?

ACROSS
1 1974 hit album, and British supergroup
11 Many
15 Man on the street
16 Old Milan money
17 Unusual delights
18 First family child
19 Cost of a dozen?
20 Mischief by Bart Simpson
22 Quenches
25 Lean to the extreme
26 Hard-hearted
29 Rap sheet item
32 Pepper or Preston, e.g.
35 Communication prefix
36 Cat's-paw
37 Finishes a complex project
42 Commedia dell'___
43 Corddry on "Mom"
44 Bishopric
45 Caprine comment
47 Chilling out
49 Covered (in)
51 "Goodness!"
55 Smear campaign spots
59 On the sheltered side
60 Bird feeder food
61 "Not hardly!"
64 Pot part
65 Bathroom flooring installer
66 "Faint heart ___ won . . .": Cervantes
67 Asked nicely

DOWN
1 Poets of old
2 Be of use
3 Yiddish sausage
4 Runnels
5 Scone grain
6 Corp. boss
7 Secret glimpse
8 Open a tad
9 Nary a one
10 Binary kind of question
11 Buffet alternative
12 Potent potables
13 Pitcher Hershiser
14 Like many runway models
21 The Colonel's place
23 Start of Caesar's last question
24 Flow slowly
27 Annex
28 "A Fistful of Dollars" director
30 Fashion
31 Otherwise
32 Wild guess
33 Boy-band fan
34 Sit-down session
38 Most abundant liquid
39 Henley competitor
40 Part of a wine glass
41 Counting-out word
46 Second of three X's
47 Twain with a "Now" album
48 Old phones and TVs, e.g.
50 "SNL" segments
52 Soul singer Adams
53 Monica on "The X-Files"
54 Big name in tractors
55 Wise ___ owl
56 Ditty
57 "Inventions of the Monsters" painter
58 Hurried along
62 Comcast, e.g.
63 Take shape

147 THEMELESS by Brian E. Paquin
The answer to 23 Down can be found in Genesis 8.

ACROSS

1 Amusing
10 Big name in little blocks
14 Not too bright
15 X, Y, or Z
16 Zoned out
17 Pell-___
18 Proofread
19 Intrinsically, in law
21 To a certain extent
24 Copier need
25 Japanese soup
27 Inventory of words, briefly
31 Valley of song
35 Indiana Jones hat
36 Defense lawyer, at court
37 Hockey great Jagr
38 Musical alley
39 Mathematical points
40 Beelzebub
41 Web locations
42 Oxidizes
44 Molded
49 Minnow merchants
53 Main part of a church
54 R&B singer Braxton
55 Self-involved
58 Spaniard's "some"
59 Bad feelings
60 Dispatched
61 Takes the Hollywood bus tour?

DOWN

1 Notable acting family
2 In darkness
3 Opposite of o'er
4 Org. with Penguins and Ducks
5 Nay's opposite
6 Liberian linebacker Tamba
7 Conversion gizmo
8 Kermit's creator
9 Browser extra
10 Laker who married a Kardashian
11 Corp. bigwig
12 Gold-leafed
13 Munch Museum city
14 Oktoberfest offering
20 Feeling the flu
22 Neighbor of Orion and Taurus
23 Ark's first disembarker
26 Le Coeur de la ___ ("Titanic" gem)
28 Stupor
29 Seed case
30 Outlaws
31 Bus. papers
32 "On the Waterfront" director Kazan
33 Bumper blemish
34 Jay-Z, e.g.
35 Features of some cards
37 Shade of black
39 Get rid (of)
41 Cheap cigar
43 Outbuildings
45 "Sweet Love" singer Baker
46 Standardbred horse
47 Chris in "The Iceman"
48 Shoulder muscle, briefly
49 HVAC measures
50 Top-notch
51 Aware of
52 Puts on the dog?
56 911 at sea
57 Amatol ingredient

39 Across was the fifth female Best Director Oscar nominee.

ACROSS

1 Band aids
5 Like some prescriptions
15 Rockets' Anthony, familiarly
16 "My Boo" singer
17 "My stars!"
18 Vehicle with a braying puller
19 2004 Jamie Foxx film
20 Doctor's office fees
21 French for "born"
22 Slack communiqués, for short
23 First-year law student
24 Sit for a shoot
25 Single-named "Goodies" singer
27 Flora and ___
31 "Black Panther" actress
35 Dollar General, e.g.
37 Galapagos creature
39 "Lady Bird" director Gerwig
40 "The show is starting!"
41 Phone-seller's proposal
44 Autograph
47 Plus-or-minus stick, for short
48 Up in the ___
49 Non-dairy Yuletide quaff
51 Michael of "SNL"
52 Menu section
55 Magic wand tip
56 Googling #1
57 Fitting toy for a child?
58 Does a cleanse
59 Dad in "Thor: Ragnarok"

DOWN

1 Fourth word of the poem "I, Too"
2 Metro Man's enemy
3 Performs on tour
4 Grub's home
5 Gas often tested for
6 Skip the shower?
7 Video game threequel of 1990
8 Yukky
9 "Balderdash!"
10 Place gently
11 U.S. dog registry: Abbr.
12 Gas-X alternative
13 U-shaped instruments
14 Eponymic Lauder perfume
20 CSX hopper found in West Virginia
24 Bottom, slangily
26 Leave work early?
28 Regarding
29 Losing "Miracle on Ice" team
30 Mosquito protection
32 Top of the line
33 Cigarette discard
34 Cut in three
36 Pipe organs?
38 Commence
41 Like some aprons
42 Feudal boss
43 Cant
45 Sophomoric
46 They're suspended for loud music
49 Indian wedding attire
50 "Prometheus" composer Carl
53 Spanish for "that"
54 Nickname of Linux's penguin logo
55 Not fast, for short

149 THEMELESS by Erik Agard

31 Down is the home of Louisiana Hot Sauce.

ACROSS

1 1987 protest when linemen walked the picket line
10 "Yuri!!! on Ice" genre
15 1968 album with the single "Think"
16 Break down
17 "Think again!"
18 "Headlines" rapper
19 Part of the fam
20 "Odyssey" sea nymph
21 Painter inspired by Courbet
22 Sarajevo citizen
24 Grip comparison
27 ___ Tomé
28 Custard treat
30 Moody rock genre
31 Obvious choice
33 Come upon
34 Complains about
35 Around quitting time
37 On the road
38 Seniors under 70?
40 Get the point
41 Funny jokes
42 Org. for those going through the motions?
43 Second-oldest Jackson brother
44 Italian cheese, for short
46 Amazon founder
48 Arrangement of ti leaves
50 It added "EGOT" in 2018
52 "The Three Sisters" sister
53 Star schema, for one
56 SF gridder
57 Unnamed netizens
58 Many Manxmen
59 Maine river

DOWN

1 Mum's mum
2 Bushy dos
3 "Elmer Gantry" novelist
4 Expert in grooming
5 "America, the Beautiful" possessive
6 Prime Minister of India (1984–1989)
7 A party to
8 From Pristina, say
9 She sounds like you?
10 Facebook friend request
11 Nephew of Claudius
12 "Yeah, that's plausible"
13 Get into a food fight, e.g.
14 Large canine
23 Site of Akbar's Tomb
25 Mad
26 Monk's discipline
29 Swiss watchmaker Charles-Félicien
31 City SW of Lafayette, LA
32 Oprah Winfrey covers it regularly
33 Going places?
34 "Easy peasy!"
36 Farmiga of "Bates Motel"
39 Like many roads
43 Rulers of yore
45 Battle cry?
47 Scott Turow title
49 College founded in 1440
51 Art ___
53 Skip stones
54 Texter's "Butt out!"
55 Netball?

150 MERGE AHEAD   by Steven E. Atwood
Original portmanteau words are featured below.

ACROSS

1 Current law
5 Big-___! (props)
8 Criticized abusively
14 Grounded in reality
16 "Get Me to the Church ___"
17 Spirited loathing?
18 At all
19 Probable cost of a loan?
21 Outlaw
23 Marquee letters
24 What those in favor say
25 Box: Abbr.
26 October birthstone
28 Dillydally
30 Give an edge to
31 Narcotic drug
34 September birthstone
37 Inmate wear at country club prisons?
39 Fabulous
42 Drumstick target
46 "Armageddon" author
47 ___-de-chaussée (street level)
49 Therefore
50 Angling float
51 Liberace's nickname
53 Jungfrau or Piz Bernina
56 Homophonic promise
57 Feigning tennis elbow?
61 Steer snarer
62 Offensive defensive lineman?
65 Slothful
66 Jazz trumpeter Wynton
67 Sneak preview
68 Pre-AD
69 Putin's refusal

DOWN

1 Chicago airport code
2 Japanese affirmative
3 Where Moses talked with God
4 Subscribe
5 Al with four Indy 500 wins
6 Walk a beat
7 Gin flavoring
8 Spoils
9 "Sweet Dreams" singer Lennox
10 Goblets feature
11 Tailgate party cooker
12 Quasar, for one
13 Cold War thaw
15 Excuses
20 "The Dragons of Eden" author
21 Halloween sound
22 Google Play download
27 Velcro predecessors
29 Sotto voce
30 "What did I do to deserve this?"
32 Cargo unit
33 Rob Gronkowski's position
35 Muscle next to a delt
36 Use a crowbar
38 Shot
39 Story within a story
40 Divide fairly
41 West African republic
43 In a vigorous manner
44 Way back when
45 "Two Faces Have I" singer Christie
48 Heartburn drug
51 GM contract
52 Key in
54 A little over a quart, in Quebec
55 School volunteer orgs.
58 Padre's hermanos
59 Pentameter unit
60 Sam Smith hit "Like ___"
63 Factor in deciding which golf club to use
64 "In the ballpark" no.

151 REPS FOR A MENTAL WORKOUT   by Steven E. Atwood
The voice of 6 Down can be heard in the classic hit "Georgy Girl."

ACROSS

1 Is wearing
6 Kid
10 Hawaiian food fish
14 "Ole!" cousin
15 Sevier Lake locale
16 Gyro wrap
17 "The Man Without a Shadow" author
18 One and ___
19 ___'acte
20 Delivery room bed?
23 French pointillist
24 Golf pencil's lack
26 Web page for reports of UFOs?
29 Sales pitch
32 Nullify
33 ___-line (aerial ride)
34 Common investment
35 They're in hypertext
37 Note
38 List-ending abbr.
39 Talus or phalanx
40 Yields
41 First Amendment guarantee?
45 Clapboards, e.g.
46 Double positive?
49 Prize for the best buttinski?
52 Songwriter Mitchell
53 Stimulus used in aversion therapy
54 "___ bleu!"
56 Start of a fairy tale
57 Prunus spinosa
58 Not earth, air, fire, or water
59 Word with bleary or googly
60 Trike rider
61 Deity with a nymph mania

DOWN

1 Bill Maher's network
2 Riyadh residents
3 "Sarabandes" composer
4 Done to death
5 Dragon's smoke outlet
6 The Seekers vocalist Durham
7 Berkshire college town
8 ___-froid
9 Decompression sickness
10 La Scala events
11 Diminutive
12 Then
13 Kramden laugh syllable
21 Malicious old woman
22 "Cogito, ___ sum": Descartes
25 Consequences of defaults
27 Pitchpipe user
28 Press coverage
29 Lots and lots
30 Inheritance
31 Rate of occurrence
35 Not heard from in ages
36 Bach's "Minuet ___"
37 Cross references, e.g.
39 Pickle
40 Gouda and Gruyère
42 Put in order, with "up"
43 "You're right"
44 Fitness room
47 Key West boat
48 Elvis, to his Spanish fans
50 To no avail
51 Recess
52 Montana, for one
55 Stray

152 LEAVING ON A YET PLANE by Anna Carson
Alternate clue for 36 Down: Blake Shelton hit.

ACROSS

1 Irons role in "The Lion King"
5 Daytime dramas
10 Corp. recruits
14 Daly of "Judging Amy"
15 Overplay
16 "Stupid me!"
17 Part of UAR
18 Butler's lady
19 Dextrose source
20 Ivy League dorm song?
23 Cookbook author Prudhomme
24 Was wishy-washy
27 Iditarod racer
30 Do a cobbler's job
31 Give the slip
34 Ticks off
35 Complaint heard from an oxen span?
40 Pump it
41 Went off course
42 Diet food word
45 Samuel Beckett play
50 Shows contempt for
53 Carnation holder
54 Streisand remix of a Glen Campbell hit?
57 Tiger Hall-of-Famer
59 Ladies' man
60 English saint
61 Pitcher Hershiser
62 In front
63 Covers cakes
64 Source of pollen
65 Phony pearls
66 Reason to cram

DOWN

1 Didn't budge
2 Playwright de Bergerac
3 Handy watch?
4 Defies authority
5 "Go on!"
6 Pearl Harbor locale
7 Build up
8 Turn to mush
9 More scanty
10 Soft shoe
11 Bibliophage
12 Spring mo.
13 1040 ID
21 "Roots" author
22 Verb ending
25 Sommer in "Jenny's War"
26 Montreal's Place ___ Arts
28 Rock trigram
29 Coach K's team
32 Austrian article
33 Land of Yeats
35 High-tech suffix
36 Melittologist's study
37 Deprive of strength
38 B. Obama, in 2005
39 Not as expected
40 HMO concern
43 Valiant son
44 Woman's shoe style
46 Sacrificial move
47 Per unit
48 Sergio of easy listening
49 Firstborn
51 Honolulu greeting
52 Scholarly books
55 Bar request
56 Prevailing style
57 Simple sack
58 HHS program

153 "FANTASTIC VOYAGE" by Anna Carson
It's funny how the film "Fantastic Voyage" ties in with the quote below.

ACROSS

1 Omar of "ER"
5 Genesis maker
9 Supermarket section
14 Gets rid of
16 Kilmer simile phrase
17 Frayed so
18 Fable feature
19 **Stanislavski quote: Part 1**
21 Carney
22 Legionnaire Beau
23 Quick bites
27 Marx or Malden
29 Bk. before Jeremiah
31 Van Pelt with a blanket
32 Makeshift swing
33 Scribbles
34 Face defacer
35 **Quote: Part 2**
36 Phrase before instant
37 Fail to grip the road
38 Sticks figure
39 Nominee list
40 "That's rich!"
41 Urban region
42 Whoop
43 Ocean motions
45 Jiffy
46 **Quote: Part 3**
53 Ross of Motown fame
54 More than several
55 Sleek swimmer
56 Sabotage
57 Baseball's "Little Colonel"
58 Like sharp cheddar
59 School near Windsor Castle

DOWN

1 Prep for publication
2 Phnom ___, Cambodia
3 Best or Townshend
4 Practice for a boxing match
5 Indian instruments
6 Wield
7 "First Knight" actor
8 Part of WNBA
9 Fair maiden
10 Molecule constituents
11 Like unfounded fears
12 Grounds and such
13 Raise a ruckus
15 Chophouse fare
20 Grimm monsters
23 Lower, as prices
24 Where to find "Friends"
25 Wipe out
26 Helped with a line
27 Puckett of baseball
28 Johnson of "Laugh-In"
30 Former SAG president
32 Without give
33 Nursery rhyme tumbler
35 Light bender
39 Type of mom
41 Lucrezia Borgia's brother
42 Put in the microwave
44 Force units
45 Try to avoid a tag
46 Polecat's calling card
47 Blue tint
48 Air bag
49 Domesticated
50 "Never heard ___"
51 Clinton's DOJ head
52 Nasty computer worm

154 THEMELESS by Harvey Estes

There's a mini-theme at 19 and 43 Across.

ACROSS

1 When Romeo meets Juliet
5 Head turner
9 Less fumbling
14 "I'm Sorry" singer
16 Substantiate
17 Potluck dish
18 Sat
19 Tale about the so-called Headless Horseman? (with 43-A)
21 Deck's highest quartet
22 Regular hangout
23 Told jokes to, maybe
26 Let
29 Sonny and Chaz
30 Parson's place
31 Feathers adhesive
32 Product of sifting
33 Japanese car company
34 Atlantic ___
35 Giant outfielder
36 Things to crack
37 Arcade attractions
38 Like one who appears drawn?
40 Least plausible
41 Stack by the copier
42 "Catskill Mountains" painter
43 See 19 Across
48 Solemn ceremonies
49 Ordinary people
51 "___ you the clever one!"
52 Yerevan citizens
53 Resulted in
54 Put on a peg
55 Opening bet

DOWN

1 "The Bachelorette" network
2 Ending for auto
3 "Angels in the Snow" pianist
4 Harvest time
5 Was even after 18 holes
6 Neatniks' opposites
7 Ward in "The Fugitive"
8 Holden Caulfield, for one
9 Make concessions
10 Wing-tip shoe
11 Make haste
12 Happens finally
13 He played Fred the junkman
15 Low pair
20 Sacred city of Lamaism
23 Top Trappist
24 High-arcing barrage
25 Not corroborated
26 Bummed around
27 Brings to a close
28 Rendezvous
30 Put together
33 Archie's musclebound pal
34 Alabama state flower
36 Wakes up
37 Milk measure
39 Scout's pursuit
40 Kept playing over and over
42 Sound on the hour
43 Type of history
44 '90s slang for "awesome!"
45 Days of old
46 Pearl Buck heroine
47 Refuses to
50 Expert finisher

ACROSS

1 Androgynous
8 Classic exile site
15 Lower shackle
16 Mild, weatherwise
17 Totally trust
18 Administrations
19 Sextant predecessor
21 Marsh bird
22 Dr. of the rap world
23 Vintage wheels
25 "At Last" singer James
26 Al of Grandpa Munster fame
29 "Sister Act" setting
31 That hombre
32 Bieber trial?
35 Hearing range
38 Make poisonous
39 Work slogan at a container company?
41 Alley animal
42 Let
43 Salad ingredient
45 Type of board or joint
47 AARP members
48 "Men ___ from Mars . . ."
49 Spot for a mike
51 Utmost extent
56 Musically monotonous
58 Mental pictures
59 Mason creator
60 Fill to the brim
61 Mama's boys
62 Laughed with disgust

DOWN

1 Snow Queen of Arendelle
2 Basilica benches
3 "Now ___ it!"
4 "How Does a Poem Mean?" author
5 Diamond flubs
6 Like argon or krypton
7 "Storms in Africa" singer
8 It plays a role in getting roles
9 Duct tail
10 Asks for alms
11 High rank
12 Mail-in payment
13 Not up to the task
14 In a fog
20 Some sibs
24 Like some folds
26 "12 Angry Men" actor Cobb
27 Seesaw sitter of verse
28 Congregation
29 Economize
30 Pt. of SASE
32 Bobby of golf
33 In order (to)
34 They're welcome at pileups
36 Dollars for scholars
37 That ship
40 Czech Rep. neighbor
43 Dream up
44 "Mr. October" Jackson
45 Drain problems
46 Maui neighbor
48 Employee of Sterling Cooper
50 "WKRP" actress Anderson
52 Fuse sound
53 It's in back
54 Art Deco name
55 Got a load of
57 Driving area

156 "O CAPTAIN! MY CAPTAIN!" by Bruce Venzke

There's a "Star Trek" tie-in at 20 Across.

ACROSS

1 Completely confused
5 Back muscles, for short
9 Canine cries
14 Dichromatic cookie
15 Aleve may relieve it
16 Off-Broadway awards
17 Newspaper notice, briefly
18 Cauterize
19 "The Last Tycoon" director
20 One of four in diving
23 Warehouse worker
24 Heretofore
25 Short-lived sensation
28 Television and radio
31 Priced to go
33 Financing abbr.
36 Small rodent leaper
38 "Eins, zwei, ___ . . ."
40 Cord or Ford
41 Alien combiner
42 It's burned before finals
47 Instrument for 51 Across
48 "Beats me!"
49 Initiate a break-up
51 Jazz legend Beneke
52 Doughnut amt.
54 Utterly ridiculous
58 Downtown Julie Brown et al.
61 Complete chaos
64 Archerfish do it
65 High rocky hills
66 Praise greatly
67 Kipling's "Rikki-Tikki-___"
68 Blackthorn fruit
69 Measures (out)
70 Obi-Wan's portrayer
71 Smacker

DOWN

1 Air show stunts
2 Revolve around
3 Timex competitor
4 For the prescribed time
5 Longtime Dodgers manager
6 Quick Isner points
7 Tom yum kung's cuisine
8 Simmons sister company
9 "I'm Moving On" singer
10 "Voice of Israel" author
11 Garfield's vet
12 Shell-game accessory
13 Target of ID thieves
21 It sometimes involves a keyhole
22 Borodin's "Prince ___"
25 Lyft charges
26 De la Garza of "Law & Order"
27 Place to dry out
29 Creep (along)
30 Banded marble
32 Red or White team
33 Take in, as patients
34 Group that roars
35 Updike's "Rabbit ___"
37 Caleb's brother in "East of Eden"
39 Holiday stopover
43 Charges formally
44 The Beach Boys' "___ Vibrations"
45 See 54 Across
46 Case in "Route 66"
50 "For shame!"
53 Keebler cracker
55 Garlicky mayo
56 Peter and a Wolfe
57 Pothook shapes
58 Field mouse
59 Translucent birthstone
60 1940s jazz
61 Stitched skirt edge
62 "The Shining" door buster
63 Napa Valley tank

157 DOUBLE THE HOMEWORK? by Bruce Venzke

A double dose of 56-Across things here.

ACROSS

1 Ring
5 Brunch, e.g.
11 Place to get hot, but not bothered
14 "The Times They ___-Changin' ": Dylan
15 Morning warnings
16 Toy taken out for a spin
17 An old one may have a due-date stamp
19 Become rancid
20 Three nautical miles
21 Wisconsin's Fond du ___
22 Racer of fable
23 Near the core
24 Hard-hat areas
26 Cloud function
28 Apprehensive feeling
29 Gossip
30 Not quite right
32 Ream elements
33 Regular group at a jazz club
36 Like some fingerprints
39 Haversack
40 "Washington Week" airer
43 Web commerce
44 Frankenstein's wear
47 A regressive one favors the wealthy
51 Lethal tree snake
52 Temperamental tizzy
53 Anthem preposition
54 Sluggishness
55 "Darn that sweater!"
56 Time for intramural activities
58 Central Honshu city
59 Grateful Dead founder
60 American hotel chain
61 Ganem of "Devious Maids"
62 Soapbox speaker
63 Soft attention-getter

DOWN

1 What female models tend to be
2 East, in Ecuador
3 Tripoli locale
4 Bulkier
5 Like the Florida panther
6 Bridge authority Culbertson
7 Cubist artist Picasso
8 Really noisy, as a crowd
9 Painter's wear
10 Reproachful utterance
11 Idiosyncratic
12 Most needy
13 College Boards
18 Saintly radiance
22 Sharp
24 Altars one's status?
25 Author of the "Thrawn" trilogy
27 Toe woe
31 Ball girl
32 Lengthy chronicle
33 It takes a thief
34 "For Your Eyes ___" (1981)
35 Soothing application
36 Words of reflection
37 Finished
38 Pre-takeoff tarmac
40 Cheerleader's accessories
41 Terrestrial monkeys
42 Like a bright night
45 Columbia lion?
46 Server on skates
48 As yet
49 Neon ___
50 Stiff-backed
54 Autocratic ruler
56 Back in time
57 2016 Olympics city

158 MISSING CLUE   by Roger & Kathy Wienberg
. . . and that missing clue can be found at 31 Down.

ACROSS

1 It's a plus
6 Mini-map
11 Auction action
14 Rado product
15 Giant of the parrot world
16 Put away
17 Napoleon's fate
18 Picture editor
20 Song written by Bowie and Lennon
22 Sleeveless woman's garment
23 Natural talent
25 Sweeper's need
28 Like every other integer
29 Short tune
30 Avalon, for one
34 Pothole filler
35 Italian stratovolcano
36 Money-saving prefix
37 Bridal registry category
39 Final curtain
41 Stomping ground
42 Fine-tuned
43 Slaw seller
45 Man-child
46 "Jeopardy!" contestant
47 Turf chunk
48 Alkaline solution
49 Assent from an hombre
51 Have an off day?
52 5, 6, 7, 8, and X
55 Mild oath
57 "Lost Horizon" land
60 Golden calves
63 Allow
64 Urged (on)
65 "Wow!"
66 Lanolin source
67 Pulls apart
68 Bump-out

DOWN

1 Wonderment
2 Kenny G's instrument
3 *
4 Flamboyance
5 Not us
6 Little devil
7 "Nope"
8 "Enterprise" engineer
9 Really enjoy
10 *
11 Thailand currency
12 Myself included
13 Johnny in "Transcendence"
19 Roman philosopher
21 Work on a draft
23 "Tricked you!"
24 Potatoes
26 Quarterly magazine
27 *
29 *
31 BLACKJACK OPTION
32 Bugs
33 "Are we there?" response
38 Liam in "Run All Night"
40 "Whip It" band
44 Oral tradition
47 Think up and plan out
50 Twill fabric
51 Basement hazard
52 Land in the sea
53 "That was a close one!"
54 Ill will
56 City on the Nile
58 Supervised
59 Wraps on buses
61 Fish story
62 Kind of symbol

159 SHAKE 'N QUAKE   by Roger & Kathy Wienberg
Starts of clue* answers can be found at 57 Across.

ACROSS

1 Thereabouts
5 IRS investigator
9 Supernatural wizard
13 Be desperate for
14 "Barracuda" rock band
15 "Sounds like a plan!"
16 Way of thinking*
18 Rip apart
19 Summer cooler
20 ___-European
21 "Precisely!"
22 Pewter element
23 One who looks for text trouble*
26 Gives the lowdown
28 Projecting windows
29 Ballyhoo
30 Morsel
31 Color changer
32 Rockettes' music hall*
37 Org. for Federer
40 Ice skating jump
41 Fireworks reactions
45 Bead of dew
47 Typically
50 Set of morals*
52 Homeland Security agcy.
53 Without exception
54 Sun Bowl stadium sch.
55 Type of baseball bunt, briefly
56 Hindu noble
57 Lesser tremor
60 Drill parts
61 Toe woes
62 Sunburn soother
63 Window shutter piece
64 "Gadzooks!"
65 Cut down

DOWN

1 Performing sentinel duty
2 With no hesitation
3 Popular "uncola"
4 Poem of homage
5 Achilles, for one
6 Toon prone to squinting
7 High school elective
8 For the ___ time
9 Sister of Moses and Aaron
10 Changed a bill
11 Like some snaps
12 Give approval
14 Toulouse-Lautrec
17 Syncing parts?
21 Floppy topper
24 Savings acct. insurer
25 Indian flatbread
27 Always, poetically
30 Pen name of Dickens
33 Where you can hear pins drop
34 Club charges
35 Minuscule
36 Slangy greetings
37 Then and there
38 Trial and tribulation
39 Creamy Italian side dish
42 Shoe part that typically wears first
43 Goes ballistic
44 Relax
46 Uncompromising sort
47 Make an appearance
48 Palm readers, supposedly
49 USTA officials
51 Buddhist scripture
57 Par-3 hole eagle
58 Haze or daze
59 "Fat chance!"

ACROSS

1 Bunco squad concern
5 Snake and worm, for two
10 "Pardonnez-___!"
13 Sit
14 Update an atlas
15 Clan clash
16 ___-lock brakes
17 Scacchi in "Beyond the Sea"
18 Texas Hold'em stake
19 2001 Brooks & Dunn hit
22 Homer Simpson's friend
24 Roker and Gore
25 "The Devil ___ Prada" (2006)
26 Without assistance
31 World's largest democracy
32 Range animal, in song
33 Cozy spot
34 ESPN figures
36 Wingding
40 Lake bird
41 "Park" in Silicon Valley
42 Dover fishmonger?
47 Emeril's coverup
48 Talent for music
49 TLC provider
50 Nickname of Alice's home
55 Armenia's chief river
56 Marble
57 Bellicose god
60 Last team managed by Stengel
61 "When hell freezes over!"
62 Nevada resort
63 Suffix for verb
64 They look ahead
65 Christian Science founder

DOWN

1 Mineral spring
2 Hoodwink
3 Flabbergasts
4 Chicken chow ___
5 Diamond sock pattern
6 Succumb
7 Foretoken
8 Some bank contents
9 Hormel product
10 Like drudge work
11 Public protest
12 Notions
15 Turned out
20 "___ Land" (2016 film musical)
21 Still-life subject
22 S ___ Sam
23 Carry a torch for
27 "Vamoose!"
28 Hersey bell town
29 It often comes between Venus and Serena
30 ___ Plaines
34 Soak up
35 Craggy crest
36 Nectar collector
37 Like female reindeer
38 Feed the pigs
39 Didgeridoo, for one
40 Glass eye
41 Sorvino of "Like Dandelion Dust"
42 Mushroom seeds
43 Flowery
44 Rich soil
45 Bug
46 Yelp users
47 Cottonwood
51 Earthy hues
52 "A Death in the Family" author
53 Four-star review
54 Scale button at the deli
58 Cessation
59 Kikkoman sauce

161 RIGHT ON CUE   by Pam Klawitter

Ryan Gosling had to learn how to play piano for his role in 18 Across

ACROSS

1 Jupiter's composition
4 Griffis in "Runaway Jury"
9 Cocoon resident
13 Acting coach Hagen
14 Peeping Tom
15 Parched
16 Counterpart of none
17 Restaurant of song
18 "___ Land" (2016)
19 "Sweeney Todd" event
22 Day-spa features
23 Slave leader Turner
24 Lt. factory
25 French liqueur
30 Department store feature
34 "Gotcha!"
35 Word heard before a snap
36 "___ my brother's keeper?": Cain
37 Seville sounds of support
38 Solothurn's river
39 Money that's not reimbursed
43 Pamplona bull, at times
45 Business letters
46 Complex ending
47 Tracker, of sorts
50 Disney World's busiest time
55 Ride in a glider
56 Burnt pigment
57 Bosun's reply
58 Game on a 300-yard field
59 Effusive one
60 Wait partner
61 Unoriginal one
62 Valjean escape route
63 Cassandra's curse

DOWN

1 U.S. Pacific territory
2 Calypso's father
3 Mexican chip dip
4 Let go of
5 Executor's concern
6 Willy in "Free Willy"
7 Monopoly card
8 Whodunit weapon
9 Taste tester's asset
10 Siberian river
11 Pain in the neck
12 "The Piano" pianist
14 Lift-off
20 Bid price
21 Catch some rays
25 Shining suit
26 Wide-eyed sort
27 TV show genre
28 The old "you"
29 White House room
30 Gabfest
31 Deceptive one
32 Creole stew
33 Render replete
37 Come about
39 Ocular prefix
40 James Joyce work
41 Word on a lager bottle
42 Sign of poor reception
44 Type of image
47 "À votre ___!" (French toast)
48 Do a hairdresser's job
49 Garfield's predecessor
50 Poultry pen
51 Fit as a fiddle
52 It waits for no man
53 Word from Garfield
54 Castle stronghold
55 Hot tub

ACROSS

1 Letters from Camp Pendleton?
5 "Two ___ up!"
11 Commandment pronoun
14 Seehorn in "Better Call Saul"
15 Had no more left to sell
16 Down-and-dirty tool?
17 Butler's last word
18 Edward VIII's act of 1936
20 Thick Japanese noodle
21 Sound lovey-dovey
22 Small stands at the mall
23 "Star-cross'd" lover
25 Dominates, in gamer lingo
26 Eric Clapton classic
28 Not very exciting
30 Fusses
34 Say positively
36 What gawkers might be in
37 In days of ___
38 Overly
39 Home of the banh mi sandwich
42 Bedridden Adrian's plea to "Rocky"
43 Underground resource
45 Ohio's busiest airport: Abbr.
46 Heavy British weights
48 Website language
49 Hannah Montana's bodyguard
51 One tapped for sap
52 Soon, poetically
54 Taste unlike salty, sweet, sour, or bitter
56 Hang out with the elite
59 Springfield's "Jolly Bengali"
60 "There's more . . ."
63 "Bang! Bang!" westerns
65 Czech or Croat
66 Exchanges w/ emoticons
67 1964 Tippi Hedren film
68 Prized book
69 Matey's reply
70 Did some film splicing
71 Kool-Aid pitcher

DOWN

1 Pakistani tongue
2 River herring
3 Mattress material*
4 Pastry with a ricotta filling
5 Cheat at freehand drawing
6 Violent sandstorm, from Arabic
7 Nullify
8 "Pardonnez-___!"
9 "Our Gang" character*
10 Inevitability on a baby's bib
11 The one right here
12 Catchy part of a song
13 Wants it badly
19 "I've nothing else ___"
24 Former Bills coach Levy
25 One of sixteen in chess
26 Metal fastener you can flip open
27 Get ___ in the door
29 Chicle source
31 Feather-filled sleeping aid (and what each clue* answer is?)
32 Bay window
33 Get a feeling of
35 Plastic particle and water pollutant*
40 SpaceX founder Musk
41 Home of "The Starry Night"
44 Argentine plain
47 Hindu greeting
50 Hipster's 1980s cousin
53 Response to "Who made this mess?"
55 Thought (about)
56 First Chinese dynasty
57 Words of pleasant surprise
58 It makes Waves
59 Grandma's daughter
61 Equivalent
62 Terminated
64 CAT-scan alternative

163 "YOU CAN . . ." by Greg Johnson
A fill-in-the-blanks challenge from the Keystone State.

ACROSS

1 Rain delay roll-out
5 "Saving Private Ryan" depiction
9 Bathtub toys
14 Butt
15 Oil company with a "diamond spark" logo
16 Rye field fungus
17 Sal's canal, in song
18 Name on Nutrish pet food
20 ___ ("Gone!")
22 Take care of
23 P before X
24 Start of something special?
27 ___ ("I tried!")
32 Rating related to UV light
35 Part of TGIF
36 Recycled stuff
37 Arizona desert
40 "I don't need that many"
42 Pointer
43 Non-PC wear
44 Barely out
45 ___ (with 56-A) ("Big bully!")
50 Superlative ending
51 Like some Fr. verbs
52 In a way
56 See 45 Across
61 Rhode Island license plate words
63 Prefix with skeleton
64 Leafy green
65 Keynesian study, briefly
66 Harlem Globetrotter Curly
67 Measurement for fitting a backpack
68 DOJ division?
69 Floor trader's shout

DOWN

1 Migrations
2 Cliff home
3 Be aggressive in Texas Hold'em
4 Magician's cry
5 Cricket game piece
6 Move, but not quite carry
7 Agreements promising peace
8 Pirate song chant
9 BBC, familiarly
10 Air France hub
11 Come to terms about a price
12 Toast beginning
13 Place for a mud bath
19 Disturbances
21 Positive particle
25 Part of the act
26 Molelike creature
28 Make a perjurous statement
29 Financial report abbr.
30 Mil. exercises
31 Place to exercise
32 "The Maltese Falcon" sleuth
33 Achilles' killer
34 Like One L students
38 Yokohama drama
39 Prefix meaning "double"
40 Protrude (out)
41 City area, for short
43 Amana product
46 Twitches
47 Spoke from a soapbox
48 "Queen of the South" network
49 Obsolete NYC subway fare
53 Zellweger of "Chicago"
54 Like some pools
55 Dot on a map of the Pacific
57 Eight's eight
58 Command following an "Uh-oh!"
59 Sunroof cousin
60 Shelter with flaps
61 31-day mo.
62 John in "Star Trek Beyond"

164 INTERNATIONAL BLEND   by Gary Larson
19 Across was an early rival of Tide.

ACROSS
1 Cogitate
5 Dundee denizen
9 Didn't dawdle
14 Between a rock and a hard place
16 Saunders novel "Lincoln in the ___"
17 Prague DJ's playlist?
18 Conception
19 Bygone detergent brand
20 Legislate
22 Beetle, e.g.
23 Harvest goddess
24 Warsaw polka band selections?
27 It never starts with an 8 or a 9: Abbr.
28 Bewail
29 A chip, maybe
32 Amounted (to)
36 Unrefined
40 Pyrenees natives getting a tan?
43 Capital on the Han River
44 Can't stomach
45 Began, with "off"
46 Mineral suffix
48 Asner and Begley
50 Helsinki Cruises, e.g.?
56 Sweetheart, slangily
59 Mama bear, in Madrid
60 Auto part
61 Airs
63 Old Glory's land, for short
65 Bangkok barrette?
67 "Network" director Sidney
68 Beat walkers
69 Capture
70 Dagger in "The Mikado"
71 Junior in 12 Pro Bowls

DOWN
1 Prefix for manage
2 Open, as a jacket
3 Composer Camille Saint-___
4 Computer keys
5 AARP members
6 Caravan beast
7 Express
8 Paris resident
9 Sort of annoying
10 Panthers QB Newton
11 Hint
12 Mystery writer's award
13 Go-getters
15 Whacks
21 Blackguard
25 A long time ago
26 Artiste toppers
27 Disk-shaped bead
29 Tummy muscles
30 Dumfries denial
31 Late Qing dynasty general
33 Fire remnant
34 Ronan Farrow's mom
35 Suffix with absorb
37 Consume
38 Give the devil his ___
39 Boundary
41 Contact game involving a frisbee
42 Adult-to-be
47 Pamplona pronoun
49 Battery brand
50 Court infractions
51 Any "Time"
52 Osaka of tennis
53 Certain address starter
54 Lindsay of "Mean Girls"
55 All worked up
56 Hold responsible
57 Confused
58 College sports channel
62 Misfortunes
64 Casbah headgear
66 Embitterment

165 OFF THE WALL   by Gary Larson
The famous father of 62 Across founded St. Jude Children's Hospital.

ACROSS

1 Jennifer Saunders sitcom
6 Limitless quantities
10 Play group
14 Blogger in "State of Play"
15 French girlfriend
16 Utah ski resort
17 Member of the wedding
19 "Frozen" reindeer
20 Fort Bliss town
21 Atlanta Braves symbol
23 Unhurried
24 Commodities at hand
26 Horse sense
31 May honoree
34 Cleave
35 Make aware
36 Was humiliated
38 No sense of history
40 Priceless violin
41 Request
42 Stocking stuffer
43 Mechanic's tool
47 Like some jacks
48 "Neither snow nor rain nor heat . . ." org.
52 Tex-Mex snack
55 Kitt of song
57 "Enchanted" girl in a 2004 film
58 Written documentation
60 "___ Rainbow": Box Tops
61 Baseball's Hershiser
62 "That Girl" girl
63 Ski lifts
64 Math column
65 Satin quality

DOWN

1 Commercial charge
2 "Twilight" heroine Swan
3 Turkeys
4 Inevitably
5 Significant others, slangily
6 2012 AFTRA merger partner
7 Radiated
8 Put it on the line?
9 Diamond and Blair
10 Non-credit deal
11 Peace Nobelist Myrdal
12 Dish cooked in a pot
13 Aquarium
18 Lion heard from afar
22 Reference work
25 Red coin?
27 Poseidon's staff
28 Lie
29 Duet plus one
30 Mast support
31 Sunday service, for some
32 Camp Swampy dog
33 Soldier of fortune, briefly
37 Pierre people
38 Safe, on board
39 Mr. Fix-it
41 Jimmy
44 Bag holder
45 Message in a corporate image ad
46 "Whoopee!"
49 Gaze
50 Suffix for Franco
51 Receiving room
52 Dispatched
53 Pat on the buns?
54 "Orinoco ___": Enya
56 Bill producers
59 2011 World Golf Hall of Fame inductee

166 THEMELESS by Tucker Smith
The state flower at 24 Down is easy to remember.

ACROSS

1 Like the White Rabbit
5 Packs tight
10 Dilly
14 Smallest amount of gold
15 Airport fleet
17 Bit of theater litter
18 Just a guess
19 "Pardon me" from a computer
21 Dishwasher cycle
22 Port vessel
26 Like a block of lava
31 Mead research site
32 Fall flower
33 Held
35 Suit material?
36 Sinus, for one
38 Fruit seen in Peter Paul Rubens' "The Fall of Man"
39 "Picnic" playwright
40 Conga feature
41 Limited intake
43 Lacrosse team quorum
44 Heaps of, slangily
46 Cause to lose hope
48 Injury addition
50 Hayek of "Frida"
52 Revised manuscripts
57 Figures seen in "The Fall of Man"
60 Take the edge off
61 Order newbies
62 Teen fave
63 Just right
64 Stylish
65 Re or so

DOWN

1 Tool for light work?
2 Assigning
3 Basketball season enders
4 Adorn in relief
5 Blondie drummer Burke
6 Mezzo Stevens
7 Tsp. and tbsp.
8 Month, in Marseilles
9 Shrub that may be poisonous
10 Intelligentsia
11 Ed Sheeran song from his "+" album
12 Melissa of "Wayward Pines"
13 Blue Angels' org.
16 Large accounts
20 Part of ROM
23 Sherry in a Poe title
24 Alaska's state flower
25 Eroded, with "away"
27 Starring role
28 Neither hot nor cold
29 JFK Library designer
30 Boston team, in brief
32 Prefix for meter
34 Adele's "Rolling in the ___"
37 Turn in again
42 File holder
45 ___ once
47 Gorp morsel
49 Mediterranean capital
51 Confuse mentally
53 Red rind contents
54 Anti-fur org.
55 Even a single time
56 Snug retreat
57 Aardvark appetizer
58 End of a Flintstone yell
59 Gardener on screen

THEMELESS   by Tucker Smith
Alternate clue for 15 Across: Detroit Tigers legend.

ACROSS

1 Navy helicopters
9 Unlikely donors
15 Detroit slugger
16 Swathe
17 Mother painter
18 Part in a song
19 Seminary subject
20 Designer Cassini
21 Kind of moment
22 Purdue team
24 Decks out
27 Galley mover
28 Photo tint
29 Eartha Kitt hit
35 PC competitor
36 Hindu outergarment
37 Fall (in)
38 Peter, Paul, and Mary tunes
40 Yak's home
41 Turn to the driver's side
42 Uses indelicate language
43 Warehouse job
49 Sniggling experts
50 Melodramatic cry
51 Sound of relief
54 1974 Mocedades hit
55 Easily moved
57 Walked like a tosspot
58 School sound system
59 Mysore music makers
60 Can't stand

DOWN

1 "Money talks" and more
2 Designed for all grades
3 Like, with "to"
4 "Morning ___ Broken"
5 Central Pennsylvania city
6 "Die Hard" star Bruce
7 Use a prie-dieu
8 Suit fabric
9 Bragg breakfast buddy
10 Visibly moved
11 Elegant
12 "Shark Tale" jellyfish
13 Blade holder
14 Warship booms
22 Building block
23 Pasadena float flowers
24 "Get real!"
25 Music sampler
26 Harlequin
29 "Oh please, let us!"
30 Bit of energy
31 Slicker in the winter
32 Small rum cake
33 In charge of
34 Clears after taxes
36 Bubble bath sight
39 Less protracted
40 Ballroom dance
42 Gets the ball rolling
43 Eyes thighs, e.g.
44 "Able was ___ . . ."
45 Admiral's concern
46 Elon Musk's car
47 Celeritous
48 With no other
51 Basic principles
52 Emollient source
53 Clothes lines
56 Where Jackie got her "O"

ACROSS

1 Banjo ridge
5 Buffalo females of song
9 1987 Peace Nobelist
14 Longtime "Hollywood Squares" regular
16 Kravitz in "The Hunger Games"
17 Slanting
18 Tex-Mex snacks
19 Jersey cousin of "y'all"
20 One score after deuce
21 Wight, for one
22 Head doctor
24 Lots and more
27 Place to wallow
28 E's on down the road to Athens
30 Dr. Hartman of "Family Guy"
31 Herring type
32 Harness part
33 LBJ beagle
34 Pays no mind to
37 Marseilles Mrs.
38 Côte d'___
40 Some August babies
41 Hamelin musician
43 Ruination
44 Musophobiac's cry
45 In demand
46 Better companion
48 Dryer residue
49 Rock genre
50 Synonym for sheep's clothing?
55 Of service
56 They identify dispatches
57 Mules and such
58 Round of cordials
59 Varieties
60 Oxygen container
61 To a degree

DOWN

1 Wear
2 Prefix for tiller
3 A geminus in Genesis
4 Stretchable
5 Tall and awkward
6 Bicker
7 Collins in "The Last Tycoon"
8 Reacts to a haymaker
9 Baptismal area
10 Less unprepared
11 How a judge may hold you
12 "La Dolce Vita" actress
13 Pt. of DOS
15 Leaders in pits
23 "Fifty Shades Darker" villain
24 Physical therapy
25 Shakespeare's queen
26 Magazine contents
27 Upset, with "up"
29 Edgar Bergen dummy
31 Showed disdain for
35 Lea Michele series
36 Sprinkle with glitter
39 Showed a really good time
42 Senses
45 Most prudent
47 Daly's "Cagney & Lacey" costar
48 Open the door to
49 Cologne scent
51 Wind down
52 Grooving on
53 Look like
54 In ___ (actually)

169

ACROSS

1 1997 Spielberg film
8 Congests
15 Like nonviolent resistance
16 Spartan, for example
17 "Too Big to Fail" star
18 Country in the Pyrenees
19 Union opposer
20 Run in
22 Ball game purchase
23 "___ Three Lives"
25 Cambodia's 1939 neighbor
26 Kind of colony
27 Domino, e.g.
28 Jr. naval officer
29 Stands in a studio
30 Marina site
32 Sondheim musical
34 Cintra Wilson's "fashion road trip" book
40 To-do
41 Glare deterrent
42 Director's cry
46 Affirmatives
48 Something to cast
49 Sports transaction
50 Vegetable soup bean
51 Sparkle
52 "Aqualung" group Jethro ___
53 Tiffany weights
55 Attorney's org.
56 "Peekaboo" followers
58 Had faith in
60 Put away
61 Every last person
62 Covered wagon figure
63 Baseball and basketball, e.g.

DOWN

1 Sherry, often
2 Kahn of "Blazing Saddles"
3 Backer of Columbus
4 Teakettle sound
5 Cohen-Chang on "Glee"
6 Strongly opposed
7 Heroics
8 Deep rift
9 Mardi Gras follower
10 Dated
11 Orbs
12 Collected
13 "Awesome!"
14 Units of wisdom
21 Comfy spot
24 Fast-moving game?
26 Cable, e.g.
29 That, in Toledo
31 Resort lake
33 Schoolyard chums
35 Rouen refusal
36 Drone's home
37 Quarantine imposer
38 "Read this!"
39 "Pineapples" of WW2
42 Cocklofts
43 "The Water Horse" monster
44 Scout's concern
45 Most lazy
47 Persian ruler
50 Former "Today" anchor
53 "Follow me"
54 Similar things
57 Oscar winner Brynner
59 Elle, in English

170

3 Down has been on the cover of 59 Across twice.

ACROSS

1 Mausoleum on the Yamuna River
9 Cold War threat
15 907, to Alaskans
16 Acid neutralizer
17 "Blue Bayou" singer
18 Decaying metal
19 Shrimp
20 Largest Saudi city
22 Moon vehicle
23 Nationality suffix
24 Pigeonhole
25 Haliaeetus albicilla
26 Get by reasoning
28 Party card game
29 Former queen of Jordan
30 Prefix for profit
31 Home-run swing
32 Betty's "Golden Girls" role
33 Of a bygone empire
36 The gal
37 Did a lawn job
38 Fowl place
39 1988 Meg Ryan film
40 Slight jerk
41 To be, in Toulon
42 Ransom ___ Olds
43 Perches
47 Dylan's "I ___ You"
48 Entrance barrier
50 Irish breakfast
51 Rocket interceptor, briefly
52 Made a touchdown
53 Loads
54 Swarmed
56 Seasoned crew
58 Facilitate
59 General Mills product
60 Runs with sticks
61 "Donkey Kong" creator

DOWN

1 Spread feather adhesive
2 Build a fire under
3 1976 Olympic decathlon gold medalist
4 Crow's-nest location
5 Work on a stage
6 Become raspy
7 ___ Ababa
8 "Whoop it up, Rapunzel!"
9 Roof for a roof rack
10 Lacking panache
11 Green-lighted
12 Post processing place
13 Puritanical person
14 Fermented
21 "L.A. Law" lawyer
24 Mary Kay rival
25 Physicist Fermi
27 Sulking
33 Vein contents of the cool-headed
34 "Read this!"
35 Spoon bread ingredient
36 Wise old Athenian
37 Mufasa, for one
39 Gay Nineties et al.
40 Trampled
44 Russian leader at Yalta
45 Camped out
46 Gives confirmation
49 Indian metropolis
52 Cromwell's portraitist
53 Significant other
55 Wharton grad
57 Emulated Jack Horner

171

ACROSS

1 Kind of sax
5 Bit of help
9 "Go ahead, ask"
14 Labor Party constituency?
16 Goes bad
17 Augustine's "The City of God" et al.
18 Series opener
19 Baton holder
21 Subj. for some aliens
22 Frozen Wasser
23 Baptism of fire
24 Prefix with occupied
25 Lighter choices
26 Put the kibosh on
28 Make-up artists?
31 Pitch properly
32 Just go knee-deep
33 Not taken in by
34 Wined and dined
35 Susan of "Nikki"
36 Cut short
37 Mare fare
38 "I'm outta here"
39 Line of dresses
40 Japanese beverage
41 ProFlowers parent
42 Top of an i
44 Title for Tor
45 "Leaving ___ Jet Plane"
48 Baton holder
51 "The Wreck of the Mary ___": Innes
52 Hubble Space ___
53 Fired up
54 One incident too many
55 Crockpot meals
56 Time line divisions
57 Iwo Jima, e.g.

DOWN

1 Sentient
2 Runs easily
3 Newsgroup troublemaker
4 Ark. neighbor
5 Immobilize, at a rodeo
6 Dodge model
7 SEC overseer
8 "State Fair" setting
9 Part of a ballpark
10 "Amadeus" star Tom
11 "Annie" setting
12 Vacationing
13 Nicholas or Peter
15 Vestibules
20 Like rainbows
24 Stage item
25 Montana metropolis
27 Lucy Lawless role
28 Burns may feed it
29 Pulling out
30 It started in 1945
31 Steamer on the range
32 Roundup target
34 Stable youngsters
38 Burnout cause
40 Holds the wheel
41 Boneless entrées
43 Hurled
44 Burrito topper
45 Secret targets
46 Everest is on its border
47 "___ there yet?"
48 Lofty tributes
49 Bumper area
50 Stage starter

172 FROM HAIR TO ETERNITY by Marie Langley
Speak of the devil . . . or not.

ACROSS

1 2009 Beyoncé hit
5 Jazz singer James
9 Instrument with tuning beads
14 Dash
15 Eisenberg of "Deep Space Nine"
16 Duck out from under
17 Set down
18 Budget item
19 Interview format
20 **Start of a quip**
23 Take a break
24 "The Greatest" boxer
25 Oil can letters
28 **More of quip**
31 Swallow up
35 Harrison or Tillerson
36 Adidas alternative
37 Thoroughly trounces
38 Bruin teammate of Espo
39 Partner of dined
40 Beatles' meter maid
41 Mil. drop site
42 Bay of Bengal feeder
43 **More of quip**
46 King of Spain
47 TiVo ancestor
48 "But of course!"
53 **End of quip**
55 Muscle Beach dudes
58 Just right
59 Goofing off
60 Dodge model
61 Rafa Nadal's uncle
62 Link up
63 Way around Paris
64 Added factors
65 Big diamonds?

DOWN

1 Toss call
2 Dispense carefully
3 "Mule Train" singer Frankie
4 "___ of Old Smokey"
5 One of a warming pair
6 Picks up the tab
7 Rummy game
8 Colony attacker
9 Glittery bit
10 Tennis great Lendl
11 Catch some rays
12 Tack on
13 Stephen of "V for Vendetta"
21 Garage items
22 Linen source
25 Oscillated
26 Name that means "beloved"
27 Curse of Camelot
29 "One way" symbol
30 Washer cycle
31 Slip-up
32 Word after bête
33 Brave
34 Great Salt Lake state
38 Light work for musicians
39 Look for him in children's books
41 Bend over
42 Larynx opening
44 Just the same
45 Away from the shore
49 Spiritualist's board
50 "What's ___?" (1972 Streisand film)
51 Prove otherwise
52 Young voters
53 Suds
54 "On Golden Pond" bird
55 Son of Noah
56 "Able was I ___ . . ."
57 "Good Will Hunting" setting

ACROSS

1 Wise guy
6 Back street
11 Alicia of "Romero"
14 Family wheels
15 "It's a waste of time!"
16 Vixen's home
17 Give counsel to stagehands?
19 Fairy tale figure
20 Easter blooms
21 Track events
23 Wrap a baby
26 Pet shop squawker
27 San Diego team
28 "Aw, c'mon!"
30 Hot blood
31 Uneasy feeling
32 Striking sound
35 Maryland athlete, briefly
36 Beyond well-done
37 Green Lantern's foe
38 Nationality ending
39 Composure
40 Double agents
41 Tawdry stuff
43 They're passed in some races
44 Playing hooky
46 Elude capture
47 Varnish ingredient
48 Mideast hub
50 Post-op stop, for short
51 Music source for a garden party?
56 Word after "poli"
57 Be worthy of
58 Word on a campaign button
59 Fuel up
60 Kool-Aid holders
61 Icy forecast

DOWN

1 Fed. benefits agency
2 Take the plunge
3 Adj. modifer
4 One way to send large files from iCloud
5 Source of a hot tip
6 Tennis star Kerber
7 Traditional knowledge
8 Pitcher Tiant
9 Medium skill
10 Polite response
11 Stick to the bottom?
12 "Great!"
13 Uptight feeling
18 Some pipe joints
22 Hosp. trauma centers
23 Sudden outpouring
24 They're peddled
25 Proper attire when giving a speech?
26 Throw stuff at
28 Race winnings
29 Pool division
31 Interrogate
33 Contest venue
34 Like slippery rocks
36 Dugout, for one
37 "Am I imposing?" answer
39 Saki, for one
40 Grows up
42 Luau necklace
43 Soil embankment
44 Come to mind
45 "Life Goes On" daughter
46 Crèche scene trio
48 Ready to streak
49 Islamic leader
52 Drops in the grass
53 Hollywood ending?
54 U.S. immigration org.
55 Baseball's "Master Melvin"

174 "OO-LA-LA!" by Richard Silvestri
2 Down was laughingly referred to as "The Thief of Bad Gags."

ACROSS

1 Construction beam
5 Time, metaphorically
10 Chaucer chapter
14 Son of Agrippina
15 Keep from happening
16 In the thick of
17 Comprehensive guide to animal parks?
19 Bit of wampum
20 Einstein's birthplace
21 Neat thing?
22 Stonework
24 Not so far
26 Scrap
27 Water, for one
29 Clothing scenter
33 A/C condenser base
36 Spelunking spot
38 Overcharge
39 Eyelashes
41 Prepare to drag
42 "Enigma Variations" composer
43 In the entourage
44 Barbershop request
46 Moon of Jupiter
47 Some church donations
49 Kauai "hi"
51 "Paper Moon" Oscar winner
53 Crosshairs image
57 Key
60 It borders Fla.
61 Ring great
62 Served perfectly
63 Antibiotic ointment container?
66 No great shakes
67 Blake of jazz
68 "Young Frankenstein" role
69 In the know about
70 Cuts, perhaps
71 The latest

DOWN

1 For laughs
2 "Uncle Miltie"
3 Kitchen drawer?
4 CD-___
5 Like the Golden Raspberry Awards
6 River near Stonehenge
7 ___ Perce (Western tribe)
8 Hippo tail?
9 Brown ermines
10 Arrest that was frowned upon?
11 Prayer period
12 Truth twister
13 Countercurrent
18 Pinnacle
23 Show place
25 Sherwood Forest jinx?
26 A bunch of
28 Pub projectile
30 Mammoth
31 Old oath
32 Mega- times a million
33 Do a dooby-doo
34 Reinhart on "Riverdale"
35 Over and over
37 Satanic doings
40 FBI employee
45 Words to live by
48 Navy worker
50 Divine light
52 Meant to be heard
54 Dash feature
55 It's bent at the bar
56 Stadium sections
57 Part of UTEP
58 Screen symbol
59 Kevlar product
60 Somewhat
64 Kimono belt
65 Canterbury can

175 TEN MORE   by Richard Silvestri
The clue at 57 Across is a bit of a tongue-twister.

ACROSS
1 Jacks, e.g.
5 Con jobs
10 Try
14 Ere long
15 "Adam Bede" author
16 Butler's quarters?
17 Shabby knickknack?
19 Help for the hapless
20 Cambridge campus
21 Verb for you
22 George and Mitt of politics
24 Off the ship
26 Called for
27 Up to
29 Opinion pieces
33 Fedora fabric
36 Neighbor of Col.
38 Carousal
39 Notice in passing
40 Liquid medicine
42 Official proceedings
43 Iron clothes?
45 New Delhi wear
46 Dilute
47 Lets go
49 Island west of Maui
51 Polynesian carvings
53 Madison Avenue product
57 With head held higher
60 Kingston Trio hit
61 "Hold On Tight" band
62 Set the pace
63 Two parts hydrogen to one part oxygen?
66 Thesis starter
67 Piano piece
68 Competes
69 Pirate's cry
70 Young turk
71 The last Stuart

DOWN
1 Kind of ray
2 Diarist Nin
3 Billing period
4 Pt. of OED
5 Works like a gland
6 Tipoff
7 Football filler
8 Shearer of ballet
9 Fine role?
10 Cookout locale in the bleachers?
11 Account
12 Defense force
13 Pitched low?
18 Skein stuff
23 Laurel and Hardy situation
25 Where retired artists are put?
26 Men and women, e.g.
28 Summer treats
30 St. Louis sight
31 Himalayan legend
32 John and Yoko's son
33 Stable youth?
34 River through Aragon
35 Long ride?
37 Surrounding glow
41 Medieval musician
44 The Lone Ranger's real identity
48 Spit in the meat?
50 Banned apple spray
52 Hot
54 Invitation to a hitchhiker
55 UFO crewman
56 Lariat feature
57 The thing, to Hamlet
58 Slots spot
59 Inauguration highlight
60 Persian of yore
64 Popcorn buy
65 Clark's "Mogambo" costar

176 PREPOSITION REPETITION by Richard Silvestri
The answer to 9 Down can be found in Genesis 2.

ACROSS

1 Doorway sidepiece
5 Snail trail
10 "Mamma Mia" group
14 Conditioner additive
15 Like a milquetoast
16 Job opening
17 Prefix follower
18 Sheepish
19 Do a washday job
20 Work out with the Colts?
23 Checkers choice
24 Banana oil, e.g.
25 Miscellaneous
29 Barely sufficient
32 In the center of
33 Split
34 Home of the Horned Frogs
37 Army brass satire?
41 Superlative suffix
42 Emergency signal
43 X and Y, on a graph
44 On the ball
45 Time to hibernate
47 2009 Peace Nobelist
50 Storage place
51 Was upright in the chair?
58 The gamut
59 Adjustable loop
60 House site
62 Atlantic City game
63 Tammany symbol
64 Peter or Nicholas
65 Port of Yemen
66 Gray
67 Bar Mitzvah dance

DOWN

1 Honey holder
2 Gobs
3 Medieval invader of Spain
4 Frat letter
5 Squiffed
6 More than miffed
7 Poker declaration
8 Series starter
9 Locale of the Pishon and Gihon rivers
10 Set up a goal
11 Swell
12 Carried
13 Petal product
21 Hot blood
22 Tooth, in combinations
25 Carnation container
26 Band aids
27 Mob scene
28 Bachelor's last words
29 Wear
30 Alfresco eatery
31 Peke's squeak
33 Out there somewhere
34 Email alternative
35 Hudson Bay tribe
36 Cold War monogram
38 E equivalent
39 Bullring bravo
40 Warhol subject
44 Wonder Woman, for one
45 Napa Valley sight
46 Bad stat for a QB
47 Honshu city
48 Reduced in intensity
49 Make amends
50 Plagued
52 Red army?
53 Plug away
54 Forum wear
55 Septennial phenomenon
56 Pasta used in soups
57 Hard by
61 Chapter of history

177

THEMELESS   by Brian E. Paquin

21-D was written by Paul while waiting for John at the Penny Lane Bus Station.

ACROSS

1 "We have some breaking news . . ."
11 Make a design on glass
15 Was unrepentant
16 "The Good Dinosaur" dinosaur
17 TVs, slangily
18 "And so it ___"
19 Restoration, briefly
20 1966 Frank Sinatra hit
22 Male ducks
25 Political matter
26 Like a punk's coif
28 Pickled veggies
32 Dawdler
36 Accumulates
37 Pub entertainment
38 Is so inclined
39 Bob Dylan's "Tangled Up ___"
40 Fails entirely
41 Wear for bank jobs
42 PGA Masters champion Watson
43 Boutique
45 To some extent
50 Big dogs
54 NBA coach Kokoškov
55 "Good Luck Chuck" actress Jessica
56 1973 energy crisis trigger
59 Hidden "Survivor" object
60 Joe Jackson hit song
61 Highland dance
62 Muddy shades

DOWN

1 Bronze position
2 Bill in "Trainwreck"
3 "Glee" actress Menzel
4 Caribbean food fish
5 Write quickly
6 Flash drive port
7 Wild guess
8 Unpopular political move
9 Song from "Nashville"
10 Straw homes
11 Sharp lookouts
12 "Star Trek" counselor Deanna
13 Score symbol
14 Rinse off
21 "There beneath the blue ___ skies . . .": "Penny Lane" lyric
23 Wedding
24 Orated
27 Operation Overlord's overlord
29 "Tiger-in-your-tank" gas
30 Skirt for Pavlova
31 The Munsters' pet dragon
32 Milk type
33 Clark's high school sweetheart
34 Heavenly bodies
35 Shows self-confidence
36 Thumper's friend
38 Corn core
40 Clumsy one
42 Madonna's "La Isla ___"
44 Unattached
46 Schroeder's instrument
47 "Glee" actress Dianna
48 Anna Paquin's "X-Men" role
49 Hambletonian heats
50 Like Monday's child
51 Ye ___ Curiosity Shoppe
52 Descendant of a crumhorn
53 Days in a Dunkirk week
57 Dashboard initialism
58 Comedy routine

THEMELESS by Victor Fleming
Lawyers will know the answer to 34 Down.

ACROSS

1 Fled to be wed
7 University life
15 Moolah
16 The Police drummer
17 Free of charge
18 Lipstick shade
19 For an action, in law
21 Cool light
22 Pro response
23 Musical staff symbol
24 Nuzzles or nozzles
26 Memo tablet
27 "You're ___ Man, Charlie Brown"
28 Goes after
30 Like big kahunas (with 38-A)
34 Rochester's insane wife
35 Environmental science
36 Hit the hay
37 Zedonk, for one
38 See 30 Across
39 Puniest pups
40 Satisfy a thirst
41 Wood-finishing tool
42 Unwavering
43 Time out of mind
47 Lust or gluttony
48 Yvette's affirmative
49 Baked Italian dish
51 Foot vis-à-vis yard
54 Cause of freezing
55 Site of an 1861 battle
56 Cut some slack
57 Does a fine job?
58 January rains

DOWN

1 Annual literary award
2 "Royals" singer
3 Doctoral hurdles
4 ___ four (teacake)
5 Discharge
6 Put in neutral
7 The Hokies conference
8 Lost heat
9 "___ moi, le déluge": Louis XV
10 Qumran's sea
11 Pipe angle
12 "The Maltese Falcon" star
13 Words best not said to a bear?
14 Puts together
20 Woolgathering
25 Grass in a roll
26 Richard E. Byrd's coat
27 Really long stretches
28 Anne of "Men in Trees"
29 Darrin's boss on "Bewitched"
30 Ogle
31 Familiarizes
32 Circularity
33 Razzle-dazzle
34 Enters nunc pro tunc
36 Symbol of slowness
38 Caught a bug
40 Big do
42 Sweat or wet followers
43 Analyze grammatically
44 Avoid making waves
45 Aardvark feature
46 Rain-delay rollouts
47 Place for a sleeper
48 Electrical units
50 Barking sea creature
52 Calendar watch abbr.
53 Kildare and Strangelove

179 THEMELESS by Victor Fleming
A 17 Across of a puzzle by an 11-Down puzzler.

ACROSS

1 Home in Havana
5 Bigwig in temple
10 Capture a chess piece
14 Hannibal's hurdles
15 Corby of Grandma Walton fame
16 Dire sign
17 Whimsical undertaking
18 Thoroughly dislikes
19 Follow
20 Stays motionless
22 Africa's ___ Faso
24 Word with mass or mixed
25 "The Simpsons" creator Groening
26 LBJ's Supreme Court appointee
30 Silvers and Simms
33 Spice rack seasoning
36 Gyeongbokgung Palace site
37 One of Henry's Catherines
38 Came to a conclusion
40 Enormous
41 Govt. security
43 Like some House hearings
45 "Space Is the Place" jazzman
46 ___ stand (field sobriety test)
47 Vinegar eel, e.g.
49 Little laugh
52 Wives and husbands
55 Crooked
57 Bard's foot
58 Video game pioneer
60 Orchestral "tuning fork"
61 Irish Spring alternative
62 Schlepped
63 Campaign worker
64 Flying fish-eater
65 Shoots out
66 Title document

DOWN

1 Young rhino
2 Burglary deterrent
3 Spending binge
4 Played with fire
5 Run through lines
6 Word said with a sigh
7 Eatery order, briefly
8 English channel (with "The")
9 "To recap . . ."
10 Traveled the Leh–Manali Highway?
11 Aspiring
12 Sharp-eyed
13 "The River Sings" singer
21 Hill in Jerusalem
23 Smart blows
27 Pro ___ (to a certain extent)
28 Mayflower Compact signer John
29 Engraved marker
31 Winter Games vehicle
32 Winter Games vehicle
33 Waffles no more
34 Mork's "goodbye," when doubled
35 Female triathlete winner
39 Bodybuilder's concern
42 Head set?
44 Quick change of direction
48 Packinghouse products
50 Jazzman Blake
51 Poem with couplets
52 "Us" or "them"
53 Low poker hand
54 "Go no further!"
55 Construction group
56 Like some high balls
59 Devoured

BAND BOOKS by Erik Agard
In 1971, 17 Down won the NCAA Men's Soccer Championship.

ACROSS

1 "You play too much!"
7 Most scarce
13 Coatings on old metals
15 "Queen Sugar" actor Kofi
16 Louis MacNeice book
18 Siphons off
19 Lake rainbows
20 Ron Weasley's Scabbers, for one
21 Yoke attachments
23 Midsections: Abbr.
24 2016 Disney film princess
27 ___ Permanente
30 Upper-left keyboard key
31 Turn suddenly
33 Pictures
37 Alice Randall book
40 Greet someone
41 Remus Rabbit address
42 G&T half
43 Asian peninsula
45 Partner of services
47 Arm holder
50 Dutch graphic artist M.C.
52 Do something
53 PO part
55 Tel ___
59 James Baldwin book
62 Fix
63 Indian appetizers
64 Tee privilege at Spyglass Hill
65 Emulate Ryan Coogler

DOWN

1 Decides
2 "Funny stuff!"
3 "Stomp the Yard" dance form
4 Affixes with string
5 Ants ___ log
6 Second half, maybe
7 Mob-law
8 Radius sites
9 Rita Ora song
10 "Your Movie Sucks" author
11 Sun-related
12 Finals Week ordeals
14 Caressed
15 "Pardon me, Leonardo . . ."
17 Washington, D.C., college team
22 X-Men founder
23 Rock formation
24 Willie Mays' 1972 team
25 Labor Dept. agency
26 ___-deucy
28 Trig ratio
29 Come to light
32 Mononymous Irish singer
34 Chuck Brown's music
35 Oklahoma city
36 Ottawa team, briefly
38 "¿Que?"
39 Prophets
44 Bordeaux cap
46 Speechifier
47 Drawback
48 Sound of a sneeze
49 Severe
51 Group of six
53 Seaside structure
54 Story structures
56 Tough grip comparison
57 Desktop Apple
58 Sleeveless garment
60 Kaepernick do
61 "Eww, no more!"

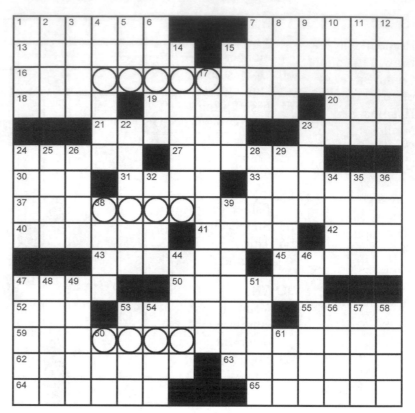

181 STRAIGHT TALK by Erik Agard

The straight at 58 Across is considered non-standard in poker circles.

ACROSS

1 Animal associated with bachelors
5 Unblushing
11 First dynasty of Imperial China
14 Lei-clad dance
15 String of prayer beads
16 Article in español
17 Smashed bit
18 Fated
20 Venice International Film Festival award
22 Walking pace
23 Day of celebration, for short
24 "___ Tunes"
26 Wind-powered extreme sport
32 "Let's do it!"
33 "Je ___" ("I love you")
34 ___ de tête (French for "headache")
37 The Pope's residence
41 Sizzling sound
42 Apt rhyme for "efface"
43 Termini
44 Dulce de leche, for one
47 EGOT winner Rita
50 Hi-___ image
51 Wired blade
52 Backstabbing
58 Straight seen in circled letters
61 Schreiber in "Spotlight"
62 Lil dude
63 Colorful shirt variety
64 Green Gables gal
65 Not quite there
66 Make beloved
67 Elopes, say

DOWN

1 Cager who wore size 22 shoes
2 Hippo's skirt in "Fantasia"
3 Burn aid
4 Cornish fowl
5 Purveyor of pads
6 Rice-a-___
7 On the subject of
8 Steve on "Treme"
9 Blake's "before"
10 Washington Square locale
11 Imam's holy book
12 Sundance debut
13 Very inclement
19 Barely containing excitement
21 Unfairly deprive
24 Like wet noodles
25 ___-Day vitamins
26 Sportage and Stinger
27 Mischievous moppets
28 Abuela's sons
29 Calypso's father
30 Heighten
31 Cubist, of a sort
34 Ex-Spur Ginobili
35 "Thunderstruck" band
36 ___-majesté
38 Archie Andrews, for one
39 Hedger's words
40 Restraining order for boxers?
44 Bottomless
45 White elephant party?
46 Brief moment
47 Cat cacophony
48 Deborah Lacks portrayer
49 Rough partner
52 Even-___ ungulate
53 Etiquette-starved
54 "Only Time" singer
55 Cologne article
56 Tear into pieces
57 Designer Saint-Laurent
59 Took tea
60 ___ Tin Tin

47 ACROSS   by Jim Holland

"People" magazine named 27 Down "Sexiest Man Alive" on November 5, 2018.

ACROSS

1 Sired
6 Common campaign tactic
11 Rubbish
14 Undue rueful behavior
15 Lope
16 Rock genre
17 Luau attire
19 Meadow sound
20 Keeps calm
21 Buckeyes
23 Deighton or Dawson
24 Lively wit
25 Contractor's proposal
31 Count Basie's "___ Darlin' "
32 "___ Little Love My Way": Murray
33 Acquires, in a way
37 "Fantastic Four" star Jessica
39 Spreads one's wings
41 Piece of cake
42 Thunder units
44 Jazz groups
46 Deuce, for example
47 Poker hand
50 Holly Golightly's creator
53 Ramon's relative
54 Feeling low while high?
56 Indigestion remedy
60 Kissing in the park, e.g.
61 WABC, e.g.
63 Bolted
64 Pose to propose
65 Is inclined
66 Press coverage
67 Carell in "The Big Short"
68 Acrylic fiber

DOWN

1 Captures
2 Raison d'___
3 Spur
4 Priced to go
5 Proctor's concerns
6 Fifth Avenue store
7 Romanized "Space Odyssey" year
8 Zaragoza's river
9 Court great Gibson
10 Holds back
11 Concrete support
12 Saudi neighbor
13 History, in a way
18 Has an inkling
22 Some tournaments
25 To-do
26 Tick off
27 Idris in "The Dark Tower"
28 It takes two to ten years to mature
29 "___ you to do it!"
30 Prada who founded Prada
34 Start to freeze
35 Make a closing effort
36 Zoomed
38 Choir section
40 Easy touch
43 Comedy routines
45 Normandy city
48 Take back
49 Teacher portrayed by Kaplan
50 Blue Grotto locale
51 Quinn of "Elementary"
52 Practical joke
55 "The Mocker Mocked" painter
56 Srta., in 45 Down
57 Marsh duck
58 Cubist Rubik
59 Part of YMCA
62 Tolstoy's nickname

183 EQUILATERAL QUADRILATERAL   by Sarah Keller
Knowledge of plane geometry is not required here.

ACROSS

1 "Bye-bye!"
5 "Gross!"
8 Grease gun's cousin
14 "Once ___ a time . . ."
15 Cow or sow
16 Ethically neutral
17 Hair line
18 World's best-selling toy*
20 Heart chambers
22 Approached quickly
23 Sound sensor
24 Knights' battlefield*
27 Transgression
28 Madame Butterfly, e.g.
32 Neighbors of quads
35 Largest Finnish company
39 Bleacher feature
40 Place to write letters*
44 Pack down
45 "Na zdorovie!"
46 Org. concerned with global warming
47 "Fifty Shades of Grey" protagonist
50 School fund-raiser
52 Its days are numbered*
59 Res followers
62 Stunner
63 Part of a stage
64 Geometry class handout*
67 Snaky swimmers
68 Viral zoonotic disease

69 Title for a Turkish leader
70 Legal rights org.
71 Equilateral quadrilateral found in clue* answers
72 "The Longest Day" ship
73 Comedienne Martha

DOWN

1 Rapper Shakur
2 "___ Out of the Desert": Pollack
3 Yankees manager (1996–2007)
4 Capers
5 Loc. of Ben Gurion airport
6 Grasshopper's trill
7 Skewered entrée
8 Poster board
9 Words after a tough workout?
10 ___ cit. (footnote abbr.)
11 Rock's Motley ___
12 "Stopping by Woods on a Snowy Evening" rhyme scheme
13 NY Met or SF Giant
19 Rescuer of Odysseus
21 Claude of "Lobo"
25 Sufficient, old-style
26 Airhead

29 King or queen, e.g.
30 Fab Four film
31 Neighborhood
32 Book after John
33 Bart Simpson, e.g.
34 A few
36 Many Conor McGregor wins
37 Annoy
38 Hustle and bustle
41 Blueprint stat
42 ___ John's Pizza
43 Extremist
48 Barbershop foam
49 Go by
51 Become visible
53 That, in Tijuana
54 View from Everest
55 They're at the bottom of the barrel
56 Tropical palm

57 "Gee whiz!"
58 Come to pass
59 Bus. directors
60 Mesopotamia today
61 He played Mowgli in "Jungle Book"
65 News anchor Lindström
66 Double-crosser

GETTING REORGANIZED   by Pam Klawitter
45 Across was the first movie to top "Titanic" at the box office.

ACROSS

1 Size at Starbucks
6 Sarcophagus symbol
9 Chile's ___ de Pascua
13 Perrier rival
14 Casino card holder
16 Money hole
17 Florida Gulf Coast city
18 Bandit-faced varmint
19 Takes to court
20 SOURCE
23 What children should be?
24 Yakov Smirnoff's birthplace
25 SWORD
30 Impressive display
31 Salon choices
32 Spanish saint
35 Eisner's Disney successor
36 Zooms upward
38 Advantageous race position
39 Captained
40 Do a bit of boxing
41 Apple-pie ___
42 BROAD
45 Futuristic James Cameron film
48 "Hamilton" star Leslie
49 CREATIONS
54 Bamboo Curtain continent
55 Tuscany island
56 Declivitous
58 Kindle competitor
59 Lose on purpose
60 Wild ducks
61 Toning targets
62 Hot time on the Riviera
63 Some Latinas: Abbr.

DOWN

1 Check for accuracy
2 Remove to a MASH unit
3 "The Secret of ___" (1982 film)
4 Where to enjoy empanadillas
5 Without reason
6 Gain altitude
7 "Get along!"
8 [It's gone!]
9 They're often debated
10 Speaks drunkenly
11 Rich soil
12 Befuddled
15 Concert extensions
21 It's found in gin
22 Morning-line figures
25 Monopoly corner
26 It might be hard to resist
27 Equine role of Rocky Lane
28 Where to tie one on?
29 First word in "The Lord's Prayer"
32 Part of some floats
33 Blue Jay or Oriole
34 Sheldon Cooper, e.g.
36 Urged
37 Inept one
38 Concert drummer?
40 Hudson River fish
41 They're among the reeds
42 Texas Roadhouse orders
43 Pinpoint
44 FL summer hours
45 Whirlpool subsidiary
46 Sun stopper
47 You can believe it
50 "Night" author Wiesel
51 Drive getaway
52 Sans mixer
53 Emmy winner Ward
57 Letter addenda

185 SOUNDS FAMILIAR by Pam Klawitter
The speaker of 6 Across is Antonio in "The Tempest."

ACROSS

1 Pepper 400 times hotter than Tabasco
6 "What's ___ is prologue": Shak.
10 Chase baseballs
14 Kind of ray
15 Minutes
16 "Fixing a ___": Beatles
17 What the nose knows
18 Lacerate
19 Shawkat of "Arrested Development"
20 Colorado annual 10K run
23 Aboveground mole
25 Yearning
26 Golfers Dutra and Browne
27 Oracle's bottom line?
32 Place on the beach
33 Plaint from Porky
34 Mad as ___ hen
35 Europe's longest river
37 Hemingway sobriquet
41 Yorkshire river
42 Squad car sound
43 Chicken quailed?
47 "Yes, there ___ bananas . . ."
49 Half a laugh
50 Cambridgeshire isle
51 Sells bicycle parts
56 Red in the middle
57 Tribal history
58 Bar mitzvah et al.
61 Of the ear
62 Iowa State U. city
63 Give a heads-up
64 Bill who wrote "Secretariat"
65 Kick back
66 "Things We Said ___": Beatles

DOWN

1 Team execs
2 Smithfield meat
3 Single file
4 D-Day town
5 Fox hunt cry
6 Type of attorney
7 Maple genus
8 Guess from left field
9 Miss in "Dr. No"
10 "Do you want me to?"
11 "Stop right there!"
12 "Falling Skies" invader
13 Clockwork, mostly
21 Aberdeen river
22 Lexington sch.
23 Refuge for strays
24 Frigate front
28 Seattle summer hrs.
29 Punted, in a sense
30 18-wheeler
31 Three ___ match
35 En route
36 Bruin Hall-of-Famer
37 Trivial Pursuit piece
38 Caught on "CoPS"
39 Marmalade ingredient
40 Raggedy Ann's brother
41 Army absentee
42 Cuss out
43 Diggory of Hogwarts
44 Next to bat
45 Words said with a smile
46 Massive UK reference
47 Raggedy Ann's wear
48 Bick Benedict's ranch
52 It flies over the Holy Land
53 "Brave New World" sedative
54 White House sobriquet
55 "___ and Stitch" (2002)
59 The Big Band ___
60 Sloppy digs

186 "THIS WILL ONLY TAKE A MOMENT" by Steven E. Atwood
In "The Angry Birds Movie" 49 Down is the voice of King Mudbeard.

ACROSS

1 The ___ economy
4 "Portnoy's Complaint" author
8 Ancient epic
13 Tie up
14 Matty or Moises of baseball
15 Pin a medal on
16 Suffix for Henri
17 Punch
18 Midwest hub
19 Film about the "Pequod" captain?
21 They get belted
22 Traditional knowledge
23 Trojan War hero
24 Range
27 A truckload
29 Situation for a server
30 Study of an Iranian religion?
36 Hydrous magnesium silicate
37 Butler of fiction
38 Neighborhood
39 Peyton Manning's signal-calling cries
41 Vehicle in a 1980s Chrysler line
42 Proceeds
43 Male Amish feature
44 Get on board
48 Former Iranian ruler
50 Former "Jeopardy!" announcer
51 Sitcom time slots?
56 Bungled situation
57 Apple product
58 Applications
59 "The Centipede" poet Nash
60 Large volume
61 Go over
62 Bottle-___ dolphin
63 Railroad siding
64 Dr. Rhine's field

DOWN

1 Theodoric the Great, for one
2 Bit
3 Have a quick meal
4 Grooming tool
5 Branch of peace
6 Collette in "Hitchcock"
7 Giant
8 "May it come to pass!"
9 "Mean Girls" star Lindsay
10 Lacking sense
11 Left ventricle exit
12 Slip cover?
13 HBO's "Show ___ Hero"
20 Le ___ juste
23 "Hotel du Lac" author Brookner
24 Ratón chaser
25 Oldest son of Ben Cartwright
26 Kunis in "Black Swan"
27 Oakland team, familiarly
28 Inaugural culmination
30 Trout type
31 Expression of resignation
32 Waterfront abode
33 Quint's boat in "Jaws"
34 Rig
35 Distance between hash marks
40 Beached
43 Scoffer's cry
44 Printer maker
45 Tropical fruit
46 Small fasteners
47 Spot charge
48 Early SeaWorld performer
49 Star of HBO's "Barry"
51 Scoreboard column
52 Each
53 Mail org. with an eagle logo
54 Operate a combine
55 Obj. of identity theft

187 HOLDING BACK NOTHING   by Harvey Estes
58 Down is a hint to the puzzle's theme.

ACROSS

1 Put out
5 Black billiard ball in Baja
9 Glowing remnant
14 Part of UTEP
15 Linguist Chomsky
16 Biscayne Bay city
17 Shout to a DJ
20 Noonday naps
21 Entrance keeper
22 Tasha of "Star Trek: TNG"
23 Take it from me
24 Fed. Rx watchdog
27 Monopolizes
30 Cookie sellers
34 Court strokes
36 Takes a bough?
38 Davis of "King"
39 Virtual helper
42 Chukka boot material
43 Bullwinkle, for one
44 Catch a wave
45 Broadcasts
47 NFL officials
49 Ends of letters
50 Jimmy Choo design
52 Green
54 Beach protector
57 Large primate
61 Hekla and Hood
63 Wishful words
64 Moon of Endor dweller
65 Anticipatory nights
66 Jury group
67 Puts in stitches
68 Laura of "Recount"

DOWN

1 Omar of "House"
2 One of the Sandwich Islands
3 Words after "woe"
4 ___-turvy
5 Conditionally out
6 Sacks that fold
7 "That'll show 'em!"
8 Last character in "Lysistrata"
9 Cyberspace face
10 Route markers
11 Oz creator
12 Flaubert heroine
13 French goose egg
18 Beach near Omaha
19 Winery equipment
24 Clean with string
25 Sinker
26 Less fumbling
28 Poli sci subj.
29 Bloodhound's clue
31 Finish off
32 Levels at the playing field
33 They did the lord's work
35 Hit, but not butt
37 Gin flavoring
40 Connecticut college town
41 Strips of ecclesiastical authority
46 One and only
48 "Gravity" singer Bareilles
51 Garden statues
53 ___ and dined
54 Came out with
55 It wakes Alexa
56 The whole nine yards
57 Look elated
58 "Nothing" held back in three answers
59 Lustful look
60 Pt. of PGA
62 "I ___ you big time!"

ACROSS

1 Birthplace of St. Francis
7 Place in a familiar role
15 Doubles' jobs
16 "Angelic Salutation" prayer
17 Distribute, with "out"
18 Giver of testimony
19 Abominable Snowman's home
21 Social grace
22 Darth, as a boy
23 WSW opposite
24 Mortar accessory
26 Below expectations
28 Explorer Vasco
31 "There you ___"
32 Tough trips
34 Wide-awake
36 **Everest expedition cry: Part 1**
39 Showing anxiety
42 "Unsafe at Any Speed" author
46 Mao's successor
47 "Be right with ya"
50 Golden Globe winner Ward
51 Activity before war
53 Ed of "The Honeymooners"
55 Hebrew letter after lamed
56 Soft ball
57 **Expedition cry: Part 2**
60 Cap with a tail
63 Makes up
64 Classic Caddy
65 Like tears
66 Predetermines
67 Puts on the books

DOWN

1 Arthur Ashe Stadium surface
2 Dye user
3 Conjecture
4 Machu Picchu builder
5 Inscribed column
6 No man, to John Donne
7 "So there!"
8 Part of YSL
9 Zing
10 Modern music genre
11 Poem part
12 Space between buildings
13 Heartfelt
14 Dropped a dime on
20 Oral vote
24 Certain Feds
25 Wouldn't stop talking
27 Ione of "Say Anything"
29 NHL enforcers
30 Showery mo.
33 Attach, as a patch
35 Schedule guesses, briefly
37 Part of a grabber
38 Kerry loc.
39 Happened (upon)
40 Light ring
41 Muzzleloading tools
43 Possessed
44 Ag or Fe
45 Yul role
48 Attention
49 Result of ironing
52 Otherwise
54 Tennessee footballer
57 Duck down
58 Mireille of "The Killing"
59 Fizzy drink
61 Mumbai title
62 Neighbor of Okla.

189 ADDITIONAL ATTEMPTS by Anna Carson
If at first you don't succeed, attempt, attempt again.

ACROSS

1 Cause of power outages
9 "Key Largo" star
15 Arm of the Atlantic
16 Mimosa tree, for one
17 Where to catch some rays
18 Slipped into
19 Line of kitchen furniture from Neverland?
21 Lisa, to Bart
22 "___ that the truth!"
23 Prague populace
27 Eyeglass frames
28 Bank offerings
31 "Good Times" actress Esther
32 Handmaid's story
33 Hawaii's "Valley Isle"
34 Possible site of water pollution?
37 Queen album "At the ___"
38 Meander
39 Typewriter type
40 Old Russian map abbr.
41 Cleans the floor
42 "Venus" singer Frankie
43 Health store offering
44 Big diamond
45 Wall hangings in the Museum of Obsolete Media?
51 Like Wonder Woman or Superman
52 New Testament letters
54 LP track
55 More animated
56 Accessed, with "into"
57 Like grapes that don't crunch

DOWN

1 "Survivor" survivors
2 Chicken pen
3 First name in detective stories
4 "At once!" in the OR
5 Beats wheat
6 Underworld boss
7 Commits to another hitch
8 Baby's first word, perhaps
9 Life's valleys
10 Squirrel's stash
11 "Not another word!"
12 Teen concern
13 Fibber's stories
14 Little shaver
20 Used hammers
23 Baby beds
24 Some basketball defenses
25 Kind of statesman
26 Driver or putter
27 Wet season events
28 Find fault with unnecessarily
29 Because of
30 Squad car sound
32 Foil
33 Kunis of "Jupiter Ascending"
35 Double-dealing
36 Did a 180
41 Why you do it
42 On the go
43 Scout unit
44 Easy ___ (effortless)
45 Miles of film
46 Cut short
47 Slippery swimmers
48 "___ never work!"
49 Peace Nobelist Wiesel
50 Lays eyes on
51 Elev.
53 AARP members

ACROSS

1 Panhandle
4 Unwelcome surprise
8 Checkers moves
13 Third-longest river in Europe
14 Like some shoppes
15 See 44 Across
16 Steroid Era suspensions, e.g.?
19 Made level
20 Second person
21 Condensation
22 Sign of an infection
24 Ecotourist's journey
27 Falafel bread
29 NFL VIPs
33 Square with reality
37 Lavish
39 Weird and scary
40 Demeanor of the bride and groom?
43 Terse concession speech
44 Basketball's "The Big Aristotle" (with 15-A)
45 Before long
46 Large chamber groups
48 Sit next to
50 13 Down competitor
52 Incredibly arid
57 Swear words
60 Place to have a pint
62 Without a friend
63 Did some housekeeping for Harry?
67 Skateboarder's feat
68 Big fish
69 County town
70 Rhone city
71 Hotel visit
72 Morn's counterpart

DOWN

1 Unafraid
2 Went slowly
3 First American in orbit
4 You can read this while driving
5 In toto
6 Without purpose
7 Stopping point
8 Garfield's owner
9 Spanish article
10 Heal up
11 Exhibit nervousness
12 Didst kill
13 50 Across competitor
17 Little horn sound
18 Spanish coin
23 Antlered beasts
25 Meadow moms
26 Knocking joints?
28 Initial letter
30 Rubik of cube fame
31 Anti-crime act of 1970
32 Not missed
33 Castor or Pollux
34 Move, to Century 21
35 Asian soup noodle
36 Henry Ford's only son
38 Fiery horses
41 Bitty lead-in
42 One goal of feminism
47 Nob Hill force
49 Asgard bigwig
51 University in Medford, MA
53 Five-spice spice
54 Zellweger of cinema
55 Highway through the Yukon
56 Russian denial
57 Worshiped object
58 "___ noted"
59 Viking Ship Museum city
61 Period
64 ___ lizzie
65 Some Va. Tech grads
66 Genetic letters

191 THE CARPENTER by Mark McClain
"If it doesn't fit, try a bigger hammer."

ACROSS

1 Have the chutzpah
5 "Not now!"
10 Cross over
14 Slugger Gattis
15 Farsi speaker
16 Emilia's murderer
17 Carrie Fisher role
18 Where your heart is
19 Laced up
20 I grew worried after hearing the tongue-in-groove carpenter I hired was ___.
23 Segovia's instrument
24 Tithonus' abductor
25 Cerastes
28 Morn's counterpart
29 "Water for Elephants" novelist Gruen
32 Takes the edge off
34 My fears were put to rest when I saw the ___ job he did on the entranceway.
36 Both: Prefix
39 Lucy in "Charlie's Angels"
40 "Freedom ___ free!"
41 I liked his work and paid him more than he asked for. Unmoved, he appeared ___.
46 More scrawny
47 Malamute's meal
48 Vacation location
51 Pop the question
52 Court
54 Sitcom luminary
56 After he left, I asked myself if he was simply ungrateful or ___.
60 Beginning on
62 Prolonged battle
63 Nymph who loved Narcissus
64 Annoying ___-calls
65 "Trick" joints
66 Supply/demand subj.
67 Ornery character
68 Green lights
69 Founding editor of "The New Yorker"

DOWN

1 Result of global warming, perhaps
2 Connecticut in Washington
3 Gorp element
4 Pass, on the Hill
5 Not idiomatic
6 Get one's ducks in ___
7 Infield cover
8 Happen next
9 1970 John Wayne western
10 In ___ (undisturbed)
11 Compadres
12 Mature, in a sense
13 One of Wynken's pals
21 Toothy file
22 1952 Winter Olympics host
26 Shock or awe
27 ["I'm over here!"]
30 Informal move
31 Santa ___ Park
33 "Topaz" novelist
34 Apple assistant
35 Go head-to-head
36 "I Do, I Do, I Do, I Do, I Do" group
37 Bossy comments
38 Illegal money transfers
42 Mountain ___ (sodas)
43 Stalin banished him
44 Suitability
45 Play the hobo
48 Siding alternative
49 Sympathetic feeling
50 Destructive felonies
53 Venture a view
55 Offensive look
57 Some radar blips
58 Cask dregs
59 "A Death in the Family" novelist
60 Hail Mary path
61 Worthless bit

HEAVY BLOWS by Gene Newman
47 Across is Spanish for "devil."

ACROSS

1 Fishing foul-up
5 Generic's lack
10 Comedian Carolla
14 Great Depression vagabond
15 Hawaiian porch
16 Rake
17 Code type
18 Behaves
19 Mrs. Dithers
20 Straits of Magellan wind
22 Wind over the Persian Gulf states
24 Tactful summons
25 Devastate
26 Like a pact with the Devil
29 Feudal farmers
33 Lariat section
34 Sudden attacks
35 Caught stealing
36 Brookings, for one: Abbr.
37 "Common Sense" author
38 Unlike Miss Manners
39 Canadian Thanksgiving mo.
40 Ore deposits
41 Scorpion secretion
42 Locale of the simoom wind
44 Gentlemen: Abbr.
45 Relaxation
46 Place for a frog
47 San Francisco Bay Area wind
50 Baja California winds
54 The lowdown
55 On drugs
57 Cambodian capital
58 Name up in lights
59 Jury
60 Hudson Bay tribe
61 Chile's cape
62 Alfred Nobel, e.g.
63 London park

DOWN

1 "Arms and the Man" playwright
2 Sushi wrap
3 "Green Mansions" hero
4 One of an end zone pair
5 It rhymes with frowsy
6 Capital near Casablanca
7 Once again
8 Dissenter's vote
9 Advise against
10 Specialized knowledge
11 Condemnation
12 Distinctive atmosphere
13 American plan amenity
21 Emerald ___
23 Serpent's warning
25 Bit attachments
26 Coalition
27 The time being
28 Shade-tolerant perennial
29 Comanche colt
30 Buy and sell, at times
31 Elizabeth I's house
32 Mushroom parts
34 Poker challenge
37 Thick fogs
38 Partner of development
40 Saltimbocca meat
41 Ed Norton wore one
43 Getting a second chance
44 Clothes press
46 Like windmills
47 Spoon's running mate
48 Division preposition
49 Way off
50 Trig function
51 Well-ventilated
52 Requirement
53 Protected side
56 Sententious saying

193 THE KING IN THE JUNGLE   by Gene Newman
The king can be found at 17 Across.

ACROSS

1 Speck
5 Test results
10 Heroic narrative
14 Gaelic name for Scotland
15 Cation opposite
16 Always
17 Star of "Red Dust" and 40 Across
19 Rajah's consort
20 Apollo Theater locale
21 So-called
23 Auburn heads?
26 Turner in "Homecoming"
27 Fire extinguisher gas
30 Lord's Prayer opener
32 Members of the lower feudal class
35 Road shoulder
36 Poisonous shrubs
38 Martini request
39 Billy goat's bluff?
40 1953 remake of "Red Dust"
41 Martin in "Goodbye, Columbus"
42 Welding type
43 Lessens
44 Bigger than a ding
45 Small bony fish
47 Musical syllable
48 Birdcage fixture
49 Franklin's research tool
51 Roast beef ___
53 "Rocket" of baseball
56 Pricy Swiss watches
60 Part
61 "Red Dust" star
64 Without enthusiasm
65 "The Hunter" constellation
66 Bluefin or yellowfin
67 Ottoman governors
68 Gridiron gains or losses
69 Appear

DOWN

1 Speed-of-sound ratio
2 Pueblo jar
3 Ski lift
4 Royal bailiwick
5 Molten rock
6 Japan's JAL rival
7 Tease
8 Caffeine source
9 Fishline leader
10 Peaceful
11 Star of 40 Across
12 Kelly or Autry
13 Desiccated
18 Enthusiastic
22 Roundup rope
24 Milky Way component
25 Island west of Java
27 Arafat's successor
28 Mobilize anew
29 Star of 40 Across
31 "Castor et Pollux" composer
33 Bygone French currency
34 Elec. instrument
36 Weep loudly
37 "Survivor" network
40 Lusterless surface
44 Abandons
46 Lord Nelson's crewmen
48 Nike rival
50 Take pleasure in
52 Glynis in "Mary Poppins"
53 Nursery bed
54 Comstock's discovery
55 Evening, in Roma
57 Epoxy
58 First-class
59 Dog-paddled
62 "Londonderry ___"
63 Tacit agreement

ACROSS

1 Grungy one
5 Court room?
8 Tree ocelot of rain forests
14 Monkey puzzle, for one
15 River inlet
16 "Relax, recruits!"
17 Wedding reception song
18 Nail polish brand
19 Eucalyptus eaters
20 Drummer's hat?
23 8 Across, for one
24 Get-go
25 Stable section
28 Sticker in your sock
29 Miss America accessory
33 Lawyer's drawers?
37 Female in a hutch
38 Oblivious
39 Movie munchie
41 Citi Field slugger
42 Hiker's jacket?
44 Burgoo or ragout
46 Stand-up comic Jo
47 "Monkey see, monkey do"
48 Fairylike
51 K1 and K2: Abbr.
52 Dad's three-piece attire?
57 "Slumdog Millionaire" setting
58 Donaldson dragon of kiddie lit
59 Clark thinks she's super
61 "___ Mr. Postman": Carpenters
62 Couch topic
63 Emulate Rembrandt or Durer
64 Sci-fi and fantasy
65 Grass that comes in a roll
66 Drink after saying "Kampai!"

DOWN

1 Intelligence seeker
2 Like a bad handshake
3 Start of a fairy tale
4 Almond pastry
5 Tiler's mortar
6 Golfer's jitters
7 "But of course, Camille"
8 Fierce sharks
9 Right a wrong
10 Shows emotion
11 Swanky gathering
12 "Get on it!"
13 "Owner of a Lonely Heart" band
21 Visit in person
22 As a response
25 Urban eyesores
26 Ideology
27 Colorful mineral
28 Burglary
30 Napping
31 More in need of a massage
32 "Give me liberty, or give me death!" source
34 "I'm frrrreeeezing!"
35 Watch chain
36 Water balloon fight sounds
40 Alternative to tablets
43 Loses electrons
45 Hotel suite amenity
49 Legal demise
50 Wendy's order
51 "Good gravy!"
52 Act the crybaby
53 "I couldn't agree more!"
54 For take-out
55 Tiny bit
56 Lyme disease carrier
57 Fuel-efficiency meas.
60 Pronoun for the sea

195 DOUBLE HOCKEY STICKS   by Lee Taylor
. . . sixteen double hockey sticks, to be exact.

ACROSS

1 Anne in "The Brave"
6 Christmas tree
9 Part of Tel Aviv
14 Stonehenge worshiper
15 Wedding words
16 Enjoyed with relish
17 Bridge fees
18 ___ canto
19 Russian pancakes
20 Beach sport
23 Whistler's mother
24 One of the primary colors
25 Table protector
27 Coffeehouse connection
30 Some golf tourneys
32 Stallone, to pals
33 Stroll around
35 Mel who voiced Bugs Bunny
37 "Do tell!"
38 No. on a business card
39 Windy City airport
43 Sing "The Lonely Goatherd"
45 Scrabble pieces
46 Give it ___
49 Constabulary
52 Genie holder
53 Keep an eye on
55 Barrister Clooney
57 Coleslaw, e.g.
58 Leading public opinion survey
63 Cybercafe denizens
65 Small, to rappers
66 "Twilight" vampire Biers
67 Enter a freeway
68 Summer sign
69 "Coronation Ode" composer
70 County near London
71 Setter that's not a dog
72 Quench

DOWN

1 Home theater component
2 Smack or switch ending
3 Select the best
4 Jed Clampett, for one
5 Detroit dud
6 McGee of radio days
7 Fresh thought
8 Attendance check
9 Boxer's punch
10 Rand McNally book
11 Deceptive moves
12 Tornado shape
13 It's buzzing with activity
21 "Fer sure!"
22 Texas mesa
26 Often ___ (half the time)
27 Has been
28 Little terror
29 Comey's former org.
31 Manuscript marks
34 Skip the big wedding
36 Take this to cool down?
38 Juicy memoirs
40 Menu words
41 "Everybody Hurts" band
42 Cassandra's curse
44 "The Whistling Season" author
46 Take for granted
47 False appearances
48 Directives
50 Choose, in class
51 Big bird
54 Brink
56 After, à la française
59 Place or stead
60 Fonda on "The Vampire Diaries"
61 Security breach
62 Ancient harp
64 Mae West play

196 THEMELESS by Erik Agard
33 Across hosted the Jeux de la Francophonie in 2005.

ACROSS

1 Side wager
8 Went long
15 Consequence
16 Season opener
17 Play-fight with open hands
18 Yellow raisin
19 Fish used in Nitsume sauce
20 "American Tragedy" setting
22 Acadia automaker
23 Animals in a Baha Men hit
25 Silly
26 Order in the court
27 "Code Geass" art form
29 33% of Rin Tin Tin
30 "We ___ Overcome"
31 Magazine holder on planes
33 Niger's capital
34 2016 Rihanna hit
35 "Godmother of Punk" Joan
36 "___ touch!"
39 Holy water creature?
43 Make whole
44 ___-Boy recliner
45 Estée Lauder subsidiary
46 Some border areas: Abbr.
47 Reeling
49 Bed support
50 "That's show ___!"
51 It's found in a freezer or bathtub
53 Port-au-Prince pal
54 Vocalist on "Use Your Illusion"
56 Test that it's okay to get an E on?
58 Chew toy?
59 Order for the court jester
60 Ancestor of 4K
61 Lies

DOWN

1 Pretended to be
2 "First and foremost . . ."
3 Earache
4 "Angel dust"
5 Circus clown Barnett
6 Smiley, e.g.
7 Phone-induced affliction
8 Tree substances
9 Waters of Rome
10 Valueless
11 Blotto
12 Make Wil Wheaton hit a new low?
13 Shipping metric
14 "Amen!"
21 Foul
24 Calendar line
26 "See if I care"
28 Dark hardwood
30 Alaska's first capital
32 Life imitates it
33 Japanese IT giant
35 Popular Salt Lake City mascot
36 Spa treatment
37 Neat, at the bar
38 Buffet restaurant chain
39 Hedgerow puzzle
40 Chills
41 Sushi bar appetizer
42 West Coast paper
44 Horse house
47 Medicated
48 Self-congratulatory cry
51 Capital home to Souq Waqif
52 Take another hitch
55 Map path: Abbr.
57 That, in Tejas

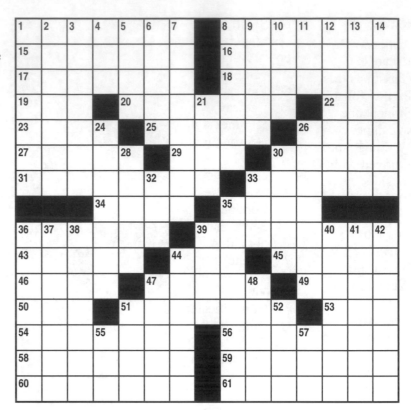

ACROSS

1 Italian white bread
9 This isn't their first rodeo
15 Bank deposit?
16 "___, My God, to Thee"
17 Creole dish
19 Number of monosyllabic U.S. states
20 Stack of chips at the table
21 Wax despondent
22 Sel source
23 Zucchini's British cousin
24 Impress
25 Source of inedible acorns
26 Like a spork
27 How one should shake
28 Passover feasts
29 Comedian ___ Howery
30 Notre Dame's patron
31 Convince of
32 Zebra giraffes
33 "Humble" rapper
34 Key for Still's "Song of a New Race"
35 State until 1991
36 Moves unproudly
37 One-named "Love Galore" singer
40 Boxing Day mo.
41 Masonry finish
42 Dark Magic spell
43 Rival successor of Babel Fish
47 Travel option in France
48 Newfangled
49 Unforested grassland
50 Orderly quality

DOWN

1 Bounce
2 "The L Word" creator Chaiken
3 Cabinetry wood
4 Kiddo
5 Forum farewell
6 Beijing's "Gate of Heavenly Peace"
7 Maki dish
8 "Git!"
9 Currently airing
10 Some Christmas lights
11 ___ es Salaam, Tanzania
12 Chain gang group
13 Splashdown operation
14 Rock strata
18 "Now I see"
23 Follow suit
24 Aloft
25 One of five in Islam
26 Paces
27 Incidental music
28 Grammy-winning Outkast album
29 Let
30 Cosmetology study
31 Unappealing liquids
32 Greek vowel
34 Surplus
36 Monumental slab
37 Battier of basketball
38 Relative vorticity symbols
39 Rink feats
41 Mess up
44 Cumberland ___
45 Alvin York's rank: Abbr.
46 Vietnam Memorial designer

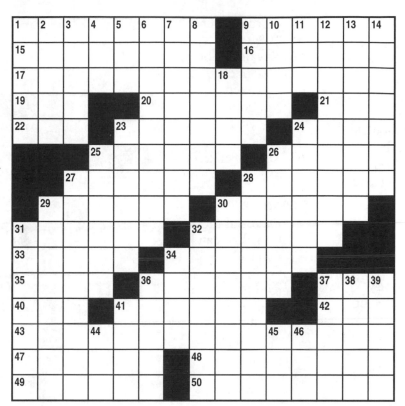

198 THEMELESS by Erik Agard
10 Down was written by Smokey Robinson and Ronald White.

ACROSS

1 Small earthquake
11 La Jolla school
15 Singer with four Grammys and 24 Junos
16 Perambulate perturbedly
17 Word on a loading screen
18 Try
19 Show
20 Take on slopes
21 Irene of "Sparkle"
22 Honorary adjective on campus
25 More genuine
27 Timely hands-free device
30 Holders
33 Computer that's a garment backwards
34 Printer Estienne
35 Followers of "walk" or "slip"
36 It comes after ex
38 Channel that's "Positively Entertaining"
39 Wolverine relative
41 Canadian loonies
42 A Tribe Called Quest rapper Phife ___
43 Compete in a digital strength contest
46 Mythical figure in the Versace logo
47 OK people
51 City on Utah Lake
52 Word of silence
55 "Well . . ."
56 Navajo endonym
57 Meteor showers?
60 ___ noche
61 Not going anywhere
62 In case
63 They open a lot of doors for you

DOWN

1 Flavor of much Canadian candy
2 Legalese for "with respect to a thing"
3 Benjamin Franklin in "Prison Break"
4 Contents of sleeves
5 Subtitle of the 1978 horror film "Damien"
6 Wild boar genus
7 "The Resident" sets, for short
8 Peeper part
9 Swished or holed
10 The Temptations' first #1 hit
11 Fancy-schmancy
12 Declarer of independence in 2017
13 Batman baddie
14 Abandoning ship
23 "Weekend! WHOOO!"
24 Aspire to
26 Reminder
28 French critic Hippolyte
29 What passwords provide
30 One seen in Dr. Scholl's ads
31 Increasing
32 Some honor roll members
36 Spheroids
37 What ":" can mean
40 Beef taste-alike
42 One end of the Oresund Bridge
44 Iroquoian strings
45 Wear out your welcome
48 Ooky
49 "___ Day People": Lightfoot
50 Sudden obstacles
53 Wing bone
54 Gaping mouths
58 Turner of Southampton
59 Emmy-nominated role for Sandra Oh

199 BROKEN by Erik Agard
Sing along with cowboy Scruggs while solving this one.

ACROSS

1 Purple-red hybrid fruit
8 Roughs up
13 Like some doctorates
15 Topped a golf ball
16 From the beginning
17 Take for granted
18 Camping shelters
19 Jingoistic dichotomy
21 Pizza request
24 ___ out a living
26 Tennis Hall-of-Famer since 2009
27 Drive
32 Like unfilleted haddock
34 Android counterpart
35 "Who knocked out Laila Ali?" reply
36 Birdie whacker
40 Super Tuesday word
41 School near Utah Lake
42 A side on Abbey Road?
43 Pops, to tots
44 Jeans label
46 World's shortest river
47 Joey Bishop's frequent "Tonight Show" role
50 Virtual house cat
54 Source of a shot from the hip?
57 Truck meet
58 Wikipedia is this
61 Country singer Jason
62 Prepaid Verizon arrangement
63 Device holder
64 Angela in "Malcolm X"

DOWN

1 "Awesome!" in '90s slang
2 Cerebral division
3 Accidental
4 One is named after Maia
5 Midlife ___
6 Breakfast morsel
7 Prefix for pod
8 Knowles clothing line
9 Coadjutant: Abbr.
10 "Not so fast"
11 It's ripe when green
12 Spoon handle
14 Taunt to Scruggs and circled grid words?
15 Dallas cagers
20 Shady, in (palindromic) slang
22 Dresden denial
23 Turn into curds
24 Left the beach?
25 Symbol of Australia
28 ___ turtle soup
29 Place for pots, but not pans
30 Calendario leaf
31 Don't mess with
33 Wedding reception song
37 "Don't you love this?"
38 Novgorod negative
39 "What's the ___?"
44 "Well, wow!"
45 Muslim theology students
48 Au courant
49 Open-handed rebukes
50 Get ready to pass in a hurry?
51 Texter's "carpe diem"
52 "Bag Lady" singer
53 Where Eve got snaked
55 Crate part
56 Ohio college town
59 Cam Newton's dance
60 Diminutive suffix

1 and 62 Across share clues, but not answers.

ACROSS

1 Drove home
9 Epicure's pride
15 A bit much
16 Arthurian paradise
17 Trust
18 Brush up on
19 TV beatnik Maynard G. ___
20 Bad lighters?
22 Aussie colleges
24 Russian Orthodox saint
25 Stuck in a scrapbook
28 Forest canopy
32 Truck routes
34 Spile a maple tree
35 Mireille of "World War Z"
36 "Strange Magic" group
37 Amazon's origin
38 "Hey Diddle Diddle" creature
39 Like many newlywed couples
43 Le monocle de mon oncle, for example
45 Lint locales
46 Tick off
47 Eighteen-wheeler
48 Anti-clog device
52 Surefooted animals
56 Weasel out
57 Summer vacation place
59 "The nerve!"
60 Kinda
61 X-ray vision and such
62 Drove home

DOWN

1 Attack through the media
2 Say so
3 Prompt beginning
4 Testimonials
5 He was Capt. Davies in "Roots"
6 Slip into
7 Atahualpa's people
8 At no time, in verse
9 One with convictions
10 Pays back
11 Calf catcher
12 Malt beverages
13 Just right
14 Tips
21 Rather
23 Fingers
25 Gun, to a gumshoe
26 Needle
27 Vermont ski resort
28 Anklebone
29 Funny Cheri
30 Cole Porter title city
31 Taters
33 Advertising tactic
37 Teaches a lesson to
39 Codependent one
40 Tops on the beach
41 "A pox upon thee!"
42 All together
44 Feel sorrow
47 All gone
48 Faucet fault
49 City N of Carson City
50 De novo
51 Sale words
53 Male issue
54 Highlands tongue
55 Open position
58 Rhine tributary

201 THEMELESS by Harvey Estes
There's a clue pair at 30 and 41 Across.

ACROSS

1 Biting, as wit
5 Breaks new ground
10 Difficult situations
14 Superman's lady
15 Back to the present
16 "Flying Scotsman" Liddell
17 Barge feature
19 Sommelier's offering
20 Foil giant
21 Look at
23 Tripping and clipping
25 State of high alarm
26 Bubba Blue's friend
28 Ecclesiastic robe
29 Queen Aleta's son
30 'Fraid so
36 Procedural units
39 "Culpa" starter
40 Wheel turners
41 Frayed so
44 Poet's before
45 Las Vegas roller
46 Powell in "Born to Dance"
49 Woo with music
54 Barbecue sites
55 Up to the belt
57 Thin pancake
59 Maine, to Monet
60 Vision type
62 Kind of base
63 Prankster in "The Tempest"
64 Brief moments
65 Catchall abbreviation
66 Down and out
67 Genealogist's diagram

DOWN

1 Sports car, briefly
2 Elicit
3 Where a boxer sits
4 Bypass road repairs, e.g.
5 Golf tutor
6 "Why don't we!"
7 Playful aquatic critter
8 Put pen to paper
9 Down the road
10 Compact disk case
11 Heed the alarm
12 Insignificant
13 Hint for a hound
18 Barn dance seat
22 Crimean seaport
24 Puncture sound
26 Fleet
27 Grant's ___
31 Stephen in "Blackthorn"
32 Highly unusual
33 Olive, vis-à-vis Nana Oyl
34 Rocket science industry
35 River in NW Belgium
37 Place for a bust
38 Superdome star
42 Poker-faced
43 Cambridge isle
47 Unit price word
48 Run in
49 Garbo, for one
50 Sandwich-board words
51 Rope with a loop
52 Model A tractor maker
53 Like many a Poe tale
56 Patchy in color
58 Additional
61 Keep the vodka flowing

ACROSS

1 Sired, in the Scriptures
6 2016 First Family member
11 Scrabble 3-pointers
14 Official under Caesar
15 Phoenix origin
16 Caldron
17 Fictional cottage dwellers
19 USBP sister org.
20 Mafia code of silence
21 Groan provoker
22 Rapper Flavor ___
23 Augusta tournament
25 Pinochle's cousin
27 "Hud" director
29 Brand of spaghetti sauce
30 Air-gun ammo
33 Drum type
35 Flanders capital
38 Eric in "Hulk"
40 German folklorist brothers
42 Trillion: Comb. form
43 Chew noisily
45 Graphic puzzle
47 Nod off
48 Thready streak
50 Morse code "T"
51 Soft and fluffy plus
54 Litmus paper, for one
59 Yodeler's response
60 Oft referenced iceberg section
62 Muse of astronomy
63 Floral neckwear
64 Enchanted device of 11 Down
66 Do needlework
67 Seawater
68 InDesign company
69 Brittany burro
70 Augment
71 Big name in briefs

DOWN

1 Cleaning tool of 32 Down
2 Swelling
3 Bestows
4 Danger signal
5 Jamboree participants
6 Timberjack tool
7 In short order
8 Landscaper's planting
9 "Playboy" founder
10 Pack animal
11 32 Down's nemesis
12 Major Asian gaming center
13 Carell in "The Big Short"
18 Adventurous
22 "Fifty-four forty or ___"
24 First Super Bowl MVP
26 Zig's pal
28 Gave it a shot
30 "Doctor Who" network
31 "Phooey!"
32 Surprise guest of 17 Across
34 Put in jail
36 PAC that's packing
37 Spile a maple tree
39 Organic acid
41 The Hirshhorn, for one
44 Air-pump letters
46 Islamic law
49 Loud firecracker
51 U.S. airline
52 "All Is Lost" setting
53 Unyielding
55 Italy's largest lake
56 Former home of the Astros
57 Zeus turned her to stone
58 Container weights
61 Pub order
64 Wharton School deg.
65 Corporate VIP

1	2	3	4	5		6	7	8	9	10		11	12	13
14						15						16		
17			18									19		
20						21				22				
23					24		25		26					
				27			28		29					
30	31	32		33					34		35			36	37
38			39		40					41		42			
43				44		45					46		47		
			48			49		50							
51	52					53		54				55	56	57	58
59					60		61		62					
63					64				65					
66				67							68			
69				70							71			

203

MUSIC MAN by Gene Newman
. . . and that music man can be found at 10 Down.

ACROSS

1 Carefree play
5 Shout of joy or hunger
11 Dit dit dit, dah dah dah, dit dit dit
14 Declare under oath
15 Roughen
16 "Horton Hears a ___": Seuss
17 Teamster's wheels
18 More revered or expensive
19 It's crude to begin with
20 "Shall We Dance" number*
22 Church council
24 ___ creek without a paddle
25 Slough off
26 AC inventor
29 Humdingers
32 Greenish blue
33 Waikiki wear
36 Uncomfortably damp
37 Bottom line
38 Medical school model
39 Reproach of yore
40 Beret's kin
41 Widely revered
42 England's Wash tributary
43 "My Day" author Roosevelt
45 Tote: Var.
46 Pluvious precip
47 At a right angle to the keel
50 Clothes fanciers
52 "A Damsel in Distress" song*
56 Asian waist wrapper
57 Demanding
59 "Name of the ___": ABBA
60 Huck's pal
61 Ne'er-ending
62 Portent
63 Ball bearing item?
64 Make a lawn lusher
65 Hibernation habitats

DOWN

1 Coarse file
2 [see other side]
3 Office directive
4 Cowslip genus
5 "I ___ thought of that!"
6 Jamaican black magic
7 Swap
8 Challenge
9 Elgar's "Coronation ___"
10 Music man linked with clues*
11 Song from "Funny Face"*
12 One of Pittsburgh's three rivers
13 Auctioneer's word
21 Anti-pollution gp.
23 Bronx Bombers network
25 Hedgehog of video games
26 It may be acquired
27 Same as
28 "Porgy and Bess" song*
29 Internet reference, informally
30 Boost
31 Win an entire series
33 Breakfast side
34 "Are you ___ out?"
35 Family
38 Clergyman
42 "Heavens!"
44 "How relaxing!"
45 Droop
47 In flames
48 Maid of Orleans
49 Did some Halloween mischief
50 Suffragette Lucretia
51 "Bolero" instrument
52 Gives the boot
53 Jane Goodall, for one
54 "You said it!"
55 Longings
58 Brunched

QUARTERLY REPORT by Gary Larson
21 Down was named after the covered wagons used to migrate west.

ACROSS

1 Broadway's "Five Guys Named ___"
4 AstroTurf alternative
9 Show place
14 Its point is to make holes
15 Blockhead
16 Speeder's bane
17 MSNBC rival
18 Propensity for imperfection
20 Garage sale warning
22 Alaskan islander
23 Mint flavor
27 Function
30 Rat
31 Deliver
33 Fish-eating bird
36 Nobleman
37 Certain retriever
42 Natural soother
43 Escargot
44 Insinuates
47 Proves false
51 Sweet drink
52 Basic gymnastics move: Var.
55 Mogul emperor of India
56 Animal shelter
57 Vivaldi subjects/TITLE
63 Magic org.
64 ___-frutti
65 Antique shop item
66 Dump
67 Dress up
68 Upright
69 Cut out

DOWN

1 Amazon parrots
2 Takes pride in
3 Pacific phenomenon
4 Image-file format
5 Nutritional inits.
6 Be indisposed
7 Green energy
8 Attendance counter
9 Like the Godhead
10 "Stop right there!"
11 "Big Daddy" Amin
12 Vole relative
13 Moistureless
19 Cold one
21 Cigars
24 Gusto
25 Boxing venue
26 Family hand-me-downs?
27 Smoothie fruit
28 Fix
29 Be a snitch
32 Erotic
34 West end?
35 18th Hebrew letter
37 Heroic tale
38 Argued
39 Some learning
40 Docking spot
41 Priestly garb
45 Invites to enter
46 It follows You online?
48 Shade
49 "Cat" cartoonist
50 Hair piece
53 Bodyshop franchise
54 1976 Raffi song
55 Museo holdings
57 Uploading initials
58 Lord's Prayer starter
59 Shoshonean
60 Vein stuff
61 "Delta of Venus" author
62 Settler's building material

1	2	3	■	4	5	6	7	8	■	9	10	11	12	13
14			■	15					■	16				
17			■	18				19						
20			21		■	22					■			
23			24	25	26					■	27	28	29	
30						■	31		32					
■	■	33			34	35		■	36					
37	38	39					40	41						
42				■	43					■	■	■		
44			45	46	■	47				48	49	50		
51		■	52		53	54		■						
■	■	55				■	■	56						
57	58	59			60	61	62	■	63					
64			■	65			■	66						
67			■	68			■	69						

205 THEMELESS by Harvey Estes
Most forget about Amazon's humble beginning at 20 Across.

ACROSS

1 Fur tycoon
6 Start of a Shakespeare title
10 Like a dungeon
14 Western director Sergio
15 Nothing, in Nantes
16 Weapon fer shootin'
17 Bar serving
18 Flat formation
19 Pennsylvania city
20 Amazon's beginning
23 Made to seem better than it is
24 Ozone layer pollutant, briefly
27 Theology topic
28 Miami team
29 Battle axe
31 Perfume sources
35 Colorful seed cover
36 John work
37 Gets ready to return home from vacation
41 Mistake
44 Mop of a sort
45 Baba flavoring
46 "Bambi" character
47 Impossible to refuse
52 One who moves a lot?
56 Domed church recess
57 Grip on a sword
58 Heep of fiction
59 Makes a doily
60 Carbonic compound
61 Not windy
62 Young falcon
63 Fit to stand trial
64 Letter opener, at times

DOWN

1 As well
2 Penn name
3 Crossing charge
4 Studio alert
5 Clown accessory
6 It encircles a limb
7 Rest atop
8 South African monarchy
9 More sinuous
10 Nutrition expert
11 Ricardo's rice
12 Bête ___
13 Hit below the belt, perhaps
21 Gulf leader
22 "The Lion King" lout
24 Blacken
25 Ticket to ride
26 Cut coupons
30 Not responsible
32 Fries, maybe
33 "The Dragons of ___": Sagan
34 Lee of baking
38 Big beer buy
39 Potato noshes
40 Six-stanza verse form
41 Crisp candy
42 Service accompanying an oil change
43 Mötley Crüe duo
47 Mad as hops
48 Wreak vengeance
49 Dreadlocks wearer, for short
50 Goshawk nail
51 Everglades habitué
53 Home of hurling
54 Ride org.
55 1954 sci-fi film

ACROSS

1 Pull an all-nighter
5 Pro ___ (in proportion)
9 Part of the Mass
14 "It's ___ vu all over again!"
15 Big party nights
16 "The Audacity of Hope" author
17 Seal in the juices
18 Leave at the alter
19 Try to bite
20 **English learner's mnemonic said to Alexa: Part 1**
23 Sendai sash
24 "You bet," in Monte Carlo
25 **Mnemonic: Part 2**
33 "Thank God ___ Country Boy"
34 Attention
35 One with lots of bills
37 Cookout locale
40 Put a halt to
42 It helps you see plays
43 Taco holders
45 Feedbag morsel
47 The "Not interested, thanks" competition?
48 **Alexa's response: Part 1**
52 ISP option
53 Bake sale sponsor
54 **Alexa's response: Part 2**
61 Gulf War ally
62 Makes do with
63 Mermaid feature
65 Shenanigan
66 Shout to a line
67 Philanthropist Cornell
68 Raid targets
69 Catches on to
70 Escape slowly

DOWN

1 Boom box inserts
2 Coral habitat
3 Cracked open
4 Strand on an island
5 Jump for joy
6 Old Hebrew month
7 Prefix with prompter
8 Minute Maid Park team
9 Bounded area
10 Somewhat
11 Puppy pickup point
12 Dorsey in "Django Unchained"
13 "Unforgettable" Cole
21 Some degree of control
22 Czech Rep. neighbor
25 Market corrections
26 Largest cornhusker city
27 Do a greenhouse job
28 "Insecure" star Issa
29 ". . . then again"
30 Conduit bend
31 "Merrily, we roll ___ . . ."
32 Let up
36 Fantasy baseball
38 Notre Dame is on one
39 Seoul event of 2018
41 Patriotic woman's org.
44 5, on a scale of 1–10
46 Key employees?
49 Like some heroes
50 Simpson trial judge
51 City on the Loire
54 Window piece
55 Wheel-worn ways
56 Ready for press
57 Revelatory cry
58 Passage of scripture
59 Hedgerow puzzle
60 Land of Yeats
61 Pine flow
64 Indy 500 unit

207 HOW AN AQUARIUS APOLOGIZES   by E.G. Harris
This is the dawning of the adage of Aquarius.

ACROSS

1 Movie promo
7 On the QT
15 Rub the wrong way
16 Less respectful
17 Threads
18 Absolutely isolated
19 **Start of an Aquarius apology**
21 Deighton of spy thrillers
22 Suffix with law
23 Even once
27 One of the Waltons
29 Cover with graffiti
34 Cakes' partner
35 Casual Friday wear
37 One covering a hanging
39 **More of apology**
41 Brillo, basically
44 Put on display
48 Barn swallow?
49 Put on
51 Hosiery shade
52 Past partners
54 Carol contraction
56 BB propellant
57 **End of apology**
63 Person of interest?
66 Husk content
67 Like a ghost town
68 The one that got away
69 Large rabbit
70 Becomes compost

DOWN

1 Fished with a net
2 Truck-stop sign
3 Justice Scalia
4 Vaudeville bit
5 George Jetson's son
6 Moved unsteadily
7 Noncommittal phrase
8 Brief plea
9 Takei role
10 Coup d'___
11 French fashion house
12 Carnival setting
13 Ending for velvet
14 Three, in Torino
20 "Don't count on it"
24 Winery fixture
25 Lilly of drugs
26 Camcorder abbr.
28 Cairo artery
30 Banned refrigerant
31 Olympics participant
32 Heart ward, for short
33 Misses the mark
36 Vulcan mind merger
38 "Aren't ___ lucky one!"
40 Lowest birdie
41 "That's all ___ wrote!"
42 Take a toll on
43 Tuber bump
45 Song of the north
46 Field of Chicago
47 Baby bottles
50 Cut calories
53 Actor Max von ___

55 Aesop was one
58 Rembrandt works
59 Bonneville Salt Flats locale
60 Magazine section
61 Let loose
62 Apple not for eating
63 Some savings accts.
64 Animated dog
65 Anka's "___ Beso"

SOUTH OF THE BORDER by Pam Klawitter

The film at 18 Across is based on a 1980s television series.

ACROSS

1 Pistol pop
5 Across-the-board
10 Future CFOs, perhaps
14 Sheltered on the sea
15 Marco Island bird
16 It might be hard to resist
17 "Phooey!"
18 Liam Neeson film (with "The")
19 Balanced
20 Feeling poor
23 Hawaiian diet staple
24 Pitchfork features
25 Area not to hit
31 "Double Stuf" cookies
32 Near East VIPs
33 Phone card
36 Landline feature
37 Debussy subject
38 Tailpipe emission
39 "Darn tootin'!"
40 Publisher Funk
42 Turf grabber
43 "Bottoms up!"
45 Yael's "Orange Is the New Black" role
47 Malleus locale
48 Thoroughly repugnant
55 Cathy in "East of Eden"
56 Roger Rabbit's friends
57 Toni Morrison novel
58 "The Sting" tunes
59 Blasé state

60 One with the keys?
61 Command to Fido
62 Not the brightest bulb
63 Bog fuel

DOWN

1 Grammy winner Erykah
2 Severus Snape portrayer Rickman
3 Howard Wolowitz, for one
4 Source of many an inheritance
5 Michael Jackson hit
6 Piglike "Jabberwocky" creature
7 Gothic arch
8 What there oughta be?
9 Persephone's mother
10 Taboo word
11 Astronomer Tycho ___
12 Choreographer de Mille
13 Crystal-baller
21 Knock-down-drag-outs
22 Isn't up to snuff
25 Whodunit discovery
26 Toledo's lake
27 Perform an axel
28 Muscular guy
29 Gershwin's "Let ___ Cake"
30 White tree
33 Feeder filler
34 1998 computer debut

35 Drug made in labs
38 Reoccurs with a vengeance
40 Hebrides island
41 Hit one out of the park
42 Tête-à-tête
43 Chic
44 Weensie partner
45 Paul of "Lonesome Dove"
46 Europe's second-largest lake
48 Carrie Nation targets
49 Sharpen
50 Take the helm
51 Load to bear
52 Guiding spirit
53 Kind of bargain
54 Like some cherries

2,000 POUNDS OF FUN   by Pam Klawitter
61 Across is based loosely on "The Snow Queen" by Hans Christian Andersen.

ACROSS

1 Spiced milk tea
5 Hardly a he-man
9 It's sometimes certified
13 Deserve
14 Transoceanic ship
15 It's all around you
16 Costume designer's job at the "Abbey"?
19 Graphics file extension
20 Range with llamas
21 Do right by, with "for"
22 Sticks in a recipe
23 Finished off
24 Superhero Atom's favorite sport?
32 Author of "Rosemary's Baby"
33 It controls a pupil
34 Pitcher Halladay
35 Some Rosetta Stone letters
36 Thin-shelled nut
38 Ark unit
39 Pump output
40 Lose zip
41 Leaf of "Ferdinand" fame
42 Gem City daycare centers?
46 Nickname for Isaac
47 Bachelor chaser?
48 Harmony
51 Come to terms
53 Droll one
56 Panther QB Cam hit paydirt?
59 Comet feature
60 Bangor's neighbor
61 "Do You Want to Build a Snowman?" was sung to her
62 "A Little Night Music" heroine
63 Unruly dos
64 Give the go-ahead

DOWN

1 Give up claim to
2 Instrument for a Marx
3 Hera's bellicose son
4 Entrance signs
5 It may be double-hung
6 "Picnic" playwright
7 Prescription drugs, commonly
8 She's paid to play
9 Trophy spot
10 Falcon or Skylark
11 Smooth things out
12 Place for a strike
14 Type of closet
17 Where to make waves
18 Suburb of L.A.
22 Musical Redding
23 Z ___ zebra
24 Argue a case
25 Nerve networks
26 Pistil part
27 Houston campus, for short
28 The ___ of Good Feelings
29 Afghani neighbor
30 Bête ___ (bane)
31 Greek sandwiches
36 Turpentine source
37 Directional suffix
38 Like the driven snow
40 "Lost in Translation" setting
41 Doled out
43 ___-tattle
44 MeTV fare
45 Kind of pad
48 Chinese rival of Nike
49 Average
50 Tape-breaker's cry
51 It might give you a big head
52 It may tame 63 Across
53 Constitutional
54 Italian news agency
55 Outback "howdy!"
57 Pierre, par exemple
58 Neighbor of Virgo

ACROSS

1 Maker of holes
5 Beach in California
10 Bakery buy
14 Gumbo vegetable
15 Excited
16 Hand lotion ingredient
17 TV series on waterpark chutes?
19 Swabs
20 Unlikely Oscar winner
21 French impressionist
22 "Titanic" previews?
25 Keepsakes
28 A while back
29 1996 Madonna musical
30 Headed
31 Myanmar ethnic group
34 C-SPAN offerings?
39 Social connections
40 Collision sound
41 College culinary choice, often
42 Just
44 Downtown sign
45 One-reelers about horse racing?
50 Became an issue
51 Broken up
55 Babushka
56 Low-budget oaters?
58 Prince's school
59 Illegal firing
60 Soba alternative
61 Prefix with byte

62 "Frida" star
63 Chest muscles

DOWN

1 Type of pit
2 Neighbor of Mo.
3 Barber's job
4 Ate
5 Penne and ziti
6 Summer gripe
7 Display
8 Kitten's cry
9 ER drug cases
10 Steamed dish
11 Companionless
12 Rodeo performer
13 Hospital work
18 Prius or Tesla
21 It's often open
23 Big laugh
24 ___ Domini
25 Bank offering, briefly
26 All square
27 Tops
30 Dashboard abbr.
31 Censure
32 Home of Iowa State
33 Ain't correct?
35 Well
36 Potato chip brand
37 Cheesy crust
38 Elevated
42 Olympic skater Baiul
43 Originally
44 Buscemi's "Reservoir Dogs" role
45 "The Rocky Horror Picture Show" heroine
46 Emulate Cicero
47 UFC star McGregor
48 Temper tantrum
49 Like prima ballerinas

52 Murderous suffix
53 Fair-hiring org.
54 Tax info
56 "Do ___ Diddy Diddy" (1964 hit)
57 Notable period

211 BIG AL'S by Gary Larson
The Crimson Tide elephant mascot inspired this theme.

ACROSS

1 Tear channel
5 Not even
11 "Gee whiz!"
14 Morales of "NYPD Blue"
15 Whacky
16 Get older
17 Where an HOV can be found
19 Jazzman
20 In the past
21 Walker, briefly
22 Bowling alley features
24 Nice woman
26 Go over again
27 Where carts may be found
32 Coen brothers Christmas movie
35 Gist
36 Self-proclaimed psychic Geller
37 Beauty parlor
40 Part of TGIF
41 Bette's "divine" nickname
44 Suffer disgrace
47 Where Japanese slot machines can be found
50 Olympic marathoner Joan
51 Hungers (for)
55 Stuck song syndrome
57 Nonalcoholic drink
59 Prankster's projectile
60 Wasikowska in "Albert Nobbs"
61 Where a mosh pit can be found
64 Aggravate
65 Stick together
66 Service station?
67 Cross-shaped
68 "Dwelt ___, forty-niner . . ."
69 Timetable, slangily

DOWN

1 Coffee preference
2 Grammar topic
3 Squash rebound
4 Pinnacle
5 Moisturizer additive
6 Auction cry
7 Chat room abbr.
8 Asian wild ass
9 Poverty
10 Driver's license requirement
11 Balkan republic
12 Thickening agent
13 New Jersey five
18 La Scala offering
23 London art gallery
25 Classic sports cars
26 Distribute differently
28 Switch ups?
29 Windy City transit org.
30 Campus military org.
31 Emerald Isle language
32 Road sign warning
33 Met song
34 Source of a car squeak
38 "How exciting!"
39 Hush-hush govt. group
42 Ed Sullivan had a "really big" one
43 Spanish vacation isle
45 Barkin in "Palindromes"
46 Winter bug
48 Nativity inn problem
49 Seoul food
52 Say something
53 Brusque
54 Filled up
55 Give off
56 Suffix for billion
57 Israeli seaport
58 Activist
62 Author Kesey
63 "Survivior" network

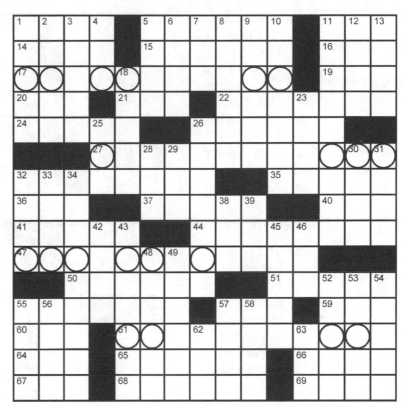

ACROSS

1 Climate change concern: Abbr.
5 Show disrespect
9 Low female singers
14 "But, wait . . ."
15 Bitty partner
16 Tom Clancy's "The Sum of All ___"
17 "Hawaii Five-0" actor
18 One on the move
19 Spy mission
20 Household budget woe
23 Heron's habitat
24 They ring, at times
25 Finished off
28 Put the pedal to the metal
31 R.E.M.'s "Murmur" label
34 Vein pursuits
35 Concerns on the Hill
36 Part of a modern movement
38 Southwest, for one
41 On ___ (comparable)
42 BP subsidiary
43 Finger Lakes loc.
44 NCAA tourney nickname
49 Part of TBS: Abbr.
50 British isles
51 Did a sous-chef's job
54 Merchant ship
57 Girl Scout cookie
60 Fortune's friend
61 Winningham of "Hatfields & McCoys"
62 Montana and Maryland, in Marseilles
63 Peru neighbor: Abbr.
64 Parti-colored
65 Sections off
66 Alpha wave charts
67 Sorts

DOWN

1 Per capita
2 Prospector's filing
3 Honshu port
4 Introverts
5 Endorser's instructions
6 Astride
7 Where to find tweeters
8 Aleppo resident
9 All over again
10 Jeans brand
11 Sea-___ Airport
12 Guatemalan gold
13 Phishing catch
21 Sandbox comeback
22 Display screen
25 "I'll have another!"
26 Lion-colored
27 Aussie couple
29 Part of MPG
30 Level edge
31 Mosque officials
32 Settle an IOU
33 Dallas hockey team
37 Tolkien creature
38 Valiant son
39 Starbucks orders
40 "Cracklin' " girl of song
42 Website revenue source
45 Engage in bullying
46 Swimsuit model Kang
47 PIN money
48 Shrimp dish
52 Digital dispatch
53 Jacobi in "I, Claudius"
54 Schlep
55 Full of oneself
56 Cincy team
57 "___ who?"
58 Essandoh in "Django Unchained"
59 Dame Edna, for one

"WHY BOTHER?" by Pam Klawitter
Whirlaway and Citation are the horses at 55 Across.

ACROSS

1 Mater
4 Japanese motorcycle
10 Body cam wearer
13 "La Bohème" number
15 Wiped out
16 Strand in biology class
17 Humdinger of a jam?
19 Computer key
20 Lissome
21 "A Boy Named Sue" songwriter Silverstein
22 Crossword pirate
23 "Lion King" song "Hakuna ___"
25 Wry superhero?
27 Nashville record label
28 Get one's goat
30 Most miffed
31 Ancient Chinese capital
33 "A Star Is Born" star
36 Ill-mannered
37 Kick-ass training venue?
40 "Freebie and the Bean" star
42 "Slate," for one
43 Ward of "Graves"
47 "Gunsmoke" star
49 Part of some portfolios
51 Soft shoe, briefly
52 Camper's complaint?
55 Jockey with two Triple Crown horses
57 Unveils, poetically
58 Gather in the field
60 Merfolk mermaid
61 Hagen of Broadway
62 Waitstaff's nickname for singer Joel?
64 Creature of habit?
65 "Fighting" Big Ten team
66 Goosefoot relative
67 MLB fielding stats
68 Most like a fox
69 "___ Fledermaus"

DOWN

1 Sargent portrait of a French socialite
2 Creased creations
3 Bunker Hill fighters
4 Ozarks assent
5 "For Your Eyes Only" villain
6 Yeager's breakthrough
7 Inquiring sort
8 Friendly greetings
9 Soda alternative
10 Studied all night
11 Rented out
12 It's often pending
14 Pasta ___ Bolognese
18 Sherpa bugaboo
22 Sugar shack products
24 Acastus sailed on it
26 Regular at Cheers
29 Petruchio's wife
32 Cagers on the sports page
34 Court house?
35 Purple superfood
38 "... wrong ___ many levels!"
39 Home of the Taj Mahal
40 Approached sneakily
41 People of La Paz
44 Sent with a click
45 Rhine siren
46 Altar server
47 Be prevalent
48 Peruse the screen
50 Part of UAE
53 Barbie's sister
54 Kavanaugh, as a collegian
56 Cheat sheet
59 "Iron Chef" props
62 "___ for Deadbeat": Grafton
63 Brand to dye for?

"I MUST BE GOING . . ." by Marie Langley
The clue at 34 Down says it all.

ACROSS

1 Like Alex Forrest's attraction
6 Horse halter
10 Fairy-tale bad guy
14 Loveliest poem, to Kilmer
15 Put up
16 Singer with "The Gang"
17 Bonnie Blue's father
18 First name in mystery writing
19 Curling locale
20 Weight gained from angry eating?
23 Executor's concern
24 Toothpaste letters
25 Start of MGM's motto
28 Sound of a tossed fruit peel?
32 Like most pages
36 Valuable collection
37 Ufa's mountains
38 "Take 2" author Gibbons
41 ___-Day vitamins
42 Bible book after Jonah
44 Adopt a healthy lifestyle
46 Butter measure for a cookout?
49 Kosugi in "Enter the Ninja"
50 1971 McCartney album
51 Tidbits for Fido
56 What termites do in the dugout?
60 M or G
62 Snowman prop
63 Do blackboard duty
64 Freedom from pain
65 Bear up there
66 Charlotte ___ (dessert)
67 TV trophy
68 Sniff out
69 Disparaging look

DOWN

1 Travesty
2 Dumas dueler
3 River from Staffordshire
4 Allstate rival
5 Tribute in song to "Mother Mary"
6 Put an edge on
7 Mata ___
8 From another museum, maybe
9 It may be hidden
10 Bayou soup ingredient
11 Fly solo
12 "Splash" director Howard
13 Antlered animal
21 June birthstone
22 Ultimate crash diet
26 Come undone
27 Swipe
29 Bridal bio word
30 "Million Years Ago" singer
31 Figurehead's place
32 Desensitizes
33 Bathsheba's first husband
34 Everything in existence
35 Give away
39 Get-up-and-go
40 "___, me hearties!"
43 Deli sandwich
45 Acid users
47 Google grounds, e.g.
48 Crew chief
52 It's new if you haven't seen it before
53 Put down
54 Yesterday's news
55 Handle the helm
57 Vietnam War chopper
58 Cathedral nook
59 Furniture wood
60 Young batter's ball supporter
61 Stage hog

215 SLEEPING QUARTERS by Harvey Estes
We suggest you take Harvey's title literally.

ACROSS

1 High, in Le Havre
6 Send sprawling
10 Pained cry
14 Bert's annoyer
15 Dr. Hadley of "House"
16 Catcher Narváez
17 Retailer's come-on
19 Capable of performing
20 Groan elicitors
21 Proceeds slyly
23 Court cry
24 Seesaw sitter of verse
25 Made tracks
26 Combined
28 Parry
30 Dice throw
32 Iowa State location
34 Most mockingly amusing
35 Tropical fruit
39 Put to use
40 Not digital
41 Actress Lollobrigida
42 Junkyard material
44 They're rigged
49 "We hold ___ truths . . ."
50 "The Heat and the Clouds" artist
52 Muscat site
53 Political commentator Reagan
54 Fleet runners
56 Cathedral nook
57 The "A" in NEA
59 Bridge in "A View to a Kill"
61 Essence
62 Enchanted girl of film
63 Gulf ship
64 Without purpose
65 ER imperative
66 Gives a hand

DOWN

1 Elf, to Santa
2 Stir up
3 Open with a pop
4 What you offer when you say "Hail, sneezer!"?
5 Slithery swimmer
6 Wanders about
7 Looks embarrassed
8 Fillipino footwear fashionista
9 ". . . our love become a funeral ___": Doors
10 Accuser's cry
11 One on the payroll
12 Lack of punctuality
13 Some demonstrations
18 Curve shape
22 Rugged chains
27 No in Nuremberg
29 Expose
31 "Crazy Rich Asians" novelist
33 Wise men
35 Deli meat
36 Ran last in
37 Kind of consent
38 Wistful word
39 Alluded to
41 Vegetarian ape
43 Sicken
45 Hero from Philly
46 Serengeti grazer
47 Subdued shade
48 Evidence of contempt
51 Vane dir.
55 Processes wine or cheese
58 Babe's home
60 Show agreement

CHANGING ONE'S MIND   by Bruce Venzke

In the Netherlands, 17 Across are called Speculaas.

ACROSS

1 Lofting shots
5 Foxworthy of "Blue Collar TV"
9 Extremely important
14 Childlike sci-fi people
15 See 5 Down
16 Hogwarts professor Severus
17 Classic treats with a Dutch history
20 Gift recipient
21 Stylish elegance
22 Law degrees
23 MIT degree
25 Youngest Manning brother
27 A doozy
34 New York City PBS station
36 Sleek, informally
37 Mescal source
38 Do tailoring work
39 Bon mot
41 "___ dieu!"
42 Mystical board
44 Truman's was Fair
45 Nuthatch food
46 Eric Clapton classic
49 "Prufrock" auth.
50 Scene of a mulligan
51 "Raiders of the Lost Ark" reptiles
54 Canter, e.g.
58 Transmission repair chain
62 Artful deception
65 Grandiose, as rhetoric
66 Rip
67 Its hub is Ben Gurion
68 Nuke event, briefly
69 Made a putt
70 Audition tape

DOWN

1 Beyond risqué
2 Eclectic assortment
3 Rhine River city
4 Secondary wager
5 World's fastest sport (with 15-A)
6 "Legally Blonde" blonde
7 Come a cropper
8 Tax that funds Soc. Sec.
9 Brandy label letters
10 Slight hunch
11 Kite trailer
12 Acted the copycat
13 "One ___ Bell to Answer"
18 Arizona's third-largest city
19 Linear
24 Thunder sound
26 Neeson in "Run All Night"
27 Pay or pardon
28 Model Klum
29 Lobbied for
30 Capone's Irish Gang rival
31 Entire scope
32 Bacchanal cry
33 Flat fee
34 Giddyap's opposite
35 Trois squared
39 Spock's pointy features
40 Landed
43 Kawasaki watercraft
45 Clipped an alpaca
47 Big prefix
48 Paraphernalia
51 "The Thin Man" pooch
52 V-chips block it
53 Juicy fruit
55 Pangolin's meal
56 New approach, perhaps
57 IRS agent
59 Embassy spy
60 Pack in
61 Kon-Tiki Museum site
63 Vermont summer hrs.
64 Bug

217 FROSTY'S RELATIVES   by Bruce Venzke
A winner of four Olympic golds, 33-A was nicknamed the "Czech Locomotive."

ACROSS

1 Grenada girlfriend
6 ICE agents
10 Audition for a role
14 Leased again
15 Irish actor O'Shea
16 Fanning in "Maleficent"
17 "Leave, and fast!"
19 Comes down with something
20 Stay glued to
21 Appears to be workable
23 "Spanish Eyes" assent
25 Famous Indy 500 family
26 "Poplars" and "Water Lilies"
30 Family head?
32 Monogram element: Abbr.
33 Czech runner Zátopek
35 Casino cap
40 Dressing-down
42 Not trustworthy
44 Sport with many traps
45 Super-narrow shoe size
47 Org. with a "Speak Freely" blog
48 Original Starbucks drink size
50 Hit on the noggin
52 Force
56 On one's uppers
58 Thomas Hardy's "___ Blue Eyes"
60 Lester Holt's domain
65 Hoodwink
66 Frosty's relatives
68 Post's opposite
69 African succulent
70 Not skillful
71 Globe Theatre king
72 Have confidence in
73 Does a household chore

DOWN

1 Hand holders
2 Ravioli filling
3 Chase in "Now, Voyager"
4 Grandpa Walton portrayer
5 Swear, in a way
6 Exams for MBA hopefuls
7 Karaoke need
8 Certain lodge members
9 Plane's landing position
10 Office orders
11 Name in a Beethoven title
12 "It's ___ nothing!"
13 Office fixtures
18 Charity fund-___
22 Springer's sister of Sherlock
24 ___ on parle français
26 Wire-thickness measures
27 Race of 0.62 miles
28 Côte d'Azur city
29 Miniaturizing suffix
31 ___-Seltzer
34 Military mess
36 Name of six tsars
37 Head Stone?
38 Jersey or Guernsey
39 Lead balloon sound
41 Downright
43 Plutocrats
46 The Matterhorn, e.g.
49 Sandy or Roberto of baseball
51 Lady's slipper, e.g.
52 Intriguing group?
53 Venture a view
54 Home of Hammett's falcon
55 Tightwad
57 In tune
59 Email attachment
61 Mork's sign-off, when doubled
62 Barely squeaks by, with "out"
63 Had a bawl
64 Retired fleet, briefly
67 IM guffaw

THEMELESS   by Bruce Venzke
A masterful construction with eight intersecting 15-letter answers.

ACROSS

1 Do art on mirrors, say
5 West African capital
10 Election prize
14 "Get lost!"
15 Lotus roadster
16 Water hazard?
17 Where Quechua is spoken
18 Rochester, to Benny
19 Covers
20 Almost a chance encounter
23 Grease ___
24 Ribbed fabric
25 Result of the subprime mortgage debacle
34 Sicilian resort
35 Sign held by a waver
36 Spicy Spanish stew
37 Myrmecology study
38 One of the Horae
39 Trident-shaped letters
40 Parisian streets
41 1998 De Niro spy thriller
42 Play rambunctiously
43 50-yard-line markings
46 The Hague tribunal: Abbr.
47 Vietnamese river
48 1962 #1 hit by The Four Seasons
57 Hunt's "___ Ben Adhem"

58 Erasable memory chip
59 Country Crock product
60 When doubled, a cry of approval
61 Like tumblers
62 One year in a trunk?
63 Gyroscope part
64 Caravel features
65 Shake alternative

DOWN

1 "Pardon the Interruption" airer
2 Fifth word of "America"
3 Countess on "Downton Abbey"
4 Great shape?
5 Scone go-with, often
6 Half a Basque game
7 Baking chamber
8 "Be with you in just ___!"
9 Assisted-living residences
10 Many small business owners
11 Moran of "Happy Days"
12 "Highway to Hell" rockers
13 Hit with a charge
21 Implement for Willie Mosconi
22 Pearl Harbor mo.
25 Fortify anew
26 It comes with low interest
27 Paid to play
28 Austrian alpine region

29 Change, as a motion
30 Braxton and Tennille
31 "Matter of Fact" columnist
32 Viscous stuff
33 Padlock adjuncts
44 Here, to Héloïse
45 String of pocketed balls for Willie Mosconi
48 Island band The ___ Men
49 Goat seen in 28 Down
50 Part of a hat trick
51 Lydia Ko's org.
52 Hindu honorifics
53 Doofus
54 Copywriter's award
55 Divide by tearing
56 It leads to nirvana

219

MANTRIC MUTTERINGS by Bonnie L. Gentry
44 Down was the primary filming location for "Fast Times at Ridgemont High."

ACROSS

1 Prefix for trooper
5 Nobel Peace Center city
9 Octagonal sign
13 Part of OTC
14 Measure the depth of
16 "Wonderful Town" song
17 Rip
18 China Clipper airline
19 News story opener
20 Marge Simpson's parody of a Beatles song?
23 Napped leathers
24 "A Wrinkle in Time" director DuVernay
25 Beatles' early record label
28 Mini border
29 November 11 honorees
32 Kind of appliqué
34 Tabloid headline on 103-year-old George Kirby's wedding?
36 Be dependent
39 Senior tech exec
40 Kerflooey
41 Dark Arts principles?
46 Have a playful romp
47 Reinforcing beam
48 Prescott–Phoenix dir.
51 Kilt size
52 Garnet's mo.
54 King who counseled Agamemnon
56 Exposé on misleading infomercial claims?
60 Neverland pirate
62 "___ Beautiful Doll"
63 Bone on the pinky side
64 Hill of Irish kings
65 Fool
66 One of eight in V8
67 Choice assignment
68 Pro shop purchases
69 Film in which Insectopia is sought

DOWN

1 Cornfield fertilizer
2 Word on 17 "Monopoly" spaces
3 "___ and weep!"
4 Extra Dry deodorant
5 "No" voter
6 Pole or Bulgarian, e.g.
7 Moon over Montmartre
8 "Gate City of the West"
9 Fish served meunière
10 "No need to be so sad"
11 Suffix for fact
12 "A Descent into the Maelström" author
15 Low-budget film
21 Denim magnate Strauss
22 Helgenberger of "CSI"
26 Early Alcazar castle resident
27 "Never ___ wildest dreams . . ."
30 Soft or crunchy snack
31 Dystopia genre
33 Like a salutatory
34 Texter's "Stay out of my affairs"
35 "Underdog" singer Lisa
36 Crusader Rabbit's pal
37 ACT is one
38 Capital founded by Pizarro
42 Personal magnetism, slangily
43 Hit the brakes hard
44 Los Angeles neighborhood
45 More than annoyed
48 Like diamond bases, at times
49 14-line poem
50 Like a $10 Rolex
53 Pitch perfectly
55 Explore reefs
57 Juice a lime
58 End of a 12/31 song
59 Start of a Welk intro
60 NASCAR sponsor
61 Baudelaire's "Les Fleurs du ___"

ACROSS

1 Granny or half-hitch
5 Kitchen accident
10 Demand for seconds
14 Site of the Pearl Mosque
15 Ragtime piano legend Blake
16 Appropriate for kids K–12
17 Make fun of the seer's foretelling?
20 Gives the go-ahead for
21 Perot who ran for president
22 "Mon ___!" (Edith Piaf song)
23 Tom yum ___ (Thai soup)
24 Angry herds of sheep?
30 Oscar nominee for "A Beautiful Mind"
31 Slips that promise payment
32 Old World cont.
34 "The Magic Mountain" novelist
35 Prone to bungling
37 Gave the once-over
38 "Don't forget about . . ."
39 Slight hitch in one's plans
40 In Britain they're called thieves' kitchens
41 Patrolman on the sunny side of the street?
45 Mil. mailing address
46 Give, and expect back
47 Nixon's Agnew
50 Mollycoddling
55 Similarity between Arial and Calibri?
57 Sampling of views
58 Epitome of hardness
59 Friend of Rat and Mole
60 Mule-drawn vehicle
61 Michaels of "SNL"
62 Guesstimates at ATL

DOWN

1 "___ Sutra"
2 CARE and Save the Children, e.g.
3 Humanoid hobbit foes
4 Dismantle a swing set
5 Composition for seven
6 Follow doggedly
7 "Like that would ever happen!"
8 Venice Film Festival site
9 Award for Miss Hawaii
10 Like liters and kilos
11 A little of this and a little of that
12 Letters before sigmas
13 Zwei ÷ zwei
18 Galliano flavoring
19 Utter pandemonium
23 Flood the market
24 Pre-2002 Calais coin
25 Symphonic finale
26 Dora the Explorer's cousin
27 Dandily dressed dude
28 Become tense
29 "You don't like it? Tough luck."
30 Award for Sugarland
33 Map lines: Abbr.
35 Help desk offering
36 Track hayburner
37 Stretch out
39 Lethargic state
40 "We ___ overcome . . ."
42 Adverb in weather forecasts
43 "Grumpier ___" (1995)
44 Stiff drink
47 Haight-Ashbury law gp.
48 "___ Richard's Almanack"
49 On Ventura Blvd., say
50 Phrase in a ratio
51 When pigs fly, poetically
52 When NHL shootouts take place
53 Elite Eight org.
54 Nonschool diplomas
56 Class for U.S. immigrants

221 "YOU LIKE POTATO . . ." by Bonnie L. Gentry
". . . and I like potahto"

ACROSS

1 Far-reaching
5 Letter flourishes
11 Bungle badly
16 Beautiful Wells race
17 Bigger-than-life, perhaps
18 Play ___ in (be part of)
19 "These regulations shouldn't be made fun of!"?
22 Corporal or sergeant, e.g.
23 Medium for a medical sample
24 Profs' classroom helpers
25 Playground comeback
29 Tax-form fig.
30 Adam's Biblical mate
31 What Helvetica has vis-à-vis Arial?
35 Hapless victims
36 Products sold with earbuds
37 Baylor's URL suffix
38 Org. that doesn't allow traveling
39 Purchase from Vanna
40 Imminent grads
42 "In a bottle" alternative
46 Sneeze-causing substance
49 Removes a sticker
51 De Niro costar in "Raging Bull"
52 Baste or hem
54 Class for some immigrants, for short
55 JPEG file
56 Hijack-prevention org.

58 Bonnie who sang "Something to Talk About"
60 Fragrant evergreens
61 Skater Hamilton in a precarious situation?
65 One in the legislative biz
66 Scrap for Bowser
67 Mailer-___ (bounce email source)
68 Like Haydn's Symphony No. 12
69 Toodle-loo, in Turin
71 Outline for a business meeting
75 Make sure every exec has insurance!?
80 Swiss watch that sounds Greek
81 Type of family tree connection
82 There's two in a sch. year
83 Divination deck
84 "You can say that again!"
85 Galbraith's subj.

DOWN

1 Shrimp removal
2 Gucci of fashion
3 In next to no time
4 Destroyers, in naval slang
5 Barely boiling
6 Prefix with "sphere" or "friendly"
7 Avian elephant eater of myth
8 Confident crossword solver's medium
9 What spoiled kids often throw
10 Charles of Wall Street
11 Jodi Benson's "Toy Story 4" role
12 Tulsa sch. with a Prayer Tower
13 Quetzalcoatl worshiper
14 Split asunder
15 Author of "Siddhartha"
20 Suit material?
21 Remarkable golf score
26 Conical dwellings
27 Barcelona bruin
28 Multivolume ref. sets
31 Aesopian narrative
32 Milky white gems
33 No. on a new car sticker
34 Missionaries of Charity members
35 Breeze, so to speak
39 House of Lords member
41 Boil with anger
43 Message board thread
44 In need of extinguishing
45 Some boot camp grads
47 Plasm opener
48 Claudius I's successor
50 Worthy of respect
53 Hogwarts graduation gift
57 Skylighted areas
59 "Don't make ___ habit!"
60 Skill plus delicacy
61 Wine center near Napa
62 Ingenious
63 Hems and haws
64 Aborted, as a launch
65 Small embroidery loop
70 Miscellaneous mix
72 One sixty-billionth of a min.
73 Aspiring musician's offering
74 Pt. of PGA
76 Narcissist's problem
77 Wile E. Coyote's Acme purchase
78 Hurricane pronoun, maybe
79 Dijon thirst quencher

19 Across played the role of Daniel Morales in seasons 7–8 on "L.A. Law."

ACROSS

1 Store
5 Competing team
9 "Tombstone" setting
16 Star salmon?
17 Poet Sandburg
18 Tennis commentator Mary
19 "Profiler" star
21 Peter Benchley thriller
22 Bavarian dance
23 Archaeological site
25 ___-day vitamins
26 Claus von Bülow's attorney
32 Head-butt
35 Make things up
36 Be parental
37 "___ you not!": Paar
39 "When in Rome, ___ . . ."
42 Ovid work
47 Roman javelin
48 Cop on "NYPD Blue"
50 Sophisticated
52 Geneva-based UN org.
53 Where Hercules battled a lion
54 George Tobias role on "Bewitched"
59 List extending abbr.
60 Chewbacca is one
61 In ___ (consecutively)
62 Jimmy of Led Zeppelin
63 Like elbows at the bar
65 Thing, in law
67 Part of a fault line?
68 The last to photograph John Lennon
75 Not long from now
76 Manning in Super Bowl XLII
77 Mr. Goldfinger
81 Links group
85 Child actor in "Home Alone 3"
88 Made money hand over fist
89 Fervency
90 Soil Conservation Service org.
91 ___ Rockefeller
92 Goes astray
93 Blacken beef

DOWN

1 Lose it
2 Human genus
3 Lap path, often
4 Tundra jacket
5 Bill Nye's subj. on TV
6 Kinsler of baseball
7 Judicial Stallone role
8 Olive Oyl's creator Segar
9 Mo. of masks
10 ___-di-dah
11 Dr. on "The Chronic"
12 "The Merry ___ Waltz": Lehár
13 1983 Nicholas Gage book
14 Winter hazard
15 November birthstone
20 Lofty
24 Rottweiler warning
27 Ethiopian princess of opera
28 Diner sign, often
29 ET–seeking org.
30 Complain
31 Constellation with a belt
32 Lumber mill fixture
33 Hands-on-hips
34 Lombardia capital
38 Jeter of the Marlins
40 1998 Sarah McLachlan hit
41 Regional forest trees
43 The 2007 World Series was one
44 1958 Kentucky Derby winner
45 The big chill?
46 Ornamental shrub
49 Nice night?
51 Levi or Asher, e.g.
55 Ship spine
56 Glass designer Lalique
57 Actress Anna on "Fringe"
58 German couple?
64 Casual Friday castaway
66 Dutch city ending
68 "Champion" rapper
69 "You've gotta be kidding!"
70 Partners of crannies
71 Map blowup, often
72 Sudden outburst
73 Gretzky was a great one
74 Boer fighters
78 Soufflés do it
79 "___ Club" (50 Cent hit)
80 Drug-fighting authority
82 Wheatley's "___ to Neptune"
83 Former space station
84 Nav. rank
86 Hammer locale
87 Big T-shirts: Abbr.

RETRONYMS* by Ray Hamel
"Acoustic guitar" and "hard copy" are two examples of retronyms.

ACROSS

1 "Magic Man" group
6 Cold-meat glazes
12 Charleston and Dover: Abbr.
16 "Call to Greatness" author Stevenson
17 Mars feature
18 Weight allowance
19 Not yet ignited
20 Bob Newhart prop*
22 Yellow Teletubby
24 RuneScape pots
25 Downy duck
26 Proper "thank-you"*
29 Sizable, as a sum
30 Like a single sock
31 Killer snake
34 Radii parallels
37 A large amount of
42 It turns heat into work*
45 Took chances
46 Spun toys
47 "Como ___ una Mujer" (Lopez album)
48 TriBeCa neighbor
49 Canadian lout
51 Reusable nursery item*
55 Inscription in memoriam
57 Baseball's Garciaparra
58 Some NFL receivers
59 Holstein holler
60 CEO resume items

62 Grammy Awards show feature*
70 Capri, e.g.
71 Check detail
72 Color, as a T-shirt
75 Nikon product*
78 Black cattle breed
79 Tent support
80 Womb
81 Physicist Bohr
82 Rise high and fast
83 Frankenstein et al.
84 Mass of loose rock

DOWN

1 Do teamster work
2 Aunt in "National Lampoon's Vacation"
3 Muhammad's god
4 Denounce
5 Golf club metal
6 Basketball center?
7 Use steel wool on
8 Lab dish name
9 Terse refusal
10 Richard of "Bleak House"
11 Clandestine agent
12 Fleetwood Mac's "Walk ___ Line"
13 Famous resident of Bag End
14 Poet Stephen Vincent ___

15 Metric unit of volume
21 Hung fire
23 Mix up
27 Keenan in "Dr. Strangelove"
28 Nigerian language
31 ___ crow flies
32 Deign
33 Classic cola
35 ". . . ___ in Kalamazoo"
36 "The X Factor" judge
38 "First Man" org.
39 Let fall, in poetry
40 Tittering sound
41 Sensory stimuli
43 "I'd hate to break up ___"
44 Intl. defense group
50 Flutist Jean-Pierre

51 Phylum of humans
52 "Let me think . . ."
53 Sponge gently
54 Persians
56 "Star Wars: The Force Awakens" pilot
61 Like some landscapes
62 Does a Sylvester impression
63 "How much ___ much?"
64 Proud cry
65 River of NW Germany
66 Hall of ___
67 White Sands' county
68 Brother of Linus and Lucy
69 Lawn neatener
73 Log time

74 Latin infinitive
76 Young den denizen
77 Source of Samson's jawbone

ACROSS

1 Latticed bower
6 Lay off
11 Bluish gray
16 Speedy Gonzales, e.g.
17 Ishmael's half brother
18 Arena walkway
19 Head of costume design
20 Backstroke movement
22 Unhand
24 Otherworldly
25 One teaspoon, maybe
26 Took care of
28 In the distance
32 MADD target
34 2011 Owen Wilson movie
36 Town Car, for short
37 Holiday ___
38 Suspicious
39 Plantain lily
40 Morocco neighbor: Abbr.
41 Cables
42 Excoriate
44 Pen point
45 Cowboy Gibson
46 Crossbow arrow
47 Temper
49 Empire State capital
51 Newfoundland discoverer
52 Tuck's partner
53 Preface
54 Ganders and cobs
55 House party
56 How LPs are reissued
57 Managing editor's concern
60 ___-80 (classic PC)
61 Suggests, as a price
62 Dreadlocked one
63 Cape near Lisbon
65 School group
67 Skillfully made, to Brits
70 Bracelet clasp
75 Jack in "Call of the Wild"
76 Clarinet wood
77 Slack-jawed
78 Felt bad
79 Final Jeopardy act
80 Water garnish
81 Shift

DOWN

1 Part of ACLU: Abbr.
2 Badgered
3 Cornerstone, e.g.
4 Prefix for path
5 Unoriginal story
6 "Mikey likes it" cereal
7 Subj. for some aliens
8 Greek consonant
9 Arched opening
10 Musical groups
11 Wraparound garment
12 Enjoy greatly
13 "Softly ___ Leave You"
14 RN specialty
15 Cartoon squeak
21 Greek god or asteroid
23 Pacific barker
26 Hail cousin
27 Loan stats
29 Hook, line, and sinker
30 Frontal
31 1986 GE acquisition
32 Primatologist Fossey
33 Disremembers
35 "NCIS" hero
39 Rev. W. Awdry's Sir Topham ___
41 "Freedom" rock duo
42 On the wagon
43 Sense of finality
46 Glider wood
48 Omar of "House"
50 Romantic film excerpt
51 Role players
53 Bluegrass genus
54 Phone playback
57 Entreat
58 Rogue
59 Type of mutual fund
64 Debussy's "___ de Lune"
66 Interstellar dist.
67 Reporter's question
68 Turnarounds, slangily
69 Cruz and Nugent
70 Put in stitches
71 Arabic robe
72 Mental mist
73 Duncan's cap
74 Naval noncom

ACROSS

1 Strunk & White subject
6 Bern's river
10 Muldaur song "Midnight at the ___"
15 "Water Lilies" painter
16 "Awakenings" drug
18 Dante's "La Vita ___"
19 Floor it (with 28-A)
21 Addison composition
22 Steamed state
23 Split to get joined
24 Exam for high school jrs.
26 Speed readers?
28 See 19 Across
33 Month before Yom Kippur
34 Prefix with gram
36 Jug handle shape
37 Ellen ___ Barkin
38 Plant part
40 As to
42 Be lenient
44 Star-___ tuna
46 Home insulation site
48 Airport code for McCarran Int.
49 Go flat-out
53 Justice Dept. division
54 Apt anagram for seats, in bridge
55 Caesar's "vidi"
56 Dana of "China Beach"
58 Embroidery need
60 Met soloists
64 In ___ (bored)
65 Messy quarters
67 News World news agcy.
69 One of the tides
70 Get away quickly
73 Dynamic opening?
75 Post-curfew
76 ___ prosequi
78 "Down in front!"
79 Yuletide candy shapes
82 Gallop
85 "What ___ baby!"
86 Yarn coil
87 Recumbent
88 Roughly a yard
89 "Signs of the Zodiac" artist
90 More balanced

DOWN

1 Ballpark figures
2 Belgian brew
3 Paid to play
4 Understand
5 Former anesthetic
6 Mighty Dog alternative
7 Highly skilled at
8 Drive through Beverly Hills
9 Cabinet-level dept.
10 When "SNL" signs off
11 Stark
12 "___ yer old man!"
13 Mrs. Miles Archer
14 Recite
17 "Brave New World" caste
20 Ultimatum ending
25 Mendes and Garcia
27 "Go jump in ___!"
29 Pearly whites
30 "___ the Girls I've Loved Before"
31 Vase handles
32 Ruffles rival
35 Kernels
39 White sale goods
41 Rizzo in "Midnight Cowboy"
43 Ennead less one
45 Patronizes a hotel
47 Lewinsky's taper
49 "SNL" alum Cheri
50 Jo Ann in "M*A*S*H"
51 Grain alcohol
52 Lightweight cord
53 A wife of Esau
57 One in training
59 In la-la land
61 Part of KJV
62 Hundred Acre Wood creator
63 Tumbling "catcher"
66 Hippodrome sections
68 "___ cost you"
71 Electroshock gun
72 Circle or city preceder
74 Pitches in
77 Moon over Paris
79 Quarterback Newton
80 It's never returned
81 "BattleBots" trophy
83 Island strings
84 Madrigal syllable

226 GOLD RUSH by Harvey Estes
Four answers are a little different.

ACROSS

1 Puts a question to
5 Barbecue entrée
9 Gateway for the gold rush to 3 Down
15 Wallpaper roll
16 Irish pop singer
17 Desk item
18 The Three Musketeers, e.g.
20 Designer's studio
21 Conductor Boulanger
22 Meteor, e.g.
24 Cornhusker, for one
27 Unappetizing mush
29 Lille buddy
30 "No Country for Old Men" setting
31 Source of irritation
32 Los Angeles athlete
35 Hudson Bay prov.
36 Long-eared pet
37 Say again
40 One that gives up
42 Cinque less due
43 Sets free
46 "There you are!"
49 Wastelands
50 It's covered on the street
54 Shaping machines
56 Duke's conference
58 Gist
59 Crimson-clad
60 Dinnertime proposal
63 Maui finger food
64 First governor of 9 Across
65 9 Across, in other words
69 Euphoric
71 Trooper's device
72 Uncertain
73 Smiles of some characters
77 Zany trio
78 Saxophonist Coltrane
79 Lena of "Chocolat"
80 Frolicked
81 Spots
82 Succeed at pitching

DOWN

1 Workout targets
2 Boar's beloved
3 Gold rush region of the Yukon
4 Soda insert
5 Avoid a temptation
6 Man in the can
7 Last word
8 Team named for a gold rush group
9 Let out a seam
10 Pop singer Lisa
11 Library section
12 Least disturbed
13 Collapse
14 LAX letters
17 Like a skinny-dipper
19 JFK's predecessor
23 Pump part
24 West African country
25 Your disposal opening
26 Prefix with skeleton
28 Townshend of The Who
31 Pop, for one
33 Poet's before
34 Caused a fender bender
36 Software test version
38 Southwestern resort
39 Rocker Brian
41 Beaver construction
44 Ready to ship
45 Elle, in English
46 "You can't pray ___"
47 Keep possession of
48 Haphazardly
51 Out of the cooler
52 Ill-gotten gains
53 Buffalo's lake
55 Poultry farm structure
57 Dog or tooth
61 Worked hard
62 "I mean . . ."
65 Where sleepy people go
66 Shacks
67 Cold war prog.
68 Fiesta fare
70 Erin Hamlin's sled
72 Tel Aviv's nat.
74 Investors' Fannie
75 It's nothing
76 "Live" NBC show

227 INTERNAL INDIFFERENCE   by Harvey Estes
. . . and that indifference can be found at 81 Down.

ACROSS

1 "Walking in Memphis" singer Cohn
5 Family art display site
11 Sound reasoning
16 Silica stone
17 "Creature From the Black ___" (1954)
18 An ex of the Donald
19 Like many traditions
21 Beg off
22 Greek messenger
23 Speaker's platform
25 Take a load off
26 Author Umberto
27 Medium strength
29 Emperor's Cup sport
30 Where the Mets met, once
31 "Get ready!"
34 Machu ___
36 Put in piles, perhaps
38 Kentucky title
41 Rapidity ratio
44 Domestic
46 "All hat and no ___"
47 "Xanadu" band, for short
48 Request from one in the dark
51 Christmas costume
52 Fats of "Blueberry Hill" fame
54 "I Shot Andy Warhol" star Taylor
55 Get uptight
56 Say again
58 Untimely end
61 Navajo lodges
63 Voice of Inspector Gadget
67 Bit of change
69 "Gotcha"
71 Ruin the appearance of
72 Upholstery problem
73 Lake Wobegon Protestant: Abbr.
74 Kidney-related
76 Handle ineptly
78 Vermont's Allen
80 Swiss chalet, e.g.
82 Golden 1 Center, for one
83 July birthstones
84 Librarian's advice
85 Like Dilbert
86 Some tree dwellers
87 Hieroglyphic snakes

DOWN

1 "Your ___ Should Know": Beatles
2 Pricing word
3 Muzzle-loading tool
4 Red Skelton's hayseed
5 Scrapes enamel
6 Turned tail
7 Composer Stravinsky
8 Rock's "Pillow Talk" costar
9 Uses a ski lift
10 Native to a region
11 Slangy hat
12 Went past
13 Guy on a safari
14 Busy
15 Magna ___
20 Loaf ends
24 Excessively ornate
28 Bit of hype
32 "What a relief!"
33 Fish with a net
35 Falcon feature
37 Like a wallflower
39 Fanning out on a movie set
40 Skipped town
41 Care beginning
42 Oodles
43 Like inviting looks
45 Took out
48 Hose trouble
49 Empty talk
50 Words mouthed to a camera
53 Bismarck ruled with one
55 G-man or T-man
57 Brings close
59 All fouled up
60 Miles of film
62 Wicked
64 Joins the debate
65 Country singer Ronnie
66 Blender settings
67 Unarmed, to a cop
68 Beyond the fringe
70 "Grand Hotel" star
75 Milk, in Metz
77 "Brothers & Sisters" matriarch
79 Vocal objection
81 Word of indifference

228 MATH THEOREM by Richard Silvestri
An original math theorem by Professor Silvestri.

ACROSS

1 Begin
6 Not exactly tactful
11 Fancy neckwear
16 Country star Tucker
17 Fast finisher?
18 Clue room
19 **Math theorem: Part 1**
22 Holy
23 Big rig
24 Swing to and ___
25 Chatroom chuckle
26 Carry on
29 Chi follower
31 "Giant Brain" of 1946
34 **Theorem: Part 2**
40 Part of a circle
42 In the buff
43 Low joint
44 Greeting from Mufasa
46 NHL venues
49 Let go
50 Gone
54 T-t-talks?
56 Screw up
57 Three-time French Open champ
59 Black-and-white snack
60 Wildly excited
62 PC picture
64 Like a good steak
68 **Theorem: Part 3**
72 Rub the wrong way
73 South African golfer

74 Summoned the butler
76 Command to Spot
77 Woolly mama
80 Fall birthstone
83 Expensive spread: Var.
86 **Theorem: Part 4**
90 Mete out
91 City on the Loire
92 Observes, Biblically
93 Financial wherewithal
94 Silly
95 Knave of Hearts' loot

DOWN

1 Belmont buildings
2 Highball, e.g.
3 Very sweet
4 Bread and whiskey
5 Keep ___ on (monitor)
6 What raindrops do on wax
7 House work?
8 Hagen of the stage
9 Loch of note
10 It leaves in the spring
11 Saintly city
12 Farm structure
13 Sleeve end
14 Something in the air
15 Newcomer
20 KO counter
21 Sound equipment
27 Sixth man, in the NBA
28 Sail support

30 Contents of some cartridges
32 Gillette razor brand
33 Miller alternative
35 2001 Judi Dench film
36 Slowly, on scores
37 Enough, perhaps
38 Globe Theatre king
39 Scout units
41 Be worthy of
45 Dig find
47 Conductor Masur
48 Hard to climb
50 Letter opener
51 For that reason
52 "Carrie" setting
53 Hexa- plus four
55 Time signal
58 Off-key
61 "Golly!"

63 Hush-hush org.
65 Forensic expert
66 Peak higher than K2
67 College board members
69 Causes to swell
70 Catch a glimpse of
71 Sheathe
75 Guy's companion
77 It may be made up
78 Corduroy ridge
79 "Enchanted" Hathaway role
81 Spot of wine?
82 Spanish province
84 Life jacket
85 Concept
87 Took the gold
88 Sine ___ non
89 Decorative vase

229 ORE ELSE   by Richard Silvestri

The final match at 83-A was decided by a penalty-kick shoot-out in overtime.

ACROSS

1 Loamy deposit
6 Up at the stadium
11 Latches onto
16 Make like Cicero
17 "From the Terrace" author
18 Track event
19 Sing in the snow
20 Ideal for dieters
21 Fiery fragment
22 Male chauvinist pig, e.g.?
25 Juanita's uncle
26 Finished
27 Taurus mo.
30 Make a hem
32 Siberian river
33 Off in the distance
37 Sanitation workers
40 Ambient music composer Brian
42 Colgate's wall greenery
43 Heavy reading
44 Wind, in combinations
47 Pool problem
49 Approaching a quartet?
53 Mediterranean capital
54 Hale and Hari
55 Kind of coffee
57 It's all the rage
58 Gives birth to
61 Bit of stage scenery
63 Cantina coin
65 Springs for drinks?
68 Course standard
69 Drops in the grass
70 Associates
73 Holiday in Hanoi
75 What the expelled West Point cadets were?
81 Diamond measure
82 Soviet prison camp
83 2006 FIFA World Cup winner
84 Tequila source
85 Put up
86 Squelched
87 Not as ruddy
88 Some TVs
89 Make up?

DOWN

1 Places
2 Setting of "The Plague"
3 Dumbo's wings
4 Guinness product
5 Not at all altruistic
6 Top-rated
7 Actress Birch
8 "Key Largo" star
9 Fit for farming
10 Brewski
11 Diving bird
12 Sucker fish
13 Goya's duchess
14 Max of the ring
15 Neighbor of Leb.
23 Enemy
24 Rachel Wood on "Westworld"
27 Pub. defender
28 Gain
29 "Blitzkrieg Bop" band
31 Former "NY Times" puzzle editor
34 Calculated
35 Miser's sin
36 Pocket filler?
38 Sixteen-wheeler
39 Barclays Center team
41 Galoot
45 Swabbie's swab
46 Elevator pioneer
48 California wine city
50 Qualifying suffix
51 Dickens clerk
52 Will matter
53 Piece of advice
56 Place to pray
59 1975 Wimbledon winner
60 Counter cleaners
62 On the money
64 From C to C
66 Maestro Toscanini
67 Hot
71 Riverine mammal
72 Hollis of the LPGA
74 It all adds up to this
75 Sitar tune
76 Spoken
77 Driver's lic. data
78 Pro follower
79 Something to build on
80 January 1 word
81 Bottle top

ACROSS

1 Glossy seashell
7 Invitation foursome
11 Smokeless tobacco
16 New York lake
17 Colorful eye part
18 Jonas Kaufmann, e.g.
19 Artful Dickens character
20 Twisted
21 Word before coast or tower
22 Advice for a drapery shop owner?
25 Personal records
28 What the feds enforce
29 Grassy
33 Take a part
34 Dr. Dolittle's wife
35 Overturn
36 Elegant hairstyle
39 Those born in early August
41 Taj Mahal site
42 ___ than thou
43 Tennis drop shot
44 "Like a Rolling Stone" singer
45 Escapist
47 Choose A, for example
49 Serve a bar mitzvah
51 Sissy
53 Emulate Earhart
56 Italian wine region
57 Interest accumulator
58 Raglan and dolman
59 Gymnast's assistant
61 Fidel Castro's brother
63 Special sight
64 Attack violently
65 Valuable place
66 Oh-so-delicious
68 Advice for Mr. Limpet?
71 Hawaiian spirit
74 Feeble
75 In flames
79 Libreville is its capital
80 Footnote abbreviation
81 Layette item
82 Leaves the stage
83 Manage
84 Pop artist Johns

DOWN

1 Barnstable's cape
2 Lennon's second wife
3 Tied the knot
4 Triangle type
5 Notions
6 Take home
7 Precious gems
8 Maleficent manipulator
9 Lets off steam
10 Way
11 Foment
12 Advice for an EMT?
13 Children's card game
14 All ___ one
15 Baby fish
23 Cheshire cat feature
24 O'Hare postings
25 "Toccata in D minor" composer
26 Platform for Alexa
27 Sexy shoes
30 Garden of Eden attire
31 Modernist poet Pound
32 "Watchers" novelist Koontz
34 Ned Stark of Winterfell, e.g.
35 Classic soft drink
37 Advice for the punch bowl server?
38 Approach
40 They justify the means
43 Defeat soundly
44 Submarine maneuver
46 Frequent still life subject
48 Umpire's utterance
49 Honduras home
50 Egyptian snakes
52 Rhetorical fallacy
54 Try
55 Glimpse
57 Place to order a hoagie
58 Bird feeder staple
60 Goliath gods
62 Off the beaten path
65 Perform a salchow
66 Fibula neighbor
67 Rand McNally book
69 Musical symbol
70 Muslim pilgrimage
71 Long time
72 Loosey-goosey
73 Geisha's sash
76 Snapchat or Pandora, e.g.
77 A maze has one
78 To do so is human

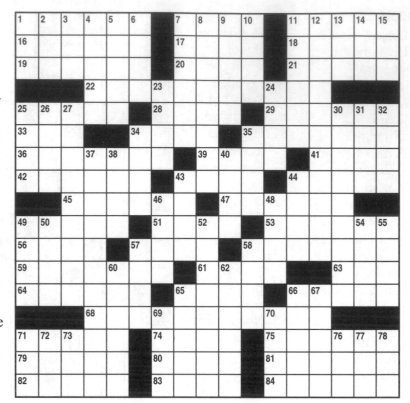

231 A STEEP PRICE TO PAY   by Bruce Venzke
73 Across had a stellar eighteen-year career . . . and all with the same team!

ACROSS

1 Acknowledged applause
6 Brings down the house?
11 Target of trolls
15 Unfathomable
17 Bacterial strain
18 Hindu royal
19 Japanese crime syndicate
20 **Quote: Part 1**
22 2000 World Series site
23 Like erbium or terbium
25 Sonny Corleone's sister
26 Cup in Cannes
28 Fail to name
30 Hightail it
33 Sugar container
35 Wall St. abbr.
39 **Quote: Part 2**
42 Terk in Disney's "Tarzan"
43 Martin in "For Love of Ivy"
44 Popular bread
45 Kind of renewal
46 Basswood tree
48 PX customers
49 "Mother Goose & Grimm" cat
50 Bridal path's end
51 Guitar man Paul
52 French painter Jean
53 Thus, in Latin
54 **Quote: Part 3**
58 Hilton luxury rms.
59 Sanford's son
60 Austrian actress Berger
61 "___ the word!"
62 Heroic adventure
64 Backup
68 Evening in Roma
69 JFK's secretary of state
73 **Source of quote**
76 Restrain
78 Certain line crosser
79 Bittern relative
80 Habitual thief, slangily
81 Cornwall gallery
82 Auditions for a part
83 Nickname of 73 Across

DOWN

1 Green Mountain ___
2 Silvery fish
3 Pacific island
4 Where it's 0 degrees
5 Old detergent brand
6 Secluded place
7 Workout aftereffect
8 Muppet Elmo's friend
9 "Xanadu" rock gp.
10 Las Vegas nickname
11 Baritone Terfel
12 Croquet venue
13 California's ___ Valley
14 Motown's Marvin
16 Mousketeer hat
21 Filmmaking area
24 Rockies resort
27 Rueful bunch
28 Sanctions
29 Allocate
30 German POW camps
31 Cockpit figure
32 Like some pumps
34 "Wrap" artist
35 Rudely abrupt
36 "Only the Lonely" singer
37 Pragmatist
38 It'll cure what ails you, they say
40 Transport for 55 Down, often
41 Remote military base
47 Root beer brand
48 Mysophobe's worry
49 Humorist Buchwald
51 Organic soil
52 Sunflower relative
55 Snake handler of a sort
56 Takes in
57 Less trusting
61 Mystery writer Rita ___ Brown
63 Cutty ___
64 For fear that
65 Toothed whale
66 Airborne pest
67 Sailing maneuver
68 Agenda, informally
70 Potentially offensive
71 As found (with "in")
72 Bureau projection
74 Scotch price factor
75 Brady Bill opponent
77 Bay State's official tree

TAIL OF WOE   by Theresa Yves
. . . when drama critics bark up the wrong tree.

ACROSS

1 Go along with
7 Send to the canvas
11 Make fast, at sea
16 Church fund-raiser
17 Some
18 Hit the decks
19 **Start of a riddle about a tail of woe**
21 Rifles
22 Leporidae members
23 Ken of "Brothers & Sisters"
24 Stirs up
25 Pupil's place
26 Rescue, with "out"
27 Jenny in "Love Story"
28 Brother of Rahm Emanuel
29 Catch some rays
30 **More of riddle**
33 Gives power to
35 Lilly of drugs
36 Mix up
37 BB propellant
38 Insurance ploy
40 Turn over
41 Brooch part
44 **More of riddle**
45 Break down
46 Towel tetragram
47 Word of parting
48 Gladys Knight backer
49 Toward the speaker
50 Burns most powerful role?
51 Carmaker Maserati
55 **End of riddle**
59 Chewbacca's friend
60 "Far out!"
61 Concern on the fairway
62 Crusader Rabbit's pal
63 "___ we go again!"
64 Wellspring
66 Stone of "Easy A"
67 Marseilles menu
68 Looked at lasciviously
69 **Riddle answer**
71 "Now We Are Six" author
72 Justify, e.g.
73 Duds
74 Dundee denizens
75 Ward of "Sisters"
76 Higher than a kite

DOWN

1 "Charlotte's Web" author
2 Parched
3 Russian ruler's wife
4 "Bellefleur" author
5 Colorado State team
6 Pod opener
7 Mystical writer Gibran
8 "Scourge of God" Hun
9 Display of disinterest
10 Lyrical lines
11 Like Lithuania
12 Switch tail
13 Take care of
14 Ceres and Eros
15 "Works for me!"
20 Ends
24 Rolling in the aisles
26 Bodine portrayer
27 Let
30 Kind of art
31 Cancún cash
32 Emulate Andy Dufresne
34 Scent hound
38 Broadway whisper
39 P, on a fraternity jacket
41 Online hangouts
42 Sluggish
43 Armored animal
44 Be silly over
45 Unwelcome motor sound
47 From the top
48 NFL members
51 Mystery writer's prize
52 ___-Williams Paints
53 Served raw
54 Like the king of diamonds
56 Water park fixtures
57 Firewood amount
58 Inverted-V letter
63 "Couldn't get out of it"
65 Chap
66 Art Deco name
67 Suffragette leader Carrie

69 Pack animal
70 Western treaty org.

233 "STAR TREK" MEETS "STAR WARS"   by Theresa Yves
Another clue for 45 Down could be "incense."

ACROSS

1 Request before a shooting
6 Former teen idol Cassidy
11 Beach Boy Wilson
16 Window pieces
17 ___ Rica
18 Cup fraction
19 Open bottles
20 Attacked, in a way
21 Meet prelims
22 4th "Star Trek" feature film
25 Ikhnaton's successor
26 Sound quality
27 Gulf leader
28 Ethically neutral
30 Trains in Chicago
31 Infielder's pad
32 Remove by suction
34 June portrayer in "Walk the Line"
36 Foolish fellow
38 Mammy Yokum's lad
39 Roughly
42 Uncooperative words
44 Sound investment
45 The "Enterprise" crew searched for this mammal in 22-A
49 GI address
51 Manchurian border river
52 Presidents' Day event
53 Show to be false
56 Cleo's guy
58 "Saturday Night Fever" music
62 Launder with chemicals
64 Georgia's continent
67 Spike Lee's "___-Raq"
68 Debate subjects
69 First homicide victim
70 Russian sea
71 Dot follower
72 Name of 45-A in the "Star Wars" version?
76 Positive pole
78 Pride sounds
79 Ripped off
80 No longer available
81 Achieve harmony
82 Athena's shield
83 Campaign button word
84 Reduces the fare
85 To be specific

DOWN

1 Failing engine sound
2 Access up to the street
3 Tick off
4 Skip town
5 Orr teammate Phil, familiarly
6 Makes tracks
7 Big sandwiches
8 Moore's TV boss
9 Four Corners state
10 Eur. defense alliance
11 Arty area
12 Regret bitterly
13 Under
14 Got going
15 They like to snuggle
23 Oral vote
24 Travel guide
29 Royal ball
31 Wall of earth
32 In a frenzied state
33 Gushes
35 Slightest bit of money
37 Bring upon oneself
40 Practice intelligence
41 "Time" 2008 Person of the Year
43 Doo-wop syllable
45 "Goodness gracious!"
46 With 47 Down, "M*A*S*H" star
47 See 46 Down
48 Oahu garland
49 Step down
50 Like ad hominem attacks
54 Critical hosp. area
55 Krypton, for one
57 1972 Minnelli musical
59 He repents in "A Christmas Carol"
60 Chardonnay alternative
61 Most unctuous
63 Placido's "that"
65 Touch and taste
66 Variety
69 Not in a fog
70 Put in a chip
73 Country singer Paisley
74 Cartoon bear
75 Lou's "La Bamba" costar
77 Wintry mo.

234 GRIDIRON PLAY by Erik Agard and Alison Ohringer
The smallest dog in recorded history was a 60 Across.

ACROSS

1 Gridiron play seen in clue* answers (with 36-A)
7 Concert boosters
11 Follow an actor?
14 Casting director?
15 Place
16 Diminutive Italian suffix
17 "Hurry!"
18 Type of exposure
20 NWA biopic "Straight ___ Compton"
22 Grinch portrayer
23 Shrimp dishes (trick PIN)*
26 Interest ceiling (rogue PETS)*
27 Leeds river
28 Inspects
30 1999 futbol World Player of the Century
31 Pearl, essentially
33 Dabbed
35 Homer's howl
36 See 1 Across
39 Figure in black, perhaps
42 Hilary Hahn's instrument
44 Hoopster Maya
46 Tridents made of ink
48 Fund
51 Words of clarification
52 Stoic reassurance (sick DAB)*
54 Bronx Bombers (pull TOPS)*
56 Un-unknot
57 Reform Party founder
58 Bullheaded quality
60 Dog breed from England
64 "Avatar" FX
65 Units for Michael Phelps
66 Nation in the Iroquois Confederacy
67 Yearning
68 "Ur 2 funny!"
69 Birdseed holder (wage WAR)*

DOWN

1 Bumstead's nickname
2 Artist, musician, and antiwar activist
3 Sheepskin boot brand
4 Late ___
5 Bit of extra help
6 Like Anaïs Nin's "Little Birds"
7 K2 site, broadly speaking
8 K2, for one: Abbr.
9 Studio recordings
10 ___ equity
11 Facial feature with at least 3 holes
12 Temper
13 2014 Rae Sremmurd hit
19 Sweet or savory pancake
21 Pat-down org.
23 True grit
24 "Adios!"
25 Joker, for one
26 Stern
29 Drop
32 Ranch addition?
34 Pro ___
37 Checkout time, perhaps
38 Sarsaparilla, e.g.
40 Lake that borders four states
41 Hamiltons
43 World's second-largest religion
45 Symbol on the Warriors "The Town" jersey
46 Taking pictures?
47 Heavy hammer
49 Santana's "___ Como Va"
50 Onto
53 "___ Your Name": Beatles
55 Tsar after Nicholas II
57 Chihuahua coin
59 Tax pro
61 Rib
62 Suffix for cyan
63 Organ with an anvil

235 FOR WHAT IT'S WORTH   by Holden Baker
Peter Weller played the title role in 27 Across.

ACROSS

1 Bloke
5 Richard Burton historical drama
11 World map in 3-D
16 Campus building
17 White-coated weasel
18 Crowd sounds
19 Diva's solo
20 Met soprano Mitchell et al.
21 Have ___ (shoot the breeze)
22 Patching plaster
25 Moral attitudes
26 St. Andrews pothole
27 1984 sci-fi romcom, for short
36 Prefix for metric
39 ___ hers (unisex)
40 Team booster
41 Central Honshu city
42 Governor in Mogul India
43 Select a new jury
46 Buys the farm
49 Côte d'Azur resort
50 Pearly whites
51 Baggage tag for the Rays
52 Aspiring atty.'s exam
53 Cheer for the diva
54 Bok ___ (Chinese cabbage)
55 M's secretary
60 Burn somewhat
61 Low-cost prefix
65 Gordon Gekko's god?
73 Home of MSU-Northern
74 "Eek!"
75 "Nasty" Nastase
76 Cub Scouts pack leader
77 Blythe in "Alice"
78 Bucolic structure
79 Part of a dovetail joint
80 Shows disdain
81 Trueheart of "Dick Tracy"

DOWN

1 Great divide
2 Julius : Groucho :: Arthur : ___
3 "Are you calling me ___?"
4 Control pill
5 It may be in a tower
6 "I kiss'd thee ___ kill'd thee . . .": Shak.
7 "Let's go!"
8 "The Green Mile" author
9 Legislator
10 Don Benito's treasure
11 Italian brandy
12 Cuckoo in Cozumel
13 Island known as "The Gathering Place"
14 Fiber One fiber
15 Cornerstone abbr.
23 Golden Flashes school
24 "Romeo and Juliet" queen
28 MLB infielder Utley
29 New Zealanders
30 Simile center
31 Field of interest to Isaac Asimov
32 Childish taunt, when repeated
33 George F. Babbitt's hometown
34 One of the two largest cities in Syria
35 "You're absolutely right!"
36 "Don't panic!"
37 Spider-man of Caribbean folklore
38 Bob and Ziggy Marley, for two
42 Bobolink beak
43 "The Canterbury Tales" pilgrim
44 ¿Dónde ___? (Where are they?)
45 Hwy. through Malibu
47 Singles, e.g.
48 Tide type
53 "Cries and Whispers" director
54 Tour de France racer
56 "American Pie" singer

57 Eponymous German physicist
58 Water nymphs
59 Mr. Anderson in "The Matrix"
62 Friend of Fran and Kukla
63 Filed things
64 Nabisco bestsellers
65 "___ Lucky Old Sun"
66 Cod's relative
67 Not odd
68 Folk singer Guthrie
69 Perfect one's skills
70 Tin Pan Alley product
71 River of Belgium
72 "Workaholics" character

ACROSS

1 Dudley Moore classic
7 Piece of snail mail
13 Bentley of "Ghost Rider"
16 Of sea gulls
17 Second-largest of seven
18 Q–U links
19 Coming across by accident*
21 "Give ___ whirl!"
22 Sugar suffix
23 Piglet's plaint
24 Lath clinger
26 The Irish have it
27 Ruffle the feathers
29 Mephisto's realm
30 Adirondack rentals
33 Measure (out)
34 "Ici on ___ français"
35 Basenji, for one
36 "Adios, Enzio"
37 Western spectacle*
38 "The Chalk Garden" playwright Bagnold
39 Steel production units
40 Old violin
41 "___ blu, dipinto di . . ."
42 Sporty convertibles*
44 Overflow point
47 Dispirit
49 Langley letters
50 Mule parent
51 Like jacket weather
53 Nuncupative
54 "Death of a Salesman" salesman
55 Swinging-door feature
56 Forest creature
57 Traveled like a monopode
58 Microsoft Web browser
59 Wait upon
60 "___ Only Just Begun"
61 New enlistee
63 Bubkes
64 "Love ___ Many Faces"
67 Reset reading

68 Sprinter's brace (and a hint to starts of clue* answers)
72 Arabian lute
73 Cut the baloney
74 Cuthbert in "House of Wax"
75 Two make a fly
76 Connect
77 The Dwarfs, e.g.

DOWN

1 More than that
2 Hamelin's problem in 1284
3 Indisputable
4 An LBJ dog
5 "Prometheus ___": Shelley
6 Items in a shrine
7 Slab-sided
8 D–H links
9 Play about writer Capote
10 Hit the sauce
11 Where an élève studies
12 Frog genus
13 Notetaker's woe?*
14 Girl's name meaning "star"
15 Hollywood hopeful
20 Sign a contract
25 Battier of basketball
26 "Swedish Nightingale" Jenny
27 Restored confidence
28 Judge in the '95 news
30 YouTube cofounder Steve
31 Start of a Welk intro
32 Contractor's concern*
33 Intellect
34 Sites for some trivia quizzes
36 Checked garment
37 Bondservant
39 Onstage "Maria" singer
40 Not an act
42 Parameter
43 Pre-Lenin ruler
45 "Dies ___"
46 Convalesce
48 "Tattered Tom" author

50 Pout
51 Cigar
52 Appalling
53 Wine prefix
54 Sweet and attractive
56 Isolated fact
57 Beats around the bush
59 Contender's pursuit
60 Pallid
62 1984 L.A. Olympics boycotter
63 Pheasant nest
64 Party-giver
65 Rubdown target
66 Game for three hands
69 Letters after Sen. Nunes' name
70 Lunar New Year holiday
71 Piercing site

237 DOOMSDAY by Pam Klawitter
80 Across is a hint to clue* answers.

ACROSS

1 Mobile sculptor
7 Place for tea and silk
12 Domino
16 Not agreeable
17 Honshu port
18 Tip more than a few
19 Alternative to a bank loan*
21 Panache
22 First name in espionage
23 Cereal bran
24 Map of Hawaii, often
26 Marines known as 31's*
32 It's big at McDonald's
35 Precinct squad
36 Passepartout, for one
37 Sets out neatly
39 Kind of fit
43 Bambi's mother-in-law
44 Uses a rotary phone
45 "Three stripes" sportswear company
47 It's out on a limb
48 K-9 unit specialty*
51 Fortune's friend
53 They mind your business
54 "Time in a Bottle" singer
57 Polished off
58 Grammarian's concern
59 Fabric that bleeds
60 A place to begin
62 Imperial
65 Waze, for one
66 Extraterrestrial*
71 Early computer
72 Sports org. founded in 1894
73 Henry James' biographer
77 Demanding letters
80 Doomsday
83 Lie out in the sun
84 Garage opener?
85 Aslan's realm
86 Joust verbally
87 Super-G tracks
88 They're perfect

DOWN

1 Sailboat stopper
2 Sports shoe company
3 Time of penitence
4 Night vision?
5 Paul Anka's "___ Beso"
6 Get back on track
7 Heart valve
8 Missouri–Florida dir.
9 Hawkins of Dogpatch
10 Fit for ___
11 East China Sea island
12 Sicilian peak
13 "The Huffington Post" acquirer
14 Balneotherapy spot
15 Quiz whiz Jennings
20 "Let It Snow" lyricist
25 "Green" sin
27 Bottomless pit
28 Baseball rarities
29 Tragedienne Duse
30 Major at Little Bighorn
31 RN's imperative
32 Certifiable
33 Singer Grande, in fanzines
34 Kind of cocktail
38 Hyacinth cousin
40 Invention impetus
41 Black Hawk's people
42 Former British Airways jet
45 Arabian Sea gulf
46 Man caves
47 "What Price Glory?" director
49 Offline farewell
50 Poker declaration
51 Africa's Burkina ___
52 Aleutian isle
55 Dental crown
56 Seer's gift
58 Online farewell
59 "Father of Radio"
61 Ebert's partner after Siskel
63 Southfork family
64 Like "no news"
67 Sabbath contribution
68 Horselaughs
69 "Ace of Cakes" workers
70 Raison ___
74 Meyer in "Star Trek Nemesis"
75 Jannings in "Quo Vadis"
76 Bucolic expanses
77 Crunch targets
78 Gullible one
79 Wanted poster abbr.
81 Netherlands city
82 Mood ring, for one

238 CLUE SHARING by Harvey Estes
Read aloud the first two clues in caps to get the third one.

ACROSS

1 "Sing, Sing, Sing" composer
6 Strike down
11 Make a minister happy
16 Perfectly clear
17 Pluto's realm
18 Civil War side
19 Change the constitution
20 Dizzying design
21 Ars ___, vita brevis
22 TACK
25 "Double Fantasy" artist
26 Minn. neighbor
27 At the peak
28 "Got ya!"
31 Old camera need
33 Pro Bowl side
35 Cartoon frames
36 Fan setting
37 Grow faint
38 Glabrous to the max
40 Ariana Grande, for one
41 Wall Street bear
43 Solitary sort
44 TICKLE
50 Centennial State resort
51 Prevailed
52 Food fish
53 40 winks and more
56 Exiled Ugandan
60 Half score
61 Sweeping story
62 Xeroxed ms., e.g.
63 Auctioneer's cry
64 Wind up
65 Kind of glasses
67 Public image, briefly
69 Expose, in verse
70 TACTICAL
74 "Follow?"
76 Round of fire
77 Everest is on its border
78 Cara of "Fame"
79 Hears a case
80 Once and again
81 "A Boy ___ Sue"
82 Have a hunch
83 Mrs. Peel's friend

DOWN

1 Postseason game
2 Black Sea country
3 Freezing
4 Ho Chi ___ City
5 Expand upon
6 Deficit
7 Glove compartment items
8 State o' potato
9 Stamp of "Valkyrie"
10 Spreads across the land
11 Dutch export
12 Part of, as a plot
13 Type of butterscotch cookie
14 Harley-Davidson's NYSE symbol
15 Bambi's aunt
23 Give power to
24 Chowderhead
29 Miserable dwelling
30 Fully informed
32 Goofed off, with "around"
34 Bevans in "Saboteur"
39 Audibly overwhelm, with "out"
40 Collar attachment
42 Fabric name ending
43 Lucy of "Kill Bill"
44 Social group
45 Ghostly pale
46 "Rise and shine!"
47 Polliwog's parent
48 Deliberately
49 Sacred music genre
53 Guitar neck attachment
54 Discriminating types
55 Steak order
57 S'more's sister
58 How to go from church
59 Got under the skin of
61 Put in piles
66 Dog-tired
68 What Sam made too long, in song
71 Break bread
72 Part of YSL
73 Eye source in "Macbeth"
74 Card player's cry
75 Sale stat

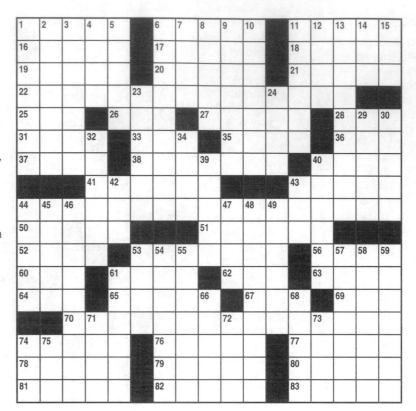

239 DOWN THE BRAIN by Harvey Estes
For people who like to play ducks and brakes.

ACROSS

1 Volleyball smash
6 Cerberus guards its gate
11 M-16, for one
16 Israeli dances
17 "Ready or not, here ___!"
18 Transmitting
19 "Pygmalion" heroine
20 "The Female Eunuch" author
21 Spa offering
22 Bench-clearer at the Iron Bowl?
25 Sonar principle
27 Golf champ Ernie
28 Cube with pips
29 Assassination accusation
32 Road guide
33 Astronomical altar
34 Small batteries
36 Strike out
37 Arms company deeply in debt? (with 40-A)
40 See 37 Across
42 Language of Livy
43 Football plays
45 Fencing move
46 Slips by
48 "No kidding!"
49 Bicycle built for two
50 Sydney sidekick
51 Tarzan, or one of his hairy friends
54 Iodine source
55 Ad prefix for winter products
56 The verge of a food regimen?
58 "Baloney!"
59 Harper Lee's lawyer
60 Transfer
62 Image site
65 Pottery glaze
69 Uninspiring
70 Business
76 "___ grip!"
77 Boast as you drain the swamp?
80 Puts to sleep
81 Off-limits
82 Destroy gradually
83 Steamed
84 Warning signals
85 Ruhr industrial center

DOWN

1 "That's all ___ wrote!"
2 Seat seeker
3 Famine of 1845–1849
4 Toy instrument
5 Twin in the Torah
6 Park that's a city in Detroit
7 Field units
8 Procrastinator's opposite
9 Correct words, perhaps
10 Belgrade residents
11 French artist Bonheur
12 Agape, maybe
13 Nitpicker
14 Wai in "Tomorrow Never Dies"
15 Chapter of history
23 Polo of "The Fosters"
24 Care for
25 Coat of arms and others
26 Desert procession
30 Grapefruit hybrid
31 Disheveled
33 "A Little Night Music" newlywed
35 Ward of "Once and Again"
38 Off the mark
39 Accompany
40 Private
41 Dip a doughnut
44 Sonogram area
47 Source of Popeye's strength
49 Old kind of variety store
52 Camcorder abbr.
53 Draw
56 Huge racket
57 Okla. neighbor
59 Act jittery
61 Carlsberg brews
62 Synagogue leader
63 Typo, for one
64 Princess topper
66 Office notes
67 Piano exercise
68 Weighed down
71 "Here ___ go?"
72 Linguist Chomsky
73 Sugar unit
74 "Ghostbusters" character
75 Peloponnesian P's
78 Monogram of Prufrock's creator
79 Part of a bray

240 PLAYERS UNION by Richard Silvestri
57 Across is a uniform color of the San Jose Sharks.

ACROSS

1 Unable to escape
6 They may be screened
11 Special skill
16 Ingraham with an "angle"
17 Like some kites
18 Oktoberfest drink
19 Moving
20 Swedish port
21 Football-shaped
22 Encountered golfer Cabrera on the links?
24 Gutsy Romano?
26 Rock group
27 The gamut
29 Morn's counterpart
30 Squared things
32 Rubbed the wrong away?
37 Columbus Day event
41 River to the Rhine
43 Cameo, e.g.
44 Got up
45 Doubles
47 Word of regret
48 Research rooms
49 Act Bossy?
50 Poetic preposition
51 Use a scale
52 Up to snuff
53 Put in a crate
55 Standardbred horse
56 Stadium section
57 Shade of blue
58 Can't stand
59 Egg-roll time
61 Rooming-house resident
64 Lend a hand
66 The O'Hara estate
67 Home of Iowa State
71 Zoo newcomer
76 Arcturus, for one
78 Type of squash
79 Knight spot?
81 Get a smile out of
82 Caribou kin
83 First sign
84 "Taming of the Shrew" locale
85 Through
86 Down-at-the-heels
87 Make hard

DOWN

1 San Antonio attraction
2 Shocking weapon
3 Western sight
4 Kathleen Battle solos
5 Kitten's plaything
6 Totalled
7 Arthurian paradise
8 "Dallas" aunt
9 Irish stew meat
10 Dorm sound
11 Forage plant
12 Go on a tirade
13 Thickening agent
14 Spanakopita ingredient
15 Deuce topper
23 Slalom marker
25 Disinclined
28 Round number?
30 Fruity drink
31 Coastal high spots
33 Biblical peak
34 Comfort
35 Buoys up
36 Leave in the lurch
37 Epicure's asset
38 World's largest peninsula
39 California oaks
40 State with confidence
42 Where you are
45 Roadwork marker
46 Union unit
49 Like liters
54 Tons
55 MPH middle
58 Exhausted
60 Was worthy of
62 Moved suddenly
63 Covered with gunk
65 Creator of Edmond Dantès
67 Draw a bead on
68 Sitcom set in Tuckahoe, NY
69 Come next
70 Lift
71 Tone down
72 Revered statue
73 Fair beater?
74 Ancient Irish language
75 Bring to light
77 Lacunae
80 Tell it like it isn't

HITTING THE SLOPES   by Richard Silvestri
Would Liechtenstein fit the scenario below?

ACROSS

1 "Friendly" cartoon character
7 Like some drones
12 Bump suddenly
16 Video-game haven
17 Spear's kin
18 Lamb by another name
19 **Start of a Steven Wright quip**
21 Try to locate
22 Derby entrant
23 Put on a happy face
24 Make things right
25 Biblical exchange unit?
26 Musical Rimes
28 Drink with bangers
29 Civil suit subject
31 **Part 2 of quip**
37 Nick and Nora's pet
39 Met melody
40 Be contrite about
41 "A Chorus Line" role
44 Staff members?
46 Theater area
47 Modify
48 Mass-transit problem
49 Dilate
50 Serve the tea
51 Holey roll
52 Bread plant
53 16.5 feet
54 Far from ruddy
55 Seaside soarer
56 **Part 3 of quip**
60 Splashy resorts
64 Well filler
65 Crete's highest pt.
67 Vaudevillian Tanguay
68 Gut
71 St. Teresa's city
73 Pick up an option
75 It may be made up
76 **End of quip**
78 Take measurements
79 Jewish sect member
80 Woman's top
81 British carbine
82 Bone, in combinations
83 Evening bell

DOWN

1 Official seal
2 Dry gulch
3 Tally keeper
4 Make the grade
5 Ford named after a Ford
6 Kind of hall
7 Diploma holders
8 Grilled sandwich
9 Pt. of IHOP
10 Lot unit
11 Marshal under Napoleon
12 Court entertainer
13 Pat on the buns
14 Mortgage, e.g.
15 Let the pitch go by
20 Japanese port
24 Pond organism
27 Noble name of Italy
28 Sale stipulation
30 Electric-dart firer
32 Dating from birth
33 Neutral colour
34 Destroy by degrees
35 Drilling tool
36 Wee
38 Dubbed one
41 Blue Grotto locale
42 Emotionally distant
43 Hit the books
44 Mideast hot spot
45 Flamenco cry
46 Takes to
48 Spanish surrealist
49 Sickly
51 Mound mistake
52 Thin nail
54 Small and weak
55 Computer of the 1940s
57 Well-invested industrialists?
58 De Ravin in "Remember Me"
59 "That's good enough"
61 Kept inside
62 Loath
63 Aunt Polly's nephew
66 As ___ (usually)
68 First lady after Eleanor

69 Highway sign
70 Pass time idly
71 Second of a Latin trio
72 Seemingly endless
74 Grandson of Eve
76 HBO alternative
77 "Heads" side of a coin: Abbr.

"WHAT I MENT TO SAY . . ."   by Anna Carson

Pee Wee King wrote the music to the song classic at 26 Across.

ACROSS

1 "I Do, I Do, I Do, I Do, I Do" group
5 Sieve bottom
9 Model
16 Indoor ball
17 Two-tone cookie
18 Warship fleets
19 Guernsey and Jersey
21 Fact facer
22 Pleasure from eating sweets?
24 Bk. before Jeremiah
25 "Why don't we!"
26 "Tennessee Waltz" lyricist Stewart
29 Work with a wok
33 Ark. neighbor
37 Mil. mail letters
38 "Cheers" regular
39 A shadow falls across it
41 Ghost town saloon?
44 Extends a finger
45 Moxie
46 "Wake Up Little ___"
48 Pitch properly
49 Road leveler
51 Website suffix for opinions?
54 O'Neal's "Love Story" costar
56 Chutzpah
57 Pilot with five kills
58 Hook's ally
59 Second edition
61 "___ Little Tenderness"
62 Gets set
63 Letter before sigma
65 Cry of "Don't smudge the window"?
74 Its capital is Abuja
75 Pneumatic tool
76 Pass receiver that lines up wide
77 Baylor's home
78 "___ Lonesome I Could Cry"
79 Bernstein musical
80 Narrow margin of victory
81 Right on a map

DOWN

1 Added factors
2 Bridges of Hollywood
3 Sailor's cooler
4 Shaking in your boots
5 Soft shoe
6 Switch suffix
7 Pieced together
8 Monstrance display
9 Paycheck recipients
10 Decorate
11 Mosque leaders
12 Handmaid's story
13 Valhalla VIP
14 It's rigged
15 NY winter hrs.
20 Soph. and jr.
23 Polar helper
26 Luftwaffe counterers
27 Wit bit
28 Greyhound event
30 Skin designs, for short
31 Preparing to bloom
32 Whys and wherefores
33 Intense hatred
34 Greg in "As Good as It Gets"
35 Dormant state
36 Gore and Green
38 Put off
40 "Didn't do it!"
42 Moose's girlfriend in "Riverdale"
43 Bar mitzvah and baptism
47 Hose hue
49 Diamond execs
50 Like the upper atmosphere
52 Foot protection
53 Leaves beverage in the bag
55 Prosperity
60 Ideology
61 Agee of the Miracle Mets
62 Word on a Russian map
64 "Isn't ___ bit like you and me?": Beatles
65 Kind of monster
66 Popeye Doyle's prototype Eddie
67 Watch over
68 Display of disinterest
69 Siena "See ya!"
70 Jumps electrodes
71 Flaubert heroine
72 Capone's nemesis
73 Brisk pace
74 Grp. of Saints

243 CIRCULAR THINKING   by Anna Carson
. . . for those who don't care to do the math.

ACROSS

1 St. Louis brewery founder
6 Get in the way of
11 Jackie's predecessor
16 Cry of defeat
17 Rust or lime, e.g.
18 "You ___ kidding!"
19 Dale Earnhardt's number
20 Battlefield cry
21 Get through to
22 **Start of a math student's protest**
25 "Star Trek: ___"
26 Hula shakers
27 Introduction to sex?
28 "Shop ___ You Drop"
29 Fried Italian veggie
32 Nutrient in almonds
34 Puts in new clips
35 Charge per unit
36 "You said a mouthful!"
37 Poem with a pastoral setting
38 Trojan beauty
39 Forfeit
40 **More of protest**
44 Letters at Camp Lejeune
48 Credo
49 Wishful words
54 Org. that sanctions schools
55 Sucrose source
56 Latin revolutionary Simón
58 Give notice to
60 Informants
61 Neither Rep. nor Dem.
62 Old witch
63 "Star Trek: TNG" empath
64 Poet Armantrout
65 **End of protest**
70 Strikeout-king Ryan
71 Message board?
72 Ovine sign
74 Digital dinosaur
75 Arm bones
76 Passover dinner
77 Not bright
78 Hammer heads
79 Donne and Bradstreet

DOWN

1 Except
2 Out of one's mind
3 Like a five o'clock shadow at nine
4 "Buffy the Vampire Slayer" demon
5 Pay attention to
6 Stomping grounds
7 Welcome word after "tax"
8 Wave makers
9 Cut film
10 Tried to bring on board
11 Prosecutor Clark
12 Kind of code or rug
13 Grace period?
14 Not level
15 Fruit-ripening gas
23 "If only ___ known"
24 Deeply focused
25 Garr in "Dumb and Dumber"
30 November runner
31 French composer Édouard
32 Clothing rack
33 Fleetwood ___
35 Bowling lane button
38 Perfected one's craft
41 JFK's "109"
42 Pressure source
43 Rembrandt works
44 Like the "Mona Lisa"
45 Entr'acte follower
46 Troubadour instrument
47 Callous heel
50 Batter's success
51 Veto
52 Avian squawker
53 Highland dialect
56 Renewable energy source
57 Ronny Howard role
59 From what source
60 Like an infamous gift horse
63 Now it's yours
66 "Serpico" author
67 Season to be jolly
68 Cicada killer
69 Sandwich cookie
73 This year's grads

244

THEMELESS by Brian E. Paquin

"The early bird gets the worm — which is what he deserves." —20 Across

ACROSS

1 Not bug-free
8 Things to block
17 "Rent" actress Dawson
18 Start studying
19 Freezing
20 Muppet who practices karate
21 Mouth, slangily
22 How Tiny Tim strolled through the tulips?
23 "The Old Curiosity Shop" girl
25 Suffix for hobby
26 Gym class
30 Hold title to
32 Bothers no end
38 Kind of ticket
39 Coen brothers movie
41 West on "Salem"
42 Sommer in "The Prisoner of Zenda"
43 Itsy-bitsy
44 Settled a score
46 Big rig engines
48 Tiny surveillance tool
49 "You can't be serious!"
50 Swing dance
51 Wide-eyed
53 More exact
54 "The Maltese Falcon" sleuth
56 Fashion
57 Maine raptor
59 Fringe-toed lizard genus
60 Snake, at times
61 Cauldron
63 Appealed (for peace)
65 Moon phases
71 Prepare for a big game
76 Like Redford's 2013 film hero
77 "Piece of cake!"
78 Helpers
79 One bringing flowers and candy
80 "Isn't this the place to be?"
81 How herds move

DOWN

1 Stagehand
2 Exact positions
3 Shrink's words
4 RPM gauge
5 Sang like Michael Bublé
6 Like Rome's landscape
7 Tyrolean tune
8 Former Dallas QB Tony
9 Offering a thought
10 Defeats
11 Like mobile windshield replacements
12 Moonbeam McSwine's creator
13 Not much
14 Team picture?
15 Opera box
16 "The ___ the limit!"
24 Bank deals
26 Game starter
27 Field goal enablers
28 Have some laughs
29 Cynic
31 Dryly humorous
33 ___ Spumanti
34 "Let's Go" group
35 Barbaric types
36 Fish or flower
37 Jack's neighbor
39 Inflates
40 Pointed arch
43 Nonexplosive gunpowder
45 "Ready Player ___" (2018)
47 Parched
48 The original golden boy?
49 Pontiac muscle car
50 Wing it with a band
52 E. Berlin was its capital
55 Green clubs
56 Pretty penny
58 Mimieux in "The Picasso Summer"
60 "Ben-Hur" Oscar winner
62 Adams exhibited at MoMA
64 Locale for a slap shot
65 Talon
66 ___ Hashanah
67 To be, to Titus
68 Ruckus
69 Matter for Mason
70 Freelancer's enc.
72 Michael in "Juno"
73 "___ Off to Larry": Del Shannon
74 Puts into action
75 Funeral fire

245 THEMELESS by Brian E. Paquin

The grapes for 73 Across are allowed to dry for 120 days before crushing.

ACROSS

1 Chart-busters
10 Best Picture of 1970
16 Fragrant bowl of petals
17 Ham Fisher's boxer
18 Blatant
19 Sojourn of the self-absorbed
20 Keyed up
21 After deductions
22 Signifies
23 Focus of a chimney inspection
26 Half a Samoan port
30 Eyes in the sky
31 Lifesaver Schindler
36 Pie option
38 1939 epic movie, briefly
40 Edge of a roof
41 Clemson team
42 Contemplates the universe
44 Lightfoot offerings
47 Plum liqueur
48 Speeding out of control
50 Join forces
52 Paid newspaper notice
53 Earth Day subj.
54 Close friends
55 Parsonage
57 Chintzy
59 Once, once
60 "Welcome Back, Kotter" setting
63 Made it to first
67 Tessio of The Godfather
68 Sportscaster Rashad
73 Italian dry red wine
74 Collection of Hemingway short stories
76 Hockey teams, e.g.
77 Cowlicked "SNL" character
78 Scarlett O'Hara's maid
79 Frumpy

DOWN

1 Blemish
2 Pouter's expression
3 Memo abbr.
4 Fashionable resorts
5 Sharpens
6 1963 Paul Newman role
7 "Edmund Fitzgerald" cargo
8 Faithful concerning
9 Portrait sessions
10 Beeps
11 Fictional king of Naples
12 Small Oz visitor
13 Civil injustice
14 Dust Bowl refugee
15 Siestas
17 Place of esteem
24 In all probability
25 Little amphibians
26 Androgynous "SNL" character
27 Woodcutter in a den of thieves
28 First man in space
29 Frittatas
32 Ocean channel
33 Avant-garde artist Malevich
34 "Monopoly" purchases
35 Hi-___
37 Shield border
39 Contacted, old-school
43 The Bee ___
45 Gives commands
46 Blankets the North
48 ORG alternative
49 Shiny color photos
51 L.A. clock setting
54 Louis Pasteur's forte
56 Reverberates
58 German chancellor Willy
61 Like dryer filters
62 Madame Curie
63 Express surprise
64 Period after Passover
65 Roll down a runway
66 Cultural pursuits
69 Web language
70 Country distance?
71 Leon in "Peggy Sue Got Married"
72 Former Turkish rulers
75 WWW address

THEMELESS by Bruce Venzke and Victor Fleming

Hint: "Don't talk back" followed 37 Across in the 1958 Coasters hit.

ACROSS

1 Prone to use selfishly
13 Links
17 Yellowish-brown
18 Ginger ___
19 Micronutrient
20 Prominent do
21 Title for Edith Evans
22 Embarrassing display
23 Praying figure
24 Skillful
27 Blood component
29 Abbr. before 10 digits
30 Ft. Bragg cops
33 Part of a tooth
35 Commonsensical
36 Application
37 The Coasters 1958 hit
40 Steel helmets
42 Stand for a hot dish
43 Man of many words
45 Cash sources
46 BVD competitor
47 Estate splitters
48 "___ in the House" (2006 documentary)
49 Pitcher Daal
50 Intermediate, in law
51 ___ and the same
52 More in need of a brushoff
54 Precious group
56 From earlier
57 Applies artistically
59 Judges follower
60 Part of DOS
61 Male cat
62 Tweaks a manuscript
64 Develop
66 "___ you so!"
68 Lowlands, to poets
70 Fred's portrayer on "Sanford"
74 Water-to-wine village
75 Sign of things to come
78 Warlike god
79 Without certainty
80 Disintegrate, as cells
81 American Law Institute publications

DOWN

1 Tavern sign abbr.
2 Bonus, in ads
3 Tottenham tot's transport
4 Streaked with color
5 Have an unpaid balance
6 Diamonds, to thieves
7 "War and Peace" writer
8 Jamesir in "Murder by Death"
9 Ponderous texts
10 Dunne and Ryan
11 Regards with respect
12 Summer hrs. in Charleston
13 Bygone Russian leader
14 Youthful crushes
15 Buyer's deposit
16 Goal of a Felix Unger type?
23 Sign of things to come
25 Popular Deco lithographs
26 Four-time Indy 500 winner
28 Education division
30 Thunderbirds, e.g.
31 Like the National Guard
32 Scrawny
34 Bitter vetches
38 Turn inside out
39 Conor McGregor specialty
41 Winnie the Pooh's greeting
44 Garson of Hollywood
47 Triceratops, e.g.
48 Even if, for short
50 Viking quaff
51 Cosmology sci.
53 Checked a birthday
55 Rap sheet accompanier
58 Bart, Ringo, and Ken
63 Wintry phenomenon
65 Stayed in touch
67 Shoot a light gun
69 She, in Sicily
71 Bremner in "Wonder Woman"
72 Shoulder muscle, for short
73 Prohibitionists
75 Hemlock relative
76 Draft pick
77 "Dragnet Theme" syllable

247 BIG APPLE CORE   by Ray Hamel
Alternate clue for 63 Down: Con artist in "The Usual Suspects."

ACROSS

1 Dangerous download
8 Creator
13 What dry ice + hot water creates
16 Sound of a trumpet
17 "What's in ___?": Shakespeare
18 River of Spain?
19 Animated conscience
21 Keebler cookie maker
22 Earth's pull, briefly
23 Ask for
24 "Goosebumps 2" director Sandel
25 Marienbad, notably
26 Arctic sightings
28 Work perk
31 Song
33 Party person
34 Hyperbolic timespan
35 "Some Like It Hot" star
41 Cologne article
43 "___ Daba Honeymoon"
44 Birth of a notion
45 Canine in the comics
49 "Stay back!"
55 Protection
56 Mother of the Titans
57 Source of royal insomnia
58 Keg device
60 Inexpensive sweets
63 Itinerary preposition
65 Ride at a stand
67 Aggregate
68 Weight Watchers alternative
72 Sixteen make a cup: Abbr.
76 Cyberspace address
77 Rarebit ingredient
78 Huffy state
81 Applebee's acquirer
82 Adam Silver's org.
83 Carlo Rizzi's brother-in-law
86 Juice container
87 Insipid
88 Incubator occupant
89 Immemorial
90 Ready for use again
91 Stopped fidgeting

DOWN

1 Work for a burger flipper
2 Dress with flare
3 Not as believable
4 Unable to sit still
5 Eastern French department
6 Rogers and Bean
7 Suffix with differ
8 Apprentice geisha
9 RSA political party
10 Nocturnal New Zealand parrot
11 Green beryl
12 ___-A (wrinkle reducer)
13 Wall painting
14 Bottom of a crankcase
15 Be a huge success
20 Amusement, for short
27 Plant pouch
29 AWOL arresters
30 Type of question often asked in court
32 Bygone Serbian car
35 "And here it is!"
36 Symphony member
37 Da ___ (Vietnam port)
38 Dream sleep
39 Quattro less uno
40 Politico's concern
42 "The Joy of Signing" subj.
46 Scott Van Pelt's network
47 Bassoonist's buy
48 Breakfast-in-bed need
50 Industry bigwig
51 Richmond was its cap.
52 John Masefield's "The Tragedy of ___"
53 Feminine energy
54 Great Barrier Reef lagoon sights
59 IBM knockoff of the '80s
60 Kegling org.
61 "That's a wrap!"
62 Kind of lighting
63 SAT section
64 Like the Caspian Sea
66 Some Olympic venues
68 Snowbird
69 Co-Nobelist of Yitzhak and Shimon
70 "The best ___ to come!"
71 Health supplement chain
73 River hazard
74 Bridge, in Bologna
75 Sandra Bullock film
79 Solar wind particles
80 Cashew or pecan, e.g.
84 One-eighty from SSW
85 Sodom survivor

248 EXISTENTIAL ENDING by Marie Langley
In the end, just live.

ACROSS

1 Disco Era hairdos
6 Ireland's patron, briefly
11 Not-for-profit music org.
16 Not exactly excited
17 Bootlegger's product
18 In the know
19 "The old gray mare ___"
22 Yellowstone denizen
23 Brian who managed the Beatles
24 Sportscaster Andrews
25 One of seven in the Constitution
27 Gets back in business
29 Italian tabloid
30 "General Hospital" network
33 Big heart?
34 Those in control
38 "Foiled again!"
40 Drop off
41 Is indebted to
42 Buffoon
45 Ahab, in a Ray Stevens song
47 Broom companion
49 "Young Frankenstein" role
50 #1 Beatles hit of 1970
52 In a lather
53 "Hallelujah!"
54 Accompany
56 Stooge with a bowl cut
57 Pay tribute to
58 "I'm so stupid!"
59 Donovan's daughter Skye
61 College list keeper
63 Do road work
64 In vigorous health
65 French toast ingredients
67 U.S. Army slogan
74 Pastry ingredient
75 Like Conor McGregor
76 Studied, with "over"
78 African language group
79 Wedding site
80 Where the elated walk
81 "Hedda Gabler" playwright
82 Black, in Bordeaux
83 LPGA golfer Korda

DOWN

1 Rhyme scheme
2 Small handbill
3 Charged
4 Swift-running bird
5 Stitch up
6 Physical condition
7 Little ones
8 Military station
9 Feel compassion
10 Not our
11 ___ in aardvark
12 Popeye's "infink"
13 Leadership group
14 ". . . who ___ heaven"
15 Unappreciated workers
20 Rooftop landing place
21 Still on the plate
26 Process a bite
28 "Draft Dodger Rag" singer
30 "Far out!"
31 Existential ending of five answers
32 Cut
34 Make a straw roof
35 Heavy burden
36 Influence
37 Dress up
38 Reacted to canoe leak
39 "You ___ right!"
43 It comes straight from the heart
44 McDonald's machine
46 Irving Stone speciality
48 Lao-tse's "way"
49 Taking a sick day
51 Shakedown cruise
53 Overwhelm with numbers
55 Kind of bridge
57 Starchy stuff
60 Novak Djokovic, for one
62 Pooh's grumpy pal
64 ___ cuisine
66 Light biscuit
67 Rat
68 Just about forever
69 2009 Beyoncé hit
70 Curtain-raising time
71 Whar the whale is?
72 One-time "Sea of Islands"
73 Justice Gorsuch
74 Fox Mulder employer
77 Martini request

249 PICKY FOR A REASON   by Marie Langley
A good one to solve while you're waiting to get your ears lowered.

ACROSS

1 Rain check, e.g.
5 Island near Sicily
10 Shuffling dance
16 Elizabeth of "La Bamba"
17 Tear producer
18 Choice word
19 Dr. Jones' nickname
20 Parade
21 Flight
22 **Start of a barbershop joke**
25 Seam bonanza
26 Female fowl
27 Sarah's "Walking Dead" role
28 FICA funds it
31 Victoria's Secret purchase
33 Hooked to the wrecker
36 Ice cream utensil
38 **More of joke**
41 Large low digit
44 Duel tools
45 Sea near the Caspian
46 Turkish title
47 Bus. card abbr.
49 Scoundrel
51 Season abroad
52 Cellar pump
54 Marshal's group
58 Trojan hero
60 **More of joke**
63 The blahs
64 "NCIS" actor Joe
65 "On Beyond Zebra!" author
69 Reagan was president of this
70 Lineage chart
72 Sandra in "Tammy Tell Me True"
74 Bottom-line
75 **End of joke**
79 Welding wear
82 Hirsch in "The Emperor's Club"
83 Blue shade
84 Take a chill pill
85 Black bird
86 Browse without posting
87 Cartoon canary
88 Edgar Bergen dummy
89 Golf pegs

DOWN

1 Keg feature
2 Campus security
3 Like a natural blond
4 Howls at the moon
5 Israeli leader Dayan
6 Madonna's "Evita" costar
7 Old Italian coin
8 Take the show on the road
9 Chamois, for one
10 Joker portrayer Romero
11 Revenge roster
12 Minimally
13 AL or NL team, on scoreboards
14 Ship pronoun
15 Pirate interjections
23 "I see no problem with this"
24 Derby hat
28 Gathering in the evening
29 "Moonlight ___": Beethoven
30 Turns aside
32 NYPD rank
34 Pahrump, Nevada, county
35 Cooking meas.
37 Elhi org.
39 Tired Cherokees?
40 Old Testament patriarch
41 Blowouts
42 Galápagos lizard
43 Nevada revenue source
48 Let out
50 Service, of a sort
53 Boston tower, with "the"
55 Vatican City basilica
56 Doo-wop syllable
57 Fabric name ending
59 U-turn from SSW
61 "Pipe down!"
62 "The Lonely Goatherd" singer, e.g.
66 Peerless
67 Safe from break-ins
68 Saltgrass orders
71 Out of practice
73 Make corrections to
75 "Anything Goes" writer Porter
76 IRS agent
77 House of wax
78 White on "Breaking Bad"
79 "___ your age!"
80 Cartoon sound effect
81 Sevruga delicacy

250 SCALE MODEL   by Harvey Estes
. . . in honor of Paul McCartney's instrument.

ACROSS

1 Freshness symbol
6 Insignificant ones
11 Cymbals sound
16 Gilbert Grape's brother
17 Greek column style
18 Bob Marley, for one
19 **Comment heard at a Phish concert**
22 Mean mutt
23 Not fantastic
24 Don Juan's mother
25 Klee contemporary
26 Sale words
28 Slow movement
30 Grave
31 Alamo patron
33 **More of comment**
34 Basket maker, e.g.
36 Award for Dick Francis
37 Tea type
39 Listens to
40 Cons do it
42 Portfolio components
44 **More of comment**
51 Take back
52 Small batteries
53 Rose
55 Indivisible
56 Pitcher's place
59 Back from now
60 Hardly fast-food fare?
63 Sudden halt
66 Ignore Polonius
67 Scratch a dele
68 **End of comment**
75 Ram in the night
76 Temporarily put aside
77 Mata Hari was one
79 Jessica of "Feud"
80 It flows through the fridge
81 Brief fight
82 Hightails it
83 Lobby greenery
84 City on the Ruhr

DOWN

1 Children's program
2 Stirred up
3 Getting tougher
4 Attack word
5 Wine list datum
6 Moon of Saturn
7 Aspiring
8 B&B
9 Connect with
10 Hardly any
11 Penelope of "Vanilla Sky"
12 "Love Story" composer
13 He danced in "Silk Stockings"
14 Had top billing
15 Bazaar type
20 At the ready
21 Thou and more
27 Pigeon hangout
29 Ocean diver
30 Knocks off
32 Jong or Kane
35 Rub the wrong way
37 White House souvenir
38 Article written by Merkel
41 Bad-mouths
43 Info to analyze
44 Cravings
45 Crude bunch
46 "Mr. Republican" president
47 Mai ___
48 Played for a sucker
49 Right away
50 Science fiction award
51 Sturgeon delicacy
54 Coach Warner
57 Dozes
58 Flags
61 Assert without proof
62 Hershey's brand
64 Knock down
65 Loses freshness
68 Caspian feeder
69 Five after four
70 About
71 Rank
72 Click here
73 Is in session
74 Stuff to the gills
75 Kjellin in "Ship of Fools"
78 Prince George, to Kate Middleton

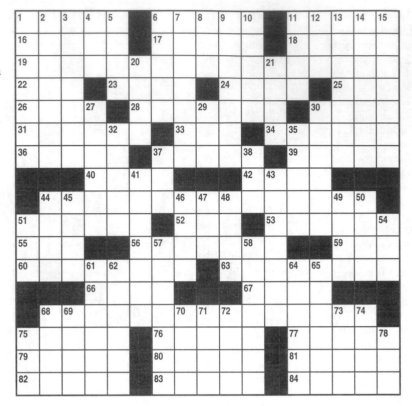

251 WATCH THE BATHROOM SINK   by Harvey Estes
There's a hint about the theme at 79 Down.

ACROSS

1 Flyers with narrow waists
6 Cowboy's date
9 Avon or Cornwall
14 Aimée of "La Dolce Vita"
15 Kate's sitcom partner
17 Mild word for a hot place
18 Two-inch putt, e.g.
19 Run off
20 Eurasian chain
21 Certain balloon fight?
24 German wheels
26 Krypton, for one
29 Salem's st.
30 '60s McCoys song encouraging a mole?
34 "___-hoo!"
35 Many a saint
37 "Double Fantasy" artist
38 ___ City (Chicago)
40 Sneaky maneuver
41 Tries to lose
43 Tinted
44 Cruise quarters
47 Favored few
50 With 52-A, ruling family on the horizon?
52 See 50 Across
55 Changes political strategy
56 Escaped
58 "True that!"
59 USA alternative
62 Brother of Curly and Shemp
64 Pump part
65 Easter beginning
66 First name in courtroom fiction
67 Man of Oman
69 Law, to Lucretius
70 Bar where they drink to a fault?
74 Peach pit
76 Fritter away
77 Waters of the sound
80 In one's salad days
81 Unmitigated
82 Latin for "I believe"
83 Airport worry
84 Loud bursts
85 "Couldn't avoid it"

DOWN

1 Witty one
2 Darth, as a boy
3 It has a wide brim
4 Mountain carnivores
5 Lacking detail
6 TV series set in a high school
7 Food on the floor
8 Willingly
9 Sleep
10 Sultan's palace area
11 Words to bait the foolhardy
12 Meth., e.g.
13 Tough turn
15 "Over the Rainbow" composer
16 Cary of "Robin Hood: Men in Tights"
22 Over yonder
23 Range in which the von Trapps sang
24 Partner of circumstance
25 By word of mouth
27 Zip
28 Sondheim's Sweeney
31 Auctioneer's warning
32 Smallest bill
33 Picked up on
36 Business big shot
39 They may hold your drawers
41 Huge racket
42 Kind of dog
45 Invoice no.
46 Calais café
48 Ready to roll
49 Way of the East
50 Long car, for short
51 Emerson essay, with "The"
53 Where rakes may be hung
54 Kind of log
55 Harsh review
57 Cowboy moniker
60 Hit the roof
61 Group at Caesar's last meeting
62 Shelf above a hearth
63 Info for waiters
66 Lines of lament
68 Tree with smooth bark
71 Wife of John Bates on "Downton Abbey"
72 Hollywood canine
73 Gillette brand
74 Barrett of Pink Floyd
75 It may test the waters
78 D.C. summer hrs.
79 Bathroom that sinks in and out of four answers

"YOU DON'T SAY!" by Joel D. Lafargue
Here's a hint to 14 Down: Cavity Sam has a red light bulb for a nose.

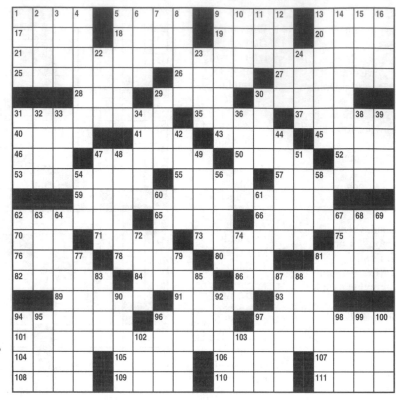

ACROSS

1 Helgenberger in "Erin Brockovich"
5 College math, for short
9 Green-winged duck
13 Swabbie's swabs
17 Ben Gurion carrier
18 Butterine
19 Moon ring
20 Samoan capital
21 **Start of a quip**
25 Talk like Porky Pig
26 Adjective for Granny Smith
27 Group of four
28 Offensive of 1968
29 Leo's locks
30 Stretchy fabric
31 **86 Across cartoonist**
35 "An Inconvenient Truth" author
37 Spend time in rehab, say
40 Winged god
41 Summer mo.
43 Whitecap crest
45 "New Look" couturier
46 Agrippa's 52
47 Aspen activity
50 Gator's cousin
52 "Black Widow" singer Rita
53 Low-flying cloud
55 St. Louis landmark
57 Self-confident
59 **Middle of quip**
62 Angel
65 You, among Friends
66 Settles the score
70 Judge in the 1995 news
71 Trouser section
73 Like matryoshka dolls
75 Dedicated piece
76 High throws
78 Met or Cub, for short
80 Charlotte of sitcoms
81 Last writes?
82 Prepare to be knighted
84 Talk to God
86 **Comic strip source of quip**
89 Invasions
91 Small projections
93 Stumblebum
94 Drive creatures
96 Fairy-tale heavy
97 Overdue debts
101 **End of quip**
104 One on a pedestal
105 Pedro's pet, perhaps
106 Sutherland solo
107 "Torch ___ Trilogy"
108 Philatelic sheet
109 When both hands are up
110 Russo in "Outbreak"
111 Waffles brand

DOWN

1 Just what the doctor ordered
2 Plenty
3 Prego competitor
4 Scintillate
5 Recover
6 Wing-shaped
7 Super Bowl IV MVP Dawson
8 Spain's ___ Brava
9 In regards to that
10 Word after Far or Near
11 Catwalker Carol
12 Highfalutin
13 Bistro employee
14 Game featuring Cavity Sam
15 ___ colada
16 Anti-DUI org.
22 Stick in the mud?
23 Pistol pop
24 Shipping rm. stamp
29 Hawaii's "Valley Isle"
30 Regan's father
31 Ladies
32 Give forth
33 Monte Carlo roulette bet
34 Ballet teacher Struchkova
36 Valium maker
38 Cloud named after a Dutch astronomer
39 Superman's vision
42 Chew peanuts
44 Great Basin desert
47 Procedure segments
48 Torte relative
49 Eco-friendly
51 Like UFC fighters
54 Org. that rates judicial nominees
56 Support the team
58 Mil. branch
60 Verbalize
61 Marathon handout
62 Hose material
63 Hugh Laurie's alma mater
64 Britt in "Under the Dome"
67 Mongolian wasteland
68 Make a long story short
69 Org. seeking life in outer space
72 Rhine's source
74 Droops down
77 "Frasier" setting
79 Burma's largest city
81 Side with the football
83 Oscar winner Kedrova
85 Mongol tent
87 Vital vessels
88 Casino card game
90 Lower oneself
92 Joy of "The View"
94 Intel product
95 Verdi heroine
96 Wised up
97 S ___ Sam
98 Open-mouthed
99 Ladder piece
100 Mormon State flower
102 Mekong River language
103 Dander

253 FASHION STATEMENT   by Joel D. Lafargue
Start of a quip by 101 Across: "You've probably noticed already that . . ."

ACROSS

1 Bed board
5 Uncouth type
9 Track, in a sense
13 Pet rescue org.
17 Hokkaido native
18 "___ kleine Nachtmusik"
19 Early NBC host
20 Experts
21 **Quip continues**
24 Exasperate
25 School piano, usually
26 Begins to move
27 Hospital supply
29 Switch ending
31 Forum greeting
32 Used up
33 **Quip continues**
38 Mrs. Peter Griffin
40 Tempted a ticket
41 Mallory Keaton's brother
42 Word of refusal
43 Ortiz of "Devious Maids"
44 French bread?
46 Hit the + key
47 Le Moko or Le Pew
48 Lead in the pit
50 Trigger
52 However, briefly
54 **Quip continues**
58 Manipulate
59 Where Singaraja is
60 Sambuca flavoring
63 Bert in "Zaza"
66 It pays the rent
67 Flanders river
68 Turn on the waterworks
69 Pink Floyd label
70 Snowmobile
72 Pampering places
74 Give a rap
75 **Quip continues**
80 Nantes decree
81 Replaceable joint
82 Nike rival
83 Rock salt
85 Firth of Clyde island
87 "Where the Wild Things Are" author
91 Gallimaufry
92 **Quip ends**
95 "Pull-down" item
96 German admiral

97 Bone: Comb. form
98 Shoppe descriptive
99 They're sold in dozens
100 Audio receptors
101 **"Moonstruck" star**
102 Greet the judge

DOWN

1 Je ne ___ quoi
2 Like some dishrags
3 "___ Love Her": Beatles
4 Right takers
5 Grant
6 Start of Grafton's 15th title
7 Till compartment
8 Bureaucratic runaround
9 Flowering shrub
10 Mitchell's Twelve ___
11 Scots negative
12 Wrestle (with)
13 Leapt
14 Untainted
15 Irish actor Meaney
16 Between ports
22 Gateway Arch's Saarinen
23 Ready to spit nails
28 Pope defied by Luther
30 Like some inspections
32 Last word at Sotheby's
33 Hagrid is half this
34 "Moesha" network
35 Mission priest
36 Microwave quickly
37 Peacock feather feature
38 Insect secretion
39 The Plastic ___ Band
44 Partners of calls
45 Throbbing sensatioin
46 Autobahn auto
47 Lyrical Lily
49 Sullen
50 Picket line pariah
51 Homeboy
52 Newcastle river

53 Cowsills tune
55 Domicile
56 Principal mountain mass
57 Suitcase sticker
61 Miscalculate
62 Congo red, e.g.
63 Ring around the collar?
64 Roadie's burden
65 Menial worker
66 Joke about
67 Sun ___-Sen
70 In love, old-style
71 Wallet item
72 Method of cooking 99 Across
73 Duvalier nickname
74 Loud ringing sound
76 Contemptible
77 Unlucky match numbers
78 "The Virginian" author
79 Intestinal parts
83 Hopscotch space
84 Shake ___ (hurry)
85 Say for sure
86 Bite to eat
88 Artist to say hello to?

89 Helpful items
90 Tot's perch on daddy
93 Air-quality agcy.
94 Believer

254 "DON'T BLINK" by Joel D. Lafargue

Ferris Bueller is the speaker of the quote below.

ACROSS

1 Bangkok currency
5 "Picnic" playwright
9 Emulate Ella
13 Not quite dry
17 Gallic girlfriend
18 Toon explorer
19 Long-haired sheepdog
20 Composer Siegmeister
21 **Start of a quote**
25 "Un Ballo in Maschera" aria
26 Greek sandwich
27 Robberies
28 "Sicko" targets
31 Do better, market-wise
34 **More of quote**
39 Toon skunk
43 Menial laborer
44 Mute swan genus
45 In a ___ (dour)
47 Wonderland bird
48 R-V hookup?
49 Transgressions
51 Memorable nights
53 Baccarat wager
54 Atelier stands
56 Soon, poetically
58 Regards as true
60 ___ Dhabi
61 **More of quote**
63 Centennial number
64 Argue
67 Autograph
68 Sinkers
71 Cologne connective
72 Vic Cathedral muralist
74 Philip Pullman's shape-shifter
76 Christogram letter
77 "Take ___ from one who's tried . . .": Dylan
79 Cello's ancestor
81 Behind the scenes
82 Barbra's "A Star Is Born" costar
83 General Mills cereal
85 **More of quote**
88 Straighten out again
90 Cannon in "Deathtrap"
91 Lawmakers
94 Not working
97 Unpackaged
101 **End of quote**
106 Start of a Welk countdown
107 Harvey's "Hairspray" role
108 "So that's how it's done"
109 Corona
110 What you used to be?
111 Ducky color?
112 Put in the mail
113 Adam Trask's favorite son

DOWN

1 Bruce Wayne's portrayer
2 "The Kite Runner" hero
3 Old-school sound system
4 Cut one's ___ (gain experience)
5 Start of an ABBA song title
6 Fall mo.
7 Gutfeld of Fox News
8 Hardly a challenge
9 Brussels ___
10 Prompter's offering
11 Ctrl-___-Delete
12 Church donation
13 Contaminated
14 Hamlet's lament
15 Atomizer contents
16 Favorites
22 Hawaiian dress
23 They know their stuff
24 Shout
29 Airwick targets
30 Recital numbers
32 Pitch
33 "Meet the Press" originator
34 ___ dixit (no proof needed)
35 Spanakopita cheese
36 "Amen, brother!"
37 "Time and tide wait for ___"
38 Pollster's discoveries
40 Mixed bag
41 Cut a movie
42 Problems
46 Dick Tracy, for one
49 Black suit
50 Firm
52 Descendant
55 Slacken
57 "No pain, ___"
59 Unfathomable time
61 Rabbit ears
62 Continuously
64 Four, to a pharmacist
65 "Render ___ Caesar . . ."
66 Third OT book: Abbr.
68 Most of "Happy Days"
69 Wispy
70 Sluggin' Sammy
73 "To Venus and Back" singer Amos
75 Temperament
78 Former inmate
80 Making sense
82 City S of Milwaukee
84 Everest climber Gammelgaard
86 Option for the typo-prone
87 Colombian tourist city
89 To date
91 Ruth's sultanate
92 "This isn't good . . ."
93 Series of wares
95 San ___ Obispo
96 Besides
98 Glacial ridges
99 Pastoral tower
100 Harrow's rival
102 Metrical tribute
103 Stubbs of "Sherlock"
104 Bear lair
105 Big Apple slugger

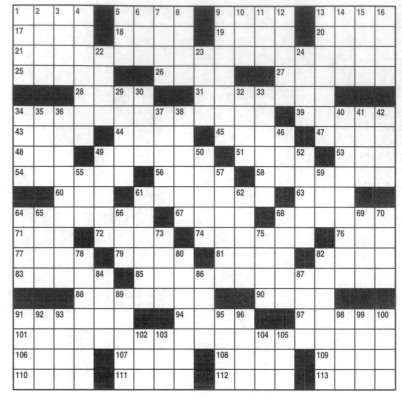

255 ARTISTIC LICENSE by Joel D. Lafargue
27 Across can be found in the comic strip "Shoe."

ACROSS

1 Cy Young Award factors
5 Orbital period
9 Does summer work?
13 Bumper ___
17 Prior pickleworm
18 Ye ___ shoppe
19 Bona fide
20 It works best when tired
21 **Pablo Picasso quote: Part 1**
25 Sightseer's transport
26 Tabloid, slangily
27 Batson D. Belfry, for one
28 Broadway lyricist Rice
29 Came to attention
31 Hebrew letter
32 Dog food brand
35 Anderson and Sue Martin
37 CB, to a CBer
41 **Pablo Picasso quote: Part 2**
46 Part of the Crown Jewels
47 Top-flight
48 Rival of 32 Across
49 Inlet
50 Acts the dilettante
52 Chopin's "___ Sylphides"
55 This "will make it so"
57 Arced throw
58 Kristen's "Twilight" role
60 Grade that doesn't make the grade
61 VIP board member?
64 "Mountain Music" band
66 Headlight bulb
70 Pakistani tongue
71 **Pablo Picasso quote: Part 3**
73 Yorkshire valley
74 Workplace for a boniface
75 "___ and bells for fools": Cowper
76 Belted out
78 Pet detective Ventura
79 Mindful letters?

81 Word on a Chance card
84 Like LeBron James in 2003
86 College URL suffix
87 Marsh birds
89 Prefix for metric
90 **Pablo Picasso quote: Part 4**
96 Sun language
97 Iranian coin
98 Move slowly (along)
99 Potting soil
101 Skating jump
102 Model Macpherson
103 Small particle
104 Resort NNW of Syracuse
105 Quant's skirt
106 Spotted
107 Saharan
108 Legal paper

DOWN

1 Give off
2 Newspaper section
3 Aleutian island
4 In low supply
5 Dogpatch family name
6 "Shady Lane" trees
7 Suffix for cannon
8 Pose another way
9 Peppery salad green
10 Berlin article
11 "Those were the ___"
12 February forecast
13 Ship with lateen sails
14 Reddish brown
15 "Beetle Bailey" bulldog
16 On one's uppers
22 Kyoto cummerbund
23 Gabby Hayes movie
24 Japan's JAL rival
29 Behalf
30 "Big ___" (David Ortiz)
32 Footless animal
33 Mrs. Eric Trump
34 Mr. who was a pop star?
35 John Cena wins

36 "Saint Joan" playwright
38 Bomb shelter
39 Wrack's partner
40 Harry Potter's Patronus
42 Claw
43 "Hurricane" singer Lisa
44 In with
45 County on the North Sea
51 Chicken Cordon ___
52 Nissan model
53 Cuxhaven river
54 Crate component
56 Take note
58 Electronic sound
59 "The Rachel Papers" novelist
61 Witticism
62 Banquet hall dispensers
63 Tracy's "Hairspray" mom
64 "Regrettably . . ."
65 "Diary of ___ Housewife"
67 "Cool!"

68 "___ bitten, twice shy"
69 More than want
71 Becomes an owner
72 Added value to
75 Po tributary
77 Deep cut
80 Katmandu resident
81 Common allergen
82 Uris protagonist
83 Columbia tributary
85 "Curses! ___ again!"
87 Like knock-knock jokes
88 Man of La Mancha
90 Vehicle for hire
91 "MasterChef" prop
92 Longest river in the world
93 Play opener
94 Unpartnered
95 Jutlander
96 Studio session
100 "Spy vs. Spy" magazine

CROSS WORDS by Steven Atwood
Brazilian walnut is another name for 6 Down.

ACROSS

1 Tachometer letters
4 Be petulant
9 Time and a half, e.g.
13 "___ have to do"
17 Battery size
18 Unenthusiastic
19 College in North Carolina
20 El quinto mes
21 Cross
23 Workplace regulating agcy.
24 "___ Excited": Pointer Sisters
25 Château chambers
26 Cross
28 Lyons learning site
29 Early Microsoft product
32 Indeed
33 Cross
35 Inferred
37 Libation with sushi
38 Left speechless
39 Cross
43 Appliance manufacturer
44 New workers
45 Sound of a rubythroat's wings
46 Cross
50 Last word at Sotheby's
51 Exiled queen of 48 BC
52 Frequent fliers
53 Space
54 Bidding
56 Serve some more
57 Driver in "The Last Jedi"
59 Cross
61 Bank amenity
62 Singapore's peninsula
64 Wachter of MSG Networks
65 Cross
67 Give (in)
68 Minor
72 King of Rock
73 Cross
75 "Twelfth Night" duke
78 Foe of Bilbo Baggins
79 Actor Max von ___
80 Cross

83 Stars
84 New Mexico city
85 Prefix with "sol"
86 Cross
89 Neutral color
90 Pack in
91 NYSE members
92 "It ___ far, far . . .": Dickens
93 Second person in the King James Bible?
94 Competitor of 58 Down
95 Daisy type
96 Like Marvell's mistress

DOWN

1 Aggressive poker players
2 Answer to everything
3 Andy Griffith role
4 Actor with the most Oscar nominations
5 Promontory
6 Decking hardwood
7 French peak
8 When to spring forward in CT
9 They attract fish
10 Hebrew "A"
11 Punch or gouge
12 Ring
13 Make like
14 Sri Lankan language
15 Disinfectant spray
16 On the fringe
22 Dr. Sattler of "Jurassic Park"
26 MSN alternative
27 Tops off a room
29 Environmentalist Farley ___
30 Backdrop
31 Movement in art
34 Harold of "Ghostbusters"
35 Like rice paper
36 River in Switzerland
39 Tomahawk ___
40 Maple Leaf, for one
41 Surmise
42 Overact
43 Nova Scotia hrs.
46 Harpo Productions founder
47 Devoutness

48 Take soundings of
49 "Alley ___!"
50 Social visit
51 Fidel's amigo
53 Motown's Marvin
54 Sherlock's street
55 Foam used in wrestling mats
57 Hawaiian royal
58 Häagen-___
59 Fishing net
60 Other side
62 Creator of the heffalump
63 Champion
64 ___ boomers (millennials)
66 Stamp again
68 Choreographer Tharp
69 Like a photographic memory
70 1962 Paul Anka hit
71 Long Island tabloid
73 Three, in Terni
74 Crossword fly
75 Eight-member band
76 House pest
77 Saw logs
78 Car roofs with removable panels

81 Process words
82 Land force
83 It's made of blocks
86 Seeking, in classifieds
87 Latin for "king"
88 "Insecure" star Issa

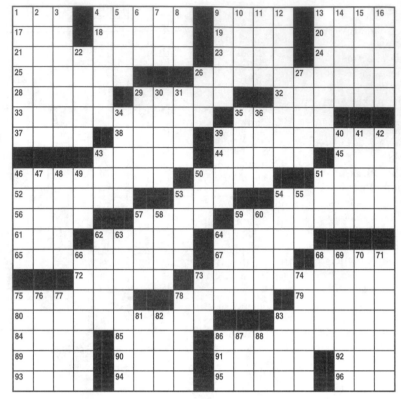

ACROSS

1 Make cents
5 Begin a triathlon
9 Absurdist art movement
13 Vanishing Asian sea
17 Dermatologist's concern
18 Sunday Silence's sire
19 Ready for recycling
20 Dressy event
21 **Start of a riddle**
25 Military attacks
26 Capacity
27 Wiped clean
28 Melon throwaway
29 More than superficial
30 Root problem
31 Movie part
33 The way things are going
34 Secondary wager
38 Mountaineering hazard
39 Pageant prize
40 Fine china
41 Star of the pitching staff
42 Flying start?
43 Toe woes
44 Criticize cleverly
45 Whale of the dolphin family
46 Bottled note
48 Capitol Hill figure
49 Make fit
50 **Middle of riddle**
55 Katmandu locale
58 Tag players
59 Meantime
63 Farm team
64 Puzzle with blind alleys
66 Is a sign of
68 Sorority letter
69 Place to be pampered
70 One for the book
71 Seven-time AL batting champ
72 Bus. course
73 Health-care facility
75 Tricky problem
76 Mimicry
77 Gametes
78 Personal records
79 Fall preceder
80 Contributing element
83 Sol–do bridge
84 Prop for a bridge
87 **End of riddle**
90 Penn name
91 Old auto
92 Play the siren
93 Fill with freight
94 Bakery purchase
95 Tiny, to a tot
96 Long, long time
97 Danube tributary

DOWN

1 Cornfield cacophony
2 ___ Rios, Jamaica
3 Behind with payments
4 Bug protection
5 Did livery work
6 Means partner
7 1969 Peace Prize Nobelist
8 Wake attendees
9 Fought for one's honor
10 Autumn flower
11 Drops in the grass
12 Sticking
13 Paternally related
14 Tampa Bay nine
15 Shampoo additive
16 Sing the praises of
22 Enjoy a meal
23 About to, informally
24 Eat into
29 Turkey's neighbor
31 Fleecing activity
32 Manitoba native
33 Four on the Ford
34 Trinity member
35 Springfield brat
36 Behold! to Brutus
37 Sign of sadness
39 Nancy Drew's dog
40 Swindle
43 Track legend Lewis
44 Wildlife park
45 Merrie ___ England
47 Look for blips
48 Sleepwear
49 Red army?
51 Tag number
52 Had a bite
53 Down source
54 From the start
55 Snack
56 Convention Center event
57 They get shelled
60 Wedding party
61 "Believe ___ Not!"
62 Umpteen
64 Feather in Yankee Doodle's cap
65 Get on
66 Historic French prison
67 Metallic rocks
70 Slue
71 ___ del Sol
72 Letter from Paul
74 Packing a punch
75 Keen pal?
76 Aphrodite's love
78 Heavenly joy
79 Pear and plum
80 Secured
81 Geometric calculation
82 Burn a little
84 Go bad
85 Item of interest
86 Outer limits
88 Scapegrace
89 Status ___

CELEBRITY COOKBOOK by Jeff Eddings
61 Across was the voice of Big Bird and Oscar for fifty years.

ACROSS

1 Walleye prey
6 Pairs
11 Broadband connection
14 Medicinal salts
19 Minor role
20 Charge
21 Magilla, for one
22 Chef's chapeau
23 Flu strain
24 Fashion apparel founder Mario
25 "I ___ your pardon"
26 Activist Sojourner
27 Recipe from the Walrus of Love?
31 Avatar people
32 Sermon
33 "Aladdin" parrot
36 Portal best run on IE, probably
39 Recipe from the Reverend?
44 Grammy winner Khan
47 Bladed sea implement
48 California's ___-Parks
49 13th Spanish letter
50 Recipe from the Godfather of Soul?
57 Federer's rival
59 Like some high heels
60 Refuges
61 Puppeteer Spinney
62 It may be a twin
63 Isopod's fourteen
66 Scottish Parliamentary votes
67 Stiff collars
68 Recipe from the "Unforgettable" singer?
72 Jerk
74 Ham's dad
75 "I've got this"
76 Kooky
79 Quickly
80 Presses
82 Soaring cost?
85 They've got bugs
86 Recipe from Eddie Vedder's group?
89 Item ID
90 Roof finial
93 Apple core?
94 WW2 torpedo craft
95 Recipe from the "Calypso" singer?
103 Mercedes models
104 Ancients, for instance: Abbr.
105 Peace Nobelist Peres
106 Act of faith?
109 Recipe from Boy George's group ?
117 TCBY product, casually
119 Russian for "peace"
120 Edge
121 "Pretty in Pink" heroine
122 Creative accountings?
123 Trig pre-req
124 Doc of "Gunsmoke"
125 Glitter rock?
126 Abstained
127 Born
128 Like Thor
129 Henry Ford's son

DOWN

1 Unpopular union label?
2 Tamale dough
3 Mideast title
4 Get
5 Dr. Zhivago's wife
6 Show launched by Harpo Studios
7 Cosmonaut Gagarin
8 Coroner's subj.
9 Miami county, informally
10 Hipster's handlebar
11 Great, slangily
12 Coins
13 Orlando's "Lord of the Rings" role
14 Contralto James
15 "The Merchant of Venice" heroine
16 Whistle-blew
17 It might be forced on a base
18 [Shrug]
28 It's NE of Ky.
29 Babe
30 Coal miner's daughter Loretta
34 Mubarak and Nasser
35 Beckham Jr. of the NFL
36 Low-level gig
37 Craft
38 Specified
40 Slime
41 Green
42 Cubist Rubik
43 Beethoven work
45 Rosewall of tennis
46 Labrador hrs.
51 Michael who sang "To Love Somebody"
52 Exude
53 Stock owner
54 Japanese golfer Aoki
55 Half of Gnarls Barkley
56 Birthplace of Big Bertha
58 Lined up
61 Welsh, for one
64 Artificially inflate
65 Hibernation sound
68 Dragsters' org.
69 Tickled
70 Cray-cray
71 Southeast Asian exonym
72 Crush underfoot
73 Pick up something common?
76 Great white relatives
77 Common font
78 411
79 Nigeria's capital
81 Slight
83 Nemo's original home
84 Car remote
87 Plumber of 2008 debates
88 Palm reading?: Abbr.
91 ___ control
92 Cruel
96 Common Vietnamese surname
97 Manly
98 Show
99 Pitt panther
100 Checked out
101 Pass
102 Total knockout
107 Saw
108 Trounced a noob
110 Came home with silver
111 Ctrl-Z
112 Yellowstone omnivore
113 Totals
114 Rite answers
115 Derby winner Funny ___
116 Bread end
117 Teleflora alternative
118 Bollywood star Aishwarya

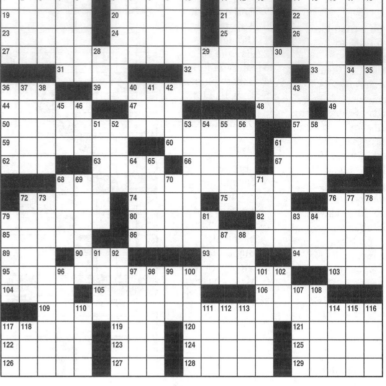

259 "I'M STUCK!" by Robert W. Harris
These crossword solvers are stumped. Can you help them?

ACROSS

1 Make whole
5 Sparkling Italian wine
9 Boat or plane
14 "The Virginian" actor Gulager
17 Aquatic plant
18 Llama relative
20 Cliffside abode
21 Han Solo's son Kylo
22 "What's another word for 'hurl'?" asked Bacall
24 "What's the name of a 'SpongeBob' whale?" asked Owens
26 Engine without spark plugs
27 Knock down
28 Czech-German river
29 Prefix meaning "bone"
30 Typed data
32 "Born from jets" automaker
34 Ulmus americana
35 Animated Betty
36 Matter, in law
37 Son of Aphrodite
39 "What's the name of Cecil Fielder's son?" asked Brooks
42 Melancholy
44 Help
45 Formerly
46 "What's another word for 'haystack'?" asked Mandela
52 The Crimson Tide, briefly
54 Overused
58 Brody in "Houdini"
59 Give way to stress
61 Earth, in many sci-fi stories
63 "Funny!"
64 Milkmaid's handful
65 Group of four
67 Ready for the scrap heap
69 Bring down
70 "What's the Latin word for 'king'?" asked Ford
73 Honolulu Zoo bird
74 In question
76 Temporary shelter
77 Whodunit award
78 Beginning of civilization?
79 Past or future
82 ___'acte
83 Sabotage
84 Bacon piece
86 Diamond's "Song ___ Blue"
88 "What's the name of a preprandial prayer?" asked Ripa
90 ___-mo
92 Tree trunk
94 Fusses
95 "What's the capital of Texas?" asked Boothe
100 Ingredient in many skin lotions
102 Windy City transit org.
105 Peugeot tire
106 Spanish 101 verb
107 Part of QEF
109 Hooch
111 Send forth
112 Portable shelter
114 Drummer Van Halen
116 Deep secrets
117 "What's New York's state flower?" asked Osmond
119 "What's the name of a 1969 rock opera?" asked Carlson
121 Dot partner
122 WME employee
123 Unit of electrical current
124 Cuckoopint genus
125 Not mine, in a text
126 Rock shelf
127 Long periods
128 "National Geographic" bonuses

DOWN

1 South African mullet
2 Famed NYC restaurateur Kaufman
3 Lace ends
4 Temporary failure
5 In the manner of
6 Idaho baker
7 Container weights
8 Most of Greenland
9 Toro's target
10 Incumbent's plea
11 Ready to cultivate
12 Blaze battler
13 Bus. card datum
14 Fictional castaway
15 Scriptures reader
16 Broken, as promises go
18 Wheat, for some
19 Capital of Turkey
23 "Take this"
25 Stripped-down motorcycle
31 "Satin ___"
33 Lettuce variety
38 Spaniel breed
40 Unlike Oscar Madison
41 Allow access to
43 One is named after Mars
46 Daily grind
47 Comes up with solutions
48 Duke University's "Cameron ___"
49 Soaring birds of prey
50 Game console of the '80s
51 Pro-choice org.
53 C-3PO's cohort, phonetically
55 Sunday shopping was once this
56 Something to clip
57 Getting along in years
60 The City of Light, in song
62 Oscar winner Howard
65 Many skateboarders
66 Sturm und ___
68 Holland in "Selma"
70 Regret
71 Prefix meaning "within"
72 Fiat model
75 Engraving implements
77 "Yikes!"
80 Persuading one to commit perjury
81 Sufficient, to Shadwell
83 Like a moonscape
85 Shrewd
87 Joy
89 Fast-food beverage
91 Treading the boards
93 Corrigenda
95 Insight
96 Weigh anchor
97 Earth tremors
98 Looked intently
99 Richard Strauss opera
101 Grayish yellow
102 Energy center in yoga
103 Firm one's muscles
104 Causes to become agitated
108 Largo, for one
110 Philosopher of "razor" fame
113 Lyon head
115 Mutant superheroes
118 Evil computer on "Captain Planet"
120 Many mos.

ACROSS

1 Fasten jeans
5 Kettle emission
10 Like some gloves
15 Feign
19 Oliver's request
20 "Where's ___?"
21 Start of a Neapolitan song
22 Dermal opening
23 Brand sold at PetSmart
24 Tokyo motor company
25 Got the fire going again
26 2017 cat 5 hurricane
27 "Happy Together" group
29 "Runaway" singer
31 Getty of "The Golden Girls"
32 "Asi ___ vida" (such is life)
34 "Ghost ___ in the Sky"
35 Ghostbuster in "Ghostbusters"
36 Caulking material
38 Goblin's cousin
40 Gossamer
43 "Hats Off to ___" (1961 hit by 29-A)
44 Nice nothing
45 Harrow rival
49 Ice-cream preference
50 Sorta
51 Rescue
53 Sister channel of Cinemax
54 Mausoleum vessel
55 "You Can't Hurry Love" group
57 "Fuzzy Wuzzy was ___ . . ."
59 Moment of enlightenment
61 Millstone
62 Job for a roadie
63 CNN's Burnett et al.
64 Checkout jar coins
66 Dennehy in "Cocoon"
67 Those wanting answers
69 Get bluffed out
70 Diatribe
73 Lincoln's in-laws

74 "Brown Eyed Girl" singer
77 Reptilians, e.g.
78 Low in the lea
79 1969 Classics IV hit
81 Down source
82 Give it up
83 Rumba or mambo
85 Hill group
86 "The World Is Not Enough" director
87 Like some jobs
88 Ram near a bull
90 Afflicts with ennui
91 Clause connectors
92 "Monster" Oscar winner
95 Supporting plinth
96 1960s musical invasion
100 "Hold On, I'm Comin' " duo
103 "Space Oddity" singer
106 Rah-rah
107 Indira Gandhi's son
108 Serviceable
109 Single ___ Scotch
110 Djokovic's nickname
111 Yemeni's neighbor
112 Ballroom dance
113 Son of Rebekah
114 "Top Gun" pilots
115 Dijon dads
116 Georgia of "Hot in Cleveland"
117 Speak harshly

DOWN

1 Bible belt?
2 "In Search of ___ Ark" (1976)
3 Camelot helmet
4 Noodged
5 Forming spiral patterns
6 There's no accounting for it
7 Month in Tel Aviv
8 Logger's tool
9 Agatha Christie play (with "The")
10 Imperious
11 "___ bad moon rising . . .": CCR
12 Coach with four Super Bowl wins

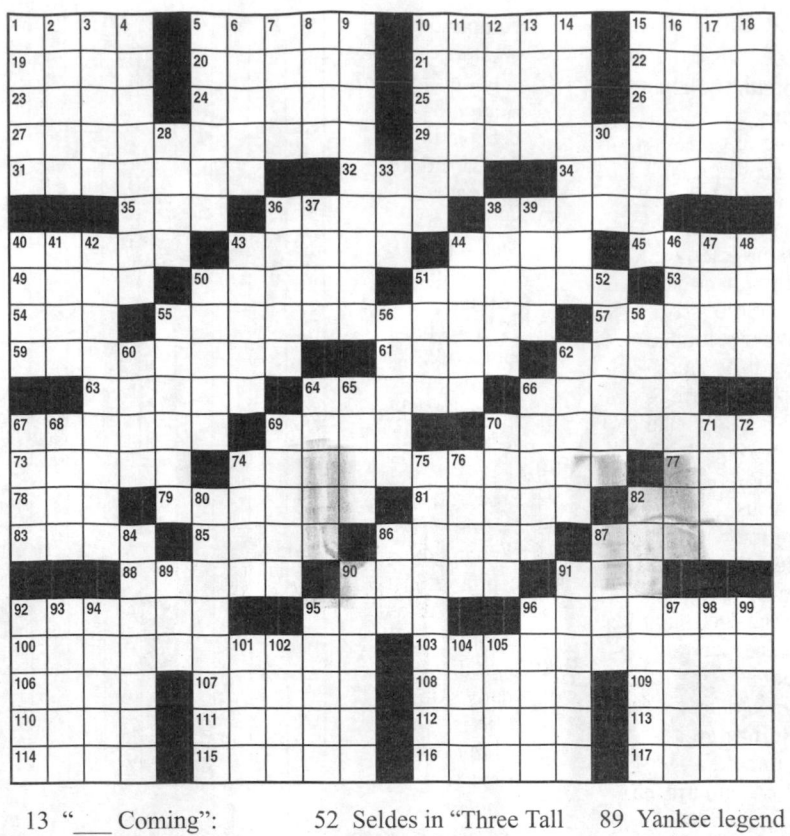

13 "___ Coming": Three Dog Night
14 Unseat a king
15 Spinning wheel part
16 Mezzo Marilyn
17 Mail from way back
18 "By all ___!"
28 Ending for cell
30 Feel lousy
33 Wallowing place
36 Violet variety
37 Pakistani tongue
38 Bay of Fundy attractions
39 Roger of "Cheers"
40 "CSI" actress Elisabeth
41 Symbol of Eire
42 "Mother-in-Law" singer
43 Bank claims
44 Hogwarts professor Lupin
46 "My Boyfriend's Back" group
47 Firth of Lorn resort
48 "L'etoile du ___" (Minnesota motto)
50 Genghis and Kubla
51 Dollars for quarters

52 Seldes in "Three Tall Women"
55 Desire for drink
56 Symphonic finale
58 Healthy cereal
60 Nashville NHLer, to fans
62 Field trip?
64 Cotton candy holders
65 Graceful trees
66 Stationed
67 Dough dispensers
68 Smudge on Santa's suit
69 Sgt. Friday's quest
70 Avoids being "it"
71 State with a three-word capital
72 Outstanding Team Award
74 Wind indicator
75 Clone
76 Ceremonial act
80 Japanese cake
82 Subscriber
84 Greenwich Village Halloween events
86 MapQuest's parent for 16 years
87 Nursery fixture

89 Yankee legend Guidry
90 Ars longa, vita ___
91 Boot camp, e.g.
92 Blue Nile source
93 Devastation
94 Microphone inventor Berliner
95 Kind of like ewe
96 ___ water (nonsense)
97 James Taylor's "___ Fool to Care"
98 "The Da Vinci Code" villain
99 All atwitter
101 Baronet's wife
102 Almost closed
104 "This weighs ___!"
105 Rhames in "Dawn of the Dead"

ACROSS

1 Home to some lilies
5 Wealthy "Titanic" casualty
10 Capital of Morocco
15 Spicy Sichuan sauce
19 Sarah McLachlan song
20 Joe of "NCIS"
21 Like Crusoe before Friday
22 Kingsley who wrote "Girl, 20"
23 Bank (on)
24 British trio Johnny ___ Jazz
25 Jumble
26 Upshot
27 1970 Jackson 5 hit
29 1971 Rolling Stones hit
31 Mercury astronaut Deke
32 Track legend nicknamed "Lightning"
34 Short vocal solo
35 Rostov river
36 Bruce of Gotham City
38 Hardship
40 Tethys, e.g.
43 Hooded killer
44 Bathe
45 U2 guitarist The ___
49 In need of ibuprofen
50 Two-time MLB All-Star Erstad
51 Horny toad, for one
53 Sale stat
54 Springfield bartender
55 1973 Marvin Gaye hit
57 ___ Bell (Emily Brontë)
59 Inborn behavior
61 Higher
62 Like coach dogs
63 Extra inning
64 Following
66 Polish wedding dance
67 "The Best of Both ___": Van Halen
69 "Souls on Fire" author Wiesel
70 Bagel-shaped
73 "Set Fire to the Rain" singer
74 1971 Melanie hit

77 Rose in "Burlesque"
78 Favorable position
79 Chuck of "Walker, Texas Ranger"
81 Built-out window
82 Did the trudgen
83 Pseudonym of H.H. Munro
85 "It's ___ a hard day's night . . ."
86 Use a mano
87 Slant-cut pasta
88 Bottle-___ dolphin
90 Suite prices
91 Tuned in
92 Loblolly leaf
95 Friends and neighbors
96 Haydn wrote over 50
100 1974 John Denver hit
103 1973 Ringo Starr hit
106 Punchcard info
107 "Fallen" singer McLachlan
108 Like some galleys
109 30% of Earth's land area
110 "I completely agree!"
111 President-___
112 Loot
113 Jazz or Blues
114 Old money of Italy
115 Study pieces
116 Striped antelope
117 Britain's largest eagle

DOWN

1 Michael Jackson's daughter
2 "Jubilee Road" singer Tom
3 Nabisco wafer
4 1972 "Godspell" hit
5 Kutcher on "The Ranch"
6 Brave pitcher in the Hall of Fame
7 NFL wide receiver Golden
8 Individualist

9 "Instant Family" actress
10 Kid Ory's "Muskrat ___"
11 At the ready
12 Western tie
13 "___ Day Has Come": Dion
14 One who thinks 30 is old
15 Tobey in "Spider-Man"
16 Puebla pal
17 "Mona ___ and Mad Hatters": Elton John
18 The Jetsons' dog
28 Peter Wimsey's alma mater
30 Socko sign
33 Soap-___-rope
36 As bad as it gets
37 "It's ___ world out there!"
38 Five o'clock shadow remover
39 Cat in "Peter and the Wolf"
40 "Ashes to Ashes" author Hoag
41 Windows image
42 1974 Ray Stevens hit

43 Shoestring ___
44 Cubic decimeter
46 1972 Tanya Tucker hit
47 Gumption
48 1977 Commodores hit
50 Makes a bad impression on?
51 Aired when it's happening
52 Set battle lines
55 Basswood
56 Schlepped
58 Tricky Norse god
60 "The William ___ Overture"
62 Julien of "The Red and the Black"
64 Delon in "Once a Thief"
65 Swimming aids
66 Reproved a snorer
67 ___ and Means Committee
68 Concert halls
69 Botched
70 Similar siblings
71 Composer Hovhaness
72 1949 Welles role
74 Vampire Tanner
75 Toy capital of the world?

76 Weird canal?
80 Tormented by
82 Sever
84 Wyandotte Cave locale
86 Hood's gun
87 Big name in golf clubs
89 Fiesta-taurina cheer
90 Bill of ___
91 Like the cobra
92 2018 French Open winner
93 As a friend, to Jules
94 "Welcome!"
95 Flair
96 Daniel in "C.H.U.D."
97 Electroshock gun
98 Bee-fitting description?
99 Disgrace
101 Price-reduction event
102 Mined-over matters
104 It may follow U
105 SeaWorld showoff

262 SOAPS by Jim Holland

Eight soaps are hidden in the answer grid. Can you find them all?

ACROSS

1 ___ decisis (legal precedent)
6 An Everly brother
10 Cameron Champ's org.
13 Jazzercise cousin
18 Trickery
19 Sierra Nevada resort
20 What a gumshoe might do
21 Pentathlon blades
22 "I'm going all in!"
25 "Cut me some ___"
26 Synthesizer inventor
27 Yossarian's tentmate in "Catch-22"
28 Between 12 and 20
29 Summits in Crete and Turkey
30 Verdi opera set in Egypt
32 Sage, for one
33 Get ___ the mat
35 Click the clicker
40 Request to a bartender
44 Concealed
45 1992 NBA #1 draft pick
46 Gleaner of tossed tickets at the track
48 Eggs
49 Choose
51 Position for 10 Across
53 Drop a few keys?
55 In high spirits
60 Devoid of meaning
61 Hook's bosun
62 Some roulette results
63 Help-wanted abbr.
64 Electrician on the set
66 A ___ apple
68 "Fresh Air" airer
69 A lot of pizzazz?
70 Engraved pillars
72 Suffix for Gotham
73 Season, in tweets
74 "Enchanted" Levine heroine
78 First name in cosmetics
80 Whispered words to one on the lam
84 What teachers often have students do
86 Former United rival

87 ___ worse than death
88 Like some Fr. verbs
89 St. John, notably
92 Machu Picchu residents
95 Cambodian coin
96 1973 Al Pacino title role
98 Historical transition
101 "___ Kick Out of You"
103 Before Baker and Charlie in a series
104 Only child of Elvis
105 Fetches
108 Accipitrine feature
110 These or those along the Seine
111 Bed size
115 Smart outfit?
116 Go with the flow
119 "___ Frutti": Little Richard
120 Paris plane destination
121 Without ice
122 Oscar winner Zellweger
123 Flatware item
124 14th Greek letters
125 ___ English Bulldogge
126 Avarice

DOWN

1 Flutter-kick
2 Mambo king Puente
3 Moreover
4 President known as "Dutch"
5 Night school subj.
6 Divide proportionately
7 Monsieur, in Munich
8 ___-Out Burger
9 Went on a pillaging spree
10 French bread
11 Knife pitched on TV
12 Mor. neighbor
13 Joie de vivre
14 Raise the spirits
15 Drink for Beowulf
16 Mitchell of "Pitch Perfect"
17 NASDAQ quotes

20 Thayer's "Casey at ___"
23 Waterproof coat material
24 Garr and Hatcher
29 Do-re-mi
31 "___ Pieces": Peter & Gordon
32 Indy 500 winner Castroneves
34 Some shooting stars?
35 "Chopped" contestants
36 Seed scar
37 "Love in the Dark" singer
38 Saintly symbols
39 Easy stride
41 "Laughing All the Way" author
42 Steven's partner
43 Facing extinction
47 Russian actor Menshikov
50 Like baseball shoes
52 Blissful
54 Egoist's concern
56 Laurel, to Hardy, e.g.
57 Totally deteriorated
58 Own up

59 Contract adverb
65 Swampy stretches
67 What a dieter might do on Black Friday?
70 Whitewater prosecutor
71 Padlocked
73 It's taken by a witness
75 Pad paper?
76 Casual goodbye
77 Cleveland's "The Q" is one
78 Greek goddess of discord
79 Like the Dust Bowl
81 Blue-pencil
82 Strain of flu
83 Baja dwellings
85 Spikes the punch
90 Shilly-___
91 2007 Heisman Trophy winner
93 "Gigi" author
94 "___ Called Wanda" (1988)
97 Attaches, in a way
99 Weather influencer
100 Talk idly
102 "Pong" parent

105 Italian ___ (Subway subs)
106 Enlist again
107 Excited about
109 Is bedbound
110 Punch card dangler
112 Kind of cellar
113 Thought from Voltaire
114 Require
116 Fenway nine, briefly
117 ___ Aviv
118 Work unit

ACROSS

1 Elite group
6 "Brave New World" caste
11 Scarlett's home
15 Dirty political tactic
19 Country crooner Gill
20 Hastily
21 Type of ID
22 Stick or comics character
23 Where Gawain alcohol was discovered?
27 Nova ___
28 Replay option
29 Elsa in "Born Free"
30 Creep
32 Natural coverings
35 Sally Field role that had her flying high
36 Requirement for security clearance in Prague?
42 Bank take-backs
46 Bar none
47 Kin of -trix
48 Gulager in "McQ"
49 "___ my case"
50 IHOP serving
53 Greek moon goddess
56 Auspices
58 JFK inspection group
59 Wheel crafter in need of a trim?
61 Sassy legatee?
63 Get going
64 Gold and silver
66 Balaam's rebuker
67 1914 battle site
68 Alliance of 1954–1977
71 Tenn. athlete
72 ___ und Drang
74 Roadie's responsibility
77 Calif. neighbor
78 Word for poor Yorick
80 Endless ages
82 Guy gets in some sparring practice?
85 Network news stars taking some time off?
90 George's lyricist brother
91 ___ nous

92 Substance once thought to fill all of space
93 Prince Valiant's wife
94 Type of show often found boring
96 Byrnes who played Kookie
97 "A horse is a horse" horse
99 "All systems go!"
100 1965 Arthur Hailey novel
101 License to shoot "The Naked Gun" films?
107 Use a straw
109 "John ___ Tractor": Judds
110 Letter opener
111 Intern
115 Viking alphabet
118 Military command
122 Why the Saloon Singers tour was canceled?
126 Something you might smell
127 Diamond cover
128 European ermine
129 Blakley in "Nashville"
130 Workout units
131 Merry ___ England
132 2013 Johnny Depp role
133 Editorial instructions

DOWN

1 Enterprise competition
2 Clarence played him on "The Mod Squad"
3 Fascinated with
4 Comic's bit
5 Starting (off)
6 Rod in a gangster flick
7 Paris pals
8 Modern day agora
9 Address used on "Downton Abbey"

10 Lacking social purpose
11 When repeated, a mild admonition
12 Mary Kay of cosmetics
13 React in horror
14 Yossarian's portrayer in "Catch-22"
15 Trolling lure
16 Seating section
17 Some pun reactions
18 Spoils
24 "___ bleu!"
25 "Happy Days" character
26 Foster
31 1953 John Wayne movie
33 Non-jittery libation
34 Eye membranes
36 Whoop-de-do
37 Utah ski resort
38 "The Cosby Show" mom
39 Outfit
40 "Groovy!"
41 Most expansive
43 ___ Wicked Ale

44 Actor and activist Davis
45 First Super Bowl MVP
51 Sports stick
52 NASCAR racer Petty
54 Roman emperor before Trajan
55 Spaces between veins of a leaf
57 Bank on a credit card
60 Expect a given situation
62 Where to find "Rock of Ages"
65 Bias
69 Writer who's all thumbs?
70 Went too far too fast
73 Parks on a bus
74 Some men in black
75 Thomas on "That Girl"
76 Longstocking braid
79 Dolt
81 Give one's word
83 Direct route
84 Papyrus, e.g.
86 ___ Robert (wild geranium)

87 Companion of Artemis
88 Emmy Award depiction
89 Some milk producers
95 Holds up
98 Rev. King had one
102 Marshall's Thundering ___
103 Most accurate
104 Be so inclined
105 Bib wearers
106 Schoolyard retort
108 Trattoria sauce
111 This will lift you up
112 Grill order
113 On the double
114 Airline that serves kosher meals
116 Harrow rival
117 One type of team
119 Steak sauce brand
120 Bird feed
121 "Vous ___ ici"
123 Glen ___ Scotch
124 Mimic
125 Great Plains tribe

ACROSS

1 ___, Baker, Charlie
5 "Will that ___?" ("Anything else?")
10 Nurses a drink
14 Genesis verb
19 Pivotal point
20 Rajah's wife
21 "It's ___": Pet Shop Boys
22 Quicklime, for one
23 Pack firmly
24 Eight maids a-singing
25 Natalie Wood's sister
26 Merchandise
27 Road going in all directions?
30 Air Force Academy team
32 Bequest recipients
33 No walk in the park
34 Make the grade
35 Took the World Series in four
38 Sign between Virgo and Scorpio
40 Write on the cover
44 Long lock
47 On the ___ (at large)
49 Antelope of the steppes
51 Wandflower
52 Get better
53 "Times" delivery route?
55 Climbed out of bed
56 EGOT winner Moreno
57 Hindu sage
58 Word before loose or down
59 Vichyssoise veggies
60 Ad nauseum
62 Preacher's target
66 High regard
67 Soon, in Calais
69 Abide by
74 Pasta strainer
76 Country bumpkin
77 "Madonna and Child Enthroned" painter
81 High train lines
82 Arafat's successor
85 Check for ID
86 Crosswise, on a schooner
87 Road named after a speedy superhero?
90 Cornfield unit
91 Jordan's Great Temple site
92 2013 Depp role
93 "To a Skylark" is one
94 Asparagus piece
95 Hialeah housing
97 Smile factor
99 Hogwarts' potion master
101 Opinion pieces
103 Takes on a romantic getaway
105 Skin layers
109 It's read with feeling
112 Private access to Qantas Airways?
115 She plays Romana on "Doctor Who"
116 Wolfish expression
118 Cranky pants
119 Put the spurs to
120 Native Mexican
121 Mr. Rogers
122 Disgorge
123 50-50 guess, maybe
124 Daniel of "Ugly Betty"
125 Salon goals
126 Work stations
127 Looked up and down

DOWN

1 Had a part
2 "Vanderpump Rules" channel
3 Light measure
4 Fast road?
5 Window-shop
6 "To ___ his own"
7 Contra equivalent
8 Mooch
9 Beyond harmful
10 Steakhouse feature
11 Brit's "Well, well!"
12 ATM code
13 Major mess-up
14 Road on the Brooklyn side?
15 Bus driver's demand, at times
16 Aircraft in "You Only Live Twice"
17 Capital of Yemen
18 "Ocean's Twelve" heroine
28 Their boughs make bows
29 Carpal tunnel site
31 Completed a course
34 Most cunning
36 Bagel choice
37 Reveille counterpart
39 Historic bridge on the Grand Canal
41 Lotion ingredient
42 Whiskey barrel
43 New singles
44 Violent spasm
45 Holds one's horses
46 Gnaw away
48 "Does nothing for me"
50 Low voice
53 Film trailer
54 In a lather
61 Pointed road?
63 Smallest bill
64 Yo-Yo Ma's Davidov cello
65 Imperial decree
67 Election forms
68 Utterly foolish
70 Road to get away from it all?
71 Sixties sign
72 ___ firma
73 More out on the fringe
75 One side of the aisle
76 Safe harbor
77 Places for napkins
78 "Yeah right!"
79 Anti-fur org.
80 Half-cooked
83 Dude
84 Auction actions
88 Wine servers
89 Enthusiastic about
94 Contractor's detail
96 Sushi selection
98 Refused to share
100 Gets a shelter dog
102 Vermeer's "View of ___"
104 Boot camp drillmaster
106 Beach Boys' manager Wilson
107 Lock horns
108 Knight's mount
109 "Kapow!"
110 Tear down
111 Utah ski resort
112 Wail like a banshee
113 Has second thoughts
114 Trans-Siberian Railway stop
117 Tom Seaver's 2.86

FORERUNNERS   by Lee Taylor

At an altitude of 11,450 feet, 65 Across is one of the world's highest cities.

ACROSS

1 Pursued
7 Queens stadium
11 Fraction of a kilo
15 Sound from the belfry
19 Maleficent's victim
20 Perform an Appalachian folk dance
21 Have a repast
22 President Coin of "Hunger Games"
23 Trimmed branches
24 ___-deaf
25 Centre Court cry
26 Trim nails
27 Alabama congresswoman Martha
28 Voicemail forerunner
32 Agog
34 Conspicuous
35 Disinfectant brand
36 Freely admits
38 Bops on the noggin
39 It once was "cool"
40 Symbolic figures
43 Swampy wetland
44 Old Spanish coins
48 Polio vaccine developer
49 Trunk contents
51 Memory card forerunner
54 Tonsorial touch-up
55 Corn syrup brand
56 EWTN anchor Raymond
57 Catty comment
58 Award for "Bluebird, Bluebird"
60 "Mastermind" game piece
61 Men's dress shoe
63 Some Tuscans
65 City on the Tibetan Plateau
67 Escaping
72 Joker
74 Business card abbr.
76 Of ebb and flow
77 Prepares to fire
81 Move from side to side
82 A spider has eight
84 Congressional staffer
85 CD-ROM forerunner

87 Hebrew "A"
88 Pork cut
89 Updates connections
90 Sneaky
91 Hindu monkey god
93 Leaf or Bolt
94 Own up
97 Deck out
98 On frequent occasions
101 Kept going
103 Sold-out show
107 Netflix forerunner
110 "Hang ___ your hats!"
111 Early caucus state
112 HOMES member
113 Pull apart
114 Yard dividers
116 Himalayan hike
117 Carol
118 River to the Caspian
119 Egg dish
120 All-Star Red Sox pitcher Chris
121 Valedictorian's gown
122 Cut costs
123 Goes along with

DOWN

1 Ischia neighbor
2 HOMES member
3 Caribbean cruise stop
4 iPod forerunner
5 "End ___ I do begin": Shak.
6 Man Ray's movement
7 Represents
8 Decelerates
9 Nectar collector
10 Taron in "Kingsman: The Secret Service"
11 Solidarity birthplace
12 Features of Ruffles
13 "Dragon Ball Z" genre
14 Suvari in "American Reunion"
15 Rhinoceros, for one
16 Museum of Immigration site

17 Acid in meat
18 Place for a boutonniere
29 Craigslist forerunner
30 It carries a charge
31 Wear stripes with polka dots
33 Night before
37 Trans-Siberian Railroad hub
39 Display horror
40 Adlai's 1956 running mate
41 Day before Mercredi
42 Grammy winner Mary J. ___
43 Not a favorite food of Kermit's
44 Cell forerunner
45 Low digit
46 Spanish word of love
47 Patch up, perhaps
50 It's often after you
51 Kardashian matriarch
52 In a flowery manner
53 Animal on show at Westminster
56 In the loop
59 Whistle blower?
62 Expressed

64 Twain protagonist
66 "Incredible" superhero
68 Wi-Fi forerunner
69 "Cool as a cucumber," e.g.
70 Tennis player Petrova
71 First American to orbit the Earth
73 "Frozen" FX
75 Center of Florence
77 Landmass south of Eur.
78 Paris island
79 Do yard work
80 Dessert with a cream cheese frosting
83 Thick rug
86 "Punk'd" feature
87 Emollient ingredient
90 Place for a cowboy boot
92 Greek N's
94 Sausage skin
95 Nicaraguan president (1985–90)
96 Palm Treo successor
97 Take baby steps
98 Final notices

99 Botanist's forte
100 Locker room item
101 Collectible
102 Bahrain banknote
104 Part of WASP
105 Take the helm
106 Party people
108 Blue-ribbon
109 "Call on me!"
115 Apteryx relative

CLASSICAL CROSSOVERS by Elizabeth C. Gorski
Here's a puzzle for your next sorority or frat party.

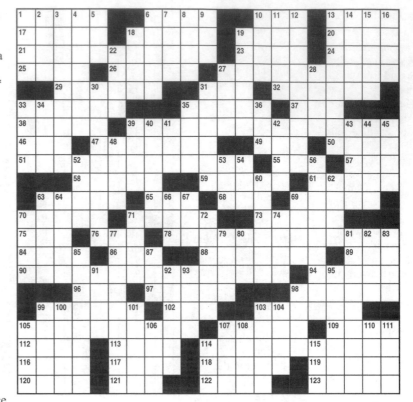

ACROSS

1 Unisex garment
6 Bygone fliers
10 Dept. of Justice org.
13 Shock
17 Hello from Hilo
18 Page in "Inception"
19 "In a cowslip's bell ___": Shak.
20 ___ about
21 Billy Ray Cyrus album*
23 Cambodia's 1939 neighbor
24 Chair designer Aarnio
25 Egg on
26 Dove's perch
27 Antiterrorism legislation of 2001*
29 Family cars
31 Six, in Sicily
32 Luanda's land
33 It's a thought
35 "Rumor has it . . ."
37 Suffix with cash
38 Borneo anthropoid
39 Bread-basket classic from a Boston hotel*
46 Before B–Q or none
47 Organic energy option
49 Mohawked "A-Team" actor
50 Duel tool
51 Dead drunk*
55 AOL, for one
57 Prof's aides
58 "The Father of Physics"
59 "Gadzooks!"
61 Top invitees
63 Pirate's pal
65 Motel rentals: Abbr.
68 Young bloke
69 Robert of "Spenser: For Hire"
70 Allayed
71 Threw in
73 Blows off steam
75 SSE's opposite
76 Cardinal cap letters
78 Project beginnings*
84 "Arrivederci!"
86 With it, once
88 Miser's sin
89 Tennis club instructor
90 Hawaii, as named by Captain Cook*
94 "___ say more?"
96 Insult
97 Rosie the Riveter's hairnet
98 Hobo transportation
99 Universal
102 Boxer
103 Observed in the area of
105 Paints the town red*
107 Reside
109 Bivouac
112 Fed. fair-hiring org.
113 "Truthful" James creator Harte
114 What's hidden in each clue* answer
116 Pitching no-no
117 Frozen desserts
118 Key West trees
119 Stag
120 Aromatherapy settings
121 Leg, in slang
122 Norms: Abbr.
123 Neophytes

DOWN

1 Go by
2 Hanging loosely
3 Frank request?
4 Occupying that place
5 Droop
6 Winter coasters
7 Dross
8 Prefix for gram
9 NBC weekend show
10 Landed
11 Pageant crown
12 Supporters of equal rights for women
13 Former Yankee skipper
14 Ryan in "Oliver's Story"
15 "Poet in New York" poet
16 Jog
18 Squared
19 Biblical prophet
22 Conductor Gilbert
27 Equal
28 Curved molding
30 The AKC divides these into seven groups
31 Civil War historian Foote
33 Celebrity chef Matsuhisa
34 Algerian port
35 Furniture brand
36 Nog's dad on "Deep Space Nine"
39 "The Far Shore of Time" author
40 Apprehensive, to some
41 Boring routine
42 "Topaz" author
43 Eye-related
44 Rover's restraint
45 For fear that
48 Teeny
52 Diminutive suffix
53 Like Abner
54 Ecol. watchdog
56 Acropolis temple
60 "The Scream" painter Munch
62 Emmy winner Kudrow
63 Craze
64 Dam on the Nile
66 Roman 1501
67 Capitol Hill VIP
69 Offensive and not cool
70 Env. contents
71 "Aloha" actor Baldwin
72 Script lines
74 Fans of the Bulldogs
77 "Have I got news for you!"
79 Spot on ABC
80 Baseball's Kinsler
81 One who's a real looker?
82 "Siegfried" role
83 Evening in Paris
85 Singles in the laundry room
87 Acidity measures
91 Weakling
92 Scans into a scanner
93 Gazpacho, e.g.
95 "Bingo!"
98 First telephone caller
99 Stingy
100 Alley Oop's lady
101 See 20 Across
103 Appears
104 BPOE members
105 Haunted house sights
106 Abound
107 "Phooey!"
108 Use a blowtorch
110 ". . . tell ___ lies"
111 Bop pioneer Young
114 Family docs
115 Dig in

DOWN FOR THE COUNT   by Elizabeth C. Gorski
A theme inspired by "Hidden Figures."

ACROSS

1 Har-___ (tennis surface)
4 Battery fluid
8 Origami bird
13 Prized Prado hangings
18 Denis Leary TV show
20 Betty Ford program
21 Take offense at
22 How to learn to dance?
24 1955 union merger
25 Maestro's pace
26 Do in, as a vampire
27 Place for antifreeze
29 Workout clothes
31 The Judds sang in it
35 Filbert, e.g.
36 Noise from a hammock
37 Soon-to-be grads
38 Weep loudly
41 Memorandum
44 Mexican money
46 Ruse
51 Ella Fitzgerald song
57 Bagel feature
58 "Snow Angels" author Stewart
59 "Understood, dude!"
60 "Baby Hold On" singer
62 VIP on Air Force One
64 Picasso's first wife
66 Victory sign
67 "Mayday!"
68 Colin Powell's April 4, 1989 promotion
75 Before
78 Mao ___-tung
79 "Scarface" drug lord
80 Doesn't hold water
84 Botches things up
89 Places in the heart
92 Dobrev of "The Vampire Diaries"
93 Appearance
94 Stubble beard
97 Venomous viper
99 "Typee" sequel
100 Harper Lee's "Go ___ Watchman"
101 Wheat bristle
102 Trouble

105 "The show is starting!"
108 Genetic letters
110 Hexagons
116 Most eccentric
120 "I'd like you to leave"
121 Press
123 More pallid
124 Milk curdler
125 1964 Ava Gardner film
130 Sanctify with oil
131 Obliterate
132 Chills beforehand
133 Camp shelters
134 Claire in "Homeland"
135 American tennis star
136 2005 Prince hit

DOWN

1 Sulky races
2 Ask for more "Money"
3 1972 Bill Withers hit
4 Off-key singer's best friend
5 Bee follower
6 Rapscallions
7 Did a deck job
8 Wax pastel
9 Like 68-A
10 Sushi fish
11 Ice star Naomi Nari ___
12 Germany's first president
13 Eager kid's demand
14 Imam's faith
15 Verso's opposite
16 Horse that beat Secretariat
17 Shaggy-dog ___
19 Senate broadcaster
21 Doppler device
23 Shooting marbles
28 Spa sounds
30 Grey Goose rival, for short
32 Bishop of Rome
33 "___ there yet?"
34 Lay down a new lawn
38 Halt

39 "It can't be!"
40 Eric Cartman, for one
42 Kang of "The Mentalist"
43 Set of values
45 Glen ___ Scotch
47 Sorority letter
48 Charged bits
49 Nile queen, familiarly
50 Jailer's janglers
52 Ample, in dialect
53 Lean to one side
54 Lexi Thompson's org.
55 Jackknife, for one
56 Crystal-gazer
61 Repast
63 High society?
65 "___ Poetica"
69 F-16 wing letters
70 Do-___ (money)
71 Polo score
72 This, to Pedro
73 Dealer's foes
74 Sultry Horne
75 Austen heroine
76 Incursion
77 Scratched (out)

81 Disney Broadway musical
82 Have down
83 Like lumber
85 Away from WSW
86 Bolivian president Morales
87 Big rigs
88 Truth, of yore
90 Taj Mahal's "Sounder" role
91 Houston player
95 ___ Nostra
96 Select carefully
98 Oatmeal add-ins
103 Dog tags, for short
104 Sleeping stork's support
106 Chimes in
107 Dweeb
109 Town in a Hersey novel
110 Young herring
111 "Empire" producer Chaiken
112 Headlight gas
113 Municipal dept.
114 Medicated
115 "Guiding Light" and others

117 Saint ___ fire
118 Navy frogmen
119 Secret rendezvous
122 "Stoney End" songwriter
126 Notable time
127 Pianist Cliburn
128 Beirut–Damascus dir.
129 Moment

WEATHER FORECAST by Norm Guggenbiller
Billy Dee Williams played 127 Across in "Brian's Song."

ACROSS

1 Tiny fraction of a min.
5 Namesake awards of Poe
11 Opal ending
15 Inc. relative
19 Bank of the Tiber
20 Beat to the tape
21 Hesitant speaker
23 1961 space chimp
24 General feeling of wrongdoing
26 Mideast appetizer
28 Millionths of a meter
29 Bridge play
30 Off-road wheels
31 A narcoleptic may take it often
33 Portuguese saint
34 Philanthropist Hogg
36 Indisposed
37 Ace an exam in record time
43 ___ say (regrettably)
44 Monogram of Van Halen's front man
45 "Get outta here!"
46 Escorts to the penthouse
50 It's needed for lawns
53 Plane part
55 Purina competitor
56 Large bay windows
59 Tumultuous outburst of disapproval
63 French refusals
64 "___ Done Him Wrong" (1933)
66 Indelicate
67 Sharpens
68 Sister of Helios
69 Dump
70 Treats an icy road
71 Peking or Siam suffix
73 "Nonsense!"
74 10th-century Holy Roman Emperor
76 Walnuts on "The Sopranos"
78 Safe investments
79 Miss Gulch's dread
80 Choice seat location
83 January birthstone
85 Faulkner's "Requiem ___ Nun"
86 Heisman Trophy winner Walker
87 Fake fat
89 "A Streetcar Named Desire" role
91 ___ de gallo (Mexican salsa)
94 Can. province
95 Cheapskate
99 It's impossible to catch this
103 13th Greek letters
106 A woman named Arthur
107 Hindemith's "Mathis ___ Maler"
108 Way off
109 Thing, in court
110 Lauder who made scents
112 Progressive
116 Emulate Icarus
118 What Bill and Jo had in "Twister"?
121 Reebok rival
122 Passbook user
123 Big commotion
124 HBO comedy series
125 Mine finds
126 Senator's stint
127 Bear nicknamed the "Kansas Comet"
128 To be, to Brutus

DOWN

1 Homes built off-site
2 Gardner's third husband
3 Took shape, in a way
4 House in Spain
5 Epoch in the Cenozoic Era
6 Clods
7 Sporty Pontiac
8 Calla lily, e.g.
9 Salad veggie
10 Arctic transports
11 It's pumped in Ottawa
12 Phaser setting
13 Othello's lieutenant
14 Part of HRE
15 Gospel singer Winans
16 Small African antelope
17 Fix the squeaks again
18 Gearshift sequence
22 Fata Morgana
25 Latte topping
27 Pasta in "That's Amore"
32 Covered with fine hair
35 Thoughtful type
38 Major add-ons
39 Nerve
40 Tee privilege at Augusta
41 Mouth tops
42 Toffee candy bar
47 Think about, for a night
48 Albany, to Manhattanites
49 Criticism out of left field
51 "Over here . . ."
52 Story setting
54 Tempo
56 Singular events
57 Pansy disease
58 Forthcoming
60 1998 De Niro film
61 Forced
62 Be light
65 Sleep: Comb. form
69 Perch
70 Dupe
72 Air Force NCO
75 Firing ___ cylinders
77 Go with the flow
78 Richard in "Rambo III"
79 Mannerism
81 Saw
82 "The Time Machine" race
84 Weapons depot
88 Senior officer's vehicle
90 Smears
92 Halloween drink
93 Irksome
96 Shoots for
97 Sad poems
98 Change, as the future
100 Rock salt
101 Dad's dad, to kids
102 Haying machines
103 Part of a makeover
104 Escort
105 Michael of R.E.M.
111 Love god
113 "___ out, kitty?"
114 Apartment ad abbr.
115 Detroit Lion great Yale ___
117 Eat
119 Swift quality
120 San Francisco valley

ACROSS

1 Bath bathroom
4 Former "Meet the Press" host Marvin
8 Coloring media
15 Miracle site in John 2:1
19 Org. for Zverev
20 Assert
21 Enters carefully
22 Islands off Ireland
23 Hwy.
24 **The electrician felt like he was going ___**
27 "Drive fast!"
29 Shaping tool
30 Mother-of-pearl source
31 Somalian supermodel
32 How LPs are reissued
33 Medicated
36 Scottish golfer Montgomerie
37 **His usual methods weren't working so he decided to ___**
40 Get noticed
41 Lloyd of silent films
42 Peking or Siam suffix
43 Plastic item banned in San Francisco
45 Retirement agcy.
46 Stadium level
48 Sports car gauge
51 Daggoo's captain
53 Grand Canyon discoverer
57 **Not sure if that was going to work, he decided to just ___**
63 Rita in "Fifty Shades Freed"
64 ___-Siberian Orchestra
66 Starting
67 "Am I the problem here?"
68 "___ five" (actor's cue)
70 **. . . lest he ___ of meeting his deadline**
73 Stud site
74 Spanish inn
77 Shows curiosity
78 Vanishing sounds
81 "No ___ intended"
82 **All this was tiring, but fortunately he had ___**
85 Emphasizes
87 Cruising
88 Belgian river
90 Plummet
91 Co. decision makers
94 Arctic jacket
97 Japanese IT giant
99 Western financial coalition
103 Overdue debt
105 **. . . and tried desperately to sneak ___**
109 Blue clay of England
110 "___ laughing matter"
111 Outdoor bite preventer
112 Third-generation Genesis figure
113 Bugs
115 Alaska natives
117 Whitecap feature
118 **Alas, he finished the job late and no doubt would ___**
122 Dodger great Hodges
123 Mine passage
124 The eyes have them
125 Goose that's a state bird
126 NYC's Park or Madison
127 PC hookups
128 Bears witness to
129 "___ in the Clowns"
130 Taylor Swift album

DOWN

1 Sizable
2 Iowa city on the Des Moines river
3 Like a concert in the park
4 Southpaw Jim with 16 Gold Gloves
5 Dow Jones stat
6 Picked up, at Eton
7 Sweet bun
8 "___ la vie!"
9 Like "Toy Story"
10 They were first to have a dome
11 Mumbled assent
12 Sugar suffix
13 Battery type
14 Give the cold shoulder to
15 "The Bourne Ultimatum" villain
16 Spaces on leaves
17 Tot attendants
18 Dish not for food
25 One getting lots of exposure
26 Trotter tracks
28 Entirely
32 "Mercy!"
34 Hog genus
35 First-trimester exam
38 Country singer Black
39 Half-moon tide
40 Religion of Iran
44 Damp and chilly
47 Dietary figs.
49 Reunion groups
50 "Zip it!"
52 Cricket crossbar
53 Brooding places
54 "Believe it ___!"
55 Gorbachev's first lady
56 Slated
58 Gunk
59 "Hair" hairdos
60 Some Corvette roofs
61 Permeate throughout
62 High schoolers, mostly
65 Mediocre
69 Spring water from Quebec
71 Landscaped rd.
72 Little ones
75 Send out a cab
76 Close, in verse
79 Kind of wig
80 Pick up on
83 Fish with toxic roe
84 Shred
86 Criticize sharply
89 Emend further
91 Like Harry Potter's world
92 The Alhambra site
93 Count on
95 The Phantom's first name
96 Yvette's years
98 Canea citizenry
100 Cider product
101 Like the wind
102 Tucked in
104 Puts in office
106 Their chapters aren't meant to be read
107 Diet-friendly
108 One in final jeopardy?
110 Key
114 Neighbor of Twelve Oaks
116 Takes advantage of
117 Emailed a dupe
119 Giant with 511 homers
120 Cause of sudden death
121 ___-Out Burger

270 LEADING UNIVERSITIES   by Lou Sabin
Be sure and give this one the old college try.

ACROSS

1 Energetic burst
6 Medical coverage, for many
10 Belt piercers
14 "In" things
19 Soprano Lehmann
20 Roof repair site
21 Short life stories
22 Fridge label
23 It's helpful for dating vintage clothing
25 Baked apple dessert
27 Conked out
28 Hyderabad royals
30 Houston eleven
31 Rigatoni, tufoli, etc.
33 Ray-headed blooms
35 Gram or graph connection
36 Basilica section
39 "What ___!"
41 Soul sister Franklin
43 Historic U.S. auto racing trophy
47 Debate side
48 Short month?
51 Hank of court renown
52 Toon frame
53 Cassius, per Shakespeare
54 Gridiron maneuver
56 Mountaineer's challenge
57 "You're ___ to talk!"
58 Grain appendage
61 Nutsy
62 Profitless deal
64 Genesis craft
66 Grain or ounce, e.g.
69 Render useless
71 Nod's meaning, perhaps
72 Early race leader
76 Mamba's warning
77 "Don't sweat it!"
81 Missing from action
82 Hunkpapa or Oglala
84 EMT effort
85 Cacophany
86 Williams of "Ugly Betty"
89 "Mottke the Thief" author
91 Furrow maker
92 Enlarge, in a way
93 Cyclopean characteristic
94 Family
95 Aerie lingerie parent
98 Snowball holder, often
100 Marisa of "What Women Want"
101 Target of 91 Across
102 Wire-haired cine star
105 Seasonal mall figures
107 Make champagne
110 Snazzy bar order
112 Morning fare, usually
114 Dealer's offer
118 Julianne Moore feature
120 "Psycho" shower scene setting
122 Far from peppy
123 Ensign producer?
124 "1776" responses
125 Strut and fret
126 Air vents?
127 Asks for it?
128 Dictatorial decisions
129 Dumb and dumber

DOWN

1 Bad-mouth
2 Corn concoction
3 Off-balance
4 Deigned, in a way
5 "The Brainy Bunch"?
6 Bride and groom's seating
7 Fairy queen
8 Push really hard
9 Ward of TV note
10 Monastery heads
11 Evidence source
12 Not so uptight
13 Way the wind blows, briefly
14 I.I. ___ Nobel winner, 1944
15 Aviatrix Earhart
16 Off-limits, like some communities
17 ___ nous (for our ears only)
18 Final word
24 Guitar master Paul
26 Cosa ___
29 Auto racing name since 1948
32 Beauvais buddy
34 Vintage TV fare
36 For the birds
37 Chilean poet ___ Neruda
38 Play openers, for 30 Across
40 Sandwich meat
42 Fashionable
44 Lyon learning centers
45 Whist flub
46 Part of ICU
48 Potential prince?
49 Every's partner
50 Backgammon sacrifice
55 Like A-teams
59 Short Spanish ladies?
60 Deep-six
63 Bless, long ago
64 "___ girl!"
65 Sulphuric acid distinction
67 Combat requirement
68 Banquet course
70 Turner Field's city
72 Set cobblestones
73 Game for visiting teams
74 Lane marker
75 Buffalo do it!
76 Bone specialist's comb. form
78 "That's life!", e.g.
79 Move like a crab
80 Closed
83 Winged bloodsucker
84 Standing room only explanation
87 Compete at Kitzbuhel
88 Subs, at a jazz festival
90 Mt. Everest's range
95 Poker requirement
96 Middle mark
97 "Wow, dude!"
98 Ready for plucking
99 Prepare for shipping
102 Full force
103 Room with reduction potential
104 Umbrian river
106 Polonius' hiding place
108 Ancient Roman money
109 Broke, in a way
111 Camp activities
113 Basic rhyme scheme
115 "Let's get ___!"
116 Takes home
117 ___ club
119 Central point
121 Many a fifth-grader

271 TRAIN OF THOUGHT   by Lou Sabin
A good one to solve during a layover at Grand Central Terminal.

ACROSS

1 Throws home
5 Gaiters
10 Ballerina's handrail
15 Quahog
19 Laura's "Brief Encounter" love
20 Summer camp boat
21 Red-haired mermaid
22 Originate
23 Sam Huff was a great one
25 Cross-country events
27 "Too Fat ___": Yankovic
28 Dew-catcher
30 A port in a storm, say
31 Commuter computers
34 Rings out
35 Skittles ennead
37 Ginsberg and Leech
38 Not too bright
39 "Barefoot" Gardner role
43 French river to the Moselle
44 Large steak cut
46 Lobster's leg count
47 "Grey's Anatomy" extra
48 Climbs, in a way
50 Toward
51 Diplomat's skill
52 Tip one's hat
54 Goes to pot?
56 Quarry
57 ___ Grosso, Brazil
58 Emulates W.J. Bryan
60 Old as the hills
62 Dole out
63 On display
65 Boy of song
66 Joseph Conrad work
67 Horn-___ glasses
68 "Impression, Sunrise" painter
69 Basis of belief
70 Apothecary measures
71 Copped
72 It may be flying or running
74 Follow instructions
77 Crossed D's in Old English
78 Time immemorial
79 Gladstone, to Disraeli
81 Map abbr.
82 Opposite of paleo-
83 "12 items or less" area
87 Crosswise, nautically

89 Bridge supports
91 Ga'hoole sounds
92 Minor to-do
93 Biblical pronoun
94 Cleo's carrier
95 Captured back
96 "Oops!"
99 George who played Sulu
100 Early computer language
101 Slugger's power zone
104 Grand theft auto
109 Minion
110 Brando's drama coach
111 The varsity
112 It's found in HOMES
113 2017 Streep film (with "The")
114 "The Time Machine" author
115 River of forgetfulness
116 Galaxy message

DOWN

1 Sidekick
2 Part of REO
3 ___ X
4 Symbol of imperial power
5 Tonsure areas
6 Lupine groups
7 "My Way" songwriter
8 Oxford area
9 Sinuous firework
10 Gladiator
11 Rich tapestry
12 Coin worth 100 dinars
13 TiVo button
14 Hartford Insurance logo
15 Hockey goal area
16 Polygraph spikes
17 Poor man's champagne
18 Private dinner
24 MLB manager Aaron and family
26 ___ Cassino, Italy
29 With relative ___

31 Performed light surgery
32 Southwestern poplar
33 Lady Gaga's footwear of choice
34 Midnight blue
35 Acting sulky
36 ___ many words
38 No-no's
39 Brooklyn island
40 Program interuption
41 Zone
42 Marc of old Rome
44 Longed (for)
45 "Move it!"
49 Detested
51 Herve Villechaize role
53 Sets up
55 Leg
56 Hip-huggers
57 Rainwear, for short
59 Approving words
61 Ace value in cribbage
62 Rope on the range
63 Burning with desire
64 Melee member
65 Lorna ___ cookies
66 Liveliness
68 Ties up
69 Claude in "Casablanca"
71 Dakota dwelling
73 Timeworn

75 Tour de France stage
76 Republic on the Gulf of Aden
78 Undercarriage bar
80 Milk acid
83 Grain alcohol
84 Millennial Church members
85 Bruised
86 "Makes sense!"
88 Tournament seeding
90 See 92 Down
92 Locale of Hooper's Store (with 90-D)
94 Swiss city on the Rhine
95 Rogers Hornsby's nickname
96 Quid pro quo
97 Fallen Timbers locale
98 MLB's oldest team
99 "Aqualung" group Jethro ___
100 Brother of 24 Down
102 Half a bray
103 Carole King's "Tapestry" label
105 Took tea
106 High dudgeon
107 Put the kibosh on
108 "People ___ Ready": Impressions

ACROSS

1 Shoot the breeze
5 Camp Swampy dog
9 ABC News anchor
13 Lady's bonnet, back in the day
19 Pantomine dance
20 Farm butter?
21 Buck end
22 "___ Fideles"
23 Western song by Johnny Mercer
26 Staff sergeant, e.g.
27 "Way to go!"
28 They're on your side
30 2007 Peace Nobelist
31 Dinner service
34 Tankard filler
35 Like most Beatle songs
38 Santa's suit coat?
39 Code red, for one
41 "Ow!"
42 Bemoaned
43 Rubs the wrong way
45 When house lights dim
48 Ran into
51 "The Hobbit" beast
52 "The Task" poet
54 Cheer for Real Madrid
55 Invitation initials
56 Ehrenreich in "Solo"
57 Brother of Prometheus
58 Uruguay's Punta del ___
59 Thoreau book
61 Base neutralizers
62 Bowling Green athlete
64 Hustler
66 Irani coins
67 Concord
68 Married
69 Green, to da Vinci
70 Scopes Trial attorney
71 River feeding the Colorado
72 Kate Middleton's sister
73 March city of 1965
74 Suffix for secret
77 Online guffaw
78 "Blue Juniata" poet
81 Dorothy diminutive
82 Cockney cacklers

83 Ancient Macedonian capital
84 Afghan bigwig: Var.
85 "Fixer Upper" city
86 Vicinity
87 "Dee-lish!"
89 Lauren on "Whiskey Cavalier"
90 Displayed displeasure
95 "Told ya!"
96 Piscine groups
98 Algerian university city
99 In a chop shop, say
101 Sobersided
102 Premarital activity
105 NSC Advisor under Bush 41
110 Season starter
111 Commedia dell'___
112 Sheet of stamps
113 It's blown in the winds
114 When 1 + 1 = 1
115 Rorschach ___
116 Like fine Scotch
117 Clean the counter

DOWN

1 McBride in "Mercury Rising"
2 Play a kazoo
3 After a fashion
4 2010 animated Disney film
5 Creepy starer
6 "Things We Said ___": Beatles
7 Diplomat's forte
8 Word form of "ear"
9 "The Song of the Earth" composer
10 Narodnaya's range
11 Column order
12 Drive through Beverly Hills
13 Half a dance
14 Ruckus
15 Talked at ___
16 Sporty scarf
17 Chain member
18 Muscle Beach dudes
24 Mine extract
25 1983 Peace Nobelist
29 Dives like an osprey
31 St. John's bread
32 Loan shark's practice

33 "Indian Lake" singing group
34 Texas Hold'em bet
36 Gandalf's letter
37 Bakery artist
39 L-shaped wrench
40 Palpable
43 Like Notre Dame University's dome
44 Cabinetry wood
46 Viral ailments
47 Start of "Jabberwocky"
48 Gem State university town
49 "Rocket Man" subject John
50 Miniscule
52 2008 Pixar film
53 Pavement material
58 Sailor's saint
60 "___ way to go!"
61 Time on the radio
62 Sodbuster
63 Deck out
64 Retreat sounder
65 Credit ___
66 Some auctioned autos

67 Berry in "Cloud Atlas"
69 Trader ___
70 Upset loser of 1948
72 Argues a claim
73 Where the Red Baron met his death
75 Outspoken
76 Preppy jackets
78 Keyboardist Saunders
79 "Zip-___-Doo-Dah"
80 Dental fixative
85 Call in "Lonesome Dove"
86 Café sunshade
88 Giganews product
89 In vogue
90 Biblical sin city
91 Crinkly fabric: Var.
92 Hopalong Cassidy vehicle
93 Poised to hit and run
94 Yankees manager (1996–2007)
96 Backgammon piece
97 Crowed
100 Wimbledon do-overs
101 Heroin, slangily
103 Premaritally named

104 Lab warning
106 Where losing can be fun
107 Kyoto cummerbund
108 Clotheshorse
109 Kicker's aid

ACROSS

1 Become liquid
5 Fire results
10 Backless sofa
15 Jack Benny's catchword
19 Improv sound
20 "The Real Slim ___": Eminem
21 "Love in the Dark" singer
22 Exchange premium
23 Israeli vacation spot
24 Commandeered
25 Extend a lease
26 Oscar-winning Alfonso Cuarón film
27 BEAN
29 GARRY
31 Showy Scandinavian rugs
32 Obedience school command
34 "Something I cannot use, but you can?"
35 Sting's "fields of gold"
38 "Friendship 7" pilot
40 Georgia city and river
45 "Farewell, amigo"
46 Bearded animals
47 Subject of reinvention
48 Suffix with señor
49 Nuts or crackers
50 Iranian language
51 Slugger Judge
52 He speaks with a burr
53 Speedometer letters
54 KIMBERLEY
56 Shoulder wrap
57 Stirrup-shaped ear bones
59 Tiny diving bird
60 Hermione Granger's expertise
61 Pinker in the middle
62 Gallows reprieves
64 Small groove
65 Symbols of authority
67 German mountain
68 What every feller needs?
71 Lucifer, once
72 WROUGHTON
75 Stars and Bars org.

76 Road closing?
77 Time-share unit
78 "___ Day's Night": Beatles
79 Hustler in "The Hustler"
80 Paving crew goo
81 Heartaches
82 Adventurer Fossett
83 Debra in "Love Me Tender"
84 Writers of poetic laments
86 Department and river of France
87 Longfellow rider
88 Superdome shout
89 Diner "sea dust"
90 Prefix for sol
91 GÉZA
96 KARUNA
102 Flock females
103 Book for un élève
104 Donald Duck's twin sister
105 Tall Corn State
106 Some pipe joints
107 Wicker willow
108 Walter Disney's middle name
109 Of two minds
110 Woody's owner in "Toy Story"
111 Cardiff locale
112 Secret store
113 "It's in the Rain" singer

DOWN

1 Kansas City Royals ballpark
2 Parhelic circle
3 Starbuck's skipper
4 Napoleon met his on June 18, 1815
5 Off the beaten path
6 Rebellion of 1786
7 Maori war dance
8 "The Garden of Earthly Delights" panel
9 Motor oil type
10 "Never ___ my door again!"
11 Unflawed
12 Steam hole

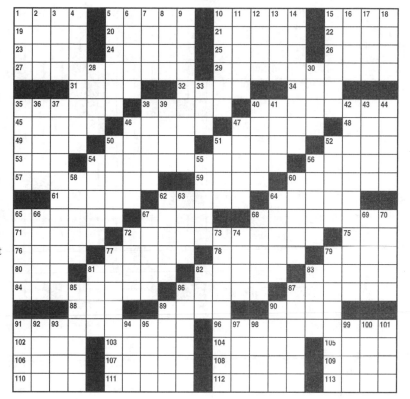

13 Windward's opposite
14 Yale Bowl site
15 Jailer
16 Vanity cases?
17 Wedding rental
18 Shark's offering
28 Brief farewells
30 Kazakh river
33 Dining couple?
35 Aromatic oils
36 Vote to accept
37 TIFFANY
38 Horns in?
39 Girl
40 Petruchio's wife, e.g.
41 Time immemorial
42 KIM
43 Ebon or Bikini
44 Despises
46 "Call of Duty" player
47 Is up the creek?
50 Bets against the shooter
51 Kind of brat
52 Friend of Alice B. Toklas
54 Tiara sparkler
55 "August: ___ County" (2013)

56 Holly piece
58 Beeping device
60 Undemonstrative
62 Emails
63 Ping, Pang, and Pong, e.g.
64 Quota
65 Sew big stitches
66 Conductor Dorati
67 Pageboy feature
68 Desire deeply
69 It blooms late in the season
70 Result of haste
72 "Stop!"
73 Horse ___
74 "Clueless" protagonist
77 Liquidity factor
79 Darling
81 "La Vie en Rose" singer
82 Fa follower
83 "Kon-Tiki" launch site
85 Like an infamous Dallas knoll
86 Staples Center team
87 Go back over

89 Loose rock at the base of a slope
90 Brother of Prometheus
91 Beet genus
92 Bremner in "Wonder Woman"
93 Essential item
94 A Simpson
95 Dr. of Austin Powers films
97 Become slush
98 Amman's Queen ___ Airport
99 "Apollo 11" destination
100 Out of whack
101 Visitor in "Deep Space 9"

274 DIVINE OCTET   by Brenda Cox
Eight gods are lurking in the squares below.

ACROSS

1 Challenging
5 Bundle of papers
10 Spider sensors, e.g.
15 Hummus bread
19 Epithet of Athena
20 Worshiper in a fire temple
21 "Sing, Sing, Sing" composer
22 In good time
23 Gainsay
24 "Empire March" composer
25 Paquin and Pavlova
26 Pulmonic organ
27 SEAL missions
29 Elm Street ordeals
31 Pummel
32 Nipper
34 Superlative for 6E boots
35 Ukraine river
36 Cannes clerics
38 "Once Were Warriors" people
40 "Magic in the Moonlight" director
43 Butter wannabes
44 Head of a family
45 Puma rival
49 Former Notre Dame coach Holtz
50 Gold Rush mill owner
52 McMurtry's "Streets of ___"
54 Zero, in soccer
55 Music, dance, etc.
57 McCullough novel (with "The")
59 State Fair attractions
61 Goes over again
63 Sacred Buddhist mountain
64 Philippines capital
65 PC key
66 Frequent hangout
68 Baked, in Bologna
69 Workaholic's concern
71 Take it very easy
72 ___ instinct
75 Regardful
76 "Bosh!"
79 River of Switzerland
80 Start of many film sequel titles
81 Feigned
83 "Gunsmoke" star
85 Enlisted man's club
86 "Anything ___?"
88 Mr. Potato Head parts

89 Peeve
90 Pyromaniac's act
92 White-and-yellow lily
94 Henry VIII's house
95 LOL or OMG, e.g.
96 Where teams like to play
99 Mackerel shark
100 Miracle scene in Exodus
104 Humongous herbivore
107 Wombats, bandicoots, etc.
111 Wine prefix
112 E.C. Bentley detective
113 119 Across is one
114 "I don't give ___"
115 Ski turn
116 Maternally related
117 Zeedonk's father
118 Behind schedule
119 Duck soup
120 Covered stadiums
121 Ruhr Museum site
122 "Kung Fu Panda 2" villain

DOWN

1 Verb with thou
2 First Hebrew letter
3 Avoid a cancellation
4 Preschool facility
5 Gets the word out?
6 Lecture site
7 "Tantum ___": Aquinas hymn
8 Right away!
9 Prince William, e.g.
10 Paddywhacks
11 Heisman winner Davis
12 Chime sound
13 Rajah's governess
14 "Mystic River" director
15 White knight
16 Caseharden
17 Ambient music sounds
18 Ill-at-ease feeling
28 Religious artworks
30 Plummeter to Earth in March 2001

33 "Sure!"
36 Bay Area city Los ___
37 Ballpark beverage
38 Tuesday, in Paris
39 King Kong's subjects?
40 Pesticide of puzzles
41 Traditional knowledge
42 Church of Denmark members
43 Catchall checkbox
44 Emoticon symbol
46 Hoosiers
47 Jaws portrayer in "Moonraker"
48 "Lohengrin" heroine
51 King Arthur's father
52 Describe in words
53 Give a stemwinder
56 More balanced
58 French bread shape
60 Half of IV
62 Brew oolong
64 Former woolly bears
66 Grappling grips
67 "Fantasy" singer Nova
68 Mudville slugger
69 Accusative, for one
70 Over the hill
71 Carmichael of "Downton Abbey"
72 Lordly home

73 Bowed, in the pit
74 Painter Bakst
76 Small college in Bangor, Maine
77 Arrange haphazardly
78 Ursula Andress film
82 Picked out
84 Ground orchid tubers
87 Cheap way to fly
89 Arctic diving bird
91 Bridgestone products
93 Rihanna song "Te ___"
94 Samples
95 President from Missouri
96 Came to be
97 Letter from Athens
98 Cheryl of "Curb Your Enthusiasm"
99 Sidewalk scam
101 Diva Brightman
102 A-listers
103 Quaking tree
105 Composer Dohnányi
106 Paper order
108 Picnic coolers
109 Umbrella parts
110 Sensitive

FROM HAND TO FOOT   by Brenda Cox
Clue hint: The answer to 4 Down is not "director."

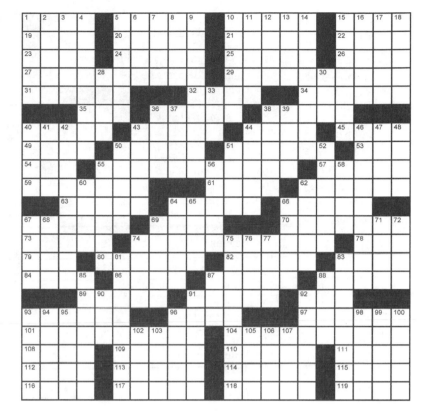

ACROSS

1 Brit's brolly
5 First-stringers
10 Hair braid
15 Once upon a time
19 Eisner's Disney successor
20 "Eleanor Rigby" instrument
21 Cafeteria event
22 1980s pesticide
23 Relative of -ville or -town
24 Stan Lee's type of role
25 Architectual piers
26 Lizard Fuel company
27 Short-term bank offering
29 Games that go down to the wire
31 "Beetlejuice" setting
32 "Shoulda, woulda, coulda" speaker
34 Adds to the pot, say
35 Alice's Snowdrop
36 "A Dissertation Upon ___ Pig": Elia
38 Boxy Toyota
40 Like spy messages
43 "Mary Poppins" family
44 "Hanging" 2000 election concern
45 Basilica section
49 Swan genus
50 Request of Mr. Bojangles
51 Library cubicle
53 Essandoh in "Hitch"
54 Dallas NBAer
55 Upstate New York wine region
57 Stephen Foster's "___ Bayne"
59 Dracula's uptime
61 "Look, ___ day has begun" ("Memory" lyric)
62 "Forever" USPS issues
63 Commencement clothes
64 Grandma of art
66 Address in "Gunga Din"
67 Preposterous
69 "Slumdog Millionaire" costume
70 Stonehenge is on one
73 "Mother ___ Suite": Ravel
74 Steven Wright pitch
78 "Classified" info
79 "Oh, bloody ___, what 'appened 'ere?"
80 Flatware items
82 "Three Times ___": Commodores
83 Cottontail tail
84 Slumgullion
86 Flash foe ___ Kadabra
87 "Rebel-'Rouser" guitarist Eddy
88 A black tea
89 "Hollywood Squares" answer
91 "The Christmas Song" composer
92 Old French coin
93 Smelting residue
96 Hogwarts librarian Pince
97 Appeases (with "to")
101 Sneakernet storage
104 Falling apart
108 Life of Riley
109 Herbert Hoover, by birth
110 Phishing spot
111 Killarney language
112 Red salamanders
113 Respect the anthem
114 Esther in "Driving Miss Daisy"
115 Time-honored practice
116 Cockroach, e.g.
117 "A Modest Proposal," e.g.
118 "Copy that"
119 Egg holder

DOWN

1 "Dance With Me Henry" singer Georgia
2 Hundredth of a shekel
3 Deserve
4 Oscar recipient for Best Picture
5 "La Bohème" has only one
6 $100 bill background color
7 Mr. Noodle's friend
8 "Guantanamera" codirector
9 1979 Roger Moore film
10 Krypton, for one
11 Like the Sea of Serenity
12 Tom Waits record label
13 Suffix for period
14 "Father of ___" (1991 Steve Martin film)
15 Italian wedding soup ingredient
16 Fugard's "A Lesson From ___"
17 "Light Brigade" weapon
18 "The Rape of the Lock" concern
28 Homecoming comer
30 Maui's ___ Needle
33 "Arizona" letters
36 "You ___, sir?"
37 Start of a fairy tale
38 Smallest mammal
39 Jam ingredients?
40 "___ and Get It": Beatles
41 Patron saint of Norway
42 Prized food fish
43 Feature of a Dutch bob
44 They're made for weddings
46 Mar-a-Lago locale
47 Baby's first ___
48 "Like, forever"
50 Took some courses?
51 Walking stick
52 Like sarin
55 London threads
56 Alternative to contacts
58 Café au ___
60 "Entre ___" (1983 film)
62 Porsche in "Cars"
64 Hawaii's ___ Loa
65 "Dungeons & Dragons" creatures
66 Groundbreaking tool
67 ". . . and children of all ___!"
68 Runner with nine Olympic gold medals
69 Rattle bunkmates
71 "For two," on sheet music
72 Arthur Ashe Stadium inits.
74 Japanese beef
75 "Big Little Lies" star
76 Jack of oaters
77 Cause of ruin
81 Blissful setting
83 From Dixie
85 Closest, in a guessing game
87 Suffix for star
88 Windjammer, e.g.
90 Tomcat
91 In style
92 Attempted Jungfrau
93 Like Jungfrau
94 Abrade
95 Dethrones
96 Eric Trump's mom
98 Willies-inducing
99 Has an off day?
100 "Wintry mix" stuff
102 Becomes compost
103 "___ a Teenage Werewolf" (1957)
105 "Typee" sequel
106 "Pogo" creator Kelly
107 "Aida" backdrop

PERFECT GAME HALL OF FAME* by Elizabeth C. Gorski
Follow the asterisks to find nine pitchers that made baseball history.

ACROSS

1 Minnesota hockey team
5 Beach "hermits"
10 Dinah Shore's label
13 Drink for an ant
16 Brock of Modest Mouse
18 Maid of paradise
19 "Your Song" singer
20 Cocktail party food
21 Los Angeles Dodgers pitcher (9/9/65)*
23 Assist a con
24 Stratford river
25 Op-Ed contributor
26 Cincinnati Reds pitcher (9/16/88)*
29 Cheer for el toro
30 Towed boat
32 "This is all ___ to know!"
33 Philadelphia Phillies pitcher (6/21/64)*
38 Tax write-off
41 Reynolds Wrap maker
44 Chefs Ducasse and Passard
45 "___ oui!"
47 Mannerisms
49 Spring sound
50 Gossip sheet
51 Sarah McLachlan hit song
53 Eckersley or Martinez
54 Cherry variety
55 Tex-___ food
56 Bean counter's deg.
57 Psychedelic drug
59 Tierney in "Laura"
60 Sanctioned
62 Purveyors
65 Pitcher Halladay
66 Oakland A's pitcher (5/8/68)*
68 Global Wi-Fi network
71 Astonishing
72 Catherine the Great, e.g.
74 Pinkett in "Ali"
78 Brooks Koepka's org.
79 Wrath

80 Enero, for one
81 Lacking width and depth
82 My Lord, in Hebrew
84 Auntie of Broadway
86 Daisy of Dogpatch
87 553, in letters
88 Women, in quaint literature
90 Futurist
92 Edie Brickell song
93 Rented out anew
94 You might bounce it off someone
96 New York Yankees pitcher (5/17/98)*
98 Beautify
100 Storage area
102 D.C. VIP
103 Adirondack vacation spot
107 High-rated investments
112 Carnality
113 Within earshot
114 Texas Rangers pitcher (7/28/94)*
117 Eastern arch
118 Coffee grind
119 Bolshevik leader
120 Frailty's name, to Hamlet
121 Take the pennant
122 Craving
123 "You ___ Beautiful": Cocker
124 Pixels

DOWN

1 Sage
2 "Beauty___ beauty does"
3 Office hookups
4 Max Ernst's movement
5 Picked
6 Drubbing
7 "___ Wiedersehen!"
8 Playtex product
9 54 past the hour
10 AnnaSophia on "The Carrie Diaries"
11 Hit song by "The Association"
12 "Star Trek" actor Yelchin

13 New York Yankees pitcher (7/18/99)*
14 Wellington's alma mater
15 Former "NY Times" puzzle editor
17 Boston Americans pitcher (3/5/04)*
19 Pickle
20 1960s wall covering
22 Pottery ovens
27 Shakespeare's "night's herald"
28 Make rugs
30 Catch a liner
31 "Transformers" FX
33 Kareem in "Airplane!"
34 Panay seaport
35 "The rain in Spain stays ___ . . ."
36 Dog of song
37 Giant screen format
39 Eastern sash
40 Enclose securely
42 "Little Shop of Horrors" dentist
43 South African fox
46 Blue birthstones

48 Driver's license datum
50 Clearance label
52 Novelist du Maurier
55 Mrs. Lovett's pastry in "Sweeney Todd"
56 Ramadan faster
58 Foyer item
61 London lavs
62 "Have a seat"
63 Schlep
64 Madrilenian Mrs.
67 Like Roger Rabbit
68 Dome ornament
69 "Strange Interlude" playwright
70 "The Young & Restless" theme
73 "Good Times" star Esther
74 Hockey great Jaromír
75 "Zip-___-Doo-Dah"
76 New York Yankees pitcher (10/8/56)*
77 Precede in time
80 Ex-Met Throneberry
83 TV chef Brown

85 "The Shining" door buster
86 "Beowulf" beverage
87 Violin sheet music marking
89 Earnest
91 Netherlands piano center
92 "___ Cassio!": Shak.
95 Interrogate
97 "Forget it!"
99 Pitcher Johnson
101 Icelandic volcano
103 Unhurried
104 Start of a summer mo.
105 Had reclined
106 Dada sculptor
107 ___ del Mono (Spanish liqueur)
108 "___, Our Help in Ages Past"
109 Disney clownfish
110 "Blast!"
111 Numerical IDs
115 Auction ending
116 Paris–Amsterdam dir.

BASEBALL TRIVIA   by John M. Samson
The hero of "Damn Yankees" is named after 55 Across.

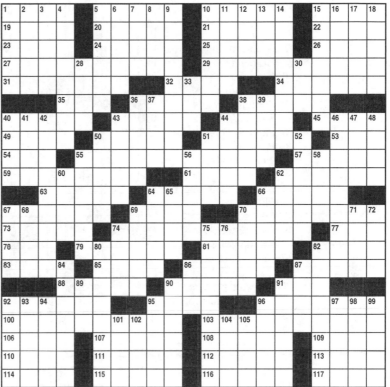

ACROSS

1 Peak projection
5 Skiddoo
10 Prohibit
15 Speak with a rough voice
19 "A Question of Mercy" playwright
20 South Korean city
21 College town near Bangor
22 Dragonfly wings
23 Whitehorse's tribe
24 Charcoal wood
25 Git-go
26 Vole cousins
27 Baseball's "Chairman of the Board"
29 Pesky's Pole stadium
31 Plays a trick on
32 Birds with deep drumming calls
34 Makes one's hair stand on end
35 What the irate see
36 Subject of HBO's "61*"
38 ___ concern
40 Bouncers, as a rule
43 Tumult
44 Don's man
45 Resort NNW of Siracusa
49 Woeful cry
50 Sixties protest
51 Gourmand's pastime
53 Taylor Swift's "___ Song"
54 Mount Olivet loc.
55 Black Sox Scandal figure
57 Brother of Dido
59 Spring home of the Detroit Tigers
61 Russia-China border river
62 Christopher Walken's birth name
63 Member of the camel family
64 All-clear sounder
66 Pleiades' number
67 Wade Boggs' retired Tampa Bay number
69 Kunis of "Jupiter Ascending"
70 Materialized
73 Friend in the 'hood
74 Giant pitcher nicknamed "The Meal Ticket"
77 "Whoopee!"
78 Rocky Mountain deer
79 Puffs on
81 Mary Poppins, e.g.
82 Give a darn
83 ___-do-well
85 Peerless pitchers
86 Speed, to a base runner
87 Betrothal notice
88 Dana in "The Sting"
90 He sits in a lot of laps?
91 Rorqual school
92 Sissy in "Carrie"
95 Blacken beef
96 Justin Bieber album
100 World Series MVP Award eponym
103 Baseball's "Mr. Cub"
106 Dominican baseball family
107 "Fiddler on the Roof" role
108 Vacation segments
109 "Rhyme Pays" rapper
110 Bottom of the barrel
111 Charlton Heston title role
112 "The Lego Movie" hero
113 Giddy happiness
114 Latin infinitive
115 Gazpacho server
116 Opportunities, so to speak
117 Lets touch them

DOWN

1 Ballpark throng
2 Early-blooming
3 In a state of excited activity
4 Motions
5 Hung in there
6 ___-foot jelly
7 Salon correction
8 Stress, so it's said
9 Certain homicide, in police lingo
10 Homer Simpson's persona
11 Oceanic raptors
12 Warrant officer, briefly
13 Over again
14 Starting-pitcher sequence
15 Run amok
16 The Babe, for one
17 "___ bleu!"
18 Steals a glance
28 First lady's home
30 Sushi money, maybe
33 "Mission to ___" (1997 documentary)
36 Subdued
37 Nutmeg husk
38 Ron Guidry's nickname
39 Mayberry minor
40 Word to the chief
41 Snow Queen of Arendelle
42 Brave who batted .417 in the 1991 World Series
43 Shrek's wife
44 Like some Louisiana fare
46 Pitcher with 5,714 career strikeouts
47 Legally invalid
48 His 25 grand slams broke Lou Gehrig's record
50 Disesteem
51 Salinger title girl
52 Bootlick
55 Odalisques, e.g.
56 "Fallen" singer McLachlan
58 First flat, first floor
60 She outwrestled Thor
62 Email option
64 Begets
65 Misfortunes
66 Went on a buying binge
67 "___ He Kissed Me": Crystals
68 Playwright Soyinka
69 Constructor
70 Baseball's Doubleday
71 Win by effort
72 They can get in your hair
74 Colombian cash crop
75 Removed a light bulb
76 Result of a walk
80 Kind of sky or shark
82 Crusade
84 Serious homebody
86 Major minor league?
87 Carping comment
89 Luau memento
90 Have a place to call home
91 They make a party a party
92 Low marshy tract
93 Accumulations of dirty dishes
94 "A Lesson From ___": Fugard
95 "Downton Abbey" daughter
96 Cheapskate
97 Le frère de père
98 Olympic shooting sport
99 Shawn with a plaque on the Giants Wall of Fame
101 ___ fide (not genuine)
102 "Alphabet Song" start
104 Drum set company
105 Disney clownfish

278 THEMELESS by Raymond C. Young
Beatle fans have the edge at 56 Down.

ACROSS

1 Liquid plastic?
9 Emperor who finished the Colosseum
14 En ___ términos (in other words)
19 University of Michigan city
20 Slim Shady's alter ego
22 Christopher in "Morning Glory"
23 Turkey locale
24 Cheesy chip
25 Chelmsford's county
26 Chipped meat
28 Streaming app
29 Cheri heard in "Shrek the Third"
30 Hidden hiker in children's books
31 Ginger Spice, formerly
33 New York's Carnegie ___
34 Salmon eggs
35 Banksy, for one
37 Mosquito repellant
39 First-aid plant
40 2018 French Open champ
45 Unanswerable queries
47 Flying Spur or Bentayga
48 Arthur ___ Courage Award
50 Gets in the way of
51 Peers
52 "MMMBop" group
54 ___ row exercise
55 Ski jumper Görlich
56 Showy yellow flower
58 NYC sub letters
61 Mother of Artemis
62 Tufted flexible wire
63 You make them up
64 2015 Payne Stewart Award recipient
65 First American political party members
66 Decibel measures
67 Be the father of
68 Many AC units
69 Search for water beneath

70 Southern denial
73 Obeys, as a dog
74 Like a tryst
75 Going for bigger
77 Golden hair color
80 Give gratis
81 Not so much
83 Public hissy fits
84 Stealing: Prefix
86 Part of the loop
88 Benz of Mercedes-Benz
89 See 69 Across
94 Nutritionist Krieger
95 Flub
97 Cause a ruckus
99 "Inside the Actors Studio" topics
100 Capital of Punjab
102 Have one whiff
103 Live and breathe
104 Japanese mushrooms
105 Dissipate
106 Simple song
107 And the next: Abbr.
108 One missing from formation

DOWN

1 Saloon music, briefly
2 "It's the end of ___"
3 Slo-o-ow mover
4 Sprinted, to Brits
5 Words to live by
6 Rhyme structure
7 Subdued pink shade
8 Muppet keyboardist
9 Chaough of "Mad Men"
10 "My turn!"
11 Hardly perky
12 As a collective
13 Makes a home of
14 BK shake ingredients
15 Student hand-in
16 Applied more caulk
17 Exhausted
18 Eye-candy quality
21 IMDB listings
27 Chilly, in Chile
32 Lesser Antilles native
35 Dunkirk donkeys
36 Creates a mosaic
38 Pinterest rival
40 Sophomore album
41 Canadian Arctic natives

42 Kyushu volcano
43 Cantina stew
44 Dial a no-show
46 Org. that started film ratings
47 Snoopy's sister
49 Box eggs
52 It springs eternal
53 Recall announcements
56 Book mentioned in "Rocky Raccoon"
57 Myrmecology study
58 It holds 20 minutes of audio
59 Microscopic
60 Black-ink item
62 Alexander the Great conquest
63 The ___ Spoonful
65 John Amos role on "The West Wing"
66 Forage storage
67 Sassy to the max
69 Shared Microsoft Windows files
70 Exhausted (with "out")
71 Historic space flight of 1969

72 Comment regarding an unseen skunk
74 Frankie Laine hit
76 Hogarth's "Beer Street" print partner
78 First or reverse
79 Furious
82 Coolio song from "Gangsta's Paradise"
85 Easily irritated
87 Quaint corners
89 Revolutionary patriot Silas
90 Deep yellow
91 Love handles locale
92 ___ that time
93 Large computer key
96 ___-dieu (kneeler)
98 MTA stops
101 Atty.'s honorific

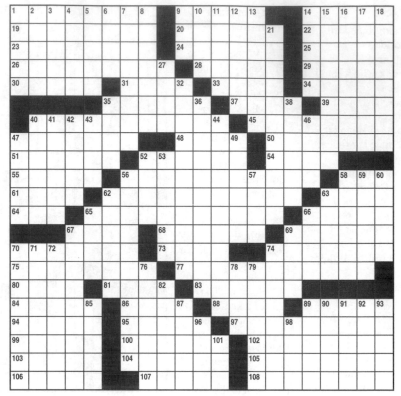

279 "IT'S COZY INSIDE" by Elizabeth C. Gorski
This theme is really for the birds!

ACROSS

1 A couple of laughs?
5 Sing "shooby-doo"
9 Morning joe
13 Lunar stages
19 Nobel Prize subj.
20 Come clean
21 Coldplay's "___ Love"
22 ___-Hungarian Empire
23 2017 U.S. Open Champion
26 Under control
27 Dine at nine
28 Mental spark
29 Retail outlets that are a click away
31 See socially
33 "Das Lied von der ___"
34 Avoid capture
35 Tribe of Canada
36 Verso opposite
38 Roxy Music founder
39 2005 Prince hit
42 Well-versed writer?
43 Not far
48 ___ Bator
49 "Mr. Palomar" author Calvino
50 Spanish gold
51 Dastardly looks
52 Deli sandwich request
54 Shoelace holders
57 Make over
58 Quadrennium's four: Abbr.
59 "Sad to say . . ."
62 Slowly, to Sibelius
63 Nonviolent protest
64 Binding job-cost proposal
68 Catch ___
71 Incendiary crime
72 King Prawn of the Muppets
73 A billion years
76 "___ cost you"
77 Scorn
80 Brain twister
82 "Sweet ___": Rolling Stones
85 South Pacific parrot
86 Less dated
89 Award for "The Band's Visit"
90 Pump locations
93 Biol. and others
94 Ordinal suffix
95 Winter sculpture medium
96 French styling goo
97 Iowa college city
98 Of an eye part
100 Caspian Sea feeder
101 Claim on a home
102 Center of attention in a cast
106 Man-goat deity
108 New Deal power proj.
111 Prehistoric tool
112 Osteology study
115 Fictional Interpol agent
116 Go ___ great length
117 Robin Williams role
118 iPhone assistant
119 Aware of the joke
120 Sleuth Wolfe
121 Noncommittal reply
122 Read a bar code

DOWN

1 Name on a toy truck
2 Rights advocacy org.
3 1994 basketball documentary
4 "Fifty Shades Freed" heroine
5 Björn Borg, for one
6 Job for Sherlock
7 Dashiell's dog
8 Word ignored in indexing
9 Mr. X, in court
10 Anoint with oil
11 Caesar's "I came"
12 River of France
13 Palermo pals
14 Locate through detective work
15 ". . . woman who lived in ___"
16 Drawing card
17 Seabird
18 Lays down the lawn
24 Evening, in ads
25 Philip Roth's "kvetcher"
30 Always
32 Vulcan's home
33 School for Pierre
35 Use a crayon
36 Trio before U
37 Greek vowel
39 Sour partner
40 Eponymous NYC restaurateur
41 "Iron Mike" of boxing
42 Hardly brawny
43 Garlicky mayo
44 Brogue bottoms
45 Ontario river
46 "Can't lose" advice from a railbird
47 Nest on Mount Marcy
53 Knitter's purchase
55 Violinist Semenova
56 Vague quantity
60 Slightly
61 Ump's cry
63 British firearm
64 Word after "Roger"
65 Ogee shapes
66 Greet silently
67 Mimics
68 Netflix-watching spree
69 Annoyed persistently
70 Splish-splash
73 Solipsistic
74 They got out of Dodge
75 Unfavorable votes
78 Sobbing
79 Sam in "Jurassic Park III"
81 "Yoo hoo, ___, my name is Pinky Lee . . ."
83 Typewriter King wrote "Carrie" on
84 Fairway compliment
87 Sorrow
88 Opposite of WSW
91 Tidy
92 Settle on
97 "___ We Got Fun?"
98 Schenectady college
99 Simon of Duran Duran
100 Of a forearm bone
101 Like PowerBall winners
102 Start of finals
103 Bourbon ingredient
104 "Tickle Me" Muppet
105 First-rate
106 Word on a gift card
107 Radiant glow
109 "Up in the Air" actress Farmiga
110 Alphabet book phrase
113 Texter's "Enough details!"
114 Intrepid letters

ACROSS

1 "La Boheme" girl
5 A slew
10 One of 30 Down
14 Ascetic holy man
19 Polecat's protection
20 Snowy-white wader
21 Promise, for one
22 "Let me reiterate"
23 Singer Cantrell
24 More detached
25 Great quantity (with "of")
26 Add a little color
27 Shy, Spanish idealist?
31 Miso ingredient
32 Dele a dele
33 C.W. and Emily
34 ___ trumpet
35 Sound at a shearing
37 Montreal team
39 Little Jack Horner's last words
40 Use henna
41 Two or three priests?
48 Ragweed, e.g.
49 Is plural?
50 Conger line
51 Zhivago's love
55 Theater backdrops
56 Pouchlike structures
58 Rock to and fro
59 Tabloid no-no
60 Last letter of words?
61 Freshwater fish
62 Cove
64 Picture palace
65 Judy carried gratuitously?
68 Loath (with "to")
71 Fiat or ukase
72 The ___ Duke (Wellington)
73 It can be a gift
76 Put a lid on it
77 It was sacred in ancient Egypt
78 Distort
79 Small combo
80 Start of a conclusion
81 John Deere competitor
82 Clark's "Mogambo" costar
84 Take another look at a test paper
86 Cowgirl cooling off?
90 Salsa, for example
93 What teacher's pet got
94 Diacritical mark
95 Kimona go-with
96 Existing
98 Analyze syntactically
100 Outer prefix
103 MacGregor topper
106 Play a card game above Doral?
110 Type of syrup
111 At the summit
112 Disappear bit by bit
113 Elevator man
114 Bushed
115 Two over Paar?
116 Japanese liquors
117 Part of SAT
118 City on the Aire
119 Work units
120 Winter wheels?
121 Like an unswept hearth

DOWN

1 Sheds skin
2 Baking potato
3 Safes, sort of
4 Neighbor of Jordan
5 Make like new
6 Correspond
7 Worried excessively
8 Abound (with)
9 Giant of a man
10 Behemoths
11 In the sky
12 Elite Navy group
13 It's sometimes jerked
14 "The ___ Verses": Rushdie
15 Mellowing
16 Tripped the light fantastic
17 Extremely
18 Malaise
28 Convention
29 Not a soul
30 "Monday, Monday" half
36 Hole punching tools
38 Brief holiday?
39 Comrade in arms
41 Projection on a basilica
42 Visitors, to the home team
43 Done here
44 Japanese metropolis
45 More novel
46 1950s nonconformist
47 Curtis' costar in "A Fish Called Wanda"
52 Maggie Simpson's grandpa
53 ZZZ letters
54 King's intro?
57 Brain prefix
58 Cash-dispenser?
59 It may be on the house
61 Subtle signal sound
62 Cow-horned diety
63 Tom Brokaw's network
64 Gloated
65 Side-splitting
66 Dialect
67 Jacques, in song
68 One at Spyglass Hill
69 Far from monotony: Abbr.
70 Chang's twin
73 Moves toward
74 West Wing worker
75 Afrikaner
77 Hawkeye state
78 True grit
79 Feeder: Abbr.
81 Fundamental principle
82 Unequal prefix
83 Wickedness
85 Stable worker
87 Hotfoots
88 One of the Fates
89 Enkindle once again
90 Depressing
91 Sniff the air?
92 Inhabit
97 Unbroken
98 The pumpkin eater
99 In the company of
101 Surrendered formally
102 Ringlet of hair
104 Mennonite
105 Erroll Garner classic
107 Senior golfer Irwin
108 Mouthy?
109 Letter after theta

UNITED NATIONS   by Edgar Fontaine
A good one to solve on October 24.

ACROSS

1 Pass over
5 Leg of lamb
10 Part of Nasdaq: Abbr.
15 Apple cores?: Abbr.
19 Yemeni port
20 One possessed?
21 Hottie
22 Tennis's Mandlikova
23 Caboose, figuratively
24 Indonesian island
25 Ottoman title
26 All in the family
27 Three United Nations members?
30 Ekland of "The Wicker Man"
31 "The Sweetheart of Sigma ___"
32 Bonheur and Ponselle
33 Asia's shrinking body of water
35 Fungi
39 Met expectations?
42 Med. school class
43 Babylonian sky deity
44 Ancient Greek marketplace
47 Not more than
49 Spanish appetizer
52 Any of the Bee Gees
54 Three United Nations members?
57 Gawk (at)
59 Stuffed shirt
60 Loser's place?
61 Bullion unit
62 Blow off steam?
64 Scrub
67 Good thing to break
69 Hart Trophy winner (1970–72)
70 Three United Nations members?
76 She played Blanche opposite Marlon's Stanley in "Streetcar"
77 Battleship letters
78 Bixby and Murray
79 Monument Valley feature
80 Startled
82 Be-bopper
85 Flight data, briefly
87 Dot's twin on "Hi and Lois"
90 Three United Nations members?
95 Allege as fact
96 Capitol Hill worker
97 Valedictorian's last role
98 Rips apart
100 Pique
101 Nobel Prize ceremony site
103 Trig functions
105 Aggregates
107 Deform
110 La ___ opera house
113 Sushi treat
114 Stay sleeping
115 Three United Nations members?
122 As well
123 Pageant prize
124 Sidestep
125 Cop's collar
126 Bit attachment
127 Kind of wrench
128 Number of deadly sins
129 Dates
130 Baseball stats
131 Skirt fold
132 1545 council site
133 Advantage

DOWN

1 Close to guessing
2 Brain popper
3 Sound of thunder
4 Improve, in a way
5 They don't conceal much
6 Pelvic bones
7 Player
8 Convex molding
9 Mother with a Nobel prize
10 Relevant
11 Airplane assignment
12 Cummerbund
13 Recently retired Lorena
14 When repeated, a Latin dance
15 Impostor

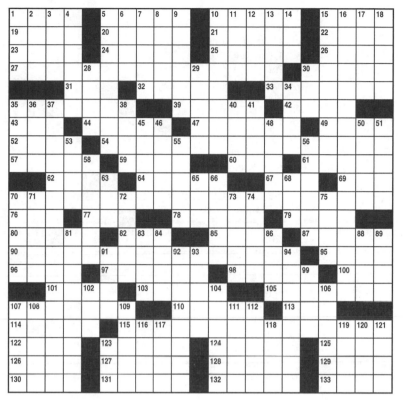

16 Three United Nations members?
17 Connect
18 Clement Moore character
28 2000 World Series locale
29 See-through wrap
30 Exclude
34 Have status
35 Falls behind
36 "What's ___ for me?"
37 Three United Nations members?
38 Propagates
40 Rock concert apparatus
41 Ivory legally sold?
45 Kidney-related
46 Marinated Philippine dish
48 High-fives
50 Light, flat cake, popular in Pakistan
51 Bone cavity
53 Get-up-and-go
55 Microwave explosive
56 Purred, as a motor
58 Cape Verde money
63 Physics and chemistry, e.g.: Abbr.
65 Jeter stat
66 Masonic doorkeeper
68 Bread box?
70 Houseflies
71 Tenth-century Holy Roman Emperor
72 Half of the Odd Couple
73 Hitching post?
74 Electric bill datum
75 Where most people live
81 Excretions
83 Literary collections
84 South American monkey
86 Phoenix squad
88 Guam or Yukon: Abbr.
89 Valuable deposits
91 Locale for a werewolf attack?
92 Like pi
93 Betel palm
94 Follower
99 Old World duck
102 First name in horror films
104 Least wild
106 Pass, as time
107 ___ Boothe Luce
108 Crude workman?
109 Govt. security
111 Giblets part
112 Tequila source
116 Senior golfer Irwin
117 Carbamide
118 Churchill's successor as prime minister
119 Must
120 Remnant
121 Basilica section
123 Bojangles' genre

ACROSS

1 Rival rival
5 Job safety org.
9 ___ de résistance
14 Yucatán stuffed cheese
18 Mean companion?
19 Oddly funny
20 Press on
21 Fallon's late-night predecessor
22 1965 Glenn Yarbrough hit
25 Queen Maud ___
26 Ship to remember
27 Pocket ___
28 At the hub of
30 1963 Polo Grounds player
31 Dealer's query
33 "Robot Wars" robot: Abbr.
36 L'chaim, e.g.
39 Mtn. stat
40 2011 Adele hit
43 Bollywood wrap
45 First word spoken by Scrooge
47 Like Schönberg's music
48 Odist's "prior to"
49 Put trust in
51 Mustangs of Dallas
53 Open-source reference entry
55 2009 Luke Bryan hit
58 Gives the slip to
59 Duke Ellington's monogram
60 Film director Herzog
61 Somewhat
64 "Hacksaw Ridge" hero
66 Popular sandwich cookies
67 Vocational school tool
68 Jane Addams' org.
72 Admits a mistake
74 Former Yankee Mariano
75 All systems go!
76 Tawdry
79 1965 Peter, Paul and Mary hit
83 Coffee whiteners
86 "Gangnam Style" singer
87 Protected inventor
88 Parlor letters
89 Union contract?
91 "I ___ a Name": Croce

92 Some Sugar Ray wins
93 1970 Creedence Clearwater Revival hit
97 M1 motorway sports cars
98 Half a Kingsmen title
99 Key lime pie ingredient
100 City 60 miles southwest of Seattle
103 Lighthouse view
106 Accident-probing grp.
108 Hoarse speech
110 Golf's "Big Easy"
112 Max Ernst's movement
114 1971 Carpenters hit
118 Sign word
119 ___ toilette
120 Peeta's "Hunger Games" weapon
121 Besides that
122 Nimble
123 Judicial gowns
124 "The Plague" setting
125 Natalya's negative

DOWN

1 Picture book
2 Pad paper
3 "Blue Ribbon" beer
4 "Word" suffix
5 Informal bridge bid
6 Pasta cooker's need
7 Self starter?
8 Big name in contact lenses
9 Heinz Field team
10 "My vote is yes!"
11 Org. that registers pesticides
12 Animation unit
13 Cinders of old comics
14 "Mama" Cass
15 "Coming right up"
16 New England cape
17 In vogue, in the '60s
19 Smidgeon, in recipes
23 Some detective work
24 Small paving stone
29 Pickle company or its NC home
32 Kyrgyzstan city
34 Magpie relative
35 Start of Caesar's boast
37 Sportcoat material
38 On-the-job learners

39 Living space
41 Follower of Pan
42 Cheer up
43 Timex competitor
44 Locales of bishop thrones
45 Jeer leaders
46 Nobelist Sakharov
49 Completely spent
50 Perform miracles
51 "___ Always a Woman": Billy Joel
52 Satellite that deorbited in 2001
54 Law firm aide, for short
56 Certain security, briefly
57 Boat contents
62 Resume speed, musically
63 Food channel?
65 Ice-cream drink
67 Easter bloom
69 Major division of a long poem
70 Really good seats
71 Poland neighbor
73 Female headdresses
74 Four "Monopoly" properties: Abbr.
76 Grumpy glare
77 Weed B Gon company
78 Hoopster, at times

80 Date bk. entry
81 Profit
82 Signs
84 Fibrous network
85 Canoodle, in Canterbury
90 Software improvement
91 Pebbly
94 Liturgical chant
95 One of the Cartwrights
96 Marty Robbins signature song
97 Kind of chord
101 Jason's sorceress wife
102 Spin doc
103 Posturepedic company
104 "Family Ties" mom
105 Definite plus
107 "That's a no-___!"
109 Pro group
111 Course at St. Andrews
112 "U.S.A." author John ___ Passos
113 Google Play download
115 Former NBA star Ming
116 Confer knighthood on
117 "Fresh Air" network

283

"ABSOLUTELY!" by Victor Fleming and Tracy Bennett

"Belgian painter" is the usual clue for 12 Down.

ACROSS

1 Upscale hotel chain
6 Mennen aftershave
10 Autobahn auto
14 Hilltop
19 Whether by land ___
20 Place
21 Russo onscreen
22 Ganja smoker
23 "Absolutely!"
25 Wagner role
26 Sting's "Kate & Leopold" song
27 Dancing on air
28 Alterations expert
30 Heart-pounding episode
31 Four-legged father
32 "Absolutely!"
34 Most of the world
37 Start to press?
38 Never existed
39 O'Donnell or O'Grady
40 Anticipatory feelings
41 Mafia chieftain
44 Knotted
45 Speech issue
46 Bart's grandpa
47 "La Dolce Vita" star Anouk
52 Before, for poets
53 Invitation ender
56 "Absolutely!"
58 They're checked at LAX
59 Brook
61 Blood feud
62 Winning QB of Super Bowl VIII
65 Put in solitary
67 Sandy Koufax's manager
68 Summarized the main points of
70 Okla. or Dak., once
71 ___-à-porter
72 "Absolutely!"
74 Loud and wild
76 First word of "Nowhere Man"
79 Ram near a bull
80 "Insecure" star Issa
81 Word before Orange or Lyme
82 "Absolutely!"
83 Magical herb given to Odysseus

84 Change colors, again
86 Havana's ___ Castle
87 Kellogg's Honey ___
92 Deep sleeps
93 Soup or salad, e.g.
94 "Absolutely!"
98 Electronic synthesizer
99 Opposing forces
100 "___ I Would Leave You"
101 They're pulled when jumping
105 Garden center purchase
106 North Sea feeder
107 "Absolutely!"
109 "The Old Wives' Tale" playwright
110 Teri of "After Hours"
111 Dorm designation
112 Handle, as an axe
113 It's driven in a cattle drive
114 Sportscast tidbit
115 Unagi, in a sushi bar
116 Doesn't bolt

DOWN

1 Brain division
2 Gemsbok genus
3 "My Brother ___": Grateful Dead
4 "Absolutely!"
5 Cracker for Brie
6 Coeur d'___ Lake
7 Maserati parent
8 Half a score
9 Strait-laced
10 Brand of frozen fries
11 Window company
12 Lorna Doone's grandfather
13 Profit from a lecture
14 Friday's rescuer
15 Ill will
16 Expansive residence
17 Pudding recipe directive
18 Natural ability
24 M&M's inventor
29 Treaty concern

32 "Absolutely!"
33 Tango requisite?
34 Johnson of "Laugh-In" fame
35 Nice evening?
36 "Aha"
37 Upscale
40 Charted records
41 Warhol subject
42 Too refined for
43 Small dog, familiarly
45 Folklore tale
47 Discombobulates
48 Clarifying phrase from Cato
49 Kitchen glove
50 Inner, in combinations
51 "Sleepy Time Gal" lyricist
53 Tubs
54 Attica uprising
55 "Oklahoma!" aunt
57 Stultified
58 Prove otherwise
60 Flynn Boyle in "Twin Peaks"
62 "Naked Maja" artist
63 Regretful sort

64 "You're looking at him!"
65 Paragon
66 "Absolutely!"
69 The younger Saarinen
71 Struck thing
73 Bengal tiger mascot Who ___
75 Islets
76 German "mister"
77 Dumbo's are jumbo
78 Rockport product
82 "Absolutely!"
83 Bulldogs of the SEC
84 Tom Rakewell, for one
85 Show of affection
86 Sources of baby's milk
87 Overloads
88 Bach's "___ in G"
89 Churchill's successor
90 Gum base
91 On the up and up
92 Clandestine
93 Cairo Christian
95 Supermodel Cheryl
96 G-sharp equivalent

97 Winger in "Rachel Getting Married"
98 "Great ___ think alike"
101 Bobbin
102 Seehorn in "Better Call Saul"
103 Tim on "Madam Secretary"
104 Norms, for short
108 Springfield barkeep

BAND OF BROTHERS*: PART I   by Steve Davies
The answers to 60 Across and 81 Down combine to form a Pete Seeger song.

ACROSS

1 Dull as dishwater
5 Sacred poem
10 Put in ___ word for
15 Sponsorship
19 San ___ (Riviera resort)
20 Perfume scent
21 Dante's "La Vita ___"
22 "Enterprise-D" android
23 Bautista of tennis
24 Green lizard
25 "___ Nuthin' " ("Oklahoma!" song)
26 Pechora's mountains
27 President on the Purple Heart*
29 "The Misfits" star*
31 Jumper's lack
32 Grand-slam results
34 Site of draft picks
35 Long-tailed rodent
36 Jake in "Lonesome Dove"
38 George Burns film
39 Japanese noodle dish
42 Like Swiss cheese
43 Uncovered
44 Dos cubed
48 Perry's "Diary of ___ Black Woman"
49 Malone in "The Hunger Games"
50 Medium-dry sherry
53 ___ Hamoed (Passover period)
54 Whereas
55 Composed
57 Differently
58 Squeezed
60 "Land of Opportunity"
62 Like some gloves
64 Bargnani of the NBA
65 Cutthroat fish
66 Grilling grippers
67 Akin to jejunal
68 Skyline sights
70 Denny of the Moody Blues
71 Rock's Jefferson ___
74 Lower in esteem
75 Whale schools
76 Civil War buttons, e.g.
78 Film-noir actress Lupino
79 Nero's 1002
80 Hits the books
83 Scrawny
84 Rorschach Test feature
85 Sicily's "Burning Mountain"
87 Brooklet
88 Talking Stick, for one
90 Scrooge's one-time fiancée
91 "Moneyball" subject Billy
93 Norfolk jacket feature
94 Law degree
95 Effectuate
98 Lodge group
99 Thai neighbor
103 Patriotic silversmith*
105 "Salomé" playwright*
108 Winter coating
109 "The Stepford Wives" author
110 Valence river
111 Theoretical
112 Hamadan home
113 Found
114 Hackneyed
115 It, in Italy
116 Like the Texas star
117 Olympic race
118 Final approval
119 Escalator part

DOWN

1 Some chess endings
2 Majestic
3 Bring a smile to
4 Annoyed
5 "Daily" Metropolis paper
6 Goes caroling
7 Slew
8 "Symphonie Espagnole" composer
9 1999 Tennis Hall of Fame inductee
10 Motrin alternative
11 Marina birds
12 "Return of the Jedi" character

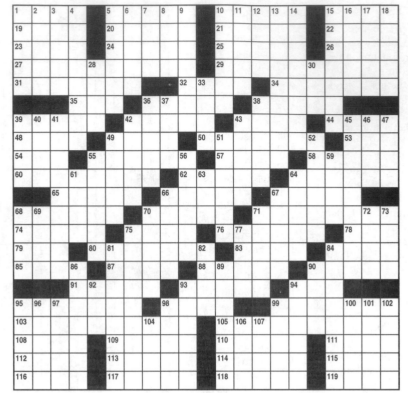

13 Topple
14 Fall of Rome aftermath
15 Facebook cofounder Saverin
16 Greta in "Grand Hotel"
17 Novelist Calvino
18 Massachusetts harbor town
28 Composer Caryll
30 Central mail bureau
33 Perth lad
36 Decibel measures
37 Schematize
38 Competed at Henley
39 Nadal's nickname
40 Youngest god
41 "The Innocents Abroad" author*
42 Afghan city
43 A human has 206
45 Yalta Conference attendee*
46 Give an edge
47 Picasso's mad wife
49 "Godspell" role
51 German golfer
52 Manager hirers/firers
55 Nasal sounds

56 Kay Thompson title
59 Dietary figs.
61 Apollo's half brother
63 "Holiday ___" (1942)
64 "Woe is me!"
66 It's spoken in India
67 To put ___ nutshell
68 Bust broncos
69 Newspaper bio
70 Minestrone server
71 Angle
72 Pedestal occupant
73 Cocktail party food
75 Keira's "King Arthur" role
77 Where Zeno taught
81 One who's going places?
82 Polio vaccine
84 Story hours
86 Kansas city of song
89 Honeymoon spots
90 Make a mess of
92 Sonnet addendum?
93 David Hare play
94 Rio Grande port
95 "___ Fools": Warwick

96 Muhammad Ali Mosque site
97 Maugham's "Of ___ Bondage"
98 Susan's "All My Children" role
99 Where strikes occur
100 Words of concession
101 ___ of one's own medicine
102 Indian-to-Pilgrim greeting
104 Memorable Knievel
106 Some Muslims
107 NHL goalie Schneider

BAND OF BROTHERS*: PART II   by Steve Davies
. . . and that band is revealed at 97 Across.

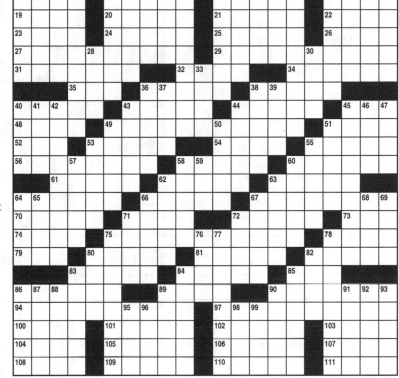

ACROSS

1 Bookbinding tools
5 Paired socks
10 "___ Ev'ry Mountain"
15 Boston orchestra
19 Kaput
20 "I'm looking ___ four-leaf . . ."
21 Café client
22 Mince words?
23 Olympic queen
24 "Commitment" singer Rimes
25 Childish retort
26 Jean in "Mission: Impossible"
27 Justice appointed by Eisenhower*
29 Battle of San Jacinto general*
31 "Forever Young" singer
32 Big Bang theory matter
34 Swanson in "Buffy the Vampire Slayer"
35 Colorado NHL team, to fans
36 Heckled
38 "24 Hours from ___": Pitney
40 Goldwater or Gibb
43 What "Mac" or "Mc" means
44 Dr. Zhivago's wife
45 ___ Anne de Beaupré
48 Upheaval
49 "Fair Deal" president*
51 Temple
52 Horror novelist van Belkom
53 Marisa in "Welcome to Sarajevo"
54 Des Moines suburb
55 Italian sub slices
56 "Mystic River" director
58 "Home Alone" boy
60 "Why, Juan?"
61 Swedish model Linder
62 Like starbursts
63 Military salute
64 Two make a sawbuck
66 "24" hero
67 Loaded down
70 "Get ___ job!"
71 Ending for Louis
72 Strike zone
73 Prior, poetically
74 Quarterback McCoy
75 "Ramblin' Rose" singer*
78 Strike out
79 "The Last Ship" network
80 Nigerian seaport
81 Thereabouts
82 Tenderloin cut
83 "Barefoot in the Park" playwright
84 Sponge features
85 Model A or T
86 Mumford in "Fifty Shades of Grey"
89 Galileo's birthplace
90 Advances
94 Second man on the moon*
97 Brothers revealed in clue* answers
100 Eleven, in Paris
101 Flare up
102 Special talent
103 Teri in "Young Frankenstein"
104 Pride Lands abode
105 Sandpiper relative
106 Implant
107 Take in less
108 Trojan ally in the "Iliad"
109 Submarine tracker
110 Like pumpkins, but not jack-o'-lanterns
111 Mouseketeer cap

DOWN

1 Edvard Munch painting
2 Source of gluten
3 "Casablanca" actor
4 Sturdy
5 Back biters
6 Deflect
7 Eye drop
8 Maritime eagle
9 Song sung at Irish funerals
10 Broke off
11 Anaheim Stadium footballer
12 Big-ticket ___
13 A net or hammock, e.g.
14 Home of the Nets
15 Realm of Xerxes I
16 "Awake and Sing!" dramatist
17 Wine grape
18 Like Lincoln's Mt. Rushmore countenance?
28 Permanent adjective
30 Polaris bear
33 Out in ___ field
36 Like some Pamplona runners
37 Crucifix letters
38 "Peace on earth, good will ___!"
39 Race in "Stargate SG-1"
40 Talking horse of Narnia
41 Opera set in Memphis
42 President in office 4,422 days*
43 Where Stevenson wrote "Catriona"
44 Bombastic
45 "The Big Aristotle" of basketball*
46 Odette's wear
47 Failing that
49 Errant golf shots
50 Actress Kim of "24"
51 Do time
53 Pirouette
55 Like Roquefort
57 Pick up the tab
58 Hawaii's "Garden Island"
59 Spud sprout
60 ". . . after they've seen ___"
62 Pecking orders
63 Julius Caesar's predecessor
64 Almanac entry
65 Age after Bronze
66 It's passed on the track
67 Political coalitions
68 Canal of song
69 Shoulder muscle, briefly
71 Cassio's rival
72 Building lot
75 Like Banksy
76 Noncoms
77 They sleep while standing
78 Like 42 Down's chats
80 Sax-playing Simpson
82 Bean used in falafel
83 Egg-sorting machines
84 "The Homecoming" playwright
85 "As You Like It" is one
86 Virus named after an African river
87 Kind of eclipse
88 Rick Nelson's dad
89 Prince William's sister-in-law
90 Doled (out)
91 Justice Sotomayor
92 Lemmon's "Odd Couple" role
93 Jr. exams
95 SPECTRE villain
96 Wrack partner
98 City of the Seven Hills
99 Kathryn of "Law & Order: CI"

"PAR EXCELLENCE!"   by Jim Leeds
A clever challenge from an enigmatist extraordinaire.

ACROSS

1 Still
5 Inning segment
9 A galleon has three
14 "Gymnopédies" composer
19 Occupation
20 Gannon University locale
21 While, briefly
22 "Right Place ___ Time": Dr. John
23 Excellent crime scene clue?
25 Bird that builds a hanging nest
26 Positive pole
27 "___ on Indolence": Keats
28 Tampa Bay team
30 Orthodontist's goal?
32 Cautionary tales
35 Scabbards
37 Lhotse challenge
38 Gene mutations
40 Like NCOs
41 Sleuth (out)
43 Part of A&E
44 "Good buddy" of the road
45 Fiddlesticks
48 Friend of Aramis
50 A skosh
51 Nuthatch food
52 Thrown ___ (stunned)
54 Jungle swinger
57 First-rate dinnerware dishes?
59 Ring combos
61 Convent head
64 Discount rack abbr.
65 Catchall Latin abbr.
67 Hasty Pudding event
68 Soup kitchen sound
69 "The Jungle Book" python
70 "M*A*S*H" roles
71 Bob up
72 Depend on
73 "The Superannuated Man" essayist
75 Black Hawk, for one
76 Pavarotti's were high
77 International alliance
79 Praise for a cabbage farmer?
82 "___ for Noose": Grafton
83 Wisdom
85 Hotel chain
86 New Zealand parrot
89 Deeds of derring-do
90 Saharan rodent
92 Jump for Shoma Uno
93 "Fortune Favors the Brave" musical
96 South Beach locale
98 Cereal box info
99 National Museum of Indonesia site
101 Tweeter output
103 Head wreaths
106 Lament
107 A-1 invoice service?
109 Piglike "Jabberwocky" creature
111 "Final Space" network
112 Toughen
113 Firebox feature
115 Epithet for Caroline Wozniacki?
119 America's first saint
120 John Landy, e.g.
121 Grey often in hot water
122 Playing on the road
123 Subject of Pope's mock-heroic poem
124 Strong suit
125 Switcheroo
126 Stuffing herb

DOWN

1 Rapscallion
2 Trial-by-jury amendment
3 Conferred honors upon
4 Heckler
5 2013 Joaquin Phoenix film
6 Bust ___ (laugh hard)
7 Roache on "Vikings"
8 Chased a stick
9 Big D hoopster
10 Red-carpet group
11 Detroit beer
12 Regular's bar order
13 "Later!"
14 Q-Tips, e.g.
15 Sunflower family members
16 Whistle blower
17 Use the tab key
18 Disgorges
24 Paint may do this
29 Summon
31 2012 All-Pro safety Goldson
32 Actuality
33 August in "Becoming Astrid"
34 Like "Punk'd" stunts
36 Tolerate
39 Malaysia's Chin ___ Caves Temple
42 Seats at Cheers
46 Heart septum
47 Oilman Halliburton
49 Modus ___
51 Hitchcock specialty
53 Stellar
54 Be on call
55 Rapper's entourage
56 Kefauver who ran with Stevenson
57 Worsted suit fabric
58 Sauté, then simmer
60 Fiat pickups
61 Pale
62 Shrovetide pancakes
63 Diamond sacrifices
66 News head
69 Conform with
74 Sheaf bristles
75 Lissome
76 Cambridge student
78 Mortarboard dangler
80 Online greeting
81 Basic guitar chord: Abbr.
84 Followers of Aga Khan IV
86 "Stray Dog" director
87 Singer James
88 Muslim call to prayer
89 "Black granite" rocks
91 Courtroom compensation
92 Letters after kappas
93 Bear witness to
94 Pressing job
95 Name, as a proxy
97 Archival documents
100 Etta of old comics
102 Mortgages, e.g.
104 Come to terms
105 Barn bedding
108 Prayer wheel user
110 Goddess of marriage
114 Clubber Lang portrayer in "Rocky III"
116 Innsbruck peak
117 "Camptown Races" winner
118 Needle feature

287

THEMELESS by Elizabeth C. Gorski

In 1962, Barbra Streisand made a popular recording of the song at 66 Across.

ACROSS

1 "Waterloo" group
5 Madonna's "Take ___"
9 Zilch
13 Touring Italy, say
19 Thunderous
20 Song of India
21 Milky gem
22 At hand
23 Long distance, it's not
25 Jack Bauer's "24" wife
26 Pickup artist?
27 Ham's refuge
28 Bygone Ford
29 Sonia in "Empire"
31 Play groups
32 Monet's brainstorm
34 Say the rosary
36 Dracula's best hours
38 Walking sticks
40 Charlatan
42 CSA soldier
43 LAPD alert
46 Pond growth
47 Book jacket parts
48 Sailboard rider
52 "Unh unh"
53 Heckles
54 Barcelona bruin
55 Jones of Kentucky Derby fame
56 Needing variety
58 Recruit through deception
61 Competes
62 Army doc
64 "Little" Bahama island
65 PC shortcut
66 FDR's campaign song
72 Missouri mountains
73 Witherspoon of "Wild"
74 Out of bed
75 Island near Java
76 Brunch melon
79 Moore of "Arthur" fame
82 James Michener novel
84 Green Day album
85 Smoothing undergarment
88 Honolulu's ___ Wai Canal
89 Last week, say
91 Man of La Mancha
92 Understood
93 ___ kwon do
94 Always, in verse
95 Streep of "The Post"
96 Tufnel of Spinal Tap
97 Passover dinner
99 Posh
100 Raw linen color
101 Chose
104 Measured (up)
106 "One of Ours" author Cather
109 Director DuVernay
112 High nests
114 Flaccid
115 Game suitability stats
117 Increases
118 Needle case
119 Mediocre
120 Monthly expense
121 Tramples heavily
122 Tragic
123 ___-bitty
124 Europe's neighbor

DOWN

1 Penne ___ vodka
2 Rude dude
3 Locale of many London garden parties
4 Oklahoma city
5 ___ Triomphe
6 Cote calls
7 Leer at
8 Decorating material that's on a roll
9 Pretty good
10 Mimic's forte
11 Olympic swimmer Torres
12 Set straight
13 Mandela's org.
14 2019 McConaughey role
15 Morocco's capital
16 Spheres
17 Slightly
18 Salon jobs
24 Sediment
30 "Little Knell" author
33 Jean-Sébastien of the NHL
35 Rene in "Get Shorty"
37 Bas-relief medium
38 Kid's plea
39 Bates in "Duet for One"
40 Ga. neighbor
41 Dorm VIPs
43 Swahili and Yoruba, e.g.
44 "Great" Russian tsar
45 "A Walk in the Woods" author
47 Malodorous
48 "___ unto thee, O Moab!": Jer. 48:46
49 NBA Hall-of-Famer Thomas
50 Present purpose
51 Devastated
53 Alan of "Suburgatory"
57 Frank Sinatra label
59 Cut expenses
60 Air pressure measure
63 Verdi's "___ nome"
65 Maestro Kurt ___
66 Tasmanian capital
67 Colorful shrub
68 Busybody
69 Prophets
70 To date
71 Steller's duck
76 Abhorred
77 Bill Haley's first label
78 Question after a digression
80 General Robert ___
81 Two-masted ship
83 Heavily involved in
86 Whatever
87 Cracow loc.
90 Lester Young of bop
92 Cassis cocktail
95 Rich, chocolaty dessert
96 Nonprofit sports org.
97 Earth tremor
98 Worked (up)
99 Madagascar critter
100 "The Jetsons" son
101 Rowboat duo
102 Bog fuel
103 Small chamber group
105 Tubular pasta
107 "___ Rhythm"
108 For fear that
110 Caesar's "I came"
111 Skippy's canine film role
113 Radiator sound
116 Wayne LaPierre's org.

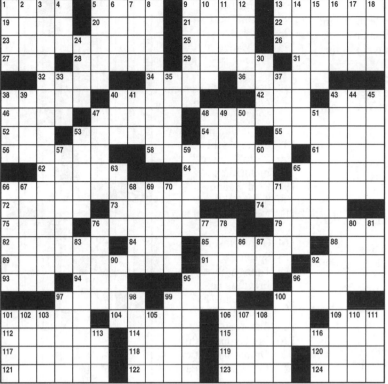

288 POSSESSIVE CASES by Elizabeth C. Gorski
68 Across can be viewed at New York's Museum of Modern Art.

ACROSS

1 Gabrielle in "Scent of a Woman"
6 Nothing out of the ordinary
12 Gomer Pyle's org.
16 Metric ruler amts.
19 "Forget You" singer Green
20 Bird with a hanging nest
21 Well-groomed
23 Heavenly body to return in 2061
25 Scold sharply
26 "Das Lied von der ___"
27 List-ending abbr.
28 NAACP ___ Awards
30 Lure
31 Joyce DiDonato album "___ & Peace"
33 Egg-shaped
36 Envelope abbr.
37 Where Hope remained
40 Lose big time
46 Oktoberfest drink
47 Ski lodge quaff
49 Globe Theatre king
50 ___-color pasta
51 Bol. neighbor
52 "Blondie" paperboy
55 Frank McCourt memoir
58 Entre ___
60 Outlying community
62 "Harry Potter" actor Rickman
63 Reuben cheese
64 Tyler or Rice
65 Suffix for billion
66 Whatever
67 Have mercy (on)
68 Andrew Wyeth painting
73 Encourage
76 Here, in Dijon
77 Aachen article
78 Diminutive suffix
82 Tax-form part
83 ___ Domini
85 "___ at 'em!"
86 Lat. noun gender
87 Movement of Grieg's "Peer Gynt Suite No. 1"

90 Fringe benefit
92 Ordinal suffix
93 Actor Brynner
94 De Matteo of "Joey"
95 "Love Story" author
97 ___-gritty
99 Dessert with a cream cheese frosting
102 1992 Nolte/Sarandon film
105 Silent assent
106 Bette's "divine" nickname
108 Really annoy
109 Senate aide
111 Ashe, on the UCLA courts
114 Gridlock sound
116 Sprint
119 Thoroughbred breeding costs
121 Alaska, in 1867 headlines
125 Experienced
126 Goolagong with 14 Grand Slam titles
127 "Your 15 minutes of fame ___!"
128 ___ Aviv
129 Lugosi in "The Raven"
130 Looked after
131 Canal vessel

DOWN

1 Dull pain
2 Close
3 Tool used for steel sculptures
4 "The House of the Spirits" author
5 Shad product
6 Cosa ___
7 Bates painted by Jamie Wyeth
8 1970 John Wayne western
9 Pop's mate
10 Hearty brew
11 "___ ride"
12 Flo-Jo's alma mater
13 Dross
14 Viral GIF
15 Car with a checkered past?
16 2007 AL Cy Young winner

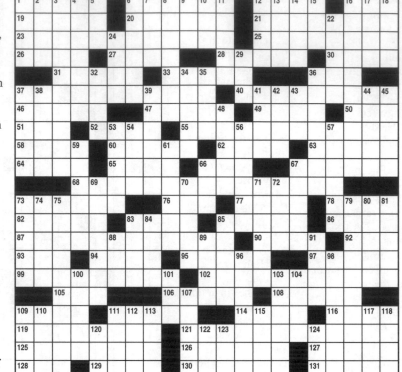

17 Maestro Riccardo ___
18 Undo a dele
22 Bigwig
24 Revolutionary time?
29 Hail-fellow-well-___
32 Sported
34 Word knowledge, briefly
35 Neural transmitter
36 Mai Tai accessory
37 First course of action
38 Super Bowl XLV MVP Rodgers
39 Uses steel wool
41 Penne ___ vodka
42 New Jersey governor (1982–1990)
43 ___ in "elephant"
44 Lock of hair
45 Like Parseltongue word sounds
48 Guam capital
53 Absorb
54 DVI doubled
56 Palais de Paris
57 ABBA's homeland
59 The untold story?
61 Wrinkle reducer

66 "Joyful Girl" singer DiFranco
67 Feminist Germaine
69 Collected compulsively
70 Windows symbols
71 Nun's head covering
72 "My treat!"
73 Knocks 'em dead at the comedy club
74 Calendar girl
75 Speaking only one language
79 One likely to pass the bar
80 "___ Frutti": Little Richard
81 Grain alcohol
83 Within the Bermuda Triangle
84 Minn. neighbor
85 Toys for tots
88 Semicircle
89 Animation frames
91 Shoelace snarl
96 You wear it on your sleeve
98 "Fear of Flying" heroine
100 Future alumnae

101 Virgin ___ Records
103 Required
104 Microwaves
107 Map within a map
109 Whispered "Hey!"
110 Suit to ___
111 "Stand By Me" singer King
112 Stagger
113 Fed. food inspector
115 Coastal raptor
117 Punch
118 Pre-event buzz
120 Watch chain
122 Marie Curie's daughter
123 Triumphed
124 "Terrif!"

289
TOMFOOLERY*   by Elizabeth C. Gorski
It's unlikely you'll hear 100 Across played at a feminist rally.

ACROSS

1 Yale Bowl sounds
5 Chowder head?
9 Notoriety
13 Carve, in a way
18 Now, on a memo
19 Circle dance
20 "The Haj" author
21 Ogle
22 1996 biopic starring Liam Neeson*
25 Thistle-eating Milne character
26 LPGA Tour player Se Ri ___
27 Morays
28 Capital on the Mediterranean
30 Enzyme endings
31 Poses
33 Old portico
34 Unethical lender
36 Insect-eating gray bird*
40 Supine protest
41 Barbera's animation partner
42 Ireland
43 Acting independently
47 Words to a backstabber
48 2017 World Series winners
50 Hosp. hookups
51 Some July babies
53 Pronoun in a Hemingway title
54 Iranian money
55 Campus near Beverly Hills
57 Giving in
59 Bench for Kavanaugh
61 Aachen article
63 Money drawer
65 Hogwash
66 Recede
69 1972 hit song by Billy Paul*
72 Start of a hissy fit?
73 Nay nullifier
74 "Money ___ object"
75 As found, after "in"
76 Raised
78 Burns with hot coffee
80 General ___ chicken
82 Niger neighbor
84 Olympic skater Lysacek
88 Poi base
89 Fiscal VIP
90 As a whole
92 Fraction
93 1992 Olympics host city
97 Margarine
98 Brother of Prometheus
99 Do-nothing
100 1966 Rolling Stones hit*
103 Ida of "High Sierra"
105 No-win situations
106 ___-daisy
107 Carpenter's holder
108 Unconscious
111 Zany Imogene
113 One of the Cratchits
116 2000 pounds
118 Vacation on a floating casino*
121 Parma playhouse
122 Spoken
123 Michael in "Juno"
124 2018 Alden Ehrenreich role
125 No-brainer in school
126 Portal
127 Tribe known for their beadwork
128 "___ Day Has Come": Dion

DOWN

1 Wheelchair access
2 Actress Argento
3 Breaks a computer code
4 Figure in geom.
5 Tostada topping
6 Lounge
7 Curved lines
8 Olympic skater Asada
9 Replete with
10 Japanese "thanks"
11 Diminutive
12 Being, to Brutus
13 Observe
14 Nickelodeon series about a fourth-grader*
15 "That which we call ___ . . .": Shak.
16 Vegetable knife
17 Le Marais seasons
21 One with a flat
23 MetLife competitor
24 Like the ALMA Awards
29 Rome tourist attraction
32 "This is a complete shock!"
33 Moved in a vortex
35 Sue Grafton's "___ for Undertow"
36 Rawhide dog toy
37 Biblical verb
38 Sammy Davis Jr. book
39 Young lady of Sp.
40 "Here We Go Again" singer Demi
44 Zero
45 Small dams
46 Taboos
48 "Gunsmoke" star
49 Stirring time of day?
52 Boot camp bosses
56 "___ la vie!"
57 Servant of God
58 Otherwise
60 During
62 "___ Excited": Pointer Sisters
64 Flowering
66 Right on the map
67 One way to cross town
68 ___ resemblance to (look like)
70 Bob Dylan's "If ___ You"
71 Scrambled word puzzles
77 Ocean bottoms
79 "Orange Is the New Black" actress*
81 Junior
83 Mariner, for ex.
85 Assessment
86 Composer Khachaturian
87 Govt. travel watchdog
89 Rival of Pericles
91 "All bets are off!"
94 Form of 401
95 Warm ocean current
96 Horn & Hardart eatery
98 How some stocks are purchased
101 Agile
102 Painted Desert flowers
103 Tax form starter
104 "___ directed" (Rx warning)
107 Hold a referendum
109 Awestruck
110 Model Delevingne
111 Tech-news website
112 Shrek, for one
114 Fair ___ (sweater pattern)
115 Cat call
117 Rita in "Fifty Shades of Grey"
119 "ER" setting
120 Dos Passos trilogy

Eight Taylor Swift songs are playing below.

ACROSS

1 Second feature?
5 Judicial seats
10 Bluff
15 Mary's pet
19 Marion's sister in "Psycho"
20 "Water Under the Bridge" singer
21 Easter Bunny, for one
22 "Little Things" singer
23 Yours, in Monaco
24 Lama land
25 Mariner's rescuee in "Waterworld"
26 Number of Beethoven symphonies
27 Take a hit and move on*
29 Start over*
31 Alaskan bears
32 Greek P's
34 Hose shade
35 Metric weights: Abbr.
36 One to avoid
38 Super-impressed
42 "Let's Dance" singer David
45 Colonial town reporter
46 Palm smartphone
47 Time past, time past
48 Superdome shout
49 1986 Indy 500 winner
51 Downton Abbey worker
52 Barbra Streisand film
53 Suffer loss (with "take")
55 Erich Segal bestseller*
58 Beats by ___
59 Honeybun
61 Of letters and such
63 Apollo in "Rocky"
65 Home of the Ewoks
66 Thai kebab
67 Winner of the longest Wimbledon match
69 "Darn!"
71 Grandchild of Japanese immigrants
73 How Berg composed "Wozzeck"

76 Taoism founder ___-tse
77 "The Blind Side" star*
79 Mother of Hermes
80 Eliot's cruelest month
83 Drinks slowly
84 Bond villain Blofeld
86 New Orleans–Baton Rouge dir.
87 Puccini opera
88 Japanese apricot
89 Wander off
91 Touring car
93 Adjective for the Ents
95 Paper-chase runners
96 Homie
97 "Let's see now, where ___?"
98 Unexciting, party-wise
99 Like 98 Down
103 C.W. drives one in "Bonnie and Clyde"*
107 Margin*
110 Do this for the home team
111 Haying machine
112 Jargon
113 Bibliography abbr.
114 Play money?
115 Barely manage
116 Like oak leaves
117 Dido's "Life for ___"
118 River of Flanders
119 Big wheels for big wheels
120 Work for a body shop
121 Sonic boomers of yore

DOWN

1 Football fan's bottle
2 Collectible print
3 "Get ___ of this!"
4 Honolulu beach
5 Hand-dyed fabrics
6 Mine entrances
7 Mount climbed by Moses
8 Symbol on a staff
9 Liberate
10 Cyndi Lauper hit
11 Cheryl of "Suburgatory"

12 "Me and You and ___ Named Boo": Lobo
13 Breathing easier
14 Strut about
15 Barrier for some world travelers
16 Song from "Tosca"
17 BMW marque
18 "Love's ___ Good to Me": Sinatra
28 Chomping at the bit
30 Wide selection
33 2013 Rooney Mara film
36 Thirst for
37 Churn up
38 Language of E India
39 Mock Turtle's home*
40 ___ nous (confidentially)
41 Edited out
42 Bric-a-___
43 "Hawaii Five-O" setting
44 Good guy's mount*
45 Lofty groups?
46 GOP's end?
50 Ken-L Ration competitor
51 Tiled artwork

54 Arena or Turner
56 Muscular jerks
57 It has a pole position
60 Brother of JFK and RFK: Abbr.
62 Tedious account
63 Jim Acosta's network
64 Stationery unit
66 Long-billed shorebird
68 Scatters seed
69 Oliver in "Frost/Nixon"
70 Distinctive taste
72 Grisham's "___ To Kill"
73 Flemish tapestry
74 2011 French Open winner
75 ["Bo-o-o-ring!"]
78 Richard in "MotherFatherSon"
81 It comes free with dinner
82 NBC's Emmy-winning legal drama
83 1963 Kyu Sakamoto hit
85 Pre-Lenin leaders

89 Walmart founder Walton
90 Increased threefold
92 Lovebirds in flight
94 "Eva Luna" writer Allende
95 Connick Jr. and Sr.
96 Sri Lankan teas
98 Martial arts–based workout
99 High anxiety
100 Maine college
101 "___ Let Go": Ronstadt
102 Isle of Man inhabitants
103 Overcast
104 Forever, or close enough
105 Bag with handles
106 Blondie drummer Burke
108 Trevi Fountain coins from yesteryear
109 Mr. X, for short

291 "VIVE LA FRANCE!" by John M. Samson
A good one to solve on Bastille Day.

ACROSS

1 "The Hurt Locker" setting
5 "Common" complaints
10 Flight part
15 Cass Elliot's nickname
19 Diamond Head locale
20 Thumb-twiddle
21 Tubular pasta
22 Legend
23 Like the Magi
24 They parallel radii
25 Lascivious
26 Late-night TV host for 22 years
27 Sunblock ingredient
28 Left Bank river rat?
30 See 91 Across
31 "No way, Sergei!"
33 Another name
34 Win–draw go-between
36 Applied paint in spots
39 Drift
40 Like some networks
44 "Snowy" wader
45 Where a breaker breaks
46 Casper's witch friend
47 "Big Daddy" Amin
48 Buffy Sainte-Marie, for one
49 Lip cosmetic
50 Jewel case inserts
51 "Dream Children" essayist
52 Lien's "Star Trek: Voyager" role
53 Sports
54 Florentine bridge
55 Leisure suit material
56 Volleyball position
58 Japanese comic book genre
59 Square-shooting
60 T.S. Eliot work
61 Legatee
63 In the center of
64 Things to toss
66 Borden bovine
67 Watusi weapons
70 Senior group
71 Epsom sailors?
72 Number in a pool
75 Quarrel
76 "Sounder" director
77 Spritz
78 Former New York governor
79 Like a robin's egg
80 Xena's daughter
81 Puts a lid on it
82 Not italicized
83 1/100 of a rupee
84 Wayne's world?
86 Wampum
87 To the ___ born
88 Classical work
89 Short-handed hockey ploy
90 Give in
91 Lift weights (with 30-A)
94 Gave counsel to St. Martin's city?
97 Source of Evian water
101 "Don't move!"
102 "Ode to a Baby" poet Nash
103 Jamaican citrus fruits
104 First name on the moon
105 "Breaking Bad" lawyer Goodman
106 Like 11 Down
107 Schoolbag item
108 Frequent babysitter
109 For whom the bell tolls
110 Sitar ridges
111 Gets warmer?
112 Like Montmartre

DOWN

1 Tall Corn State
2 Belmont fence
3 Comment of understanding
4 Royal jelly eater
5 Brought about
6 Fledging hooter
7 Hall of Brasil '66
8 "Love Hangover" singer
9 Heinz Field team
10 Centerfold
11 Crocodile ___
12 Landers and Lee
13 Sloth
14 Ryan in "Green Lantern"
15 Environs
16 Packard Bell parent
17 Kissing disease
18 Shortly
29 Source of pesto nuts
32 On the other hand
35 Foxy
36 Shoe holdings
37 Jibe
38 Brittany dishes?
39 Thursday's eponym
40 Jai-alai racquets
41 French remix of a Count Basie standard?
42 "Ciao, Carlos!"
43 Gleeful
45 City of NW Morocco
46 "Band on the Run" band
49 Lysol targets
50 Gifted one
51 Muppet in a striped shirt
53 Herbicide targets
54 "La Ville Lumière"
55 That certain something
57 "Sláinte!" is one
58 A bit foggy
59 Harvard's ___ Pudding Club
61 A squid has three
62 Greek name for Greece
64 Hinge holder
65 Still kicking
68 Work up
69 Take an oath
71 Cotton candy
72 Huey P. Long, for one
73 McGregor in "Moulin Rouge!"
74 Writers' org.
77 Dismiss disdainfully
78 Decrease
79 Biker headwear
81 Thirty-day mo.
82 2018 Kansas City Chiefs coach
83 T-Fal item
85 Overthrow
86 Movie makeup
87 Gentlemen: Abbr.
89 Akin to exempli gratia
90 Prickly plant
91 "Ahem"
92 Mormon State
93 Wry face
95 Having an off day
96 Secretary in "The Producers"
98 Father of Cordelia
99 Guinness serving
100 Leave in stitches

UNITED PRESS INTERNATIONAL by Jim Page

... not to be confused with the news agency.

ACROSS

1 Ends a case
6 Prone
12 "An American in Paris" studio
15 Lump of gum
19 Remove a bowler
20 Laundry employee
21 Malachite, e.g.
22 Dutch model Stone
23 Hollywood A-list list?
25 Reviewed
27 Novak Djokovic, for one
28 Statue with limitations
30 "Love in the First Degree" group
31 Mountain nymphs
32 Steadfast
33 Fix a pump
35 Historical account of a spelling competition?
39 L. Frank Baum princess
43 Cartoonist Larson
46 Poor grades
47 Medical school test
48 Terrestrial monkey
50 "I thought so!"
51 Volleyball winner
52 Rental paper
53 Still in the outbox
54 "___ Show" (2000 mockumentary)
56 Non-alcoholic brew
58 Know-how
59 Gutenberg Bible's language
60 Tired Cherokees?
62 Stairlike
64 Cheeseboard choice
65 Album under the Universal Music label?
67 Panel trucks
71 Pass out?
73 Sleepyhead's need
74 The king of Champagne
75 Good earth
78 Queen Aleta's son
79 Café bottle
80 Does a front-end garage job
81 Alhambra locale
85 Stand ___ by
87 QB Roethlisberger
88 Dance in 3/4 time
89 Knit one, ___ two
90 Height: Prefix
91 Whale watching
92 "Storms in Africa" singer
93 Usher in the dawn?
96 Hamlet's weapon
99 Be overdrawn
100 Memory trace
104 Not barefoot
107 Popular half of a 45
110 Fallen reign?
111 Defensive barrier
113 Message board mod?
115 Space
116 Boxing trainer D'Amato
117 Kickoffs
118 2015 Lauren Daigle song
119 Dodge model
120 Fair Deal pres.
121 Chain links
122 Firebugs

DOWN

1 Rene in "Lethal Weapon 4"
2 Enroll
3 Divide up
4 Toni Morrison novel
5 Track coach's concern
6 Autograph
7 S Korean political party
8 Collectibles for cinephiles
9 As a whole
10 ___-do-well
11 Is human
12 Groom Witch Hollow
13 "You're the One I Want" musical
14 Edison's "Park"
15 Spectator at a London theatre?
16 Hot issue on the Big Island in 2018
17 City near Provo
18 Theda of silent films
24 Entered gradually
26 Jazz guitarist Farlow
29 Killer whales
32 Windbreaks
34 Fashionable reading
36 Cartoon frame
37 Valley of San Francisco
38 Stage actor Aldridge
40 Akins and Caldwell
41 Olympus ___ (Martian volcano)
42 Poker stake
43 Clark in "Mogambo"
44 Down the road
45 Follower of Selassie
48 Physique
49 Whistler's mother
51 Family
52 Columbo's employer
55 Game clock official?
57 Meals for seals
58 Growing business
60 "Piano Man" singer
61 Span. lady
62 Mufasa's brother
63 Rolls-Royce model
65 Place for a manacle
66 Enthusiasm
68 Fiery horses
69 Like some checking accounts
70 Tuscan town
72 Auctioneer's final word
74 Henhouse order
75 Docile
76 Lena of "Alias"
77 Like a Maine forest
79 Narrow the gap
81 WW1 German admiral
82 Manx murmurs
83 Astral altar
84 Ailing
86 "2001" track "Still ___"
90 RNC chairman (1989–1991)
91 In a fit of pique
93 Most Indians
94 Argument phrase
95 Break apart a dam
97 Some are full-page
98 Dahl's giant fruit
101 "And where he ___ fly they know not whether": Shak.
102 Old Olds
103 Rummy laydowns
104 Attention ___
105 Fabled also-ran
106 It's sold in bars
108 Nasdaq newcomers
109 Word of warning
110 Pickle
112 "Dulce et decorum ___": Horace
114 Sault ___ Marie

PRODUCT PLACEMENT by Tracy Gray
Leading brand names have been subtly embedded in seven films.

ACROSS

1 John Irving title character
7 Some are bookmarked
12 Zoe in "Avatar"
19 More devout
20 Digs
21 Itemized bills
22 Comfortable with
23 Threshold
24 Place for a welcome mat
25 2000 Nicolas Cage movie
28 Astor Library's NYC locale
29 Danish novelist Dinesen
30 Makes do
34 1995 Michael Douglas movie
42 Flat-broke
43 Noodle
44 Tam-tam or tom-tom
45 Hewson in "Robin Hood"
46 1987 William Hurt movie
53 Autograph marker
55 Contrail maker
56 "The Polar Express" figures
57 Weisshorn, for one
59 Appointed
60 Bill de Blasio, for one
61 Stitches
65 BFFs
66 2002 Parminder Nagra movie
69 Houston Astros symbol
71 "Too Big to Fail" star
72 Parade vehicle
73 It's said to be small
75 RSVP encl.
76 Barbarian
77 Cruise ship amenity
80 Took in or let out
83 1967 Albert Finney movie
87 Dietary guideline letters
88 Some draft picks
90 Cambridge tutor
91 A lo-o-ong time

92 2002 Nia Vardolos movie
100 Cheeky talk
101 Wallop but good
102 Pennsylvania's "Flagship City"
103 2006 Meryl Streep movie
113 Middling
116 Swing states?
117 Katie in the Television Hall of Fame
118 Cause of many eagles
119 Singly
120 Poised and polished
121 Old-school inkwell locale
122 Dominant figure at Roland Garros
123 Did hairy work

DOWN

1 Gorilla
2 See 113 Across
3 Type of plaid
4 ___-de-camp
5 Optic membrane
6 Nous or vous, in Paris
7 Messiah
8 Cliff-dwelling goat
9 Civil wrongdoing
10 High-strung
11 Does a butler's job
12 Hoodwinks
13 River to the Severn
14 Baltimore, for one
15 Bad-mouthed
16 Shtick
17 Michelle Obama, ___ Robinson
18 Cerastes
21 Security checkpoint request
26 ___-crab soup
27 Cassandra's curse
31 Zip one's lips
32 Begrudged
33 Noble mounts
34 Ran like Usain Bolt
35 Owl's yowl
36 Kyle Hendricks stat
37 Negative QB stats
38 Charlatan

39 Teddy's Mt. Rushmore neighbor
40 Ndamukong of the NFL
41 One-named supermodel
42 Sandwich for lactarians
47 Horror fiction writer Koontz
48 Basketball Hall-of-Famer Drexler
49 Circumvent
50 Some bedroom queens
51 Grog ingredient
52 Soft lump in yarn
54 Moroccan capital
58 Lean toward
60 Dandridge on "Greenleaf"
61 Tendon
62 George Harrison played one
63 Dazzling effect
64 Smidgen
66 Tavern tallies
67 Aspiring DA's exam
68 Kind of crime

69 Multitudes
70 "Shoulda listened!"
74 Wet blanket
76 Comic strip sound effect
77 Coming right up
78 Twinge of remorse
79 Some banners
81 Santa's sleigh loader
82 Public USB flash drive
84 Poetic tribute
85 Antagonist
86 Outdoor gear retailer
89 D or C, in D.C.
93 Cry after throwing a gutter ball
94 Surrey "sir"
95 One skilled at driving home
96 Renege, with "out"
97 Louse up
98 Summer Olympic event
99 Expatriate
104 One having an affair?
105 Alexa-enabled speaker

106 "Copacabana" showgirl
107 Termite treat
108 "The Cider House Rules" nurse
109 July's gem
110 World's fourth-largest lake, formerly
111 Sup in style
112 Nailed an exam
113 Central
114 Long lead-in
115 Toledo tango number

NOT ACCORDING TO WEBSTER   by Gary Larson
21 Across was once a haven for pirates, including Bluebeard and Blackbeard.

ACROSS

1 Terrycloth item
10 Rugby union variant
16 "Guys and Dolls" doll
20 One might wait for it to drop
21 Charlotte ___, Virgin Islands
22 Missouri River tribe
23 Not fond of candid photography?
24 Talk smack about a magic trick?
26 More wan
27 Hold forth
29 City near Sacramento
30 Busiest
31 Future atty.'s exam
32 "The Swallow's Tail" et al.
34 ___ at the wheel
37 Salty solutions
39 Miner's load
42 Pat on the back?
46 Publish screenplays on the web?
48 "Ars amatoria" poet
49 Cheap way to travel
51 Swim-meet units
52 Tampa neighbor, for short
54 Seaport in E Mexico
55 Bob of the Kingston Trio
57 Aired again
58 "Caught you!"
59 Less significant
61 "The English Patient" setting
64 Private vacation?
65 Corporate-speak for rehiring a former employee?
68 ___-Magnon
71 WW2 graffiti name
73 Leg bones
74 Listening device
75 Body build
77 Entices
79 Analyze
81 Crimson Tide rival
83 2018 World Series pitcher
84 Crooked
85 Pandora's boxful

86 Fraternity hazing, for one?
90 CIA operatives
91 "Pioneer Woman" Drummond
92 Stirs
93 P.F. ___ (Chinese restaurant chain)
95 Chronic nag
96 Mower maker
97 John Zogby specialty
101 "Brokeback Mountain" director
104 "___ Needs to Know": Shania Twain
106 Gawk
109 It should be heeded while on the golf course?
112 Time for students to put away their calculators?
114 Bust
115 Twain of country
116 Yuletide salutation
117 Units of resistance
118 Convictions
119 Divided like a grapefruit

DOWN

1 Hale's comet co-discoverer
2 "Watch out! It's ___!"
3 Not these
4 Numerical prefix
5 Horse-drawn vehicle
6 Bone: Comb. form
7 Blender sound
8 Huge time frame
9 Box of blocks
10 1978 Peace Nobelist
11 Broadcast
12 Arrangement holder
13 First name in pharmaceuticals
14 Lacking value
15 Altruistic
16 Exodus leader
17 Williams of the Temptations
18 Nutcase
19 Lantern-jawed celeb
25 "Battle Cry" author
28 Emulates Eminem

31 Suffix for Congo
32 Business slumps
33 Zoc, for one
35 Deeper into la-la land
36 Access, in a way
37 Breakfast staple
38 Opportune
39 Done with role-playing?
40 Comic Rudner
41 Heaven on earth
42 Rigel or Spica
43 Provo native
44 Like dry-erase boards?
45 Energy
47 Like drawn butter
48 0 on a phone: Abbr.
50 "Batman Forever" baddie
53 Firebird muscle car
55 Round Table address
56 Be indecisive
60 Chief
61 "Rugrats" dad
62 Wing part
63 April 1 activity
66 Lousy egg?
67 Workout targets

69 Charged
70 German autos
72 Deejay Don
75 So-so
76 Decree
77 Structure near a silo
78 " 'Tis a pity!"
80 Soccer star Hamm
82 Turkey's locale
83 Brood
84 Amalfi adieu
87 Classic Jaguar
88 Computer image
89 Clothes, slangily
92 "That was close!"
94 Lean
95 Coasters
96 "Animal House" party wear
98 Financial guru Suze
99 Inclined
100 Espresso variation
101 Big do
102 Japheth's father
103 ___ Reaper
104 "The Mudville ___"
105 Not procrastinating
106 Groom-to-be party
107 Proviso

108 Sen. Cochran of Mississippi
110 Scoreboard trio
111 One of the Bobbsey twins
113 Honorarium

DIAGNOSING HISTORY by Christopher Liebel

77 Across was the first American president to appear on televsion.

ACROSS

1 Lake at the foot of McKenzie Mountain
7 Commercial names
13 Hood Range
20 Comfort
21 Have a shortage
22 Williams on "Girls"
23 Like Yellowstone Park
24 Bring into harmony
25 Played pat-a-cake
26 **Historic quote by 77 Across: Part 1**
29 Canter, gallop, and 45 Down
30 Crichton novel about deadly nanobots
31 Weep
34 Military branch est. 9/18/47
38 John André, e.g.
39 Stymie
42 Creole dish ___ choux
44 Emulates an Airbnb host
46 Faints at the sight of
47 Crimson Tide rival
48 Stopgap
50 Toothy wheel
51 Come as a result of
52 **Quote: Part 2**
58 Political org. founded March 20, 1854
61 Stretched membrane
62 World's fair
63 Musical transition
64 "We Try Harder" company
66 Meddle
67 "The Nutcracker" step
68 Droughty
69 Honors in a big way
71 Made some beds
73 Pliable
76 Abaia of Melanesian mythology
77 **"Arsenal of Democracy" president**
81 Devout
82 ___ meridiem
83 Let up
87 Col. Hogan's prison
89 Strikes down
91 Brought down
92 "___ California": Eagles
93 Twilled pants
94 "Hooray!"
96 Tony winner Hall
97 "You got it!"
98 Extended family
99 ASIMO, for one
101 **Psychiatric diagnosis of quote**
110 Two-time gold-medalist decathlete
113 Cherry red
114 "Hoist with his own ___": Shak.
115 Wife of Dionysus
116 Ardent admirer
117 "Bobby" director Estevez
118 Plains dwellings
119 Forwarded on
120 Break

DOWN

1 "Hey!"
2 Morar or Maree
3 Wheelhouse direction
4 Robinson of baseball
5 Short-handed NHL act
6 Make nonconfidential
7 Childishly impudent
8 Doctor and the Babe
9 Naysayer
10 Person, place, or thing
11 Organic fertilizer
12 Jambalaya pot
13 Prestige
14 Relieve
15 Tchaikovsky, for one
16 U.S. Chamber of Commerce affiliate
17 Sarcophagus symbol
18 No-name surname
19 Terminus
27 Chihuahua cry
28 Sins
31 Window wiper
32 Taylor Swift's "___ Song"
33 Movie rat
34 Rhody the Ram's school
35 Yen fraction
36 Spacebar neighbor
37 Features of some old bathtubs
39 "Don't!" singer Shania
40 "___ tricks?"
41 "The Right Stuff" author
42 Obligations
43 Misuses
45 See 29 Across
46 Spritzed
47 Singer DiFranco
49 Home of Tigers and Grizzlies
51 Like many acids
53 Parking area at JFK
54 Reveals
55 Hurriedly
56 Tackle box item
57 Sense
58 Weapon in "I Know What You Did Last Summer"
59 On top of
60 Sounds of rain on the roof
65 Doddering
70 Copenhagen toast
72 Empty
73 Fawns
74 Crop menace
75 If not
78 Tote
79 Aware of
80 Legendary bowman
84 Fiesta-taurina cheer
85 Morass
86 It banned THG in 2001
87 Short
88 Low digit
89 Pres. Ford's cat
90 Shriner parade vehicle
93 Shuts
94 Max portrayer in "Cape Fear"
95 Native Aussie
98 Ichabod of Sleepy Hollow
99 Fragrant flowers of Frankfurt
100 Subject
101 Bloke
102 Screen
103 Give in
104 Tour players
105 Recruit
106 Auricular
107 Batman actor
108 Tennessee state flower
109 Hubbubs
110 Pin cushion?
111 Word for you, but not for me
112 ___ fighter of "Star Wars"

ACROSS

1 Owns
4 Hunky guy
8 Silky fabrics
14 Place to get clean
19 "___ Maria"
20 River under the Ponte Vecchio
21 Observes Yom Kippur
22 Oranjestad's island
23 Perlman in "Hellboy"
24 Just in case
25 Flashy flier
27 Common solvent
29 Devours
30 Robin resting places
31 Burst of new energy
33 It's morning in Paris
35 Eminem song featuring Dido
36 Creep
37 Said grace
39 Exceeded the limit
43 SAT for grad school
45 Begin gently
47 Big Mac ingredient
49 Largest American cat
52 Really good time
53 Calm down
54 They're blown in the winds
55 One-celled organisms
57 "Forrest Gump" author
58 Arrive
60 Balkan native
61 Curse
62 Stash on board
63 "Ode on a Grecian Urn" poet
66 Go-ahead
68 President and Chief Justice
71 Like Dumbledore
73 Little foxes
75 More blurred
77 Big hit
79 Final words
82 Flourless cake
83 Fan of talk radio
86 Bull-riding event
87 Cut some slack
88 Got out of line
89 Lumbermill tool
90 Little devil
91 Samuel Adams, for one
92 Delaware statesman and family
94 Half-moon tide
96 World's largest fashion magazine
100 Layered minerals
101 1984–85 Prince tour
103 Biblical holy land
107 Positive
110 One type of 91 Across
111 Blue Angels' rivals
113 Folk singer Mitchell
114 "But ___ Love You": Rimes
115 Spanish seashore
116 Condor nests
117 Like thrift-shop wares
118 Col. neighbor
119 "Monopoly" building
120 Revolutionary War general Nathanael
121 "American Gigolo" star
122 It follows you, at times

DOWN

1 Bedevil
2 Wading bird
3 Roman Stoic
4 Place for a Mohawk
5 Even more hip
6 Without a stitch
7 Morse "E"
8 Vegan dish
9 Busily engaged
10 Duds
11 Ghoulish
12 Take home amount
13 ID thief's target
14 Went long
15 Therefore
16 O'Hare and LAX
17 Lie beside
18 Carry-ons
26 Rainbows
28 It's hard to say
29 Surround with light
32 Northern Sea Route convoy escort
34 Fender guitar
37 Mexican dollars
38 Crackers with seven holes
39 "Star Wars" soldiers
40 Play the snob
41 Amazon smart speaker
42 Consider
44 Devil-may-care
46 Watched kids
48 Attire for Augustus
49 Goes for a run
50 Drive getaway
51 Rot
53 Party with a pink or blue theme
55 ___-existing condition
56 "R.I.P." singer Rita
59 Scratch (out)
61 Anonymous John
64 15–20% is a standard one
65 Recipe instruction
67 Text mess.
69 Soiree
70 Toledo train
72 Lose a winter coat
74 Milk runs have many
76 Unit of matter
77 Pound cake serving
78 Cursor controls
80 Spots
81 "Snickers" ingredient
84 Young and attractive
85 Monumental
87 Cosmetic item
89 Breathe
93 Amateur painter
95 Juxtapose
97 El Niño's counterpart
98 Schubert songs
99 Cover up
100 One of Michael Phelps' 28
101 So last week
102 Say "gonna"
103 Have a hankering
104 "Get lost!"
105 "Diamonds and ___": Baez
106 Kitty feed
108 Creamy cheese
109 Original sin location
112 Scott Joplin piece
113 Cider container

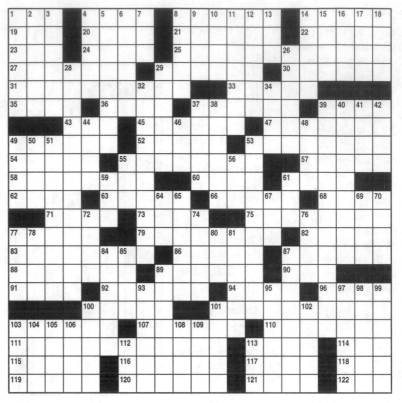

297 ADVERTISING MIX*   by Joel D. Lafargue
19 Across spent his entire baseball career playing for the Minnesota Twins.

ACROSS

1 Rebound
6 Keyboard bar
11 Invite
14 Swift steeds
19 1964 AL Rookie of the Year
20 ". . . some tarts, ____ a summer's day"
21 Springfield bartender
22 Gambling mecca
23 Siphon off profits?*
25 Club VIP
27 Severe to the max
28 England's FBI
30 Hems in
31 Thrice, in the pharmacy
32 Musical transition
34 Kurosawa epic
35 Lady of pop music
38 Prima donna taking a break?*
43 1999 Matthew McConaughey film
47 Aleutian island
48 Robert's "Untouchables" role
49 Lawn decoration
51 West Sumatra district
52 Jacobi in "The Odessa File"
54 Bird of the Outback
55 Billy Blanks' regimen
57 "Nick of Time" singer Bonnie
59 Jurassic, in a way
60 Asks an alum over?*
63 Boston's Charles ____
64 Conical home
66 Practice like 8 Down
67 Forest female
69 Terrible
70 Djokovic of tennis
72 Valuable earth
73 Suze of finance
75 Place for an icicle
77 Breeziness
79 Smith of "Dick Tracy"
81 "American Idol" hopeful
84 Tackle heights
86 Numbers put up by a Baltimore team?*
90 Common Core exam
91 Wonder Woman's weapon
92 Eastern Rift Valley lake
93 Life often imitates it

94 Parboil
96 Friend of François
97 Actor Bakula
99 Angola antelope
101 Where most people live
102 Little ones
104 Board fees at the public pool?*
107 End of the road?
108 Word heard on Talk Like a Pirate Day
110 Lowe and Everett
111 ____ Alamos, NM
113 Operatic antagonist's voice
118 Position at Winged Foot
119 Baby's game
124 Be thrifty
126 Attempted to 124 Across?*
128 Bird in the "Buckles" strip
129 PAC that's packing
130 Little Dipper School pupil
131 Start to noster or familias
132 Steel plow inventor
133 Interlaken river
134 Gosling and Seacrest
135 Plant fiber used in bagging

DOWN

1 Cape ____ (cottages)
2 On fire
3 Split apart
4 Catch up to and pass
5 Château-Thierry's river
6 Droops down
7 Form preceder
8 Olympic torch bearer in Atlanta
9 Fanciful idea
10 Pulver's rank
11 Elec. unit
12 Ticked, but not tocked
13 Razor-sharp
14 "The Town of Stones and Saints"
15 Made over
16 Broadway's "Rock of ____"

17 Batman's muscular foe
18 Planes in the no-fly zone?
24 Italian Riviera's Cinque ____
26 To-go order
29 Understood a hipster?
32 Dark brews
33 Lawn tool
35 Gal in "Wonder Woman"
36 "Someone Like You" singer
37 Swing by a Knicks home game?*
39 Map abbr.
40 California valley
41 Out of favor, informally
42 Haitian practice
44 Tooling from Oregon to Maine?*
45 Spud
46 "A ____ sante!" (French toast)
50 Drop a stitch
53 Ukraine's "Mother of Cities"
55 Anastasia, for one
56 Said "yes"
58 Quinn of "Practical Magic"

61 Low high tide
62 Lyrical verses
65 Ted Kooser writings
68 Once, once
71 Greek pottery rings
74 It's as good as a mile
75 Brilliance
76 "The Cradle of Texas Liberty"
78 Premium channels, in general
80 Miss World crowns
82 Manny's "Ice Age" love
83 Airspace monitor
85 Aurochs genus
87 Prophetic
88 Sandpaper feature
89 "Let ____": Beatles
95 Staple foods of Nigeria
98 Software box item
99 Hospital worker
100 Queen of the Misty ____ (Aleta)
103 Fight "souvenir"
105 Islanders' org.
106 Lower leg covering
109 Observe Yom Kippur
112 Striped giraffe
113 Necklace unit
114 One of the "back forty"
115 Took the "A" Train

116 Hirschfeld hidden name
117 Rock's Better Than ____
119 Peasant worker
120 "Slow Churned" ice cream
121 Vertical post on a ship
122 Scott Turow book
123 Fairy-tale heavy
125 Cochlea site
127 Glass of NPR

298 INSIDE MAN by Robert H. Wolfe
Chiromancy would be another clue for 24 Across.

ACROSS

1 Buddhist memorial dome
6 Moose order
10 "Julius Caesar" conspirator
15 Retained
19 Signs (an agreement)
21 "___ and his money . . ."
22 Skating star Kulik
23 Paving vehicle
24 A bit of fortune telling
26 Row
27 North Carolina river
29 Attorney Boies
30 Stillwater school
33 McGwire's 1998 rival
34 "I tawt ___ a puddy tat . . .": Tweety
36 Tort
39 Nursery rhyme couple
41 Vivaldi's "___ Dominus"
43 Part of IPA
45 Mall anchor of yore
47 Rips apart
49 Kidney combiner
51 XIX x VIII
52 McKellen and Holm
53 Mongolian tent
55 "The Hateful Eight" star
58 Father of Moses
59 Elton John's sign
61 Peru capital?
62 City east of El Paso
63 ___ Park, Queens
64 One bringing two sides together
66 "Crepuscule" poet's monogram
67 Big night
69 Swampy stretch
70 Cylindrical cake
72 Not very bright
74 Soldier at Cold Harbor
76 Ultimatum words
78 ___ Trucking Company
79 Place to go in Leeds
81 TV palomino
83 Fishy
85 At hand
87 Pier loved by James Dean
89 The Way, in Mandarin
90 Slangy fun
93 Aquatint
94 Mad Hatter's table item
95 Tenets
97 Editorial "never mind"
98 Ubiquitous bag
99 Blanket with a hole in it
101 Job seeker
103 Social climber
105 ___ diem
106 Painter Holbein
108 Ring around a pupil
109 Wolverine's kin
111 "___ magnifique!"
113 "The Temple of Dullness" composer
115 2013 McCartney album
116 Lesser of two ___
118 Don Draper's secretary
119 Place for a corsage
121 Rump roast cut
125 Steadfast resoluteness
130 Larson in "Kong: Skull Island"
131 Davis of "Evening Shade"
132 Political theories
133 Tapster's draw
134 Control knobs
135 Rocker Rundgren
136 "What's ___ like?"

DOWN

1 Amazon cloud-based email service
2 Tequila-tonic drink
3 Bear Dance tribe
4 "I eat my ___ with honey . . .": Nash
5 Sofa sides
6 Tunes
7 Given temporarily
8 Suffix for Capri
9 Tenon's mate
10 Goat genus
11 Airline stewards union
12 Realtor's sign
13 Vladimir's friend
14 Advil alternative
15 Power Wheels wheels
16 Father of Phinehas
17 Brooch
18 Swiss watch, familiarly
20 "In other words . . ."
25 Has something
28 Alert and expectant
30 Ancient Roman port
31 "Hunger Games" weapon
32 Power source
35 Hearty homecoming
37 Quiet contemplation
38 ER priority systems
40 Prefix for element #33
42 Form 10-Q, for one
44 "Gigi" playwright
46 American gymnast Biles
48 Brazil native
50 It's search target
54 "When You're Hot, You're Hot" singer
56 "Prufrock" poet's monogram
57 Mayhem
60 Window part
65 Parade vehicle
68 Gaston Leroux's phantom
70 Jackson and Leigh
71 Paint solvent
73 Breakfast fruit
75 Slant
77 Maroon
80 Hurricane category
82 Eighty-sixed
84 "Brave New World" sedative
86 Instrument for measuring viscosity
88 Look amazed
91 Staffordshire university
92 Stall bedding
96 Sporting dog
100 Throws a hissy
102 Keep slogging
104 "Time shifting" DVR
105 Speaker Ryan's successor
107 Seethed
110 Hunting son of Cush
112 State fair fare
114 Old rifle adjunct
117 Capital of ancient Elam
120 Nancy Drew's dog
121 Consumer protection org.
122 Pay dirt
123 SpongeBob wears one
124 Zippo
126 Union meeting words?
127 Squiffed
128 Verify a manuscript
129 That, in Leòn

299 BREAKING NEWS* by Charles M. Deber
A clever theme from a Toronto biochemist.

ACROSS

1 C ___ Charles
5 Corp. money execs
9 Web sights
14 Supplicate
19 Faye Kellerman heroine Lazarus
20 Rabanne of fashion
21 Sentient
22 ___ de Mayo
23 Response to the cub reporter's query*
27 Pang
28 Viewpoint
29 Powell pup
30 Shivering fit
31 Well-being
33 Short-horned buffaloes
35 2013 Kentucky Derby winner
37 Game piece
38 Response to the cub reporter's query*
43 Alabama island near Florida
44 Mirren in "The Queen"
45 "The Deuce" network
46 Eschew chewing
50 Hyogo capital
53 "The Huffington Post" acquirer
55 Pianist Maisenberg
59 Response to the cub reporter's query*
66 Super bargain
67 Type of acid in proteins
68 Latin love
69 "Goody!"
70 Has in stock
73 "This is only ___"
75 Travel agents at work
77 Son of, in Arabia
78 First Dominican MLB manager
80 "The ___ Fugue": Bach
82 Evening, in 4 Down
83 Response to the cub reporter's query*
88 Ringo Starr's "Oh ___"
89 Say "You're it!"
90 Cider type
91 Not as much
92 Grimley and Norton
95 Gelett Burgess slobs
99 A/V staple
101 Response to the cub reporter's query*
111 Socialite
112 "Don't ___ spoilsport"
113 Anna Paquin's "X-Men" role
114 "On ___ Day You Can See Forever"
115 CCIV + CCCIII
117 He did "My Way" his way
120 "… spirits from the ___ deep": Glendower
122 Vieux ___ of New Orleans
123 Remark on the cub reporter's employee performance evaluation*
127 NBA 1999–2000 MVP
128 Compete in a contest
129 Past time
130 "Last one ___ a rotten egg!"
131 Let slip away
132 Folks at Arhus
133 Cert. tournament round
134 Shrewdly cautious

DOWN

1 "Queen of Soul" Franklin
2 Took a deep breath
3 Grammy winner James
4 Citta in Campania
5 Coast Guard noncom
6 They come and go
7 Of an eye site?
8 Schoolyard rejoinder
9 Indulge
10 Lou Gehrig's disease
11 "Dennis the Menace" girl
12 Twilight times
13 Pie chart slice
14 They do Windows
15 Homer Simpson's issue
16 Mystery
17 Real
18 Senior members
24 Back to the present
25 Methuselah's father
26 Planet not in Holst's "The Planets"
32 Tom aboard "Apollo 13"
34 Member of the scale
36 Tiny Tim's dad
39 "Keep me in the ___"
40 French menu meat
41 Fictional sister of Sherlock
42 Fast Eddie's game
46 "Tea With Mussolini" subject
47 "Way to go, son!"
48 Breastbone
49 "There's gold in them ___ hills!"
51 Cry from 54 Down
52 "At Wit's End" columnist Bombeck
54 March 31st animal
56 Infant outfit
57 Euchre cousins
58 Yellowstone attractions
60 24-book epic
61 Saturn's largest moon
62 Nonreactive
63 Spain's ___ Brava
64 Christopher Robin's playmate
65 Trident feature
71 "Telephone Line" group
72 Squishy
74 Nottingham nonsense
76 German chancellor (1982–98)
79 Wear and tear
81 Kissimmee loc.
84 Dmitri's demurral
85 Excited times ten
86 Troop group
87 Bollywood's Goswami
93 Neophyte socialite
94 Lipstick slip
96 Word of belonging
97 Killdeer and dotterel
98 "Broca's Brain" author
100 Staph and strep agents
101 "You're telling me!"
102 Devotion to St. Jude
103 Spoonbill relatives
104 Had broad scope
105 Herd cattle to a fence?
106 Life-threatening
107 Russian's language family
108 Star close to Venus?
109 Scary "Night Gallery" bug
110 Like Oscar Night attire
116 "___ first you don't …"
118 Big Island coffee
119 Envelope wd.
121 Sherpa sighting?
124 Bravo!
125 Simon Cowell's shirt of choice
126 French noun gen.

ACROSS

1 "Have you ___?"
6 Panama, for example
11 Symphonic conductor Ernö
16 "Now more ___!"
18 Lazy Marley of rhyme
19 Houdini's birthplace
21 Front page stories, as a rule
22 Longest river in France
23 Hearst's middle name
24 Site for a cinephile
25 Held a candle to
27 Gmail folder
28 "Time" singer Amos
29 Ephron and Roberts
31 Pulls a Halloween job
32 HST's party
34 Ergate
35 "Myst" sequel
36 Hummocks
38 RAF award
40 Kind of scholarship
42 Hide-and-___
43 Frog pond sounds
45 Betrothed
47 ___'acte
48 Get lit
50 Northern California peak
53 Catches off base
56 Likely Emmy nominee
57 Gets creative (with 70 & 81 Across)
58 Recyclable item
61 ___-scarum (reckless)
63 "Dulce et decorum ___": Horace
64 Bit for a busker in Brussels
66 "Raiders of the Lost Ark" villain
68 Quitter's words
70 See 57 Across
73 High point in Exodus
74 Blue bloods
76 Leakes of "The New Normal"
77 Partner with vigor
79 Cordelia's sister

80 Banjo location of song
81 See 57 Across
83 Large fishing boat
86 Kind of job
87 Sportscaster Ahmad
88 "Hmmm . . ." sayer
90 "Unto us ___ is given": Isa. 9:6
92 "Runaway Train" singer Cash
94 Astromancers
97 "Be ___ Your School": Beach Boys
98 Eye surgery
99 Chang's twin
101 "___ under your hat"
103 ___ trot (eager)
104 Singer Damone
105 Zinger
107 One of two NT books
109 Bygone Crayola color
110 "Time ___ the essence!"
111 Seeding
112 Low-risk wager
115 Antioxidant berry
116 Uncool Kool stimulant
118 Up and about
120 Cause for a Gotcha Day celebration
122 Olympic skater Nancy
123 "Tsk, tsk!"
124 Hesitant start to a question
125 Damask rose oil
126 Mideast capital at 7,500 ft.
127 "Dilbert" secretrary

DOWN

1 Earring shape
2 Off-the-wall sport
3 CA–FL hwy.
4 "When pigs fly!"
5 "I was right!"
6 Body's bug battler
7 With a saintly glow
8 Mole
9 Popular depilatory
10 "Fish Magic" painter Paul

11 AWOL student
12 "I ___ thought of that . . ."
13 Where to tap an app
14 Heir hirer
15 React dramatically to bad news
16 ___ rye (deli order)
17 Sent regrets
19 Data portrayer Spiner
20 Buying binge
26 Give a thumbs-up
27 Broke the ice
30 Word with mail or coin
33 Tilly in "The Big Chill"
35 "Oxford Blues" heroine
37 Polish companion
39 First flat, first floor
41 Like a horse after a visit to the farrier
42 "On your mark, ___ . . ."
44 Innings for stretching
46 Waterproof fabric
49 CIA forerunner

51 "___ Quiet Flows the Don"
52 ATM hazards
53 Eckhart in "I, Frankenstein"
54 Widespread waterfowl
55 "Wake Up" girl of song
57 Checks for fit
58 Let out a yell
59 Danny of the Boston Celtics
60 March tourney, for short
62 Wire measure
65 "Anchors Aweigh" org.
67 Original "Dungeons & Dragons" co.
69 Lee competitor
71 "Wooly Bully" opening lyrics
72 Sue Grafton's "E"
75 "Uh-huh"
78 Ending for hero
82 Joe's 2012 running mate
84 Feminine suffix
85 Smell of smoke

87 Fantasy baseball
88 Lahore local
89 Nemo's home
90 Dictator
91 Begin a journey
93 Penguin Crosby
95 Reunion member
96 A Kellogg's cereal
97 Riveter of WW2
98 Alb fabric
100 Turn to the dark side
102 Golfer Aoki and namesakes
104 Joan on "Knots Landing"
106 "Stardust" novelist Neil
108 Censor for security reasons
111 Mikhail Baryshnikov, by birth
113 Go ape
114 Temple scroll
117 Reddish monkey
118 DA's associate
119 Persian king
121 "Frasier" actress Gilpin

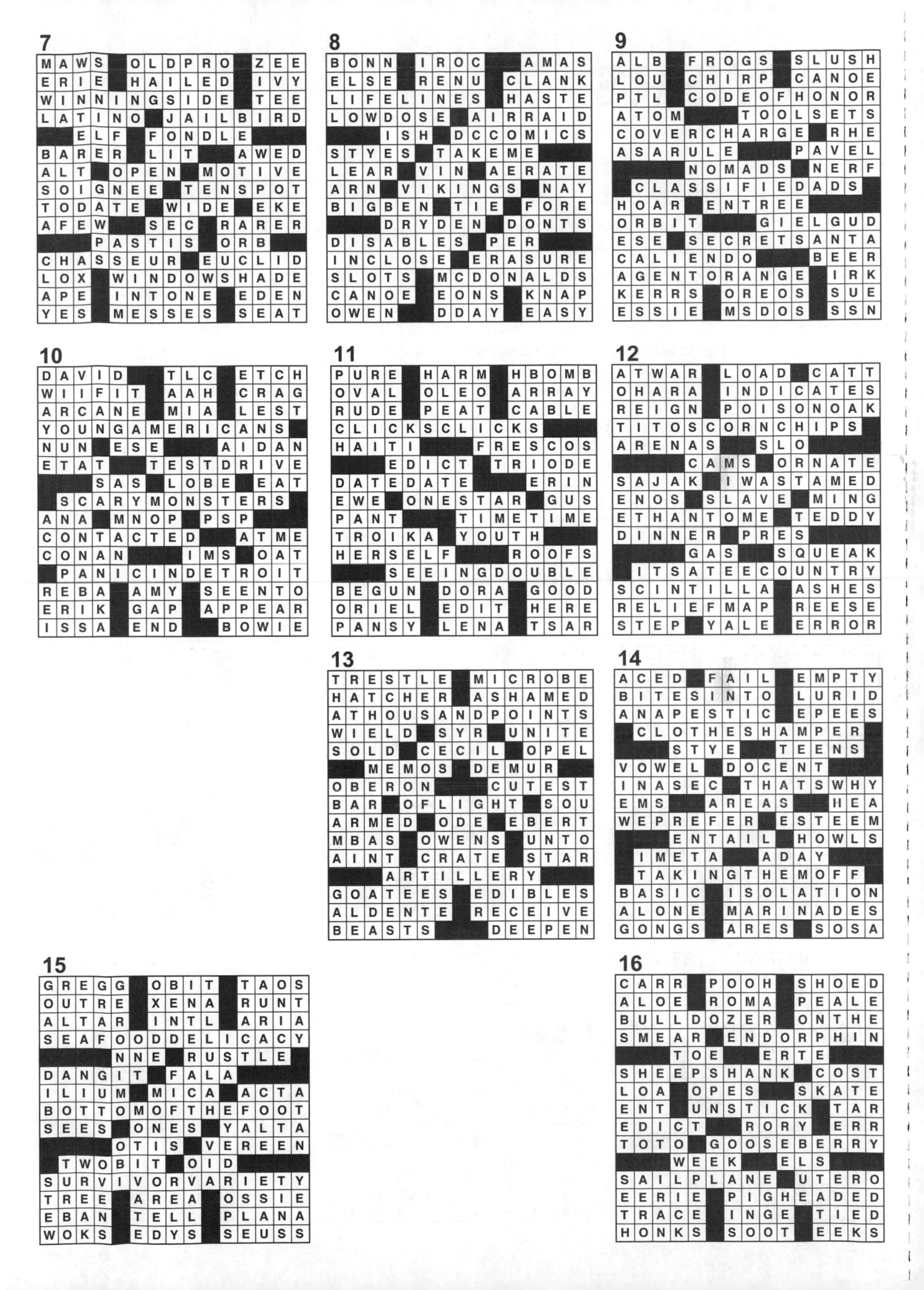

7
```
MAWS  . OLDPRO . ZEE
ERIE  . HAILED . IVY
WINNINGSIDE  . TEE
LATINO . JAILBIRD
 . ELF . FONDLE .
BARER . LIT . AWED
ALT . OPEN . MOTIVE
SOIGNEE . TENSPOT
TODATE . WIDE . EKE
AFEW . SEC . RARER
 . PASTIS . ORB .
CHASSEUR . EUCLID
LOX . WINDOWSHADE
APE . INTONE . EDEN
YES . MESSES . SEAT
```

8
```
BONN . IROC . AMAS
ELSE . RENU . CLANK
LIFELINES . HASTE
LOWDOSE . AIRRAID
 . ISH . DCCOMICS
STYES . TAKEME .
LEAR . VIN . AERATE
ARN . VIKINGS . NAY
BIGBEN . TIE . FORE
 . DRYDEN . DONTS
DISABLES . PER .
INCLOSE . ERASURE
SLOTS . MCDONALDS
CANOE . EONS . KNAP
OWEN . DDAY . EASY
```

9
```
ALB . FROGS . SLUSH
LOU . CHIRP . CANOE
PTL . CODEOFHONOR
ATOM . TOOLSETS
COVERCHARGE . RHE
ASARULE . PAVEL
 . NOMADS . NERF
 . CLASSIFIEDADS .
HOAR . ENTREE
ORBIT . GIELGUD
ESE . SECRETSANTA
CALIENDO . BEER
AGENTORANGE . IRK
KERRS . OREOS . SUE
ESSIE . MSDOS . SSN
```

10
```
DAVID . TLC . ETCH
WIIFIT . AAH . CRAG
ARCANE . MIA . LEST
YOUNGAMERICANS .
NUN . ESE . AIDAN
ETAT . TESTDRIVE
 . SAS . LOBE . EAT
 . SCARYMONSTERS
ANA . MNOP . PSP
CONTACTED . ATME
CONAN . IMS . OAT
 . PANICINDETROIT
REBA . AMY . SEENTO
ERIK . GAP . APPEAR
ISSA . END . BOWIE
```

11
```
PURE . HARM . HBOMB
OVAL . OLEO . ARRAY
RUDE . PEAT . CABLE
CLICKSCLICKS .
HAITI . FRESCOS
 . EDICT . TRIODE
DATEDATE . ERIN
EWE . ONESTAR . GUS
PANT . TIMETIME
TROIKA . YOUTH .
HERSELF . ROOFS
 . SEEINGDOUBLE
BEGUN . DORA . GOOD
ORIEL . EDIT . HERE
PANSY . LENA . TSAR
```

12
```
ATWAR . LOAD . CATT
OHARA . INDICATES
REIGN . POISONOAK
TITOSCORNCHIPS .
ARENAS . SLO .
 . CAMS . ORNATE
SAJAK . IWASTAMED
ENOS . SLAVE . MING
ETHANTOME . TEDDY
DINNER . PRES .
 . GAS . SQUEAK
 . ITSATEECOUNTRY
SCINTILLA . ASHES
RELIEFMAP . REESE
STEP . YALE . ERROR
```

13
```
TRESTLE . MICROBE
HATCHER . ASHAMED
ATHOUSANDPOINTS
WIELD . SYR . UNITE
SOLD . CECIL . OPEL
 . MEMOS . DEMUR
OBERON . CUTEST
BAR . OFLIGHT . SOU
ARMED . ODE . EBERT
MBAS . OWENS . UNTO
AINT . CRATE . STAR
 . ARTILLERY .
GOATEES . EDIBLES
ALDENTE . RECEIVE
BEASTS . DEEPEN
```

14
```
ACED . FAIL . EMPTY
BITESINTO . LURID
ANAPESTIC . EPEES
 . CLOTHESHAMPER .
 . STYE . TEENS
VOWEL . DOCENT .
INASEC . THATSWHY
EMS . AREAS . HEA
WEPREFER . ESTEEM
 . ENTAIL . HOWLS
IMETA . ADAY .
TAKINGTHEMOFF .
BASIC . ISOLATION
ALONE . MARINADES
GONGS . ARES . SOSA
```

15
```
GREGG . OBIT . TAOS
OUTRE . XENA . RUNT
ALTAR . INTL . ARIA
SEAFOODDELICACY
 . NNE . RUSTLE
DANGIT . FALA
ILIUM . MICA . ACTA
BOTTOMOFTHEFOOT
SEES . ONES . YALTA
 . OTIS . VEREEN
 . TWOBIT . OID
SURVIVORVARIETY
TREE . AREA . OSSIE
EBAN . TELL . PLANA
WOKS . EDYS . SEUSS
```

16
```
CARR . POOH . SHOED
ALOE . ROMA . PEALE
BULLDOZER . ONTHE
SMEAR . ENDORPHIN
 . TOE . ERTE .
SHEEPSHANK . COST
LOA . OPES . SKATE
ENT . UNSTICK . TAR
EDICT . RORY . ERR
TOTO . GOOSEBERRY
 . WEEK . ELS .
SAILPLANE . UTERO
EERIE . PIGHEADED
TRACE . INGE . TIED
HONKS . SOOT . EEKS
```

ANSWERS

FOREWORD

I have noticed that (in poems, slim) people are seldom mentioned.
    Simple Simon

When he walks into (the room, egos) begin to need massaging.
    Mother Goose

I found the captain's (log locked in) a file cabinet.
    Old King Cole

I tend to (resist smarmy) sales pitches.
    Mistress Mary

I heard everyone in (my ward rage) against the proposed tax increase.
    Margery Daw

If you hear the (pope belittle) himself, it is an act of humility.
    Little Bo Peep

They sent (my truck to me) without charging for the driver.
    Tommy Tucker

The person who is (godly mourns no) action of his own.
    Solomon Grundy

Where Robert Downey (Jr. sat, pack) animals could be seen moving about.
    Jack Sprat

Placing a corn (cob in rock) salt prevents insect infestation.
    Cock Robin

1

A	M	A	S	S		V	I	N	E		G	L	O	W
R	E	B	U	T		I	R	O	N		E	A	C	H
T	R	A	V	E	L	V	I	S	A		O	T	T	O
I	R	S		P	O	I	S	E		I	D	E	A	L
E	Y	E	S	O	R	E			E	M	E	R	G	E
			T	U	N	N	E	L	V	I	S	I	O	N
B	E	R	E	T		V	E	I	N		S	N	O	
A	M	E	N		E	M	A	I	L		H	E	A	T
T	P	S		A	N	O	N			B	E	R	L	E
H	O	T	E	L	V	I	S	I	T	O	R			
S	W	A	M	P	Y			N	O	T	A	B	I	T
H	E	R	B	S		S	P	E	N	T		A	N	I
E	R	T	E		S	W	I	V	E	L	V	I	S	E
B	E	E	R		P	A	C	E		E	E	L	E	R
A	D	D	S		A	G	A	R		R	E	S	T	S

2

T	A	G	S		D	R	A	T		S	P	A	S	M
O	L	E	O		I	A	G	O		C	I	S	C	O
M	E	N	U		S	N	I	T		R	E	T	R	O
	C	A	L	A	M	I	N	E	L	O	T	I	O	N
			M	C	A	N			H	O	A	R	D	S
S	T	M	A	R	Y		B	R	A	G				
H	A	U	T	E		W	E	A	S	E	L	O	U	T
A	X	L	E		S	O	F	I	A		O	R	S	O
D	I	E	S	E	L	O	I	L		S	W	E	E	P
				S	A	L	T		V	A	P	O	R	S
A	D	D	I	C	T			G	A	R	R			
Q	U	I	C	H	E	L	O	R	R	A	I	N	E	
U	N	T	I	E		E	S	A	I		C	O	L	E
A	S	K	E	W		E	L	S	E		E	V	I	L
S	T	A	R	S		R	O	S	S		S	O	S	O

3

J	O	E	S		B	L	O	B		T	O	W	I	N
A	X	L	E		R	A	M	A		E	V	A	D	E
N	O	S	E	D	I	V	E	S		R	A	F	E	R
				P	A	G	A	N	I	N	I		F	A	D
A	C	T	A	S			L	E	G	A	L	L	Y	
G	E	R	S	H	W	I	N		W	A	K	E		
N	E	A	T		W	O	O	S		R	A	I	D	S
E	L	F		P	I	N	E	T	A	R		R	A	W
S	O	F	A	R		A	L	A	N		B	O	N	E
	I	M	A	C		S	R	I	L	A	N	K	A	
I	N	C	I	T	E	S			A	S	S	E	T	
W	A	S		T	O	U	R	I	S	T	S			
I	N	T	E	L		C	O	N	E	H	E	A	D	S
S	C	O	R	E		K	I	T	E		T	I	R	E
H	Y	P	E	R		S	L	O	P		T	R	E	X

4

C	R	E	W		A	U	R	A	L		F	A	T	S
O	A	T	H		S	T	E	V	E		I	V	A	N
P	I	T	A		T	U	N	E	S		V	A	S	E
S	L	U	M	B	E	R	O	R	S	I	E	S	T	A
			E	R	N			R	A	T	E	D		
L	I	S	T	E	N		C	L	A	I	M			
O	S	L	O		T	H	O	R	N		E	L	F	
S	L	I	P	P	E	R	O	R	S	A	N	D	A	L
S	E	T		L	O	O	S	E		A	I	D	A	
			D	A	N	T	E		K	I	T	T	E	N
S	T	O	A	T			T	I	M					
C	Y	P	R	E	S	S	O	R	S	P	R	U	C	E
O	P	E	N		C	A	V	E	S		A	B	O	Y
W	E	R	E		A	L	I	V	E		J	E	T	E
L	E	A	D		R	E	D	I	D		A	R	E	S

5

R	U	B	E		S	P	A	T	S		S	A	C	S
A	N	O	X		E	L	I	O	T		C	R	A	W
I	D	E	A		V	A	N	N	A		R	O	V	E
D	O	R	M	L	E	T	T	E	R		A	M	I	D
			O	R	E			T	A	M	A	L	E	
S	E	R	E	N	E		C	L	E	M				
E	L	I	T	E		D	A	I	R	Y	T	A	L	E
N	O	N	O		S	O	R	E	S		O	K	A	Y
D	I	G	N	E	W	T	O	N		J	U	I	C	E
				G	A	E	L		W	A	R	N	E	D
C	A	R	B	O	N			S	O	D				
A	R	I	A		D	U	L	L	N	E	L	S	O	N
R	U	G	S		I	L	I	A	D		A	C	R	E
O	B	I	T		V	A	L	V	E		M	A	Z	E
M	A	D	E		E	N	T	E	R		P	R	O	D

6

T	E	S	L	A		L	A	S	T		S	W	A	P
U	T	T	E	R		E	T	N	A		L	A	L	A
R	H	E	A	S		G	O	A	R	O	U	N	D	S
B	E	E	F		J	U	M	P	S	T	R	E	E	T
O	L	D	C	H	A	P		P	A	T		D	R	Y
			L	I	V		B	E	L	O	W			
S	A	B	O	T	A	G	E	D		E	X	A	M	
O	L	I	V	E		R	N	A		S	E	E	D	S
S	I	Z	E		A	T	T	A	C	K	D	O	G	
			R	O	A	N	S		D	O	S			
A	C	E		D	U	D		F	A	T	L	I	P	S
G	A	L	L	O	N	D	R	U	M		A	T	O	P
E	N	T	E	R	T	A	I	N		A	T	A	L	L
N	O	O	N		I	D	I	G		F	E	L	L	A
T	E	N	D		E	S	S	O		T	R	Y	S	T

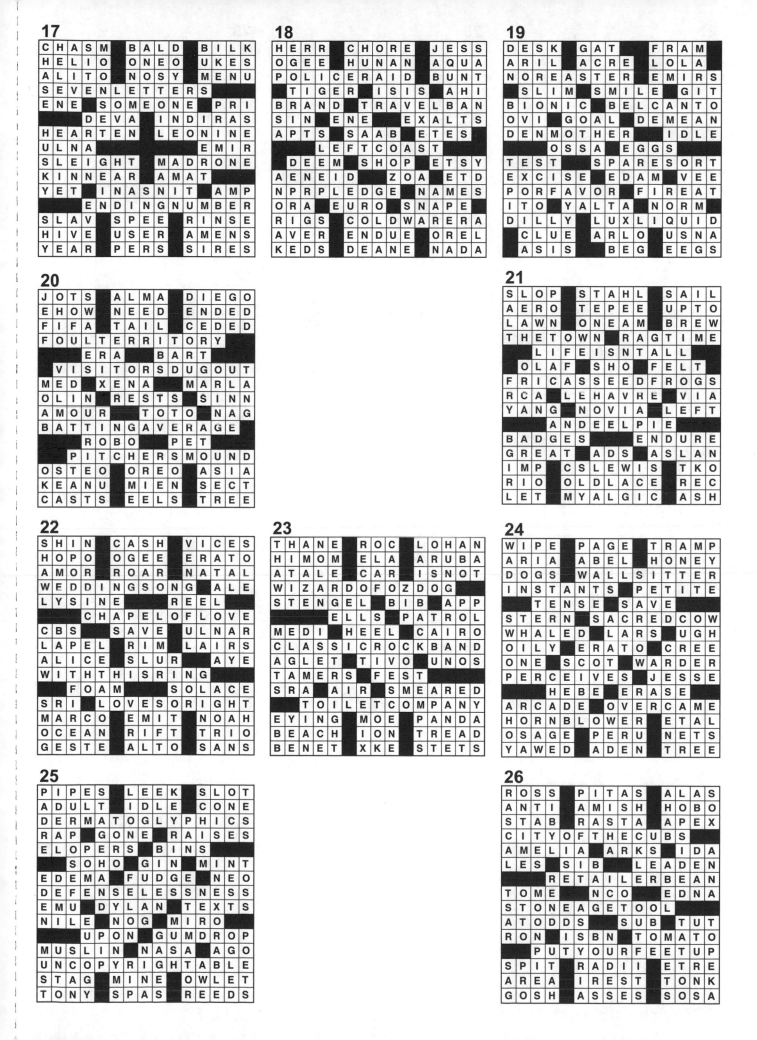

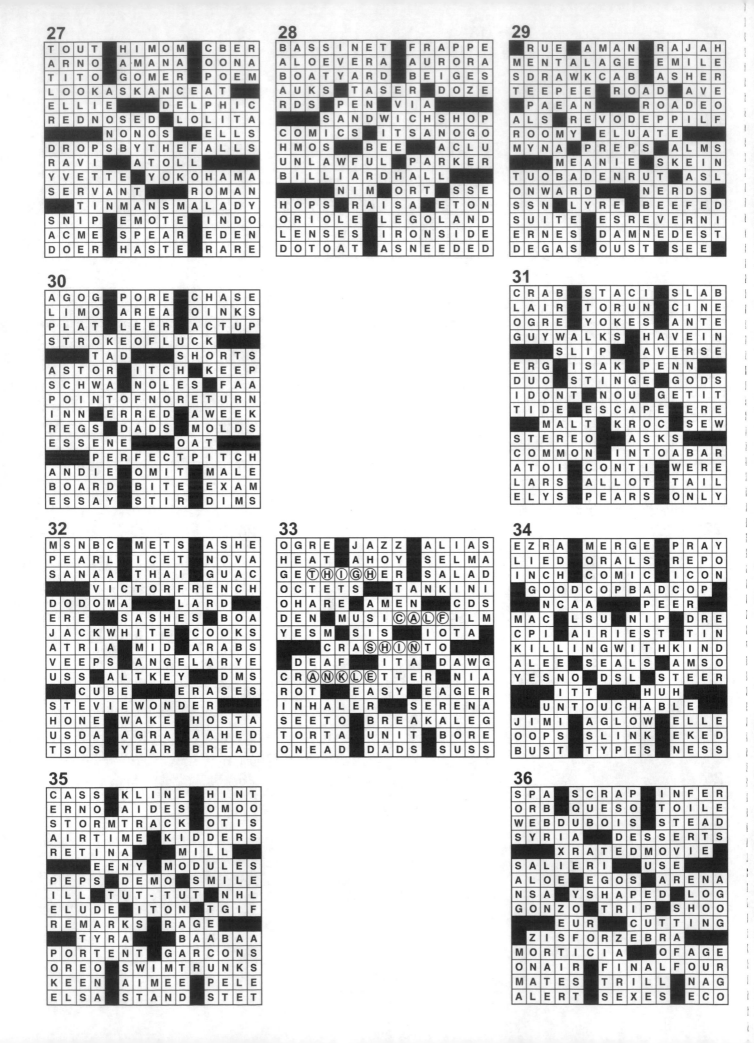

27

TOUT · HIMOM · CBER
ARNO · AMANA · OONA
TITO · GOMER · POEM
LOOKASKANCEAT
ELLIE · · DELPHIC
REDNOSED · LOLITA
· · NONOS · ELLS
DROPSBYTHEFALLS
RAVI · · ATOLL
YVETTE · YOKOHAMA
SERVANT · · ROMAN
· TINMANSMALADY
SNIP · EMOTE · INDO
ACME · SPEAR · EDEN
DOER · HASTE · RARE

28

BASSINET · FRAPPE
ALOEVERA · AURORA
BOATYARD · BEIGES
AUKS · TASER · DOZE
RDS · PEN · VIA
· SANDWICHSHOP
COMICS · ITSANOGO
HMOS · BEE · ACLU
UNLAWFUL · PARKER
BILLIARDHALL
· NIM · ORT · SSE
HOPS · RAISA · ETON
ORIOLE · LEGOLAND
LENSES · IRONSIDE
DOTOAT · ASNEEDED

29

RUE · AMAN · RAJAH
MENTALAGE · EMILE
SDRAWKCAB · ASHER
TEEPEE · ROAD · AVE
· PAEAN · ROADEO
ALS · REVODEPPILF
ROOMY · ELUATE
MYNA · PREPS · ALMS
· MEANIE · SKEIN
TUOBADENRUT · ASL
ONWARD · · NERDS
SSN · LYRE · BEEFED
SUITE · ESREVERNI
ERNES · DAMNEDEST
DEGAS · OUST · SEE

30

AGOG · PORE · CHASE
LIMO · AREA · OINKS
PLAT · LEER · ACTUP
STROKEOFLUCK
· TAD · SHORTS
ASTOR · ITCH · KEEP
SCHWA · NOLES · FAA
POINTOFNORETURN
INN · ERRED · AWEEK
REGS · DADS · MOLDS
ESSENE · OAT
· PERFECTPITCH
ANDIE · OMIT · MALE
BOARD · BITE · EXAM
ESSAY · STIR · DIMS

31

CRAB · STACI · SLAB
LAIR · TORUN · CINE
OGRE · YOKES · ANTE
GUYWALKS · HAVEIN
· SLIP · AVERSE
ERG · ISAK · PENN
DUO · STINGE · GODS
IDONT · NOU · GETIT
TIDE · ESCAPE · ERE
· MALT · KROC · SEW
STEREO · ASKS
COMMON · INTOABAR
ATOI · CONTI · WERE
LARS · ALLOT · TAIL
ELYS · PEARS · ONLY

32

MSNBC · METS · ASHE
PEARL · ICET · NOVA
SANAA · THAI · GUAC
· VICTORFRENCH
DODOMA · LARD
ERE · SASHES · BOA
JACKWHITE · COOKS
ATRIA · MID · ARABS
VEEPS · ANGELARYE
USS · ALTKEY · DMS
· CUBE · ERASES
STEVIEWONDER
HONE · WAKE · HOSTA
USDA · AGRA · AAHED
TSOS · YEAR · BREAD

33

OGRE · JAZZ · ALIAS
HEAT · AHOY · SELMA
GET(THIGH)ER · SALAD
OCTETS · TANKINI
OHARE · AMEN · CDS
DEN · MUSI(CALF)ILM
YESM · SIS · IOTA
· CRA(SH)INTO
DEAF · ITA · DAWG
CRA(NKLE)TTER · NIA
ROT · EASY · EAGER
INHALER · SERENA
SEETO · BREAKALEG
TORTA · UNIT · BORE
ONEAD · DADS · SUSS

34

EZRA · MERGE · PRAY
LIED · ORALS · REPO
INCH · COMIC · ICON
· GOODCOPBADCOP
· NCAA · PEER
MAC · LSU · NIP · DRE
CPI · AIRIEST · TIN
KILLINGWITHKIND
ALEE · SEALS · AMSO
YESNO · DSL · STEER
· ITT · HUH
· UNTOUCHABLE
JIMI · AGLOW · ELLE
OOPS · SLINK · EKED
BUST · TYPES · NESS

35

CASS · KLINE · HINT
ERNO · AIDES · OMOO
STORMTRACK · OTIS
AIRTIME · KIDDERS
RETINA · MILL
· EENY · MODULES
PEPS · DEMO · SMILE
ILL · TUT-TUT · NHL
ELUDE · ITON · TGIF
REMARKS · RAGE
· TYRA · BAABAA
PORTENT · GARCONS
OREO · SWIMTRUNKS
KEEN · AIMEE · PELE
ELSA · STAND · STET

36

SPA · SCRAP · INFER
ORB · QUESO · TOILE
WEBDUBOIS · STEAD
SYRIA · DESSERTS
· XRATEDMOVIE
SALIERI · USE
ALOE · EGOS · ARENA
NSA · YSHAPED · LOG
GONZO · TRIP · SHOO
· EUR · CUTTING
· ZISFORZEBRA
MORTICIA · OFAGE
ONAIR · FINALFOUR
MATES · TRILL · NAG
ALERT · SEXES · ECO

37

L	S	D		J	A	C	K	S		R	U	S	S	O
A	H	I		A	T	R	I	A		E	N	N	U	I
N	O	N		C	H	O	C	K	A	B	L	O	C	K
D	O	G	G	O		S	K	E	W		E	U	R	O
		A	R	B	Y	S		S	E	N	A	T	E	S
M	I	L	E	S	O	F	F		D	E	S			
E	C	I	G		D	I	O		S	H	R	U	G	
T	E	N		R	A	T	A	T	A	T		O	B	E
A	L	G	A	E		M	O	W		E	P	E	E	
	L	E	D		S	M	O	L	D	E	R	S		
S	T	U	C	K	U	P		P	L	A	N	A		
N	I	N	O		D	O	Z	E		S	A	D	I	E
E	T	C	H	A	S	K	E	T	C	H		O	P	T
A	L	L	O	W		E	S	T	E	E		P	A	T
K	E	E	L	S		S	T	Y	E	S		E	D	U

38

T	E	A	R		S	T	O	M	P		A	S	P	S
R	I	S	E		W	I	P	E	R		S	C	O	T
I	L	S	A		E	N	E	M	Y		H	E	R	A
F	E	E	D	B	A	G	C	O	N	T	E	N	T	S
L	E	S	S	O	R		S	N	O		A	A	H	
E	N	S		F	O	P	S		E	M	E	R	G	E
			E	F	F	E	C	T		V	I	E	D	
	B	O	X	O	F	C	H	E	E	R	I	O	S	
W	A	N	G		K	E	R	N	E	L				
A	T	T	I	R	E		D	I	R	T		A	B	S
T	W	O		A	N	S		I	R	O	N	O	N	
T	O	L	L	H	O	U	S	E	C	O	O	K	I	E
A	M	O	I		U	R	I	A	H		M	A	L	E
G	A	G	S		G	L	A	R	E		P	R	E	Z
E	N	Y	A		H	Y	M	N	S		H	A	R	E

39

P	L	O	D		C	O	B	B		P	R	M	A	N
L	O	S	E		O	N	E	I		H	Y	E	N	A
A	H	A	B		U	T	E	P		Y	E	A	T	S
T	A	K	I	N	G	A	B	O	W	L		L	E	A
O	N	A	T	E	A	R		L	I	L	A	C		
			T	R	I		A	N	I	M	U	S		
P	I	C	A	S	S	O		R	E	S	U	L	T	S
T	R	U	E							S	P	A	S	
L	A	P	S	E	R	S		A	C	R	E	A	G	E
	S	O	I	R	E	E		B	R	A				
	F	R	I	D	A		S	O	U	P	S	O	N	
A	D	J		C	O	W	L	C	O	L	L	E	G	E
R	O	O	D	S		A	E	O	N		A	L	D	A
C	R	E	D	O		L	I	N	E		I	M	E	T
H	A	L	E	N		L	A	D	D		N	A	N	O

40

S	A	F	E		C	R	A	S	S		P	R	E	Z
A	L	L	Y		H	E	I	S	T		I	A	G	O
S	L	E	E	P	A	P	N	E	A		S	P	A	N
H	O	U	S	E	C	A	T		F	A	C	A	D	E
A	T	R	O	P	H	Y		A	F	T	E	R		
			R	E	A		A	C	C	O	S	T	E	D
O	K	I	E		S	C	R	A	M		I	R	A	
H	E	P		L	E	T	T	E	R	S		S	I	S
N	E	A		I	V	I	E	S		E	T	C	H	
O	N	D	E	M	A	N	D		R	E	X			
	D	R	I	N	K		C	O	M	P	E	T	E	
K	A	R	A	T	E		H	A	M	I	L	T	O	N
A	R	E	S		S	H	O	P	A	R	O	U	N	D
R	I	S	E		C	A	N	O	N		I	D	E	A
L	A	S	S		E	D	E	N	S		T	E	S	T

41

O	N	U	P		A	S	C	O	T		A	B	C	D
L	U	N	A		P	H	O	N	Y		G	E	R	E
I	D	L	Y		O	I	L	E	R		O	L	E	G
V	I	A	L	A	S	V	E	G	A	S		L	E	A
E	S	C	O	R	T	S		H	O	C	K	S		
S	M	E	A	R		B	A	T	H	T	U	B	S	
			D	I	C	T	A	T	E		T	R	E	E
E	C	G		D	O	E	B	A	R	S		E	D	S
S	U	R	E		C	R	E	D	I	T	S			
S	T	A	R	W	A	R	S		R	E	T	R	O	
E	L	Y	S	E		V	O	U	C	H	E	R		
N	O	B		S	E	E	N	S	A	M	U	R	A	I
C	O	O	S		A	L	L	I	S		R	I	S	E
E	S	A	I		S	I	E	G	E		E	C	O	N
S	E	T	S		Y	A	R	N	S		D	E	N	T

42

F	E	S	S		B	R	A		D	E	P	A	R	T
O	N	T	H	E	R	U	N		E	M	I	N	O	R
S	C	O	R	S	E	S	E		P	U	R	S	U	E
S	O	R	E	P	A	T	R	O	L		A	W	L	S
I	R	E	D		D	I	A	N	A		T	E	E	
L	E	D		P	E	C		I	N	S	E	R	T	S
		C	A	D	S		T	E	A	S	E	T	S	
A	P	T	L	Y				T	I	D	E	S		
R	E	R	O	U	T	E		A	T	I	P			
C	R	I	S	P	E	R		T	R	E		L	A	I
	S	A	E		A	G	I	L	E		S	I	B	S
T	O	N	S		S	O	W	A	N	D	T	E	L	L
E	N	G	A	G	E		I	N	T	E	R	N	E	E
S	A	L	V	E	R		S	T	O	N	I	E	S	T
S	L	E	E	T	S		H	A	N		P	E	T	S

43

T	A	R	I	F	F	S		G	R	I	E	V	E	S
O	B	A	D	I	A	H		A	I	R	T	I	M	E
N	E	V	E	R	B	E	E	N	D	I	S	S	E	D
S	L	E	D		R	I	D	G	E	S		I	R	A
			L	I	L	I	E	S		S	T	A	T	
D	I	T	T	Y	C	A	T	S		S	T	O	L	E
A	C	O	R	N	S			A	W	A	R	D	S	
R	O	M	A	N		L	E	A	D	I	N			
T	M	E	N		K	I	T	H	A	N	D	D	I	N
H	E	S	S		A	C	E	S		D	E	R	M	A
			P	O	L	E		S	L	E	E	P	S	
C	I	T	I	Z	E	N	D	A	N	E		A	L	A
A	G	O	R	A		S	A	G	E		E	M	I	L
L	O	N	E	R		E	V	E	R		N	O	E	L
F	R	I	S	K		D	E	E	D		A	N	D	Y

44

B	I	B	B		T	A	B	B	Y		G	E	M	S
I	D	O	L		A	T	R	E	E		I	M	O	K
T	I	N	A		P	E	A	R	L		J	I	M	I
	G	E	N	E	R	A	T	E	P	O	O	L	S	
		C	R	O	S	S	F	I	R	E				
S	I	P		R	O	E		T	N	T		O	A	T
G	R	A	H	A	M			G	E	R	U	N	D	
T	A	R	O	T		T	E	X		G	A	T	E	S
	A	L	A	M	O	D	E	R	A	T	E			
A	L	M	A		I	N	A	N	E		E	R	M	A
G	E	E		A	N	I	M	A	L	S		S	U	B
A	T	T	E	N	D			A	D	O	P	T	S	
T	H	E	L	I	F	E	O	F	P	I	R	A	T	E
H	A	R	M		U	L	N	A	S		E	C	O	N
A	L	S	O		L	O	O	S	E		S	E	N	T

45

B	O	P	S		E	M	I	L	E		B	I	L	L
I	N	R	I		L	I	C	E	N	S	E	F	E	E
S	E	E	N		I	N	B	A	D	T	A	S	T	E
H	O	M	E	R	S	I	M	P	S	O	N			
O	F	I	W	O			S	U	L	T	A	N	S	
P	U	S	S	Y	C	A	T		P	E	O	R	I	A
S	S	E		K	U	D	O	S		W	E	P	T	
			H	O	L	D	U	P	M	A	N			
A	N	N	E		S	T	A	I	R		H	A	S	
T	O	R	A	H	S		S	T	A	M	P	E	D	E
A	V	A	R	I	C	E		O	R	L	O	N		
		T	H	E	V	O	N	T	R	A	P	P	S	
H	A	V	E	A	N	I	D	E	A		I	O	T	A
I	D	E	N	T	I	T	I	E	S		S	U	E	T
T	A	G	S		C	A	N	T	S		E	T	R	E

46

A	C	A	I		I	S	U	Z	U		T	H	A	T
B	A	E	R		N	O	T	I	N		N	E	R	O
E	P	S	O	M	D	O	W	N	S		T	A	R	P
L	E	O	N	E		T	O	G	A	S		D	A	B
		S	P	I	N	E			I	T	A	L	I	A
			C	U	S	T	O	M	D	E	S	I	G	N
P	F	C		S	P	A	N	O		W	A	N	N	A
E	L	E	V		O	P	E	R	A		P	E	E	N
G	O	N	E	R		E	T	A	I	L		R	D	A
B	O	T	T	O	M	D	O	L	L	A	R			
O	R	I	O	L	E			S	M	O	C	K		
A	S	P		E	N	A	C	T		E	A	R	N	S
R	H	E	A		S	T	O	R	M	D	R	A	I	N
D	O	D	D		C	R	E	E	D		A	N	T	I
S	W	E	D		H	A	D	E	S		T	E	S	T

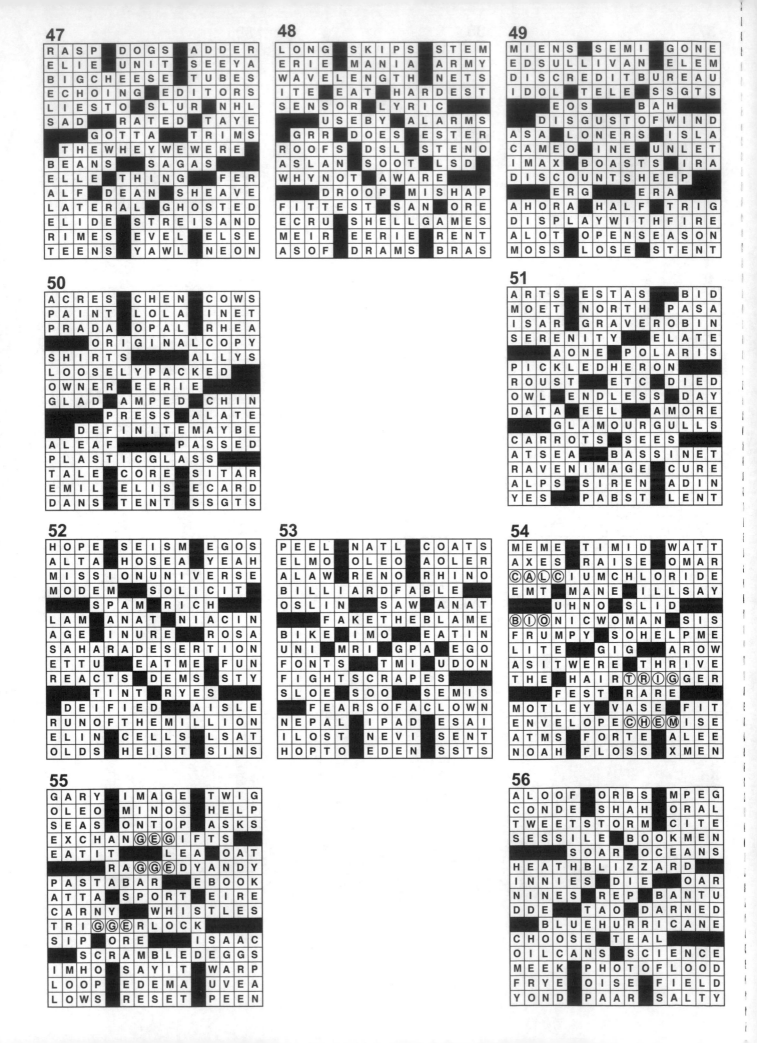

47

RASP · DOGS · ADDER
ELIE · UNIT · SEEYA
BIGCHEESE · TUBES
ECHOING · EDITORS
LIESTO · SLUR · NHL
SAD · RATED · TAYE
· GOTTA · TRIMS ·
THEWHEYWEWERE
BEANS · SAGAS ·
ELLE · THING · FER
ALF · DEAN · SHEAVE
LATERAL · GHOSTED
ELIDE · STREISAND
RIMES · EVEL · ELSE
TEENS · YAWL · NEON

48

LONG · SKIPS · STEM
ERIE · MANIA · ARMY
WAVELENGTH · NETS
ITE · EAT · HARDEST
SENSOR · LYRIC ·
· USEBY · ALARMS
GRR · DOES · ESTER
ROOFS · DSL · STENO
ASLAN · SOOT · LSD
WHYNOT · AWARE ·
· DROOP · MISHAP
FITTEST · SAN · ORE
ECRU · SHELLGAMES
MEIR · EERIE · RENT
ASOF · DRAMS · BRAS

49

MIENS · SEMI · GONE
EDSULLIVAN · ELEM
DISCREDITBUREAU
IDOL · TELE · SSGTS
· EOS · BAH ·
· DISGUSTOFWIND
ASA · LONERS · ISLA
CAMEO · INE · UNLET
IMAX · BOASTS · IRA
DISCOUNTSHEEP ·
· ERG · ERA ·
AHORA · HALF · TRIG
DISPLAYWITHFIRE
ALOT · OPENSEASON
MOSS · LOSE · STENT

50

ACRES · CHEN · COWS
PAINT · LOLA · INET
PRADA · OPAL · RHEA
· ORIGINALCOPY
SHIRTS · ALLYS
LOOSELYPACKED
OWNER · EERIE ·
GLAD · AMPED · CHIN
· PRESS · ALATE
· DEFINITEMAYBE
ALEAF · PASSED
PLASTICGLASS ·
TALE · CORE · SITAR
EMIL · ELIS · ECARD
DANS · TENT · SSGTS

51

ARTS · ESTAS · BID
MOET · NORTH · PASA
ISAR · GRAVEROBIN
SERENITY · ELATE
· AONE · POLARIS
PICKLEDHERON ·
ROUST · ETC · DIED
OWL · ENDLESS · DAY
DATA · EEL · AMORE
· GLAMOURGULLS
CARROTS · SEES ·
ATSEA · BASSINET
RAVENIMAGE · CURE
ALPS · SIREN · ADIN
YES · PABST · LENT

52

HOPE · SEISM · EGOS
ALTA · HOSEA · YEAH
MISSIONUNIVERSE
MODEM · SOLICIT
· SPAM · RICH
LAM · ANAT · NIACIN
AGE · INURE · ROSA
SAHARADESERTION
ETTU · EATME · FUN
REACTS · DEMS · STY
· TINT · RYES
· DEIFIED · AISLE
RUNOFTHEMILLION
ELIN · CELLS · LSAT
OLDS · HEIST · SINS

53

PEEL · NATL · COATS
ELMO · OLEO · AOLER
ALAW · RENO · RHINO
BILLIARDFABLE ·
OSLIN · SAW · ANAT
· FAKETHEBLAME
BIKE · IMO · EATIN
UNI · MRI · GPA · EGO
FONTS · TMI · UDON
FIGHTSCRAPES ·
SLOE · SOO · SEMIS
· FEARSOFACLOWN
NEPAL · IPAD · ESAI
ILOST · NEVI · SENT
HOPTO · EDEN · SSTS

54

MEME · TIMID · WATT
AXES · RAISE · OMAR
(C)ALCIUMCHLORIDE
EMT · MANE · ILLSAY
· UHNO · SLID
(B)IONICWOMAN · SIS
FRUMPY · SOHELPME
LITE · GIG · AROW
ASITWERE · THRIVE
THE · HAIR(T)(R)(I)(G)(G)(E)(R)
· FEST · RARE
MOTLEY · VASE · FIT
ENVELOPE(C)(H)(E)MISE
ATMS · FORTE · ALEE
NOAH · FLOSS · XMEN

55

GARY · IMAGE · TWIG
OLEO · MINOS · HELP
SEAS · ONTOP · ASKS
EXCHAN(G)(E)GIFTS ·
EATIT · LEA · OAT
· RA(G)(G)EDYANDY
PASTABAR · EBOOK
ATTA · SPORT · EIRE
CARNY · WHISTLES
TRI(G)(G)ERLOCK ·
SIP · ORE · ISAAC
· SCRAMBLEDEGGS
IMHO · SAYIT · WARP
LOOP · EDEMA · UVEA
LOWS · RESET · PEEN

56

ALOOF · ORBS · MPEG
CONDE · SHAH · ORAL
TWEETSTORM · CITE
SESSILE · BOOKMEN
· SOAR · OCEANS
HEATHBLIZZARD ·
INNIES · DIE · OAR
NINES · REP · BANTU
DDE · TAO · DARNED
· BLUEHURRICANE
CHOOSE · TEAL ·
OILCANS · SCIENCE
MEEK · PHOTOFLOOD
FRYE · OISE · FIELD
YOND · PAAR · SALTY

57

```
EZRA  AHAB  CELEB
KEEP  SOFA  IVORY
GREENHORN   VERGE
SOLDO  SOGGINESS
    ONCE  LILT
CHAMPAGNEFLUTE
FIT  CLOG  YAWLS
OPAL  SWAIN  LAIC
SPLIT  IRAS  NSA
 OLFACTORYORGAN
   ETUI  ISLA
REATTEMPT  VIOLS
AUDIO  BRAKEDRUM
PRIMO  ROTE  ESAU
TOTES  EDEN  ROUT
```

58

```
SCAM  SMITE  SEWS
COTY  PEARY  WRAP
OOHS  ALGAE  IOTA
FLEETWOOD  UNDER
FINLAND  EATDIRT
STAFFERS  BALBOA
   FRACAS  ELAN
GABBY  MAC  TREKS
APAR  LANCER
SPRUCE  SOLUBLES
SLOSHES  RETRIAL
TENSE  ANDCHEESE
OPIE  TRAIT  ANTE
VIAL  VAPOR  KELP
EELS  SHANA  SEAS
```

59

```
PSALMS  WAGS  CPR
STRAIT  ACRE  HOE
TATTLE  INACTION
 GENE  TENTACLE
ROAREDAT  DSL
ELLA  SLIME  ODOR
PILLS  CLOUDNINE
EVE  IRONORE  EWE
AIRTRAVEL  IOTAS
TAYE  TEXAS  WARE
  SST  THEBIRDS
FOULPLAY  DENY
ALKALINE  ANGLES
DEE  ANNA  NOTARY
SOS  YGOR  STOWED
```

60

```
NAHS  ROCA  AHEAD
ALEE  ENOS  MECCA
ROADSTERS  APORT
DOREMI  FAST  SEA
OFTRANQUILITY
   RUE  LOVESET
EXCITED  SWEETIE
CRAW      MERE
CANARDS  BATSMEN
EYESHOT  ISH
 BAYSATTHEMOON
ERR  MEMO  ATONCE
LEASE  PAYMASTER
MAKER  ODIE  SHAD
SPEWS  NYPD  YENS
```

61

```
ASIS  SABU  PHASE
SEMICOLON  LINEN
PLUGALONG  AGNES
 ASHTONKUTCHER
   HEE  LEER
SCORED  PASSERBY
TONER  BUTT  GERE
EKED  MERES  ARIA
RIBS  ORES  GRIDS
NECKBONE  GADGET
   EELS  TON
 WOLFATTHEDOOR
CANTO  EYESHADOW
ACTOR  INTUITIVE
BOONE  NEAP  HEED
```

62

```
FAWN  RABID  SCAR
ALOE  ARARA  LACE
HERMITCRAB  ETCH
DEMENTO  CIERA
 SMASHANDGRAB
ACTION  AWASH
FLOSS  EBAN  TSAR
RAM  TAXICAB  TIE
OWES  GETS  ACIDS
 UHURU  ARARAT
CONCRETESLAB
IROCS  UPCLOSE
DATE  SHISHKEBAB
ETES  IONIA  TOMB
REDS  RENES  VEES
```

63

```
BOWE  SHASTA  RET
AKIN  PASTES  EVE
CENTRALPARK  VEX
HYDRA  AIRS  GERM
 DOUBLEREVERSE
HOOPLA    INBOX
DEWY  SAFEBET
LON  LAIDLOW  FAY
  VILLAIN  FUSE
ATEIT  EGRESS
GENDERNEUTRAL
ALDA  ITEM  ATLAS
SLO  SCENICDRIVE
SOW  CASINO  ONIT
INS  INTENT  WEDS
```

64

```
SODA  INSP  PAGAN
AMAN  TETE  ELOPE
KICKBOXER  ABASE
STALE  TAILGATED
   ESC  ROAR
RAP  TRENDSETTER
AMID  AWS  VERONA
DINETTE  GENOMES
ANGLEE  TAG  TEMP
RESEARCHLAB  SYS
   PELE  SAC
PIAZADORA  SHAKE
HOVER  ROCKHOUND
INERT  OCHO  PRIG
LEROY  XKES  SATE
```

65

```
FETA  STET  PRIMP
OPAL  URGE  REPAY
SETDESIGN  ETAIL
SEEALSO  SATIDLE
ESS  REDEEMER
 BOXENDWRENCH
CAGEY  GUAM  ERA
ALOE  HARPY  DREW
SEA  TAMA  BIDEN
TELLYSAVALAS
 SPARERIB  SRI
LUDDITE  ABETTOR
EDITS  TUBESTEAK
DONAT  TALL  ONME
SNOBS  ORES  PTSD
```

66

```
JOSE  USED  IMPS
UNPC  ETAPE  DIAL
SEAT  DEFICIENCY
TAT  AIRE  ORATE
SCIENTIST  ALICE
ORANGS  ESQ  NAT
 ELAL  CAPE  MGRS
  CONCIERGE
SCAT  ELSE  ADDS
IAL  SEE  RUINED
DRURY  FINANCIER
 IMING  KITT  EKE
CONSCIENCE  APED
FLUE  LEEKS  BERG
LESS  LOWS  ERSE
```

67

```
. A C M E . . B O P . U M P S
C L E A N S H A V E . N O O K
1 A N D 2 M U S I C . T O N E
S S T . E E L S . A I N T I .
. . R E E L I N A N D 1 I N .
G A L A . . . E D G Y . . . .
A G E N D A . G A E L . O E D
S H A K E R A T T L E A N D 2
P A D . P E N S . A R L E N E
. . L U N K . . . . P A A R .
. 1 I N A T T H E H O P S . .
S O A P Y . D I N O . I B N .
A N D S . C H U C K B E R R Y
L I E U . P I C K P O C K E T
T A R P . A P E . Y O S T . .
```

68

```
S T A F F . C L U B . E A S T
R U B L E . M U S E . L I A R
O N A I R . A R M S . A D U E
. . P R O J E C T S P E C S .
V A S S A R . . B O S S E S .
E N T I R E . S C E N E . . .
S T U D I O F L A T S . M S U
P E T E . I A M . D O O R . .
A D Z . H E R M I T C R A B S
. P O L E S . U R A N I A . .
A S H O R E . . N E W A G E .
F L Y I N G S Q U A D S . . .
L I P S . I O U S . I O T A S
A G E E . E D I E . T U R B O
C O R D . S A D D . S T I E S
```

69

```
U S H E R . T O R S . S M U G
S C A L E . H E A T . H E L L
E A G L E . R O M O . A N N A
F M R A D I O . J V S Q U A D
U P I . . S T R E E T . . . .
L I D S . A T I T . R A M P S
. . L A Y L A . V E N U E S .
O R N U R S E . L A W O M A N
S E I S M O . H O L S T . . .
O M A H A . F U S I . E A R S
. . D O U B T S . . R O Y . .
N C S T A T E . P E C L A S S
A R E A . A L E E . L I M I T
V E A L . R E N T . A L I N E
Y E L L . U D O S . M I S S M
```

Puzzle 67
1 = ROCK
2 = ROLL

70

```
Y O R E . T U B A . I M A M S
A X E L . A R A T . N E P A L
L E A P T I N T O . E A S Y A
E N L A I . . S N A P T O I T
. . S N I T . C I T I . . . .
. B L O W D R I E D . E L B A
T O E . A S A N . E S S A Y S
E S T E R . P T A . A T S E A
S O I S E E . O M A N . S A P
T M N T . L O W B I D D E R .
. . I T A L . I R M A . . . .
D I A M O N D S . . A F L A C
U N J A M . P O T E N T I A L
O R A T E . R A N T . E C H O
S E X E S . O P T S . R E S T
```

71

```
M A I L O R D E R B R I D E S
S M O O T H O P E R A T O R S
N I C O T I N E L O Z E N G E
. . . T O N N E . S E R . . .
L I C E . O A S T . . A M M O
S H O R T . . O V A T I O N .
H O R S E S . S L I C E D U P
A P B . N O T A L O T . I S A
P E E R S O U T . L E T R I P
E S T E E M S . . D R O N E .
D O T S . . H A C K . E N G R
. . T O Y . L A N G E . . . .
P I R A T E S T R E A S U R E
S P I R I T U A L L E A D E R
T O O T S I E R O L L P O P S
```

72

```
H O O D . T O A D . R A J A S
A L F A . H A L O . O V O L O
J E F F E R S O N . N I H I L
. . . F R E T T E D . A N N A
T A B O R S . . E A R T H E N
H E E D . H E P . S H E A . .
E R N I E . L I T H O . N B R
R I F L E . B O A . M C C O Y
E E R . R H E U M . B R O O D
. A R I A . S E A . A C N E .
G E N O E S E . . D O C K E R
A L K Y . H A Y F O R K . . .
M I L A N . G E O R G E I I I
U T I L E . L A C E . R O O F
T E N S E . E R I S . S U N S
```

73

```
T E S T . D I E T . S T E A L
A R A B . E R A S . P I X I E
F I R S T B A S E . E L I D E
T E A P A R T Y . B A T T E R
. . . H I E . H E R E . . . .
C R I S I S . H E L . D A M E
H U R S T . B A L L . S E X .
A M E R I C A S P A S T I M E
N O N . H I T S . A R D O R .
G R E G . E Z E . S L Y E S T
. . E L S E . D N A . . . .
P U T O U T . D I A M E T E R
I N E R T . S A C R I F I C E
S T A G E . A N T E . G E R E
H O M E R . L E A D . H A U L
```

74

```
A A R O N . R O P E . E M M Y
S C E N E . I H O P . D O U G
T H E T O R N A D O W A S S O
R E F . C O S I . N E T H E R
. . G O M E R P Y L E . . . .
A R S I N E . . R M S . Q B S
D E A L S . S H U S H . U R I
B A D A . H E N . . L A I D .
I D I . A D O R E . P A Y N E
Z E E . N A W . K I O S K S .
. J I M N A B O R S . . . .
A T C A M P . T U N A . V I N
T H E S A M E E G G T W I C E
R E D O . O V A L . E S S E X
A M E N . P A T E . D W E L T
```

75

```
S O R E . C H A R T . R O L L
H A H N . P E T E Y . A L O E
A T I T . O N T A P . M I R V
D E N I S . R I D O F . V E E
E S O T E R I C A . L I E S L
. . L E E K . B L O N D . . .
C O W E R S . J L O . O R A L
U N I . S I D E E Y E . A L I
P O K E . S I T . O R E B E D
. . I N S T A . G L U T . . .
R S P C A . S C R A P H E A P
H I E . P A P U A . T I B I A
Y O D A . C O M T E . C O L T
M U I R . D R I E D . A L E C
E X A M . C A N D Y . L A S H
```

76

```
S T E M S . D A T A . R O I L
A W A I T . O P U S . E C R U
W A R M O N G E R S . S H A M
. . M E R E . . F A S T O N E
S M A . M A K E S I T R A I N
P O R T . T A S . L E A . . .
E L K E . O P T S . P I P I T
A D E L E . P E T . S N A R E
R Y D E R . A V O W . T S A R
. P A C . E L I . S S T S . .
E M P A T H I Z I N G . W E E
D E L T O I D . . K A R O . .
U T A H . C R O S S W O R D S
C A N I . H I L L . K U D O S
E L E C . I S A Y . Y E S E S
```

77

A	F	R	O	S			P	A	R	T	D		T	W	A
I	L	E	N	E		A	M	E	R	A	S	I	A	N	
L	A	M	E	R		S	T	V	I	N	C	E	N	T	
	N	O	S	A	L	T			M	O	U	R	N		
A	N	D		P	A	Y	T	V			M	A	A	M	
D	E	E	M	E	D		R	I	D	I		C	B	S	
E	L	L	A		R	A	T	S	N	A	K	E	S		
		C	A	K	E	W	A	L	K	S					
P	I	N	E	A	P	P	L	E			S	A	D	E	
E	K	E		S	H	O	E		P	I	N	C	E	R	
N	E	W	T		T	R	E	E	S		O	S	S		
	B	E	R	E	T		P	R	O	W	L	S			
M	A	D	E	S	E	N	S	E		B	A	Y	E	R	
O	N	E	S	T	R	I	K	E		A	S	T	R	O	
B	A	N		A	N	A	I	S		R	H	E	T	T	

78

T	O	N	A	L		F	O	G	G		J	A	D	E
E	M	O	T	E		L	I	R	A		A	L	O	T
M	A	N	T	A		A	L	A	S		B	O	L	T
P	H	O	E	N	I	X		P	H	I	B	E	T	A
S	A	S	S	E	D		P	E	E	V	E			
				T	R	Y	T	O		D	A	R	I	N
W	A	D		S	L	E	E	T		N	E	P	A	L
A	R	I	D		S	A	T	E	D		D	O	V	E
R	E	B	E	L		M	I	M	I	C		D	I	N
P	A	S	T	E	S		C	A	C	H	E			
			O	A	T	E	S		T	A	M	A	L	E
F	A	U	X	P	A	S		F	U	M	B	L	E	D
I	N	R	I		S	T	A	R		B	R	I	N	G
L	O	A	F		I	O	T	A		E	U	B	I	E
O	N	L	Y		S	P	A	Y		R	E	I	N	S

79

S	T	A		W	A	G	E	R		D	A	M	U	P
C	A	R		A	D	A	G	E		E	L	I	Z	A
A	L	M	O	N	D	L	O	V	E	A	G	A	I	N
L	E	A	V	E	S			I	S	L	E			
E	N	D	E	D		P	S	S	T		R	A	J	A
S	T	A	R		B	A	L	E	E	N		B	A	Y
			S	A	U	T	E			I	S	E	R	E
	M	E	E	T	T	H	E	B	E	T	E	L	S	
V	I	D	E	O			P	A	S	S	E			
I	C	E		P	A	C	E	R	S		T	R	A	M
Z	E	N	O		F	O	R	K		T	H	E	T	A
			C	H	E	R			W	O	R	S	E	N
C	A	S	H	E	W	S	I	F	Y	O	U	C	A	N
A	G	R	E	E		E	V	E	N	T		U	S	E
B	E	A	R	D		T	E	E	N	S		E	E	R

Puzzle 77
ALMOND crescent
PINEAPPLE upside down cake
CINNAMON roll
SNOW ball
BANANA split

80

O	B	O	E			S	H	O	P		S	I	R	E
R	A	I	N	S		P	U	M	A		K	N	O	X
C	A	N	D	I	D	A	T	E	S		I	D	L	E
A	S	K	S	T	O		U	N	T	I	D	I	E	R
				S	U	B			B	O	A	S	T		
C	O	N	F	I	G	U	R	A	T	I	O	N		
A	G	A	I	N		R	E	B	U	S		C	B	S
E	L	S	E		A	L	E	R	T		B	L	O	T
N	E	T		B	R	A	V	O		T	R	U	L	Y
		U	N	I	M	P	E	A	C	H	A	B	L	E
C	A	R	E	T			D	E	I					
O	U	T	S	T	R	I	P		T	S	T	O	P	S
B	R	I	T		S	L	I	M	E	B	A	L	L	S
R	A	U	L		V	E	N	D		E	L	L	E	N
A	S	M	E		P	S	A	T		C	A	D	S	

81

E	Z	R	A		F	A	N	G	S		C	H	I	C
D	O	O	R		E	N	I	A	C		O	O	O	O
Y	O	U	C	A	N	O	N	M	E		T	U	T	U
S	T	E	A	M		S	E	I	N	E		S	A	N
				R	I	A		E	E	R	I	E	S	T
O	F	M	O	N	T	E	C	R	I	S	T	O		
P	R	O		O	O	N	A			T	O	R	T	E
T	E	N	T		Z	O	N	E	D		O	G	R	E
S	E	E	R	S			A	R	I	A		A	I	L
		Y	O	U	R	B	L	E	S	S	I	N	G	S
N	O	M	I	N	E	E			C	A	N			
A	B	A		S	A	M	O	A		D	A	I	S	Y
S	A	K	E		D	O	W	N	F	O	R	T	H	E
A	M	E	N		T	A	N	N	A		U	T	E	P
L	A	R	D		O	N	S	E	T		T	O	M	S

82

S	C	A	R		H	A	Z	E	S		J	E	R	K
H	A	L	E		E	N	I	A	C		A	D	E	E
I	V	A	N		I	N	T	R	O		L	U	N	G
R	E	S	T	O	R	E	I	N	P	E	A	C	E	
T	A	K	E	N			S	E	E	P	A	G	E	
S	T	A	R	E	D	A	T			G	E	T	A	T
			O	U	T	R	A	N		N	O	D	S	
	M	E	A	N	D	M	Y	G	A	L	O	R	E	
F	U	S	S		S	E	S	A	M	E				
Y	E	C	C	H			T	R	E	N	C	H	E	S
I	N	A	R	U	S	H			D	O	O	N	E	
S	L	I	P	P	E	R	Y	E	L	M	O	R	E	
S	T	A	B		O	N	E	A	L		I	D	O	S
P	E	T	E		C	R	A	W	L		C	O	L	T
A	R	E	S		K	I	L	N	S		S	O	L	O

83

L	A	G	S		S	U	S	H	I		S	P	A	M
A	T	O	P		I	M	E	A	N		T	U	N	A
S	O	L	O	N	G	A	N	D	T	H	A	N	K	S
E	N	D	R	U	N			L	A	R	I	A	T	
R	A	I	T	T		C	C	S		U	S	E	R	S
	L	E	S	S		A	H	A		T	Y	R	A	
			P	O	R	P	O	I	S	E	S			
A	L	M	A		Y	O	U	T	H		T	O	M	E
H	O	A	G	I	E	S		H	O	W	E	V	E	R
A	S	N	E	R				O	M	E	N	S		
B	E	T		M	A	B		W	Y	O		R	T	E
	F	O	R	A	L	L	T	H	E	F	I	S	H	
F	A	M	E		P	O	R	E	S		D	O	O	R
A	C	A	I		H	O	Y	L	E		L	U	L	U
B	E	N	D		A	D	A	M	S		E	L	S	E

84

J	E	D	I		J	A	W	S		Q	U	A	L	M
I	R	A	Q		O	R	A	L		U	N	T	I	E
M	I	S	T		E	T	T	U		A	C	R	E	S
	C	H	E	M	I	S	T	R	Y	C	L	A	S	S
				S	A	S			P	E	K	E		
M	I	S	T	R	U	S	T		A	S	S	E	S	S
A	R	M		I	Z	A	A	K			A	M	M	O
J	E	A	L	O	U	S	P	A	R	A	M	O	U	R
O	N	L	Y			H	E	T	U	P		T	R	E
R	E	L	I	S	H		D	E	B	R	I	E	F	S
			N	C	A	A			N	O	D			
I	V	E	G	O	T	M	Y	I	O	N	Y	O	U	
H	E	L	L	O		P	E	N	S		L	U	N	A
A	E	S	O	P		L	A	T	E		L	C	D	S
D	R	A	W	S		E	R	O	S		S	H	O	P

85

B	O	R	G		F	L	I	P	S		M	B	A	S
A	R	A	L		R	E	N	E	E		O	A	T	H
R	I	T	A		E	A	G	E	R		O	B	E	Y
D	O	E	S	S	H	E	H	A	V	E	A	N	Y	
O	L	D	S	A	W			E	N	N	O	B	L	E
T	E	X		V	I	C	I		A	D	R	O	I	T
		D	E	L	A	N	O			B	O	N	A	
	S	K	I	L	L	S	A	S	A	M	I	M	E	
L	O	A	M			E	L	L	I	O	T			
E	U	R	E	K	A		L	O	R	N		L	A	B
O	P	E	N	E	R	S		S	T	R	I	D	E	
	N	O	N	E	T	O	S	P	E	A	K	O	F	
S	H	I	V		T	E	P	E	E		N	E	R	O
H	O	N	E		H	A	I	L	E		U	S	E	R
H	E	A	L		A	D	E	A	D		P	O	S	E

86

I	R	A	N		S	P	A	R	E		S	P	I	T
M	I	L	I	T	I	A	M	E	N		O	H	N	O
P	A	L	B	A	T	R	O	S	S		B	O	N	O
E	T	O		S	S	E		I	L	L		T	E	N
L	A	Y	I	T	O	N		S	A	I	L	O	R	
			D	E	U	T		T	V	T	A	B	L	E
B	R	E	A	S	T	S		S	E	E	T	O	I	T
R	E	G										M	F	A
A	P	O	S	T	L	E		A	E	R	O	B	E	S
S	U	S	T	A	I	N		C	U	E	S			
	D	U	P	O	N	T		O	N	G	U	A	R	D
F	I	R		S	D	I		L	U	G		L	O	O
R	A	F	F		S	T	A	Y	C	A	T	I	O	N
I	T	E	R		A	L	L	T	H	E	S	A	M	E
Z	E	R	O		Y	E	S	E	S		E	R	S	E

87

```
VICTIMS  SALLIES
IDAHOAN  CHOOSES
VERANDA  OEUVRES
EASTERPARADE
    EBBED RIGS
EPOCH EER ASSET
NATIONAL INLIEU
GLEASON CADENZA
ALLOTS MANEATER
GOLFS CUR SPORT
EROO AANDE
  REFRIGERATOR
MAGNATE ALAMODE
OPPOSES METERED
DRAWERS ERASERS
```

88

```
FRAT COLA PLAZA
ROME ENOS OILER
ODOR LENS SPENT
NEUROLOGISTS
DOREMIFASOW STA
   OSU TRACTOR
TEAPOTS STREAMS
IAGO      OREO
STEREOS PHASEIN
HINTSAT YAM
ANT CHAIRMANMAO
 YOURWILDOATS
ASTOR MATE TUSK
SKIRT ASIT IDEA
KINKS PACS NEAR
```

89

```
NITTI SHAMELESS
EGRET CAMISOLES
VOILA ANASTASIA
 ROLLINGSTONES
   MIN   SEN
INSECRET DISMAY
DOOM EDYS ALONE
ERNO DEPOT EONS
STARR NONO EDIE
THREED SYNOPSES
   GRE    ITT
 SATIESFACTION
TABULATOR AGLOW
AMENDMENT WHERE
NETASSETS ATOMS
```

90

```
RPMS TILE AMMOS
ARIA OLAY CORNY
PENNYWISE AUDEN
THESINAI   NEMO
OER NICKELODEON
RAVAGE  RUNSDRY
STAN REACT SEM
  DIMENSION
MCA NOFEE ADAM
COMPILE SINISE
QUARTERBACK SPA
URSI IVEEATEN
EASED COINAWORD
EGEST STAT ERSE
NESTS IANS STER
```

91

```
ARCO GRIPS AMPS
SOAP RATIO DERN
HIPPOINTER OGEE
 ROAD  TERRACE
GUEST LAYRUBBER
ASSESSED BSIDE
BEER PASSEL TED
  STUDPOKER
GAM ONSALE EBBS
ALAIN CADILLAC
BIGDIPPER DEATH
RAILCAR SEAN
ISLE NOSYPARKER
EELS ENTER NERO
LSAT LENNY STAT
```

92

```
ALSO RATS FAKER
RUED EXIT ALINE
INDEWTIME SITON
EGG HIS FATTEST
SEESIN AFRO
 PRUSSIANBLEW
SAFE ERA PEYOTE
LURES ITA SLANT
ORACLE EBB AMAS
WITHOUTACLEW
  TRIM ALSACE
APRICOT ETA COG
RIATA HEWANDCRY
ANGER EVEN TRAP
BEAMS DART SALT
```

93

```
ROSE HORAS MASS
ABLE ELUDE ERIC
DEALORDEAL LIZA
ASS VEE GLADDEN
REHEAT SIEG
 ALISTORALIST
MBAS CHA STATUE
AERIE ETA EDEMA
STEENS ISM IMOK
CHARDORCHARD
  AMOS TOASTS
INASTEW FRA CIA
CAPE WELLORWELL
OVEN ANION ONEA
NEXT YATES NERD
```

94

```
REDO HASH ANIME
OTIS UNTO SEXES
ANTSINYOURPANTS
DAZING PRE RARE
  FAR  PREYON
BUGINYOUREAR
AGREE KNELT JOG
SLID WAITS CUKE
SYD SAPOR QATAR
 MUDINYOUREYE
SCRAPE   SAT
IRON ILK ILLEST
FOOTINYOURMOUTH
TAMER LONI AREA
STYLE EKES DOWN
```

95

```
WILLA THEM MIST
ICEAX EURO INTO
THERE ASIS LUAU
 GLASSCEILING
ACAI LEI SNITCH
FALSESTEP NOSES
ASTHMA SATON
RHO ACT YEW LAO
  KNEEL EASELS
ILONA DIRTYPOOL
NONETS NIH ONTO
 CASSETTEDECK
ODES ROME AERIE
METE AGAR BUNNY
ERST PANS SPADE
```

96

```
TRAP READE IMAC
HOPE URGES NOGO
EWES NIELS TURN
REMORSE LEARNED
ONESEC SANMATEO
NAN DARC ONAIR
 AURORAS SINS
 BINGEWATCHING
SANK DETROIT
PSALM CART ANA
RESEARCH EAGLES
ICEDTEA OCTOPUS
TONE ARENA FIRE
EASE COLOR ANON
STEP TBIRD RENT
```

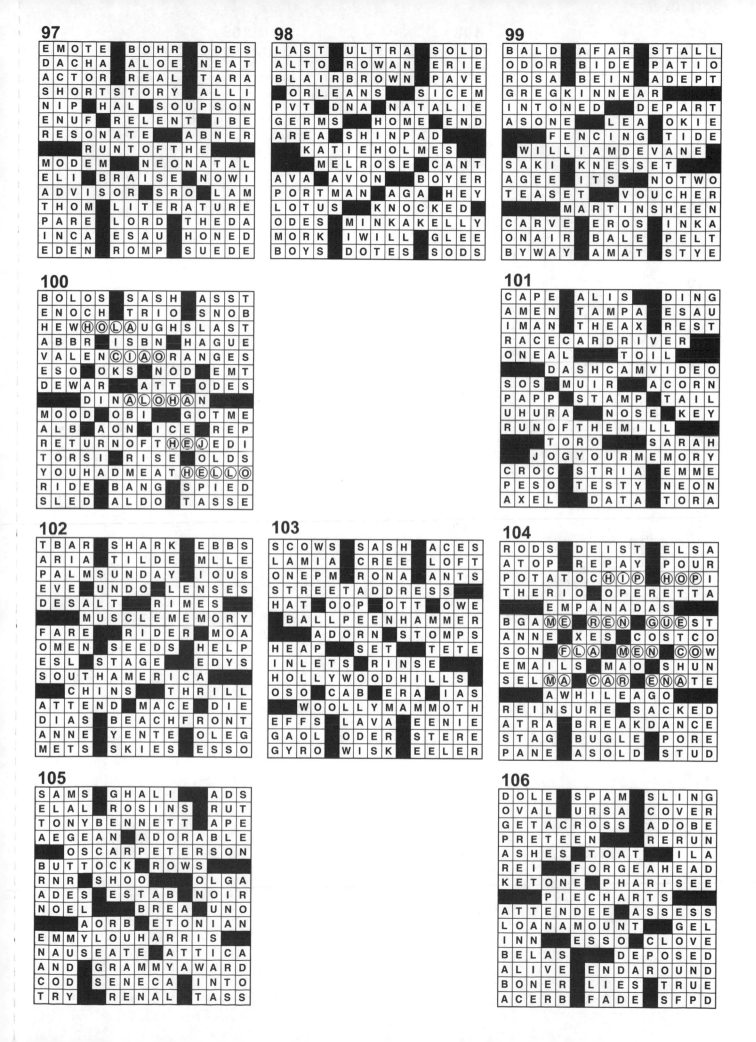

97

E	M	O	T	E		B	O	H	R		O	D	E	S
D	A	C	H	A		A	L	O	E		N	E	A	T
A	C	T	O	R		R	E	A	L		T	A	R	A
S	H	O	R	T	S	T	O	R	Y		A	L	L	I
N	I	P		H	A	L		S	O	U	P	S	O	N
E	N	U	F		R	E	L	E	N	T		I	B	E
R	E	S	O	N	A	T	E		A	B	N	E	R	
		R	U	N	T	O	F	T	H	E				
M	O	D	E	M		N	E	O	N	A	T	A	L	
E	L	I		B	R	A	I	S	E		N	O	W	I
A	D	V	I	S	O	R		S	R	O		L	A	M
T	H	O	M		L	I	T	E	R	A	T	U	R	E
P	A	R	E		L	O	R	D		T	H	E	D	A
I	N	C	A		E	S	A	U		H	O	N	E	D
E	D	E	N		R	O	M	P		S	U	E	D	E

98

L	A	S	T		U	L	T	R	A		S	O	L	D
A	L	T	O		R	O	W	A	N		E	R	I	E
B	L	A	I	R	B	R	O	W	N		P	A	V	E
	O	R	L	E	A	N	S		S	I	C	E	M	
P	V	T		D	N	A		N	A	T	A	L	I	E
G	E	R	M	S		H	O	M	E		E	N	D	
A	R	E	A		S	H	I	N	P	A	D			
		K	A	T	I	E	H	O	L	M	E	S		
			M	E	L	R	O	S	E		C	A	N	T
A	V	A		A	V	O	N		B	O	Y	E	R	
P	O	R	T	M	A	N		A	G	A		H	E	Y
L	O	T	U	S		K	N	O	C	K	E	D		
O	D	E	S		M	I	N	K	A	K	E	L	L	Y
M	O	R	K		I	W	I	L	L		G	L	E	E
B	O	Y	S		D	O	T	E	S		S	O	D	S

99

B	A	L	D		A	F	A	R		S	T	A	L	L
O	D	O	R		B	I	D	E		P	A	T	I	O
R	O	S	A		B	E	I	N		A	D	E	P	T
G	R	E	G	K	I	N	N	E	A	R				
I	N	T	O	N	E	D		D	E	P	A	R	T	
A	S	O	N	E		L	E	A		O	K	I	E	
		F	E	N	C	I	N	G		T	I	D	E	
	W	I	L	L	I	A	M	D	E	V	A	N	E	
S	A	K	I		K	N	E	S	S	E	T			
A	G	E	E		I	T	S		N	O	T	W	O	
T	E	A	S	E	T		V	O	U	C	H	E	R	
		M	A	R	T	I	N	S	H	E	E	N		
C	A	R	V	E		E	R	O	S		I	N	K	A
O	N	A	I	R		B	A	L	E		P	E	L	T
B	Y	W	A	Y		A	M	A	T		S	T	Y	E

100

B	O	L	O	S		S	A	S	H		A	S	S	T
E	N	O	C	H		T	R	I	O		S	N	O	B
H	E	W	H	O	L	A	U	G	H	S	L	A	S	T
A	B	B	R		I	S	B	N		H	A	G	U	E
V	A	L	E	N	C	I	A	O	R	A	N	G	E	S
E	S	O		O	K	S		N	O	D		E	M	T
D	E	W	A	R		A	T	T		O	D	E	S	
		D	I	N	A	L	O	H	A	N				
M	O	O	D		O	B	I		G	O	T	M	E	
A	L	B		A	O	N		I	C	E		R	E	P
R	E	T	U	R	N	O	F	T	H	E	J	E	D	I
T	O	R	S	I		R	I	S	E		O	L	D	S
Y	O	U	H	A	D	M	E	A	T	H	E	L	L	O
R	I	D	E		B	A	N	G		S	P	I	E	D
S	L	E	D		A	L	D	O		T	A	S	S	E

101

C	A	P	E		A	L	I	S		D	I	N	G
A	M	E	N		T	A	M	P	A		E	S	A	U
I	M	A	N		T	H	E	A	X		R	E	S	T
R	A	C	E	C	A	R	D	R	I	V	E	R		
O	N	E	A	L				T	O	I	L			
			D	A	S	H	C	A	M	V	I	D	E	O
S	O	S		M	U	I	R		A	C	O	R	N	
P	A	P	P		S	T	A	M	P		T	A	I	L
U	H	U	R	A		N	O	S	E		K	E	Y	
R	U	N	O	F	T	H	E	M	I	L	L			
			T	O	R	O			S	A	R	A	H	
		J	O	G	Y	O	U	R	M	E	M	O	R	Y
C	R	O	C		S	T	R	I	A		E	M	M	E
P	E	S	O		T	E	S	T	Y		N	E	O	N
A	X	E	L		D	A	T	A		T	O	R	A	

102

T	B	A	R		S	H	A	R	K		E	B	B	S
A	R	I	A		T	I	L	D	E		M	L	L	E
P	A	L	M	S	U	N	D	A	Y		I	O	U	S
E	V	E		U	N	D	O		L	E	N	S	E	S
D	E	S	A	L	T		R	I	M	E	S			
		M	U	S	C	L	E	M	E	M	O	R	Y	
F	A	R	E		R	I	D	E	R		M	O	A	
O	M	E	N		S	E	E	D	S		H	E	L	P
E	S	L		S	T	A	G	E		E	D	Y	S	
S	O	U	T	H	A	M	E	R	I	C	A			
	C	H	I	N	S		T	H	R	I	L	L		
A	T	T	E	N	D		M	A	C	E		D	I	E
D	I	A	S		B	E	A	C	H	F	R	O	N	T
A	N	N	E		Y	E	N	T	E		O	L	E	G
M	E	T	S		S	K	I	E	S		E	S	S	O

103

S	C	O	W	S		S	A	S	H		A	C	E	S
L	A	M	I	A		C	R	E	E		L	O	F	T
O	N	E	P	M		R	O	N	A		A	N	T	S
S	T	R	E	E	T	A	D	D	R	E	S	S		
H	A	T		O	O	P		O	T	T		O	W	E
	B	A	L	L	P	E	E	N	H	A	M	M	E	R
		A	D	O	R	N		S	T	O	M	P	S	
H	E	A	P		S	E	T		T	E	T	E		
I	N	L	E	T	S		R	I	N	S	E			
H	O	L	L	Y	W	O	O	D	H	I	L	L	S	
O	S	O		C	A	B		E	R	A		I	A	S
	W	O	O	L	L	Y	M	A	M	M	O	T	H	
E	F	F	S		L	A	V	A		E	E	N	I	E
G	A	O	L		O	D	E	R		S	T	E	R	E
G	Y	R	O		W	I	S	K		E	E	L	E	R

104

R	O	D	S		D	E	I	S	T		E	L	S	A
A	T	O	P		R	E	P	A	Y		P	O	U	R
P	O	T	A	T	O	C	H	I	P		H	O	P	I
T	H	E	R	I	O		O	P	E	R	E	T	T	A
			E	M	P	A	N	A	D	A	S			
B	G	A	M	E		R	E	N		G	U	E	S	T
A	N	N	E		X	E	S		C	O	S	T	C	O
S	O	N		F	L	A		M	E	N		C	O	W
E	M	A	I	L	S		M	A	O		S	H	U	N
S	E	L	M	A		C	A	R		E	N	A	T	E
			A	W	H	I	L	E	A	G	O			
R	E	I	N	S	U	R	E		S	A	C	K	E	D
A	T	R	A		B	R	E	A	K	D	A	N	C	E
S	T	A	G		B	U	G	L	E		P	O	R	E
P	A	N	E		A	S	O	L	D		S	T	U	D

105

S	A	M	S		G	H	A	L	I		A	D	S	
E	L	A	L		R	O	S	I	N	S		R	U	T
T	O	N	Y	B	E	N	N	E	T	T		A	P	E
A	E	G	E	A	N		A	D	O	R	A	B	L	E
		O	S	C	A	R	P	E	T	E	R	S	O	N
B	U	T	T	O	C	K		R	O	W	S			
R	N	R		S	H	O	O		O	L	G	A		
A	D	E	S		E	S	T	A	B		N	O	I	R
N	O	E	L		B	R	E	A		U	N	O		
		A	O	R	B		E	T	O	N	I	A	N	
E	M	M	Y	L	O	U	H	A	R	R	I	S		
N	A	U	S	E	A	T	E		A	T	T	I	C	A
A	N	D		G	R	A	M	M	Y	A	W	A	R	D
C	O	D		S	E	N	E	C	A		I	N	T	O
T	R	Y		R	E	N	A	L		T	A	S	S	

106

D	O	L	E		S	P	A	M		S	L	I	N	G
O	V	A	L		U	R	S	A		C	O	V	E	R
G	E	T	A	C	R	O	S	S		A	D	O	B	E
P	R	E	T	E	E	N		R	E	R	U	N		
A	S	H	E	S		T	O	A	T		I	L	A	
R	E	I		F	O	R	G	E	A	H	E	A	D	
K	E	T	O	N	E		P	H	A	R	I	S	E	E
		P	I	E	C	H	A	R	T	S				
A	T	T	E	N	D	E	E		A	S	S	E	S	S
L	O	A	N	A	M	O	U	N	T		G	E	L	
I	N	N		E	S	S	O		C	L	O	V	E	
B	E	L	A	S		D	E	P	O	S	E	D		
A	L	I	V	E		E	N	D	A	R	O	U	N	D
B	O	N	E	R		L	I	E	S		T	R	U	E
A	C	E	R	B		F	A	D	E		S	F	P	D

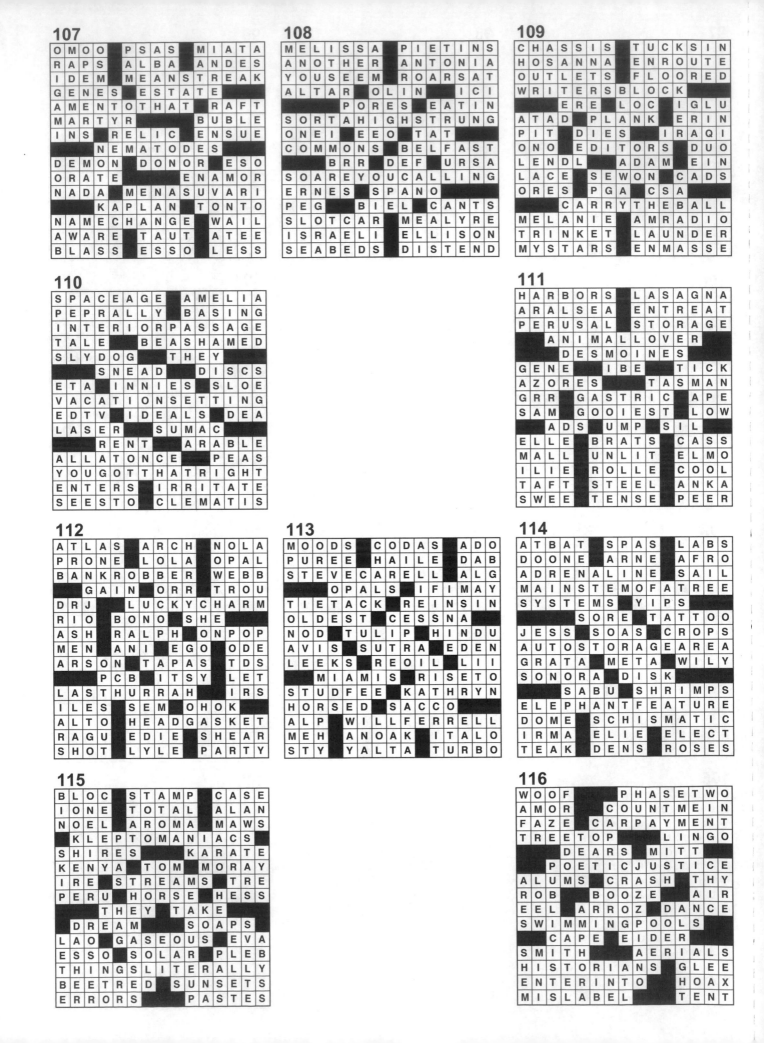

107

OMOO·PSAS·MIATA
RAPS·ALBA·ANDES
IDEM·MEANSTREAK
GENES·ESTATE··
AMENTOTHAT·RAFT
MARTYR··BUBLE
INS·RELIC·ENSUE
··NEMATODES··
DEMON·DONOR·ESO
ORATE··ENAMOR
NADA·MENASUVARI
·KAPLAN·TONTO
NAMECHANGE·WAIL
AWARE·TAUT·ATEE
BLASS·ESSO·LESS

108

MELISSA·PIETINS
ANOTHER·ANTONIA
YOUSEEM·ROARSAT
ALTAR·OLIN·ICI
··PORES·EATIN
SORTAHIGHSTRUNG
ONEI·EEO·TAT
COMMONS·BELFAST
·BRR·DEF·URSA
SOAREYOUCALLING
ERNES·SPANO··
PEG·BIEL·CANTS
SLOTCAR·MEALYRE
ISRAELI·ELLISON
SEABEDS·DISTEND

109

CHASSIS·TUCKSIN
HOSANNA·ENROUTE
OUTLETS·FLOORED
WRITERSBLOCK··
·ERE·LOC·IGLU
ATAD·PLANK·ERIN
PIT·DIES·IRAQI
ONO·EDITORS·DUO
LENDL·ADAM·EIN
LACE·SEWON·CADS
ORES·PGA·CSA·
·CARRYTHEBALL
MELANIE·AMRADIO
TRINKET·LAUNDER
MYSTARS·ENMASSE

110

SPACEAGE·AMELIA
PEPRALLY·BASING
INTERIORPASSAGE
TALE·BEASHAMED
SLYDOG·THEY··
·SNEAD·DISCS
ETA·INNIES·SLOE
VACATIONSETTING
EDTV·IDEALS·DEA
LASER·SUMAC··
·RENT·ARABLE
ALLATONCE·PEAS
YOUGOTTHATRIGHT
ENTERS·IRRITATE
SEESTO·CLEMATIS

111

HARBORS·LASAGNA
ARALSEA·ENTREAT
PERUSAL·STORAGE
·ANIMALLOVER
·DESMOINES··
GENE·IBE·TICK
AZORES·TASMAN
GRR·GASTRIC·APE
SAM·GOOIEST·LOW
·ADS·UMP·SIL·
ELLE·BRATS·CASS
MALL·UNLIT·ELMO
ILIE·ROLLE·COOL
TAFT·STEEL·ANKA
SWEE·TENSE·PEER

112

ATLAS·ARCH·NOLA
PRONE·LOLA·OPAL
BANKROBBER·WEBB
·GAIN·ORR·TROU
DRJ·LUCKYCHARM
RIO·BONO·SHE
ASH·RALPH·ONPOP
MEN·ANI·EGO·ODE
ARSON·TAPAS·TDS
·PCB·ITSY·LET
LASTHURRAH·IRS
ILES·SEM·OHOK
ALTO·HEADGASKET
RAGU·EDIE·SHEAR
SHOT·LYLE·PARTY

113

MOODS·CODAS·ADO
PUREE·HAILE·DAB
STEVECARELL·ALG
·OPALS·IFIMAY
TIETACK·REINSIN
OLDEST·CESSNA·
NOD·TULIP·HINDU
AVIS·SUTRA·EDEN
LEEKS·REOIL·LII
·MIAMIS·RISETO
STUDFEE·KATHRYN
HORSED·SACCO··
ALP·WILLFERRELL
MEH·ANOAK·ITALO
STY·YALTA·TURBO

114

ATBAT·SPAS·LABS
DOONE·ARNE·AFRO
ADRENALINE·SAIL
MAINSTEMOFATREE
SYSTEMS·YIPS··
·SORE·TATTOO
JESS·SOAS·CROPS
AUTOSTORAGEAREA
GRATA·META·WILY
SONORA·DISK··
·SABU·SHRIMPS
ELEPHANTFEATURE
DOME·SCHISMATIC
IRMA·ELIE·ELECT
TEAK·DENS·ROSES

115

BLOC·STAMP·CASE
IONE·TOTAL·ALAN
NOEL·AROMA·MAWS
·KLEPTOMANIACS
SHIRES·KARATE
KENYA·TOM·MORAY
IRE·STREAMS·TRE
PERU·HORSE·HESS
·THEY·TAKE·
·DREAM·SOAPS
LAO·GASEOUS·EVA
ESSO·SOLAR·PLEB
THINGSLITERALLY
BEETRED·SUNSETS
ERRORS·PASTES

116

WOOF·PHASETWO
AMOR·COUNTMEIN
FAZE·CARPAYMENT
TREETOP·LINGO
·DEARS·MITT·
·POETICJUSTICE
ALUMS·CRASH·THY
ROB·BOOZE·AIR
EEL·ARROZ·DANCE
SWIMMINGPOOLS·
·CAPE·EIDER·
SMITH·AERIALS
HISTORIANS·GLEE
ENTERINTO·HOAX
MISLABEL·TENT

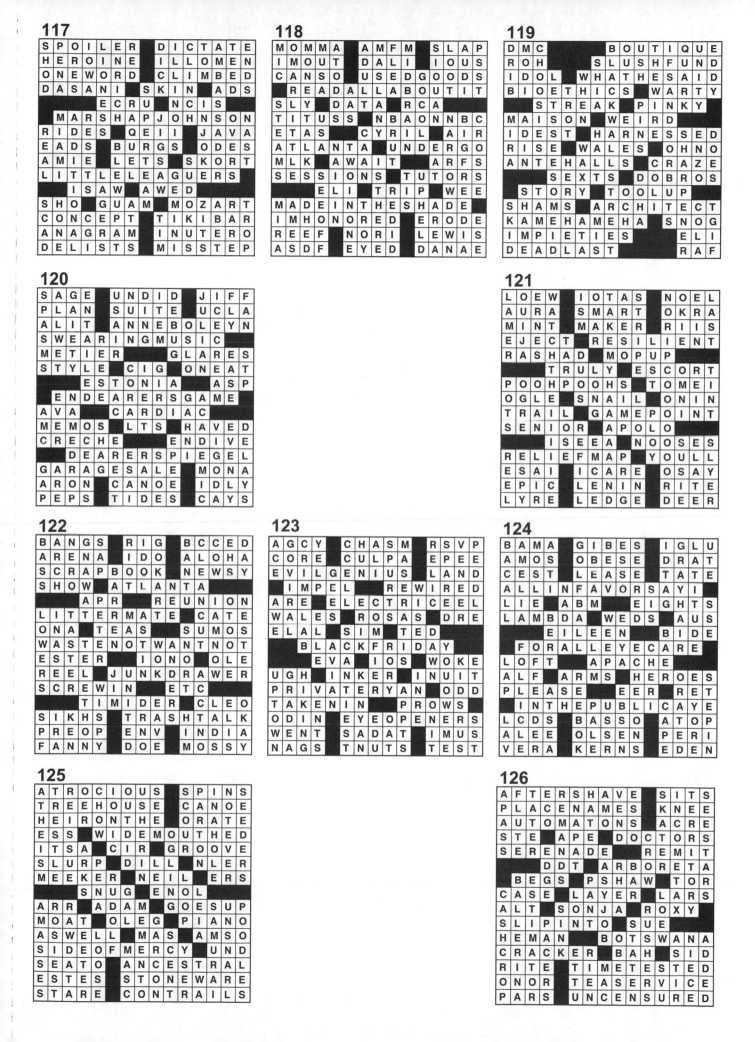

117

S P O I L E R		D I C T A T E
H E R O I N E		I L L O M E N
O N E W O R D		C L I M B E D
D A S A N I	S K I N	A D S
E C R U	N C I S	
M A R S H A P J O H N S O N		
R I D E S	Q E I I	J A V A
E A D S	B U R G S	O D E S
A M I E	L E T S	S K O R T
L I T T L E L E A G U E R S		
I S A W	A W E D	
S H O	G U A M	M O Z A R T
C O N C E P T	T I K I B A R
A N A G R A M	I N U T E R O
D E L I S T S	M I S S T E P

118

M O M M A · A M F M · S L A P
I M O U T · D A L I · I O U S
C A N S O · U S E D G O O D S
R E A D A L L A B O U T I T
S L Y · D A T A · R C A
T I T U S S · N B A O N N B C
E T A S · C Y R I L · A I R
A T L A N T A · U N D E R G O
M L K · A W A I T · A R F S
S E S S I O N S · T U T O R S
E L I · T R I P · W E E
M A D E I N T H E S H A D E
I M H O N O R E D · E R O D E
R E E F · N O R I · L E W I S
A S D F · E Y E D · D A N A E

119

D M C · B O U T I Q U E
R O H · S L U S H F U N D
I D O L · W H A T H E S A I D
B I O E T H I C S · W A R T Y
S T R E A K · P I N K Y
M A I S O N · W E I R D
I D E S T · H A R N E S S E D
R I S E · W A L E S · O H N O
A N T E H A L L S · C R A Z E
S E X T S · D O B R O S
S T O R Y · T O O L U P
S H A M S · A R C H I T E C T
K A M E H A M E H A · S N O G
I M P I E T I E S · E L I
D E A D L A S T · R A F

120

S A G E · U N D I D · J I F F
P L A N · S U I T E · U C L A
A L I T · A N N E B O L E Y N
S W E A R I N G M U S I C
M E T I E R · G L A R E S
S T Y L E · C I G · O N E A T
E S T O N I A · A S P
E N D E A R E R S G A M E
A V A · C A R D I A C
M E M O S · L T S · R A V E D
C R E C H E · E N D I V E
D E A R E R S P I E G E L
G A R A G E S A L E · M O N A
A R O N · C A N O E · I D L Y
P E P S · T I D E S · C A Y S

121

L O E W · I O T A S · N O E L
A U R A · S M A R T · O K R A
M I N T · M A K E R · R I I S
E J E C T · R E S I L I E N T
R A S H A D · M O P U P
T R U L Y · E S C O R T
P O O H P O O H S · T O M E I
O G L E · S N A I L · O N I N
T R A I L · G A M E P O I N T
S E N I O R · A P O L O
I S E E A · N O O S E S
R E L I E F M A P · Y O U L L
E S A I · I C A R E · O S A Y
E P I C · L E N I N · R I T E
L Y R E · L E D G E · D E E R

122

B A N G S · R I G · B C C E D
A R E N A · I D O · A L O H A
S C R A P B O O K · N E W S Y
S H O W · A T L A N T A
A P R · R E U N I O N
L I T T E R M A T E · C A T E
O N A · T E A S · S U M O S
W A S T E N O T W A N T N O T
E S T E R · I O N O · O L E
R E E L · J U N K D R A W E R
S C R E W I N · E T C
T I M I D E R · C L E O
S I K H S · T R A S H T A L K
P R E O P · E N V · I N D I A
F A N N Y · D O E · M O S S Y

123

A G C Y · C H A S M · R S V P
C O R E · C U L P A · E P E E
E V I L G E N I U S · L A N D
I M P E L · R E W I R E D
A R E · E L E C T R I C E E L
W A L E S · R O S A S · D R E
E L A L · S I M · T E D
B L A C K F R I D A Y
E V A · I O S · W O K E
U G H · I N K E R · I N U I T
P R I V A T E R Y A N · O D D
T A K E N I N · P R O W S
O D I N · E Y E O P E N E R S
W E N T · S A D A T · I M U S
N A G S · T N U T S · T E S T

124

B A M A · G I B E S · I G L U
A M O S · O B E S E · D R A T
C E S T · L E A S E · T A T E
A L L I N F A V O R S A Y I
L I E · A B M · E I G H T S
L A M B D A · W E D S · A U S
E I L E E N · B I D E
F O R A L L E Y E C A R E
L O F T · A P A C H E
A L F · A R M S · H E R O E S
P L E A S E · E E R · R E T
I N T H E P U B L I C A Y E
L C D S · B A S S O · A T O P
A L E E · O L S E N · P E R I
V E R A · K E R N S · E D E N

125

A T R O C I O U S · S P I N S
T R E E H O U S E · C A N O E
H E I R O N T H E · O R A T E
E S S · W I D E M O U T H E D
I T S A · C I R · G R O O V E
S L U R P · D I L L · N L E R
M E E K E R · N E I L · E R S
S N U G · E N O L
A R R · A D A M · G O E S U P
M O A T · O L E G · P I A N O
A S W E L L · M A S · A M S O
S I D E O F M E R C Y · U N D
S E A T O · A N C E S T R A L
E S T E S · S T O N E W A R E
S T A R E · C O N T R A I L S

126

A F T E R S H A V E · S I T S
P L A C E N A M E S · K N E E
A U T O M A T O N S · A C R E
S T E · A P E · D O C T O R S
S E R E N A D E · R E M I T
D D T · A R B O R E T A
B E G S · P S H A W · T O R
C A S E · L A Y E R · L A R S
A L T · S O N J A · R O X Y
S L I P I N T O · S U E
H E M A N · B O T S W A N A
C R A C K E R · B A H · S I D
R I T E · T I M E T E S T E D
O N O R · T E A S E R V I C E
P A R S · U N C E N S U R E D

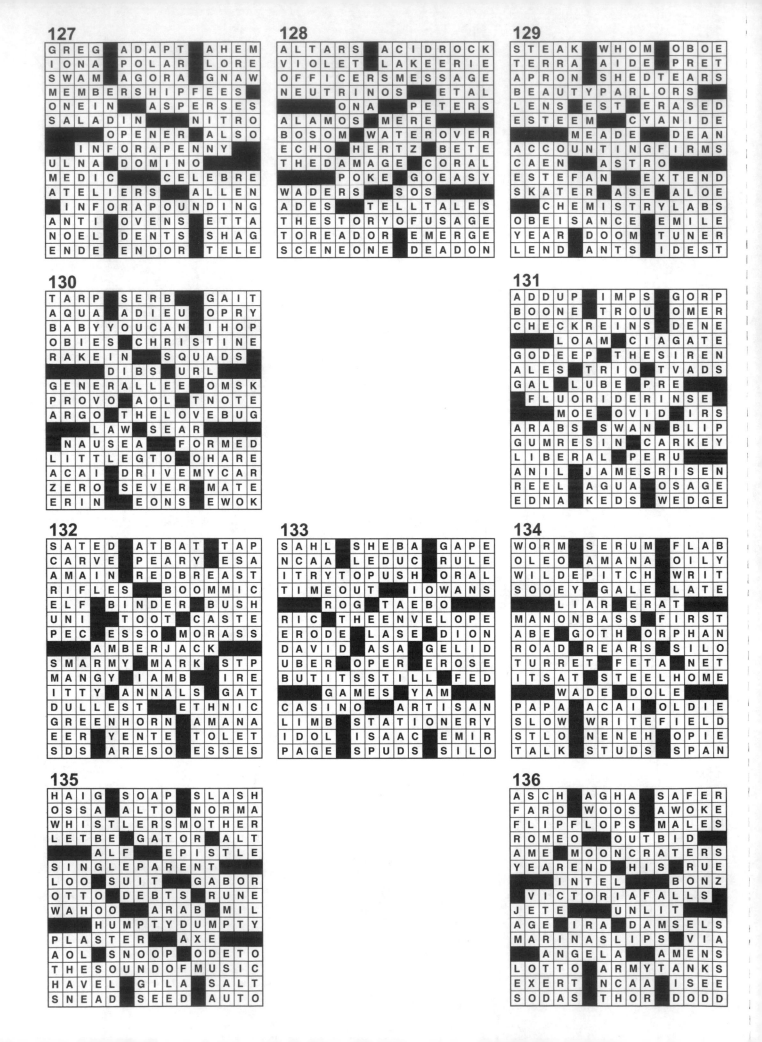

127

GREG · ADAPT · AHEM
IONA · POLAR · LORE
SWAM · AGORA · GNAW
MEMBERSHIPFEES ·
ONEIN · ASPERSES
SALADIN · NITRO
· OPENER · ALSO
· INFORAPENNY ·
ULNA · DOMINO
MEDIC · CELEBRE
ATELIERS · ALLEN
· INFORAPOUNDING
ANTI · OVENS · ETTA
NOEL · DENTS · SHAG
ENDE · ENDOR · TELE

128

ALTARS · ACIDROCK
VIOLET · LAKEERIE
OFFICERSMESSAGE
NEUTRINOS · ETAL
· ONA · PETERS
ALAMOS · MERE
BOSOM · WATEROVER
ECHO · HERTZ · BETE
THEDAMAGE · CORAL
· POKE · GOEASY
WADERS · SOS
ADES · TELLTALES
THESTORYOFUSAGE
TOREADOR · EMERGE
SCENEONE · DEADON

129

STEAK · WHOM · OBOE
TERRA · AIDE · PRET
APRON · SHEDTEARS
BEAUTYPARLORS ·
LENS · EST · ERASED
ESTEEM · CYANIDE
· MEADE · DEAN
ACCOUNTINGFIRMS
CAEN · ASTRO ·
ESTEFAN · EXTEND
SKATER · ASE · ALOE
· CHEMISTRYLABS
OBEISANCE · EMILE
YEAR · DOOM · TUNER
LEND · ANTS · IDEST

130

TARP · SERB · GAIT
AQUA · ADIEU · OPRY
BABYYOUCAN · IHOP
OBIES · CHRISTINE
RAKEIN · SQUADS
· DIBS · URL
GENERALLEE · OMSK
PROVO · AOL · TNOTE
ARGO · THELOVEBUG
· LAW · SEAR
· NAUSEA · FORMED
LITTLEGTO · OHARE
ACAI · DRIVEMYCAR
ZERO · SEVER · MATE
ERIN · EONS · EWOK

131

ADDUP · IMPS · GORP
BOONE · TROU · OMER
CHECKREINS · DENE
· LOAM · CIAGATE
GODEEP · THESIREN
ALES · TRIO · TVADS
GAL · LUBE · PRE
· FLUORIDERINSE
· MOE · OVID · IRS
ARABS · SWAN · BLIP
GUMRESIN · CARKEY
LIBERAL · PERU
ANIL · JAMESRISEN
REEL · AGUA · OSAGE
EDNA · KEDS · WEDGE

132

SATED · ATBAT · TAP
CARVE · PEARY · ESA
AMAIN · REDBREAST
RIFLES · BOOMMIC
ELF · BINDER · BUSH
UNI · TOOT · CASTE
PEC · ESSO · MORASS
· AMBERJACK ·
SMARMY · MARK · STP
MANGY · IAMB · IRE
ITTY · ANNALS · GAT
DULLEST · ETHNIC
GREENHORN · AMANA
EER · YENTE · TOLET
SDS · ARESO · ESSES

133

SAHL · SHEBA · GAPE
NCAA · LEDUC · RULE
ITRYTOPUSH · ORAL
TIMEOUT · IOWANS
· ROG · TAEBO ·
RIC · THEENVELOPE
ERODE · LASE · DION
DAVID · ASA · GELID
UBER · OPER · EROSE
BUTITSSTILL · FED
· GAMES · YAM ·
CASINO · ARTISAN
LIMB · STATIONERY
IDOL · ISAAC · EMIR
PAGE · SPUDS · SILO

134

WORM · SERUM · FLAB
OLEO · AMANA · OILY
WILDEPITCH · WRIT
SOOEY · GALE · LATE
· LIAR · ERAT
MANONBASS · FIRST
ABE · GOTH · ORPHAN
ROAD · REARS · SILO
TURRET · FETA · NET
ITSAT · STEELHOME
· WADE · DOLE ·
PAPA · ACAI · OLDIE
SLOW · WRITEFIELD
STLO · NENEH · OPIE
TALK · STUDS · SPAN

135

HAIG · SOAP · SLASH
OSSA · ALTO · NORMA
WHISTLERSMOTHER
LETBE · GATOR · ALT
· ALF · EPISTLE
SINGLEPARENT
LOO · SUIT · GABOR
OTTO · DEBTS · RUNE
WAHOO · ARAB · MIL
· HUMPTYDUMPTY
PLASTER · AXE
AOL · SNOOP · ODETO
THESOUNDOFMUSIC
HAVEL · GILA · SALT
SNEAD · SEED · AUTO

136

ASCH · AGHA · SAFER
FARO · WOOS · AWOKE
FLIPFLOPS · MALES
ROMEO · OUTBID
AME · MOONCRATERS
YEAREND · HIS · RUE
· INTEL · BONZ
· VICTORIAFALLS
JETE · UNLIT
AGE · IRA · DAMSELS
MARINASLIPS · VIA
· ANGELA · AMENS
LOTTO · ARMYTANKS
EXERT · NCAA · ISEE
SODAS · THOR · DODD

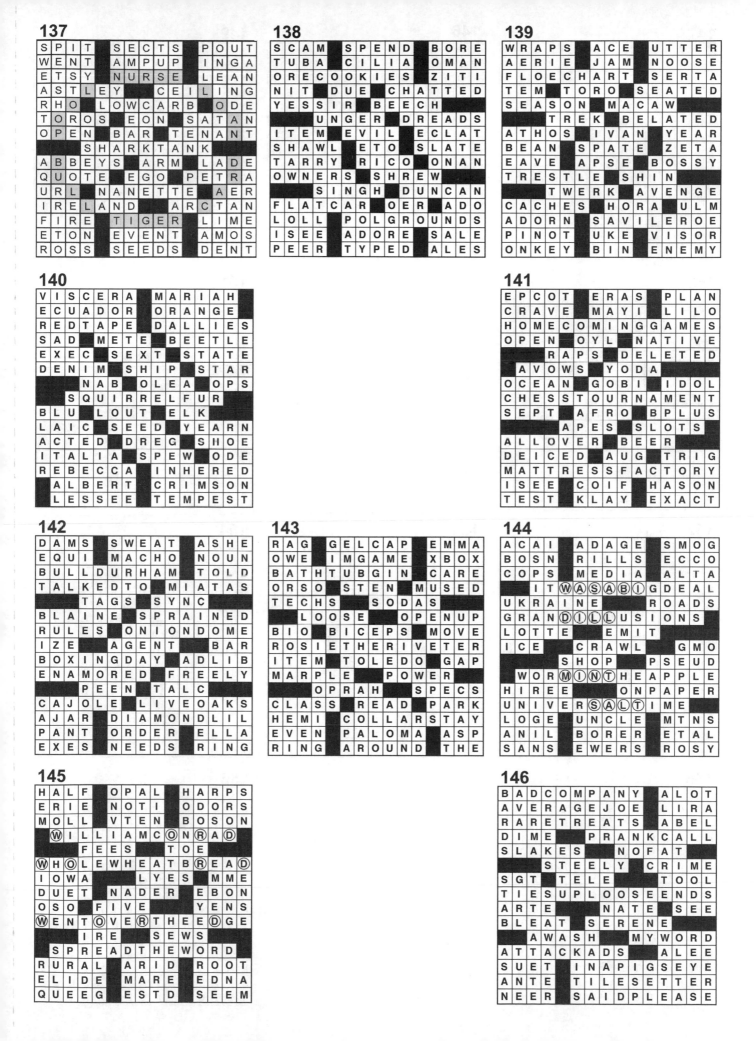

147

F U N N Y H A H A	L E G O
B O N E H E A D E D	A X I S
I N L A L A L A N D	M E L L
E D I T	I P S O F A C T O
R A T H E R	T O N E R
R A M E N	V O C A B
R E D R I V E R	F E D O R A
P L E A D E R	J A R O M I R
T I N P A N	D E C I M A L S
S A T A N	S I T E S
R U S T S	S H A P E D
B A I T S H O P S	N A V E
T O N I	E G O I S T I C A L
U N O S	D I S C O N T E N T
S E N T	S E E S S T A R S

148

A M P S	R E F I L L A B L E
M E L O	A L I C I A K E Y S
E G A D	D O N K E Y C A R T
R A Y	C O P A Y S	N E E
I M S	O N E L	P O S E
C I A R A	F A U N A
A N G E L A B A S S E T T
D I S C O U N T S T O R E
G I A N T T O R T O I S E
G R E T A	I T S O N
P L A N	S I G N	E P T
A I R	S O Y N O G	C H E
V E G E T A R I A N	S T A R
E G O S U R F I N G	L E G O
D E T O X I F I E S	O D I N

149

N F L S T R I K E	A N I M E
A R E T H A N O W	D E C A Y
N O W A Y J O S E	D R A K E
S I B	I N O	M O N E T
S L A V	V I S E	S A O
E G G T A R T	E M O
N O B R A I N E R	M E E T
B E M O A N S	F I V E I S H
A W A Y	D S T U D E N T S
D I G	H O W L E R S
A B A	T I T O	P A R M
B E Z O S	L E I	O E D
I R I N A	D A T A M O D E L
N I N E R	A N O N Y M I C E
G A E L S	P E N O B S C O T

150

O H M S	U P S	B A S H E D
R A T I O N A L	O N T I M E
D I S G U S T O	O N E B I T
I N T E R E S T I M A T E
B A N	S R O	A Y E	C T N
O P A L	L A G	W H E T
O P I A T E	S A P P H I R E
C O N F I N E R Y
S P L E N D I D	C Y M B A L
U R I S	R E Z	E R G O
B O B	L E E	A L P	I O U
P R E T E N D I N I T I S
L A R I A T	A T T A C K L E
O T I O S E	M A R S A L I S
T E A S E R	B C E	N Y E T

151

H A S O N	J E S T	O P A H
B R A V O	U T A H	P I T A
O A T E S	D O N E	E N T R
B I R T H I N G B E R T H
S E U R A T	E R A S E R
S I G H T I N G S I T E
S P I E L	U N D O	Z I P
L A N D	L I N K S	M E M O
E T C	B O N E	C E D E S
W R I T I N G R I G H T
S I D I N G	A Y E A Y E
M E D D L I N G M E D A L
J O N I	O D O R	S A C R E
O N C E	S L O E	E T H E R
E Y E D	T Y K E	S A T Y R

152

S C A R	S O A P S	M B A S
T Y N E	H A M U P	O O P S
A R A B	O H A R A	C O R N
Y A L E H O U S E R O C K
E N O L A	S E E S A W E D
D O G S L E D	R E S O L E
E L U D E	I R K S
T H E Y O K E I S O N M E
I R O N	E R R E D
N O N F A T	E N D G A M E
S N E E R S A T	L A P E L
Y E N T L O N M Y M I N D
C O B B	R O M E O	B E D E
O R E L	A H E A D	I C E S
T R E E	P A S T E	T E S T

153

E P P S	S E G A	D A I R Y
D E E P S I X E S	A T R E E
I N T A T T E R S	M O R A L
T H E R E A R E N O S M A L L
A R T	G E S T E
S N A C K S	K A R L	I S A
L I N U S	T I R E	J O T S
A C N E	P A R T S	I N A N
S K I D	R U B E	S L A T E
H A H	C I T Y	H O L L E R
T I D E S	S E C
O N L Y S M A L L A C T O R S
D I A N A	Q U I T E A F E W
O T T E R	U N D E R M I N E
R E E S E	A G E D	E T O N

154

A C T I	P S S T	A B L E R
B R E N D A L E E	P R O V E
C A S S E R O L E	P O S E D
T H E U R B A N L E G E N D
A C E S	H A U N T
A M U S E D	L E A S E O U T
B O N O S	M A N S E	T A R
B R A N	M A Z D A	C I T Y
O T T	C O D E S	G A M E S
T A T T O O E D	L A M E S T
R E A M S	C O L E
O F S L E E P Y H O L L O W
R I T E S	H O I P O L L O I
A R E N T	A R M E N I A N S
L E D T O	T E E D	A N T E

155

E P I C E N E	S I B E R I A
L E G I R O N	C L E M E N T
S W E A R B Y	R E G I M E S
A S T R O L A B E	S N I P E
D R E	R E O	E T T A
L E W I S	C O N V E N T
E S O	J U S T I N C A S E
E A R S H O T	E N V E N O M
J U S T E N C A S E	C A T
H I R E O U T	C R E S S
C L I P	S R S	A R E
L A P E L	N T H D E G R E E
O N E N O T E	I M A G E R Y
G A R D N E R	S A T I A T E
S I S S I E S	S N E E R E D

156

L O S T	L A T S	Y E L P S
O R E O	A C H E	O B I E S
O B I T	S E A R	K A Z A N
P I K E P O S I T I O N
S T O R E R	A G O	F A D
M E D I A	O N S A L E
A P R	K A N G A R O O R A T
D R E I	C A R	X E N O
M I D N I G H T O I L	S A X
I D U N N O	E N D I T
T E X	D O Z	I N S A N E
V I D E O J O C K I E S
H A V O C	S P I T	T O R S
E X A L T	T A V I	S L O E
M E T E S	A L E C	K I S S

157

```
T O L L   R E P A S T   S P A
A R E A   A L A R M S   T O P
L I B R A R Y B O O K   R O T
L E A G U E   L A C   H A R E
I N N E R   W O R K Z O N E S
S T O R A G E     A N G S T
H E N   O D D   S H E E T S
    H O U S E B A N D
L A T E N T   B A G   P B S
E T A I L     L A B C O A T
T A X S Y S T E M   M A M B A
S N I T   O E R   T O R P O R
S E W   A F T E R S C H O O L
E N A   G A R C I A   O M N I
E D Y   O R A T O R   P S S T
```

158

```
A S S E T   I N S E T   B I D
W A T C H   M A C A W   A T E
E X I L E   P H O T O S H O P
    F A M E   T U B E T O P
G I F T   D U S T P A N
O D D   D I T T Y   S E D A N
T A R   E T N A   E C O N O
C H I N A   E N D   H A U N T
H O N E D   D E L I   B O Y
A S K E R   D I V O T   L Y E
    S I S E N O R   R E S T
I P H O N E S   E G A D
S H A N G R I L A   I D O L S
L E T   E G G E D   Z O W I E
E W E   R E N D S   A N N E X
```

159

```
O R S O   T M A N   M A G E
N E E D   H E A R T   I M I N
W A V E L E N G T H   R E N D
A D E   I N D O   B I N G O
T I N   P R O O F R E A D E R
C L U E S I N   D O R M E R S
H Y P E   B I T E   D Y E
    R A D I O C I T Y
A T P   L U T Z   O O H S
D R O P L E T   A S U S U A L
V A L U E S Y S T E M   T S A
E V E R Y   U T E P   S A C
R A N I   A F T E R S H O C K
B I T S   C O R N S   A L O E
S L A T   E G A D   H E W N
```

160

```
S C A M   A P O D S   M O I
P O S E   R E M A P   F E U D
A N T I   G R E T A   A N T E
    O N L Y I N A M E R I C A
A P U   A L S   W E A R S
S I N G L E H A N D E D L Y
I N D I A   D E E R
N E S T   S T A T S   B A S H
    L O O N   M E N L O
    S O L E P R O P R I E T O R
A P R O N   E A R   L P N
L O N E S T A R S T A T E
A R A S   A G A T E   A R E S
M E T S   N E V E R   R E N O
O S E   S E E R S   E D D Y
```

161

```
G A S   R H O D A   P U P A
U T A   L E E R E R   A R I D
A L L   A L I C E S   L A L A
M A S Q U E R A D E B A L L
  S A U N A S   N A T
    O C S   A N I S E T T E
C L O T H E S R A C K   A H A
H I K E   A M I   O L E S
A A R   O U T O F P O C K E T
T R A M P L E R   I N C
  I T Y   S L E U T H
  C H R I S T M A S B R E A K
S O A R   S I E N N A   A Y E
P O L O   E M O T E R   S E E
A P E R   S E W E R   E S P
```

162

```
U S M C   T H U M B S   T H Y
R H E A   R A N O U T   H O E
D A M N   A B D I C A T I O N
U D O N   C O O   K I O S K S
    R O M E O   P W N S
L A Y L A   B L A H   A D O S
A F F I R M   A W E   Y O R E
T O O   V I E T N A M   W I N
C O A L   C L E   T O N N E S
H T M L   R O X Y   M A P L E
    A N O N   U M A M I
H O B N O B   A P U   A L S O
S H O O T E M U P S   S L A V
I M S   M A R N I E   T O M E
A Y E   E D I T E D   E W E R
```

163

```
T A R P   D D A Y   B O A T S
R E A R   A R C O   E R G O T
E R I E   R A C H A E L R A Y
K I S S I T G O O D B Y E
S E E T O   R H O   E S S
    O N L Y D O S O M U C H
S P F   I T S   P A P E R
P A I N T E D   J U S T O N E
A R R O W   F U R   N E W
D I S H I T O U T B U T
E S T   I R R   S O R T A
  Y O U C A N T T A K E I T
O C E A N S T A T E   E N D O
C H A R D   E C O N   N E A L
T O R S O   D E P T   S E L L
```

164

```
M U S E   S C O T   A C T E D
I N A S C R A P E   B A R D O
C Z E C H S M I X   I M A G E
R I N S O   E N A C T   C A R
O P S   P O L E N U M B E R S
    S S N   R U E
A N T E   C A M E   C R U D E
B A S Q U E S I N T H E S U N
S E O U L   H A T E   T E E D
  I T E   E D S
F I N N I S H L I N E   B A E
O S A   M O T O R   L I L T S
U S O F A   T H A I C L A S P
L U M E T   P A T R O L M E N
S E I Z E   S N E E   S E A U
```

165

```
A B F A B   S E A S   C A S T
D E L L A   A M I E   A L T A
F L O W E R G I R L   S V E N
E L P A S O   T O M A H A W K
E A S Y   A C T U A L S
  S T R E E T S M A R T S
M O M   R E N D   A L E R T
A T E D I R T   A M N E S I A
S T R A D   P L E A   T O Y
S O C K E T W R E N C H
  O N E E Y E D   U S P S
S O F T T A C O   E A R T H A
E L L A   P A P E R T R A I L
N E O N   O R E L   M A R L O
T O W S   T E N S   S H E E N
```

166

```
L A T E   C R A M S   L U L U
A T O M   L I M O U S I N E S
S T U B   E S T I M A T I O N
E R R O R M E S S A G E
R I N S E   C A R A F E
  B A S A L T I C   S A M O A
M U M   D E E M E D   T O R T
I T E R   A P P L E   I N G E
L I N E   D I E T E D   T E N
L O T S A   D I S P I R I T
I N S U L T   S A L M A
  B L U E P E N C I L E D
A D A M A N D E V E   S A N D
N O V I T I A T E S   I D O L
T O A T   S M A R T   N O T E
```

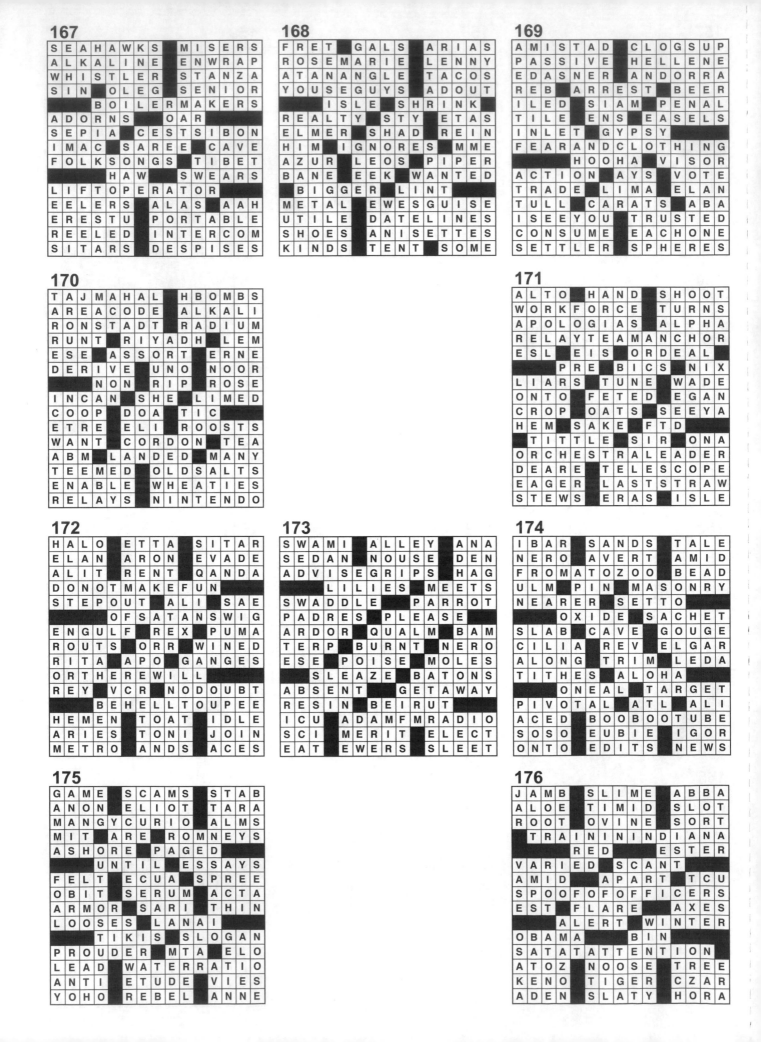

167

```
S E A H A W K S   M I S E R S
A L K A L I N E   E N W R A P
W H I S T L E R   S T A N Z A
S I N   O L E G   S E N I O R
      B O I L E R M A K E R S
A D O R N S       O A R
S E P I A   C E S T S I B O N
I M A C   S A R E E   C A V E
F O L K S O N G S   T I B E T
      H A W       S W E A R S
L I F T O P E R A T O R
E E L E R S   A L A S   A A H
E R E S T U   P O R T A B L E
R E E L E D   I N T E R C O M
S I T A R S   D E S P I S E S
```

168

```
F R E T   G A L S   A R I A S
R O S E M A R I E   L E N N Y
A T A N A N G L E   T A C O S
Y O U S E G U Y S   A D O U T
      I S L E   S H R I N K
R E A L T Y   S T Y   E T A S
E L M E R   S H A D   R E I N
H I M   I G N O R E S   M M E
A Z U R   L E O S   P I P E R
B A N E   E E K   W A N T E D
      B I G G E R   L I N T
M E T A L   E W E S G U I S E
U T I L E   D A T E L I N E S
S H O E S   A N I S E T T E S
K I N D S   T E N T   S O M E
```

169

```
A M I S T A D   C L O G S U P
P A S S I V E   H E L L E N E
E D A S N E R   A N D O R R A
R E B   A R R E S T   B E E R
I L E D   S I A M   P E N A L
T I L E   E N S   E A S E L S
I N L E T   G Y P S Y
F E A R A N D C L O T H I N G
      H O O H A   V I S O R
A C T I O N   A Y S   V O T E
T R A D E   L I M A   E L A N
T U L L   C A R A T S   A B A
I S E E Y O U   T R U S T E D
C O N S U M E   E A C H O N E
S E T T L E R   S P H E R E S
```

170

```
T A J M A H A L   H B O M B S
A R E A C O D E   A L K A L I
R O N S T A D T   R A D I U M
R U N T   R I Y A D H   L E M
E S E   A S S O R T   E R N E
D E R I V E   U N O   N O O R
      N O N   R I P   R O S E
I N C A N   S H E   L I M E D
C O O P   D O A   T I C
E T R E   E L I   R O O S T S
W A N T   C O R D O N   T E A
A B M   L A N D E D   M A N Y
T E E M E D   O L D S A L T S
E N A B L E   W H E A T I E S
R E L A Y S   N I N T E N D O
```

171

```
A L T O   H A N D   S H O O T
W O R K F O R C E   T U R N S
A P O L O G I A S   A L P H A
R E L A Y T E A M A N C H O R
E S L   E I S   O R D E A L
      P R E   B I C S   N I X
L I A R S   T U N E   W A D E
O N T O   F E T E D   E G A N
C R O P   O A T S   S E E Y A
H E M   S A K E   F T D
      T I T T L E   S I R   O N A
O R C H E S T R A L E A D E R
D E A R E   T E L E S C O P E
E A G E R   L A S T S T R A W
S T E W S   E R A S   I S L E
```

172

```
H A L O   E T T A   S I T A R
E L A N   A R O N   E V A D E
A L I T   R E N T   Q A N D A
D O N O T M A K E F U N
S T E P O U T   A L I   S A E
      O F S A T A N S W I G
E N G U L F   R E X   P U M A
R O U T S   O R R   W I N E D
R I T A   A P O   G A N G E S
O R T H E R E W I L L
R E Y   V C R   N O D O U B T
      B E H E L L T O U P E E
H E M E N   T O A T   I D L E
A R I E S   T O N I   J O I N
M E T R O   A N D S   A C E S
```

173

```
S W A M I   A L L E Y   A N A
S E D A N   N O U S E   D E N
A D V I S E G R I P S   H A G
      L I L I E S   M E E T S
S W A D D L E   P A R R O T
P A D R E S   P L E A S E
A R D O R   Q U A L M   B A M
T E R P   B U R N T   N E R O
E S E   P O I S E   M O L E S
      S L E A Z E   B A T O N S
A B S E N T   G E T A W A Y
R E S I N   B E I R U T
I C U   A D A M F M R A D I O
S C I   M E R I T   E L E C T
E A T   E W E R S   S L E E T
```

174

```
I B A R   S A N D S   T A L E
N E R O   A V E R T   A M I D
F R O M A T O Z O O   B E A D
U L M   P I N   M A S O N R Y
N E A R E R   S E T T O
      O X I D E   S A C H E T
S L A B   C A V E   G O U G E
C I L I A   R E V   E L G A R
A L O N G   T R I M   L E D A
T I T H E S   A L O H A
      O N E A L   T A R G E T
P I V O T A L   A T L   A L I
A C E D   B O O B O O T U B E
S O S O   E U B I E   I G O R
O N T O   E D I T S   N E W S
```

175

```
G A M E   S C A M S   S T A B
A N O N   E L I O T   T A R A
M A N G Y C U R I O   A L M S
M I T   A R E   R O M N E Y S
A S H O R E   P A G E D
      U N T I L   E S S A Y S
F E L T   E C U A   S P R E E
O B I T   S E R U M   A C T A
A R M O R   S A R I   T H I N
L O O S E S   L A N A I
      T I K I S   S L O G A N
P R O U D E R   M T A   E L O
L E A D   W A T E R R A T I O
A N T I   E T U D E   V I E S
Y O H O   R E B E L   A N N E
```

176

```
J A M B   S L I M E   A B B A
A L O E   T I M I D   S L O T
R O O T   O V I N E   S O R T
      T R A I N I N I N D I A N A
            R E D   E S T E R
V A R I E D   S C A N T
A M I D   A P A R T   T C U
S P O O F O F O F F I C E R S
E S T   F L A R E   A X E S
      A L E R T   W I N T E R
O B A M A   B I N
S A T A T A T T E N T I O N
A T O Z   N O O S E   T R E E
K E N O   T I G E R   C Z A R
A D E N   S L A T Y   H O R A
```

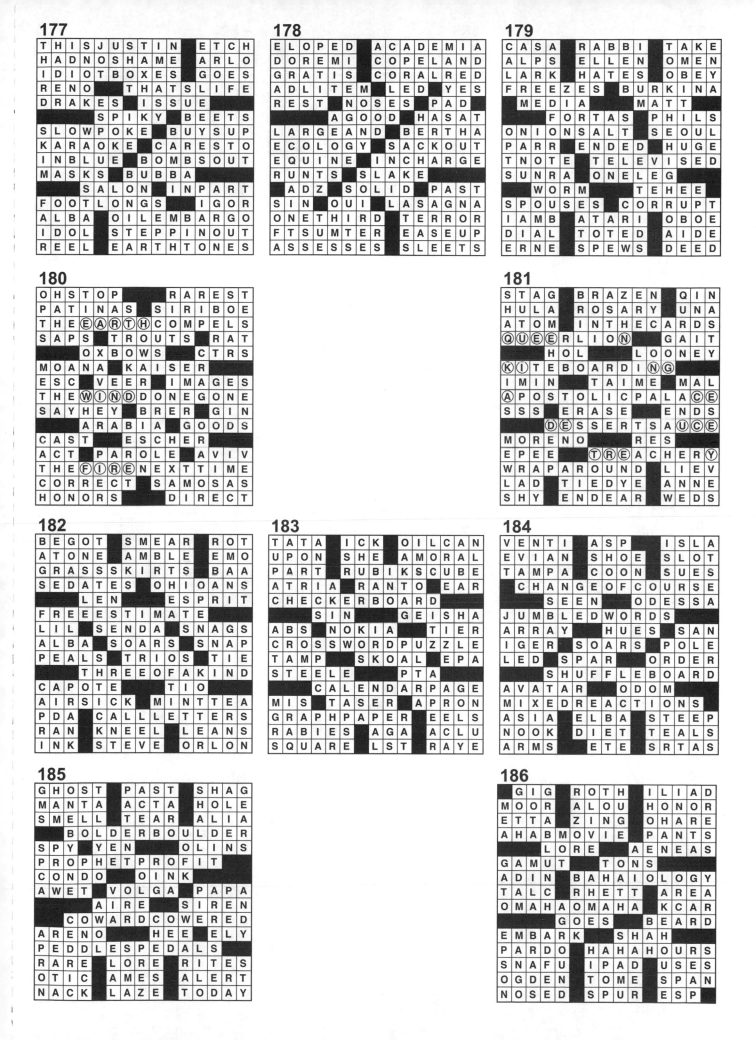

177
THIS JUST IN | ETCH
HAD NO SHAME | ARLO
IDIOT BOXES | GOES
RENO | THATS LIFE
DRAKES | ISSUE
SPIKY | BEETS
SLOWPOKE | BUYSUP
KARAOKE | CARESTO
IN BLUE | BOMBSOUT
MASKS | BUBBA
SALON | IN PART
FOOTLONGS | IGOR
ALBA | OIL EMBARGO
IDOL | STEPPIN OUT
REEL | EARTH TONES

178
ELOPED | ACADEMIA
DO RE MI | COPELAND
GRATIS | CORAL RED
ADLITEM | LED | YES
REST | NOSES | PAD
AGOOD | HASAT
LARGE AND | BERTHA
ECOLOGY | SACK OUT
EQUINE | IN CHARGE
RUNTS | SLAKE
ADZ | SOLID | PAST
SIN | OUI | LASAGNA
ONETHIRD | TERROR
FTSUMTER | EASE UP
ASSESSES | SLEETS

179
CASA | RABBI | TAKE
ALPS | ELLEN | OMEN
LARK | HATES | OBEY
FREEZES | BURKINA
MEDIA | MATT
FORTAS | PHILS
ONION SALT | SEOUL
PARR | ENDED | HUGE
TNOTE | TELEVISED
SUNRA | ONELEG
WORM | TEHEE
SPOUSES | CORRUPT
IAMB | ATARI | OBOE
DIAL | TOTED | AIDE
ERNE | SPEWS | DEED

180
OH STOP | RAREST
PATINAS | SIRIBOE
THE EARTH COMPELS
SAPS | TROUTS | RAT
OXBOWS | CTRS
MOANA | KAISER
ESC | VEER | IMAGES
THE WIND DONE GONE
SAYHEY | BRER | GIN
ARABIA | GOODS
CAST | ESCHER
ACT | PAROLE | AVIV
THE FIRE NEXT TIME
CORRECT | SAMOSAS
HONORS | DIRECT

181
STAG | BRAZEN | QIN
HULA | ROSARY | UNA
ATOM | IN THE CARDS
QUEER LION | GAIT
HOL | LOONEY
KITEBOARDING
IMIN | TAIME | MAL
APOSTOLIC PALACE
SSS | ERASE | ENDS
DESSERT SAUCE
MORENO | RES
EPEE | TREACHERY
WRAPAROUND | LIEV
LAD | TIEDYE | ANNE
SHY | ENDEAR | WEDS

182
BEGOT | SMEAR | ROT
ATONE | AMBLE | EMO
GRASS SKIRTS | BAA
SEDATES | OHIOANS
LEN | ESPRIT
FREE ESTIMATE
LIL | SENDA | SNAGS
ALBA | SOARS | SNAP
PEALS | TRIOS | TIE
THREE OF A KIND
CAPOTE | TIO
AIRSICK | MINT TEA
PDA | CALL LETTERS
RAN | KNEEL | LEANS
INK | STEVE | ORLON

183
TATA | ICK | OILCAN
UPON | SHE | AMORAL
PART | RUBIKS CUBE
ATRIA | RANTO | EAR
CHECKER BOARD
SIN | GEISHA
ABS | NOKIA | TIER
CROSSWORD PUZZLE
TAMP | SKOAL | EPA
STEELE | PTA
CALENDAR PAGE
MIS | TASER | APRON
GRAPH PAPER | EELS
RABIES | AGA | ACLU
SQUARE | LST | RAYE

184
VENTI | ASP | ISLA
EVIAN | SHOE | SLOT
TAMPA | COON | SUES
CHANGE OF COURSE
SEEN | ODESSA
JUMBLED WORDS
ARRAY | HUES | SAN
IGER | SOARS | POLE
LED | SPAR | ORDER
SHUFFLE BOARD
AVATAR | ODOM
MIXED REACTIONS
ASIA | ELBA | STEEP
NOOK | DIET | TEALS
ARMS | ETE | SRTAS

185
GHOST | PAST | SHAG
MANTA | ACTA | HOLE
SMELL | TEAR | ALIA
BOLDER BOULDER
SPY | YEN | OLINS
PROPHET PROFIT
CONDO | OINK
AWET | VOLGA | PAPA
AIRE | SIREN
COWARD COWERED
ARENO | HEE | ELY
PEDDLES PEDALS
RARE | LORE | RITES
OTIC | AMES | ALERT
NACK | LAZE | TODAY

186
GIG | ROTH | ILIAD
MOOR | ALOU | HONOR
ETTA | ZING | OHARE
AHAB MOVIE | PANTS
LORE | AENEAS
GAMUT | TONS
ADIN | BAHAIOLOGY
TALC | RHETT | AREA
OMAHA OMAHA | KCAR
GOES | BEARD
EMBARK | SHAH
PARDO | HAHA HOURS
SNAFU | IPAD | USES
OGDEN | TOME | SPAN
NOSED | SPUR | ESP

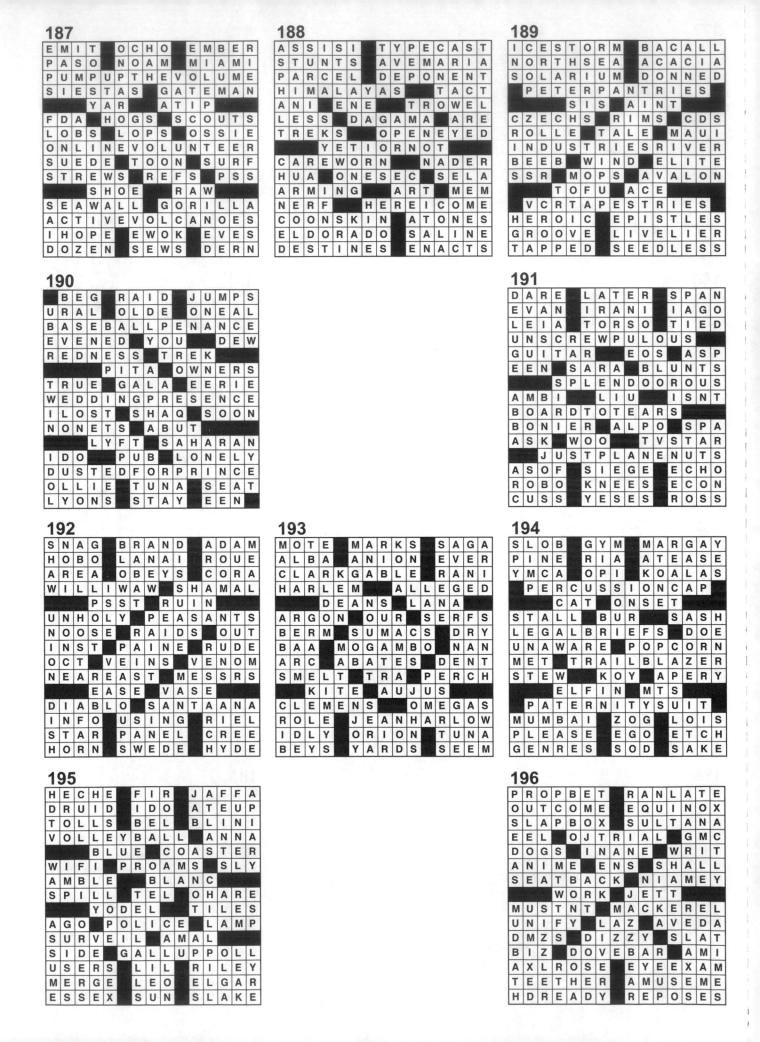

187

```
E M I T _ O C H O _ E M B E R
P A S O _ N O A M _ M I A M I
P U M P U P T H E V O L U M E
S I E S T A S _ G A T E M A N
_ _ Y A R _ A T I P
F D A _ H O G S _ S C O U T S
L O B S _ L O P S _ O S S I E
O N L I N E V O L U N T E E R
S U E D E _ T O O N _ S U R F
S T R E W S _ R E F S _ P S S
_ _ S H O E _ R A W
S E A W A L L _ G O R I L L A
A C T I V E V O L C A N O E S
I H O P E _ E W O K _ E V E S
D O Z E N _ S E W S _ D E R N
```

188

```
A S S I S I _ T Y P E C A S T
S T U N T S _ A V E M A R I A
P A R C E L _ D E P O N E N T
H I M A L A Y A S _ T A C T
A N I _ E N E _ T R O W E L
L E S S _ D A G A M A _ A R E
T R E K S _ O P E N E Y E D
_ Y E T I O R N O T
C A R E W O R N _ N A D E R
H U A _ O N E S E C _ S E L A
A R M I N G _ A R T _ M E M
N E R F _ H E R E I C O M E
C O O N S K I N _ A T O N E S
E L D O R A D O _ S A L I N E
D E S T I N E S _ E N A C T S
```

189

```
I C E S T O R M _ B A C A L L
N O R T H S E A _ A C A C I A
S O L A R I U M _ D O N N E D
_ P E T E R P A N T R I E S _
_ _ S I S _ A I N T _ _
C Z E C H S _ R I M S _ C D S
R O L L E _ T A L E _ M A U I
I N D U S T R I E S R I V E R
B E E B _ W I N D _ E L I T E
S S R _ M O P S _ A V A L O N
_ _ T O F U _ A C E _ _
_ V C R T A P E S T R I E S _
H E R O I C _ E P I S T L E S
G R O O V E _ L I V E L I E R
T A P P E D _ S E E D L E S S
```

190

```
_ B E G _ R A I D _ J U M P S
U R A L _ O L D E _ O N E A L
B A S E B A L L P E N A N C E
E V E N E D _ Y O U _ D E W
R E D N E S S _ T R E K
_ P I T A _ O W N E R S
T R U E _ G A L A _ E E R I E
W E D D I N G P R E S E N C E
I L O S T _ S H A Q _ S O O N
N O N E T S _ A B U T
_ L Y F T _ S A H A R A N
I D O _ P U B _ L O N E L Y
D U S T E D F O R P R I N C E
O L L I E _ T U N A _ S E A T
L Y O N S _ S T A Y _ E E N
```

191

```
D A R E _ L A T E R _ S P A N
E V A N _ I R A N I _ I A G O
L E I A _ T O R S O _ T I E D
U N S C R E W P U L O U S
G U I T A R _ E O S _ A S P
E E N _ S A R A _ B L U N T S
_ S P L E N D O O R O U S
A M B I _ L I U _ I S N T
B O A R D T O T E A R S
B O N I E R _ A L P O _ S P A
A S K _ W O O _ T V S T A R
_ J U S T P L A N E N U T S
A S O F _ S I E G E _ E C H O
R O B O _ K N E E S _ E C O N
C U S S _ Y E S E S _ R O S S
```

192

```
S N A G _ B R A N D _ A D A M
H O B O _ L A N A I _ R O U E
A R E A _ O B E Y S _ C O R A
W I L L I W A W _ S H A M A L
_ P S S T _ R U I N
U N H O L Y _ P E A S A N T S
N O O S E _ R A I D S _ O U T
I N S T _ P A I N E _ R U D E
O C T _ V E I N S _ V E N O M
N E A R E A S T _ M E S S R S
_ E A S E _ V A S E
D I A B L O _ S A N T A A N A
I N F O _ U S I N G _ R I E L
S T A R _ P A N E L _ C R E E
H O R N _ S W E D E _ H Y D E
```

193

```
M O T E _ M A R K S _ S A G A
A L B A _ A N I O N _ E V E R
C L A R K G A B L E _ R A N I
H A R L E M _ A L L E G E D
_ D E A N S _ L A N A
A R G O N _ O U R _ S E R F S
B E R M _ S U M A C S _ D R Y
B A A _ M O G A M B O _ N A N
A R C _ A B A T E S _ D E N T
S M E L T _ T R A _ P E R C H
_ K I T E _ A U J U S
C L E M E N S _ O M E G A S
R O L E _ J E A N H A R L O W
I D L Y _ O R I O N _ T U N A
B E Y S _ Y A R D S _ S E E M
```

194

```
S L O B _ G Y M _ M A R G A Y
P I N E _ R I A _ A T E A S E
Y M C A _ O P I _ K O A L A S
_ P E R C U S S I O N C A P
_ C A T _ O N S E T
S T A L L _ B U R _ S A S H
L E G A L B R I E F S _ D O E
U N A W A R E _ P O P C O R N
M E T _ T R A I L B L A Z E R
S T E W _ K O Y _ A P E R Y
_ E L F I N _ M T S
_ P A T E R N I T Y S U I T
M U M B A I _ Z O G _ L O I S
P L E A S E _ E G O _ E T C H
G E N R E S _ S O D _ S A K E
```

195

```
H E C H E _ F I R _ J A F F A
D R U I D _ I D O _ A T E U P
T O L L S _ B E L _ B L I N I
V O L L E Y B A L L _ A N N A
_ B L U E _ C O A S T E R
W I F I _ P R O A M S _ S L Y
A M B L E _ B L A N C
S P I L L _ T E L _ O H A R E
_ Y O D E L _ T I L E S
A G O _ P O L I C E _ L A M P
S U R V E I L _ A M A L
S I D E _ G A L L U P P O L L
U S E R S _ L I L _ R I L E Y
M E R G E _ L E O _ E L G A R
E S S E X _ S U N _ S L A K E
```

196

```
P R O P B E T _ R A N L A T E
O U T C O M E _ E Q U I N O X
S L A P B O X _ S U L T A N A
E E L _ O J T R I A L _ G M C
D O G S _ I N A N E _ W R I T
A N I M E _ E N S _ S H A L L
S E A T B A C K _ N I A M E Y
_ W O R K _ J E T T _
M U S T N T _ M A C K E R E L
U N I F Y _ L A Z _ A V E D A
D M Z S _ D I Z Z Y _ S L A T
B I Z _ D O V E B A R _ A M I
A X L R O S E _ E Y E E X A M
T E E T H E R _ A M U S E M E
H D R E A D Y _ R E P O S E S
```

197

```
CIABATTA   OLDPRO
ALLUVIUM   NEARER
REDBEANSANDRICE
ONE   NACHOS   SOB
MER  MARROW   MOVE
    PINOAK  TINED
   FIRMLY  SEDERS
   LILREL  STMARY
SELLON   OKAPIS
LAMAR   GMINOR
USSR  SLINKS   SZA
DEC  STUCCO   HEX
GOOGLETRANSLATE
EURAIL  ORIGINAL
STEPPE  NEATNESS
```

198

```
MICROSEISM   UCSD
ANNEMURRAY   PACE
PROCESSING   STAB
LETON   SKI   CARA
EMERITA   REALER
    DIGITALCLOCK
FOBS  IMAC  HENRI
ONS  OFFICIO   ION
OTTER  ONES  DAWG
THUMBWRESTLE
MEDUSA   SOONERS
OREM  MUM  IMEAN
DINE  PLANETARIA
ESTA  UNWAVERING
LEST  MASTERKEYS
```

199

```
PLUMCOT   MAULS
HONORARY  MISHIT
ABINITIO  ASSUME
TENTS   USVSTHEM
  THINCRUST
EKE  SELES  IMPEL
BONY  IOS  NOONE
BADMINTONRACKET
ELECT  BYU  KERB
DADAS  GUESS  ROE
  GUESTHOST
CYBERPET   FLASK
ROADEO  EDITABLE
ALDEAN  DATAPLAN
MOUNT   BASSETT
```

200

```
BATTEDIN  PALATE
OVERDONE  AVALON
RELIANCE  REREAD
KREBS  ARSONISTS
   UNIS  OLGA
PASTED  TREETOPS
INTERSTATES  TAP
ENOS  ELO  PERU
COW  CHAUFFEURED
EYEGLASS  INNIES
   RILE  SEMI
DRAINTRAP  ASSES
RENEGE  SEASHORE
INEVER  INASENSE
POWERS  STRESSED
```

201

```
ACID  PLOWS  JAMS
LANE  RETRO  ERIC
FLATBOTTOM  WINE
ALCOA  SETEYESON
  FOULS  REDALERT
FORREST   ALB
ARN  SORRYTOSAY
STEPS  MEA  AXLES
THREADBARE   ERE
   DIE  ELEANOR
SERENADE  YARDS
WAISTDEEP  CREPE
ETAT  PERIPHERAL
DATA  ARIEL  SECS
ETAL  NEEDY  TREE
```

202

```
BEGAT  SASHA  EMS
EDILE  ASHES  VAT
SEVENDWARFS  ICE
OMERTA  PUN  FLAV
MASTERS  BEZIQUE
   RITT  RAGU
BBS  SNARE  GHENT
BANA  GRIMM  TERA
CHOMP  REBUS  NAP
   WISP  DASH
DOWNIER  REAGENT
ECHO  TIP  URANIA
LEI  MAGICMIRROR
TAT  BRINE  ADOBE
ANE  ADDTO  HANES
```

203

```
ROMP  HOTDOG  SOS
AVER  ABRADE  WHO
SEMI  DEARER  OIL
PROMENADE  SYNOD
  UPTHE  SHED
TESLA  WOWSERS
AQUA  BIKINI  RAW
SUM  MANIKIN  FIE
TAM  ICONIC  OUSE
ELEANOR   SHLEP
  RAIN  ABEAM
MOTHS  AFOGGYDAY
OBI  TAXING  GAME
TOM  ETERNE  OMEN
TEE  RESEED  DENS
```

204

```
MOE  GRASS  THIRD
AWL  IDIOT  RADAR
CNN  FALLIBILITY
ASIS   ALEUT
WINTERGREEN  ACT
STOOLIE  RESCUE
   GANNET  EARL
SPRINGERSPANIEL
ALOE  SNAILS
GETSAT  DEBUNKS
ADE  SUMMERSAULT
  AKBAR   LAIR
FOURSEASONS  NBA
TUTTI  CURIO  CAN
PREEN  ONEND  END
```

205

```
ASTOR  ALLS  DANK
LEONE  RIEN  IRON
SALAD  MESA  ERIE
ONLINEBOOKSTORE
  ROMANTICIZED
CFC  SIN  HEAT
HALBERD  ORRISES
ARIL   AIDA
REPACKS  BLUNDER
  MANE  RUM  ENA
IRRESISTIBLE
REALESTATEAGENT
APSE  HILT  URIAH
TATS  ENOL  TERSE
EYAS  SANE  STEAM
```

206

```
CRAM  RATA  CANON
DEJA  EVES  OBAMA
SEAR  JILT  NIPAT
  FROMOVERAFTER
   OBI   OUI
DOWNACROSSNEAR
IMA  EAR  TELLER
PATIO  END  SLOMO
SHELLS  OAT  NIT
  AREYOUTRYINGTO
   MSN   PTA
  PREPOSITIONME
SAUDI  USES  TAIL
ANTIC  NEXT  EZRA
PESTS  GETS  SEEP
```

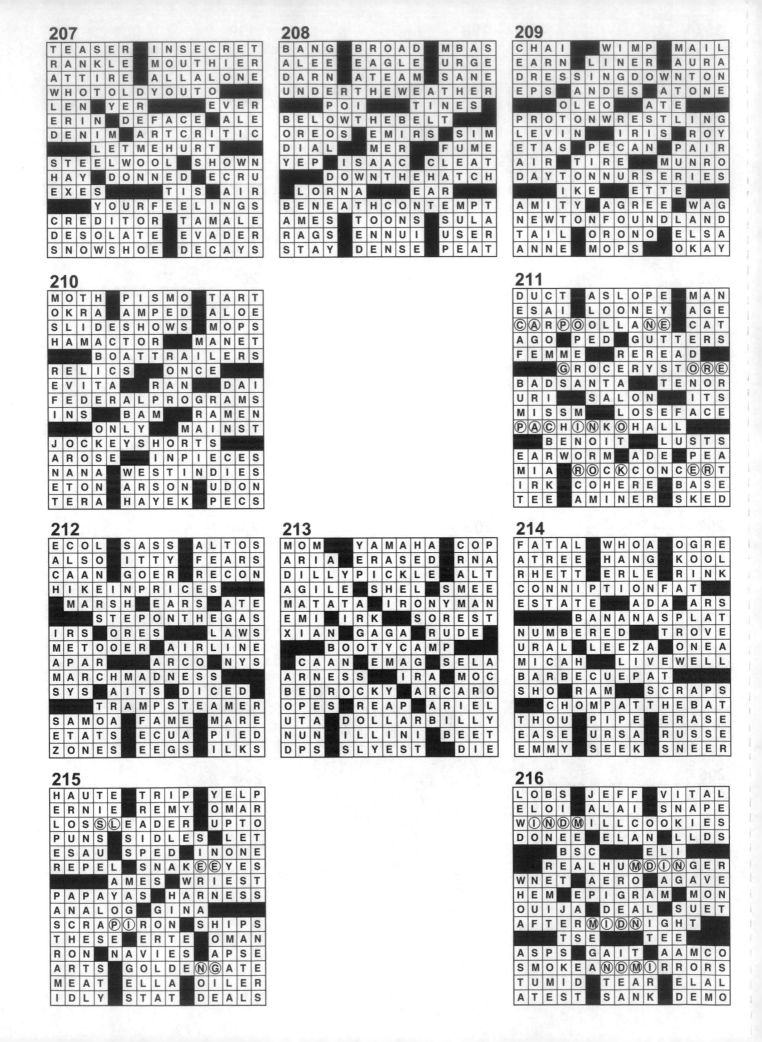

207

```
T E A S E R   I N S E C R E T
R A N K L E   M O U T H I E R
A T T I R E   A L L A L O N E
W H O T O L D Y O U T O
L E N   Y E R       E V E R
E R I N   D E F A C E   A L E
D E N I M   A R T C R I T I C
    L E T M E H U R T
S T E E L W O O L   S H O W N
H A Y   D O N N E D   E C R U
E X E S       T I S   A I R
    Y O U R F E E L I N G S
C R E D I T O R   T A M A L E
D E S O L A T E   E V A D E R
S N O W S H O E   D E C A Y S
```

208

```
B A N G   B R O A D   M B A S
A L E E   E A G L E   U R G E
D A R N   A T E A M   S A N E
U N D E R T H E W E A T H E R
    P O I       T I N E S
B E L O W T H E B E L T
O R E O S   E M I R S   S I M
D I A L   M E R   F U M E
Y E P   I S A A C   C L E A T
    D O W N T H E H A T C H
L O R N A       E A R
B E N E A T H C O N T E M P T
A M E S   T O O N S   S U L A
R A G S   E N N U I   U S E R
S T A Y   D E N S E   P E A T
```

209

```
C H A I   W I M P   M A I L
E A R N   L I N E R   A U R A
D R E S S I N G D O W N T O N
E P S   A N D E S   A T O N E
    O L E O       A T E
P R O T O N W R E S T L I N G
L E V I N   I R I S   R O Y
E T A S   P E C A N   P A I R
A I R   T I R E   M U N R O
D A Y T O N N U R S E R I E S
    I K E       E T T E
A M I T Y   A G R E E   W A G
N E W T O N F O U N D L A N D
T A I L   O R O N O   E L S A
A N N E   M O P S   O K A Y
```

210

```
M O T H   P I S M O   T A R T
O K R A   A M P E D   A L O E
S L I D E S H O W S   M O P S
H A M A C T O R   M A N E T
    B O A T T R A I L E R S
R E L I C S   O N C E
E V I T A   R A N   D A I
F E D E R A L P R O G R A M S
I N S   B A M   R A M E N
    O N L Y   M A I N S T
J O C K E Y S H O R T S
A R O S E   I N P I E C E S
N A N A   W E S T I N D I E S
E T O N   A R S O N   U D O N
T E R A   H A Y E K   P E C S
```

211

```
D U C T   A S L O P E   M A N
E S A I   L O O N E Y   A G E
C A R P O O L L A N E   C A T
A G O   P E D   G U T T E R S
F E M M E   R E R E A D
    G R O C E R Y S T O R E
B A D S A N T A   T E N O R
U R I   S A L O N   I T S
M I S S M   L O S E F A C E
P A C H I N K O H A L L
    B E N O I T   L U S T S
E A R W O R M   A D E   P E A
M I A   R O C K C O N C E R T
I R K   C O H E R E   B A S E
T E E   A M I N E R   S K E D
```

212

```
E C O L   S A S S   A L T O S
A L S O   I T T Y   F E A R S
C A A N   G O E R   R E C O N
H I K E I N P R I C E S
  M A R S H   E A R S   A T E
    S T E P O N T H E G A S
I R S   O R E S   L A W S
M E T O O E R   A I R L I N E
A P A R   A R C O   N Y S
M A R C H M A D N E S S
S Y S   A I T S   D I C E D
    T R A M P S T E A M E R
S A M O A   F A M E   M A R E
E T A T S   E C U A   P I E D
Z O N E S   E E G S   I L K S
```

213

```
M O M   Y A M A H A   C O P
A R I A   E R A S E D   R N A
D I L L Y P I C K L E   A L T
A G I L E   S H E L   S M E E
M A T A T A   I R O N Y M A N
E M I   I R K   S O R E S T
X I A N   G A G A   R U D E
    B O O T Y C A M P
C A A N   E M A G   S E L A
A R N E S S   I R A   M O C
B E D R O C K Y   A R C A R O
O P E S   R E A P   A R I E L
U T A   D O L L A R B I L L Y
N U N   I L L I N I   B E E T
D P S   S L Y E S T   D I E
```

214

```
F A T A L   W H O A   O G R E
A T R E E   H A N G   K O O L
R H E T T   E R L E   R I N K
C O N N I P T I O N F A T
E S T A T E   A D A   A R S
    B A N A N A S P L A T
N U M B E R E D   T R O V E
U R A L   L E E Z A   O N E A
M I C A H   L I V E W E L L
B A R B E C U E P A T
S H O   R A M   S C R A P S
    C H O M P A T T H E B A T
T H O U   P I P E   E R A S E
E A S E   U R S A   R U S S E
E M M Y   S E E K   S N E E R
```

215

```
H A U T E   T R I P   Y E L P
E R N I E   R E M Y   O M A R
L O S S L E A D E R   U P T O
P U N S   S I D L E S   L E T
E S A U   S P E D   I N O N E
R E P E L   S N A K E E Y E S
    A M E S   W R I E S T
P A P A Y A S   H A R N E S S
A N A L O G   G I N A
S C R A P I R O N   S H I P S
T H E S E   E R T E   O M A N
R O N   N A V I E S   A P S E
A R T S   G O L D E N G A T E
M E A T   E L L A   O I L E R
I D L Y   S T A T   D E A L S
```

216

```
L O B S   J E F F   V I T A L
E L O I   A L A I   S N A P E
W I N D M I L L C O O K I E S
D O N E E   E L A N   L L D S
    B S C       E L I
    R E A L H U M D I N G E R
W N E T   A E R O   A G A V E
H E M   E P I G R A M   M O N
O U I J A   D E A L   S U E T
A F T E R M I D N I G H T
    T S E       T E E
A S P S   G A I T   A A M C O
S M O K E A N D M I R R O R S
T U M I D   T E A R   E L A L
A T E S T   S A N K   D E M O
```

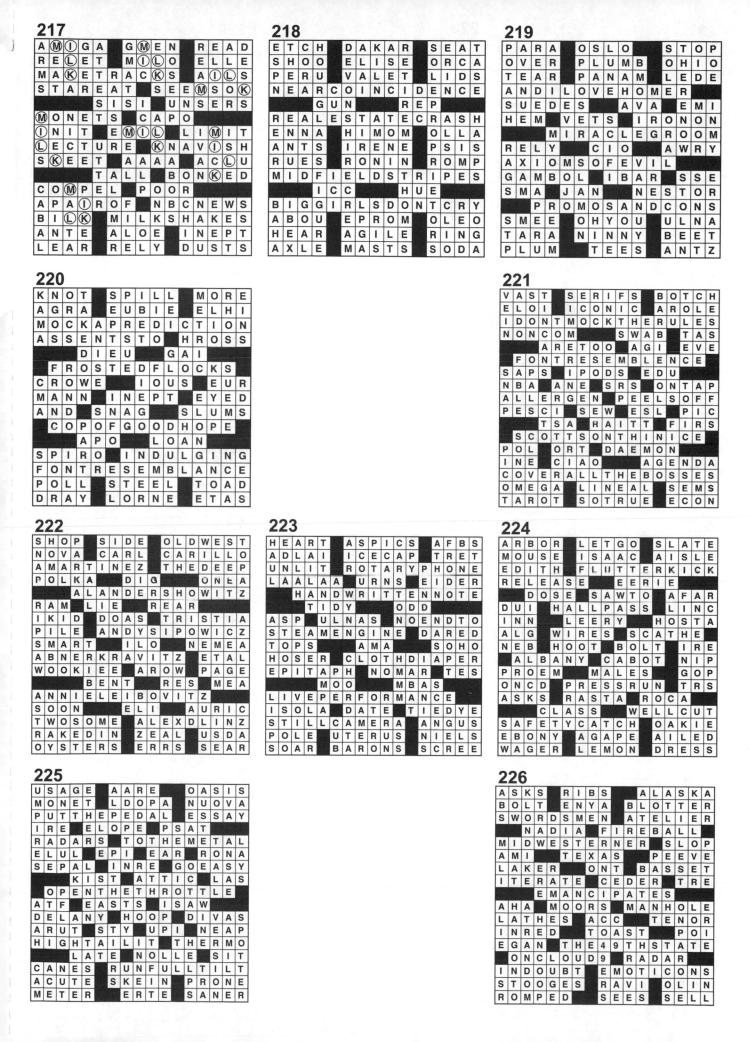

217
AMIGA · GMEN · READ
RELET · MILO · ELLE
MAKETRACKS · AILS
STAREAT · SEEMSOK
· · SISI · UNSERS
MONETS · CAPO · ·
INIT · EMIL · LIMIT
LECTURE · KNAVISH
SKEET · AAAA · ACLU
· · TALL · BONKED
COMPEL · POOR · ·
APAIROF · NBCNEWS
BILK · MILKSHAKES
ANTE · ALOE · INEPT
LEAR · RELY · DUSTS

218
ETCH · DAKAR · SEAT
SHOO · ELISE · ORCA
PERU · VALET · LIDS
NEARCOINCIDENCE
· · GUN · · REP · ·
REALESTATECRASH
ENNA · HIMOM · OLLA
ANTS · IRENE · PSIS
RUES · RONIN · ROMP
MIDFIELDSTRIPES
· · ICC · · HUE · ·
BIGGIRLSDONTCRY
ABOU · EPROM · OLEO
HEAR · AGILE · RING
AXLE · MASTS · SODA

219
PARA · OSLO · STOP
OVER · PLUMB · OHIO
TEAR · PANAM · LEDE
ANDILOVEHOMER
SUEDES · AVA · EMI
HEM · VETS · IRONON
· MIRACLEGROOM
RELY · CIO · AWRY
AXIOMSOFEVIL
GAMBOL · IBAR · SSE
SMA · JAN · NESTOR
· PROMOSANDCONS
SMEE · OHYOU · ULNA
TARA · NINNY · BEET
PLUM · TEES · ANTZ

220
KNOT · SPILL · MORE
AGRA · EUBIE · ELHI
MOCKAPREDICTION
ASSENTSTO · HROSS
· · DIEU · GAI · ·
· FROSTEDFLOCKS
CROWE · IOUS · EUR
MANN · INEPT · EYED
AND · SNAG · SLUMS
· COPOFGOODHOPE
· · APO · LOAN · ·
SPIRO · INDULGING
FONTRESEMBLANCE
POLL · STEEL · TOAD
DRAY · LORNE · ETAS

221
VAST · SERIFS · BOTCH
ELOI · ICONIC · AROLE
IDONTMOCKTHERULES
NONCOM · SWAB · TAS
· ARETOO · AGI · EVE
· FONTRESEMBLANCE
SAPS · IPODS · EDU
NBA · ANE · SRS · ONTAP
ALLERGEN · PEELSOFF
PESCI · SEW · ESL · PIC
· TSA · RAITT · FIRS
SCOTTSONTHINICE
POL · ORT · DAEMON
INE · CIAO · AGENDA
COVERALLTHEBOSSES
OMEGA · LINEAL · SEMS
TAROT · SOTRUE · ECON

222
SHOP · SIDE · OLDWEST
NOVA · CARL · CARILLO
AMARTINEZ · THEDEEP
POLKA · DIG · ONEA
· ALANDERSHOWITZ
RAM · LIE · REAR
IKID · DOAS · TRISTIA
PILE · ANDYSIPOWICZ
SMART · ILO · NEMEA
ABNERKRAVITZ · ETAL
WOOKIEE · AROW · PAGE
· BENT · RES · MEA
ANNIELEIBOVITZ
SOON · ELI · AURIC
TWOSOME · ALEXDLINZ
RAKEDIN · ZEAL · USDA
OYSTERS · ERRS · SEAR

223
HEART · ASPICS · AFBS
ADLAI · ICECAP · TRET
UNLIT · ROTARYPHONE
LAALAA · URNS · EIDER
· HANDWRITTENNOTE
· TIDY · ODD · ·
ASP · ULNAS · NOENDTO
STEAMENGINE · DARED
TOPS · AMA · SOHO
HOSER · CLOTHDIAPER
EPITAPH · NOMAR · TES
· MOO · MBAS · ·
LIVEPERFORMANCE
ISOLA · DATE · TIEDYE
STILLCAMERA · ANGUS
POLE · UTERUS · NIELS
SOAR · BARONS · SCREE

224
ARBOR · LETGO · SLATE
MOUSE · ISAAC · AISLE
EDITH · FLUTTERKICK
RELEASE · EERIE
· DOSE · SAWTO · AFAR
DUI · HALLPASS · LINC
INN · LEERY · HOSTA
ALG · WIRES · SCATHE
NEB · HOOT · BOLT · IRE
· ALBANY · CABOT · NIP
PROEM · MALES · GOP
ONCD · PRESSRUN · TRS
ASKS · RASTA · ROCA
· CLASS · WELLCUT
SAFETYCATCH · OAKIE
EBONY · AGAPE · AILED
WAGER · LEMON · DRESS

225
USAGE · AARE · OASIS
MONET · LDOPA · NUOVA
PUTTHEPEDAL · ESSAY
IRE · ELOPE · PSAT
RADARS · TOTHEMETAL
ELUL · EPI · EAR · RONA
SEPAL · INRE · GOEASY
· KIST · ATTIC · LAS
· OPENTHETHROTTLE
ATF · EASTS · ISAW
DELANY · HOOP · DIVAS
ARUT · STY · UPI · NEAP
HIGHTAILIT · THERMO
· LATE · NOLLE · SIT
CANES · RUNFULLTILT
ACUTE · SKEIN · PRONE
METER · ERTE · SANER

226
ASKS · RIBS · ALASKA
BOLT · ENYA · BLOTTER
SWORDSMEN · ATELIER
· NADIA · FIREBALL
MIDWESTERNER · SLOP
AMI · TEXAS · PEEVE
LAKER · ONT · BASSET
ITERATE · CEDER · TRE
· EMANCIPATES
AHA · MOORS · MANHOLE
LATHES · ACC · TENOR
INRED · TOAST · POI
EGAN · THE49THSTATE
· ONCLOUD9 · RADAR
INDOUBT · EMOTICONS
STOOGES · RAVI · OLIN
ROMPED · SEES · SELL

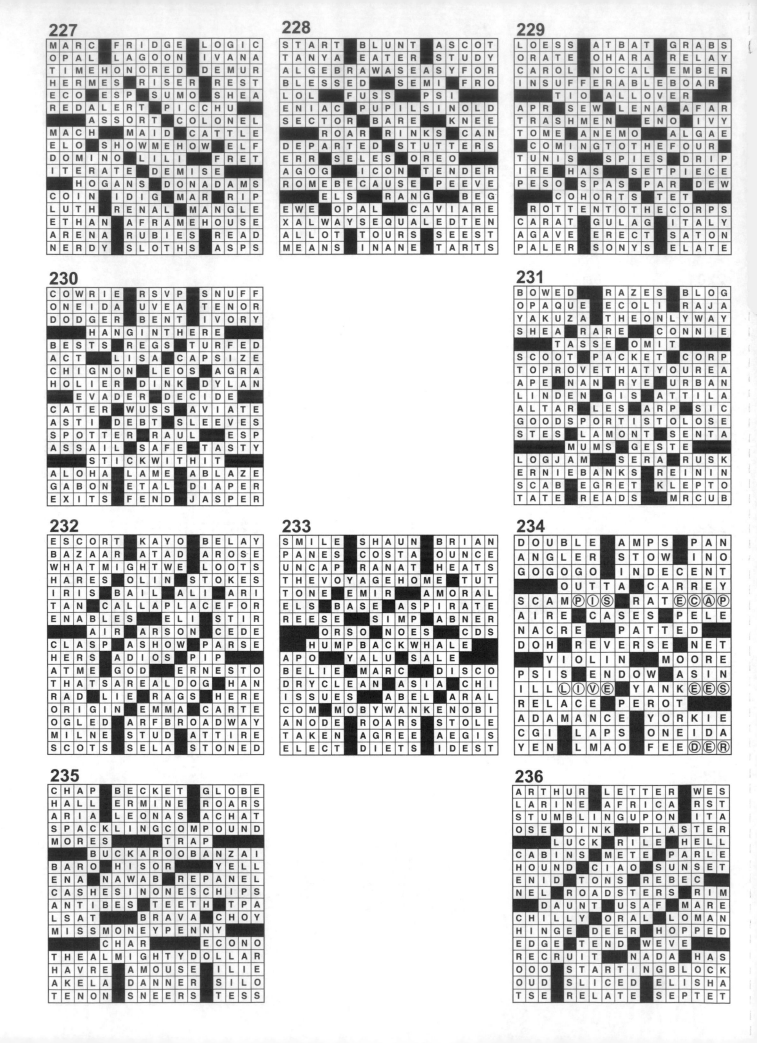

227
```
MARC  FRIDGE  LOGIC
OPAL  LAGOON  IVANA
TIMEHONORED  DEMUR
HERMES  RISER   REST
ECO  ESP  SUMO  SHEA
REDALERT    PICCHU
    ASSORT  COLONEL
MACH   MAID   CATTLE
ELO  SHOWMEHOW   ELF
DOMINO  LILI    FRET
ITERATE    DEMISE
    HOGANS  DONADAMS
COIN  IDIG  MAR  RIP
LUTH  RENAL  MANGLE
ETHAN  AFRAMEHOUSE
ARENA  RUBIES   READ
NERDY  SLOTHS   ASPS
```

228
```
START  BLUNT   ASCOT
TANYA  EATER   STUDY
ALGEBRAWASEASYFOR
BLESSED   SEMI   FRO
LOL   FUSS      PSI
ENIAC  PUPILSINOLD
SECTOR   BARE    KNEE
    ROAR  RINKS   CAN
DEPARTED   STUTTERS
ERR   SELES     OREO
AGOG   ICON   TENDER
ROMEBECAUSE   PEEVE
    ELS   RANG    BEG
EWE   OPAL   CAVIARE
XALWAYSEQUALEDTEN
ALLOT  TOURS   SEEST
MEANS  INANE   TARTS
```

229
```
LOESS  ATBAT   GRABS
ORATE  OHARA   RELAY
CAROL  NOCAL   EMBER
INSUFFERABLEBOAR
       TIO   ALLOVER
APR  SEW  LENA   AFAR
TRASHMEN   ENO   IVY
TOME   ANEMO   ALGAE
COMINGTOTHEFOUR
TUNIS   SPIES   DRIP
IRE   HAS   SETPIECE
PESO  SPAS  PAR  DEW
    COHORTS    TET
ROTTENTOTHECORPS
CARAT  GULAG   ITALY
AGAVE  ERECT   SATON
PALER  SONYS   ELATE
```

230
```
COWRIE   RSVP   SNUFF
ONEIDA   UVEA   TENOR
DODGER   BENT   IVORY
    HANGINTHERE
BESTS   REGS   TURFED
ACT    LISA   CAPSIZE
CHIGNON  LEOS    AGRA
HOLIER   DINK   DYLAN
    EVADER  DECIDE
CATER   WUSS   AVIATE
ASTI   DEBT  SLEEVES
SPOTTER  RAUL     ESP
ASSAIL   SAFE   TASTY
    STICKWITHIT
ALOHA   LAME   ABLAZE
GABON   ETAL   DIAPER
EXITS   FEND   JASPER
```

231
```
BOWED   RAZES    BLOG
OPAQUE  ECOLI    RAJA
YAKUZA  THEONLYWAY
SHEA   RARE    CONNIE
    TASSE   OMIT
SCOOT   PACKET   CORP
TOPROVETHATYOUREA
APE   NAN  RYE   URBAN
LINDEN  GIS   ATTILA
ALTAR  LES  ARP   SIC
GOODSPORTISTOLOSE
STES   LAMONT   SENTA
    MUMS   GESTE
LOGJAM   SERA    RUSK
ERNIEBANKS   REININ
SCAB   EGRET   KLEPTO
TATE   READS   MRCUB
```

232
```
ESCORT   KAYO   BELAY
BAZAAR   ATAD   AROSE
WHATMIGHTWE    LOOTS
HARES   OLIN   STOKES
IRIS  BAIL  ALI    ARI
TAN  CALLAPLACEFOR
ENABLES    ELI    STIR
    AIR  ARSON    CEDE
CLASP   ASHOW   PARSE
HERS   ADIOS     PIP
ATME   GOD   ERNESTO
THATSAREALDOG    HAN
RAD   LIE  RAGS   HERE
ORIGIN   EMMA   CARTE
OGLED   ARFBROADWAY
MILNE   STUD   ATTIRE
SCOTS   SELA   STONED
```

233
```
SMILE   SHAUN   BRIAN
PANES   COSTA   OUNCE
UNCAP   RANAT   HEATS
THEVOYAGEHOME    TUT
TONE   EMIR   AMORAL
ELS   BASE  ASPIRATE
REESE   SIMP   ABNER
    ORSO  NOES    CDS
    HUMPBACKWHALE
APO   YALU   SALE
BELIE   MARC   DISCO
DRYCLEAN   ASIA   CHI
ISSUES   ABEL   ARAL
COM  MOBYWANKENOBI
ANODE   ROARS   STOLE
TAKEN   AGREE   AEGIS
ELECT   DIETS   IDEST
```

234
```
DOUBLE   AMPS    PAN
ANGLER   STOW    INO
GOGOGO   INDECENT
    OUTTA   CARREY
SCAM(PIS)  RAT  (EC)AP
AIRE   CASES    PELE
NACRE    PATTED
DOH   REVERSE   NET
    VIOLIN    MOORE
PSIS   ENDOW    ASIN
ILL  (LIVE)  YANK(EES)
RELACE    PEROT
ADAMANCE   YORKIE
CGI   LAPS   ONEIDA
YEN   LMAO   FEE(DER)
```

235
```
CHAP   BECKET   GLOBE
HALL   ERMINE   ROARS
ARIA   LEONAS   ACHAT
SPACKLINGCOMPOUND
MORES          TRAP
    BUCKAROOBANZAI
BARO   HISOR     YELL
ENA  NAWAB  REPANEL
CASHESINONESCHIPS
ANTIBES   TEETH   TPA
LSAT    BRAVA   CHOY
    MISSMONEYPENNY
    CHAR       ECONO
THEALMIGHTYDOLLAR
HAVRE  AMOUSE   ILIE
AKELA  DANNER   SILO
TENON  SNEERS   TESS
```

236
```
ARTHUR   LETTER    WES
LARINE   AFRICA    RST
STUMBLINGUPON     ITA
OSE   OINK   PLASTER
    LUCK  RILE    HELL
CABINS   METE   PARLE
HOUND   CIAO   SUNSET
ENID   TONS    REBEC
NEL   ROADSTERS   RIM
    DAUNT   USAF   MARE
CHILLY   ORAL   LOMAN
HINGE   DEER   HOPPED
EDGE    TEND    WEVE
RECRUIT   NADA    HAS
OOO   STARTINGBLOCK
OUD   SLICED   ELISHA
TSE   RELATE   SEPTET
```

237

```
C A L D E R   A S S A M   M A S K
A V E R S E   O S A K A   T O P E
L I N E O F C R E D I T   E L A N
M A T A   O A T   I N S E T
      M A C H I N E G U N N E R S
M A C   B U N C O     V A L E T
A R R A Y S   H I S S Y   E N A
D I A L S   A D I D A S   F O O T
    B O M B D E T E C T I O N
F A M E   Y E N T A S   C R O C E
A T E   T E N S E   M A D R A S
S T A R T   R E G A L   A P P
O U T O F T H I S W O R L D
    E N I A C   I O C   E D E L
A S A P   T H E E N D O F T I M E
B A K E   H A R D G   N A R N I A
S P A R   E S S E S   I D E A L S
```

238

```
P R I M A   S M I T E   T I T H E
L U C I D   H A D E S   U N I O N
A M E N D   O P A R T   L O N G A
Y A C H T E R S H E A D I N G
O N O   O N T   O N T O P   A H A
F I L M   A F C   C E L S   L O W
F A D E   B A L D E S T   D I V A
    S E L L E R   L O N E R
C A U S E E L M O T O G I G G L E
A S P E N   W O N O U T
S H A D   C A T N A P S   A M I N
T E N   S A G A   D U P   G O N E
E N D   O P E R A   R E P   O P E
  A D R O I T L Y P L A N N E D
G E T I T   S A L V O   N E P A L
I R E N E   T R I E S   T W I C E
N A M E D   S E N S E   S T E E D
```

239

```
S P I K E   H A D E S   R I F L E
H O R A S   I C O M E   O N A I R
E L I Z A   G R E E R   S A U N A
    S O U T H E R N B R A W L
E C H O   E L S   D I E   E T T U
M A P   A R A   A A S   F A N
B R O W N I N G   I N R E D I N K
L A T I N   D O W N S   L U N G E
E V A D E S   W O W   T A N D E M
M A T E   P R I M A T E   K E L P
S N O   D I E T D R I N K   R O T
      F I N C H   D E C A L
R E T I N A       E N A M E L
A R I D   C O N C E R N   G E T A
B R A G T H R O U G H T H E M U D
B O R E S   T A B O O   E R O D E
I R A T E   O M E N S   E S S E N
```

240

```
A T B A Y   C A L L S   C R A F T
L A U R A   A V I A N   L A G E R
A S T I R   M A L M O   O V A T E
M E T A N G E L   B R A V E R A Y
O R E S   A T O Z   E V E
    A T O N E D   E R A S E D
P A R A D E   R U H R   R O L E
A R O S E   C L O N E S   A L A S
L A B S   M O O   E R E   R A T E
A B L E   E N C A S E   P A C E R
T I E R   T E A L   D E T E S T
E A S T E R   L O D G E R
    A I D   T A R A   A M E S
T I G E R C U B   R E D G I A N T
A C O R N   M A L T A   A M U S E
M O O S E   A R I E S   P A D U A
E N D E D   S E E D Y   S T E E L
```

241

```
C A S P E R   A P I A N   J O L T
A R C A D E   L A N C E   E L I A
C R O S S C O U N T R Y   S E E K
H O R S E   S M I L E   A T O N E
E Y E   L E A N N   A L E
T O R T   S K I I N G S G R E A T
    A S T A   A R I A   R U E
C A S S I E   N O T E S   L O G E
A L T E R   D E L A Y   W I D E N
P O U R   B A G E L   B A K E R Y
R O D   P A L E   E R N E
I F Y O U L I V E I N A   S P A S
    I N K   M T I D A   E V A
B E L L Y   A V I L A   R E N E W
E X A M   S M A L L C O U N T R Y
S I Z E   H A S I D   B L O U S E
S T E N   O S T E O   V E S P E R
```

242

```
A B B A   M E S H   E P I T O M E
N E R F   O R E O   A R M A D A S
D A I R Y C O W S   R E A L I S T
S U G A R C O N T E N I M E N T
      I S A   L E T S
R E D D   S T I R F R Y   O K L A
A P O   D I A N E   S U N D I A L
F I G M E N T B A R   P O I N T S
  G R I T   S U S I E   T U N E
G R A D E R   D O T C O M M E N T
M A C G R A W   N E R V E   A C E
S M E E   R E I S S U E   T R Y A
      G E L S     R H O
  G E T O F F M Y C A S E M E N T
N I G E R I A   A I R H A M M E R
F L A N K E R   W A C O   I M S O
C A N D I D E   N O S E   E A S T
```

243

```
B U S C H   D E T E R   M A M I E
U N C L E   O X I D E   A R E N T
T H R E E   M E D I C   R E A C H
  I A M D I A M E T R I C A L L Y
T N G   H I P S   U N I   T I L
E G G P L A N T   V I T A M I N E
R E L O A D S   R A T E   A M E N
I D Y L L   H E L E N   C E D E
      O P P O S E D T O
U S M C   T E N E T   I H O P E
N C A A   B E E T   B O L I V A R
S E N D W O R D   T I P S T E R S
I N D   H A G   T R O I   R A E
G E O M E T R Y H O M E W O R K
N O L A N   O U I J A   A R I E S
E N I A C   U L N A S   S E D E R
D E N S E   P E E N S   P O E T S
```

244

```
G L I T C H Y   R O B O C A L L S
R O S A R I O   O P E N A B O O K
I C E C O L D   M I S S P I G G Y
P I E H O L E   O N T I P T O E S
      N E L L   I S T
P H Y S E D   O W N   E A T S A T
R O U N D   F A R G O   S H A N E
E L K E   T I N Y   G O T E V E N
  D I E S E L S   M I N I C A M
G E T R E A L   J I V E   A G O G
T R U E R   S P A D E   T R E N D
O S P R E Y   U M A   H I S S E R
      V A T   S U E D
C R E S C E N T S   P S Y C H U P
L O S T A T S E A   I T S E A S Y
A S S I S T E R S   C O U R T E R
W H E R E E L S E   E N M A S S E
```

245

```
S M A S H H I T S   P A T T O N
P O T P O U R R I   P A L O O K A
O U T A N D O U T   E G O T R I P
T E N S E   N E T   D E N O T E S
      S O O T I N E S S
P A G O   D R O N E S   O S K A R
A L A M O D E   G W T W   E A V E
T I G E R S   S T A R G A Z E S
  B A L L A D S   S L O E G I N
C A R E E R I N G   T E A M U P
O B I T   E C O L   B E S T I E S
M A N S E   T W O B I T   E R S T
      C L A S S R O O M
G O T A H I T   S A L   A H M A D
A M A R O N E   I N O U R T I M E
S E X T E T S   E D G R I M L E Y
P R I S S Y   S T Y L E L E S S
```

246

```
E X P L O I T A T I V E   T I E S
S T R A W C O L O R E D   S N A P
T R A C E E L E M E N T   A F R O
D A M E   S C E N E   O R A N T
      D E F T   S E R U M   T E L
M P S   R O O T   S A N E   U S E
Y A K E T Y Y A K   T I N H A T S
T R I V E T   R O G E T   A T M S
H A N E S   H E I R S   A L I O N
O M A R   M E S N E   A L L O N E
L I N T I E R   G E M S T O N E S
O L D   D A B S   R U T H   S Y S
G I B   E D I T S   G R O W
I T O L D   V A L E S   R E D D
C A N A   F O R E S H A D O W E R
A R E S   I R R E S O L U T E L Y
L Y S E   R E S T A T E M E N T S
```

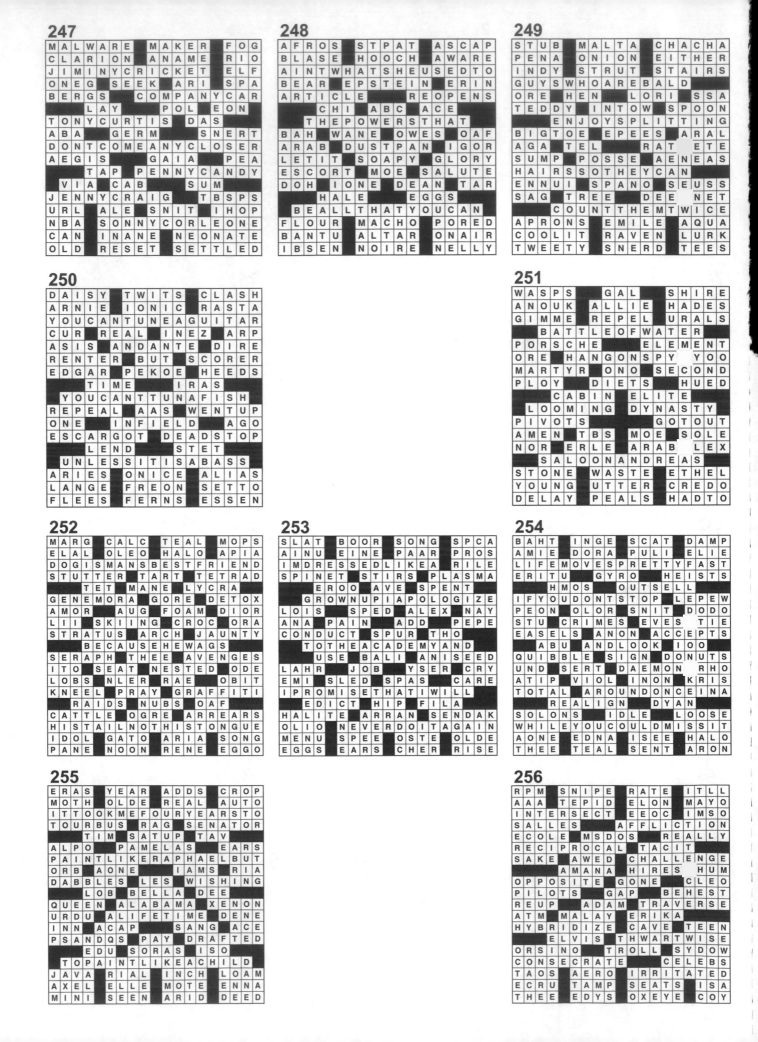

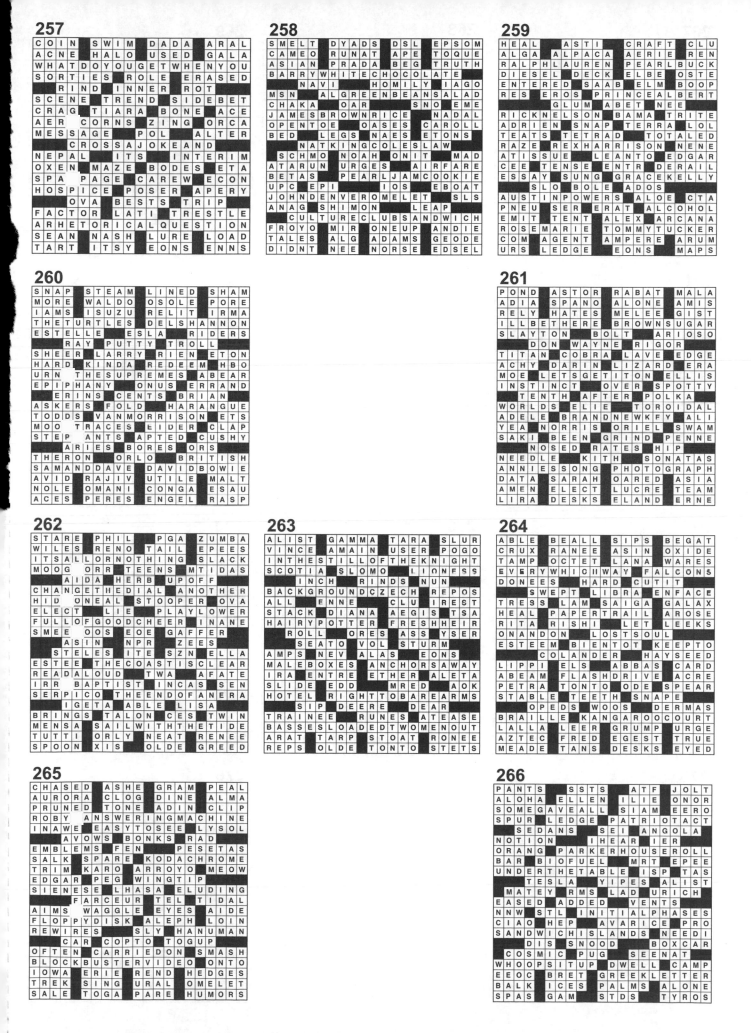

257

COIN SWIM DADA ARAL
ACNE HALO USED GALA
WHATDOYOUGETWHENYOU
SORTIES ROLE ERASED
RIND INNER ROT
SCENE TREND SIDEBET
CRAG TIARA BONE ACE
AER CORNS ZING ORCA
MESSAGE POL ALTER
CROSSAJOKEAND
NEPAL ITS INTERIM
OXEN MAZE BODES ETA
SPA PAGE CAREW ECON
HOSPICE POSER APERY
OVA BESTS TRIP
FACTOR LATI TRESTLE
ARHETORICALQUESTION
SEAN NASH LURE LOAD
TART ITSY EONS ENNS

258

SMELT DYADS DSL EPSOM
CAMEO RUNAT APE TOQUE
ASIAN PRADA BEG TRUTH
BARRYWHITECHOCOLATE
NAVI HOMILY IAGO
MSN ALGREENBEANSALAD
CHAKA OAR SNO EME
JAMESBROWNRICE NADAL
OPENTOE OASES CAROLL
BED LEGS NAES ETONS
NATKINGCOLESLAW
SCHMO NOAH ONIT MAD
ATARUN URGES AIRFARE
BETAS PEARLJAMCOOKIE
UPC EPI IOS EBOAT
JOHNDENVEROMELET SLS
ANAG SHIMON LEAP
CULTURECLUBSANDWICH
FROYO MIR ONEUP ANDIE
TALES ALG ADAMS GEODE
DIDNT NEE NORSE EDSEL

259

HEAL ASTI CRAFT CLU
ALGA ALPACA AERIE REN
RALPHLAUREN PEARLBUCK
DIESEL DECK ELBE OSTE
ENTERED SAAB ELM BOOP
RES EROS PRINCEALBERT
GLUM ABET NEE
RICKNELSON BAMA TRITE
ADRIEN SNAP TERRA LOL
TEATS TETRAD TOTALED
RAZE REXHARRISON NENE
ATISSUE LEANTO EDGAR
CEE TENSE ENTR DERAIL
ESSAY SUNG GRACEKELLY
SLO BOLE ADOS
AUSTINPOWERS ALOE CTA
PNEU SER ERAT ALCOHOL
EMIT TENT ALEX ARCANA
ROSEMARIE TOMMYTUCKER
COM AGENT AMPERE ARUM
URS LEDGE EONS MAPS

260

SNAP STEAM LINED SHAM
MORE WALDO OSOLE PORE
IAMS ISUZU RELIT IRMA
THETURTLES DELSHANNON
ESTELLE ESLA RIDERS
RAY PUTTY TROLL
SHEER LARRY RIEN ETON
HARD KINDA REDEEM HBO
URN THESUPREMES ABEAR
EPIPHANY ONUS ERRAND
ERINS CENTS BRIAN
ASKERS FOLD HARANGUE
TODDS VANMORRISON ETS
MOO TRACES EIDER CLAP
STEP ANTS APTED CUSHY
ARIES BORES ORS
THERON ORLO BRITISH
SAMANDDAVE DAVIDBOWIE
AVID RAJIV UTILE MALT
NOLE OMANI CONGA ESAU
ACES PERES ENGEL RASP

261

POND ASTOR RABAT MALA
ADIA SPANO ALONE AMIS
RELY HATES MELEE GIST
ILLBETHERE BROWNSUGAR
SLAYTON BOLT ARIOSO
DON WAYNE RIGOR
TITAN COBRA LAVE EDGE
ACHY DARIN LIZARD ERA
MOE LETSGETITON ELLIS
INSTINCT OVER SPOTTY
TENTH AFTER POLKA
WORLDS ELIE TOROIDAL
ADELE BRANDNEWKFY ALI
YEA NORRIS ORIEL SWAM
SAKI BEEN GRIND PENNE
NOSED RATES HIP
NEEDLE KITH SONATAS
ANNIESSONG PHOTOGRAPH
DATA SARAH OARED ASIA
AMEN ELECT LUCRE TEAM
LIRA DESKS ELAND ERNE

262

STARE PHIL PGA ZUMBA
WILES RENO TAIL EPEES
ITSALLORNOTHING SLACK
MOOG ORR TEENS MTIDAS
AIDA HERB UPOFF
CHANGETHEDIAL ANOTHER
HID ONEAL STOOPER OVA
ELECT LIE PLAYLOWER
FULLOFGOODCHEER INANE
SMEE OOS EOE GAFFER
ASIN NPR ZEES
STELES ITE SZN ELLA
ESTEE THECOASTISCLEAR
READALOUD TWA AFATE
IRR BAPTIST INCAS SEN
SERPICO THEENDOFANERA
IGETA ABLE LISA
BRINGS TALON CES TWIN
MENSA SAILWITHTHETIDE
TUTTI ORLY NEAT RENEE
SPOON XIS OLDE GREED

263

ALIST GAMMA TARA SLUR
VINCE AMAIN USER POGO
INTHESTILLOFTHEKNIGHT
SCOTIA SLOMO LIONESS
INCH RINDS NUN
BACKGROUNDCZECH REPOS
ALL ENNE CLU IREST
STACK DIANA AEGIS TSA
HAIRYPOTTER FRESHHEIR
ROLL ORES ASS YSER
SEATO VOL STURM
AMPS NEV ALAS EONS
MALEBOXES ANCHORSAWAY
IRA ENTRE ETHER ALETA
SLIDE EDD MRED AOK
HOTEL RIGHTTOBAREARMS
SIP DEERE DEAR
TRAINEE RUNES ATEASE
BASSESLOADEDTWOMENOUT
ARAT TARP STOAT RONEE
REPS OLDE TONTO STETS

264

ABLE BEALL SIPS BEGAT
CRUX RANEE ASIN OXIDE
TAMP OCTET LANA WARES
EVERYWHICHWAY FALCONS
DONEES HARD CUTIT
SWEPT LIBRA ENFACE
TRESS LAM SAIGA GALAX
HEAL PAPERTRAIL AROSE
RITA RISHI LET LEEKS
ONANDON LOSTSOUL
ESTEEM BIENTOT KEEPTO
COLANDER HAYSEED
LIPPI ELS ABBAS CARD
ABEAM FLASHDRIVE ACRE
PETRA TONTO ODE SPEAR
STABLE TEETH SNAPE
OPEDS WOOS DERMAS
BRAILLE KANGAROOCOURT
LALLA LEER GRUMP URGE
AZTEC FRED EGEST TRUE
MEADE TANS DESKS EYED

265

CHASED ASHE GRAM PEAL
AURORA CLOG DINE ALMA
PRUNED TONE ADIN CLIP
ROBY ANSWERINGMACHINE
INAWE EASYTOSEE LYSOL
AVOWS BONKS RAD
EMBLEMS FEN PESETAS
SALK SPARE KODACHROME
TRIM KARO ARROYO MEOW
EDGAR PEG WINGTIP
SIENESE LHASA ELUDING
FARCEUR TEL TIDAL
AIMS WAGGLE EYES AIDE
FLOPPYDISK ALEPH LOIN
REWIRES SLY HANUMAN
CAR COPTO TOGUP
OFTEN CARRIEDON SMASH
BLOCKBUSTERVIDEO ONTO
IOWA ERIE REND HEDGES
TREK SING URAL OMELET
SALE TOGA PARE HUMORS

266

PANTS SSTS ATF JOLT
ALOHA ELLEN ILIE ONOR
SOMEGAVEALL SIAM EERO
SPUR LEDGE PATRIOTACT
SEDANS SEI ANGOLA
NOTION IHEAR IER
ORANG PARKERHOUSEROLL
BAR BIOFUEL MRT EPEE
UNDERTHETABLE ISP TAS
TESLA YIPES ALIST
MATEY RMS LAD URICH
EASED ADDED VENTS
NNW STL INITIALPHASES
CIAO HEP AVARICE PRO
SANDWICHISLANDS NEEDI
DIS SNOOD BOXCAR
COSMIC PUG SEENAT
WHOOPSITUP DWELL CAMP
EEOC BRET GREEKLETTER
BALK ICES PALMS ALONE
SPAS GAM STDS TYROS

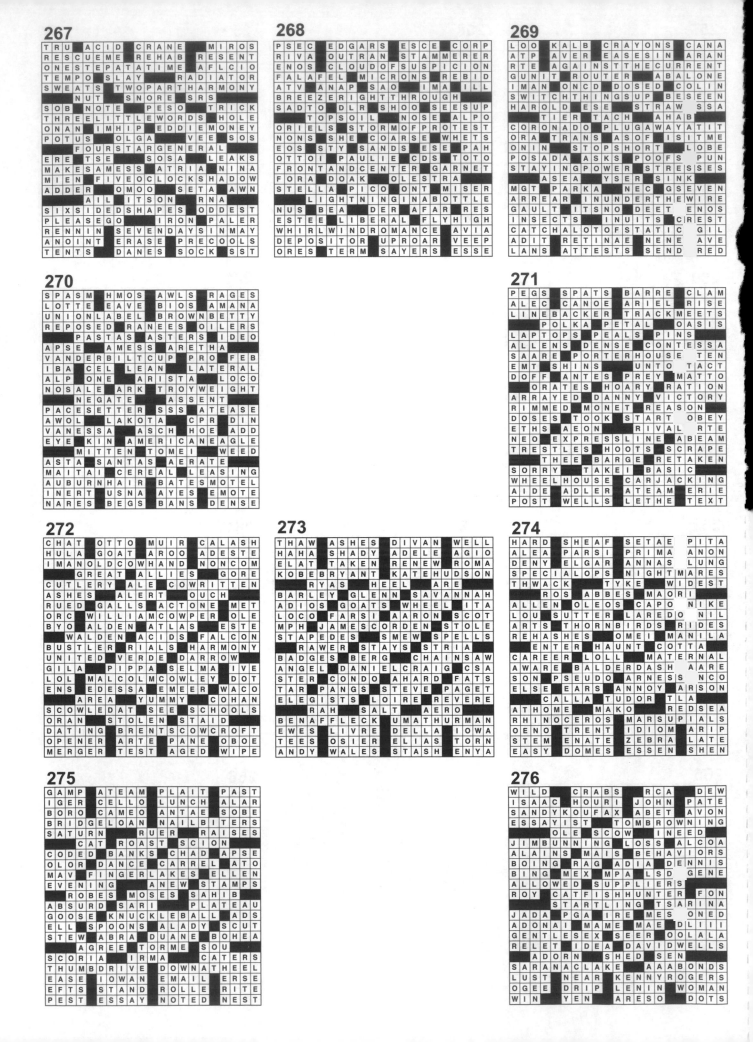

267
TRU·ACID·CRANE··MIROS
RESCUEME·REHAB·RESENT
ONESTEPATATIME·AFLCIO
TEMPO··SLAY···RADIATOR
SWEATS··TWOPARTHARMONY
···NUT··SNORE··SRS····
SOB·NOTE··PESO··TRICK·
THREELITTLEWORDS··HOLE
ONAN·IMHIP·EDDIEMONEY·
POTUS··OLGA··VEE··SOS·
····FOURSTARGENERAL···
ERE·TSE··SOSA··LEAKS··
MAKESAMESS·ATRIA·NINA·
MIEN·FIVEOCLOCKSHADOW·
ADDER·OMOO··SETA··AWN·
···AIL··ITSON··RNA····
SIXSIDEDSHAPES··ODDEST
PLEASEGO··IRON··PALER·
RENNIN·SEVENDAYSINMAY·
ANOINT·ERASE·PRECOOLS·
TENTS··DANES·SOCK··SST

268
PSEC·EDGARS·ESCE··CORP
RIVA·OUTRAN·STAMMERER·
ENOS·CLOUDOFSUSPICION·
FALAFEL··MICRONS·REBID
ATV·ANAP·SAO··IMA··ILL
BREEZERIGHTTHROUGH····
SADTO·DLR··SHOO·SEESUP
···TOPSOIL··NOSE·ALPO·
ORIELS·STORMOFPROTEST·
NONS·SHE·COARSE·WHETS·
EOS·STY·SANDS·ESE·PAH·
OTTOI·PAULIE·CDS·TOTO·
FRONTANDCENTER·GARNET·
FORA·DOAK··OLESTRA····
STELLA·PICO·ONT·MISER·
··LIGHTNINGINABOTTLE··
NUS·BEA··DER·AFAR·RES·
ESTEE·LIBERAL·FLYHIGH·
WHIRLWINDROMANCE·AVIA·
DEPOSITOR·UPROAR·VEEP·
ORES·TERM·SAYERS·ESSE

269
LOO·KALB·CRAYONS·CANA·
ATP·AVER·EASESIN·ARAN·
RTE·AGAINSTTHECURRENT·
GUNIT·ROUTER··ABALONE·
IMAN·ONCD·DOSED·COLIN·
SWITCHTHINGSUP·BESEEN·
HAROLD·ESE··STRAW·SSA·
···TIER·TACH··AHAB····
CORONADO·PLUGAWAYATIT·
ORA·TRANS·ASOF·ISITME·
ONIN··STOPSHORT··LOBE·
POSADA·ASKS·POOFS·PUN·
STAYINGPOWER·STRESSES·
····ASEA·YSER·SINK····
MGT·PARKA··NEC·GSEVEN·
ARREAR·INUNDERTHEWIRE·
GAULT·ITSNO·DEET·ENOS·
INSECTS··INUITS·CREST·
CATCHALOTOFSTATIC·GIL·
ADIT·RETINAE·NENE·AVE·
LANS·ATTESTS·SEND··RED

270
SPASM·HMOS··AWLS··RAGES
LOTTE·EAVE··BIOS··AMANA
UNIONLABEL·BROWNBETTY·
REPOSED·RANEES·OILERS·
···PASTAS·ASTERS·IDEO·
APSE··AMESS··ARETHA····
VANDERBILTCUP··PRO·FEB·
IBA·CEL··LEAN··LATERAL·
ALP·ONE·ARISTA·LOCO····
NOSALE·ARK·TROYWEIGHT·
···NEGATE···ASSENT····
PACESETTER·SSS·ATEASE·
AWOL··LAKOTA··CPR··DIN·
VANESSA·ASCH·HOE··ADD·
EYE·KIN·AMERICANEAGLE·
···MITTEN·TOMEI··WEED·
ASTA··SANTAS··AERATE···
MAITAI·CEREAL··LEASING·
AUBURNHAIR·BATESMOTEL·
INERT·USNA··AYES··EMOTE
NARES·BEGS··BANS··DENSE

271
PEGS·SPATS·BARRE··CLAM
ALEC·CANOE·ARIEL··RISE
LINEBACKER·TRACKMEETS·
·POLKA·PETAL··OASIS····
LAPTOPS·PEALS·PINS····
ALLENS·DENSE·CONTESSA·
SAARE·PORTERHOUSE·TEN·
EMT·SHINS··UNTO··TACT·
DOFF·ANTES·PREY·MATTO·
··ORATES·HOARY·RATION·
ARRAYED·DANNY·VICTORY·
RIMMED·MONET·REASON···
DOSES·TOOK··START·OBEY·
ETHS·AEON···RIVAL··RTE·
NEO·EXPRESSLINE·ABEAM·
TRESTLES·HOOTS·SCRAPE·
··THEE··BARGE·RETAKEN·
SORRY··TAKEI··BASIC····
WHEELHOUSE·CARJACKING·
AIDE·ADLER·ATEAM··ERIE
POST·WELLS·LETHE··TEXT

272
CHAT·OTTO··MUIR··CALASH
HULA·GOAT··AROO··ADESTE
IMANOLDCOWHAND·NONCOM·
···GREAT··ALLIES··GORE·
CUTLERY·ALE·COWRITTEN·
ASHES··ALERT··OUCH·····
RUED·GALLS·ACTONE·MET·
ORC·WILLIAMCOWPER·OLE·
BYO·ALDEN·ATLAS··ESTE·
··WALDEN·ACIDS·FALCON·
BUSTLER·RIALS·HARMONY·
UNITED·VERDE··DARROW···
GILA·PIPPA·SELMA··IVE·
LOL·MALCOLMCOWLEY·DOT·
ENS·EDESSA·EMEER·WACO·
···AREA··YUMMY··COHAN·
SCOWLEDAT·SEE·SCHOOLS·
ORAN··STOLEN··STAID····
DATING·BRENTSCOWCROFT·
OPENER·ARTE··PANE·OBOE
MERGER·TEST··AGED·WIPE

273
THAW·ASHES·DIVAN··WELL
HAHA·SHADY·ADELE··AGIO
ELAT·TAKEN·RENEW··ROMA
KOBEBRYANT·KATEHUDSON·
··RYAS··HEEL···ARE····
BARLEY·GLENN·SAVANNAH·
ADIOS·GOATS·WHEEL·ITA·
LOCO·FARSI·AARON·SCOT·
MPH·JAMESCORDEN·STOLE·
STAPEDES··SMEW·SPELLS·
··RAWER·STAYS·STRIA···
BADGES·BERG··CHAINSAW·
ANGEL·DANIELCRAIG·CSA·
STER·CONDO·AHARD·FATS·
TAR·PANGS·STEVE·PAGET·
ELEGISTS·LOIRE·REVERE·
··RAH··SALT···AERO····
BENAFFLECK·UMATHURMAN·
EWES·LIVRE·DELLA··IOWA
TEES·OSIER·ELIAS··TORN
ANDY·WALES·STASH··ENYA

274
HARD·SHEAF·SETAE··PITA
ALEA·PARSI·PRIMA··ANON
DENY·ELGAR·ANNAS··LUNG
SPECIALOPS·NIGHTMARES·
THWACK·TYKE··WIDEST····
···ROS··ABBES··MAORI··
ALLEN·OLEOS·CAPO··NIKE
LOU·SUTTER·LAREDO·NIL·
ARTS·THORNBIRDS·RIDES·
REHASHES··OMEI·MANILA·
··ENTER·HAUNT·COTTA···
CAREER·LOLL··MATERNAL·
AWARE·BALDERDASH·AARE·
SON·PSEUDO·ARNESS·NCO·
ELSE·EARS··ANNOY·ARSON
···CALLA··TUDOR··TLA··
ATHOME·MAKO··REDSEA···
RHINOCEROS·MARSUPIALS·
OENO·TRENT·IDIOM··ARIP
STEM·ENATE·ZEBRA··LATE
EASY·DOMES·ESSEN··SHEN

275
GAMP··ATEAM··PLAIT·PAST
IGER··CELLO··LUNCH·ALAR
BORO··CAMEO··ANTAE·SOBE
BRIDGELOAN·NAILBITERS·
SATURN···RUER···RAISES
···CAT·ROAST·SCION····
CODED·BANKS··CHAD·APSE
OLOR·DANCE·CARREL·ATO·
MAV·FINGERLAKES·ELLEN·
EVENING··ANEW·STAMPS··
··ROBES··MOSES··SAHIB·
ABSURD·SARI···PLATEAU·
GOOSE·KNUCKLEBALL·ADS·
ELL·SPOONS·ALADY·SCUT·
STEW·ABRA··DUANE·BOHEA
··AGREE··TORME··SOU···
SCORIA··IRMA··CATERS··
THUMBDRIVE·DOWNATHEEL·
EASE·IOWAN·EMAIL··ERSE
EFTS·STAND·ROLLE··RITE
PEST·ESSAY·NOTED··NEST

276
WILD··CRABS··RCA···DEW
ISAAC·HOURI··JOHN·PATE
SANDYKOUFAX·ABET··AVON
ESSAYIST·TOMBROWNING··
···OLE··SCOW···INEED··
JIMBUNNING·LOSS··ALCOA
ALAINS·MAIS··BEHAVIORS
BOING·RAG··ADIA·DENNIS
BING·MEX·MPA·LSD··GENE
ALLOWED··SUPPLIERS····
ROY·CATFISHHUNTER·FON·
··STARTLING·TSARINA···
JADA·PGA·IRE·MES·ONED·
ADONAI·MAME··MAE·DLIII
GENTLESEX·SEER·OOLALA·
RELET·IDEA·DAVIDWELLS·
·ADORN··SHED··SEN·····
SARANACLAKE·AAABONDS··
LUST·NEAR··KENNYROGERS
OGEE·DRIP··LENIN··WOMAN
WIN··YEN···ARESO··DOTS

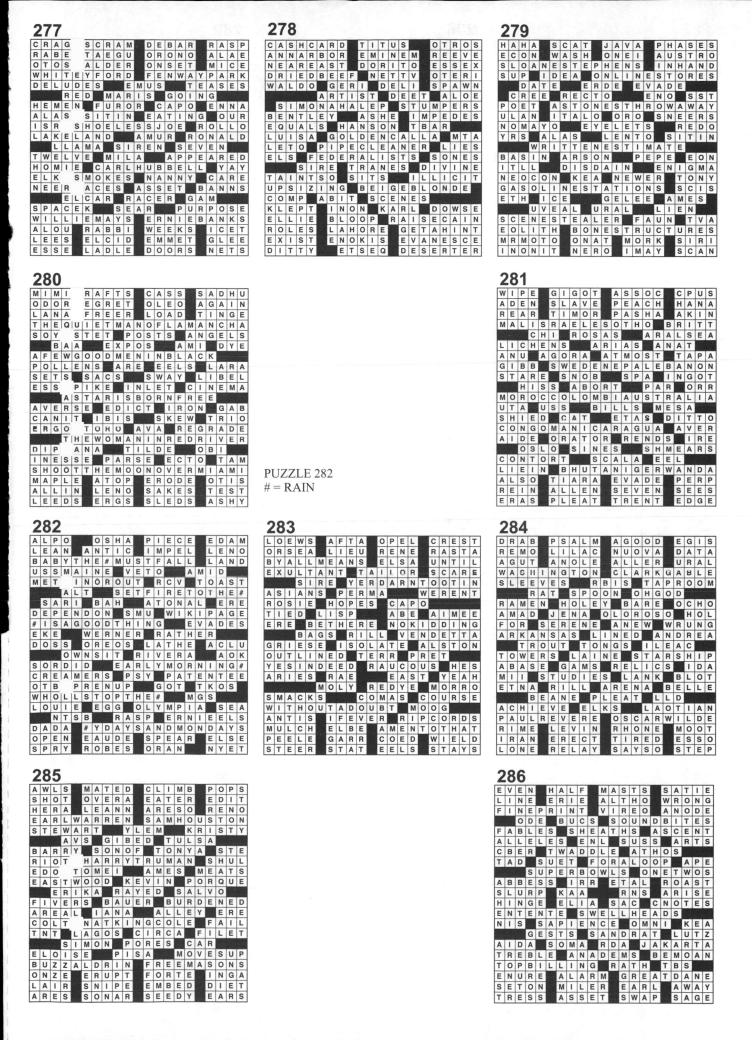

277

```
CRAG SCRAM DEBAR RASP
RABE TAEGU ORONO ALAE
OTOS ALDER ONSET MICE
WHITEYFORD FENWAYPARK
DELUDES  EMUS  TEASES
   RED MARIS GOING
HEMEN FUROR CAPO ENNA
ALAS SITIN EATING OUR
ISR SHOELESSJOE ROLLO
LAKELAND AMUR RONALD
  LLAMA SIREN SEVEN
TWELVE MILA APPEARED
HOMIE CARLHUBBELL YAY
ELK SMOKES NANNY CARE
NEER ACES ASSET BANNS
  ELCAR RACER GAM
SPACEK SEAR PURPOSE
WILLIEMAYS ERNIEBANKS
ALOU RABBI WEEKS ICET
LEES ELCID EMMET GLEE
ESSE LADLE DOORS NETS
```

278

```
CASHCARD TITUS OTROS
ANNARBOR EMINEM REEVE
NEAREAST DORITO ESSEX
DRIEDBEEF NETTV OTERI
WALDO GERI DELI SPAWN
   ARTIST DEET ALOE
SIMONAHALEP STUMPERS
BENTLEY ASHE IMPEDES
EQUALS HANSON TBAR
LUISA GOLDENCALLA MTA
LETO PIPECLEANER LIES
ELS FEDERALISTS SONES
SIRE TRANES DIVINE
TAINTSO SITS ILLICIT
UPSIZING BEIGEBLONDE
COMP ABIT SCENES
KLEPT INON KARL DOWSE
ELLIE BLOOP RAISECAIN
ROLES LAHORE GETAHINT
EXIST ENOKIS EVANESCE
DITTY ETSEQ DESERTER
```

279

```
HAHA SCAT JAVA PHASES
ECON WASH ONEI AUSTRO
SLOANESTEPHENS INHAND
SUP IDEA ONLINESTORES
  DATE ERDE EVADE
CREE RECTO ENO SST
POET ASTONESTHROWAWAY
ULAN ITALO ORO SNEERS
NOMAYO EYELETS REDO
YRS ALAS LENTO SITIN
  WRITTENESTIMATE
BASIN ARSON PEPE EON
ITLL DISDAIN ENIGMA
NEOCON KEA NEWER TONY
GASOLINESTATIONS SCIS
ETH ICE GELEE AMES
  UVEAL URAL LIEN
SCENESTEALER FAUN TVA
EOLITH BONESTRUCTURES
MRMOTO ONAT MORK SIRI
INONIT NERO IMAY SCAN
```

280

```
MIMI RAFTS CASS SADHU
ODOR EGRET OLEO AGAIN
LANA FREER LOAD TINGE
THEQUIETMANOFLAMANCHA
SOY STET POSTS ANGELS
  BAA EXPOS AMI DYE
AFEWGOODMENINBLACK
POLLENS ARE EELS LARA
SETS SACS SWAY LIBEL
ESS PIKE INLET CINEMA
 ASTARISBORNFREE
AVERSE EDICT IRON GAB
CANIT IBIS SKEW TRIO
ERGO TOHO AVA REGRADE
 THEWOMANINREDRIVER
DIP ANA TILDE OBI
INESSE PARSE ECTO TAM
SHOOTTHEMOONOVERMIAMI
MAPLE ATOP ERODE OTIS
ALLIN LENO SAKES TEST
LEEDS ERGS SLEDS ASHY
```

281

```
WIPE GIGOT ASSOC CPUS
ADEN SLAVE PEACH HANA
REAR TIMOR PASHA AKIN
MALISRAELESOTHO BRITT
  CHI ROSAS ARALSEA
LICHENS ARIAS ANAT
ANU AGORA ATMOST TAPA
GIBB SWEDENEPALEBANON
STARE SNOB SPA INGOT
 HISS ABORT PAR ORR
MOROCCOLOMBIAUSTRALIA
UTA USS BILLS MESA
SHIED CAT ETAS DITTO
CONGOMANICARAGUA AVER
AIDE ORATOR RENDS IRE
 OSLO SINES SHMEARS
CONTORT SCALA EEL
LIEIN BHUTANIGERWANDA
ALSO TIARA EVADE PERP
REIN ALLEN SEVEN SEES
ERAS PLEAT TRENT EDGE
```

PUZZLE 282
= RAIN

282

```
ALPO  OSHA  PIECE EDAM
LEAN ANTIC IMPEL LENO
BABYTHE#MUSTFALL LAND
USSMAINE VETO  AMID
MET INOROUT RCV TOAST
ALT SETFIRETOTHE#
SARI BAH ATONAL ERE
DEPENDON SMU WIKIPAGE
#ISAGOODTHING EVADES
EKE WERNER RATHER
DOSS OREOS LATHE ACLU
OWNSIT RIVERA AOK
SORDID EARLYMORNING#
CREAMERS PSY PATENTEE
OTB PRENUP GOT TKOS
WHOLLSTOPTHE# MGS
LOUIE EGG OLYMPIA SEA
NTSB RASP ERNIEEELS
DADA #YDAYSANDMONDAYS
OPEN EAUDE SPEAR ELSE
SPRY ROBES ORAN NYET
```

283

```
LOEWS AFTA OPEL CREST
ORSEA LIEU RENE RASTA
BYALLMEANS ELSA UNTIL
EXULTANT TAILOR SCARE
 SIRE YERDARNTOOTIN
ASIANS PERMA WERENT
ROSIE HOPES CAPO
TIED LISP ABE AIMEE
ERE BETHERE NOKIDDING
 BAGS RILL VENDETTA
GRIESE ISOLATE ALSTON
OUTLINED TERR PRET
YESINDEED RAUCOUS HES
ARIES RAE EAST YEAH
 MOLY REDYE MORRO
SMACKS COMAS COURSE
WITHOUTADOUBT MOOG
ANTIS IFEVER RIPCORDS
MULCH ELBE AMENTOTHAT
PEELE GARR COED WIELD
STEER STAT EELS STAYS
```

284

```
DRAB PSALM AGOOD EGIS
REMO LILAC NUOVA DATA
AGUT ANOLE ALLER URAL
WASHINGTON CLARKGABLE
SLEEVES RBIS TAPROOM
 RAT SPOON OHGOD
RAMEN HOLEY BARE OCHO
AMAD JENA OLOROSO HOL
FOR SERENE ANEW WRUNG
ARKANSAS LINED ANDREA
 TROUT TONGS ILEAC
TOWERS LAINE STARSHIP
ABASE GAMS RELICS IDA
MII STUDIES LANK BLOT
ETNA RILL ARENA BELLE
 BEANE PLEAT LLD
ACHIEVE ELKS LAOTIAN
PAULREVERE OSCARWILDE
RIME LEVIN RHONE MOOT
IRAN ERECT TIRED ESSO
LONE RELAY SAYSO STEP
```

285

```
AWLS MATED CLIMB POPS
SHOT OVERA EATER EDIT
HERA LEANN ARESO RENO
EARLWARREN SAMHOUSTON
STEWART YLEM KRISTY
  AVS GIBED TULSA
BARRY SONOF TONYA STE
RIOT HARRYTRUMAN SHUL
EDO TOMEI AMES MEATS
EASTWOOD KEVIN PORQUE
 ERIKA RAYED SALVO
FIVERS BAUER BURDENED
AREAL IANA ALLEY ERE
COLT NATKINGCOLE FAIL
TNT LAGOS CIRCA FILET
 SIMON PORES CAR
ELOISE PISA MOVESUP
BUZZALDRIN FREEMASONS
ONZE ERUPT FORTE INGA
LAIR SNIPE EMBED DIET
ARES SONAR SEEDY EARS
```

286

```
EVEN HALF MASTS SATIE
LINE ERIE ALTHO WRONG
FINEPRINT VIREO ANODE
 ODE BUCS SOUNDBITES
FABLES SHEATHS ASCENT
ALLELES ENL SUSS ARTS
CBER TWADDLE ATHOS
TAD SUET FORALOOP APE
SUPERBOWLS ONETWOS
ABBESS IRR ETAL ROAST
SLURP KAA RNS ARISE
HINGE ELIA SAC CNOTES
ENTENTE SWELLHEADS
NIS SAPIENCE OMNI KEA
 GESTS SANDRAT LUTZ
AIDA SOMA RDA JAKARTA
TREBLE ANADEMS BEMOAN
TOPBILLING RATH TBS
ENURE ALARM GREATDANE
SETON MILER EARL AWAY
TRESS ASSET SWAP SAGE
```

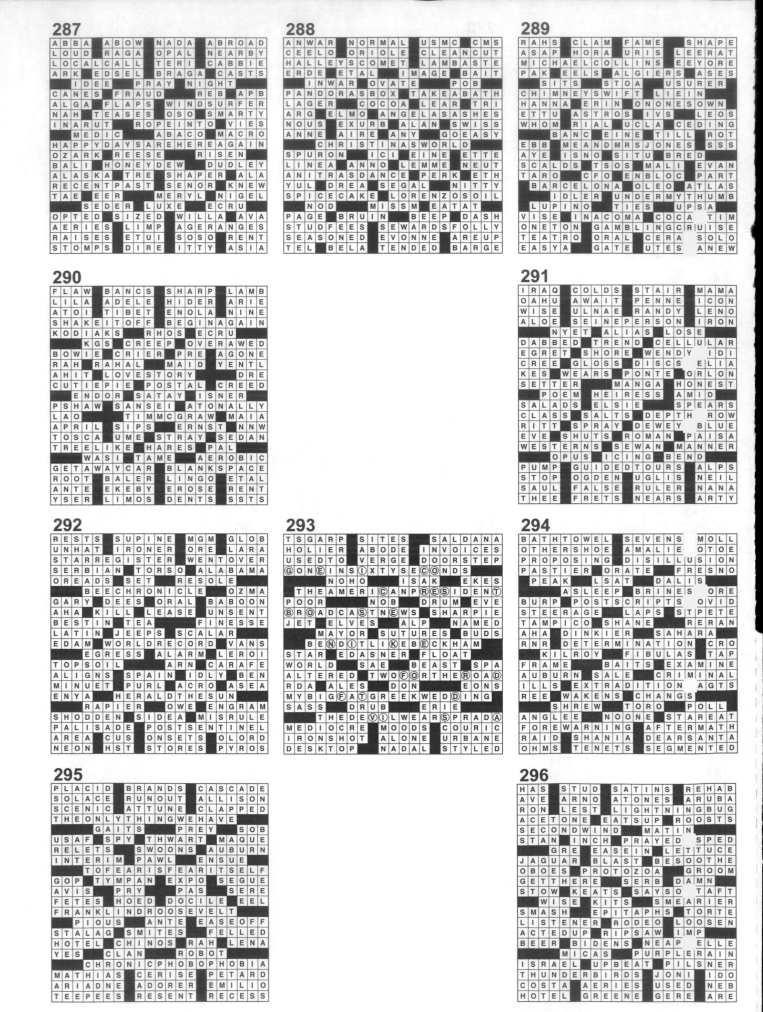

297

```
CAROM  SPACE  ASK  ARABS
OLIVA  ALLON  MOE  VEGAS
DIVERTGAINS  PRESIDENT
STERNEST  CID  ENCLOSES
     TER  SEGUE  RAN
GAGA  RESTINGDIVA  EDTV
ADAK  ELIOT  GNOME  RAO
DEREK  EMU  TAEBO  RAITT
OLD  INVITESGRAD  RIVER
TEEPEE  SPAR  DOE  DIRE
   NOVAK  ORE  ORMAN
EAVE  PEP  DIET  SINGER
CLIMB  RAVENDIGITS  ELA
LASSO  NYASA  ART  SCALD
AMI  SCOTT  ORIBI  ASIA
TOTS  DIVINGRATES  STER
    HAR  CHADS  LOS
BARITONE  LIE  PEEKABOO
ECONOMIZE  TRIEDSAVING
ARDEN  NRA  ELROY  PATER
DEERE  AAR  RYANS  ISTLE
```

298

```
STUPA  LOOM  CASCA  KEPT
ENTERSINTO  AFOOL  ILIA
STEA[MR]OLLER  PAL[MR]EADING
     SETTO  TAR  DAVID
OSU  SOSA  ITAW  DELICT
SPRATS  NISI  ALE  SEARS
TEARSAT  NEPHRO  CLII
IANS  YURT  TI[MR]OTH  A[MR]AM
ARIES  PEE  ODESSA  REGO
  UNIFIER  EEC  EVE  FEN
JA[MR]OLL  DIM  REB  ORELSE
ACE  LOO  [MR]ED  PISCINE
NEAR  ANGELI  TAO  KICKS
ETCH  TEAPOT  ISMS  STET
TOTE  PONCHO  APPLIER
SNOOT  PER  HANS  AREOLA
ERMINE  TRES  ARNE  NEW
  EVILS  IDA  WAIST
BOTTO[MR]OUND  FIR[MR]ESOLVE
BRIE  OSSIE  IDEOLOGIES
BEER  DIALS  TODD  NOTTO
```

299

```
ASIN  CFOS  PAGES  PLEAD
RINA  PACO  ALIVE  CINCO
EGGPRODUCERSNECESSITY
THROE  SLANT  ASTA  AGUE
HEALTH  ANOAS  ORB  MAN
ADMIRALRICKOVERTOPALS
    ONO  HELEN  HBO
FAST  KOBE  AOL  OLEG
ATTHISPARTICULARPLACE
STEAL  AMINO  AMOR  YAY
CARRIES  ATEST  BOOKERS
IBN  ALOU  ARTOF  NOTTE
SOUNDOFSANTASLAUGHTER
MYMY  TAG  HARD  LESS
   EDS  GOOPS  MIC
ANITEMREGULARLYTOSSED
NOB  BEA  ROGUE  ACLEAR
DVII  ANKA  VASTY  CARRE
HESFORGOTTENTHEFIVEWS
ONEAL  ENTER  LATE  INIS
WASTE  DANES  ELIM  CAGY
```

300

```
THINK      THINK      THINK
EATEN      CANAL      RAPEE
THANEVER  ELSIE  BUDAPEST
HARDNEWS  LOIRE  RANDOLPH
IMDB  RIVALED  SENT  TORI
NORAS  TPS  DEM  ANT  RIVEN
KNOLLS  DSO  MERIT  GOSEEK
PLOPS  ENGAGED   ENTR
   TIEONEON  SHASTA
TAGS  TVSTAR  THINKS  CANT
IIARUM  EST  EURO  DIETRICH
IRESIGN  OUTSIDE  MTSINAI
NOBILITY  NENE  VIM  REGAN
KNEE  THEBOX  SEINER  DESK
   RASHAD  PONDERER
ASON  ROSANNE  SEERS
TRUETO  LASIK  ENG  KEEPIT
HOTTO  VIC  DIG  COR  FLESH
ISOF  RANK  SAFEBET  ACAI
NICOTINE  ASTIR  ADOPTION
KERRIGAN  SHAME  DAREIASK
ATTAR  SANAA  CAROL
IHINK      THINK      THINK
```

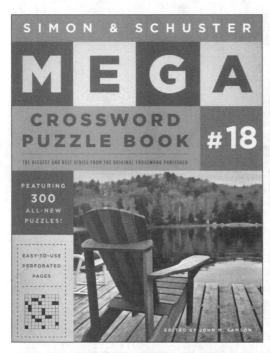
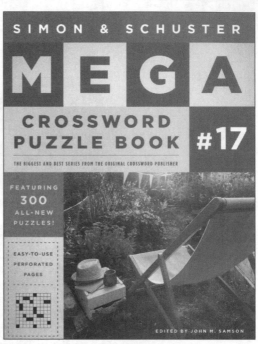

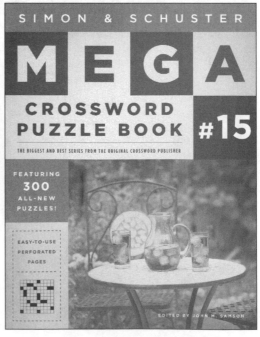